TUTORIAL

COMPUTER AND NETWORK SECURITY

Marshall D. Abrams and Harold J. Podell

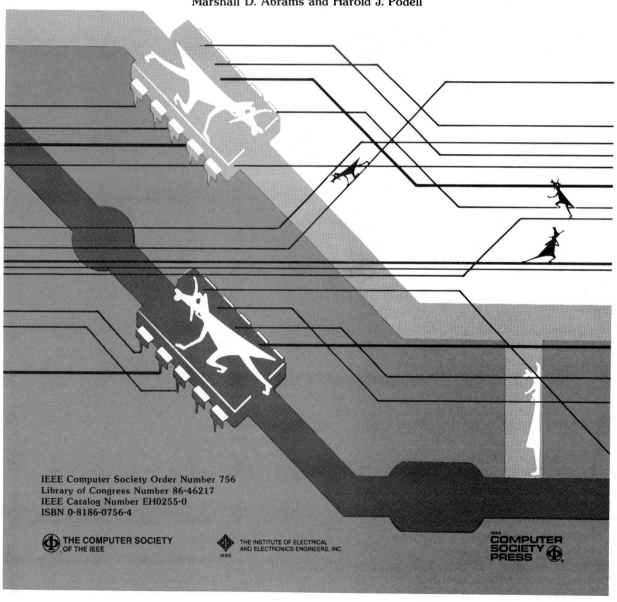

IEEE Computer Society Order Number 756
Library of Congress Number 86-46217
IEEE Catalog Number EH0255-0
ISBN 0-8186-0756-4

THE COMPUTER SOCIETY
OF THE IEEE

THE INSTITUTE OF ELECTRICAL
AND ELECTRONICS ENGINEERS, INC.
IEEE

IEEE
COMPUTER
SOCIETY
PRESS

Published by IEEE Computer Society Press
1730 Massachusetts Avenue, N W
Washington, D.C. 20036-1903

COVER DESIGNED BY JACK I. BALLESTERO

IEEE Computer Society Order Number 756
Library of Congress Number 86-46217
IEEE Catalog Number EH0255-0
ISBN 0-8186-0756-4 (Paper)
ISBN 0-8186-4756-6 (Microfiche)

Order from: IEEE Computer Society   IEEE Service Center   IEEE Computer Society
            Post Office Box 80452   445 Hoes Lane   Avenue de la Tanche, 2
            Worldway Postal Center   Piscataway, NJ 08854   B-1160 Brussels,
            Los Angeles, CA 90080   Belgium

 THE INSTITUTE OF ELECTRICAL AND ELECTRONICS ENGINEERS, INC.

Preface

This tutorial text is written for those who are concerned with security in automated systems, and those who should be concerned. We have tried to bridge the gaps between civil government, military, and private sector. Actually, we think these gaps are more apparent than real. All three groups are concerned with security policy, cost/effectiveness, risk management, and residual risk acceptance. Their emphases may differ, but the concerns are there. Different vocabularies emphasize differences rather than similarities. This book is about information system security, which includes data security, computer security, and network security. Though we often refer to information system security as computer security, we intend to imply the broader context.

We think that computer security has reached a "critical mass." *The Trusted Computer Security Criteria* (TCSEC), the *Orange Book,* has become very well known. It has also become a Defense Department Standard. The annual National Computer Security Conference has outgrown the facilities at the National Bureau of Standards. Other conferences are also experiencing growth pressures. The National Computer Security Center is working to extend the application of the TCSEC to networks and databases. The *Evaluated Products List* is growing. Many interesting and useful computer systems have been evaluated or are in the process. There should be a goodly number of secure systems available in the next few years.

The state-of-the-art is changing very rapidly. This is reflected in the literature. Textbooks rapidly become obsolete. We offer this tutorial text as one small way to disseminate knowledge about computer security. We hope you find it useful. Your comments and suggestions for the next edition will be appreciated.

The book is organized into five major sections: Introduction, Computer System Security, Network Security, Glossary, References, and Recommended Readings. The first three sections are subdivided.

Section 1.1 provides an introduction to the various concepts and considerations that constitute computer and network security. Many important subjects are covered lightly; additional treatment occurs in subsequent sections. Each section is written as a stand-alone discussion of a topic; therefore, there is some redundancy between related sections. Introductory overview papers have been selected to help establish a framework for what follows. Perhaps you will want to pass one of these papers, appropriately highlighted, up the management chain!

Section 1.2 takes a closer view of the context for our concerns with security. Issues of public policy, national defense, individual privacy, and property rights are all constituent parts.

Section 2.1 addresses management issues in computer system security. A basic framework to establish a structure for viewing computer systems security is established. Three aspects of the structure are discussed: management responsibility and authority; managerial; physical: administrative, technical, and communications controls and management decision-making for systems under development.

Formal models, the basis for proofs of correctness and trustworthiness, are discussed in Section 2.2. The concept of a formal model for computer security is central to (1) the development of trusted computer system evaluation, (2) the implementation of the controls specified by the criteria into a trusted computing base (TCB) of hardware and software, and (3) the verification and, in some cases, testing that the TCB implementation is a correct implementation of the model.

Standards provide a basis for comparison, interoperation, and evaluation. Section 2.3 provides a guide to this aspect of computer network security. The sections on standards are adapted from key papers and documents pertaining to the security standards issues. There are very few national standards and guidelines available for use in defining levels of computer and network security. Important computer security standards and guidance from the National Bureau of Standards and the National Computer Security Center (NCSC) are discussed. In addition, the security aspects of draft guidance on network security from the International Organization for Standardization Open Systems Interconnection seven-layer reference model and the Consultative Committee for International Telegraph and Telephone standards are presented.

Application requires technology and methodology. These are discussed in Section 2.4. TCB specific issues are presented by adapting selected work from the NCSC and Stanley Ames, Morrie Gasser, and Roger Schell.

Security of computerized databases is an area of current interest and is discussed in Section 2.5, where selected database security issues pertaining to NCSC criteria are presented and unresolved security issues related to DBMS are resolved.

Examples of commercially available systems and the concerns of their developers are extremely important to practitioners in separating theory from practice. Section 2.6 contains a number of such examples. NCSC publishes an *Evaluated Products List* and individual product evaluation reports. The discussion provides a sample of NCSC's activity with respect to evaluating security products against NCSC criteria.

Having achieved some degree of success with monolithic computer systems, one of the next security concerns is networks. Section 3.1 provides an overview of this topic. Issues are addressed concerning the nature of a network, network architecture, and security services.

Encryption, discussed in Section 3.2, is the most important mechanism in computer and network security. In fact, it is so important that it is often confused with a service. This section contains a cryptographic overview, including keys, single (secret) key cryptosystems, two (public) key cryptosystems, block and stream ciphers, link and end-to-end encryption, standards, network protocol security, message authentication, and the Commercial COMSEC Endorsement Program.

Access control and authentication are extended to the network environment in Section 3.3. After reviewing individual user identification and authentication, the concept is extended to messages, also discussed in conjunction with encryption in Section 3.2. Several approaches and products are discussed. Although introduced earlier, network protocols are given their own Section, 3.4. Protocol security is discussed in terms of the *Open System Interconnection Protocol Reference Model*. Specific security systems and mechanisms are identified and related to the layered protocol model. As we did with computer systems, we conclude the discussion of network security with examples and applications. Section 3.5 summarizes the importance of standards, followed by discussions of applications in financial institution key distribution, space shuttle security, and development of a multilevel secure local area network. The conclusions, which follow Section 3.5, reflect our initial observation that computer security has reached a "critical mass."

The glossary has been amalgamated from definitions in the papers considered and from several pre-existing glossaries. We believe it serves as a baseline that integrates selected computer and network security terms. The recommended readings and other references conclude the book.

Marshall D. Abrams
Harold J. Podell
Silver Spring, MD
October 1986

Table of Contents

Section 1
Introduction

Section 1.1: Overview

Why Computer Security Is Important

As a start, let's establish what computer security is and why it is important. We will discuss several of the many approaches. Consider how computers have become a standard part of the operation of many organizations. The way in which the organization conducts its business has become inseparably intertwined with computers. There are varying degrees of ability to revert to noncomputerized manual methods ranging from difficult to impossible. Given this dependence, the organization should be concerned that its computer services are going to be available when needed and to provide timely and accurate information to the end users.

The Value of Information

Computers process and store information. Value may be attributed to this information, which is an asset. The determination of value is both complex and controversial and it may be based either on the cost of developing or assembling the information or on the (potential) loss that would occur if the information were disclosed. The value may be established by the organization that created or gathered the information or it may be established by someone or something else who would like to gain access to the information. Information created by mental activity is known as intellectual property. Information gathered and organized from observation is known as intelligence. Other information consists of business records. Some information is a perishable commodity. Its value changes as a function of time, usually decreasing. Consider, for example, the latest economic statistics, crop forecasts, deployment of military forces, and business plans. This concept of information as a valuable commodity is relatively recent, often identified with a society's economic state. Recognition of this value indicates a post-industrial or information society.

Objectives

Having established that information has value, we can now consider objectives and vulnerabilities. Certain words and phrases have specific meanings in the computer security arena. These "buzz words" are italicized below; their meaning may be inferred from context or determined by consulting the glossary.

Much information is considered *secret* by its owner, whose objective is to maintain its *confidentiality* against the risk of *disclosure*. Another important property of information is its *integrity;* there should be assurance that no inadvertent changes have occurred, causing *corruption* of the information. The value of some information depends on its source. Its value is enhanced by *attribution;* it is decreased by the possibility of *repudiation*. The continuous *availability* of the information and the computer resources to process it are important; *unauthorized use* and *denial of service* to authorized users are to be prevented.

Vulnerabilities

We now take a slightly more detailed look at the vulnerabilities of automated information systems. We will add consideration of how the justice system is prepared to deal with offenders. While these vulnerabilities apply equally (at least in a taxonomical sense) to military and civil systems, mention of the justice system causes us to consider vital differences. Civil violations can be redressed by suit for compensation for damages and/or criminal prosecution of violators. The threat of punishment is a deterrent. Military systems must rely on prevention. Lost military security and advantage cannot be recovered.

Physical Property

The easiest vulnerability to contend with concerns physical property such as equipment and supplies. Physical property is susceptible to unauthorized modification, destruction, and theft. In general, the protection against these threats is also physical, involving barriers, locks, alarms, and guards. The criminal justice system has dealt with physical property as one of its basic concerns almost since its inception; there is no special difficulty because the physical objects are computer related.

One type of physical property is very vulnerable: information stored on removable media. For example, tapes, disk packs, and diskettes are all physical property potentially containing valuable and/or sensitive information. The diskettes from personal computers illustrate the problem of vulnerability. How many diskettes do you have that are important to you that are not adequately protected?

Computer Services

It is only slightly more difficult to deal with problems of computer services. Unauthorized use is combatted by *identification* and *authentication* of users. Authentication can be

3

divided into three classes: information the individual knows, such as a password; a physical possession, such as a machine readable badge; and a physical characteristic, such as a fingerprint or handprint. A shorthand for these three classes is something the person knows, has, or is. Theft of service is a reasonably solid legal concept; a value for the service can be established in the open marketplace.

Denial of service is slightly more complex to deal with. Property violations can cause denial of service as a secondary effect, but this is not the only way. Overloading access mechanisms (e.g., repeated spurious attempts to obtain access to computers or the creation of communications overloads) can result in the denial of service to authorized and unauthorized persons alike. Since nothing of value is obtained, the legal system has problems dealing with this vulnerability unless there are national security considerations or specific legislation has been enacted.

Denial of service has major organizational survival implications for a class of online information systems in service industries. For example, banks, airlines, and insurance companies strive to continually provide defined levels of service to the end users. Although the degrees of industrial sensitivity vary pertaining to the need for continuous availability of defined levels of service, each industry has its set of critical requirements for continuous availability to support continuity of operations. Consider the importance to an airline of having several thousand remote terminals at airports unable to provide continuous availability during a major holiday period. Denial of service may also affect human life. The following are examples: nuclear power/critical process control, air traffic control, and vehicle/aircraft navigation and control.

Intellectual Property

Information, or intellectual property, such as computer programs and data, is subject to unauthorized modification, disclosure, or destruction. Until recent legislation defined these vulnerabilities as criminal offenses, it was difficult to obtain legal remedies. A fiscal loss had to be shown, such as in the disclosure of a trade secret. *Audit trails* are effective for both defensive and corrective action, and provide a record of attempted and successful accesses to information, thus helping to identify the culprit.

War Stories

Like many other disciplines, this one is based substantially on experience and empirical evidence. Computer security has accumulated its share of war stories, which have considerable value for sensitization as well as cataloging known risks. Many of the reprints in this collection include such experiences; read them for their educational value as well as for their interest.

Severity of Security Risks

The following ordered list of risks is based on Courtney [COUR84] errors and omissions, dishonest employees, fire, disgruntled employees, water, and strangers. Note that this ordering is based on commercial practice; military security would undoubtedly re-order the risks. In addition, the military is interested in prevention of violation, and detection when a violation has occurred, so that code and strategy changes may be made.

Errors and Omissions

Note that the biggest risk comes from human error, and not from malfeasance! Courtney says that "criminals will never be able to compete with incompetents." Security is inconvenient. There are a number of procedures required for security that have nothing to do with getting the work done; therefore, these procedures may be viewed as dispensable, especially when not double checked. For example, the use of a password to authenticate identification presented to gain access to the computer (i.e., to "logon" or "login") is inconvenient. People do not like to have to remember a password. The first approach is to disable passwords in the computer. If that fails, the next step is to select a common, easy to remember password, such as your name or street. Failing that, you write the password on the terminal or on a piece of paper that is always near the terminal. Some security!

Other examples include keyboard entry errors, programming errors, and transmitting incorrect data as input to another process. The last example can be very expensive because the errors can be magnified rapidly. The construction of an integrated database is a process where input errors can be readily magnified. This occurs when the original databases are transmitted as input to the integrated database, which then becomes a common database for a class of software applications and users.

There must be a management response to avert these errors and omissions. Security awareness training is required. People are more likely to perform inconvenient operations if they understand the reasons for these operations. But even the best intentions go wrong. A common approach is some system of checks and balances such as division of responsibility—separation of duties. One person cannot perform all the security-related actions; two people are required to perform complementary actions.

Dishonest Employees

Most computer crime would have occurred without computers. Embezzlement, fraud, and conversion are very well known criminal acts. But now that information is contained in computers rather than on pages of a ledger, the computer gets involved in the crime. Not only do computers make it easier for legitimate business to be conducted; they also make it easier for crime to be conducted.

Dishonest employees tend to ply their trade where they are skilled. The longer they work in a particular department or on a specific set of operations, the more they know about those operations. Eventually, if so inclined, employees may discover a flaw that can be exploited for criminal purposes. The flaw might be in manual procedures or in programmed logic. For example, "data diddling" can be used to generate unauthorized disbursements, and privileged information can be used for personal gains. The point is that these people are authorized to use the computer and that they are probably not straying far from their normal duties.

The people who create the programs have additional opportunities. They can insert a special program code that violates security rules only when activated by a secret means. Colorful names such as *Trojan horse,* and *trapdoor* are applied to these program parts. Modern team methods of software development, such as structured peer review of code, can help reduce these vulnerabilities. Rigorous personnel policies, such as a *closed security environment,* also can be employed.

Organizations need an effective computer *security policy.* Violations need to be detected and punished. Non-military organizations should include computer security violations in their employee disciplinary procedures. Otherwise, computer security will not be taken seriously.

Fire

Computers do not burn, but they can be damaged by fire. The location of the computer relative to combustibles must be carefully planned. The quantity of combustibles, such as printer paper, in the same room with computers should be controlled. This is another example of a tradeoff between security and convenience. Fire extinguishing equipment, such as sprinklers, should be placed where the combustibles are. Adjacent spaces should be checked. It is not wise to locate a computer adjacent to an operation employing open flame or other hazards.

Many serious fire hazards result from locating a computer or communications facility in a building or floor that has high risk facilities. For example, if a truck loading dock is located on the first floor, all adjacent first and second floor facilities are at risk to gasoline-based fire and resulting damage.

Disgruntled Employees

Computers are susceptible to sabotage. Luddites and grudge-bearers are likely to do damage to computers whether or not the computers have anything to do with their anger. Like dishonest employees, this group is likely to do its damage where it has computer access as part of normal employment functions. For example, employees can access information after they quit if passwords are not changed. In addition, "logic bombs" of various types can be planted in the computer software that later cause disruptions in the computer operating system at a specified time. Procedures designed to protect against disgruntled employees can only inconvenience the benign worker trying to do his or her job. Personnel practices, such as employee assistance programs for substance abuse and family-affairs counseling, should be re-examined with an eye toward anticipating and preventing destructive action. Disciplinary actions, especially dismissal, offer potential for damage. Many organizations escort a dismissed employee off the premises, paying salary in lieu of notice.

One aspect of this topic bears specific mention. Systems programmers have the access to and knowledge of supervisory or control systems, such as operating systems. This access and knowledge enable them to effectively bypass many access control systems, such as a password for login. Therefore, a substantial requirement exists to carefully screen systems programmers before employment and to support these valuable employees after employment. This support includes understanding and accommodating the personal needs of each system programmer within the constraints of an organizational working environment.

Water

Electronic equipment does not like to get wet. It is difficult, almost impossible, to get computers and communications equipment to work properly after it has gotten thoroughly drenched. The prudent operations manager is prepared to keep the equipment dry. Water damage often occurs as a by-product of fire, but burst pipes and leaks are not unknown. Rolls of plastic sheeting should be stored near the equipment so that it can be quickly covered when necessary.

Strangers

Notice what is last on the list! When all other risks have been dealt with, it is time to worry about outsiders. In pre-network days, physical protection was the predominant defense. Physical access was restricted to authorized individuals. Their *identification* was *authenticated* as part of the process. Data communication networks provide access to computers and information from remote locations. Authorized users are greatly convenienced. Unfortunately, so are unauthorized adversaries. Examples of unauthorized users include hackers gaining unauthorized access and/or tampering with files or industrial espionage via eavesdropping on data transmissions. Some of the convenience must be traded-off to make it more difficult, if not impossible, for the unauthorized person to gain access to the resources. The generic name for this protection is *access control*. It will receive considerable attention in this volume.

Risk Management

To this point we have established the importance of computer security, the value of information, objectives, vulnerabilities, and the severity of security risks. Now we shall discuss how to live with these risks. Essentially, this is a management issue. Computer and network security are management responsibilities. Information is gathered and estimates made of the risks present in a system; this is known as *risk analysis*. Methods for *risk reduction* are proposed and analyzed; cost estimates are prepared. This work is performed by computer and communications analysts along with risk and computer security specialists. Finally, a management decision is made concerning risk reduction, risk acceptance, and system operation.

No system is one hundred percent safe. *Risk management* involves analysis of risk, cost-effective risk reduction, and acceptance of the residual risk. The name is well chosen. Risk acceptance is a management decision to operate the system with full recognition of the residual risk. Among the factors considered is the necessity of the system for the organization to function at a given level of performance, accuracy, and continuity of operations. *Certification* is defined in a Federal Information Processing Standard, *Guideline for Computer Security Certification and Accreditation* [GUID83] as the identification by technical managers of the level of residual risk and accreditation as the acceptance of this residual risk by senior management. In private industry, a company officer is the accreditation authority, while, in the military, the accreditation authority may be the commanding general.

Risk Analysis

Risk analysis is the most mature component of risk management. Its maturity may be a drawback in that its practitioners see it as an end rather than as a means. Sometimes there is a lack of management information in all the data reported. The fundamental considerations in risk analysis are the damage or loss that could result from an unfavorable event and the likelihood that such an event will occur. The problem becomes mathematically intractable when the value of the risk asymptotically approaches infinity and the probability of occurrence asymptotically approaches zero. This is the normal state of affairs, not an exception; hence, risk analysis and risk management are management functions, since operational decisions must be made based on insufficient information.

Risk analysis can be based on quantitative or qualitative analysis; each approach has its methods and adherents. Vari-

ous hybrids also exist. Naturally a number of computerized tools are available for assistance in performing risk analysis. Earlier tools were designed to relieve risk analysts of manual tedium; most recent ones help prevent nonspecialists from overlooking key factors. Two other Federal Information Processing Standards are often used as the basis for risk analysis: *Guidelines for ADP Physical Security and Risk Management (FIPS 31)* [GUID74] and *Guidelines for Automatic Data Processing Risk Analysis (FIPS 65)* [GUID79].

Personal Computers and Word Processors

All of the fundamental concepts of computer security were developed in the era of large centralized computer centers. Perhaps there were communications among centers or with remote terminals. Advances in microelectronics have changed that environment. Today we have omnipresent desktop, end user, personal computers, and word processors. The environment will continue to change as the market spews forth new and wondrous devices. It is prudent to examine the implications of this changing environment for security.

The major impact is the shifting of security responsibility to the individual end user and to non-ADP management. Previously, computer security was provided to the user by specialists who operated computer and communications facilities; the user was responsible for complying with their rules and procedures. The advent of distributed desktop computers has cast the end user in the role of operating a miniature computer center, responsible, among other things, for security. Recognition of this responsibility is the first step toward acceptance.

Word processors should be viewed as a specific computer application that may be accomplished by networked or standalone workstations. These workstations may be special purpose, optimized to the application, or they may be general purpose terminals or computers. Most of the cautions and concerns for personal computer security apply to word processing, but special attention should be paid to the information-related vulnerabilities. Users of word processing equipment may be among the least trained employees to deal with the technical complexities and operational procedures that proper security requires. Management must accept the responsibility to provide proper instruction and support.

Reprints

There are three reprints, which provide supplementary reading for the basics of computer security, security considerations for personal computers, and a perspective on risk analysis.

Our very first selection, appropriately entitled "An Overview of Computer Security," by Rita C. Summers, mentions many important terms in the computer security lexicon. Her purpose is to give the nonsecurity specialist an appreciation of the wide range of topics that encompasses computer security. She quickly establishes several purposes of computer security: protection of information against unauthorized modification, destruction, or disclosure; maintenance of the integrity and availability of the computing system and its applications; and protection of the hardware, software, and data from danger of loss. Her discussion of the protection of privacy introduces principles of privacy. Achievement of security is discussed in terms of access control, information flow control, inference control, and integrity; each of which requires a different type of security technique.

Fundamental security concepts introduced include fail-safe defaults, such as no-access which characterizes closed systems. Models described for introducing security control into information systems include the access matrix model and its derivative access control list and capability list; hierarchical models incorporating sensitivity levels and clearances; and information flow models. Her identification of commercial models is dated and slightly near-sighted, omitting reference to Honeywell Multics, as listed in Section 2.6. Operational approaches such as complete mediation, separation of privilege, least privilege, and least common mechanism are described briefly.

Protection techniques in hardware in support of operating systems include privilege states, virtual memory, virtual machine, capability systems, and the kernel approach. User authentication by passwords is mentioned, as is logging of events (audit trails). Encryption may be used to protect information within a computer system and in a communications system.

Administrative security is not forgotten. Physical security, data classification, personnel considerations, auditing, implementation of a security program, and risk management are discussed.

W.H. Murray's article, "Security Considerations for Personal Computers," is necessary because end users and their managers may not be aware of computer security concerns. Once informed they can decide what actions to take and which risks to accept. The simplest problems address physical equipment considerations. The personal computer is a valuable piece of office equipment requiring physical protection appropriate to the environment. However, it usually does not require special temperature or humidity conditioning, nor is it a fire hazard.

One special concern with personal computers and word processors is the information they process. As mentioned above, this information must be protected against unauthorized modification, destruction, or disclosure. Murray catalogs protection mechanisms based on the location of the working data, but all methods involve backup copies. Management of these backups is given inadequate attention. Sensitive information on media require management procedures similar to paper copies, such as filing and retrievability, fire protection, and possible off-site storage. Removable diskettes can be handled in much the same way as paper files, including storage in safes and fire-resistant containers.

As the sophistication and complexity of personal computer environments increases, so do the security concerns. Encryption is suggested to protect information in a multi-user environment. Application programs must be protected from interference or data contamination. This problem applies even more extensively to multi-user time-sharing systems that communicate with personal computers. Isolation may be maintained by resource allocation.

Since personal computers and terminals are indistinguishable via open communications lines, any communicating computer must consider personal computer induced vulnerabilities in its security plans. Personal computers can be programmed to mount exhaustive attacks; open, communicating systems cannot be assumed to exist in a benign environment. These controls are well addressed throughout this volume.

The widespread distribution of personal computers introduces a new organizational vulnerability of responsibility for an employee's actions. Much personal computer software is sold with certain restrictions on its use. Software is usually copyrighted; it may also be contractually restricted to be used on a single piece of hardware. Employees who violate these restrictions are probably placing the employer at risk. Clear guidance to employees can obviate the problem.

In his abstract "NBS Perspective in Risk Analysis: Past, Present, and Future," S.W. Katzke provides a context for appreciating the continuing debate concerning risk analysis and management. The roles of risk analysis and risk management to operational systems, requirements definition, design, and implementation are presented along with constituent concepts and terms. Experience with FIPS 65 [GUID79] has been that it was not particularly well suited for use during the entire risk management process; its "order of magnitude approach" has not been well understood. Current methods and approaches are too immature for standardization; reasons are discussed. Future National Bureau of Standards plans are sketched.

Recommended Readings

Three recommended readings are suggested to give supplementary information on the protection of information in computer systems, the total computer security problem, and a summary of key risk analysis issues.

The classic tutorial paper, "The Protection of Information in Computer Systems," by J.H. Saltzer and M.D. Schroeder provides a historical perspective from which to appreciate current work and thinking. While the areas of current research and product development have changed, you will find that the fundamentals have not. This paper concentrates on internal technical approaches to information protection from an architectural viewpoint. It starts with a glossary, followed by a discussion of basic principles including privacy, security, and protection. A hierarchy of protection progresses from unprotected through all-or-nothing (dedicated), controlled sharing, user-programmed sharing, to labeling of outputs.

The design principles, economy of mechanism, fail-safe defaults, complete mediation, open design, separation of privilege, least privilege, least common mechanism, psychological acceptability, work factor, and compromise recording continue their applicability. The technical underpinning presented is still important, but should not be considered representative of the current state-of-the-art. Descriptor-based protection systems employing separation of addressing and protection, capabilities, access control lists, and object protection are discussed.

The article by K.S. Shankar, "The Total Computer Security Problem: An Overview," presents a balanced picture of the environment, external controls, internal controls, information organization, and integrity. In presenting the user environment, he discusses threats to computer services, protection versus sharing, complexity of services, and the value of information. Brief reference to security requirements and models introduce external protection mechanisms of administrative controls and physical security. Internal protection mechanisms such as authentication, access control, surveillance mechanisms, and communications security must be complete, tamperproof, and certified.

The summary, "Summary of Key Issues (Federal Information Systems Risk Analysis Workshop)," by S.W. Katzke, may be understood as a state-of-the-art assessment of risk management, at least as practiced in the federal government, as well as an agenda for further action. A formal, structured, modular, conceptual model of risk management should be developed and will help in understanding alternative methods, tools, and approaches. Approximations for unknown functional relationships must be supported. Metrics for evaluating alternative methods are needed. Methods that combine quantitative and qualitative approaches, should continue to be developed. Inconsistent results decrease credibility. Risk management expertise should be distributed throughout the organization, especially with the assistance of automated tools.

An overview of computer security

by R. C. Summers

Presented is an overview of computer security, including concepts, techniques, and measures relating to the protection of computing systems and the information they maintain against deliberate or accidental threats. Motivations for security measures are discussed. Security strategies are considered. Actions and events that threaten security are described, along with technical problems that can prevent the computer from adequately dealing with threats. Security models are surveyed. Specific technical and administrative measures for promoting security are described. Among the technical measures discussed are design of secure systems, hardware and operating systems, identification of users, encryption, and access control packages. Administrative measures include personnel, physical security of the computing system, and auditing. Also presented is the establishment of a security program. Reviewed are special problems and their solutions, including communications and networks, data base management systems, and statistical data bases. This paper is based on a paper by the author published in The Handbook of Computers and Computing, edited by Arthur H. Seidman and Ivan Flores, Van Nostrand Reinhold Company, Inc., New York (1984).

As organizations automate their record keeping and other operations, computer security becomes more and more vital to the functioning of the organizations. The purpose of this paper is to give those who are not working professionally in the field an appreciation for the wide range of topics within computer security.

The computer has become the main repository for most of an organization's records. Some of the records represent or are used for controlling resources such as money and inventory that can be lost to the organization through manipulation of the records. Some records are essential to the operation of an organization, some contain trade secrets, and some

describe persons whose privacy must be protected. Thus one aspect of computer security is the protection of information against unauthorized modification, destruction, or disclosure.

Equally critical is the role of the computer in process control and on-line applications. Process control at a chemical plant, for example, involves the sensing of such process variables as temperature, pressure, and reaction products, followed by computation and feeding back of signals to control the process. Airline reservation systems are on-line applications that control the airline's only products—space and time. The needed data must be protected, and the computing system must be available to carry out the computations in a timely way. Thus another aspect of computing security is the maintenance of the integrity and availability of the computing system and its applications.

An additional impetus for security comes from the legal requirements of many countries and states that prescribe how personal records are to be handled. Other laws and regulations require organizations to control their assets properly. This includes assets maintained or controlled by a computing system.

The objective of computer security is to put the hardware, software, and data out of danger of loss. In this paper, the term *computer security* includes concepts, techniques, and measures that are used to protect computing systems and the information they maintain against deliberate or accidental threats. We first consider motivations for security measures, then list possible strategies for computer security, including the controlling of access to information. Next we consider actions and events that threaten security and describe technical problems that can prevent the computer from adequately dealing with the threats.

Because a conceptual framework is essential for research in security, as well as for the intelligent appli-

---

One reason for security measures is to protect the privacy of individuals.

---

cation of security techniques, formal models of security have been developed. We survey some formal models and consider informal models that are implicit in many software systems and application environments.

After developing the necessary framework, we consider two kinds of measures for promoting security: technical measures implemented within the computing system and administrative measures outside the computing system.

For measures within the system, we summarize general principles that have proved useful in designing secure systems. We describe techniques used in both hardware and operating systems to protect programs and data. We survey ways of identifying users who attempt access to a computing system. We describe encryption, a technique that can be used to guard against a wide variety of security threats. We discuss software packages that can control access to data and other resources.

Among the administrative measures we consider are those involving personnel, physical security of the computing system, and auditing and controls as they relate to computerized systems. Described next are ways by which an organization can establish a security program using the measures discussed.

Because computing systems are accessed over communication lines and are connected into networks, we review the special security problems introduced by communications and networks, and discuss the use of encryption as a security measure. Security aspects of local networks are discussed.

Data base systems have their own special requirements, which are discussed. Security features of data base management systems are introduced, and research on the security of statistical data bases is summarized.

Motivations and strategies for computer security

One reason for security measures is to protect the privacy of individuals,[1-3] so as to give them some control over information about themselves that is maintained in computerized systems. Personal information appears in the records of banks and credit institutions, doctors' offices and hospitals, taxing agencies, and in many other places. More and more, such information is being collected and kept, and wrong decisions have been made on the basis of inaccurate information, or sensitive personal data have been wrongly revealed. A number of countries now have privacy legislation. In the U.S., the Privacy Act of 1974 applies to all federal record systems, and other laws apply to specific areas of the private sector, such as credit and banking. Many states also have privacy laws. Although the various laws differ, common principles underlie them. We summarize here the principles of privacy[4] adopted by the member nations of the Organization for Economic Cooperation and Development (OECD):

- There should be limits to the collection of personal data, and the data should be obtained lawfully and fairly, with the knowledge or consent of the subject where appropriate. Here, the *subject* is the person about whom the data are being collected.
- Data should be relevant to the purposes for which they are collected, as well as accurate, complete, and up-to-date.
- The purposes for collecting the data should be specified when the data are collected and again whenever the purposes change. The new purposes must be compatible with the old ones.
- The data must not, in general, be used for other purposes.
- Data should be protected by reasonable safeguard against "loss or unauthorized access, destruction, use, modification, or disclosure...." In other words, data security should be provided.

- It should be possible to find out what personal record systems exist, their main purposes, and the names of the persons who are responsible for controlling the records.
- An individual should be able to find out whether a data bank has information about him, and, if so, to obtain access to the information. The subject should also be able to challenge the data, and, if successful, have it erased or corrected.
- A data controller should be accountable for complying with measures that implement these principles.

As another motivation for security-related controls, U.S. legislation (the Foreign Corrupt Practices Act of 1977[5]) requires all publicly held corporations to maintain internal accounting controls to ensure that transactions are executed in accordance with management's authorization, transactions are properly recorded, and access to assets is permitted only in accordance with management's authorization.

Computer-related crime as a motivation for computer security is perhaps better publicized than documented,[6] but there is reason to believe that it causes substantial losses.[7]

There is no single strategy for achieving security. One approach to security is *access control*, that is, ensuring that data are accessed by authorized persons in authorized ways only. Access control is not concerned with how the authorized person uses information legitimately obtained. Access control is concerned with access to the physical system, system software, applications, and data.

With a general strategy of access control, there is still a choice as to whether to try to prevent all unauthorized access or to allow access while at the same time detecting it and taking action against the violator. Another technique of access control is that of *information flow control*, which is the attempt to control the flow of information within the computing system and as it leaves the computing system. A longer-range goal, rarely aimed at in current systems, is that of *inference control*.[8] An inference, in this case, may be the result of combining a statistical summary with other facts one is aware of.

Another strategic approach to security is based on the concept of *integrity*. This approach, which can supplement approaches that control interaction, is designed to ensure that interactions leave data or systems in a correct or available state. *Data integrity*

means ensuring that data are neither destroyed nor improperly modified. These data are correct or reasonable and accurately reflect the real objects they describe. *Application integrity* means ensuring that an application, which is typically viewed as a system,

---

Preventing access by an unauthorized user also helps to protect the integrity of the data.

---

continues to operate according to its specifications and continues to be available. *System integrity* aims at the availability and correct operation of the entire computing system.

Clearly, these strategies require different kinds of security techniques. Information flow control, for example, is much more demanding of an operating system than is access control and may also involve special programming languages. It is also true that one security measure can contribute to more than one strategy. For example, preventing access by an unauthorized user also helps to protect the integrity of the data, because such a user may change the data improperly.

A later section of this paper discusses models of access control and information flow control. Inference control is discussed as applied to statistical data bases. Measures to protect application and system integrity are discussed later in various sections. This paper does not deal specifically with data integrity, but References 1 and 9 do introduce this important topic.

Sources of security threats

Consider threats to computer security from outside the computing system. The computing system hardware (including data storage devices) can be physically damaged by flood, fire, earthquake, sabotage, traffic accident, and so forth. The same events can likewise damage data stored away from the system on tapes, disks, or diskettes. Information may be accidentally destroyed if a wrong data volume, such as disk pack or tape reel, is used on the system. Off-line storage can be stolen or copied, as can printed

Without safeguards authorized users can perform improper actions either deliberately or by accident.

output. Communication lines are vulnerable to eavesdropping or to the insertion of unauthorized messages.

A person can gain unauthorized access to data by masquerading as a different person. An application program can be improperly modified by using the normal procedures for changing programs. If an application lacks adequate safeguards, its authorized users can perform improper actions either deliberately or by accident. An authorized user may act as a spy, passing restricted information outside the system.

The people who are sources of threats may have legitimate access to the system—such as application users, application programmers, system programmers, operators, system administrators—or they may be outsiders who succeed in penetrating the system.

Looking now within the computing system, we can have errors in application programs or operating systems, inadequate protection mechanisms in the hardware and operating system that result in failure to isolate user programs properly, or hardware failures. The immediate result is usually the unauthorized reading or writing of data in memory or on disk. That, in turn, may lead to a system crash with consequent denial of service, or theft or improper modification of data, theft of proprietary software, or other dire results.

Certain generic problems in system software may cause the system to fail in its protection against threats. One of these is known as the "TOCTTOU problem," which is derived from its longer name,

the time-of-check-to-time-of-use problem.[10] The TOCTTOU problem results from an event such as the following. Information, such as a parameter of a request to the operating system, is checked and found valid, but the information is changed by the user before the system actually carries out the request. Another class of problem is termed the "residues problem." Here, when an area of memory is released by a user or when a file is deleted, the information stored in memory or on the disk may remain there, although it is inaccessible in the normal way. With skilled programming, that information can then be read by the next user to whom the space is allocated. Another problem that is not guarded against in current systems is the passing of information by covert channels. That is, information is passed using means other than the normal channels provided by the computing system. For example, a program may convey information to the operator by varying its speed of reading a tape. Also, one program may convey information to another program by varying its amount of computation and its use of memory. Thus the intelligently modulated rate of progress of the other program is the covert channel. We conclude that threats, both accidental and deliberate, come from all types of accessors of the system.

Before discussing security measures that can be taken to counter the various threats, we introduce models of security that are useful in describing the measures.

Security models

Access matrix model. The best-known security model is the *access matrix* model, which is described by Lampson.[11] The basic elements of the model are subjects, objects, and access types. The model grew out of work on operating systems, which is why each element can be interpreted in terms of operating system concepts. A *subject* is an active entity capable of accessing objects. In the operating-system context, a subject is a *process*, which is sometimes defined as a program in execution. In a time-sharing system, for example, a number of processes run concurrently on the same computer, sharing the memory and processor. Thus each process represents a different user. An *object* is anything to which access is controlled. Examples of objects known to an operating system are files, programs, and segments of memory. An *access type* is simply a kind of access to an object. For each type of object, there is a set of possible access types. Files, for example, have such access types as Read, Write, or Erase.

An access matrix M relates the three types of elements of the model as follows. In this matrix the rows represent subjects and the columns represent objects. Each cell M_{ij} contains a list of access types permitted to subject i for object j. These are sometimes called access rights, privileges, or permissions. Figure 1 shows an example of an access matrix in which Process 1 can Read and Execute Program 1 and can Read and Write Segment A. However, Process 1 has no access at all to Segment B. Process 2 can Read Segment B, but has no access to Program 1 or Segment A. Since operating system subjects and objects can be created and destroyed dynamically, and access rights change continually, the dimensions and contents of the access matrix also change.

The elements of the access matrix model can also be given interpretations at a different level. The subjects then become the users of a computing system, and they have rights to persistent resources such as application programs or data base objects.

For implementing access control, as opposed to using a model, it is generally inefficient to represent access-control information by a matrix, because the matrix is typically sparse. That is, there are many objects and subjects and relatively few rights, with the result that the access matrix has many voids or zero elements. Two ways are commonly used to store access-control information. An *access control list* associated with an object lists all the subjects who can access the object, along with their rights. A *capability list* associated with a subject lists all that subject's rights to all objects. Figure 2 shows the information of Figure 1 in access-list form, and Figure 3 shows the same information in capability-list form.

Models using levels and compartments. A different type of model was developed by U.S. military services because they wanted systems that would enforce the military security policy. According to that policy, as described by Landwehr,[12] information is either unclassified or classified into *sensitivity levels* such as confidential, secret, and top secret. People are given *clearance* to access information up to a certain sensitivity level. Thus a person cleared for secret information could also access confidential and unclassified information, but not top secret information. The person must also have a *need-to-know* for the specific information accessed. In addition, some information also has one or more *compartment designations*, such as NUCLEAR, and access to such information requires clearance for all its compart-

Figure 1 Access matrix

	PROGRAM 1	SEGMENT A	SEGMENT B
PROCESS 1	READ EXECUTE	READ WRITE	
PROCESS 2			READ

Figure 2 Access control list

ACCESS CONTROL LIST FOR PROGRAM 1:
PROCESS 1 (READ, EXECUTE)

ACCESS CONTROL LIST FOR SEGMENT A:
PROCESS 1 (READ, WRITE)

ACCESS CONTROL LIST FOR SEGMENT B:
PROCESS 2 (READ)

Figure 3 Capability list

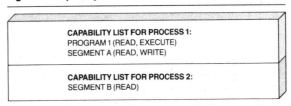

CAPABILITY LIST FOR PROCESS 1:
PROGRAM 1 (READ, EXECUTE)
SEGMENT A (READ, WRITE)

CAPABILITY LIST FOR PROCESS 2:
SEGMENT B (READ)

ments. Thus a *security level* consists of both a sensitivity or clearance level and a set of compartments.

The military policy has been formally specified as a first step toward the goal of demonstrating convincingly that computing systems correctly enforce the security policy, whatever the actions of programs and users. The best-known model is the one developed by Bell and LaPadula.[13,14] The subjects in this model again usually represent processes, and the objects represent files or other containers of information. One security level—call it A—*dominates* another level B when two conditions are true simultaneously: (1) A's classification or clearance level is greater than or equal to that of B, and (2) A's set of compartments contains those of B. The access types are the following: Read (observe only), Append (alter only), and Write (observe and alter). The state of the system is described by the following: (1) the *current access set*, where each access includes subject, object, and access type; (2) an access matrix representing need-to-know; and (3) the security levels of all subjects and objects. The system state is changed by a *request*. The system's response to the request and the new state are determined by a *rule*. If it can be proved that each rule preserves security, so that any request results in a new secure state, the system is said to be *secure*.

A secure state is defined by the *simple security property* and the *∗-property*. The simple security property is as follows: For an "observe" access type, the level of the subject dominates the level of the object. In other words, there is no reading upward in level. The simple security condition does not prevent a spy with secret clearance from reading information from a secret object and writing it into a confidential object. The star property (∗-property) prevents such writing downward, and is defined as follows:

- For Read: the subject's level dominates that of the object.
- For Append: the object's level dominates.
- For Write: the levels are equal.

A third property, *discretionary security*, requires every access to be explicitly authorized by the access matrix.

Information flow models. Landwehr points out that the Bell and LaPadula model is formulated in terms of access to objects rather than information flow. A model, termed the *lattice model*, described by Denning,[15] treats information flow more directly. The lattice model also generalizes levels and categories and their relationships. The model provides a basis for eventually analyzing source programs to determine whether they violate the information flow properties of a specific security structure.

Models implied by commercial systems. Many operating systems, data base management systems, and application systems provide access control facilities, and these usually imply an access matrix model. A user or group of users has the authority to specify the contents of the access matrix. Because the number of objects may be very great, this authorization function is usually distributed among different people. That is, for any object, some user has the right to specify the column in the access matrix or, equivalently, the object's access control list. A more de-

tailed survey of security models can be found in Reference 12.

Security measures within the computing system

This section describes technical measures that can be taken within the computing system to promote security. Some of these measures have to do with the

---

The design of security measures should be simple and small to allow careful checking of its accuracy.

---

structure and design of the system and can be called *passive measures*. *Active measures* are steps taken in addition to the usual system processing.

Principles of secure systems. Some quite general principles can be stated about how to design security measures in hardware, in various levels of software, and also in system administration. The discussion here is based on Reference 16 by Saltzer and Schroeder.

The design of the security measures embodied in both hardware and software should be simple and small so as to allow for careful checking of its accuracy.

The default situation should be of the *no-access* type in which access requires explicit permission. The implementation of this principle creates *fail-safe defaults*, which characterize a *closed* system as opposed to an *open* one.

Every access must be checked against the access-control information, including those accesses occurring outside normal operation, as in recovery or maintenance. This is termed the principle of *complete mediation*.

A lock mechanism that demands two keys for access is safer than one requiring only a single key. To illustrate this point, Saltzer and Schroeder use the analogy of the two keys required to open a bank safe deposit box. Each key can be in the custody of a different component of the system. Then a single failure does not result in a security breach. This rule is known as the *separation of privilege.*

The Saltzer and Schroeder principle of *least privilege* states that every program and every user of the system should operate using the least set of privileges necessary to complete the job.

According to Popek's rule of *least common mechanism,*[17] the design should minimize the mechanism shared by different users for their mutual security.

In practice, encryption mechanisms are not completely public.

Such shared mechanism is crucial. Keeping it small and isolated helps to keep it correct.

Security mechanisms must be psychologically acceptable. They should not interfere unduly with the work of users, while at the same time meeting the needs of those who authorize access.

A final principle differs from the others in addressing not the design of the security system itself but rather its dissemination. It is generally believed that the design of a security system should be open rather than secret. Although encryption keys, for example, must be secret, the encryption mechanisms that use them should be open to public scrutiny. They can then be reviewed by many experts, and users can therefore have high confidence in them. In practice, encryption mechanisms are not completely public, and attempts are being made to control the dissemination of encryption research.[18]

Protection techniques in hardware and operating systems. Computing systems are typically shared by many users and many applications. The needs and privileges of these users and applications vary, and they differ as a whole from the needs and privileges of such system components as the operating system.

The hardware provides protection features that isolate the executing programs from one another, protect the operating system from user programs, and allow only the operating system to perform such sensitive operations as physical I/O.

We begin our discussion with two of the most important and most universal of such features, states of privilege and virtual memory. The discussion makes use of the process concept introduced earlier in this paper in the discussion of the access matrix model.

States of privilege. Certain machine instructions are intended for use by the operating system only. These include, for example, I/O instructions and the instructions that control the protection features themselves. In most computers, these instructions are valid only when the processor is executing in a privileged state. On System/370,[19] for example, the supervisor state contrasts with the problem state, which is used for application programs. A machine can have a number of privileged states, and these states can be used for different operating-system functions that themselves vary in privilege. The VAX-11/780[20] has the following four states, called *access modes*: (1) Kernel, the most privileged state, which is used for interrupt handling and physical I/O; (2) Executive, for higher-level I/O functions; (3) Supervisor, for command interpretation; and (4) User. Multics[21] generalizes the state concept, providing a number of *rings* of privilege.

Virtual memory. Virtual memory, although its primary function is to expand the memory available to programs, is a valuable protection feature. The real memory of a computer provides a numbered sequence of cells that must be shared by all processes and all operating system components. A virtual memory is a corresponding sequence that can be used by a program as if it were real. The virtual memory seen by one process is not the same as that seen by another process. For example, the real memory might provide one million bytes, whereas each process sees a virtual memory of 16 million bytes. The virtual memories of the different processes either do not overlap at all or overlap at one end to allow the processes to share the system code that resides there. Thus one process has absolutely no access to the private data and code of another process.

The virtual memory is considered as divided into *pages*, in which the page size is 2048 or 4096 bytes on the System/370 and 512 bytes on the VAX-11/780.

The real memory is divided into *frames* of the same size. Page tables keep track of where each page is, either in a frame of real memory or on a storage device. Upon each memory reference, either the virtual address is translated by hardware into the corresponding real address or—if the page is not in real memory—an interrupt occurs. The needed page

---

A capability is a ticket that allows its holder to gain access to a specified object.

---

is then brought into real memory. Many systems (System/370, for example) also use a larger unit than the page, which is termed a *segment*.

States of privilege and virtual memory can be used together to enforce appropriate access rights for processes. In the VAX-11 the page-table entry for each page specifies the kind of access (Write, Read, or none) that is allowed from each access mode. The access mode of a process changes during execution because it calls or returns from system procedures, and different pages become accessible.

Virtual machine systems. A still more powerful concept is that of the *virtual machine*. With a virtual machine system, such as VM/370,[22] each user has the illusion of commanding an entire computer, including a processor, memory, and I/O devices. All these virtual machines, however, are implemented by a single, real computing system. This structure provides a higher degree of isolation between users than virtual memory because the virtual machines are logically independent.

Capability systems. A different approach to protection uses *capabilities*. A capability can be described as a ticket that allows its holder to gain a specified type of access to a specified object. Capability protection is usually implemented by special hardware or microcode that interprets capabilities when they are used and prevents them from being wrongly copied or manufactured. Because capabilities can be

passed around and stored, they make possible very flexible protection schemes. Flexibility, however, can also lead to difficulty in controlling and auditing the capabilities that have been given out and in selectively revoking capabilities. An example of a capability machine is the Cambridge CAP system.[23]

The kernel approach. A line of research by the U.S. Department of Defense that has resulted in several experimental operating systems is based on the concept of a *security kernel*, which is a relatively small portion of the operating system that is responsible for enforcing security policy. Inasmuch as the kernel mediates all accesses, flaws in other portions of the operating system do not threaten security. The kernel itself must be tamperproof. That is, there must be no way to modify it or interfere with its behavior. The kernel must be verifiable in that it is possible to demonstrate convincingly that the design correctly implements the system's security policy and that the programs of the kernel correctly implement the design. It is, of course, essential to the kernel approach that the security policy be concretely and formally stated. Nearly all of the kernel-based systems use the Bell and LaPadula model. At the present time, we know of no commercially available kernelized approaches to security.

One way of verifying a kernel is to prove that it is correct, and special languages and verification programs have been developed for this purpose.[24] Other ways involve careful scrutiny of the code by experts and penetration attempts by "tiger teams." From a security point of view, it is not necessary to demonstrate that the kernel is correct in all respects, but that it correctly implements security policy. Other tests, of course, are necessary to demonstrate its efficacy as an operating system component.

Hardware support for the kernel approach includes the following: the checking of each memory access and the provision of independent control for different types of access; the isolation of the kernel by such methods as a kernel mode or by implementation of the kernel in read-only memory; support for the process concept; and efficient switching between modes and between processes.

One operating system that takes a kernel approach is KVM/370,[25] which is based on the VM/370 virtual machine system. The functions of the VM/370 component that implements virtual machines—the monitor—are split between a security kernel and a set of nonkernel monitors, one per security level. Each nonkernel monitor supports all the virtual machines at its level, and the kernel enforces the military security policy. Discussions of the kernel approach can be found in References 26 through 28.

User authentication techniques. A prerequisite for almost any kind of security is the accurate identification of users. By *authentication*, the system verifies the user's claim of identity. The most widely used authentication technique is the *password*, which is a string of characters known only to the system and to

---

Often a one-way transformation is used for the stored passwords.

---

the user that the user must provide to gain access to a system. The system stores each user's password for comparison with the password presented by the user. Often a one-way transformation is used for the stored passwords, so that they are not intelligible even if they are accidentally printed. The system then applies the same transformation to the password supplied by the user before it is compared with the stored password. A password scheme is economical and acceptable to most users, and it is easy to implement.

A password scheme has a number of problems, however. Although the method depends on the secrecy of the password, it is common for users to write down passwords in exposed places or divulge them to others. Other persons can observe the keying in of a password. If the terminal is itself a computer, it can try many passwords in a relatively short time. A system can guard against this by allowing only a few erroneous attempts. Another method that has been used to learn a password is *spoofing*, by which a user of a time-sharing system writes a program that generates a display exactly like the system's sign-on display. The program is started, and the terminal is left to be used by a victim. The victim unknowingly communicates his or her password to the first user's program. With knowledge of the password, the spoofer can be authenticated in place of the victim.

Another authentication technique involves a machine-readable object possessed by the user, such as a card or badge. With such objects, there is the danger of loss, theft, or forgery of the object.

Promising techniques that are still in the research stage involve recognizing some characteristic of the user—voice, hand, fingerprint, or signature. Such a technology must be both accurate and cheap if it is to be widely used.

Logging. Logging consists of recording events so that they can be monitored at a later time. This record is called a log or audit trail. Although logging is a valuable technique for both deterring and detecting unauthorized actions, it does not prevent such actions. Logging can be performed by applications, by data base management systems, or by special access-control software. Operating systems sometimes provide basic logging facilities that can be used by these other components. A typical entry in a log might include the following: the user's identity; transaction or job identifier; name of the object being accessed (a file, for example); type of access; data values actually read or written; and date and time. Useful features in a logging facility include the following: ways to specify the events to be logged without actually programming the logging; ways to start and stop logging of selected events dynamically; and programs to generate reports from the log.

Encryption. Encryption predates computers by many centuries. The technique consists of *encrypting* or *enciphering* data by transforming them into a form that cannot be understood. The encrypted data are useful only to someone who possesses the special knowledge needed to restore them to their original form. Encryption can be used for data stored on such external media as tapes or removable disk volumes, for data transmitted over communication lines, and for data stored in the computing system.

The process of encryption takes a sequence of *plaintext*, P, applies to it an encryption procedure, E, which is controlled by a *key*, K, to produce a *ciphertext* C. To recover the original plaintext, the process applies a *decryption* procedure, D, controlled by the same key K. These processes may be expressed as follows:

Encryption: $C = E_K(P)$
Decryption: $P = D_K(C)$

In conventional encryption systems the key, K, is

secret, and the encryption and decryption procedures, E and D, are normally public.

The strength of an encryption system, that is, its resistance to being broken, can be described in terms of the kinds of attacks it can survive. The strongest type of attack is the "chosen plaintext attack," whereby the attacker can submit any amount of any plaintext and determine the corresponding ciphertext. Current encryption systems are designed to withstand chosen plaintext attacks.

In 1977, the U.S. National Bureau of Standards adopted the Data Encryption Standard (DES).[29,30] The DES uses the same algorithm for both encryption and decryption. It uses a 64-bit key (of which eight bits are for parity checking) to encrypt 64-bit blocks of plaintext. One reason for adopting a standard was to encourage the development of inexpensive implementations of the algorithm. A number of hardware DES devices are now marketed.

The DES is a *private key* system in that the keys are kept secret. One of the problems in private key systems is that of finding a way to securely distribute and maintain the keys. There have been proposed *public key* systems that make use of two keys or procedures: a public procedure, E, for encryption and a private procedure, D, for decryption. A public procedure, E, is associated with each subscriber to the system. The two procedures must have the property that for any plaintext, P, $D[E(P)] = P$. Also, it must not be possible to derive D from E. To send a message to subscriber A we encrypt with E_A. This encrypted message can be decrypted only by the possessor of D_A, namely A. Public key systems are quite promising and have important applications, such as digital signatures. However, research is still needed to develop practical algorithms that meet the requirements of the method.

Encryption, although an extremely valuable technique, does not solve all security problems. It cannot prevent destruction of data, and it is difficult to apply to data as used within the computing system. Its application in network security is described in a later section. More information about cryptography may be found in References 31–33.

Software packages for access control. A number of software packages provide access control and related functions. The market for these programs appears to be growing as users become more concerned about security. Examples are ACF2,[34] RACF,[35,36] and Top

Secret.[37] Typical functions provided by such packages are authenticating users, maintaining access control information, checking authorization to use files or other objects, logging, and producing reports.

> **A passive intruder listens to the communications and an active intruder can alter or insert messages.**

RACF, for example, allows files, storage volumes, applications, data base transactions, or user-defined resources to be specified as protected objects. RACF maintains the access control list for each object. Users may belong to groups and receive all the privileges of their groups. RACF is basically an *open system* in that resources not defined to RACF are not protected. ACF2 is a *closed system*, in which resources not defined to ACF2 are protected. RACF can, however, provide closed-system protection for any specified set of resources.

Communication and network security

Since users increasingly access computing systems from remote locations, careful attention must be given to communication security. Also increasingly important is security when connecting computers into networks. Because of their relatedness, we consider communication and network security together.

The transmission mechanisms used for data communications are vulnerable to two types of intrusion. A *passive intruder* listens to the communications, and an *active intruder* can alter or insert messages, or retransmit valid messages. Both types of intrusion can be accomplished through wiretapping, that is, by physically connecting to a communication path. Passive intrusion can be done by picking up microwave or satellite transmissions. Vulnerabilities also exist at switching centers, which are themselves computing systems, and in the interfaces of computing systems (*nodes*) to the network. These vulnerabilities are of great practical importance in applications such as Electronic Funds Transfer (EFT),[38,39] where billions of dollars are transferred daily, and a single message can involve millions of dollars.

The following are some of the objectives of network security measures: protect privacy by preventing unauthorized listening to messages; authenticate users and messages; prevent disruption of network operation (which can occur through blocking message delivery, altering messages, or overloading the network); and assist in access control. Physical security measures such as buried cables can help, but the most important measure is encryption.

Use of encryption. One issue in the encryption of messages is the level of the computing system at which the encryption is done. The most efficient place to do encryption is just before the message goes out on the communication line. At that point, encryption can be done in conjunction with other manipulations, such as compression, packet formation, or check-sum calculation. This is called *data link encryption*.[40] A weakness of this method is that either a single key must be used for all communications between a pair of nodes, or some central authority must be entrusted with all users' keys. Also, security of a message depends on correct functioning of all the levels of system software that intervene between the user and the communication line. In *end-to-end encryption* the key is chosen by the user or application and is not divulged to other system components except the encryption mechanism itself. The key can be changed whenever there has been a chance of compromise. A discussion of end-to-end security measures is found in Reference 41.

One of the greatest difficulties in managing network security is *key distribution*. Typically, with secret-key systems, a key is required for each potential pair of communicators. Thus the number of keys is large, and, at the same time, they must be distributed in some secure way. One approach is a Key Distribution Center (KDC) that maintains all the keys and by prearrangement has a special key for communicating with each node on the network. When one node wants to communicate with another it asks the KDC to send session-keys to both participants. Such an approach is vulnerable to failure or congestion of the KDC. One possible refinement might be that of distributing the key-distribution function among all the nodes.

Public-key systems have similar problems. Here there is no need to distribute secret keys, but there

is a need to keep the public listing of keys correct and up-to-date. The keeper of this listing must authenticate all changes. A sender who has been given the public key of a potential receiver needs assurance that it is correct. Key distribution is discussed in References 42 to 45.

Authentication. One of the most important communication security procedures is that of the authentication of users. For example, passwords can be compromised by passive intrusion if they are communicated in plaintext. One technique for overcoming this is for the system to call the user back by way

> **One of the most important communication security procedures is that of the authentication of users.**

of a list of telephone numbers that it keeps. This at least restricts access to authorized locations. Messages must also be authenticated. The authentication of a message means that the receiver of a message validates it in the face of possible message alteration or insertion. The use of digital signatures—discussed in the next section—is one possible way of authenticating both users and messages.

Digital signatures. A paper transaction, such as a check or order, is typically authenticated by a handwritten signature. Electronic transactions need *digital signatures*.[46] Various schemes have been developed to use encryption for this purpose. A digital signature scheme has several requirements. It should not be possible to forge a signature. The receiver must be able to validate the signature at the time the message is received and must also be able to demonstrate at a later time that a valid message was received. The sender should not be able later to repudiate the message.

Both public-key and conventional encryption have been proposed as the bases for signature schemes, and they are summarized in References 44, 45, and 47. In the public-key method, the sender encrypts the message with his own private key, and the re-

Figure 4 Employee table

NAME	DEPT.	SALARY	MANAGER
BALL	COMPUTER	35000	CHAN
CHOW	SHIPPING	18000	DIAZ
FOX	COMPUTER	39000	CHAN
KATZ	MAIL	19000	ROTH
WOOD	BUILDING	27000	LEE

Figure 5 Restricted view of employee table

NAME	DEPT.	MANAGER
BALL	COMPUTER	CHAN
FOX	COMPUTER	CHAN

ceiver decrypts it with the sender's public key. If the resulting message is intelligible, it is valid. Without additional refinements, this scheme does not prevent repudiation of messages, for example, by asserting that a key has been compromised and someone has forged the message. Neither does the method allow validation at a later time. The conventional scheme requires a central authority to encrypt and later authenticate signatures. Development of digital signature schemes is continuing. (See, for example, Reference 48.) The practical success of digital signatures depends not only on technology but also on the legal and procedural environments in which these signatures are used.

Security of local area networks. A local area network (LAN) consists of computers and related devices that are connected within a limited geographical area, such as one or a few buildings; it is usually privately owned. Although not as vulnerable as long-haul networks, local area networks cannot be regarded as secure. Cables or other transmission media are located throughout the local area and are thus subject to intrusion. Each node in the network must have a way to authenticate messages arriving from other nodes, especially if these messages are requests for data and services. Proposed security methods for LANS use encryption to provide for authentication and access control. Encryption is used to create *protected identifiers* that behave something like capabilities and that cannot be forged or used if stolen. One proposal uses public-key encryption[49] and another uses conventional encryption.[50]

Data base security

Data bases contain structured data that are maintained by a *data base management system* (DBMS). A DBMS is usually a separate software component that runs on top of the operating system and provides the additional functions to use the data base. A DBMS may also include functions to manage transactions. A DBMS assumes one or more data models upon which the data are structured, such as relations (tables), hierarchies, or networks. As an example of a data model, consider a tabular or relational arrangement as shown in Figure 4.

Data base applications typically require a fine *granularity of access control*, which means that access is controlled not according to tables as a whole but according to certain columns and rows of tables. This is sometimes called field-level access control. A DBMS usually provides its own access control, using the operating system only to protect the large containers (segments or files) in which the data are stored.

One way to provide field-level access control is through *views*, which can be constructed from one or more of the basic data base tables. A view can eliminate columns or rows. For example, the view in Figure 5 eliminates from the employee table of Figure 4 the SALARY column and all rows except those for employees in the COMPUTER department. Then each user is given access to required views only. Views that eliminate rows provide data-dependent access control, so called because the user's access to a specific row depends on the data values in that row.

Another way to provide fine granularity of access control is to encapsulate sets of allowed accesses in precompiled transactions and to grant users access to certain transactions only.

DBMS authorization facilities. Some DBMSs provide facilities that allow certain users to specify access control information. These users are termed *authorizers*, and they may be a central person or group. Alternatively, authorization may be decentralized, with each group or individual owning or controlling a portion of the total data base. For example, in Structured Query Language (SQL)[51,52] the user who creates a new table can perform any operation on that table, can grant another user any of these privileges, and can revoke the grant. The grant can also allow the recipient to grant the privileges to still another user.

Because the complex validations required in data base systems can degrade performance if not carefully implemented, considerable attention has been given to reducing overhead by designing the systems to do some of the work prior to execution time (at compile time, for example). More information about authorization and enforcement of data base security can be found in Reference 1.

Security of statistical data bases. This section summarizes research on the security of statistical data bases. A statistical data base is one that contains information about individual persons, which data

---

The threat to confidentiality in a statistical data base comes from the potential for drawing an inference.

---

must remain confidential, although statistical summaries, such as counts or sums, are freely available. Examples of statistical data bases are census data and medical research data. The threat to confidentiality in a statistical data base comes from the potential for drawing an *inference*. This means that a user may be able to correlate statistical summaries and his own prior knowledge, which may lead to compromise or disclosure.

The data model used in statistical data base research uses a set of *records* for *n* individuals. Fields of the records contain values of *attributes* (such as sex, age, or salary). Users query the data base under the assumption that there is no change to the data base between queries of a potential intruder. We now introduce the following terminology:

- *n*: the number of records in the data base.
- *C*: a characteristic formula, such as SEX = 'MALE' AND AGE < 30.
- Query: "What is the average age of all males in the data base?" for example.
- Query set: the set of records satisfying *C*.

It is easy to compromise a data base when the query set size is small. For example, one can ask for the average age where NAME = 'JOE' and learn Joe's age. User Dave can ask for the average age of Joe and Dave. It might seem reasonable to control such compromises by requiring the query set size to be greater than some minimum. Any queries with the required query set sizes would be considered *answerable*. Set size, however, is not a sufficient condition. To see why, consider an intruder who develops a formula called a *tracker*, which is a method of allowing compromise in spite of limits for answerable queries. A tracker for a specific individual can be developed quite easily if the intruder has prior knowledge of an answerable query that uniquely characterizes the individual. Even a *general tracker*, which works for anyone in the data base, can often be guessed in a reasonable number of tries.

Certain defenses can be used against compromise by a tracker. One defensive technique is to perturb the data by adding to them (either before or after computing the statistic) a pseudo-random value that depends on the data. Another defense is to release only a random sample of the original data base. This technique is used successfully for census data, but it is not practical for use in a rapidly changing data base. Audit trails can detect, but not prevent, sequences of queries that attempt compromise.

Other kinds of defense are being studied. For example, *data swapping*, a technique under research, attempts to build a new data base containing records different from the original data base that produces the same statistics as the original data base. Another technique, called *random sample queries*, randomly determines which records are in a sampled query set and computes the statistic from this sampled set. More information about these techniques can be found in References 53 to 56.

In summary, a growing body of research has revealed that most statistical data bases are subject to compromise. This same research, however, is directed toward devising useful defenses against compromise.

Administrative security measures

This section surveys security practices that are primarily administrative in nature. Administrative security practices are covered in greater detail in Reference 57.

Physical security. Among the administrative measures are physical security practices, which include controlling access to sensitive areas, such as the computing facility and the data processing department as a whole. Many organizations have a policy of not allowing anyone but operators into the computer room. Access to terminals, especially those used for sensitive applications, may also be controlled. Employee cooperation in enforcing the access restrictions is often preferable to elaborate locks and fences. Libraries for the storage of tapes and disks have a separate area with their own separate authorized personnel.

Classification of data. An organization needs an explicit policy for the confidentiality of data. Some companies define three or four levels of sensitivity

---

The auditing profession is deeply involved with security.

---

and prescribe handling and disclosure procedures for data in each level. The policy should be made known in writing to each employee at hiring and periodically thereafter.

Personnel considerations. Appropriate care in hiring and dealing with employees is of course important for security. Administrative practices[57] that can enhance individual security include the following: ensuring that vacations are taken; periodically rotating assignments, but with an unpredictable schedule; providing grievance channels to allow employees to discuss sources of dissatisfaction without jeopardizing their positions; evaluating performance periodically with supervisors trained to recognize such danger signals as refusal of vacations or promotions, alcohol, or gambling; employment termination procedures (avoiding layoffs, if possible, and carrying out terminations fairly, exit interviews, the changing of passwords, and notification of other employees). In general, these practices are directed at avoiding situations where employees are motivated to misuse computers and to interrupt their access to computers on a schedule that is not entirely within their control. Some security advisors advocate the prosecution of employees who have embezzled and the dismissal of

those who have violated security policy. Inasmuch as security is not an organization's only objective, it may be a valid choice to seek an optimum position between security and a trusting attitude in employee relations. Therefore, based on the belief that employees will do the right thing if they clearly know their responsibilities, counseling often takes precedence over immediate dismissal.

Auditing and controls. The auditing profession is deeply involved with security, and there is a specialty within auditing, called EDP audit, that deals with computerized aspects of systems. The internal auditors employed by an organization maintain the organization's system of internal controls, and one function of the external auditors is to conduct periodic reviews of those controls. Controls include a wide variety of measures, many of which can be viewed as security measures. More information about audit and control in computer environments can be found in References 1 and 57 to 59.

Computer security auditing aims at identifying and evaluating the security measures for a specific installation. Rahden[60] lists five types of computer security auditing: (1) system development audit of the procedures which are intended to ensure that only secure systems are developed; (2) application review of the security controls in the design of a specific application; (3) installation security review of all controls of the installation (administrative, technical, or physical); (4) security function review of all generalized security functions that apply to multiple departments or applications, such as those of a data base management system; and (5) controlled test or penetration study to demonstrate security weaknesses.

Implementing a security program. In this section we discuss how an organization sets up a security program. The thoughts presented are based in part on IBM security practices.[61,62]

The first step is to establish a policy about information assets and computer security. This policy serves to set direction and to guide management and all employees. The keystone to such a policy is the enthusiastic support of the chief executive officer. The policy is presented to all line and staff units, and it is reviewed regularly and updated as needs and methods change.

In content, a security policy defines broad responsibilities for functional management, owners of information, users of information, and providers of service. More detailed guidelines and instructions are covered separately.

A security management function is established, involving one or more management and staff people, depending on the size and complexity of the organization. This security management function coordinates the organization-wide security program. Direct responsibility for implementing the program belongs to line management. The security manager assists line managers in interpreting and implementing the policy for their units.

If the security program is to work, employees must understand the need for it and must support it. Therefore, an education program is designed and presented to the employees. The education program includes the training of managers, present employees, and new employees as they are hired. Employees are also updated on changes as organizational needs and security methods change.

An important step is to classify the data according to their sensitivity, and to establish a written policy on handling data of each type. Also, all data should have an *owner* who is responsible for their protection. Many organizations tend to leave the responsibility for security with the data processing organization. This is inappropriate, because it is the owners and users of the data who suffer the losses if something happens to their data.

Another important step is a *risk analysis*.[63] Risk analysis, as described in Reference 64, has two main aspects: (1) analyzing threats, and (2) identifying the undesirable events that can result. Threat analysis also identifies the security weaknesses that can permit each threat. Consider, for example, the threat that an unauthorized user may access the system from a remote terminal by means of a password found on a printout in the trash. Security weaknesses in this example are (1) inadequate physical security of the terminal; (2) failure to suppress printing of passwords; and (3) inadequate physical security of sensitive trash. These undesirable events are usually categorized as follows: unauthorized disclosure, modification and destruction of data, and denial of service.

Once the risks have been analyzed, a *risk assessment* is carried out. The undesirable events are rated and ranked according to severity. These ratings are not mathematically precise; rather, they put risks into a priority order. The likelihood of each event is then related to its acceptability. A program of security

measures is then developed, with the cost of each measure being considered in relation to the losses it

---

There has been considerable success in developing solutions to security problems.

---

is intended to prevent. All this information can then be used as the basis for management decisions about a security program. After such a program has been implemented, it must be monitored and evaluated periodically for effectiveness.

Concluding remarks

This paper has summarized the main threats to computer security. We have introduced models that provide a conceptual framework and surveyed the technology that is developing to counter the threats. Outlined are practical steps that organizations can take to protect their data and systems from unauthorized access. Discussed to a lesser degree is denial of service. We have indicated that security is a management issue as well as a technological one. As for management, it must define its expectations, explore and quantify its risks, select and implement protective measures, and follow up by continuing to evaluate the effectiveness of its policies and measures.

There is growing awareness of security, and there has been considerable success in developing solutions to security problems. However, security rarely receives the priority it warrants. Computers have become central in our social and economic lives, and rapidly changing technology is introducing new vulnerabilities along with new kinds of uses. The sponsors and designers of the new uses most especially need to foresee and avoid access and service vulnerabilities.

Cited references

1. E. B. Fernandez, R. C. Summers, and C. Wood, *Database Security and Integrity,* Addison-Wesley Publishing Company, Reading, MA (1981).
2. *Personal Privacy in an Information Society, Report of the Privacy Protection Study Commission,* U.S. Government Printing Office, Stock No. 052-003-00395-3, Washington, DC (July 1977).

3. R. Turn, *Trusted Computer Systems: Needs and Incentives for Use in Government and the Private Sector*, The Rand Corporation, Santa Monica, CA (June 1981).

4. "OECD guidelines governing the protection of privacy and transborder flows of personal data," *Computer Networks* **5**, No. 2, 127–141 (April 1981).

5. H. Baruch, "The Foreign Corrupt Practices Act," *Harvard Business Review* **57**, No. 1, 32–50 (January-February 1979).

6. J. K. Taber, "A survey of computer crime studies," *Computer/Law Journal* **2**, No. 2, 275–327 (Spring 1980).

7. D. B. Parker, "Vulnerabilities of EFTs to intentionally caused losses," *Communications of the ACM* **22**, No. 12, 654–660 (December 1979).

8. D. E. Denning and P. J. Denning, "Data security," *Computing Surveys* **11**, No. 3, 227–249 (September 1979).

9. C. J. Date, *An Introduction to Database Systems*, Vol. II, Addison-Wesley Publishing Company, Reading, MA (1983).

10. W. S. McPhee, "Operating-system integrity in OS/VS2," *IBM Systems Journal* **13**, No. 3, 230–252 (1974).

11. B. W. Lampson, "Protection," *Proceedings of the 5th Annual Princeton Conference on Information Sciences and Systems* (1971), pp. 437–443. Reprinted in *ACM Operating Systems Review* **8**, No. 1, 18–24 (January 1974).

12. C. E. Landwehr, "Formal models for computer security," *Computing Surveys* **13**, No. 3, 247–278 (September 1981).

13. D. E. Bell and L. J. LaPadula, *Secure Computer System: Unified Exposition and Multics Interpretation*, Report ESD-TR-75-306, MITRE Corporation, Bedford, MA (March 1976).

14. J. K. Millen, "Security kernel validation in practice," *Communications of the ACM* **19**, No. 5, 243–250 (May 1976).

15. D. E. Denning, "A lattice model of secure information flow," *Communications of the ACM* **19**, No. 5, 236–243 (May 1976).

16. J. H. Saltzer and M. D. Schroeder, "The protection of information in computer systems," *Proceedings of the IEEE* **63**, No. 9, 1278–1308 (September 1975).

17. G. J. Popek, "A principle of kernel design," *AFIPS Conference Proceedings* **43**, National Computer Conference (1974), pp. 977–978.

18. P. J. Denning, "A scientist's view of government control over scientific publication," *Communications of the ACM* **25**, No. 2, 95–97 (February 1982).

19. *IBM System/370 Principles of Operation*, GA22-7000, IBM Corporation; available through IBM branch offices.

20. W. D. Strecker, "VAX-11/780—A virtual address extension to the DEC PDP-11 family," in *Computer Structures: Principles and Examples*, D. P. Siewiorek, C. G. Bell, and A. Newell, Editors, McGraw-Hill Book Co., Inc., New York, 1982, pp. 716–729.

21. J. H. Saltzer, "Protection and the control of information sharing in Multics," *Communications of the ACM* **17**, No. 7, 388–402 (July 1974).

22. L. H. Seawright and R. A. MacKinnon, "VM/370—A study of multiplicity and usefulness," *IBM Systems Journal* **18**, No. 1, 4–17 (1979).

23. M. V. Wilkes and R. M. Needham, *The Cambridge CAP Computer and Its Operating System*, Elsevier North-Holland Publishing Co., New York (1979).

24. M. H. Cheheyl, M. Gasser, G. A. Huff, and J. K. Millen, "Verifying security," *Computing Surveys* **13**, No. 3, 279–339 (September 1981).

25. B. D. Gold, "A security retrofit of VM/370," *AFIPS Conference Proceedings* **48**, National Computer Conference (1979), pp. 335–344.

26. S. R. Ames, M. Glasser, and R. R. Schell, "Security kernel design and implementation: An introduction," *Computer* **16**, No. 7, 14–22 (July 1983).

27. R. R. Schell, "A security kernel for a multiprocessor microcomputer," *Computer* **16**, No. 7, 47–53 (July 1983).

28. C. E. Landwehr, "The best available technologies for computer security," *Computer* **16**, No. 7, 86–100 (July 1983).

29. *Data Encryption Standard*, National Bureau of Standards, Washington, DC, FIPS Publication 46 (January 1977).

30. W. F. Ehrsam, S. M. Matyas, C. H. Meyer, and W. L. Tuchman, "A cryptographic key management scheme for implementing the Data Encryption Standard," *IBM Systems Journal* **17**, No. 2, 106–125 (1978).

31. W. Diffie and M. E. Hellman, "Privacy and authentication: An introduction to cryptography," in *Tutorial: The Security of Data in Networks*, D. W. Davis, Editor, IEEE Computer Society, 5855 Naples Plaza, Suite 301, Long Beach, CA 90803 (1981).

32. A. Lempel, "Cryptology in transition," *Computing Surveys* **11**, No. 4, 285–303 (December 1979).

33. D. E. Denning, *Cryptography and Data Security*, Addison-Wesley Publishing Company, Reading, MA (1982).

34. D. Botnick, "Mellon Bank prepares staff to receive data security package," *Bank Systems and Equipment* **20**, No. 6, 72–73 (June 1983).

35. *OS/VS2 MVS Resource Access Control Facility (RACF) General Information Manual*, GC28-0722, IBM Corporation; available through IBM branch offices.

36. H. M. Gladney, "Administrative control of computing service," *IBM Systems Journal* **17**, No. 2, 151–178 (1978).

37. J. D. Whalen, "A false sense of security," *Infosystems* **30**, No. 8, 100–103 (August 1983).

38. B. Bosworth, "Computer and EFT system security," *Review of Business* **4**, No. 2, 9–11, 30 (1982).

39. B. Streeter, "People, more than technology, are still key to EFT security," *ABA Banking Journal* **74**, No. 7, 29–37 (July 1982).

40. A. S. Tanenbaum, *Computer Networks*, Prentice-Hall, Inc., Englewood Cliffs, NJ (1981).

41. V. L. Voydock and S. T. Kent, "Security mechanisms in high-level network protocols," *Computing Surveys* **15**, No. 2, 135–171 (June 1983).

42. S. M. Matyas and C. H. Meyer, "Generation, distribution, and installation of cryptographic keys," *IBM Systems Journal* **17**, No. 2, 126–137 (1978).

43. R. M. Needham and M. D. Schroeder, "Using encryption for authentication in large networks of computers," *Communications of the ACM* **21**, No. 12, 993–999 (December 1978).

44. G. J. Popek and C. S. Kline, "Encryption and secure computer networks," *Computing Surveys* **11**, No. 4, 331–356 (December 1979).

45. D. E. Denning, "Protecting public keys and signature keys," *Computer* **16**, No. 2, 27–35 (February 1983).

46. S. G. Akl, "Digital signatures: A tutorial survey," *Computer* **16**, No. 2, 15–24 (February 1983).

47. S. M. Matyas, "Digital signatures—An overview," *Computer Networks* **3**, No. 2, 87–94 (April 1979).

48. H. Meijer and S. Akl, "Digital signature schemes for computer communication networks," *Proceedings of the 7th Data Communications Symposium*, 1981, pp. 37–41; available from the Association for Computing Machinery, Inc., 11 West 42nd Street, New York, NY 10036.

49. J. E. Donnelly and J. G. Fletcher, "Resource access control in a network operating system," *Proceedings of the ACM Pacific Regional Conference* (1980), pp. 115–126.

50. D. M. Nessett, "Identifier protection in a distributed operating system," *Operating Systems Review* **16**, No. 1, 26–31 (January 1982).

51. *SQL/Data System: Planning and Administration,* SH24-5014, IBM Corporation; available through IBM branch offices.
52. D. J. Haderle and R. D. Jackson, "IBM Database 2 overview," *IBM Systems Journal* **23**, No. 2, 112–125 (1984).
53. D. E. Denning, "Secure statistical databases with random sample queries," *ACM Transactions on Database Systems* **5**, No. 3, 291–315 (September 1980).
54. J. Schlörer, "Disclosure from statistical databases: Quantitative aspects of trackers," *ACM Transactions on Database Systems* **5**, No. 4, 467–492 (December 1980).
55. J. Schlörer, "Security of statistical databases: Multidimensional transformation," *ACM Transactions on Database Systems* **6**, No. 1, 95–112 (March 1981).
56. D. E. Denning and J. Schlörer, "Inference controls for statistical databases," *Computer* **16**, No. 7, 69–82 (July1983).
57. L. I. Krauss and A. MacGahan, *Computer Fraud and Countermeasures,* Prentice-Hall, Inc., Englewood Cliffs, NJ (1979).
58. *Systems Auditability and Control Study,* Report of the Institute of Internal Auditors, Altamonte Springs, FL (1977).
59. R. P. Fisher, *Information Systems Security,* Prentice-Hall, Inc., Englewood Cliffs, NJ (1984).
60. H. R. Rahden, "Computer security auditing," *WESCON 1979 Conference Record* **14**, No. 3, 345–351 (1979). Reprinted in *Advances in Computer System Security,* R. Turn, Editor, Artech House, Dedham, MA (1981).
61. *Staying in Charge, An Executive Briefing for Improving Control of Your Information System,* G505-0058, IBM Corporation; available through IBM branch offices.
62. *Information Systems Security: Execution Checklist. Security is a Management Issue,* GX20-2430, IBM Corporation; available through IBM branch offices.
63. S. Fordyce, "Computer security: A current assessment," *Computers and Security* **1**, No. 1, 9–16 (January 1982).
64. R. P. Campbell and G. A. Sands, "A modular approach to computer security risk management," *AFIPS Conference Proceedings* **48**, *National Computer Conference,* AFIPS Press, Arlington, VA (1979), pp. 293–303.

General reference

K. S. Shankar, "The total computer security problem: An overview," *Computer* **10**, No. 6, 50–73 (June 1977).

Reprint Order No. G321-5227.

Rita C. Summers *IBM Los Angeles Scientific Center, 11601 Wilshire Boulevard, Los Angeles, California 90025.* Since joining IBM in 1964, Ms. Summers has designed and implemented systems for interactive applications, computer-assisted instruction, and numerical control. She has received two IBM Outstanding Contribution Awards for her work on virtual memory systems. Currently, Ms. Summers is a senior programmer and project leader for the development of a prototype resource-sharing system for personal computers. Her work in the area of computer security includes leadership of a project that developed a design for a secure data base system. She has participated in the development and teaching of courses on data base security in both IBM and universities, and is the author of technical reports, conference papers, and articles on data base security. Ms. Summers is a coauthor with E. B. Fernandez and C. Wood of the book *Database Security and Integrity,* published by Addison-Wesley Publishing Company, Reading, MA (1981). Before joining IBM, she worked as a systems analyst and programmer at the Ramo-Wooldridge Corporation. She received her B.A. and M.A. degrees from the University of California at Los Angeles.

Security considerations for personal computers

by W. H. Murray

The wide use of personal computers and general access to telecommunications links have intensified the need for computer security. Security practices as discussed in this paper relate to protecting an organization's personal computers as physical property, protecting the organization's data and applications, and protecting the organization itself. These matters are discussed from the point of view of protection from the improper use of personal computers.

Users and managers of personal computers are becoming increasingly aware of the necessity to protect the computers, their applications and data, and the organization from unauthorized or unintended events.[1-6] In this paper we deal with the identification and selection of protective practices. This process begins with the identification of the resources to be protected and the hazards to be avoided. The personal computer is itself valuable and therefore must be protected from damage, destruction, misuse, or conversion. It also contains data that must be protected from modification, destruction, or disclosure, as well as applications that likewise must be protected from tampering or interference. And, of course, the business organization, its other computers and applications and their data, must be protected from failures, errors, or malicious acts related to personal computers on the part of their users.

Protecting the personal computer

Because the personal computer is a valuable piece of office equipment, it should be protected as valuable property. As it is for office equipment, this protection is usually afforded by the normal office environment. Whereas special protection may be required for the data—as later discussed in this paper—it is not normally necessary for the equipment. However, protective shells and cabinets are available and should be used as required.[7,8]

Some people assume that because a personal computer is a "computer" it must be placed in the same kind of protective computer room environment as is normally provided for large-scale computers, including special environmental conditioning, fire suppression, and personnel access controls. Such a level of protection is not usually necessary for personal computers. First, because they are low-power devices, they generate less heat than a light bulb. Second, they are designed for use in a wider range of temperature and humidity than is usually found in an office. Third, personal computers are neither more vulnerable to fire nor more likely to cause a fire than other office equipment. Finally, personal computers are neither more valuable nor more sensitive to interference than other office equipment. Copiers, for example, often cost more than personal computers as well as having some potential for interference and abuse. In comparison with a large computer, large-scale systems incorporate highly privileged override controls. These privileged controls are reserved to management to protect one user from others. On the other hand, personal computers normally have a single user, and all controls are reserved to that user.

As for insurance, the same kind of insurance that covers other office equipment also covers personal computers.[9,10] Many large organizations self-insure their office equipment. Other companies insure under policies with broad coverage that include personal computers along with other office equipment. Although it is good practice to check, only rarely is special coverage necessary. Most homeowners' policies cover personal computers in the home except where they are used for business or are otherwise specifically excluded.

Protecting data

Data must be protected from unauthorized or unintended modification, destruction, or disclosure.[11] The consequences of such tampering with the data are more a matter of the data themselves rather than of where they are stored. The expected rate of problems, however, varies with the nature of the media on which they are stored.

In primary storage. Data in primary storage are invisible except as displayed. These data can be destroyed by a power loss, a power surge, or even a jolt of static electricity. Personal computers may be more vulnerable to static electricity than other terminals or systems. Such losses are usually only annoying, but could be costly if static were to occur several hours into a long job that had no checkpoints. The risk of static electricity can be limited by an appropriate environment. Although backup power is not often used for personal computers, it is available. Power surge protectors are also available and may be used if necessary. The best protection against data destruction is to keep copies.[11] Thus, data in primary storage should be periodically saved on secondary storage.

On diskette. All other things being equal, data are less sensitive to accidental disclosure when stored on diskette than when stored on paper. On the other hand, data stored on diskette may be considerably more vulnerable to accidental erasure than the same data stored on paper.

Data recorded on diskette are usually protected from disclosure by removing the diskette from the computer and storing it in a safe place, as though the data were on paper. Occasionally disks may be used or shared in such a way as to make off-line storage infeasible, in which case the data are protected in a manner similar to that recommended for fixed disks.

Data stored on diskette may be protected from modification and destruction by the preparation of backup copies. Usually, one or two extra copies are all that are required. Since computers are very good at preparing cheap, dense, portable copies, backup

---

Some protection from erasure can be gained by making a copy of the data on the fixed disk itself.

---

copies are not unduly expensive. Thus, the risk of destruction can be made very low by producing many copies and dispersing them widely, but this low risk is achieved through an increased probability of disclosure.

On fixed disk. Data on a fixed file must be protected from accidental erasure, from failure of the device that would make it unrecoverable, and from disclosure.

Protection from erasure. As with data on diskette, data on a fixed file are protected from erasure by making copies. Some protection from erasure can be gained by making a copy of the data on the fixed disk itself. The usual practice, however, is for the copy to be placed on a diskette.

Protection from device failure. Copies on diskette are also the usual form of protection against the failure of the device itself. This is usually done by storing on a diskette with scheduled frequency those data sets that have been opened for writing since the last scheduled backup. This capability is usually provided by the operating system (including PC–DOS).[12] The frequency of backup is selected so as to balance the time required for the backup against the updates that could be lost. Given the low incidence of failure of such devices, we have found that running the backup program at least once per day or once for each session is reasonable.

Although daily or by-the-session backup is the general method for large, fixed disks, it is limited to use with large numbers of small data sets. For a small number of large data sets, the amount of data that must be written is usually large compared to the amount of data that has actually changed. Therefore, for such applications, dumping the whole file onto a tape may be the more economical method. The added cost of the tape drive may be justified on the basis of the time savings in writing large files on tape rather than on diskette.

For systems that are connected to other systems, consideration should be given to the use of those other systems for the storage of backup copies of files. This procedure use can vary in sophistication from simply uploading a file to complete applications that provide schedule management and security.

In the worst case, when it is necessary to recover a file, the time to recover is not important in the backup decisions. Recovery is done infrequently, whereas backup is done frequently. When recovery is necessary, the fact that it can be done at all makes the time required seem trivial.

Protection from disclosure. Because fixed files cannot be removed for protective storage, it is often preferable to store confidential data on diskette. However, the greater speed and size of the fixed file may justify the use of other protective measures to protect confidential data.

Safe environment. The simplest way to protect confidential data on a fixed file is to lock the room in which the file is kept. Where it is not possible to limit access to the premises where the file is kept, smaller protective environments may be used. Cabinets for personal computers and the contents of their files are available that offer protection against theft of the device itself as well as the files.[8]

Power locks. Casual browsing in a benign environment, such as a personal office in a secure building, can be prevented by mechanisms that control access to the power to the personal computer. Such devices provide lock-and-key control over the power. They may also be used with complementary devices that sound an alarm if the device is disconnected from its intended power source. In an attended environment, these devices also offer some protection against theft of the device itself.

Access control. Where concern is limited to the data rather than the property, conventional access control

mechanisms or encryption may offer the most economical protection.[13-17] Access control may be used where the device and the data are shared by several users. Not only can it exclude unauthorized users, but it can also control sharing among users. Because there is a measurable performance penalty, such access control should be reserved for situations involving the sharing of a personal computer and data.

Access controls for personal computers may resemble those for larger systems, whereby each user receives an identifier and/or a password. However,

---

Encryption is also applicable where data on portable media pass beyond the control of the owner.

---

because all users have the ability to replace the operating system with one of their own choosing, identifier-password mechanisms rely upon encryption of the files for their integrity. A file on a fixed disk is encrypted under a key belonging to the access-control mechanism. This mechanism can deliver the file in the clear text to those specified by management as having legitimate access only. Thus, a user employing his own operating system to bypass the access-control mechanism can access the encrypted file only.

File-by-file encryption employing private keys managed by the user may have an economic advantage over full access control where only a small percentage of the data is confidential and where only the device is shared but the files are not. This kind of encryption is also applicable where data on portable media, such as diskettes, must pass beyond the control of the owner and his trusted associates and to confidential files passing across communication lines.

Protecting applications

All applications must be protected from interference or contamination from outside themselves. Most such interference is unintentional rather than malicious, and annoying rather than damaging. Nonetheless, the potential exists for one application to so interfere with another as to invalidate the results, make them unusable, or even dupe or mislead the user.

Applications on a personal computer must be protected from other applications running in the same

---

To control a communication, one must control the procedures being executed.

---

system or in communicating systems. Whenever two applications share storage, it is at least conceivable that an action of one will damage data belonging to the other.[18-20] Computers that are intended for concurrent use by two or more users often implement isolation schemes to prevent this interference. Most systems that are intended for use by a single person at a time do not provide such process-to-process isolation.

Allocation of resources to processes, programs, or tasks. Therefore, the user is responsible for protecting himself from himself by allocating his resources so as to maintain the required isolation among programs. For example, a user can place programs and data for different applications on separate diskettes. On a larger scale, one can allocate the whole machine to an untested program of which the results are unpredictable. The user may test together programs intended to run together, so as to be confident that they do indeed run properly together. After taking these precautions, if one program should interfere with another, the consequences are limited to the user himself, who is best able to correct the situation.

When a program has been written by a person other than the user, the user must protect himself against the behavior of that program. He can protect data from inadvertent modification by removal from the system, and he can protect against disclosure of the

data by limiting access to the system to himself. He can protect himself from being duped by verifying the results.

Most of these precautions continue to hold true even when the personal computer is connected to a communications link. The user continues to be in control; all program actions are visible to him and require his cooperation. Nonetheless, the user can protect himself as he does when speaking on the telephone. He talks only to whom he intends; he gives only the data he intends; and he strives to protect himself from being deceived.

Control communications. A user should know with whom he is speaking, and he should originate calls or receive expected calls only. Most systems that a user calls expect data identifying him and authenticating his identity, and the systems respond with confirming data. For example, if a user dials a number and receives the expected data tone, he has probably reached the intended system. If, however, he does not receive the expected prompt, he may wish to hang up and try again. In response to the expected prompt the user must enter his identifier and password. In return, the system transmits such authenticating data as the time and date of the user's last use of the system. If the time and date received are not those that are expected, the user breaks the connection and reports his password compromised. For systems that do not offer such authenticating data, the user may compensate by looking for data that he placed in the system (preferably in the previous session) or by inquiring for data that only he and the legitimate system are likely to know.

At all times, the user retains control of the data transmitted and, in turn, transmits only intended data. In order to control a communication, one must control the procedures being executed. Therefore, users should not execute data received during a communication with a second party. Only exceptional compensating controls or a high level of trust justify deviation from this rule.

Protecting applications from the personal computer

Likewise applications running in a communicating system must be protected from applications running in a personal computer attached to the system. In general, all the controls necessary in any on-line system are also necessary when talking to a personal computer. However, a personal computer can emulate the behavior of a terminal and that of its user, and it can be programmed to mount an exhaustive attack, such as by finding an expected answer by exhausting the set of unexpected answers. Therefore,

---

Two persons should not share the same identifier, even where they share the same privileges and data.

---

on-line system controls must be rigorously applied. For example, in a system connecting with dumb terminals only and in which passwords are changed frequently, it may be reasonable to be tolerant of user errors when signing on. However, a system connecting to personal computers or to dial-up lines to which they may be connected must be intolerant of such errors. Otherwise the system may be vulnerable.

To date, much of the software that enables a personal computer to emulate a terminal requires that the personal computer be dedicated to that emulation. That is, the software permits the personal computer to function as a terminal or as a computer, but not as both at the same time. Thus such software does not support an exhaustive attack. Inasmuch as software to permit the personal computer to function as both a terminal and a computer at the same time is both desirable and feasible, it is wishful to expect this either-or situation to persist for very long.

The controls required to protect all on-line systems operating in environments assumed to be hostile are well documented.[21-29] Those controls are sparsely and inconsistently applied in most systems. On the other hand, the environment is becoming increasingly open, and, with an exploding population of personal computers that environment is potentially more hostile. Therefore, some special cautions are in order.

User identification. To protect the organization, personal accountability is becoming increasingly important in protecting applications in an environment that includes personal computers. Therefore, each individual who uses these applications must have a *personal identifier*. Personal identifiers, together with node names if used, are like addresses that persons use when writing letters to one another. In a computer, the implicit assumption is that each addressee has been previously authenticated. Under no circumstances should two persons share the same identifier, even where they share the same privileges and data.

End user authentication. For me to use the system, I must first satisfy the system that I am who I say I am. To do this I must have my own secret *password*. My password is not my address. It authenticates me to the system, and it is known by me and the system only. Passwords should be randomly chosen, frequently changed, and long enough to resist a personal-computer-assisted exhaustive trial-and-error attack lasting the entire life of the password. Passwords of three or four characters are not likely to be able to meet this test unless chosen from a large character set or changed frequently.

Access control. Again, because of the potential for exhaustive attacks, authorization to resources should be by means of a list or algorithm that associates the resources with the user name or identifier. This procedure should be used rather than relying upon passwords or lockwords assigned to the particular resources—data sets, files, commands, transactions, or privileges. Because of the potential for high-speed browsing, access rules should have safe defaults. An access default which has been found useful is that access should be implicitly restricted except as explicitly granted, rather than implicitly granted except as explicitly denied.

Administration. Because control is likely to be widely dispersed both organizationally and geographically, administrative procedures for adding and deleting users and granting and revoking authority must be both timely and consistent.[30-32] Special consideration should be given to the procedures for revoking identities and authorities for terminated users or for accounts believed to be compromised. Management must be able to recognize attacks in progress and take prompt, effective, and efficient corrective action. This may involve the most difficult set of choices that management must make. The system itself can aid management by incorporating only those procedures that do not "cry wolf." Too many false alarms condition management to believe that most alarms are false. Therefore, alarm thresholds for denied accesses must be set low enough to permit timely intervention, yet not so low as to generate too many false alarms. Maintaining management alertness is difficult, but it is not impossible. Alertness requires constant attention to detail and adjustment of the system.

Protecting the organization

In addition to protecting the personal computer, data, and applications, the organization itself must be protected from the potential negative consequences of careless, fraudulent, hostile, unlawful, or unethical uses of the personal computer. These are acts that, although authorized in the sense that all

---

Simultaneous connection to two or more systems requires the approval of the managers of those systems.

---

the controls previously discussed are being applied, may still be unintended and damaging to the organization. For example, if the vendor of a licensed software item finds a pattern of copying of that software in violation of an agreement with the organization, he might have cause for action to recover lost revenue. From the point of view of the organization, copying may be permissible or even desirable under the controls discussed. Therefore, additional controls may be required to protect the property rights of vendors and to protect management from charges of disregarding those rights.

Policy. Most employees want to do what management intends, and, if a sufficient number do act honorably, the organization will be safe from hazards. When employees fail to do what is expected, it is often because of a failure of management to communicate the expectation properly rather than through a failure of motive or intent. Where a failure of intent is involved, it is often associated with unnecessary temptation.

Therefore, it is wise for an organization to have a clear policy about the use employees are to make of

organizational resources and the behavior expected of employees. Such a policy should be so designed and implemented that it holds the employees clearly accountable for their actions. Most organizations already have such policies in place, but the application of personal computers may so change the way people work as to obscure the intended application of those policies. Again, to use the example of a vendor's property rights, an organization may have a policy that their employees will abide by the terms of all contracts and agreements entered into by the organization with its vendors. That this policy applies to personal computer programs may not even be noticed by most employees. Therefore, management may wish to communicate explicitly that employees are not to copy programs in violation of license agreements.

Guidelines. Hypothetical or suggested guidelines for employee behavior and responsibility with regard to personal computers are presented as follows:

- Employee obligation to adhere to the spirit as well as the letter of all applicable laws, regulations, contracts, licenses, policies, standards, guidelines, business controls, security rules, and other expectations.
- Restricted use of hardware, for example, to business use only.
- Rules concerning connection to other systems. For example, a connection rule might be that personal computers are to be connected only to systems specifically authorized by the appropriate management. Simultaneous connection to two or more systems would require the knowledge and approval of the managers of those systems. Simultaneous connection to a computer of this organization and a foreign system (including user-owned personal computers) would require the approval of the director of information systems.
- Responsibility for the security of hardware, software, data, and other resources.
- Responsibility for data integrity to include correctness of computer results and updating of remote data bases via authorized software and procedures only.
- Identification of the source of data. Preparers of reports must label them properly according to their source (i.e., the identification of the preparer, the systems used, and the data used) and according to the persons who authorized the reports and who are prepared to vouch for their integrity (i.e., manager, business function, or official). Users of data are responsible for proper identification and authorization of the source of the data.

- Ownership of work products. The institution is the owner of all data used or created.
- Management responsibility for controls, supervision, and corrective action. A manager's responsibility to preserve, conserve, and control resources may include personal computers. Managers may be held responsible for authorizing the purchase and use of personal computers.[33] They may also be held responsible for the appropriateness of use and the correctness of the results produced. They are responsible for effective controls, adequate audit trail, timely detection of variances, and necessary corrective action.
- Employee responsibility to report to responsible management all variances from the expected behavior, use, or content of the system.

Of course most of these things have always been implicitly expected and in a legal and ethical sense need not be restated. Nevertheless, it may be useful or even necessary to restate them in the context of the personal computer. When batch applications were the norm, and when all computer-generated output was derived from centralized, well-controlled machines, and when all reports prepared by individuals were handwritten or typed, there was little chance that a user of data would mistake a printout for a prepared report. Labeling and checking were less necessary then than now, when it is possible to go from a mental concept to four-color slides in minutes.

Concluding remarks

Most of the uses and effects of the personal computer are expected to be benign. If this were not so, its use would be so limited as to constitute no problem. Nonetheless, users and managers must be sensitive to the potential hazards and do what a prudent individual would do in the face of those hazards. A safe environment and insurance reduce the risk to the property. A safe environment, protective storage, access control, and encryption limit the risk of loss of confidentiality. Proper copying protects against erasure or destruction. Accountability, checking, and prompt corrective action help to ensure integrity. Finally, a clear communication of policy and intent provide good protection against misuse.

Cited references

1. L. I. Krauss and A. MacGahan, *Computer Fraud and Countermeasures*, Prentice-Hall, Inc., Englewood Cliffs, NJ (1979).

2. D. Neibaur, "Micro installation requires careful planning," *Computerworld* 17, No. 13, 41–42 (March 1983).

3. M. Zientara, "DP managers encouraging personal computing," *Computerworld* 17, No. 13, 1, 14 (March 1983).

4. D. R. Brodwin, "On personal computing," *Office Administration and Automation* 44, No. 8, 92–93 (August 1983).

5. A. Goldberg, "Building micro nets—the clustered approach," *Computerworld* 17, No. 41A, 39–48 (December 1983).

6. A. Emmett, "Thwarting the data thief," *Personal Computing* 8, No. 1, 98–105, 204–205 (January 1984).

7. "Computer security: what can be done," *Business Week* (*Industrial Edition*), 126–130 (September 26, 1983).

8. B. Gilbert, "Buying computer furniture that really fits," *Personal Computing* 7, No. 9, 54–63, 194–195 (September 1983).

9. T. E. Bell, "Your insurance can ruin you," *Personal Computing* 7, No. 8, 115–119 (August 1983).

10. G. Rifkin, "Protecting your data," *Computerworld* 17, No. 32A, 59–64 (August 1983).

11. "Configure your business to protect information assets," *Personal Computing* 7, No. 7, 133–134, 136 (July 1983).

12. H. J. Hinkin, "Microcomputer and mainframe ally to bring offices new power," *Electronics* 56, No. 16, 105–107 (August 1983).

13. B. W. Lampson, "Protection," *Proceedings of the 5th Annual Princeton Conference on Information Sciences and Systems*, pp. 437–443. Reprinted in *ACM Operating Systems Review* 8, No. 1, 18–24 (January 1974).

14. *Data Encryption Standard*, National Bureau of Standards, FIPS Publication 46 (January 1977).

15. S. M. Matyas, "Digital signatures—an overview," *Computer Networks* 3, No. 2, 87–94 (April 1979).

16. A. S. Tanenbaum, *Computer Networks*, Prentice-Hall, Inc., Englewood Cliffs, NJ (1981).

17. P. J. Denning, "A scientist's view of government control over scientific publication," *Communications of the ACM* 25, No. 2, 95–97 (February 1982).

18. D. E. Denning and P. J. Denning, "Data security," *Computer Survey* 11, No. 3, 227–249 (September 1979).

19. D. W. Davies, *The Security of Data in Networks*, IEEE Computer Society, IEEE Service Center, 445 Hoes Lane, Piscataway, NJ 08859 (1980).

20. "Integrated information systems: the microcomputer explosion," *Forbes* 129, No. 9, 73–94 (April 1982).

21. D. E. Bell and L. J. La Padula, "Secure computer system: unified exposition and multics interpretation," Report ESD-TR, 75–306, Mitre Corporation, Bedford, MA (March 1976).

22. D. E. Denning, "A lattice model of secure information flow," *Communications of the ACM* 19, No. 5, 236–242 (May 1976).

23. J. K. Millen, "Security kernel validation in practice," *Communications of the ACM* 19, No. 5, 243–250 (May 1976).

24. H. R. Rahden, "Computer security auditing," *WESCON 1979 Conference Record* 14, No. 3 (1979).

25. R. P. Cambell and G. A. Sands, "A modular approach to computer security risk management," *AFIPS Conference Proceedings* 48, 293–303 (1979).

26. R. E. Johnston, "Security software packages—a question and answer comparison of the 'big 3,'" *Computer Security Journal* 1, No. 1, 15–38 (Spring 1981).

27. C. E. Landwehr, "Formal models for computer security," *Computer Survey* 13, No. 3, 247–278 (September 1981).

28. S. Fordyce, "Computer security: a current assessment," *Computers and Security* 1, No. 1, 9–16 (January 1982).

29. *Data Security Controls and Procedures*, G320-5649, IBM Corporation; available through IBM branch offices.

30. K. S. Shankar, "The total computer security problem: an overview," *Computer* 10, No. 6, 50–73 (June 1977).

31. *SQL/Data System: Planning and Administration,* SH24-5014, IBM Corporation; available through IBM branch offices.
32. B. Feezor, "Links made data available," *Computing Canada* **9,** No. 22, Personal Software Report 4 (October 1983).
33. F. X. Dzubeck, "Telecommunications," *Office Administration and Automation* **44,** No. 10, 105 (October 1983).

Reprint Order No. G321-5226.

William H. Murray *IBM Information Systems and Communications Group, 44 South Broadway, White Plains, New York 10601.* Mr. Murray is Program Manager, Data Security for the Information Systems and Communications Group, where he is responsible for advising group management on the security properties of their products. In a previous assignment, Mr. Murray managed the development of the security subsystem for the IBM Advanced Administrative System. After fifteen years, this system is continuing to operate successfully and is considered to be a model of the state of the art. Mr. Murray is the author of Reference 29 in this issue. Other articles of his have appeared in *Asset Protection, EDP Audit Control and Security, IEEE Spectrum, Computers and Security,* and *The Computer Security Journal.* He has spoken on security to SEAS and the Diebold Research Program in Europe and to the Australia–New Zealand Association for the Advancement of Science. Mr. Murray received a B.A. degree in business administration from Louisiana State University, Baton Rouge; he joined IBM in 1956.

NBS Perspectives on Risk Analysis:

Past, Present, and Future

Dr. Stuart W. Katzke

Manager, Computer Security
Management and Evaluation Group
Institute for Computer Science and Technology
National Bureau of Standards

Reprinted from *Minutes of the Federal Information Systems Risk Analysis Workshop*, 1985, The Air Force Computer Security Program Office, pages 2-3–2.5. U.S. Government work not protected by U.S. copyright.

Abstract

Risk Analysis (RA) is the cornerstone of the ADP risk management (RM)process for DP centers and computer applications. While RA can be used to estimate residual risk to operational systems, it is most useful when applied prior to requirements definition (within the development life cycle) so that the resulting estimates of potential loss can be used to define computer security requirements for the system being developed. Within the design and implementation phases, it also forms the basis for making safeguard selection cost benefit decisions.

The RM process, which includes all of the above mentioned activities, encompasses the following concepts/terms:

o   threats and threat frequencies
o   targets, resources and assets (of a threat)
o   vulnerabilities (to a threat)
o   outcome/consequence (of a threat)
o   frequency of an outcome (how often)
o   impact of an outcome (e.g., $, delay, lives, linguistic)
o   risk/estimate of potential loss/ALE
o   safeguards (to protect, detect, mitigate)
o   cost of safeguards
o   cost benefit analysis
o   subset of safeguards to be implemented

and is further illustrated in the visual material accompanying this abstract. Some observations about the RM process are also included.

In 1979 NBS published FIPS 65 which described a quantitative method for performing RA. It is not particularly well suited for use during the whole RM process since it did not specify a comprehensive approach or method for dealing with all of the concepts highlighted above. It does describe how an estimate of risk (i.e., ALE) could be obtained by estimating, for each application data file, (1) the frequency of occurrence of events that could result in the destruction, modification, disclosure or unavailability of the data file (i.e., outcomes) and (2) the impact (in dollars) that could result from each of the outcomes. Recognizing the lack of empirical data on frequency of occurrence of events and the related impacts, FIPS 65 suggested an "order of magnitude approach" to approximating the real world situation. That this concept was not well understood has been illustrated by numerous attempts to be too precise in quantifying the input data to FIPS 65 and, by the same token, interpreting the results as having more precision than they actually did.

In the years following FIPS 65, NBS searched for a candidate RM Standard (FIPS 65 was not a Standard although many seemed to think it was). After evaluating current methods and approaches we concluded that no one method or combination would serve as a candidate for the following reasons:

o   alternatives were either not fully developed (i.e., still in the experimental stage) or not widely used.

o   human interfaces left much to be desired (e.g., data entry, report generation)

o   the basic concepts/terms (highlighted above) were addressed in varying degrees of detail or incompletely.

We concluded that it was too early to standardize and that we could continue to observe new methods and approaches as they developed.

In recent years we have seen several interesting developments in alternate RM approaches, have participated in the technical evaluation and application of Los Alamos' Vulnerability Analysis (LAVA), and have obtained additional hands-on experience in both performing RM for several Federal agencies and in providing technical assistance to others. These activities have led us to conclude that:

o   There is increasing dissatisfaction with previously and currently available methods

o   a method/tool is needed which will handle all aspects of the RM process including the ability to perform iterative cost benefit tradeoff during safeguard selection

o   a more qualitative and less quantitative method is more preferable at this time then refinements to current quantitative methods

o   alternative methods must reduce the amount of time, cost and overhead of performing RM, preferably by using computers as tools for data gathering and analysis

o   alternative methods must be small systems (PC) oriented both in terms of where they execute and what they are applied to (i.e., they should be applicable to micros).

In the future, we expect to continue working with Federal agencies in both providing technical assistance with their RM activities and engaging in cooperative R & D activities that lead to practical alternative approaches to RM. We have already initiated cooperative efforts with Los Alamos National Laboratory, the DoD Computer Security Center and the President's Council on Integrity and Efficiency's Work Group on EDP Systems Review and Security. We look forward to increased Federal efforts in this area.

Section 1.2: Society and Policy Issues

Introduction

The rate of growth of technology in the United States is, according to many observers, occurring faster than our society can readily accommodate. As a result, we are experiencing inbalances in our society. We are continually working to update our organizational policies and our laws to obtain a dynamic equilibrium with our technology. The result is a series of stresses on individuals, organizations, and our society.

Four issues are presented to illustrate the trends occurring in (1) computer and network privacy, (2) electronic funds transfer (EFT) and computer crime, (3) computer and network security methods describing how the U.S. Department of Defense works with industry and (4) future directions. We conclude with a section reviewing the reprints.

U.S. Government Issues

Considerable time and space is devoted to discussions of privacy and security issues as they affect the government. There are two major reasons for this concentration. First, the government, especially the U.S. Department of Defense, has a major interest in protecting vital information. Second, the workings and policy of the government are open for public scrutiny and comment. Throughout this tutorial, we will be constantly referring to publications, regulations, policies, and laws about and by the government. An extremely comprehensive report [OTA86] addressing management of government information technology, information system security, information technology and decision support, management of government information dissemination, and opportunities for using information technology in conducting congressional oversight is discussed in the recommended reading subsection.

Computer and Network Privacy

Individual rights and privacy are fundamental to the history and tradition of the United States. We have long been concerned with protecting rights from an invasion of privacy by the federal government. This concern dates back to the founding of the United States and the English common law concept of "home as a castle." We have laws that require the owner's permission or a warrant before entering someone's home. Our concern is that the government should represent not repress peoples' rights. This is a basic building block of our heritage and society.

Conflict is inherent in assuring right to privacy. For example, freedom of the press is guaranteed by the First Amendment to the Constitution. Press freedom is also incorporated into all of the state constitutions. However, we have established a boundary for freedom as interpreted over the years in court decisions. Beyond the boundary of freedom of the press, we have laws protecting individuals from libel so that the press cannot attack reputations or invade privacy.

Concurrent investment in technology has heightened our awareness of how fragile the boundary is that protects our right to privacy. Computer and network technology has enabled U.S. society to transform manual information into electronic form. A result of this technology is that it assisted the United States in becoming an information-based society. One impact of being an information-based society is the boundary that protects right to privacy is becoming electronic and it is difficult to determine if privacy rights are being maintained. Privacy protection stemming from the benign inefficiency of manual systems is falling to advances in automation; similar protection must be explicitly designed into automated systems.

We briefly highlight some of the related trends in federal legislation concerning computer privacy. Two federal laws illustrate related aspects of our concern with privacy: the Fair Credit Reporting Act of 1969 (15 USC 1987 et seg) and the Privacy Act of 1974. After considerable public concern and congressional hearings, the Fair Credit Reporting Act of 1969 was passed. This act applies to businesses that collect, maintain, and make available credit information on individuals, and addresses individual rights. Unauthorized access to credit databases is restricted. This control depends upon effective computer and network security.

Another act concerning individual rights is the Privacy Act of 1974, which applies to federal organizations. This act is implemented in the federal government in accordance with Office of Management and Budget (OMB) Circular A-108, which was issued in 1975 (superseded in 1985 by Circular A-130). The data security program required is quoted from the Circular:

> Each agency head shall establish and maintain procedures, consistent with the Act, OMB guidelines, and related directives issued pursuant to this Circular, to . . . establish reasonable administrative, technical, and physical safeguards to assure that

records are disclosed only to those who are authorized to have access and otherwise to protect against any anticipated threats or hazards to their security or integrity which could result in substantial harm, embarrassment, inconvenience, or unfairness to any individual on whom information is maintained.

One result of the Privacy Act was to define the boundary for federal organizations beyond which disclosure of information on individuals should be limited (i.e., where substantial harm, embarrassment, inconvenience, or unfairness could occur to any individual on whom information is maintained). OMB further stressed in its guidelines to the federal agencies that each security program be tailored to an agency's specific needs and consider applicable threats and hazards. These guidelines state

> The development of appropriate administrative, technical, and physical safeguards will necessarily have to be tailored to the requirements of each system of records and other related requirements for security and confidentiality. The need to assure the integrity of and to prevent unauthorized access to systems of records will be determined not only by the requirements of this Act but also by other factors like the requirement for continuity of agency operations, the need to protect agency operations, the need to protect proprietary data, applicable access restrictions to protect the national security, and the need for accuracy and reliability of agency information.

The next section concerns additional society and policy issues pertaining to EFT and computer crime.

Electronic Funds Transfer and Computer Crime

As our information-based society processed more transactions electronically, the United States passed new federal legislation to protect the concerned parties. Two examples are discussed: the Electronic Funds Transfer Act of 1982 (15 USC 1693) and the Computer Fraud and Abuse Act of 1984 (P.L. 98-473). A basic framework that defines the rights, liabilities, and responsibilities of the concerned parties in electronic fund transfer (EFT) systems was established by the Electronic Funds Transfer Act. The customer's rights are preserved as provided for in existing consumer protection laws. Risk and liabilities between the customer and the EFT institution are defined in the Act. For example, provisions are given if the institution fails to respond accurately to the customer's instruction, losses occur as a result of unauthorized access to a customer's account, and disputes arise concerning alleged errors. The Act requires the EFT institutions to provide customers with a statement of their rights and liabilities, records of transfers, and error correction procedures. In addition, a customer's liability is limited for losses incurred from unauthorized database accesses and computer fraud.

The Act authorizes the Federal Reserve Board to develop regulations to implement the Act. There are some questions of coverage of telephones under the Act and Federal Reserve Regulation E, Electronic Transfers. The telephone or home terminal is not defined as an electronic device, which raises questions about the coverage of the Act for home banking EFT.

On October 12, 1984, President Ronald Reagan signed new comprehensive anti-crime legislation. This is the first federal law on computer crime, because there are specific provisions for the protection of information stored in federal computers. Specifically, there are penalties for persons convicted of accessing and disclosing classified information stored in federal computers.

There have been many examples of computer crime reported that do not necessarily fit the provisions of any one act. Therefore, there is a likelihood that new federal legislation will be passed. A banking example illustrates the point. In this case, a branch operations officer withheld savings deposits from customer savings accounts. He took cash or credited his own account as an offset [AICP84]. The perpetrator entered a correction charging another account with the offset, when a customer complained that a deposit had not been entered. Sometimes he took cash and offset the shortage by creating an inter-branch clearing. When no response to such entries was made after 5 to 6 days by other branches, the amounts were transferred to the branch's suspense account. The perpetrator controlled the suspense account. For the month-end balancing, they were charged to another suspense account and then transferred back after balancing. This concealment lasted 13 months during which $800,000 was taken. The fraud was discovered when the perpetrator was transferred to another branch, after a customer complaint about an unauthorized charge to his savings account.

These computer crime problems can also be international because of EFT capabilities. An example to demonstrate the point is the case of a $13.1 million EFT transfer. The EFT transfer was completed by one of the world's largest banks to a Swiss account. The EFT ostensibly was on the order of a South American government. However, the EFT order was subsequently denied as being sent. A $13.1 million loss occurred.

The U.S. Department of Defense has been a pioneer in meeting the need for combatting computer crime and improving computer and network security technology. Defense is assisting U.S. companies to improve their computer and network security. Highlights of Defense's security progress and role in assisting the commercial sector are discussed in the next section, which is followed by a section on Future Directions.

Computer and Network Security Methods; U.S. Department of Defense Working with Industry

While the U.S. Department of Defense has taken the lead in the development of many types of computer and network security methods, industrial participation and innovation are essential to utilize the prodigious technological capability of U.S. knowledge. Furthermore, the unit cost of security technology can be reduced as the commercial use of modern security systems is increased, because of the ability of spreading start-up costs over a broader market base, commercial plus Defense. An overview of selected Defense security developments is given that illustrates how Defense is working with industry. This is followed by a few highlights of the categories of commercially available security products and services. Some of these hardware/software products have been evaluated for security features by the U.S. National Security Agency's National Computer Security Center (NCSC).

Historically, computer and network security methods consisted of relatively simple managerial, physical, administrative, technical, and communications safeguards or controls. As the needs for more effective security methods increased, a demand was created for new methods to protect automated information systems.

National Computer Security Center

An example of addressing this need was the establishment of the U.S. Department of Defense Computer Security Center in 1981 (now the NCSC). The U.S. Department of Defense has invested in many technological developments in computer and network security because of its historic need for protecting information pertaining to national security interests. NCSC has coordinated and influenced much of the current federal research and development computer security activities.

Most important is the role of the NCSC in actively supporting more effective computer security for sensitive federal and private sector applications. An example of this work is the development of the U.S. Department of Defense *Trusted Computer System Evaluation Criteria* [CSCS83]. This book is often referred to as the *Orange Book* because of the color of the cover.

These criteria define standard hierarchical levels of protection for commercial hardware/software products in specific hardware/software environments, such as operating systems and access control software. Several companies are utilizing these criteria in their commercial products and have submitted these products to the NCSC for evaluation at one of the defined levels of protection. Evaluations have been given (as of 1986) for various levels of protection for products from companies such as IBM, Honeywell, SKK, Inc., and CA. The effect of these companies developing their products and submitting them for NCSC evaluation has been an increase in the technical level of computer security and an increased understanding of the development process to achieve this security.

National Security Decision Directive 145

On September 17, 1984, *National Security Decision Directive (NSDD) 145, National Policy for Telecommunications and Automated Information Systems Security,* established a broader role for the U.S. Department of Defense in providing computer and network security technology for protecting sensitive information with national security implications. An example of the effect of NSDD 145 is the broadening of the role of the NCSC to include the *Development of Trusted Network Security Evaluation Criteria* [BRAN85].

Another effect of NSDD 145 has been the establishment of the Commercial COMSEC (Communications Security) Endorsement Program (CCEP). These products will be sold commercially to the government, government contractors, and the private sector. There are restrictions on distribution and export of some, if not all, of the products of this program. See the Rosenberg paper reprinted in Section 3.2 for a description of this important program.

Electronic Funds Transfer

Other related U.S. Department of Defense network security programs include assisting the National Bureau of Standards with its work on providing a commercial data encryption standard (DES) *Federal Information Processing Standard* (FIPS), [GUID77]. This encryption standard has been implemented by a variety of companies as an algorithm in microchip form for commercial encryption-based products, such as message authentication. Message authentication is an encryption technique for use in financial applications, such as the banking industry for EFT applications. Essentially, the data in the message are transmitted in the clear and each message has a unique message authentication code (MAC) appended to it. The MAC is computed by using a secret DES based electronic key, which operates on the message which is a cryptographic checksum process. This process is discussed further in Section 3.3.

DES-based applications are limited in security effectiveness by the usable life of the DES algorithm. Any encryption algorithm that is well documented in the public domain has a limited lifespan. However, a counterveiling viewpoint in the commercial sector is that DES is better than some previous manual code book and equivalent methods.

A new commercial communications security program, *Commercial COMSEC (Communications Security) Endorsement Program*, CCEP, is offered by the National Security Agency (NSA) to assist American industry in developing highly secure encryption products [ROSE86]. The program is briefly highlighted:

Vendors interested in using standardized [encryption] subsystems or modules with the new chips in commercial products for the federal market must first approach one of the companies qualified by the NSA to manufacture COMSEC devices. Although these companies—AT&T, GTE, Harris, Honeywell, Hughes, IBM, Intel, Motorola, RCA, Rockwell, and Xerox—can provide unclassified information about chips and modules, they may provide applications information and sample parts only with NSA approval . . .

Provisions will also be made for use of some of these chips or modules in the commercial sector. Another related program is also available from NSA [ROSE86]. This program concerns secure telephones for the federal and private sector markets and is discussed next.

Secure Telephones

A third example of the U.S. Department of Defense's active role in computer and network security is its development of a classified technology for secure digital encryption of telephone conversations. This technology is essentially being offered to telecommunications companies for incorporation in their lines of secure telephones. Examples of companies that have accepted this offer are IBM, RCA (now part of GE), Motorola, and Wang [SIII85]. The Secure Telephone Unit 3 (STU3) has resulted from this program.

Industrial Roles in Computer and Network Security

In addition to the computer and network security technology being given to U.S. industry by the U.S. Department of Defense, there is a substantial amount of related and independent research and development being performed. For example, many companies offer computer security products and services based on U.S. Department of Defense, National Bureau of Standards, related, and independent efforts. Examples of the categories of commercially available security products and services are anti-theft devices, computer security consultants, dial up/network security, disaster recovery consultants, disaster recovery hotsites, encryption, environmental controls, fire protection, identification/access control, information sources, media/output protection, micro data security, microcomputer security, risk analyses, secure computer systems, security software, and training.

Examples of secure computer systems and security software that have been evaluated, based on NCSC evaluation criteria, are: (1) secure computer systems (Honeywell SCOMP (secure communications processor and Honeywell Multics) and (2) security software (access control (IBM's RACF, SKK's ACF2, and CA's TOP SECRET).

The wide variety of security products and services is reflective of the broader societal issues that will be affecting security.

Future Directions

As the United States continues its rapid technological development, a changing set of management and legal concerns must be continually assessed by each individual and organization. An illustrative set of management trends is presented and followed by a set of legal trends.

Management Trends

Maintaining data and applications integrity is becoming a more increasingly complex management responsibility because of the increasing variety and intensity of security threats. Integrity is being challenged by the continuing investment in distributed processing systems. For example, traditional separation of duties is a valuable administrative technique to assist in maintaining data and applications integrity. However, many personal computer (PC) users have downloaded (copied) selected database files from central data processing (DP) sites. The typical PC user performs the functions that are carefully controlled at the central DP site and performed by separate individuals. Although, in principle, PCs and other computers used for office automation (OA) are merely small instances of computers susceptible to the same computer security practices, the direct end-user involvement with these machines changes the way in which security must be managed. End users may not be as amenable to authorative controls as DP staff; an employee education and awareness program is probably required. These PC/OA functions may include data entry, data verification, file maintenance, application development, application testing, application *certification* (assessing its technical controls or safeguards) and application *accreditation* (management acceptance of an application at a defined level of security).

As we introduced in the overview section, "the major impact is the shifting of security responsibility to the individual end user and to non-ADP management." In effect, we are changing the way we do business because of the rapid introduction of the PC into the organization.

The challenge to management includes the development and improvement of an effective computer and network security program. Elements of this program may include senior management responsibilities, management by objectives (MBO) [DRUC54], and formal security programs.

Management trends may also be viewed on national and international levels. Computer and network security are becoming essential to the national and international operations of multinational corporations as well as the federal government. Organizations such as IBM, GM, GE, and ITT process substantial amounts of sensitive information that must be protected against national and international competitors. The federal government has the same concerns plus the requirement to protect information classified for the purposes of national security.

Management of computer and network security is becoming more difficult to maintain on a national and international level because of the growing complexity of organizational relationships. For example, the relative autonomy of the cabinet-level officers in the Executive branch of the federal government makes it difficult to establish and implement a central focus for national and international computer and network security. Variables, such as perceived levels of data sensitivity, may influence the management decisions in each cabinet-level agency. Also, there are key legislative provisions in laws, such as the Brooks Act (Public Law 89-306) and Paperwork Reduction Act (Public Law 96-511), that have a bearing on the management of automated information systems including computer and network security. In addition to the laws, there is a wide variety of recent executive guidance that affects the management of computer and network security. One such set of guidance is NSDD 145, which was introduced in a previous section on Computer and Network Security Methods: U.S. Department of Defense Working with Industry.

Management trends are continually changing with respect to organizational values and in many cases are highly dependent on other developments such as the passage of new legislation. This issue is particularly complex for international operations such as the worldwide EFT networks. Each nation may have its own set of laws and/or regulations regarding the security measures for EFT. For example, one nation may allow EFT encryption and another only allow EFT authentication by using MACs.

The related national and international issues include trends in standards, which are important for system compatibility and interoperability. The formation of the Corporation for Open Systems, which is a consortium of major users and suppliers to test and implement the *Open System Interconnection Standards,* is further evidence of the importance of system compatibility and interoperability [HORW86]. There are a wide variety of evolving standards and guidelines that may apply to each aspect of computer and network security. For example, there are national and federal standards in the United States pertaining to EFT [ANSI82][DOT85]. In addition, the security architecture from the International Standards Organization discussed in Section 3.1, could have substantial impact on network security developments [OSI85].

Legal Trends

Legal issues are also continually evolving and must be assessed for their impact on computer and network security. In addition to the basic federal and state legislation on security and privacy, the state governments and the Congress are continually reassessing the need for new legislation. For example, the Computer Fraud and Abuse Act of 1984 (Public Law 98-473) defines certain crimes against federal databases. These include certain actions of outsiders attempting access to an automated information system via a dial-in line. Other federal bills are being considered to expand the definition of crimes to private sector databases.

Other legal trends include the issue of establishing the responsibility for maintaining source code of proprietary software products. This issue is becoming more important as our organizations increase their reliance on packaged or proprietary software (e.g., ACF2 and TOP SECRET). In the event the system developer goes out of business, customers who have only object code for the proprietary product would find it very difficult to maintain the product. One alternative is a legal agreement between the system developer and a third-party custodian. The custodian would keep updated copies of the source code but would not provide them to the system developer's customers unless the developer goes out of business. Continuity of operations for customers is thereby made much easier in the event of a corporate failure affecting an important software developer.

Legal trends, such as the examples presented here, may have a substantial impact on the design and development of computer and network systems. One reason for the impact is the additional requirement for carefully defined access control methods. This applies to legal provisions specifying penalties for unauthorized access to databases by external and internal users. The system designer should consider the legal, managerial, and technical aspects of access control from a unified software engineering viewpoint.

An important requirement for effective systems design is to consolidate user needs so that one set of software controls protecting a database may satisfy needs for a wide variety of legal, managerial, and technical access safeguards or controls. For example, an access control over a credit database that complies with the Privacy Act and other legislative constraints should also protect against human error, which could accidently result in a loss of data integrity.

The concluding section discusses the reprints and suggested reading.

Reprints

A representative set of papers provides insight into current issues affecting our society. These papers concern computer privacy, NCSC, and communications security.

Privacy concerns are presented in the paper, "Computer Privacy in America: Conflicting Practices and Policy Choices," by Ben Matley. His central issue is that our high-tech nation is continually utilizing new computer and network technology without adequate consideration for personal privacy. For example, he reflects on the thought of Senator Sam Ervin during early privacy hearings. Senator Ervin observed that while we collect, with good intentions, substantial amounts of data for worthwhile purposes, we find latent adverse effects. His example is that military surveillance of civilians was directed at congressional and presidential requests. However, later concerns were raised concerning potential threats such as to Constitutional safeguards.

Matley traces privacy concerns back to colonial times and the English common law concept of "home as castle." He suggests that the basis for much of our current views on privacy can be traced to the 1980 work of Louis Brandies. Brandies observed that our modern technology, while of substantial benefit to our society, can threaten our privacy. Matley shows later events that support the Brandies observations. For example, an early Kennedy administration proposal for a National Data Bank had a worthwhile purpose, but threatened personal privacy.

The paper, "The National Computer Security Center," by Col. Joseph Greene, Jr., presents a review of the directions at the NCSC. His emphasis is on the development of consistent standards for computer and network security. These standards should be stable for periods of approximately five years to support industry by giving companies fixed targets during the product development cycle. Greene's focus on industry is key to his commitment. He states, "The standards proposed by the National Computer Security Center must be supported by worked examples that prove feasibility, clarify interpretations, and communicate the knowledge and experience of industry. . . ."

Two priorities under NSDD 145 are mentioned by Greene. The first is to strengthen the NCSC. In particular, NCSC will focus on working with industry and offering a significant security evaluation program for hardware/software products. The target is for ". . . approximately 45 new commercial product evaluations by 1990." The second priority is to improve NCSC's program for research, including industry participation. Three aspects of the research program are: near-term efforts to assist federal agencies using existing computer systems, mid-term efforts to increase the availability of trusted hardware/software products with improved security features, and ". . . long-term efforts to develop and distribute to industry the technology base needed to build much more trustworthy system[s] than we currently know how to build."

An important report, "COMSEC in Transition," is referred to by Orville Lewis concerning the need to improve federal communications security (COMSEC), in "The 1982-1983 Report to the President on the Status of Communications Security in the Federal Government." The report recommendations are that the federal government should protect critical sensitive information by more cost effective (COMSEC) equipment; improved COMSEC policy, requirements definition, priorities, and funding; increased funding for COMSEC; near-term increase in availability of secure telephones; increased computer and network security.

Lewis introduces the organizational structure established to implement NSDD 145 and improve federal computer and network security. Highlights of the structure include:

Level 1. *The Systems Security Steering Group:* Be in a leadership role for the implementation of the national policy on telecommunications and automated information systems (network and computer security) for classified and sensitive information, and review the federal computer and network security programs and budgets and give recommendations to the Office of Management and Budget.

Level 2. *The National Telecommunications and Information Systems Security Committee (NTISSC):* The operating level group that reports to the Steering Group and develops ". . . a national issuance system for promulgating operating policies, directives, instructions, and guidance."

Levels 3 & 4. *Executive Agent and National Manager:* The Secretary of Defense is the executive agent for federal computer and network (automated information systems and telecommunications systems) security, and the Director, NSA is the national manager for federal computer and network security, reporting to the executive agent.

Recommended Readings

Congressional concern with respect to the vulnerability of computer and network systems to security and privacy threats has increased over the years. An excellent example of this concern and a set of recommendations is presented by the Subcommittee report, *"Computer and Communication Security and Privacy"* by Congressman Dan Glickman, Chairman, Subcommittee on Transportation, Aviation and Materials, Committee on Science and Technology, U.S. House of Representatives [GLIC84]. The tone of the report is that there is an expanding role in computer and network security for the federal government; however, there is inadequate federal leadership. These conditions are reported next.

Condition 1. Federal Government's Role: "The Federal Government has a role in protecting computer/communications systems of national importance as well as those that are needed to support operations of Federal agencies. Traditionally, the Federal role has been limited to securing systems associated with national defense and intelligence activities; however, there is growing concern that both public and private sector critical systems such as banking, utilities, entitlement systems, law enforcement, and industrial processes need additional protection."

Condition 2. Lack of Federal Leadership: "Lack of Federal leadership is evident from the fact that there is inadequate control focus to deal with computer/communications security. There has not been a concentrated effort to identify problems nor strengthen computer/communications security programs. Historically, the Office of Management and Budget (OMB) has not conducted follow-up reviews nor overseen risk assessment efforts as required by its own procedures. It has failed to develop new directives to meet recent developments and has not encouraged the other central management agencies (General Services Administration, National Bureau of Standards, Office of Personnel Management) to develop a strong set of directives to assist Federal agencies in establishing computer/communications security programs."

There has been a series of federal activities related to subcommittee's federal leadership concerns. Briefly, the federal activities are shown with respect to two of the subcommittee's recommendations, federal leadership and technical and administrative guidance to federal agencies:

Recommendation 1. Federal Leadership: "The Administration should begin an immediate assessment of the problems and issues in order to develop a set of national policies that will ensure the protection of critical national systems relevant to government, industry, commerce and the society . . ."

Independent and Related Activities: On September 17, 1984, President Ronald Reagan signed National Security Decision Directive (NSDD) 145, National Policy on Telecommunications and Automated Information Systems Security. In addition, the Office of Management and Budget consolidated four circulars pertaining to information management on December 12, 1985, and issued OMB Circular A-130, Management of Federal Information Resources [OMB85].

Recommendation 2. Technical and Administrative Guidance to Federal Agencies: "The Office of Management and Budget should establish a central focus to provide technical assistance to agencies that are responsible for sensitive, non-national security data in selecting tools and techniques to protect their computer systems. Such a focus could, for example, be created by expanding the role of the DoD Computer Security Center or be created by establishing a civil entity patterned after it . . ."

Independent and Related Activity: The U.S. Department of Defense Computer Security Center was renamed the National Computer Security Center in 1985 and its role expanded to include technical assistance for civil agencies and selected companies in the private sector. This new charter is derived from NSDD 145.

Positive Alternatives: An ACM Panel on Hacking reported on their work concerning hacking issues, problems, and possible solutions. We recommend reading a short report of their thoughts, which is authored by John A.N. Lee, Gerald Segal, and Rosalie Steier [LEE86]. This panel developed seven recommendations to address hacker related issues. These recommendations are quoted, in part, below:

Recommendation 1. Federal and State Laws: "Federal and state laws should be passed that are consistent and enforceable. These should include consistency in the treatment of electronic information as real property, as well as in the treatment of wiretapping, EMS [electronic message systems]/EFT, and electronic records . . ."

Recommendation 2. A Code of Responsible Use: "A code of responsible use should be developed within the ACM

curriculum that can be introduced into classes and that can also be used by other youth organizations as an educational tool . . ."

Recommendation 3. Access to Real Computing Power: "Access to real computing power should be established for interested users, both students and their parents. Empowerment can lead to increased responsibility . . ."

Recommendation 4. Student Apprenticeships: "Young students could be apprenticed to local companies either part-time or on a continuing basis through club or youth organization sponsorship, or on a periodic basis, permitting students to visit for a day to work with professionals."

Recommendation 5. Proposed Organization: "An organization analogous to the American Radio Relay League (ARRL) could be created, with a charter to organize contributed resources and make them available under a program of mutual education and improvement of skills."

Recommendation 6. Computer Expert Assistance: "A central information resource of computer experts could be provided to the press and other news media through which they could obtain information on stories, and from which they could obtain insights and opinions relating to the technological aspects of the articles."

Recommendation 7. Proposed Sophisticated Technical Magazine: "A technically sophisticated magazine should be created for hobbyists beyond the level of current commercial magazines that would challenge the reader rather than give canned routines and reports."

Computer crime costs to our society are estimated in the work, "Report on Computer Crime (Executive Summary)," by Joseph Tompkins, James Jorgenson, Nathaniel Kossack, and Marcia Proctor. As a nation, we generally underreport computer crime for several reasons, including the reluctance of businesses to admit to the losses. Several studies have been completed to assess the nature and magnitude of computer crime in the United States. This nationwide study by the American Bar Association (ABA) is illustrative of these studies, addressing the nature and occurrence of computer crime.

The ABA analyzed 283 results from survey respondents representing a cross section of private industry, and federal, state, and local government agencies. A ranking of computer crime significance based on the study is (1) "Use of computers to steal tangible or intangible assets; (2) destruction or alteration of data, (3) use of computers to embezzle funds; (4) destruction or alteration of software; and (5) use of computers to defraud consumers, investors or users."

Although it is difficult to estimate national annual losses, ABA did estimate total annual losses for the survey respondents as between $145 million and $730 million. Respondents were asked for their opinions concerning total annual losses caused by computer crime in the United States: "Thus, 59% of those responding to this question believe annual losses due to computer crime exceed $500 million, 41% believe them to be in excess of $1 billion, and 14% believe the annual losses exceed $10 billion. . . ."

When asked to rank preventive methods with respect to computer crime, the respondents offered four key methods in order of importance: (1) "More comprehensive and effective self-protection by private business, (2) education of users concerning vulnerabilities of computer usage, (3) more severe penalties in federal and state criminal statutes, and (4) greater education of the public regarding computer crime . . ."

One of the most significant issues developed in the study is the respondent's assessment of future directions. Specifically, what are the major computer crime concerns for our current and future computer and network investment. The survey results show the concerns to be the following (1) "The proliferation of business and personal computers and computer users, (2) the difficulty of detecting computer crime, (3) the existing vulnerability to computer crime, lack of adequate security measures, (4) the lack of public and/or managerial awareness and concern, and (5) the growing magnitude of potential losses from computer crime."

Federal Government Information Technology: Management, Security, and Congressional Oversight [OTA86]: "Information technology—including computers, software, telecommunications, and the like—is critically important to the functioning of the U.S. Government." So begins an impressively comprehensive and quite readable report by the Office of Technology Assessment [OTA86]. It identifies "significant progress, problems, and opportunities for improvement in the management and use of this very important technology."

The chapter "Trends in Federal Government Information Technology Management," provides background on policy issues and trends and summarizes the extent of information technology use in the government. Emphasizing that management of information and technology is not an end in itself, but rather is a tool to further agency missions, this chapter includes the impact of microcomputers and networking. It addresses Information Resources Management, planning, procurement, personnel, recent issues and Office of Management and Budget activities, and provides basic data on federal information technology use.

The chapter, "Information Systems Security," observes that "while the U.S. Department of Defense, and particularly the National Security Agency, has developed a great deal of technical expertise in this area, the civilian agencies have lagged in awareness. In the last decade, however, concerns about both privacy and hackers have elevated the overall visibility of this issue." The major findings are (1) "The government faces fundamentally new levels of risks in information security." (2) "Federal policy requiring the use of appropriate information systems security measures has been ineffective." (3) "Three key factors inhibit appropriate Federal information security measures: (a) competition for resources . . .; (b) lack of awareness . . .; and, (c) absence of clear guidance." (4) "NSA and the committees guiding implementation of [NSDD 145] will play a significant if not dominant role in all aspects of information security in the Federal Government . . .; concerns have been expressed that it puts the national security community in an unusually, influential, if not controlling, position on a key aspect of the Nation's information policy." (5) "Possible actions to improve Federal information systems security include: more intensive congressional oversight, changing budget procedures with information security receiving higher priority and visibility, designating a civilian agency to be responsible for security training and technical support in the nonmilitary sector, and revising and clarifying NSDD 145."

Succeeding chapters discuss computer crime; computer modeling, decision support, and government foresight; electronic databases and dissemination of government information; and information technology and congressional oversight. Appendices include other issues, federal agency data request, and a list of contractor reports.

COMPUTER PRIVACY IN AMERICA: Conflicting Practices and Policy Choices

Ben G. Matley

Department of Mathematics and Computer Science

VENTURA COLLEGE - 4667 Telegraph Road, Ventura, CA 93003

WEST COAST UNIVERSITY - 440 Shatto Place, Los Angeles, CA 90020

ABSTRACT

American history and custom are rich with the sense of personal privacy. That sense of privacy remained so strong that when the computer became reality in daily government operations, concerns about preserving privacy were vigorously expressed. The Congressional hearings on the National Data Bank(NDB) proposal of the 1960s is illustrative. In the end, the proposal was not funded out of concern for the massive volume of personal data to be contained, transmission of it around the country in telecommunications networks not secure, a national ID system that might emerge, and computer matching schemes to follow. Today, our computer practices sometimes violate those earlier tenets on computers and privacy. Some government networks now contain more personal data than was proposed for the NDB; networks are not secure, even subject to penetration by hackers; a national ID system has been proposed, but SSN is one in effect; matching schemes for draft registration verification and debt collection by the Internal Revenue Service on behalf of other agencies, do work. Computer practices in conflict with privacy principles raise the spectre of extra-Constitutional government in America, and leave us with crucial policy choices in computing.

INTRODUCTION

There is in this high-tech world a high-tech nation that designed and built a computer controlled telephone switching system of magnificient technical capability. That telephone system had great capacity, would eventually be all digital, and was capable of automatic fault isolation. Computer control provided the capability to trace all calls instantly and to record any conversation at will. It was a telephone system to warm the hearts of leaders in even the most closed societies, where widespread use of telephones would not ordinarily be welcome. But the nation in which that system was designed and built is not a closed society. In fact, that magnificient achievement in telephonic high-tech design was not intended for use in the nation of origin, and never was it installed there. However, the nation which provided that magnificient computer controlled telephone system does have a number of other computer systems installed domestically; systems of equal magnificience. There is a system capable of following the physical movements of citizens; yet another system that tracks financial transactions for most of the population on an annual basis, with summaries of most assets; a system that is capable of complete financial and credit control of citizens; a police and intelligence system capable of complete surveillance of selected subjects. But none of these computer systems were installed for sinister purposes. All were installed for positive purposes, in telecommunications networks for reasons of utility and efficiency. The nation of these technical accomplishments is, of course, the United States.

It is as though we have been living the path predicted by Jacques Ellul in his treatise on The Technological Society. There, technological devices and techniques are continually increased and expanded by a society that sees only positive outcomes in improved living standards, efficiencies in government, and advancements in the professions. Any adverse effects are encountered in isolation, and are easily rationalized in the presence of the benefits. In the end, The Technological Society embraces any and all technology, unquestioned, always for good intent, though not always without adverse societal effects. Concludes Ellul,

> But what good is it to pose questions of motive? of Why? ... Technique exists because it is technique. The golden age will be because it will be. Any other answer is superfluous.(1)

But Ellul did not intend that his book become the blueprint for implementation of his technique society. It was to be a warning that technology is to be scrutinized.

BACKGROUND

When the first national telecommunications network for personal data was requested of Congress, there was much scrutiny of the proposal from the privacy viewpoint. Subsequently, some telecommunications systems holding personal data were approved by the Congress, but with specific limitations. Over the years, networks disapproved have been funded in different forms; limitations once imposed have been relaxed; direct computer-to-computer connections once forbidden have proven unnecessary when other techniques for data sharing accomplished the same objectives. For those who would view all of this with alarm, maybe even suspicion, much more food for such thoughts can be found elsewhere.(2) I prefer the view expressed by Senator Sam Ervin during the privacy hearings he chaired. After being told that military intelligence agencies held surveillance data on civilians not connected with the military, some

Reprinted from *Proceedings of the 1985 Symposium on Security and Privacy*, 1985, pages 219-223. Copyright © 1985 by The Institute of Electrical and Electronics Engineers, Inc.

of those data subjects being members of Congress, Senator Ervin noted that in many cases data collection efforts were begun for good purpose and with good intent, but became dangerous in the extreme somewhat later. As it turned out, the good purpose for military surveillance of civilians in this case came at congressional and presidential requests. In the aftermath of political assissinations of the 1960s, Congress voted to fund protection for the candidates. There were not available immediately sufficient numbers of trained undercover agents in the civilian agencies. Military intelligence was pressed into service for the few months of the campaigns. After several elections, considerable surveillance data on many civilians had been amassed in the computers of military intelligence agencies.

To put into effect such plans, without consideration of the potential threat to Constitutional safeguards, or without consideration of the possible ill effects afterward, is to court danger by design. The plan suspected by some to requisition civilian computer centers in a national emergency is another example of plans to do, without provisions to control during, nor plans to undo afterward.(3) Not at all unlike some computer programs - lots of DO conditions, but too few DON'T DO conditions specified. At the societal level, however, such program shortcomings are neither acceptable nor necessary.

Japan, for one example, prepared a national computer policy(NCP) study in 1972 that brought her to her present leadership position in computing. The NCP plan included a full chapter titled "Demerits" in which all planned computer projects were scrutinized for their possible negative effects of a societal nature. Privacy was much considered there. Projects such as the national telecommunications administrative data base system and the remote health care telecommunications system were not begun without consideration of the "Demerits" of those systems and mitigating designs also planned.

By contrast, the US in recent years has lunged into computer applications without consideration of potential demerits, and without incorporating into initial designs some capabilities to moderate those ill effects that can be anticipated. We run the risk of implementing Ellul's society where technique "will be because it will be." We overlook Joseph Weizenbaum's admonition that "Can does not imply ought."(4)

There is need to explicitly examine potential privacy demerits at design time, for we can no longer depend upon inate societal conditions as protections for privacy.

PRIVACY PRINCIPLES AND SOCIETAL CONDITIONS

America's history and customs about privacy can be traced to Colonial times and the English common law concept of "home as castle." Those ideas on privacy were in the vein of protecting the citizen from the sovereign more than protecting the citizen from businesses or from other citizens. The U.S. Constitution followed in like manner, protecting citizens from specific invasion of privacy acts by government and, in fact, not even mentioning "privacy" nor "invasion of privacy." The subsequent judicial extension of privacy rights as we know them today can be traced to the ideas expressed in an 1890 article in the Harvard Law Review coauthored by Louis Brandies,

later of the U.S. Supreme Court. Wrote he,

> Recent inventions and business methods call attention to the next step which must be taken for the protection of the person .... Instantaneous photographs and newspaper enterprise have invaded the sacred precincts of private domestic life; the numerous mechanical devices threaten to make good the prediction that "what is whispered in the closet shall be proclaimed from the housetops."(5)

Thus Brandies recognized the relationship between privacy and technology in his day. Technology neutralizes certain inate societal protections for privacy. So, too, does literacy. One historian, writing of privacy in Colonial America, noted that widespread illiteracy was a natural protection for privacy of the mails, and for the master of the house where illiterate servants worked.(6) It is also true that technology contributes to literacy; both the printing press and the computer are held by some to be the two most important contributions to literacy in all of history. We do hope that privacy protection through illiteracy is less effective today. We as well assure that privacy protection through inaccessibility of information is less certain in our day of telecommunications networks. The natural state of things in society thus becomes less of an aid to privacy protection.

Even in the days of electronic computers there have been some inate protections to privacy by virtue of the nature of things. Those, too, we gradually dissolve through technology. For example, first generation computers were no real threat to personal data privacy because they lacked storage capacity, alphabetic capability, and communications facilities, generally. Those were calculators for the most part. The second generation machines had some storage capacity, alphabetic capability, but no communications facilities generally, and were stand-alone machines in single departments for the most part. But those protections to privacy from machine limitations vanished with third generation systems of massive storage capacity, telecommunications facilities, and ease of access.

Given that the naturally existing conditions surrounding literacy and privacy no longer offer dependable protections to privacy, it follows that privacy protections must be designed into systems and into institutions at the policy level, not in the hardware alone. Indeed, we have done just that at times in the past, but we have defaulted on those privacy policy considerations in recent years. A few examples in each case will suffice.

COMPUTER PRACTICES WITH PRIVACY CONSIDERATIONS

The first nationwide telecommunications network for massive personal data collection and distribution was that proposed during the Kennedy administration and known as the National Data Bank(NDB) proposal. The nation had declared a War on Poverty. Human services would at last be provided to all citizens in need - housing, nutrition, medical care, education, job training, family planning. Of course, such services are very much personal services, and so personal data would have to be collected so that individuals could be served on an individual basis. Clearly, a single computerized personal data center would be the most efficient approach - one agency to collect, maintain, and distribute all personal data on citizens needed by all government agencies, thereby eliminating duplication and waste. The data could also be made available to universities across the country for purposes of social research. All personal data needed for government operations and for social reports would at last become available.

THE NATIONAL DATA BANK(NDB)

The NDB would collect socio-economic data and family histories. The histories would be important, for example, in health where future risks for individuals of known attributes might be projected and so early preventative treatment begun. The data would be collected through regional centers, each connected to the Washington D.C. center.

A series of hearings followed in the Congress on the NDB proposal during the early and mid-1960s years. The debate on "computers and privacy" was joined. Congressmen probed the minds of the social scientists who had initiated the proposal, as well as the minds of the computer experts who supported its technical feasibility. In the end, none could assure the Congressmen of the preservation of personal data privacy, nor system security. The Congressmen also perceived that an inherent aspect of such a system would be, in effect, a national ID system on citizens. It was all too much for the Congressmen. The NDB proposal was not funded, primarily out of concern for privacy. But the decision was not in the nature of policy, and neither did Congress formulate a policy position from its deliberations on NDB. Throughout the 1960s years other personal data computer centers were funded as part of operational budgets within specific departments. The proliferation continued, free of policy guidelines.

THE 1972 PRIVACY STUDY

In 1972, President Nixon ordered a study of computerized personal data centers in the federal government, and the possible need of special laws to provide protection and redress for individual citizens. The report, titled Records, Computers and the Rights of Citizens, made some suggestions for policy guidelines governing computerized personal data on citizens. Among those,

- no personal data center be kept secretly;
- no data kept unknown to the data subject;
- no secondary uses of personal data;
- organization holding the data be responsible for accuracy, completeness, security;
- data subjects should have means to have erroneous data corrected;
- no Universal Identifers on citizens.

The report went on to assert,

A permanent ID issued at birth could create an incentive for institutions to pool or link their records, thereby making it possible to bring a lifetime of information to bear on any decision about any individual. American culture is rich in the belief that an individual can pull up

stakes and make a fresh start, but a universally identified man might become a prisoner to his recorded past.(7)

Many of the recommendations in the report were incorporated into the 1974 Privacy Act, unfortunately, with sufficient exceptions to preclude the necessity for strict compliance by government.

THE 1974 PRIVACY ACT

In manner of irony upon irony, the Watergate incident of the Nixon administration motivated the Congress to implement some of the privacy study recommendations from that same administration. Known as the 1974 Privacy Act, that legislation contained some important limitations. The Act applied only to the federal government, not to the states or to businesses; restrictions on secondary uses of personal data were tempered in language prohibiting inter-departmental data sharing; and a prohibition on universal identifiers exempted the on-going use of SSN. The limitations and exemptions all but nullified the prohibitions.

The limitation of the 1974 Privacy Act to federal agencies only was never removed as the Congress never enacted the 1975 Comprehensive Right to Privacy Act(HR1984).(8) The prohibition on inter-departmental data sharing was muted by an interpretation within the Executive Branch that department meant Cabinet Department, thus permitting much computer matching within working-level departments. Of course, the SSN was indeed an effective universal ID as was predicted in the 1972 Privacy Study.

COMPUTER PRACTICES SANS PRIVACY CONSIDERATIONS

Since the hearings on the NDB proposal in the 1960s and the hearings on privacy in the 1970s, a number of computerized personal data systems and a number of data matching schemes have been implemented, all on a one-at-a-time basis, and without consideration of their collective societal effects.

NDB REALIZED

Time and technology have allowed for the installation of many specific telecommunications networks that collect, maintain, and distribute personal data. The individual projects were not scrutinized in the manner of the NDB proposal. In 1982 the General Accounting Office(GAO) reported on the proliferation of such systems and the security of them. Titled "Federal Information Systems Remain Vulnerable" the report displayed a map of the U.S. with lines for network links and dots for terminal locations, representing only three federal systems. The map appeared as a woven surface freckled with connected dots. In the twenty years since privacy concerns had defeated the NDB, much more than its equivalent had been installed - more by orders of magnitude, and no more secure.(9)

DEBT COLLECTIONS

The largest category of welfare in the U.S. is that of Aid to Dependent Children. A sizable portion of that aid goes to children whose parents(usually fathers) have moved out of state and so avoid supporting their children. Some computer matches would collect from some of those run-away parents.

The Internal Revenue Service(IRS) has begun to serve as debt collector on behalf of the states by collecting from run-away parents. After a state has obtained a court order for collection from a parent, the IRS will divert income tax refunds due the parent to the home state, if the parent can be found on the tax refund rolls. Critics claim that this process violates computer privacy principles. Advocates of the practice note that direct computer-to-computer matching is not done. Magnetic tapes and paper orders are exchanged.

ADULT WELFARE CHEATERS

Select data sharing schemes have been developed, to different degrees of completion, to locate adults who cheat on welfare by not reporting all income, or by reporting non-existant children.(10)

- "Project Match" matches welfare rolls to federal civil service rolls to locate federal employees who receive welfare;
- "Project Missing Kids" matches lists for Aid to Dependent Children with school enrollments to detect adults who report non-existant school-aged children;
- "Project Sacramento" matches California welfare rolls with Social Securiy to locate income not reported by adults who receive welfare.

Critics of these projects complain that the personal data privacy rights of the data subjects are being violated by these secondary uses of personal data, unknown to the subjects. Advocates of the practices note that much illegal activity is detected when the perpetrators are unaware their actions are being observed. But complaints do have an effect. The administration proposed a National Welfare Data Base system, then withdrew the proposal under criticism about privacy violations.

TAX COLLECTIONS

In recent years, the IRS has adopted the practice of purchasing commercial mailing lists and matching those to 1040 returns to locate persons of means who have failed to file tax returns. Since the lists are highly screened, the matching can be targeted to high income subjects.

Critics of these IRS practices claim that such matches violate personal data privacy as the data subjects are unaware of the lists. Advocates of the practice note that the lists are available to all comers, and so the government should not be denied legal products commonly available.

THE PASSIVE DRAFT

In 1979, the Congress was asked to modify the 1974 Privacy Act to permit direct computer-to-computer connections among several agencies in order to register men who would be subject to the newly authorized Selective Service. This "Passive Draft System" would have prepared lists of draftable men, by age and priority, from the computers of Social Security, IRS, the fledgling National Driver Register, Student Loan Applications, and eventually the enrollments of high schools and colleges. Congress refused to fund the Passive Draft System, not wishing to authorize such wide scale computer matching, but again without declaring a policy position.

In 1980, data were traded on magnetic tape between Selective Service, and Social Security and Internal Revenue, so that lists could be prepared of young men whose names did not appear on the Selective Service rolls. Notices were sent to those men.

PERCEPTIONS

Critics of all these nationwide personal data telecommunications systems, generally not secure, and all these personal data matching schemes, many once denied in one form or another, press the privacy issue. There is reiterated from the privacy study report these principles: personal data should be held secure; the data subject should know what is done with the data on that subject; there should be no secondary use of personal data unknown to the data subject; there should be limitations on personal data matching. On behalf of the individual, these critics raise the fairness issue: An individual cannot cope with such a powerful government and its army of machines that never sleep.

Other perceptions of fairness come down on the side of the taxpayer. Supporters of data matching schemes in particular point out that cheating on welfare and cheating on student loans have undermined public faith in such programs, and so threaten what has been rather generous support in the past. Tax evasion, too, has become so widespread that a sense of fairness on the part of the public is all but lost. It is now acknowledged that the underground economy is between 15% and 25% of GNP, and growing.(11) At that rate, the budget may be nearly balanced were all income reported. There is the view that some national crises, like these, which can now be moderated with some data matching practices may just transcend any perceived need to maximize personal data privacy rights. Privacy rights, like all rights, cannot be unbounded is the view.

Still there is the concern that unrestricted computer usage in the Executive Branch may unleash extra-Constitutional government where agencies take on functions not granted them by Congress. One example would be that of the IRS performing debt collection generally. Another example is that of the National Crime Information Center(NCIC) which was forbidden message switching capability in its initial charter from Congress some twenty years ago. Such limitations were to assure that NCIC did not begin to resemble a national police force. Recently, NCIC has acquired that message switching capability, though granted, through Congressional funding.

SOME POLICY CHOICES

We have presented to ourselves computer practices in conflict with our announced privacy principles, history, and customs. Those practices began for good purposes, with no sinister intent, and only in pursuit of better government. We have as well presented to ourselves some policy choices in the area of computers and privacy. Shall we return to the privacy principles enunciated during the 1960s in the NDB debates; principles that eventually defeated the NDB proposal? Shall we return to the privacy principles of the 1972 Privacy Study and the 1974 Privacy Act; principles that would temper our use of personal data telecommunications systems and personal data matching schemes? Some provocative additional perceptions and alternatives have been presented by other nations that have objectively considered these matters more recently than have we.

JAPAN

We earlier mentioned that Japan's national computer policy(NCP) study included a chapter addressing the "demerits" of proposed networks; privacy being much concern there. One response was what is termed the "democratization" of national personal data bases. The idea is that if citizens be given access to the same data bases as government, then all would know what data have been recorded. Each citizen can also be given access to the raw data on him/her. The Japanese NCP went a step further in stating that citizens must be educated to the view that there would be a personal obligation to learn how to use these and other computer data bases for personal development, job preparation, and education, as responsible members of an information society. Such democratization of data held by government would satisfy many of the privacy issues surrounding data secrecy and citizen awarness.(12)

COPERNICAN TURN IN PRIVACY

External of the Japanese NCP paper itself, a leading researcher and designer of that study extended the notion of democratization of data bases a step further. In his book on future information societies, Yoneji Masuda projected four stages of information society development. The final stage would bring a "Copernican Turn in Privacy" was the thesis, because the ultimate democratization of personal data bases would entail full access to all of society's data by all members of society.(13)

FRANCE

In Frances's NCP study of 1978, the matter of personal data privacy was also addressed at length. The French, too, perceived that democratization of national data bases would deter an information aristocracy. But the French study went a step further, stating that the people must be re-educated to the view that supplying all personal data to the national network would be a duty, with corresponding data rights to have access to the network. Thus developed the ideas of "a new freedom of openness" with a "a new right to access" for all citizens of the future information society.(14)

PRIVACY AT THE FLASHPOINT

In many ways, the U.S. seems to be backing into the society of the "Copernican Turn in Privacy" and the "new freedom of openness" but without the "new right to access," and not by design nor with public awareness. These can be dangerous trends were they continued and expanded, unacknowledged. The time is ripe for us to make some explicit policy choices regarding computer data privacy, even if those are choices that acknowledge and accelerate computer practices which are in conflict with our history and customs on privacy. A decision knowingly made, of whatever choice, is preferable to a path derived by default.

For one alternative, we could make explicit the manner in which we trade personal data privacy for government services, by legislating a Uniform Code of Information Rights and Responsibilities.

Such a Code could specify the type and quantity of personal data that can be collected, and the security of it, for specific purposes. Sweden passed similar legislation in 1972.(15) In addition, the US Code could specify that citizens who accept services from government(medical, welfare, loans, mortgages) incur an obligation to submit all personal data pertaining to the service. The point has been well made that citizens too frequently demand personal services of government while insisting upon the right to withhold the personal data needed to service those demands. A balance must be struck among the demands, the data rights, and the data responsibilities. Alternatively, we could impose a computer equivalent of the Environmental Impact Report by requiring that each proposal for a computer personal data system be accompanied by a Privacy Impact Report akin to Japan's "Demerits" analysis.

Technical provisions for security of data in transit will mean little if there be no cohesive public policy on computer personal data privacy.

REFERENCES

1. J. Ellul, The Technological Society. New York: Vintage Books, 1964.
2. D. Burnham, The Rise of the Computer State. New York: Random House, 1983.
3. C. L. Howe, "The Disaster Dossier," Datamation, pp. 50-56, October 15, 1984.
4. J. Weizenbaum, Computer Power and Human Reason. San Francisco: W. H. Freeman, 1976.
5. S. D. Warren and L. D. Brandies, "The Right To Privacy," Harvard Law Review, pp. 193-220, December 15, 1890.
6. D. H. Flaherty, Privacy in Colonial New England. Charlottesville: University Press of Virginia, 1972.
7. U.S. Department of Health, Education and Welfare, Secretary's Advisory Committee on Automated Personal Data Systems, Records, Computers and the Rights of Citizens. Washington, D.C.: Government Printing Office, 1972.
8. U.S. Congress, 94th, 1st Session House of Representatives, H. R. 1984, January 23, 1975. "Comprehensive Right to Privacy Act," (Goldwater, Koch).
9. U.S. General Accounting Office, "Federal Information Systems Remain Highly Vulnerable," April 21, 1982. MASAD-82-18.
10. S. Garland, "Unleashing Computers to Sniff Out Welfare Fraud," The Christian Science Monitor, July 9, 1981, pp. 1.
11. P. M. Gutmann, "Statistical Illusions, Mistaken Policies," Challenge, November/December, 1979, pp. 14-16.
12. Japan Computer Usage Development Institute, A PLAN FOR THE INFORMATION SOCIETY - A National Goal Toward Year 2000. Tokyo: Japan Computer Usage Development Institute, May 1972. (This report is out of print but a compendium is in Chapter 1 of the following reference.)
13. Y. Masuda, The Information Society As Post-Industrial Society. Toyko: Institute for the Information Society, 1980.
14. S. Nora and A. Minc, The Computerization of Society. Cambridge: The MIT Press, 1980.
15. Federation of Swedish Industries, Swedish Data Act. Stockholm: P G Vinge, 1974.

DoD OVERVIEW
COMPUTER SECURITY PROGRAM DIRECTION

Colonel Joseph S. Greene, Jr., USAF

Deputy Director, DoD Computer Security Center
Fort George G. Meade, Maryland 20755-6000

BACKGROUND

At the 7th DoD/NBS Computer Security Conference (1984), and at the IEEE Computer Security Conference this spring, a number of people expressed interest in a review of new directions for the Department of Defense (DoD) Computer Security Program (CSP). This paper responds to those interests.

The DoD Computer Security Evaluation Center (DoDCSEC) was established in 1981. DoD Directive 5215.1 assigns responsibility for computer security and provides direction for the formulation of the Consolidated Computer Security Program. The Services and the Defense Communication Agency participate through the Technical Review Group in the formulation and execution of the CSP. The Director, National Security Agency, provides central oversight and single-point accountability for the CSP. The CSP funds the operation of the DoDCSEC and the generic Research, Development, Test, & Evaluation (RDT&E) program for the Department. Generic computer security research has potential application over a very broad, generalized basis and includes experimental exploration and development of feasible and potentially useful technology that is responsive to a broad class of computer security needs. Generic computer security research is distinct from application-dependent research and development for specific DoD component systems.

TECHNOLOGY BASE

In the past, the Department has responded to security needs by including computer security requirements in selected major programs (e.g., Strategic Air Command Digital Information Network (SACDIN), Automated Digital Information Network (AUTODIN), Defense Data Network (DDN), Inter-Service Agency Automated Message Processing Exchange (I-S/A AMPE), World Wide Military Command & Information Control System (WIS)). This approach tended to work for system-high systems but became increasingly expensive for multilevel secure trusted computer systems. With the trend toward ever more pervasive use and interconnection of Automated Information Systems (AIS), the case-by-case approach becomes prohibitively expensive. Without equivalent trust for all components, interconnected systems are only as secure as the weakest component, as can be demonstrated using password grabber, garbage collection, spoofing, and Trojan Horse attacks against a multilevel secure computer with an untrusted terminal. To encourage industry to incorporate trusted computer base security features and market trusted computers as their standard commercial offerings, the Department developed a

strategy of publishing standards. encouraging industry to build trusted products, evaluating and certifying these products against the standard, and publishing the results as an Evaluated Products List (EPL). Through this strategy, the Department hopes to make trusted products available to all users and to spread the development cost over a larger segment of the industry.

Discussion of the CSP should be based on a common understanding of the several factors that define the current technology maturity of the trusted computer systems. The following treatment assumes that the reader is familiar with the basic features and assurances defined in the DoD Trusted Computer Security Evaluated Criteria[1] and the fundamental conclusion of penetration studies in the 1970's that computer security must be an inherent quality of the design and implementation of the computer. The aspects discussed next provide a partial summary of the trusted computer system technology base. Correcting and overcoming deficiency in the several areas identified will constitute part of the challenge of the CSP.

a. A recent survey of 17,070 DoD computers indicates that half should be upgraded with Discretionay Access Control (DAC) capabilities. Although about 30 major vendors, each with numerous machine/-operating system combinations, were identified in the survey, only three DAC packages have been certified and placed on the DoDCSEC Evaluated Products List. These are the International Business Machines, Corp. (IBM), Resource Access Control Facility (RACF); SKK Inc's, The Access Control Facility 2 (ACF2); and CGA, Software Products Group's, TOP SECRET, all for the IBM MVS operating system that accounts for less than 400 of the machines identified in the DoD Survey. In addition to insufficient coverage, the government is somewhat behind the private sector in employment of those security measures that are available. For example, of the 10,000 MVS licenses in the private sector, half use add-on security packages, while only about 40 percent of the 500-plus government-owned MVS systems are similarly protected. If all DoD IBM mainframes used MVS and had add-on security packages, only about 4 percent of the DoD systems needing DAC capabilities would be protected.

b. According to the May 1985 Five-Year Plan published by OMB, the Federal Government plans to spend $31 billion on general purpose computers and telecommunications in the FY86 through FY90 period. Without a major initiative with incentives for the development of DAC mechanisms for a broad range of systems, the existing and future inventory will remain largely vulnerable to attack, at least through the next decade.

c. The survey of DoD computers also indicates that about one-third should be replaced with machines that provide mandatory access control (MAC). The only general purpose computer commercially available today with such capabilities is the Honeywell MULTICS computer. Although we expect to certify MULTICS at the B2 level, the product is not yet on the EPL. Industry has been reluctant to accept the risk of developing computers with MAC capabilities. About five years usually elapses between the time a vendor decides to develop a major new product to the times that the product is commercially availabile. Changes in the security requirements and criteria for certification during the development period can be very expensive. Industry representatives often express concern about their ability to interpret the Criteria in a particular situation. For these practical reasons, many vendors tend to let others pioneer the way. The government should make a major commitment to reduce these risks in order to stimulate development of a significant number of MAC machines during the next 5 years.

d. The Secure Communication Processor (SCOMP), developed by Honeywell Inc., is the only A1-level entry on the EPL. The SCOMP has only limited applications and does not have the processing speed needed to handle the general purpose problem. The national technology base for A1-level systems is essentially non-existent. There do not appear to be even 20 people in the world that have undertaken the essential steps of building an A1 system (e.g., a security policy; a security model; a descriptive top level specification; a formal top level specification (FTLS); a detailed design; a formal verification that the design complies with the FTLS, implementation, and test). The other critical A1 technology is configuration management. Existing methods are essentially human-intensive, paper-driven approaches that are subject to many classical failures. A great deal of research needs to be done to develop and distribute critical A1 technologies to industry before there will be significant numbers of verified systems on the market.

e. The President's 17 September 1984 National Security Decision Directive[2], places great emphasis on reducing the vulnerabilities for Automated Information Systems (AIS). These systems are defined as any system that creates, processes, exchanges, and modifies information in electronic form and includes mainframes, minis, personal computers (PCs), workstations, office automation, data base management systems, local and long-haul network components, distributed operating systems, file server/receivers, and multi media (text, graphics, voice, video) processors. Although we have the Criteria for secure general purpose computers and

believe them to be sufficiently general to apply to the other areas, we are only beginning to examine the extent of their applicability to the other segments of AIS's. Because these many components are frequently connected and because security is only as good as the weakest link, a great deal of work needs to be done to understand how to certify systems or to build systems with certified components. Although we can propose ideas, technical feasibility demonstrations are needed. A great deal of research will be required before standards with clear interpretations will be available to provide consistent AIS security across the range of products that comprise a modern information system.

f. To expand on the need for significant research, consider two examples. The DoDCSEC was able to write and publish the DoD Trusted Computer Security Evaluation Criteria between 1981 and 1983, because we had a technical foundation consisting of a decade of research sponsored by the services. This foundation included numerous worked examples to prove the feasibility of concepts and experienced people. We do not have that technology foundation in other AIS security areas. For example:

1. The DoDCSEC is the System Program Office (SPO) for the new multilevel secure, host-to-host encryption device called BLACKER. BLACKER will provide one new technology basis for replacement of the DDN and I-S/A AMPE AUTODIN with multilevel secure systems. The BLACKER program to build host front-ends, Key Distribution Centers, and Access Control Centers, will involve significant RDT&E dollars through the preproduction model. The effort provides extremely important pioneering network security work. Many questions remain to be answered, however, before we can extend the capabilities to include end-to-end encryption and provide support for data transfer rates of future networks as well as provide secure digital, voice, graphics, text, fax, and video multimedia communications being requested today for the command and control of military forces in the future.

2. The ANSI and ISO committees for the Graphical Kernel System (GKS) standard and the Common Language for the Interchange and Processing of Text (CLIPT) standard have not yet considered sensitivity labels that will be needed for multilevel secure, device-independent graphics and text processing. We do not have an industry standard for the internal representation of sensitivity labels used in network devices such as BLACKER. We need research to understand these issues before we publish standards.

3. The Air Force Studies Board sponsored a summer study on multilevel data base security in 1982. Many issues needing work were identified at that time. Essential by no funding has yet been approved to work on these security issues, even though many major system acquisitions need secure distributed data management

systems.

4. Without addressing fundamental issues of trusted computer systems, there are a number of ongoing efforts in the name of security that will give the uninformed a false sense of security. For example, we see complete instructions on hacker bulletin boards for defeating many different dial-back access control implementations.

5. There is a rush to add encryption to workstations and terminals. The fact, however, that information is stored and communicated in encrypted form does not eliminate the computer security vulnerabilities. Often, the perceived benefits of encryption can be circumvented by experts exploiting computer security flaws. Because a TEMPEST tested, encrypted PC costs several thousand dollars more than the comparable "unsecure" system, the Department could invest huge amounts of money for incomplete solutions that will not provide the protection sought and will have to be replaced when more of the community understands Trusted Computer Base (TCB) security issues.

6. Many of the workstations and terminals being considered as candidates for add-on encryption use single-state processors. We know of no way to secure a single-state processor machine. The Motorola 68000 and INTEL 80286 microprocessors have two or more states; however, multilevel secure operating systems are not available for these processors. Several efforts should be started immediately in this area.

The vulnerabilities suggested by these examples also apply to almost every component area of modern AIS. A great deal of research is needed to be able to guide the industry to development of trusted systems.

g. The convergence of telecommunication and computer technolgies encourages rapid aggregation of components to provide interconnected capabilities for sharing information. The unpredicted and explosive growth in the PC market between 1981 and 1984 resulted in sales of over 9 million PC's at a cost of $40 to $60 B. Local area networks are predicted to grow at an estimated rate of 46 percent compounded annually for the next few years. These market trends point to much greater interconnectivity and information accessibility that combine to make information systems more vulnerable today than they were four years ago when the DoDCSEC was founded. Without a significant surge effort, information systems will continue to become increasingly vulnerable to unauthorized access, integrity problems, and denial of critical services.

h. For years, the Department has advocated interoperable command and control systems. Without information sharing, decision making processes crumble and large organizations have difficulty behaving as a single unit. The existence of modern AIS's has been a factor contributing to 147 U.S. industry mergers in 1984 and the emergence of 300 multibillion dollar U.S. corporations in 1985. Today's mergers tend to retain the character of individual profit centers because the heterogeneous characteristics of today's AIS's do not permit horizontal integration outside a single vendor's product line. But horizontal information integration is just the kind of interoperability the DoD needs for the services, components, and U.S. allies to operate synergistically as a single unit. In this regard, the DoD is leading the world in interoperability issues, because, as a $300 billion-dollar-annually corporation, we need horizontal information integration now. Once systems are integrated and integratable, security and integrity will become absolutely essential to corporate survival. A corporation must be able to control data reading, control data writing, and prevent denial of information service. However, the technology base for this class of secure, machine-independent interoperability does not exist today. We have the basic technology concepts, but we need critical proof-of-concept research to demonstrate fundamental protection mechanisms that will prevent unauthorized use, prevent malicious and accidental data change, and complete denial of information services. Generic research in these fundamental areas is needed and the results should be widely shared with industry.

THE CHALLENGE

Based on arguments presented above, we conclude that: (1) the Department cannot afford computer security on a case-by-case basis; (2) computer security requires a fundamental change in the way industry designs and builds computers; and (3) the Department must cause industry to include security as an inherent quality of standard commercial offerings.

The AIS industry is a major national growth industry. AT&T estimates the 1984 gross sales at $141B. IBM estimated the market to be $230-240B annually. Business week estimated 1984 gross sale at $269, growing at 20% annually.

To evaluate the sufficiency of an RDT&E program, we need to understand how the program will change such a huge national growth industry, if at all. In arriving at a decision as to what is sufficient, we need, in addition to global strategy, some metrics to judge the impact of our proposed program. Although not precise metrics, the following factors are important considerations underpinnings for the CSP:

a) Standards are absolutely essential to influence the directions of industry. We have an urgent need for many standards dealing with the various components and aspects of AIS security.

b) Development of consistent standards requires strong central oversight. The National Computer Security Center, under the Director, National Security Agency, has been charged to provide that oversight. Our first priority must be to build a strong center capable of undertaking these new responsibilities.

c) Standards must be consistently applied across the Department and government. If every program office tailors the standard to its unique mission needs, the Department will speak with a confusing voice, there will be no standard, and industry will adopt a "wait and see" attitude. The National Telecommunication and Information System Security Committee (NTISSC), in conjunction with the National Manager and the National Computer Security Center, must develop and enforce standards.

d) A clear capability to monitor compliance with established standards must exist. That monitoring should be fairly and openly applied, especially when we depend on private sector funding for product development. The evaluating organization must be staffed in sufficient quality and numbers to provide responsive and open interaction with industry.

e) The average industry time to bring a new AIS product into the market is 5 years. Standards must remain stable during development periods of this length or industry will not respond by investing private sector dollars.

f) There is little worse than a well-enforced, bad standard. The standards proposed by the National Computer Security Center must be supported by worked examples that prove feasibility, clarify interpretations, and communicate the knowledge and experience to industry. A solid research program, including exploratory and exemplory development is essential.

g) The program must have reasonable balance between near-term, mid-term and long-term objectives. Some issues will take considerable time to resolve. We must not sacrifice the future for near-term fixes, and we need to do the best we can to protect the current and planned inventory through its remaining useful life.

h) The job facing the government is that of building and distributing to industry a fundamental new technology. The job must be completed before the underlying assumptions are obsoleted by changing technology. The program must have sufficient industry participation to have a significant impact on future directions and technology decisions by industry and the private sector.

PRIORITIES

Our first priority under the President's Directive will be to build a strong National Computer Security Center. We will need a strong in-house capability to provide the technology basis for standards development, to support a significant product evaluation capability, and to foster much wider awareness of computer security needs and issues. The in-house RDT&E capability will permit the best possible progress with limited resources and in the event additional monies become available provide the technical oversight for a greatly increased industry participation. Planned personnel increases should enable the Center to support approximately 45 new commercial product evaluations by 1990. This would be a significant increase over 1985 levels and should send a strong signal to industry that will encourage investment of private sector dollars in trusted product development.

Our second priority will be to greatly strengthen the research effort by strengthening industry participation. Our strategy includes three thrusts: 1) near-term efforts to improve security of the current inventory of government computers; 2) mid-term efforts to greatly increase the availability of trusted products with much better security features than are generally used today; and, 3) long-term efforts to develop and distribute to industry the technology base needed to build much more trustworthy system than we currently know how to build.

In carrying out this strategy, we are concerned that near-term fixes do not jeopardize long-term solutions. To achieve this objective, a panel that was convened in response to a Secretary of Defense security initiative recommended that the five-year computer security research program be allocated as follows: 20 percent of the resources applied to development of C-level DAC add-on security capabilities to protect current and planned systems, 30 percent to stimulate development of B- and A1-level MAC systems and 50 percent to extend our understanding of assurances beyond A1. The Technical Review Group recommended a 30 percent, 30 percent, and 40 percent mi, repectively for these objectives in the transition year FY87. The emphasis on near-term dollars will be to develop working products that will improve security for immediate needs and encourage private sector development and marketing of similar or better products. The mid-term efort will focus on exemplary products in the public domain to greatly reduce the risk involved in interpreting standards. These exemplary multilevel secure implementations will be made widely available to industry to accelerate the availability of new products and stimulate private sector development of better products. The government expects to carry the initial research burden to extend our knowledge of beyond A1. Given the fact that formal software and hardware verification may not mature to affordable technologies for many years; given also the facts that configuration control may be our only alternative to reduce vulnerability of DAC mechanisms, will be required in any case and to extend assurances beyond A-1; and,

given the fact that configuration control
is emerging as a fundamental need of
network security not adequately supported
by current methods; we hope to significantly
increased our efforts in formal methods and
automated configuration control.

Beginning in Fiscal Year 1987, a major
RDT&E initiative is being planned to
develop a new technology base in computer
security and to distribute that base to
industry. The effort will be carried on
with broadened industry participation. Our
future program will comprehensively treat
all aspects of AIS security from the
component and the total systems view.

CONCLUSION

The Center's program provides a sound
basis for expectations that computer
security vulnerabilities could be greatly
reduced by the end of the 15-year period.
It also provides a balanced effort to
reduce vulnerabilities in the intervening
years. The research is conducted on a
schedule that would significantly
contribute to the long-term
interoperability goals of the DoD.

REFERENCES

1. DoD Computer Security Center,
Department of Defense Trusted Computer
System Evaluation Criteria, CSC-STD-001-83,
dtd 15 August 1983.

2. The White House, National Policy on
Telecommunications and Automated
Information System Security, National
Security Decision Directive 145
(Unclassified Version), dtd
17 September 1984.

COMSEC IN TRANSITION

Speaker
Orville C. Lewis
Deputy Chief, COMSEC
Policy, Doctrine and
Liaison Staff,
National Security
Agency

NO DOUBT should exist in the mind of any AFCEA member that the modern world is heavily dependent on telecommunications and data processing. Every issue of *SIGNAL* Magazine carries numerous articles on the latest developments in those fields. Yet, for all the dependence on these disciplines, for all the money spent on developing new technology and for all the trust we put in these systems with information about the nation's most vital secrets, "The 1982–1983 Report to the President on the Status of Communications Security in the Federal Government" proclaimed that it is in a perilous state. Virtually every aspect of government and private information is readily available to the United States' adversaries: Unfriendly governments and international terrorist organizations alike are finding it easy to obtain information in the flood of unprotected telecommunications and automated data processing information afloat in this country.

The report to the president recommended that a number of objectives be adopted to protect vital, sensitive government information. It called for:

● improving planning, development and production to deliver more communications security (COMSEC) equipment sooner and at a lower cost;

● reorganizing and refocusing the COMSEC policy making structure to facilitate requirements definition, determining priorities and funding;

● increasing substantially funding for COMSEC;

● increasing significantly the near-term availability of secure telephones throughout the government; and

● increasing efforts to secure computerized data networks and associated office automation equipment.

History of COMSEC

COMSEC first was declared a national responsibility by President Harry S. Truman in the 1952 Presidential Directive that established the National Security Agency (NSA). He directed that the National Security Council establish a United States Communications Security Board (USCSB) to be responsible for integrating COMSEC policies and procedures throughout the government. He also established that the Secretary of Defense would act as the executive agent for communications security for the entire government and that the Director, NSA (DIRNSA), would act for the Secretary of Defense in implementing these COMSEC responsibilities.

President Truman's COMSEC structure lasted essentially intact for 24 years. Then, in 1977, recognizing a need to strengthen U.S. posture against the hostile threat to government communications across the board, President Jimmy Carter issued Presidential Directive Number 24, entitled "Telecommunications Protection Policy," which modified the Truman structure and split COMSEC responsibilities between the Secretaries of Defense and Commerce. The National Communications Security Directive, creating the National Communications Security Committee (NCSC), was issued by the Secretary of Defense in 1979 to complete the Carter structure. The national COMSEC directive reaffirmed the responsibilities of the executive agent and DIRNSA.

Although NCSC promulgated a dozen statements of policy and more than 50 instructions and information memoranda, the increasingly challenging threat to our telecommunications required an even more visionary and broader approach. National Security Decision Directive 145 (NSDD-145), the national policy on telecommunications and automated information systems security, was signed by President Ronald Reagan on September 17, 1984. This directive confirms the basic tenet of the entire communications security process as it applies to both telecommunications and information systems security—namely that COMSEC is a national responsibility. NSDD-145 directs a reorganization and refocusing of the national COMSEC and computer security (COMPUSEC) policy-making structure.

Overview of NSDD-145

NSDD-145 provides for the safeguarding from hostile exploitation of systems that process or communicate sensitive information. That information may be classified national security information or other sensitive, but unclassified, government or government derived information, the loss of which could adversely affect the national interest. NSDD also directs the government to encourage, advise and, where appropriate, to assist the private sector to identify systems that handle sensitive nongovernment information and to evaluate its vulnerability and measures for its protection.

This directive expands the authorities of the Secretary of Defense as the executive agent of the government for COMSEC to include automated information systems security. The directive also establishes a national manager as the operating arm of the executive agent. DIRNSA is the national manager. This consolidation of COMPUSEC and COMSEC under a single government manager is indicative of the trend in technology to blur the distinctions between telecommunications systems and automated information systems. This trend already has led many organizations to establish a single senior manager responsible for both fields. The military services, civil departments and agencies of the government and U.S. Allies all reflect this trend.

Systems Security Steering Group

The Systems Security Steering Group, which was established by NSDD-145, is expected to take an active role in carrying out the national policy on telecommunications and automated information systems security and will meet at least twice a year. During the first meeting each year, the steering group will review the security status of those telecommunications and automated information systems that handle classified or sensitive government or government derived information and will develop guidance for program and budget development. At the second meeting, it will review the programs and budgets assembled by the national manager and will formulate recommendations to pass to the Office of Management and Budget (OMB) for use during OMB budget reviews.

It is expected that the cabinet level membership and the President's National Security Advisor, Robert C. McFarlane, as Chairman of the steering group, will ensure that programming and budgeting for telecommunications security and automated information systems security receive the wider high level government exposure needed to obtain the necessary resources. Under the previous system, COMSEC and COMPUSEC were not programmed and budgeted with a national perspective; and those agencies not primarily in the national security sector had little role in the decision making.

The National Telecommunications and Information Systems Security Committee (NTISSC) is the operating level interagency organization subordinate to the Systems Security Steering Group. In addition to the three military departments, NTISSC membership includes the Joint Chiefs of Staff (JCS) and the Marine Corps as voting members as well as a broad representation among other DOD and civil agencies. The committee is comprised of senior representatives who are decision makers for 21 government departments, agencies and military services. NTISSC has seven nonvoting observer representatives.

NTISSC is chaired by the Assistant Secretary of Defense for Command, Control, Communications and Intelligence, Donald Latham. The committee has an impressive array of responsibilities and has established a national issuance system for promulgating operating policies, directives, instructions and guidance. This system will be maintained by the NTISSC executive secretariat as the NTISS issuance system. It will include the policy statements, instructions and advisory memoranda developed by the former NCSC until they are replaced or updated by NTISSC.

Under Executive Order 12333, the Secretary of Defense is executive agent of the government for COMSEC. NSDD-145 expands this role to include automated information systems security. The Secretary of Defense, as executive agent, and DIRNSA, as national manager, respond to the direction of the Systems Security Steering Group, under the National Security Council. They also respond to NTISSC, which formulates policy, sets objectives and establishes priorities.

NSDD-145 mandates that, for both telecommunications systems security and automated information systems security, the responsibilities of the executive agent be carried out by the national manager. The executive agent's budget recommendations are prepared by the national manager and are subsequently reviewed and approved by the steering group.

NSA continues its national role in COMSEC and now has a similar role in COMPUSEC. DIRNSA, as national manager, acts as the government focal point for cryptography and telecommunications systems security and is the focal point for automated information systems security as well. Of the national manager's responsibilities, two are particularly important. DIRNSA prescribes and approves all cryptographic systems and techniques and is responsible for conducting liaison with foreign governments and international organizations. DIRNSA also assesses the overall security posture of the government for telecommunications and information systems, conducts or approves research and development for telecommunications and information systems security, prescribes security doctrine, operates printing and fabrication facilities and enters into procurement agreements with and for departments and agencies of the government, the private sector and foreign and international organizations.

DIRNSA's responsibilities as national manager are wide ranging and vital to the security of our nation's telecommunications and information systems security. However, they are not to be viewed in isolation for without the active participation and support of all elements of the government, and that portion of the private sector that handles sensitive government and nongovernment information, our national and private secrets will remain exposed to any adversary. The national manager is in a position to educate and assist others in understanding the threat to their security and to help with the solution by finding ways to secure sensitive information and systems.

Implementing COMSEC

While DIRNSA's COMSEC authority over systems approval is clear, implementing COMSEC remains the responsibility of each department, agency or service that uses telecommunications or automated information systems. Once a department or agency head has chosen to spend money on telecommunications security or automated information systems security, DIRNSA, as national manager, prescribes or approves which COMSEC or COMPUSEC technique, system or equipment will be used. Beginning with the development of the FY 87 budget, and because of the role designated in NSDD-145, the national manager is now participating in a meaningful way in the programming and budgeting process for the entire U.S. government—civil and defense agencies and departments. Working closely with the executive agent, the military departments and the civil agencies, the national manager will review the security requirements and the proposed solutions of those organizations and will recommend, where appropriate, alternative programs for review by the executive agent and the steering group. It is important to understand that the national manager does not prepare or defend a consolidated budget; the manager's authority is limited to reviewing and assessing individual departmental and agency input and recommending alternatives. The final decision on whether to, how much to and when to spend funds for telecommunications security and/or automated information systems security is retained by the departments and agencies involved.

NSDD-145 calls for the national manager to create and operate a central technical center for COMPUSEC. This is the National Computer Security Center, which is responsive to the needs of the entire government. It was established as the DOD computer security center to provide COMPUSEC policy framework. Technical evaluations of computer systems and network security and related technical research for DOD and DOD contractor customers. Now, as a national center, the Computer Security Center serves more than 1,000 federal departments, agencies, boards and commissions in addition to its original customers.

The center responds to a growing need for computer security within the government and to a growing recognition of the technical challenges involved in providing effective protection within a computer system. The center guides and consolidates common technical activities to provide a broad base of support to government departments and agencies.

Evaluation Process

Since NSDD-145 was signed in September 1984, many efforts have been underway to realize its direction. One of these is in response to the requirement that NTISSC submit an annual evaluation of the status of national telecommunications and automated information systems security to the Systems Security Steering Group. This will replace the old biennial report to the President, which was last submitted in February 1984.

This year's annual report provides a measure of how well the United States has done in meeting the objectives of the biennial report, spells out the challenges still faced and recommends objectives for the coming year.

The Chairmen of the two NTISSC subcommittees for Telecommunications Systems Security and Automated Information Systems Security were tasked to provide separate evaluations dealing with their respective subject areas. The Executive Secretariat consolidated the two subcommittee evaluations and submitted the consolidated report to NTISSC for review prior to it being forwarded to McFarlane, the Chairman of the steering group.

The national manager has established a National COMSEC Assessment Center in the communications security organization at NSA to provide a continuing program of assessment of the nation's communications security posture. This center already has begun to work with the departments and agencies of the government to ensure that sensitive communications are identified and provided appropriate protection. The results of this collaborative effort will constitute the national COMSEC assessment program and will provide a firm foundation of documented vulnerabilities upon which to base requirements for COMSEC resources and to put in order of priority programs for national COMSEC planning and management.

Approaches to Protection

As the need for telecommunications has grown, so has the need for new approaches to providing the security essential to protecting those communications. Government contractors can now charge back the cost of their COMSEC or protection costs to the government in the same manner as other contract security costs. The Secretary of Defense has required NSA to establish procedures to permit government contractors to procure communications security equipment directly from manufacturers. NSA has responded by negotiating memoranda of agreement with several manufacturers to form the authorized vendor program. This provides the means for contractors to obtain COMSEC and protection equipment more readily than in the past. NSA has also established the Commercial COMSEC Endorsement Program to encourage private industry to use private funds to develop secure communications and information processing equipment. These equipments may be submitted for NSA endorsement and then sold privately to authorized users.

All of you are users of telecommunications and automated information systems. Most of you will, at one time or another, have occasion to discuss sensitive information whether it be classified national security information or sensitive, but unclassified government or nongovernment information. Regardless of which category it falls in, it needs protection from those who would use it to the disadvantage of the United States or your company. It is the government's goal to make low cost, effective protection devices available as widely as possible. However, the only way security can be effective is if protection is used whenever a question of sensitivity exists in the data being exchanged—whatever the means.

NSDD-145, in establishing the new National Policy on Telecommunications and Automated Information Systems Security, is refocusing national COMSEC and COMPUSEC policy-making structure to account for the changing nature of telecommunications and automated information systems. As those technologies change, it will continue to be a goal in the policy arena to stay abreast of the changing concerns and relationships that emerge as a result. With the national authority vested in the system by the presidential signature on NSDD-145, and with broad participation within the civil and military sectors of the government, and hopefully the private sector as well, NSA is optimistic about protecting a significant portion of the data now being lost to adversaries through the telecommunications and automated information systems upon which the United States is so heavily dependent.

• • • — • —

Section 2
Computer System Security

Section 2.1: Management Issues

Introduction

This section presents a basic framework to establish a structure for viewing computer systems security. Three aspects of the structure are discussed: management responsibility and authority; managerial physical, administrative, technical, and communications controls; and management decision making for systems under development. The first two topics pertain primarily to systems in operation, while the third one focuses on systems under development. A fourth topic concludes this section, which gives an overview of the reprinted extract from a MITRE Corporation report by Frederick G. Tompkins. This is followed by abstracts of recommended readings.

Many of the concepts placed in the framework, which is developed in this section, were introduced in the preceding sections. For example, in Section 1.1, Severity of Security Risks, we introduced Courtney's ordered list of risks. This list includes the following risks (1) errors and omissions, (2) dishonest employees, (3) fire, (4) disgruntled employees, (5) water, and (6) strangers.

The important point to emphasize in this discussion is the use of the terms *computer security* and *network security*. We generally define computer security as providing protection, accuracy, and continuity of operations for a database that is controlled by a processor that may communicate with other processors and/or terminals. In a broader sense, network security may be viewed as computer security extended to the communications between many components, including processors, terminals, and special-purpose communications processors. While we are focusing on computer security in this section, there is an overlap with network security issues that are developed in Sections 3.1, 3.2, 3.3, 3.4, and 3.5. This occurs because of the widespread utilization of digital technology in all phases of computer and network investments and the trend toward integrated information systems development and operation. Management must continually reassess the role of automated information systems with respect to the objectives and vitality of the organization. We often use the term computer security to include network security. Information systems security or information security may be interpreted as including computer and network security. This occurs, in part, because of the merging of the two disciplines, computer and network technology.

Management Responsibility and Authority

Senior management is responsible for the success of the organization as it performs with respect to a set of defined and agreed to objectives. Management is responsible for the cost-effective and timely accomplishment of the organization's objectives. The balance between each manager's responsibility and authority can be best defined as management by objectives (MBO). Each manager should only be responsible for those organizational objectives that he or she has the authority to control. For example, the manager of a corporate division may be held responsible for the division's contribution to the corporate profit (or loss). However, the manager can only meet this responsibility within the constraints of certain company-wide policies, such as: (1) personnel, (2) financial management, (3) capital investment, and (4) computer and network security.

Security, as we have stated, is a management responsibility. The structure of a security management program may vary substantially from one organization to another. However, for purposes of our discussion, the following structure is used.

- *Senior management responsibility:* Senior management is responsible for overall operations, plans, and directions.

- *Management responsibility boundary:* Each manager is responsible for his/her performance versus objectives within organizational constraints such as the objectives for computer and network security.

- *Formal computer and network security program:* Each organization should have a formal computer and network security program including: security planning; security policies; personnel security; systems security officer (SSO); budget review; data and applications integrity/confidentiality; risk management; managerial, physical, administrative, technical and communications controls; training; continuity of operations; formal review procedures; and corrective actions.

Each aspect of a formal security program is briefly discussed in the following sections, which follow the order above.

We suggest that a formal security program that requires computer and network security be considered as an integral aspect of doing business. Security includes data and application system integrity and accuracy. A formal security program is managed in a manner similar to other organizational programs, including measuring performance against objectives (MBO).

Security Planning

Planning for computer and network security is a subset of organizational planning. All of the practices and procedures of effective planning apply. This includes development and approval of short- and long-range security plans with respect to agreed organizational objectives. The key to planning success is implementing the planning process. Many organizations plan separately for computer and for network security. While this may be acceptable for certain short-term objectives, we have serious reservations about this practice for long-term planning. The reason integrated security planning is becoming more critical is that major organizations are merging their computer and network operations. Therefore, security must be treated as applicable to entire automated information systems—total system security or information security.

Total systems security is analogous to the concept of end-to-end encryption, discussed in Sections 3.1 and 3.2. Briefly, the concept is that data entering the system are equally protected through the processing steps in the system. Total systems security is of particular importance for automated information systems that process sensitive data, involve large financial transactions (e.g., electronic fund transfer (EFT)), and are important to the continued successful accomplishment of one or more major organizational objectives (e.g., insurance accounts receivable and payable).

Security Policies

There are important computer and network security policies that apply generically to a wide variety of systems. The most authoritative policies are implemented in standards, such as those from the National Computer Security Center (NCSC). These policies are discussed in Section 2.3. Caution is urged when developing the computer and network security policies for an individual application or organization: We urge you to consider how well the security policies correlate with the approach suggested by NCSC. For example, NCSC suggests two fundamental computer security requirements as components of a computer security policy for access control [CSCS83]. These requirements are (1) *Security policy:* There must be an explicit and well-defined security policy enforced by the system and (2) *Marking–access control labels:* These labels must be associated with objects (generally data in a computer system).

Security policy is more complex in a network. For example, an overall policy must be defined for the network and for the components (e.g., host computers, front end processors, packet switches, etc.) [BRAN85]. Categories of security policy for a network being considered by NCSC include: secrecy, a COMSEC (communication security) issue; access control, both mandatory (enforcing hierarchical sensitivity levels) and discretionary (enforcing need-to-know); protec-

tion against compromise (e.g., interconnection rules between components, where data is transmitted within an accreditation range); integrity (for transmitted data); and denial of service (as a function of mission-oriented criteria).

Personnel Security

The most important aspect of security is integrity of the personnel processing the information, whether in manual or automated form. Programs should be developed to assist management in screening personnel to ensure a high degree of individual integrity. These programs are part of a personnel security program. Basic elements of a personnel security program include (1) new employee screening; (2) background investigations (basic checks, background investigations, special background investigations, and updates on investigations); (3) designation of special access restrictions (sensitivity or class of data and limited access); (4) security awareness (briefings, training (also listed as a separate category because of its importance), and information programs (e.g., memoranda to employees)); (5) investigations (actual/potential security risks and actual/potential security violations); and (6) exit interviews (dismissals for security reasons and security exit debriefings).

The personnel security program should be integrated into the overall organizational security program. We shall show a partial example of this in a later section on security training, which is a personnel security responsibility and a major building block of a formal computer and network security program.

One of the key aspects of a personnel security program is to coordinate personnel security with a formal designation of hierarchical and nonhierarchical levels of data sensitivity. These terms are widely used when referring to data classified for national security; they are also generally applicable to commercial data as well. Examples of hierarchically classified commercial data are company proprietary, time sensitive actions or announcements, and EFT. Examples of nonhierarchical commercial data are salary tables, performance evaluations, and technical data. Just as in national security classifications, hierarchical and nonhierarchical categories can be combined to further restrict access. When management agrees to a set of defined access control levels, a set of appropriate personnel security requirements can be established for background investigations and access rights. In general, when such investigations are coupled with specific job-related requirements, such as the data access discussed here, these investigations are permitted by labor legislation.

Systems Security Officer

There are several ways to designate system security officers (SSOs). For example, an SSO may be responsible for a facility (e.g., computer center); a function (e.g., telecommunications); and an applications system (e.g., EFT for a facility, a network, or all facilities and networks).

Although, there are several schools of thought on these designations, we suggest that primary consideration be given to the designation of an SSO for an applications or automated information system. This approach is consistent with NCSC development of *Trusted Network Evaluation Criteria (TNEC)* [BRAN85]. The major reason for this approach is to provide overall security responsibility for an integrated information system. This way management can develop a high degree of confidence that total systems or information security issues are being thoroughly addressed and actual/potential security problems are being identified and corrected. Supporting SSOs can be designated for facilities and functions.

Budget Review

There is no uniform school of thought on the best set of procedures for budgeting for computer and network security because many of the security controls are considered to be an integral part of operations. For example, electronic audit trails are essential for computer security functions, such as identification of potential and actual security violations and restart and recovery including backup operations. However, the same audit trails also are essential for most on-line systems for reasons such as monitoring accidental errors, resource accounting, and maintaining historical records.

Each organization must decide how to budget for computer and network security and how to maintain the supporting financial records. In general, there are two categories of specificity involved in this process: specific security costs and joint or shared security costs. For example, specific security costs include security costs for SSOs, hardware (such as encryption devices) and software (such as access control software). Joint security costs could include electronic audit trail costs and input processing control costs. Another example could be a case where a fiber optic network is being developed because of security requirements (no emanations). This approach may also be the most cost-effective from an operations viewpoint, independent of the security features of fiber optics.

Data and Applications Integrity/Confidentiality

A user must have confidence in the database that is supporting his application. This confidence requires a baseline capability to ensure that the database is accurate, maintained in an accurate and confidential fashion, and protected from accidental and deliberate attack. Data integrity/confidentiality is one way of describing a database that continually meets these needs.

When software applications operate on a database, data integrity/confidentiality must be maintained. This can be de-

fined as applications integrity/confidentiality. The maintenance of applications integrity should be continuous. This means that the supporting computer and network processes should do only what is intended to the database, no more or no less. Achieving this continuity of applications integrity/confidentiality is difficult because of the numerous threats that can occur. For example, system failure and the necessary restart/recovery operations may be vulnerable to accidental or deliberate attacks on the database. Further, computer program modifications such as *trapdoors* or dual purpose programs such as *Trojan horses* may be developed to either passively or overtly attack a database. Passive attacks, such as reading a sensitive database, are very difficult to detect.

Data and applications integrity/confidentiality are also highly dependent upon safe digital transmission in a network. This means protection from passive and overt attacks as well as from errors and discontinuity of transmission.

In the early computer and network applications during the 1950s, data and applications integrity/confidentiality were considered as characteristics of a benign or friendly automated environment. Consequently, much of the early investment in automated information systems emphasized computer and network checks for accidental error. More recent computer and network investments have also considered deliberate attacks because of the incidents that have occurred over the years. One result has been the gradual development of computer and network security disciplines.

Developing and maintaining data and applications integrity in an organization's computer and network systems can be viewed as a goal of computer and network security. This approach to security addresses the need for controls or safeguards to protect information against error and deliberate attack. Computer and network security can also be considered as providing controls or safeguards on a continuous basis, with secure provisions for restart/recovery and backup/recovery capabilities.

Important dimensions of security include [ANDE85] protection priorities and protection objectives, such as protection of systems and of information. We have many elements of concern, depending upon the needs of the user and the organization as well as the environmental factors. Traditionally, we balance risk controls or safeguards with production needs and costs when we resolve protection priorities and objectives. This balancing process can be referred to as risk management when the final decisions are made by senior management.

Risk Management

Risk management is an approach to balancing of the risk in developing and operating automated information systems with the need for cost-effective capabilities. Risk management involves a conflict between user friendliness and effective security. Although we can never have a perfectly secure system, management should strive to minimize losses and still meet system performance objectives. Estimates of the losses for the United States vary. One estimate is over $3 billion in 1985, with 25 percent of the *Fortune* 1000 firms experiencing verifiable losses [ANDE85]. Individual losses can be substantial, such as the 28-hour computer software outage at the Bank of New York, during November 21 and 22, 1985. As a result, the Bank had to borrow over $22 billion from the Federal Reserve System [GOLD 85].

A challenge facing management is that computer and network security are becoming more difficult to provide as we move computing power closer to the end user. This process can also involve distributing entire or partial copies of the database combined with downloading of data. As we distribute processing and decentralize accountability and safeguards, we are creating a larger need for more effective methods of maintaining computer and network security.

Risk management is essential to the success of security planning. There are many schools of thought on what constitutes effective risk management. We present an overview of a structure for the risk management process which is adapted from Fred Tompkins' work. Each organization is faced with risks, and management has a set of priorities to consider when evaluating risk. Risk management occurs informally as a normal part of the business operation. However, we stress a more formal approach for computer and network security because of the complexity and importance of this technological investment.

The computer and network risk management process may be defined as consisting of six major phases:

Phase 1. Risk analysis: There are generally four steps in risk analysis:

(1) *Define the risk environment:* We strongly recommend that the risk environment be as broad as possible to accurately focus on how the automated information system supports one or more organizational objectives. Specifically we mean the risk environment includes at a minimum all personnel, facilities, hardware, software, and communications systems that support the automated information as well as the system's database and associated software.

   The largest risk to organizational continuity of operations is generally related to data and applications software integrity and/or system availability failures. For example, the securities trading database for the Bank of New York is critical to its day-to-day operation and this database is difficult to reconstruct in the event of a hardware, software, or related failure.

(2) *Define and rank the categories of risk:* The threats to a system can be defined as unintentional and intentional.

Unintentional human threats, such as input processing errors, are generally considered to be the major cause of substantial economic losses. Environmental disasters and computer crime may receive more publicity but are generally lesser economic threats to an organization.

(3) *Evaluate occurrence of risks:* Each threat can occur with a given probability. The difficulty is that we have a limited ability to identify this probability accurately. There are two schools of thought on this issue. The quantitative school of thought, which is represented by NBS Federal Information Processing Standard Publication (FIPS PUB) 65 *Guideline for Automatic Data Processing Risk Analysis* [GUID79], uses probability of occurrence that is expressed as a number from $p = 0$ to $p = 1$. A second school of thought is the qualitative school, which is represented by Robert Campbell in *A Guide to Automated Systems Security* [CAMP80]. The qualitative school of thought represents probabilities in ranges or index form. For example, for $p = 0$ to 0.33, this could be identified as a low risk; $p = .34$ to $.66$ could be medium risk; and $p = .67$ to 1.00, high risk.

(4) *Assessment of risk occurrence impact:* The key aspect of this part of risk analysis is to analyze the impact on system cost and performance of the occurrence of each risk. We stress the "system" that includes all components that support continuity of operations and data and applications integrity.

Phase 2. Risk reduction analysis: The process of risk reduction starts with an analysis of the managerial, physical, administrative, technical, and communications controls that are available to reduce risk. An important technique is to rank in order the controls so that management reviews controls in order of their potential contribution to risk reduction.

Phase 3. Management decision: Management must make a decision and accept a certain amount of risk after selecting the controls for risk reduction. There is no risk-free system; even if the probability of failure is less than 0.000000001, there is always a first time for failure, and management should select their risk reduction choices with this in mind.

Phase 4. Development of risk reduction action plans: The risk reduction action plans identify the managerial, physical, administrative, technical, and communications controls selected by management for protection of the system. The plans provide Gantt charts (bar charts) or equivalent means of showing the schedule for phasing controls into the automated information system's life cycle. In general, the earlier in the life cycle the control is implemented, the lower its cost and the more cost-effective its contribution to effective system operation. Responsibilities for each phase in the schedule should be clearly specified. Responsibility includes accepting or rejecting progress at each major system milestone.

Phase 5. Implementation and maintenance of controls: Implementing the selected controls requires substantial advance work, depending on the sensitivity of the data in the system. Controls must be presented in training sessions and be accepted by the concerned parties, including users, and implemented accurately. For example, the controls to meet the nuclear safety requirements for the Three Mile Island nuclear reactor should have been carefully explained to all operators before the controls were implemented. Apparently, this was not the case because the operators were reported to have inadequately responded to the control room software warning. There are analysts who believe the software provision for corrective action was incorrectly overridden by the control room operators.

Maintenance of controls requires effective configuration management of changes to ensure continuity of operations, data and applications integrity, and system responsiveness. Maintenance is a dynamic process that may include system correction, modification, and enhancement. Either activity can have a substantial impact on system operation. For example, fixing module A in a program may inadvertently affect module B. This impact may only be noticed when the system fails after peak load.

Phase 6. Review and audit: Review and audit are modern terms for the basic management responsibility to keep the organization on course with respect to its objectives. The techniques available to support this function for automated information systems vary from periodic managerial reviews to in-depth system testing. After each review and audit, the risk analysis for the system should be updated to reflect the corrective action taken to keep the system on course.

A fundamental fact of review and audit is that the modern technology of automated information systems life-cycle development and operation is rapidly outpacing the traditional review and audit techniques. This dilemma is recognized, and management is continually striving to meet these needs by training review and audit personnel in the latest technologies.

A limited review of the risk management plan or audit of a systems operation may not reveal serious flaws or existing fraud. We suggest that you not accept any review or audit at a level of accuracy that exceeds the accuracy level of the review and audit techniques employed.

Managerial, Physical, Administrative, Technical, and Communications Controls

Each organization's security program requires a specific set of managerial, physical, administrative, technical, and communications controls for each automated information system. Since two or more systems may share the same computer and network facilities, many controls can be common. For example, the physical access controls to a computer center may be used by personnel working on several different applications that vary from payroll to corporate financial modeling.

Several basic categories of controls should be considered when developing a computer and network security program.

Category 1. Managerial controls: Managerial controls are defined as the set of managerial decisions that pertain to the direction and control of computer and network security. The decision-making process for managerial controls includes making appropriate decisions for each of the aspects of a formal computer and network security program, such as security planning, security policies, and so on. However, most important are those decisions that integrate security into the overall operation of the organization. These decisions pertain to planning and operational issues such as "What should the proper balance be between computer and network response time and security capabilities during peak load?" The locus of managerial controls is identifying the SSO as a management function.

The criteria for measuring the effectiveness of managerial controls with respect to computer and network security include computer and network performance and security objectives, such as reliability, availability, and continuity of operations. These criteria should be defined in quantitative terms for normal, peak and restart/recovery operations, to assist in measuring how well the organization is performing. For example, the network performance criteria for company X could include specifications such as a 2-second response time during normal operations, a 5-second response time during peak load, and a 45 minute restart/recovery time from system failure. Certain criteria can be defined in decimal form such as reliability (e.g., .9995 reliability of future operations during prime shift) and availability (e.g., 95 percent demonstrated availability during prime shift). In addition, the security criteria for the network could include a requirement for security services as defined in a Network Security Architecture as described in Section 3.1. Specifications for security services could include requirements for identification, peer entity authentication, access control, data confidentiality, communications integrity, service availability, and nonrepudiation (the ability to prove to impartial third parties that a protocol-data-unit was actually sent and received). Since security is integral to organizational success, a specific security criterion may be viewed by management as also relating to operations (e.g., availability and continuity of operations).

Category 2. Physical controls: Physical controls may be considered conceptually as a set of concentric circles around the facility being protected, such as a computer center, communications center, or a terminal room. The rings in the concentric circle from the outside in approximately are perimeter controls, facility access controls, computer or communications center access controls, terminal room or remote terminal access controls, and console or terminal access controls.

A variety of devices support the physical access control process. Examples are guards, electronic scanning, and closed circuit television, especially controlled access doors, and electronic badges for user identification (e.g., badges that are read electronically).

Category 3. Administrative controls: Administrative controls may be thought of as the procedures that are defined by the SSO and implemented by the operational organization to ensure that the managerial, physical, technical, and communications controls are not bypassed. For example, the process of providing security guards to check traffic to a computer center and requiring that passwords be changed periodically could be considered as administrative procedures. An organization should have at a minimum a security manual to document these procedures for computer and telecommunications facilities. Additional manuals may be required for specific computer and network applications, depending on the nature and size of the systems. The need for additional procedures increases with the sensitivity of the data being processed.

Category 4. Technical controls: Technical controls are those controls primarily associated with the operation of hardware and software systems. The degree of control required should be determined by the user organization through a formal process, such as certification and accreditation [GUID83]. Generally these controls should be related to the *Trusted Computer System Evaluation Criteria* (TCSEC) [CSCS83]. However, it should be noted that the higher evaluated divisions of the TCSEC, B2 or better, tend to increase the assurance that the protective mechanisms are correctly designed and implemented rather than providing increased protection.

The TCSEC establishes gradations of technical controls, but does not define which controls are appropriate to a given environment. Another Center publication, the *Computer Security Requirements: Guidance for Applying the Department of Defense Trusted Computer System Evaluation Criteria in Specific Environments* [CSCG85], provides this guidance. The guidance is based on the hierarchy of sensitivity levels, coupled with nonhierarchical compartments or categories at the upper hierarchical level. This document is discussed in the standards section; an alternative is discussed in the Landwehr and Lubbes paper [LAND85] at the end of this section. When non-national defense data are being protected, the organization will have to develop its own mapping of TCSEC evaluated divisions to the classifications and ranges of data being protected.

The TCSEC constitutes the basis for NCSC's evaluation of hardware and software products that are on the Evaluated Products List. These criteria were applied initially to U.S. Department of Defense applications; however, they are being used for commercial product certifications as mentioned previously (e.g., IBM's RACF, SKK's ACF2, CA's TOP SECRET, etc.). Over time, these criteria might be modified to more fully reflect civil agency or non-defense security needs such as found in the private sector. In the meantime, they are the most authoritative security criteria available for the hardware and software industry.

Category 5. Communications controls: Communications controls are technical controls that are primarily associated with networks and less sophisticated data communications. There is a close relationship between these controls and non-network technical controls because computers are major components in a network. The same general guidelines for determination of the degree of control apply to communications controls as to technical controls (e.g., certification and accreditation).

Work is underway to extend the concepts and approach of the TCSEC to networks. Until a document is formally issued, the TCSEC is being interpreted on a network case-by-case basis. The interested reader is advised to determine the current status of network standards or guidelines. According to [BRAN85], the network document may use a similar structure to that in the TCSEC. In 1985, there were eight issues requiring further definition for development of this network document. Briefly, the issues are policy and models, access control, accountability, network architecture, configuration management and testing, verification and covert channel (indirect access) analysis, network components, and denial-of-service.

Incorporation of technical and communications controls, such as a level of control defined in the TCSEC, should be determined by using a review process to ascertain the appropriate controls required.

Training

Security training is equally essential for computer and network system developers and users. Training should include users of all office automation equipment such as personal computers and word processors. Office automation is identified as a special case because it involves hands-on end-user control by persons who often lack a data processing orientation. Security training should be incorporated into the overall organizational training program. A formal plan for security training should include sections on computer and network security: awareness and basic issues; requirements, standards and procedures; hardware, software and communications applications; verification, validation and testing relationships to related requirements (for database accuracy and continuity of operations); and relationships to organizational objectives (for performance).

Security training is part of the overall training necessary in an organization; therefore, security training should show how each security function relates to satisfying the organization's objectives. In many cases, as mentioned previously, the same control meets a security and a system performance objective. For example, the security functions in an on-line airline reservation system for database accuracy and continuity of operations can be met by the same controls that satisfy the need for effective and timely customer service.

Continuity of Operations

Most on-line systems have specific organizational performance objectives for continuity of operations. Although the specific organizational objectives may vary, the key issue is that as we invest more in automated information systems and concentrate vital data in electronic form, the organization becomes highly dependent upon effective computer support. Therefore, continuity of operations, which is a basic security requirement, is essential for the successful performance of many organizational objectives.

A continuity of operations program should include (1) continuity of operations plan, which should include a prioritization of applications targeted for continuity in a mode of degraded functionality (the payroll application frequently is top priority); (2) procedures for periodic testing of the continuity of operations plan; and (3) special procedures and/or facilities (to assist in providing backup in the case of a major system failure).

The special procedures and/or facilities, referred to earlier, may vary from organization to organization. Two possible alternatives are (1) a standby computer system ready to take over critical functions in an on-line manner, and backed up by an uninterruptable power system (UPS) or (2) another computer center connected by high-speed telecommunications ready to take over critical functions, after some delay for set up, and backed up by an UPS (this computer center can be another one in the organization or one provided by a contingency planning service, such as Sunguard).

Formal Review Procedures

Formal review procedures are one way to assess compliance of an individual computer or network system with the applicable security criteria. The formal review should consist of at least five categories of controls: (1) management, (2) physical, (3) administrative, (4) technical, and (5) communications. The compliance should be determined with respect to the level of control specified for a specific computer or network system. First it is necessary to establish control objectives. Once the objectives have been established it is

possible to measure how well these objectives are met. Reevaluation of objectives is a frequent byproduct of this process.

The SSO should generally be responsible for the formal security review. However, other management officials may initiate a security review for a variety of reasons, such as in critical situations where a system is necessary for corporate liquidity (e.g., insurance accounts receivable and payable). Good practice favors including the SSO in all formal security reviews. The nature of involvement may range from doing the review to participating as part of an interdisciplinary team to cooperating with an external team such as an audit team.

Corrective Actions

Corrective actions must be approved by management before they are implemented. This approval can vary from informal to senior management decision-making. The nature and level of the approval is highly dependent upon the magnitude of the corrective actions required with respect to the importance of the computer or network system and the resources required. For example, if senior management of a large commercial bank decides that all of its IBM mainframe computers using the MVS operating system in each of its computer centers is not providing adequate identification and authentication access controls at several thousand remote terminals, then corporate management could make a company-wide decision to resolve the situation. The solution could involve the bank's purchase of access control software to be installed at each computer center and could include modifying the corporate security procedures and manuals.

Corrective actions are one aspect of management decision-making that support a formal computer and network security program. Another aspect that deserves special mention is management decision-making for systems under development, which was introduced in the subsection on security planning.

Management Decision-Making for Systems under Development

Organizational increases in productivity and overall competitiveness in the future are often highly dependent upon today's management decisions. Of particular importance is management's direction of the automation investment. This investment involves a continuing shift of critical and routine operations to the computer software, including certain types of decision-making. The shift includes changes from:

- Manual to automated routine processes (e.g., teller operations to automated teller machines (ATM), and eventually automated branch banks).

- Off-line to on-line processes (e.g., batch updates to on-line updates)
- Manual quantitative decision-making to automated decision-making (with human review e.g., shop foreman and plant manager decision-making to automated oil refineries, steel mills, and automobile assembly plants)
- Manual analytical to automated analytical simulations of alternatives (e.g., corporate financial modeling)
- Manual design processes to automated design processing (and potential integration of production, e.g., manual design of computer chips to computer aided design and computer-aided manufacturing (CAD/CAM) of highly complex high density chips).

Today's investment decisions for automated systems are critical because of their short- and long-term impact on organizational success. Integral to this process is the provision by management for the incorporation of the appropriate security requirements into the specification of new computer and network systems under development. The economics of retrofitting technical and communications controls in general and specifically security controls preclude extensive modification of control. The costs of retrofitting increase substantially during the later phases of system operation and maintenance. Many controls cannot be economically retrofitted after system operation because they would require a different system design or architecture.

The required security criteria for systems under development should be specifically defined along with provisions for testing the security controls and evaluating the associated descriptive and/or formal models. The required provisions for security criteria should be defined for system acceptance. The SSO should be actively involved in major milestone reviews of system evaluation and testing to ensure that the specified security controls are correctly incorporated into the system development process. Provisions should be made for rejecting a system that fails to meet the specified security criteria. One possible approach for achieving this type of management decision making is presented in a report by Tompkins [TOMP84].

In addition to decisions pertaining to systems under development, there are issues related to the differences between the computer security practices in the military and in private sectors. These topics are discussed in the next section.

Reprints

Leslie Chalmers presents an interesting perspective on the differences and similarities of military and private sector computer security in her reprinted paper, "An Analysis of the Differences between the Computer Security Practices in the Military and Private Sectors." She asserts that while there is certainly some discrepancy of requirements, there are also areas of common need. She is in general agreement with Lipner's paper, suggested for recommended reading in Section 2.2.

Chalmers summarizes military computer security policy as being focused on preventing disclosure of information; secondary objectives, such as proving that a system cannot be compromised, verifying the security policy, and exorcising covert channels, all support this policy. Commercial organizations are defined by their objective of generating income; they "acquire computers because they perceive that this will lower their costs. They secure those computers because it costs them money if the computer has incomplete or inaccurate data. . . . The cost of security must be offset by a perceived risk, . . . often based upon experience of losses." In other words, military computer security is a policy decision and private sector computer security is a business decision.

In the private sector, "the need for security varies from industry to industry. Financial institutions are generally perceived as most vulnerable to losses due to inaccurate information since their assets consist almost entirely of computer records. . . . Businesses will work to protect themselves from leakage of information which would give a competitor a chance to preempt their product line or customer base. But for the day-to-day conduct of business, modification of information is by far a greater concern." Agreeing with Courtney, Chalmers observes that "what further complicates the security problem is that most of the penetrators work within their level of authority."

Areas of common interests are identified: personal authentication, audit trails, ongoing monitoring of employees "to detect when an individual has changed from a trusted employee to a potential problem," and cost effectiveness. We observe that military budgets are not limitless; although their boundary conditions and policies may differ, they also need to make management decisions where to put their money to get the best security for the investment. Another similarity is that in some businesses there are legal requirements for protection of information from disclosure.

In his paper, "An Economically Feasible Approach to Contingency Planning," Robert Courtney introduces the concept of the contingency plan, which "describes the appropriate response to any situation which jeopardizes the safety of data or of data processing and communications facilities to a degree that threatens meaningful harm to the organizations supported by those data and facilities." Courtney's approach is to introduce a methodology for contingency planning that can serve as a baseline for the development of specific plans. His discussion of contingency plans is presented in five parts. First, he provides the major components, which he follows with a second topic that specifies the alternatives. Third, he defines the critical data processing workload and suggests how to effectively utilize this concept. His fourth point pertains to the split-site approach. Before he summarizes his presentation on contingency planning, a fifth issue concerning the future is developed.

Three essential elements of a contingency plan are introduced as the major components for a successful plan. A vital aspect of Courtney's scope is that he considers survival of the organization as an essential objective of effective contingency planning. Therefore, his suggested scope for the plans includes "communications, data acquisition, storage, and presentation." The three elements of a plan are (1) emergency response plan, (2) backup plan, and (3) recovery plan.

Principal alternatives available to the organization are developed. Courtney is careful to point out that management can utilize a combination of the basic seven alternatives. The alternatives are (1) doing nothing, (2) mutual aid agreements, (3) open (commercial) hot site, (4) closed (consortium or equivalent) hot site, (5) split sites, (6) standby facilities, and (7) data servicers (e.g., ADP or McAuto). In illustrating the concept of combinations of alternatives, Courtney suggests that an organization may use one alternative for payroll, another for mainframe backup, and a third for proof (testing) and sorting operations.

Critical data processing workload is an essential concept for effective contingency planning. Our interpretation of Courtney's definition of the critical data processing workload is that a portion of the total workload that will generate serious loss if disrupted for a period exceeding a specified number of weeks (e.g., two weeks). Expected annual loss (EAL) is defined as including the dollar consequences of an undesirable event and the probability that it will occur.

Eight commonly encountered major problems in achieving feasible back-up plans serve as an introduction to the split-site approach. Briefly, the first three problems are (1) identifying the critical workload, (2) assuring suitably prompt availability of adequate computer(s) when they are needed, and (3) establishment of enough of the normally required communications network to provide adequate "limp-along capability." Courtney develops key split-site issues relating to costs, dividing the workload, management, and locations.

Distributed processing, the growth of departmental computers and the continued proliferation of microcomputers are given as substantial contributors to the future complexity of contingency planning. However, Courtney is careful to point out that improved technology can also facilitate more responsive contingency capabilities. One example is "the advent of super-safe, underground DASD [direct access storage devices] facilities connectable to geographically-remote large and small processors through very high-speed communications facilities leaving us with the need to back up only the processors and provide alternate means of communications."

Courtney sees more internal auditor involvement in the technical aspects of data processing serving as a vehicle for more communication with management concerning critical organization dependence issues. This trend of the internal auditor community could reinforce other trends to get management more involved in the process of automation investment and supporting issues, such as contingency planning.

Recommended Readings

Checklists are useful for a preliminary "size up" of the security status of a computer system. One such checklist is offered by Peter Browne in *Security: Checklist for Computer Center Self-Audits*. This checklist is oriented to the security and accuracy objectives of a computer center. His checklist includes (1) the need for security: requirements for protection and controls and (2) Risk factors and loss: security; confidentiality; privacy; integrity; vulnerability; threat (system reliability, disasters, malicious acts); loss; risk; and protection.

A structure for determining security requirements for complex computer systems is presented by Carl Landwehr and H.O. Lubbes in "Determining Security Requirements for Complex Systems with the *Orange Book*." They focus on the hardware and software architecture of the system and the environment in which it it used. Inclusion of the system environment is a point of departure from the *Yellow Book* [GUID85]. Landwehr and Lubbes' structure, like the *Yellow Book,* does not address certain security factors. Therefore, additional analysis and interpretation is required for ". . .requirements for degaussing of removable storage, TEMPEST [emanation controls] requirements, protection from physical hazards, emergency destruction, or other security requirements. . ." beyond the scope of the hardware and software architecture.

The TCSEC, the *Orange Book,* deals only with technical security of the individual computer system. It does not provide guidance concerning which evaluated division is appropriate for a given application environment. This guidance was published in two closely related subsequent documents. The first, which contains guidance only, is the *Yellow Book,* whose formal title is *Computer Security Requirements: Guidance for Applying the Department of Defense Trusted Computer System Evaluation Criteria in Specific Environments* [CSCS85]. The second, which contains the reasoning behind the guidance, is entitled *Technical Rationale behind CSC-STD-003-85: Computer Security Requirements* [CSCT85]. These are discussed in more detail in Section 2.3.

The paper identifies three components to the structure: "[1] extraction from each system (or system design) the factors that affect the risk that its operation may lead to the unauthorized disclosure of sensitive information, [2] quantifying these factors, and [3] determining system security requirements (in terms of the levels defined in the *Orange Book*) that reduce the system risk to an acceptable level."

The risk factors are identified by considering the environment in which the system operates including local processing capability, communications path, user capability, development and maintenance environment, and data exposure. Three tables are employed to apply these risk factors to *Orange Book* evaluated divisions:

Table 1: Process coupling risk: Risk levels are identified for the local processing capability used in the computer system. This process is also performed for the communication path and related to local processing capability.

Table 2: System risk: User capability is defined and correlated with process coupling risk, which identifies ". . .how well a process in one computer can maintain its integrity in the face of attempts to subvert it from outside. A high degree of coupling represents a close degree of interaction between two processes and hence a greater vulnerability of one to the other . . ."

Table 3: Mapping system risk and data exposure to Orange Book levels: System risk is related to data exposure or clearance levels to yield a sensitivity level in the *Orange Book* ranging from a high of A1 through B3, B2, B1, C2, and C1 to a low of D. The data exposure levels vary from 0 for uncleared personnel to 5 Top Secret/Special Background Investigation.

Landwehr and Lubbes conclude their paper with an example applying these techniques to a Sea Surface Surveillance system. The authors also include a discussion of pros and cons of their approach to determining security requirements. The issue is not closed; additional work may be anticipated on this subject. Significant implementation impact on cost, schedules, and performance follow from the policy guidance, which specifies the evaluated level appropriate for a given application. The private sector is advised to study the U.S. Department of Defense approach, but to make its own determination.

Although Fred Tompkins prepared his report entitled *NASA Guidelines for Assuring the Adequacy and Appropriateness of Security Safeguards in Sensitive Applications* for NASA, his guidelines are generic and can be adapted for use in a wide variety of organizations [TOMP84]. His focus is of particular value because it is life-cycle oriented, which complements the way we (should) build and maintain automated information systems. He suggests 13 software development life-cycle security activities that support system certification. We add a 14th activity—accreditation. These activities, along with the people who should perform the activities, are (1) determine sensitivity of data/application (users and application/data processing installation computer security officer (CSO)); (2) determine security objective(s) (users and application/data processing installation CSO); (3) assess security

risks (users, system planners, and application/data procesing installation CSO); (4) conduct security feasibility study (users, system planners, and application/data processing installation CSO); (5) define security requirements (users, system planners, and approved by application CSO); (6) develop security test plan (quality assurance (QA), audit, independent verification and validation (IV&V), and review and approval by application CSO); (7) design security specifications (system developers); (8) develop security test procedures (QA, audit, IV&V, and review and approval by application CSO) (9) write security relevant code (programmers); (10) document security safeguards (programmers, system developers, and review by application/data processing installation CSO); (11) conduct security test and evaluation (IV&V, QA, and audit); (12) write security test report (IV&V, QA, and audit); (13) prepare security certification report (system developers and certification issued by application CSO); and (14) accreditation of the system (management action, accreditation is a management responsibility).

The life-cycle orientation of Tompkins' work fits well into the software engineering approach for cost-effective systems development. One interesting example is that software quality assurance factors that are important for software engineering and systems security are referenced both by Tompkins (pp. 3-6 to 3-12) and by *Military Standard: Software Quality Evaluation 2168* (briefly discussed in Section 2.3). Both documents (Tompkins and *Standard 2168*) use the software quality factors from Alfred Sorkowitz [SORK79].

One other aspect of Tompkins' work is highlighted. These are his five definitions for determining security objectives, which are essential in building an automated information system. The definitions are (1) data integrity: "The state that exists when computerized data is the same as that in the source documents or has been correctly computed from source data and has not been exposed to accidental or malicious alteration or destruction . . .;" (2) application integrity: "The state that exists when the source and object code are the same as originally developed and certified/accredited or, have been modified and tested in accordance with established standards and procedures and recertified/reaccredited, and have not been exposed to accidental or malicious alteration or destruction;" (3) data confidentiality: "The state that exists when data is held in confidence and is protected from unauthorized disclosure . . .;" (4) application confidentiality: "The state that exists when applicaton source and object code and documentation is [are] held in confidence and is [are] protected from authorized disclosure;" and (5) ADP availability: "The state that exists when required ADP services can be obtained within an acceptable period of time . . ."

AN ANALYSIS OF THE DIFFERENCES BETWEEN THE COMPUTER SECURITY PRACTICES IN THE MILITARY AND PRIVATE SECTORS

Leslie S. Chalmers

The Bank of California
P.O. Box 45000
San Francisco, CA 94145

Introduction

Experts who work to produce products to enhance computer security are often puzzled by the apparent lack of interest on the part of private sector companies in acquiring those products. Over the last decade, a number of new products have not found any substantial market even though they have elegant designs, careful implementations, and independant certification.

Since most of these products have been developed in response to requests from the Department of Defense, it is clear that there is some discrepancy between the requirements of the Military and Private Sectors. This paper examines the requirements and practices of the two sectors. While the focus of the paper is on the differences between these two groups, there are also areas of common need which have been often overlooked. Some of these areas may provide ideas for future research and product development which would benefit everyone.

Trusted Computer Systems

A major focus of Military security is to prevent information being disclosed to someone not authorized to see it. This has been a concern since long before the invention of computers. The Department of Defense Trusted Computer System Evaluation Criteria[1] documents the requirements for secure computer systems at various levels. At the highest level, systems must have a formally stated security policy, which is defined as "a statement of intent with regard to control over access to and dissemination of information" [italics mine]. The system must enforce this policy, protect itself from tampering, provide audit trails, and so forth. Objects must be marked with their classification and this marking must be included in any copies of the objects.

In order to ensure that a computer system can be trusted to enforce the security policy, techniques have been developed for proving that a system cannot be compromised. Verification

ensures among other things that no process can violate the security policy, the implementation precisely represents the design specification, and no covert channels exist which could permit a process to communicate either inadvertently or deliberately with an unauthorized process.

A formal expression of a security policy is contained in a seminal paper by Bell and LaPadula[2] which states that a process (or user) may not have read access to an object (i.e. information) with a higher classification level. The *-property further states that a process may not have write access to an object at a lower classification level. Further isolation is imposed by the latice model[3] which introduces the concept of security classes or classes of objects which are isolated from each other regardless of the classification of the objects within each security class.

The Private Sector's View of the Computer Security Problem

The Private Sector is not a monolithic entity; no one organization speaks for the entire Private Sector. However, businesses within the Private Sector do have common practices. For our purposes, the Private Sector may be loosely defined as companies or businesses which generate income through the sale of services or goods. There is a fuzzy line between the Public and Private Sectors when one looks at organizations which have government agencies as their primary or only customers, but this need not divert us. Businesses exist to make money. Any organization which fails in this primary mission will, over time, cease to exist.

A company can improve its chances for survival by increasing its profit. This can be done in two ways: increase the demand for the goods or services (allowing the company to sell more of its product or raise its prices or both) or lower the costs of delivering those goods or services. Generally, companies acquire computers because

Reprinted from *Proceedings of the 1986 Symposium on Security and Privacy,* 1986, pages 71-74. Copyright © 1986 by The Institute of Electrical and Electronics Engineers, Inc.

they perceive that this will lower their costs. They secure those computers because it costs them money if a computer has incomplete or inaccurate data. The larger the company, the larger the computer investment and, usually, the larger the amount of money available for computer security.

There are, however, very large companies which continue to hold to the belief common in the 1960's and early 70's that "it can't happen here" and even if it could, any security measures they might implement could be broken, so why bother. This attitude has been changing, but it is not gone. It is the author's belief that companies which adhere to this tend to be managed by individuals who have no significant exposure to computing. Since they couldn't figure out how to break into a computer system, they believe no one else could. Teenaged computer "hackers" have done a great deal recently to dispell this misconception.

Because keeping costs low is a driving force in the data processing function, the cost of security must be offset by a perceived risk. The perception of risk may be based upon the potential size of the loss, but more often it is based upon experience of losses. Recently, the use of automatic call back devices for dial-up port protection has grown because the perceived risk is very high and the cost of such devices is low.

Few companies use line encryption because experience to date is that no one has suffered a loss from someone penetrating a telecommunications line. Even banks which move very large sums of money via electronics funds transfer systems are more swayed by this historical fact than by the high loss potential of a single transaction. The major push for line encryption in Banking has come from the centralized service providers (e.g. the Federal Reserve's FEDWIRE system) which are beginning to require the banks to encrypt lines from the bank to the server.

The need for security varies from industry to industry. Financial institutions are generally perceived as most vulnerable to losses due to inaccurate information since their assets consist almost entirely of computer records. A bank or insurance company decides to pay out money based entirely upon the information in computers. Manufacturing companies have experienced losses where computers were used to cover up the theft of goods, but the money lost tends to be lower in such cases. Again, the higher the perceived risk, the more likely a company is to spend money on protective measures.

A major problem for computer security planners is that the protective measures which are available do not deter the usual perpetrators of computer related fraud, employees. I use the term "computer-related" because there is some dispute as to whether or not a really large computer crime has ever occurred. Salami attacks, Trojan

horses, and so forth, are rare. Rather, most frauds involve the manipulation of input or, less often, output. What further complicates the security problem is that most of the perpetrators work within their level of authority[4].

A few years ago, a large bank suffered a $25 million loss caused by a branch manager submitting phoney credits to his own account and offsetting these entries with debits against the accounts used to balance the transactions between branches. A few days later, he would credit the previously used branch settlement account and debit a new one to another branch. By moving the debit around from account to account, it never came to rest long enough for anyone to notice. He was caught when he was out sick and could not make the offsetting entries in time.

More recently, the trust officer of a bank moved $10 million out of some 20 trust accounts and covered it up by suppressing the computer generated customer statements and substituting ones which he typed by hand. Since no one was reviewing the statements prior to their being sent out and since the customers had no way of knowing that they were incorrect, the loss went undetected for a couple of years. It was discovered when the officer left the bank and customers began to complain about not receiving their statements. When the officer's replacement turned the computer statements back on and reviewed their contents, the fraud was discovered.

Note that in both of these cases, the perpetrators were working within their authorized level of authority. The branch manager was responsible for submitting entries to the branch settlement accounts as part of his job. The trust officer was legitimately entitled to turn off the printing of customer statements. No computer access rules were violated, no programs were altered, no userIDs were compromised. The presence or absence of a provably secure Trusted Computing Base is irrelevant to both of these cases.

An Analysis of the Differences Between the Two Views of Security

The objectives of the Military and Private Sectors are different because the motivating forces are different. The Military is most concerned with protecting information from leaking to an enemy. To accomplish this, great efforts are made to classify information and maintain strict segregation of people from information they are not allowed to see. The cost of protecting information is included in the cost of collecting or creating that information since the value of the information is lower if it becomes known.

Businesses are motivated by a "bottom line" philosophy, i.e. if it doesn't further the goal of making money, don't do it. Since preventing monetary loss improves the bottom line, a business will elect to take measures to control their assets, but only if the cost of the protection is less than the perceived loss potential. You don't spend a million dollars protecting a pencil! Businesses will work to protect themselves from leakage of information which would give a competitor a chance to preempt their product line or customer base. But for the day-to-day conduct of business, modification of information is by far a greater concern.

A second significant difference between the two views of security is in the model of security which each uses. Bell-LaPadula implies that it is more important to prevent unauthorized read access; businesses are far less concerned with who reads information than with who changes it. One security product in widespread use in the Private Sector codifies this difference[*]. Under this system, there is a hierarchy of access levels with read access lower than all others. Any user given a higher level of access to an object is automatically given all lower levels as well. The widespread acceptance of this product implies that businesses agree with this philosophy.

Yet another difference between the two sectors is the personnel practices. Within the Military, personnel must be cleared before they are allowed access to classified information. In the Private Sector, employees may not be screened at all. Where there are screening procedures in place, they may be completed many months after the employee starts to work. Businesses with a need for a person with a specific skill do not want to keep that person idle for as long as it takes to screen him.

In addition, businesses must be concerned with various laws and regulations which restrict their access to information about a new employee. Such a simple task as calling a previous employer for a reference check will usually be worthless. The previous employer may refuse to do any more than confirm that the individual did or did not work for them in the past. Giving additional information could cause the previous employer trouble if the individual were to sue for damages.

Because of this, many businesses do not rely on pre-employment screening. Instead, they expect managers to monitor their employees for unusual behavior which might indicate the potential for trouble. This should be an ongoing practice in any organization since people who pass all tests when hired may become problem employees in later years as their personal lives change.

In summary, the difference between the two sectors is in their overall goals: total security vs. cost effective security. Total security is rarely cost effective.

[*]   IBM's Resource Access Control Facility (RACF)

Some Thoughts On Common Interests

Although the Military and Private sectors may never agree on some basic concepts, they do have common interests. Researchers should consider some of these common areas. Everyone will benefit from the development of new approaches to these common problems.

1. Personal Authentication

One activity which is central to any good computer security system, regardless of the ultimate objectives of that system, is to properly identify each user of the system. If an individual is capable of spoofing the computer system into accepting him as a different individual, not only is the spoofer able to access information to which he has not been cleared, the computer will also collect audit trails pointing to the compromised user. Businesses have too often relied exclusively upon a user identification code (userID) combined with a secret password to authenticate the identity of an individual. Their primary motivation for this is password authentication is usually included with operating system software so there is no incremental cost.

Clearly, passwords alone are not enough. If the individual is assigned a password centrally, the person administering the passwords could compromise that password. Where the individual chooses his own password, passwords become very easy to guess. The introduction of spelling checker software for word processing systems gives the uncleared individual tens of thousands of precoded likely passwords. Programming a personal computer to use its dictionary as the source of passwords is a trivial matter. The user's only good defense is to systemmatically misspell his password or combine words with numerical data. Most users are not sufficiently motivated to go to the trouble.

New technologies are being introduced to base authentication upon characteristics such as fingerprints, signature dynamics, retinal scan patterns, and so forth. While such techniques are a major improvement over passwords, they are subject to playback attacks if the penetrator is able to record a session signon. Another drawback for the Private Sector is the high cost of many such systems. Costs on the order of $500 to $1000 per terminal make such systems unacceptable for most businesses. The Sytek Polonius system[5] represents an approach based upon one-time password concepts. Such systems are not only less expensive, they cannot be compromised with playback techniques. Further research is required to lower the costs of systems while reducing the opportunities for compromise.

2. Audit Trails

The perfect audit trail provides a security officer with a complete record of every activity by an individual. However, such trails are not useful because of the time required to review them. It is not inconceivable that one full time security officer could only review the activities of two or three individuals, not a very efficient ratio. What is required is some automated system for reviewing activities and flagging items for the security officer's attention. Possible items to look for include activity outside the individual's normal working hours, access to files which, while not restricted, are not normally associated with the individual's job responsibilities, changes to files which are more than usually sensitive, and so forth.

The more granular such scanning can be made, the more useful it becomes. For example, it is not uncommon for all programmers in a shop to be allowed to read the production copies of source code, object code, control files, etc. The security officer is not going to be able to recognize a problem if he only knows that the programmer read the source code file and he will not care if the programmer reads the source code for the programs he is responsible for. If, however, the programmer assigned to the accounts payable system one day starts to read the source code for the personnel/payroll system, the security officer should be notified.

Research into the use of artificial intelligence and pattern recognition to automate review of audit trails would benefit both the Military and the Private Sector.

3. Ongoing Monitoring of Employees

As discussed above, many of the problems with computer security involve people working within their level of authority. Techniques are needed to detect when an individual has changed from a trusted employee to a potential problem. In a free society, there are numerous legal restrictions on the kind of information an employer can access, but this does not mean that employers should not use what information they can. Some kinds of information may be readily accessable, as when a clerical person parks a high-priced sports car in the company parking lot.

Employers will also benefit from research into ways to gain and maintain employee loyalty. While much has been written by management consultants and others, the research on this has not been systemmatic, or is at least not being well disseminated.

Recently researchers have been working on typing dynamics as a technique for authenticating the identity of users. Could this same technique be applied to the problem of identifying individuals under stress? Are there behavioral patterns associated with individuals contemplating embezzlement or selling secrets to an enemy?

4. Cost Effectiveness

Finally, both the Military and Private Sector will benefit from research into ways to bring down the costs of securing computers. Security for security's sake will not work in many cases. The work in the 1960's and 70's on good programming techniques has greatly reduced the problems of programming errors. Security developers need to focus on ways to maximize security while minimizing costs.

Conclusion

Since the basic philosophy of protection is so widely different in the Military and Private Sectors, they may never agree on a definition of the ideal security system. This does not mean that they have no common interests. By focusing some efforts on these common interests, both Sectors will end up with greater security.

References

1. Department of Defense Computer Security Center, Department of Defense Trusted Computer System Evaluation Criteria, DoD, CSC-STD-001-83, 1983.

2. Bell, W.E. and LaPadula, L.J., "Secure Computer Systems: Mathematical Foundations and Model", M74-244, The MITRE Corp., Bedford, Mass., May, 1973.

3. Denning, D.E. Cryptography and Data Security, Addison-Wesley, Reading, Mass., 1982.

4. Allen, B.R., "Computer Crime: New Findings, New Insights", Eighth Annual Computer Security Conference, 1981.

5. Wong, R.M., Berson, T.A., and Feiertag, R.J., "Polonius: An Identity Authentication System", Proceedings of the 1985 Symposium on Security and Privacy, IEEE Computer Society Press, Los Angeles, 1985.

AN ECONOMICALLY FEASIBLE APPROACH TO CONTINGENCY PLANNING.

Robert H. Courtney, Jr.
Robert Courtney, Inc.
Box 836
Port Ewen, New York 12466
914-338-2525

INTRODUCTION

What is a Contingency Plan?

A contingency plan describes the appropriate response to any situation which jeopardizes the safety of data or of data processing and communications facilities to a degree that threatens meaningful harm to the organizations supported by those data and facilities. A contingency plan is not a book; it is an action plan.

The threatening situation need not be a disaster which causes extensive physical damage. The disruption may cause no damage at all to the physical facility as is often the case with a chemical spill which, by forcing the evacuation of personnel, stops data processing activities. In fact, the economic feasibility of a contingency plan may well lie in its ability to contain small problems at small cost as well as providing the ability to fare through the total loss of a physical facility.

The threats to be anticipated in devising the contingency plan need only be sufficiently great in both the magnitudes of the potential losses and in their probability of occurrence to justify the preparation of plans to avoid those losses if a course of action which costs significantly less than the anticipated loss can be devised.

It is regrettable that the term "disaster recovery plan" has become, for many, synonymous with "contingency plan". It seems somewhat more rational to consider the contingency plan to be a disaster avoidance plan rather than a way of recovering from a disaster. Most of our data processing disasters become such only because we are not prepared to cope with what might have been only an inconvenience if we had prepared properly.

Who Needs Them?

Any organization which is susceptible to significant harm if it loses its data or the facilities associated with their use needs a plan with which to respond to reasonably anticipatable disruptions to normal data processing operations. These can include labor problems as well as earthquakes, leaking roofs as well as floods, gross mistakes by loyal employees and bombs by terrorists, area-wide losses of power and vital communications lines cut by back-hoes.

The losses which mount as a consequence of system outages vary widely with the nature of supported organizations. Some major organizations will not be seriously hurt with downtimes as long as a week. Others will suffer meaningful losses, amounting to as much as two-thirds gross revenue, starting within minutes of loss of system support.

Who Has Them?

Truly workable, fully tested, economically feasible contingency plans are in place for only a small percentage of the data processing mainframe installations. There are no untested but workable contingency plans. Such tests always reveal deficiencies to be fixed.

It is our belief, based upon many discussions of the subject with DP management and others, that the principal reason for the absence of good contingency plans, at least in the private sector, but to a lesser degree in the public sector because of the many complicating factors there, is the continuing belief by much of the DP management that workable plans are far too costly or are, in reality, infeasible. Other important and more urgent issues do divert management attention from contingency planning and other security related considerations as well, but the principal barrier seems to be lack of confidence that a truly workable plan can be configured. Until more DP directors are better informed about the economic feasibility and workability of contingency plans, this situation will not change.

Our goal here is to describe an approach to contingency planning which is clearly workable in many, but certainly not all, organizations.

THE MAJOR COMPONENTS

We are addressing here contingency plans for data processing, including communications, data acquisition, storage, and presentation. Of no less importance, but not within the scope of this paper, are the contingency plans for the critical dependencies which are not DP related. Preservation of the ability to take orders and bill customers may lack importance if there is no means of making shippable product.

The essential components of a complete contingency plan are these:

1. Emergency Response Plan.- A plan to respond promptly and well to a potential disruption so as to limit the damage is highly desirable. Fire extinguishers are almost worthless if no one knows how to use them. In this category, then, are the things which should be done as soon as there is an awareness of a potential problem which might result in the invocation of the contingency plan.

75

2. Back-Up Plan.- The back-up plan provides the ability to conduct, by alternate means, the critical data processing workload. The critical workload is that portion of the workload which will generate serious loss if disrupted for a period exceeding two weeks. See our comments later here on the selection of the two week period.

3. Recovery Plan.- The Recovery Plan guides the return to full and normal data processing capability.

All three plans must be considered because all are important, but the first two, the emergency response and back-up plans, are the most difficult to put in place and, usually, are the most urgently needed. There is rarely any significant overlap of the three categories. This paper is oriented primarily toward the provision of economically feasible back-up capabilities.

THE ALTERNATIVES

Several different approaches to the provision of back-up capability can be considered. They are not all equally workable. These should be considered only under some quite exceptional circumstances. The principal alternatives, then, are these:

Doing Nothing.

There are a few organizations quite dependent upon computer-based systems which will suffer but little loss if they are without that data processing support for two weeks or so. Such loss as they might encounter if they cannot run their work will be quite small in comparison with the cost of a back-up capability. Those charged with contingency planning should consider the highly desirable possibility that their respective organizations may be in this category.

It is not wholly uncommon to encounter the absence of need for back-up in headquarters operations where computers are used primarily for planning and higher level awareness and control purposes and where accounting, payroll, order entry, inventory management and other such time-dependent tasks are provided for the enterprise by DP shops in the operating divisions. Note that these other DP shops do need back-up capabilities.

Mutual Aid Agreements.

External. Arrangements made with other, unaffiliated organizations to provide back-up data processing support by deferring some of the supporting company's less critical work can work under some circumstances. It is usually fairly easy to arrive at some informal agreement of this type with other organizations. It is more difficult to establish formal written agreements which are workable. It is usually quite difficult to establish such mutual aid agreements involving adequate, periodic tests of that back-up. In general, and as we stated rather forcefully above, untested back-up plans do not work.

These arrangements increase in workability under the following circumstances:

1. When there are unused shifts available at the back-up facility so that less work, if any, is displaced in the supporting company.

2. When the work to be backed up is primarily vanilla batch or with limited use of in-dial ports only.

3. When the CPU's are relatively small.

4. When the need for back-up is such that delays of a few days will not be very costly.

5. When the mutually supportive organizations are in the same industry areas; e.g., commercial banking. That two companies are possible competitors is often an impediment, but usually not so great a problem as a complete lack of appreciation of what the other is trying to do as when they are in different businesses.

6. When the two companies are of roughly the same size.

None of the above factors are without notable exceptions, but they should provide some useful guidance in considering a mutual aid agreement with another organization.

The most useful observation we can make here about mutual aid agreements between wholly unaffiliated organizations is that they very rarely work when they are needed.

Internal. The workability of mutual aid agreements between groups with some organizational affinity is dependent upon many factors. The more prominent of those factors are these:

1. The strength of the stated desire of the common management that the respective organizations arrange such back-up support.

2. The quality and the degree of realism reflected in the back-up plan.

3. The conduct of wholly realistic tests of the back-up capability.

4. The similarity of the mutually supportive systems.

5. The simplicity of the required communications support.

6. The physical proximity of the two sites - provided that they are not so close as to be affected by the same source of disruption.

7. The availability of time to correct deficiencies in the back-up support after disruption and before losses mount intolerably.

Many other things can be listed, but these deserve careful consideration before this option is elected.

The greatest single factor in the workability of this arrangement is the ability and willingness of the common management to require the provision of fully tested back-up. Other factors are very important, but this one is usually key.

Open Hot Site.

An open hot site is a data processing facility operated for profit by making available to otherwise unaffiliated companies a site on which they can conduct their data processing after loss of the use of their own facility. These are characterized by the facilities of COMDISCO and SUNGARD.

Monthly subscription rates are paid to preserve the ability to test the back-up plans and, when necessary and on payment of additional fees, to declare an emergency and move the critical workload onto this alternate facility.

This arrangement is indeed quite workable for a number of companies, but it is far from a universal solution. It can be a partial solution for some banks, for example, but it will not solve the problem of data capture, including the proof operations, so essential to curtailing losses through disruption to demand deposit operations.

An analysis of the economic feasibility of the open hot site as back-up for any specific facility must include careful and quantitative consideration of the speed with which key data processing functions must be restored. The feasibility of this approach clearly increases with the length of time available to move people and data, to fix unanticipated problems, and to adapt the hot site communications facilities to the peculiar needs of the using organization. The cost of repeated tests at a geographically remote location must also be considered in evaluating this alternative.

Although it may be argued that such should not be the case, we have seen too many instances in which recovery at the hot site has been deferred for an inordinately long period while attempts are made to recover at the primary location to avoid paying the fees for declaring an emergency or because there is fear that the contingency plan may not actually work. Further, if there is some reasonable possibility of a prompt recovery at the primary site, prudent management will be reluctant to send the best people available to the hot site, as will be needed to establish operations in a different location, when it is clear that operations cannot be re-established at home without those best people. This is a difficult dilemma for the DP Director to resolve when he is faced with the plethora of problems normally encountered when a busy facility is suddenly and seriously disrupted.

Closed Hot Site.

A closed hot site is a facility which is owned by a consortium or which was otherwise constructed for a specific set of companies to satisfy some less than highly general need for back-up capability. Such a facility might provide proof machines and operators and check sorters for a group of banks. It might provide unusually rapid availability of back-up for organizations which encounter serious losses beginning with the first minute of facility outage.

These facilities are rare primarily because of the heavy requirements for a peculiar combination of entrepreneurial spirit, salesmanship, technical strength, and quite substantial investment (by the participating companies) needed to get them to an operational state. They can be a highly satisfactory way of satisfying the back-up needs of enterprises which cannot afford to be down for even very short periods, but the costs are significantly greater than those seen with open hot sites. These higher costs are justified only when they are fully displaced by sum of the losses avoided by this approach and the continuing availability of the facility to the participating companies for rehearsal of back-up plans and for application development and test.

This approach is definitely not the way of the future for very many organizations. It is very good for those who need it, but it will not be economically feasible for very many others. In some of those organizations for which it would be the correct approach, the DP management will not find it acceptable to ask the corporate management for the necessary funds to participate in such a consortium.

Split Sites.

Later in this paper we discuss the determination of the size of the truly critical workload in a DP mainframe facility.
For our immediate purposes here, it is sufficient to say that it is very rare to encounter a conventional data processing facility supporting a multiplicity of applications on a mainframe where the truly critical workload approaches 50% of the total. Our definition of critical workload is that portion of the workload which, if discontinued for two weeks, would result in serious loss, not just inconvenience, to the enterprise. Most commonly, if a reasonably objective evaluation is made of critical workload, it will be less than 20% of the total.

We have found it generally quite feasible to return to a reasonable semblance of normal operations within two weeks of even a major facility loss. For this reason we use the two-week period in our definition of critical workload.

If the critical workload on a facility is significantly less than 50% of the total, then it is possible to consider splitting an existing site into two physically separate parts either of which is large enough to carry the critical workload. At least theoretically, this does not require any increase in data processing capacity. In actual practice, that is not quite correct.
However, with a split site, if either is lost, the other can carry the critical workload after shedding that portion of the non-critical workload it was carrying before loss of that other facility.

It is our contention that, while other approaches to back-up are sometimes workable, the most broadly applicable, economically feasible approach to backing up critical workloads on mainframes is the split-site arrangement.

Standby Facilities.

We noted above that it is rarely possible to provide economic justification for a whole standby facility which does nothing until the primary one is lost. It is possible to compose a scenario in which the consequences of losing a facility are so dire as to provide such justification. This is most commonly true with smaller, dedicated machines such as those driving automated warehouses.

In the whole population of computers, there are enough situations where dedication of otherwise unused back-up facilities are justified that that category cannot be excluded from any reasonably comprehensive list of alternative approaches.

Data Servicers.

Many organizations would be well-served in any attempt to reduce or eliminate the critical workload to consider taking all or a portion of it, depending on its nature, to a data servicer such as ADP or McAuto. They not only might substantially reduce the cost of operations such as payroll, they can also have advantage of the extensive facilities of the larger organizations in that business to assure a high probability of the continued support of those delegated functions. In general, however, the time to place the work with the data servicers is before and not after disruption to your facilities.

A complete discussion of the several reasons for taking payroll and some other common business functions to outside specialists is somewhat beyond the scope of this paper, but the reader should give it appropriate consideration.

Combinations of Alternatives.

It is readily apparent that some combination of the different alternatives may best suit the needs of very large organizations and

even a few of the very small ones. For example, a bank may well consider taking its payroll to ADP, using an open hot site for its mainframe back-up, and joining a consortium for proof and sorting operations. Many other equally plausible examples can be cited.

THE CRITICAL WORKLOAD.

What is the Critical Workload?

Earlier here we said that the critical workload is that portion of the total workload which would cause serious loss if it could not be conducted for periods of up to two weeks. The two weeks is fairly arbitrary but, in reality, most companies do manage substantial recovery of their data processing operations in that time even when there has been catastrophic loss of a major facility. If the two-week interval seems inappropriate to any particular environment, it is quite reasonable to pick some longer or shorter period, although much shorter might be quite risky.

Another perspective on the problem might suggest that the critical workload is that portion of the total which, if it is interrupted, would generate losses great enough to provide economic justification of a back-up capability which would obviate such losses. This view of things is not correct because is suggests an assessment of criticality based on cost of back-up. The desirability of avoiding loss does not change with the feasibility of avoiding it.

All of the potential losses which would result from an outage should be compiled, not just those which can be obviated by some current notion of the nature of an appropriate back-up capability. Only when those are available will it be possible to configure a back-up plan which is sufficiently detailed to be workable. When these potentially avoidable losses have been compiled, then we can evaluate the various approaches available to us for providing a back-up capability and select the combination which displaces the greatest potential loss for the least cost.

EAL = (Cost)(Probability of Occurrence).

The Expected Annual Loss (EAL) which is used to justify backing up a data processing function or not should be evaluated in terms of not just the dollar consequences of an undesirable event but also the probability that it will happen. It is not reasonable to base a contingency plan on an assessment of consequences alone; consideration must also be given the probability (or frequency) of encountering the interruption. It is clear that the anticipated loss must be the result of consideration of both the damage done and the chance of encountering the problem.

When doing a risk assessment for contingency planning purposes, it is usually far easier to assess the consequences of a disruption than it is to judge the probability of encountering the problem. Fortunately, quite gross estimates of which we can be reasonably certain are usually good enough. No attempt should be made to refine data beyond the point where the improved precision does not make a difference in what we do. Only when we realize that the determinant for a course of action lies in the area of uncertainty between the upper and lower bounds of the value we assign a parameter are we justified in expending the effort to further refine those data. Distinctions without differences are useless; and for there to be a difference, a change has to make a difference.

We have found fairly consistently that we are rarely hampered by difficulty in estimating probabilities of occurrence. Far more often than not, when we take the probability to a level so low that we are quite comfortable with it, the consequences are sufficiently large to provide adequate justification of corrective measures. This should not be too surprising because the things with the most dire consequences usually happen with the lowest frequencies - otherwise the world would not be habitable. On the other hand, small problems often happen with frequencies so high that they rival or exceed the EAL of the catastrophes.

If, for a particular problem, we cannot arrive at an estimate of probability (or consequences) in which we have adequate confidence, it is often best to simply defer further consideration until later. Quite frequently, the appropriate corrective action will be cost-justified by some other problem which is more readily assessable. If that does not happen, then we must do the additional work required to further refine our data.

In conducting a risk assessment, a small amount of common sense far outweighs complex methodologies. We once encountered such blind obeisance to a flawed risk assessment methodology that, in a prioritized list of critical data processing tasks for a major manufacturing company, paying suggestion awards was ranked first and higher than accepting orders, shipping product, invoicing, receiving payment, and getting out the payroll.

Who Determines the Critical Workload?

Involvement of Functional Area Managers. Our experience has been that determination of the critical workload by the information systems personnel working alone and not in close cooperation with the managements of the respective functional areas does not work. The DP people almost never have the depth of understanding of the need of the enterprise for the proper functioning of each of the essential components to the extent that they can offer a quantitative evaluation of the cost of their interruption. All too often, they don't know that they don't know and, as a consequence, make gross and seriously erroneous estimates of the tolerance of the organization to specific problems. Their assessment of the importance or criticality of particular functions as often reflects the strengths of the personalities of the persons

from that area with whom they have been working as it does the real situation.

Importance of Policy Statement. We have almost always found it more difficult to achieve the involvement of the functional area managers in any planning for computer-related security, including contingency planning, in the absence of a strong policy statement issued by the chief executive officer. The policy statement should make specific assignment to functional managers of direct responsibility for the safety of data and the means of processing them. The DP management should have custodial responsibility for data and an obligation to extend to the data and the processing means such safeguards as may be required to contain the concerns of the managements of the directly responsible functional areas. The workability of this arrangement is greatly improved if the cost of security as defined by the functional managers is charged back to them. This provides an incentive for them to balance their concern for data security, for which they are held accountable by a proper policy statement, against the cost of providing it so as to make certain that no more is spent protecting data than it would cost to leave it unprotected.

Questionnaires versus Interviews. We know of no paper survey of computer security matters with other than extremely limited scope, such as which access control method has been procured, which has yielded data which are both accurate and useful. It is far easier to acquire, by proper questionnaire design, data which seem useful than it is data which are accurate. For example, there was in the Department of Defense a contingency planning questionnaire which asked, "Is your system is subject to acts of God?" We never saw that answered by other than a "No".

A major problem with paper surveys in the computer security area is that the amount of explanatory text which must accompany the questions so badly burdens the task of preparing the surveys and answering them that either the writing or the reading (or both) of that material is too often neglected.

We have found eyeball-to-eyeball interviews with key managers of functional areas by far the most satisfactory and least time-consuming approach for everyone concerned. The skilled interviewer should be accompanied by a person from the DP area - preferably, the person who will be charged with maintaining the contingency plan after its preparation - so as to provide learning for him in the conduct of those interviews. With such an arrangement, it is usually relatively easy to reach agreement between the contingency planners and the functional managers as to the direct and, very importantly, indirect costs of losing data or the processing means as a function of the duration of such loss. As we noted above, the frequency or probability of occurrence may be a little more difficult, but it is not an overwhelming burden.

THE SPLIT-SITE APPROACH

The most commonly encountered major problems in achieving and retaining a truly workable back-up plan are these:

1. Identifying the critical workload. Not only must it be initially identified, it must be continually assessed as new applications evolve and as the organization's priorities change.

2. Assuring suitably prompt availability of adequate computer(s) when they are needed.

3. Establishment of enough of the normally required communications network to provide adequate limp-along capability.

4. Conducting realistic tests of the contingency plan in the face of opposition to the cost of the tests, to the disruption to non-critical workload and to the potential for disruption to the critical workload.

5. Assuring availability of data. With the rapidly growing size of some data bases, this problem is becoming increasingly severe if only because of the time and costs required to unload and load the amount of data required to support the critical workload. Planning and assuring the availability of back-up data has become an important and fairly costly part of good systems management. It is wholly essential to workable contingency plans.

6. Assuring the availability of the skill levels required to respond promptly to a need to back-up the critical tasks and to phase off-line gracefully the non-critical tasks.

7. Maintenance of management support for contingency planning.

8. Preservation of an awareness on the part of planners and developers that ease and cost of back-up and recovery should be weighed along with all of the other operable factors when planning new applications and the refurbishing of old ones.

The list above is not necessarily in priority sequence. The relative importance of these things will vary with the organization.

Now, given a wide variety of candidate approaches to back-up, most of which were listed earlier (with notable and generally unworkable exceptions, such as dedicated and unused floor space with no DP hardware) and given these more common difficulties, we must pick an approach that promises the greatest potential workability. More often than not, it is the split site.

While the split site is most often the most workable approach to back-up, it is not necessarily the approach chosen even when it is the most appropriate. Too often there is an unwillingness to solicit management support for any approach which will have significant cost, even when it is cost-justified. If the cost will require a diversion of resource which would otherwise be available to increase data processing services or if the implementation of a good back-up plan would require recognition by the senior management of the high jeopardy with which they have been living for some time while assuming risks about which they had not been told, the DP management may opt for a less workable, basically cosmetic approach to back-up which avoids rousing the ire of that senior management. For our purposes here, we will assume that there is a sincere, politically unfettered desire to implement the most cost-effective plan.

The split-site approach is not always the best approach, but, more often than not, it provides the most cost-effective, workable one with the least encumbrance by the several negative factors listed above. We will now attempt to support that assertion.

We stated above that it is very rare for the critical workload to exceed 50% of the total workload and, more commonly, it is in the order of 20% of the total. Even during first shift on systems with heavy interactive, real-time loads, well more than 50% of the work is usually divertable to the non-critical category. When such is not the case, the most burdensome applications should be examined to see whether some of the work done under them should not have been relegated to batch and is, instead, being done unnecessarily in the real time environment.

If less than half of the total workload is critical, then it is clear that, at least conceptually, we can convert a single facility into two without increasing the total capability and have either of the two parts be large enough to carry the critical workload. Under these circumstances, we would not need to involve the facilities of other organizations to have a back-up capability. It is clear that systems do not cut cleanly into two parts of precisely the relative sizes we might want, but that is not a major problem.

Split-Site Costs.

It is clear that one cannot divide an existing facility into two parts easily or without added cost. If it is planned carefully, however, it can be done at costs sufficiently low as to make it an attractive proposition for most organizations. The smaller the critical workload, the smaller the second facility must be and, normally, the lower the cost of establishing and operating that site.

The economies of scale dictate it to be less expensive to carry a workload in one location rather than two or more. This is not a commentary on the desirability of distributed processing or putting DP under the direct control of the functional areas supported. A given DP workload is normally less costly if it is done all at one place. Because, in this case, there is a reason for splitting the workload between locations, we want to do it in such a way as to minimize that cost.

It is reasonably obvious that the smaller the second site, the less the increase in the operating cost of the two sites over the cost of the initial single site. Thus, the second site should be as small as possible and still carry the critical workload and, of great importance, be a fully viable facility for carrying whatever normal workload is appropriate for placement there. We have found that the second site increases the operating costs of that portion of the work brought to the second site by about 20%. Thus, if 20% of the workload is moved to a new site which has a capability of about 20% of the initial facility, the increase in costs incurred by operating at the two sites instead of one will be roughly (0.20 X 0.20) or 4%. The 20% figure is useful only for initial guidance and should be confirmed by hard estimates of the costs in the specific operating environments under consideration. Many factors may influence its actual value.

If the 20% increase can be confirmed for a specific environment, then it is clear that the split-site provides a highly desirable back-up option if there are no other significant barriers to that approach.

Dividing the Workload for Split Sites.

There is probably no need to note here that, when split sites are planned, as much as possible of the critical workload should be placed in the facility which is least likely to be disrupted for any reason. This is not always practicable, but, where it is, it should be done.

Many organizations already have a split between processors handling the normal workload and those supporting development and test, although these processors are often in the same physical area and are, therefore, jeopardized by the same infrastructure disruptions. It is not uncommon to find that the test and development capability is large enough to carry the critical workload provided only that appropriate access to essential communications and DASD can be provided.

Because test and development is almost always a prime candidate for suspension when normal processing is disrupted and back-up of critical applications is required, running them in the site most likely to be used for back-up often affords an ease of transition to the critical work when that is needed.

Putting test and development at the most secure site might, because it would not be needed normally, preclude the availability of

continuing attachment of that site to those communications facilities needed to support the critical applications. Even though there might be an intent to preserve the ability to provide the communications necessary to the back-up capability at that site, it is terribly easy for that ability to atrophy unnoticed and not be available when needed. Care must be taken to avoid that problem.

If the normal workload at the second site requires availability to the communications facilities which support the critical applications, then no hardware or extensive logical shifts need be made to run those backed-up applications there. It is quite fortunate when such an arrangement is feasible.

If all facilities on which the critical applications might be run when back-up is needed are on the same SNA network, then many of the communications problems are fairly readily resolved provided only that the disruption did not incapacitate a significantly large segment of the communications network.

It is imperative that the back-up plan provide adequate means for back-up of essential communications facilities. They are too frequently neglected in our contingency plans. Each year more data processing time is lost to catastrophically damaged cables, both copper and glass, than is lost to physical damage to all other DP components.

Split Site Management.

It is almost uniformly true that success in bringing any good contingency plan to fruition is dependent upon the support of the director of data processing, by whatever title. In many companies the person in that position has fought long and hard to preserve the integrity of his fiefdom and is, quite understandably, very reluctant to see it fractionated. If the company now has but a single site under each of one or more such persons, it must be anticipated that they might well oppose the establishment of a split-site arrangement unless it is quite clear that they will retain responsibility for both sites.

This frequently encountered opposition by the DP manager to a second site unless it is also under his management is a good thing - sometimes for the wrong reason, but it is usually a good thing. It is difficult to imagine a situation in which both sites of a split-site arrangement should not be under the same management. It is important that control over the two converge at a level not too high for the common management to be fully aware of any activities at either site which might threaten the ability of each to pick up the critical applications.

It is far more likely that two sites will remain compatible if they are under common management than if they are not.

There are, unfortunately, many examples of back-up arrangements within the same organizations, many of which were fully and successfully tested in the past, but where the systems, which were supposed to be and thought by the senior management to be mutually supportive, grew in ways which negated the capability to back up each other.

In a number of the more notable examples, these differences were intentionally introduced by the DP directors to achieve for their particular facility some superior capability or service level not possessed by the other.

Site Locations.

It may not be possible to satisfy all of the desiderata appropriate to the location of split sites. The relative importance of each, and, thus, the need to satisfy it, is best judged in the light of the particular operating environment. The more important ones are these:

1. Proximity.- The two sites should be sufficiently close that it is logistically feasible for each to store the back-up data for the other. In general, this is to say that the two should be within a few hours drive by motor vehicle.

2. Physical Dispersion.- They should be far enough apart that they are not subject to the same causes of disruption provided that the probability of encountering those problems is weighed realistically.

3. Independence.- So far as possible, the facilities should be located so as to be free of dependence upon elements in the infrastructure which are known to be shaky. These include factors ranging from power, communications, water, sewer, transportation, susceptibility to tornadoes and hurricanes, flood plain problems, riot-prone neighborhoods, proximity to major highways and railroads which offer the potential for chemical spills which will require evacuation of the facilities, and other such factors.

THE FUTURE

Distributed processing, the growth of departmental computers, and the rapid proliferation of microcomputers will all contribute in large measure to the problems of contingency planning just as they contribute greatly to both the efficacy and the complexity of our information systems. We can find no reason for an assumption that they will serve to decrease the size of single-site data aggregations to which access will be required for the efficient conduct of our businesses.

The cost of data storage continues to decrease as do access times and both of which

serve to accelerate growth in the volume of data to which we want access. It is inevitable that continued growth in data aggregation size will greatly change the nature of contingency plans which are practicable in support of very large, high data-volume business systems.

We expect to see the advent of super-safe, underground DASD facilities connectable to geographically-remote large and small processors through very high-speed communications facilities leaving us with the need to back up only the processors and provide alternate means of communications.

At this time, we find very little reflection in workable contingency plans of recognition of our growing dependence on microcomputers and minis. It may well be that we will not see significant change in that until some major organization has a very serious problem as a result of being unprepared, but we have almost no confidence in that as a motivator of others. The problems of others has not been a primary source of motivation for such contingency planning as we have seen about mainframe facilities. Most such losses are not broadly publicized.

The slowly increasing competence of internal auditors in the technical aspects of data processing should serve, in the foreseeable future, to alert corporate managements to the need for better contingency planning. We expect that, rather than the grief of others, to accelerate the emphasis on contingency plans which address the whole of the data processing dependency as well as recognition that there are many other parts of our businesses other than data processing which, if disrupted, have the potential for causing great harm.

SUMMARY

A wide variety of approaches to contingency planning is available to the persons charged with designing such plans. The task requires innovation, much common sense, rejection of all cookbook approaches, and, above all, prior identification and quantification of the losses potentially averted by the proper plans. No contingency plans are so inherently desirable that they should be implemented without solid economic justification.

Contingency planning is as much dependent upon understanding human nature as it is on understanding the technical aspects of our systems. Unless people at each organizational level from which we need support, or, at least, lack of opposition, can be motivated to support back up and recovery, it is very difficult to put in place. Strong senior management support born of awareness of the need for it contributes more than any other factor to the success of contingency planning - but even that is not a guarantor.

One thing of which we are certain, because it has been demonstrated repeatedly, is that good, workable contingency plans are economically feasible.

Section 2.2: Formal Models

Introduction

How do you know that a computer system does the "right" thing? Most of the time, you do not actually "know," but you have been convinced! You have been convinced by some combination of factors such as the reputation of the hardware and software vendor, some degree of testing, and prior experience. Under some circumstances, this kind of conviction is not enough. You need proof! For example, it is not unknown for an operating system module to display a latent flaw after several years of use. This section discusses the concept of proof as applied to computer security.

It should come as no surprise to readers of this tutorial that one circumstance where you might want increased assurance that a computer system's hardware, firmware, and software are correctly implementing a desired function is when that function involves the protection of valuable resources. Put another way, computer security really should work correctly; otherwise, it is not worth having. The tone of this introduction is informal; we shall keep it that way. More formal definitions are given in the following subsection on terminology.

One of the first steps is to determine what your objectives are for technical computer security; what rules you want the computer to enforce. The U.S. Department of Defense has a very comprehensive set of policies. The policies for commercial organizations are probably very different. For the computer to enforce these policies, the policies must be translated into a mathematically precise form known as a *formal security model.* Now the fun has just begun; we need to be convinced of two things: (1) that the formal model is a correct representation of the policy, and (2) that the *implementation* is faithful to the formal model.

Establishing that the formal model is a correct representation of the policy is an intellectual exercise. Over the years a number of models of Defense policy have been proposed. After considerable intellectual scrutiny, one of these, the Bell-LaPadula (B-LP) model, has been widely accepted. It is the standard against which any proposed model will be compared. Since the B-LP model [BELL76] is basic to the development of the U.S. Department of Defense *Trusted Computer System and Network Evaluation Criteria,* we shall focus on this particular model after properly setting the stage.

We can be convinced that an implementation is faithful to the formal model by a number of different procedures. The closer these procedures are to mathematical proofs, the greater the assurance they provide. Good modern software engineering methods, such as use of strongly typed high-level languages and structured walk-through, provide an intermediate degree of assurance.

Terminology

This section deals with rather precise, and sometime arcane, terminology. Many of the terms seem similar; but there are fine distinctions. We will try to introduce terms in context, italicizing new terms when first defined. The glossary should also be consulted. One source of confusion is that we deal with theory, abstract concepts, concrete concepts, and implementations. There are subset relationships among the terms as well as refinements.

We will try to take a top-down approach. The highest concept we wish to address is security architecture. Security architecture provides a plan for the security of the computer (and possibly network) system. This plan can range from a high level of abstraction to precise definition of objectives to specification of mechanisms to implementation details. Unfortunately, there are few, if any, examples of security architecture; perhaps the field is too new for ideas to have coalesced into a coherent structure. An analogy with network architecture may be helpful; as discussed in Section 3.4, some networks have architectural reference documents, while others are defined by their implementations.

One of the most important components of the security architecture is the *security policy,* the set of laws, rules, and practices that regulate how an organization manages, protects, and distributes sensitive information. In general, the security policy will be written in a natural language such as English. While natural language is easy to understand in a general way, it is often susceptible to multiple interpretations on specific points. This ambiguity indicates the need for a precise formal language restatement in a *formal security policy model.* Formal language, in this context, means mathematical notation, an algorithmic computer programming language, or a computer language designed for specification. The implementation of the formal security policy model is known as the *trusted computing base* (TCB). The TCB is the totality of protection mechanisms within a system—including hardware, firmware, and software—the combination of which is responsible for enforcing the security policy. The TCB creates a basic protection environment and provides

EH0255-0/87/0000/0083$01.00 © 1987 IEEE

additional user services required for a trusted computer system. The ability of the TCB to enforce a security policy correctly depends solely on the mechanisms within the TCB and on the correct input by system administrative personnel of parameters (e.g., a user's clearance) relative to the security policy.

One major component of security policy is *access control,* which limits the rights or capabilities of a *subject* or principal to communicate with other subjects or to use functions or services in a computer system or network. The latter part of this definition is often stated in terms of limiting access to *objects,* passive entities that contain or receive information. Access control is enforced by a *reference monitor,* still an abstract concept, which mediates all accesses to objects by subjects. The implementation of the reference monitor is the *kernel.*

The kernel is a subset of the TCB; that is, there are constituent parts of the security policy that are implemented in the TCB but outside the kernel. Examples include identification and authentification, and audit.

Applicability

The concept of a formal model for computer security is central to (1) the development of trusted computer system evaluation criteria, (2) the implementation of the controls specified by the criteria into a trusted computing base (TCB) of hardware and software, and (3) the verification, and in some cases testing, that the TCB implementation is a correct implementation of the model. This process of formal model specification, development, and implementation for computer security usually applies to the reference monitor and the security kernel. A reference monitor mediates all accesses to objects (generally data) by subjects (generally a person or surrogate for a person, such as a software program being executed). A security kernel is an implementation of a reference monitor in the specific hardware, firmware, and software elements of a TCB. The security kernel must mediate all accesses, be protected from modification, and be verifiable as a correct implementation of the reference monitor.

The concept of a formal model for network security is a logical extension of the formal model for computer security. The nature of this extension is still a matter of research; work is under development by the National Computer Security Center [CSCD85]. The TCB concept could become the trusted network base (TNB) concept, or the network could be viewed as a system with a trusted system base (TSB), or a distributed TCB. The TNB scope could include control of all components in the network including host computers, front end processors, packet switches, and so on. A security kernel in the TNB could be an implementation of a network reference monitor in a manner similar to that described for computer security. One difference would be the increased input/output activity that must be controlled by the TNB, because of the large number of communication channels possible in a network.

Formal Security Models

Why Formal Models?

Several issues are developed to introduce the concept and value of formal security models. This discussion is based upon the extensive work of Carl E. Landwehr and adapts several of his concepts [LAND81b]. This paper is discussed further in the recommended readings section. First, the question might be raised concerning why we use formal models. One reason is that system designers must decide what "secure" means for a particular computer system. One vehicle for this process is the formal model. The formal model is essentially a computer-based representation of the security procedures that define the security requirements for a class of computer system applications. Formal models are carefully structured to represent the applicable security requirements accurately.

An important use of formal models is that computer systems can be built to the specifications in the formal models. The systems developers then can use appropriate software tools to demonstrate how, or prove that, the computer system complies with the model. As of the time this tutorial is written, very few computer systems have software that is "proven" secure (i.e., proven to comply with a specific formal model as evaluated by NCSC). But the list is growing; a number of commercial computer systems, hardware and operating system, are in the evaluation process or have made initial contact with NCSC. The reader is advised to consult the most current *Evaluated Products List* and other announcements from NCSC to determine what products have been or are being evaluated.

Basic Concepts of Formal Models

The concept of a finite-state machine model is essential for understanding computer security. Essentially, this model considers a computer system as a finite set of states and a transition function, which determines what the next state will be on the basis of the current state and the current value of the input.

Output values may also be determined by the transition function. Since transactions are considered in this model as occurring instantaneously, not all real-time information channels are visible to the model. For example, information channels pertaining to time spent in a certain state may not be visible. There are different security models that have been developed; however, the finite-state machine model is basic to many of the security models.

One class of models that is of basic interest for this tutorial is the access matrix model; it is the foundation of many of the other models that have been developed. This model presents a generalized description of operating system protection mechanisms. Users access to information is the focal point of this type of model. The model does not consider semantics of the information. Rather, the model represents controls on users' access to objects (generally data) that are checked by a reference monitor.

Extensions of the access matrix model have been required for the inclusion of the semantics of the information. One reason is to incorporate control adequately over classified information into the model. In this case, the model knows the classification of the information and the clearance of the user (i.e., right to access certain classes of information). The model contains rules concerning the classifications (e.g., hierarchical classification levels). An important example of an extension to the access matrix model is the Bell-LaPadula model.

The Bell-LaPadula Model

This description of the application of the Bell-LaPadula model is adapted from the TCSEC to illustrate the basic concept of a formal model for a computer system. Where feasible, the original wording in the TCSEC is maintained. However, this discussion of the Bell-LaPadula model is a limited overview and does not substitute for the formal documentation on the model and its application to computer security.

The Bell-LaPadula model is a formal state transition model of computer security policy that describes a set of access control rules [CSCS83]. By using mathematics and set theory, the model precisely defines the notion of a secure state, fundamental modes of access, and the rules for granting subjects (basically people and surrogates) specific modes of access to objects (basically data). A theorem called the basic security theorem is proven to demonstrate that the rules are security-preserving operations, so that the application of any sequence of the rules to a system that is in a secure state will result in the system entering a new secure state.

The Bell-LaPadula model can be used in the development of a reference monitor, which is later implemented in a security kernel. The dominance relation is the key to understanding the nature of the model, where the model defines a relationship between clearances of subjects and classifications of system objects. This relation facilitates the explicit definition for the fundamental modes of access between subjects and objects, including read-only access, read/write access, and write-only access. The TCSEC defines dominance as follows: "Security level S1 is said to dominate security level S2 if the hierarchical classification of S1 is greater than or equal to that of S2 and the non-hierarchical categories of S1 include all those of S2 as a subset."

Control of access is defined by the Bell-LaPadula model by the simple security condition, the *-(star)-property (read as star property), and the discretionary security property.

Mandatory security provisions are included in the simple security condition and the *-property, which are based on the dominance relation between the clearance of the subject and the security classification of the object. The Bell-LaPadula model is an abstract formal treatment of U.S. Department of Defense security policy; hence clearance and classification refer to hierarchical levels such as top secret, secret, and confidential.

The simple security condition is used as the method or rule of the Bell-LaPadula model to control granting a subject read access to a specific object. This condition allows a subject to have read access to an object only if the security level is equal to or greater than the object (i.e., the subject dominates the security level of the object). Write access to an object is allowed by another rule of the Bell-LaPadula model—the *-property—only if the security level of the subject is essentially equal to or less than (is dominated by) the security level of the object. There are trusted subjects (i.e., not constrained by the *-property) and untrusted subjects (that are constrained by the *-property). In addition, the *-property protects against compromise of information by software programs with additional (hidden) functions (i.e., Trojan horse attacks). Also defined into the model is the discretionary security property, which requires that a specific subject be authorized for a particular mode of access required for the state transition.

Other Models

Many formal security models have been and probably will continue to be created. Some, like the Bell-LaPadula model, were aimed at expressing Defense security policy; such a model has the best chance of being accepted by NCSC when it evaluates the system containing this model under the standards discussed in Section 2.3.

While Bell-LaPadula is currently the best established model, as long as there is research in this area, it will continue to be challenged. Landwher, Heitmeyer, and McLean propose another model for military message systems; their paper is discussed later in the recommended readings subsection. Millen [MILL84] starts out to build a model that contains only the Defense policy requirements for the A1 level, but cannot restrain himself from "an overwhelming temptation . . . to add new features in response to perceived deficiencies in other models." Concerning the Bell-LaPadula model, Millen observes "that it is unnecessarily restrictive—it includes specific 'rules' for system functions, which may be incompatible with the desired TCB functions, and it includes a Multics-directory-like object hierarchy." When computer networks are discussed, Rushby has serious reservations about the applicability of Bell-LaPadula; his paper is reprinted in Section 3.1.

When implementing a security kernel, a method is necessary to prove in a formal manner that all arbitrary sequences of state transitions are security-preserving. However, the TCSEC does not require a security kernel for certain evaluated divisions (D, C1, C2, and B1). In these cases, other approaches may be adequate such as a front-end security filter or access control software, such as IBM's RACF, SKK's ACF2, and CA's TOP SECRET.

Further discussion and examples of formal security concepts and implementations are contained in the reprint and recommended readings subsections.

Reprint

An example of proving that a computer system is secure is presented in the paper by W.D. Young, W.E. Boebert, and R.Y. Kain. The paper is abstracted as follows: "A model of a computer system written in a formal notation can be reduced to a collection of theorems in mathematics and logic. The model is proved to be secure by proving these theorems." The authors ". . . would like to show that no program running on the computer can change the values held in a few hardware registers and areas of memory to values that violate the mathematical relations expressing a security policy."

The paper observes that "A theorem in geometry can be accepted with confidence because the reasoning behind it has been examined and accepted by generations of mathematicians . . . because the reasoning is expressed in formal language." An extension is made to programming languages and, even better, specification languages that can be used to prove a program correct. Proving a program correct means that it conforms to its specification. Proving a computer secure requires first establishing axiomatically that the computer is in a secure state; then an inductive proof is used to show that all state transitions result in a secure state. The state transition rules constitute the reference monitor as implemented in the security kernel.

Owing to the complexity of computer systems, successive levels of abstraction are employed in proving the system secure. The highest most abstract level, the design specification, or *formal top-level specification,* is proven secure. A slightly more detailed model is then proven consistent with the specification. In principle, this process can be repeated *ad nausium* until the kernel is proven. There are practical problems. "The proofs of complex systems tend to be ex-tremely long and tediously detailed. Indeed, a long computer-generated proof may not be read even by the person supervising the proof. Consequently claims of correctness are often underlain by confidence in the verification system." So first we have to prove the correctness of the verification system; then we can prove the security of a system. This may be the easier job, for "it may seem harder to judge the correctness of the proof than to judge the correctness of the program itself."

Young et al. describe the approach to proving the security of a system called the secure Ada target. Additional information on the secure Ada target is provided in the reprints section in Section 2.6. The proof employs the specification language Gypsy, a Pascal derivative. The security policy is "defined as characteristics of the access matrix. . . . The security properties are represented as specification functions whose domain is the matrix. . . . The system is secure if the formal statements of the simple security policy and the *-property hold for all subjects s and for all objects o."

One of the complications is that the access matrix can be changed. In fact, every operation that can affect the security state is modeled into a series of assertions. These assertions are subjected to a set of proof rules null, assignment, if, while, consequence, and composition.

Programs are proven by using a three step regime: "(1) Annotate the program with assertions describing the program state; (2) Write the verification conditions for every execution path; and (3) Prove that for every path that if the assertion at the beginning of the path is true, and the path is executed, then the asertion at the end of the path will be true."

Recommended Readings

The survey paper, "Formal Models for Computer Security," by Carl Landwehr provides a basic background in formal models for computer security. Although the focus is military security, the formal models have a wider utility. Landwher states, "This paper reviews the need for formal security models, describes the structure and operation of military security controls, considers how automation has affected security problems, surveys models that have been proposed and built to date [1981], and suggests directions for future models."

Computer and automation aggravate old problems such as aggregation, authentication, browsing, integrity, copying, and denial of service; they also introduce new problems such as confinement, Trojan horses and trap doors, and other threats related to the electromagnetic characteristics of computers and communications. Basic concepts for formal models of computer security include

- *Finite state machine model:* Used ". . . for computation views [of] a computer system as a finite set of states, together with a transition function to determine what the next state will be, based on the current state and the current value of the input. The transition function may also determine an output value."

- *Lattice model:* Describes the structure of security levels. "A lattice is a finite set together with a partial ordering in its elements such that for every pair of elements there is a least upper bound and a greatest lower bound . . ."

- *Access matrix model:* Provides ". . . a generalized description of operating system protection mechanisms. It models controls on users' access to information without regard to the semantics of the information in question. A reference monitor checks the validity of users' accesses to objects [data] . . ."

A sequence of modeling concepts is described, progressing through information-flow models to the present ultimate form, the Bell-LaPadula model. Several models and implementations along the way are discussed, including the ADEPT-50 time-sharing system; and the access matrix model implemented in the UCLA Data Secure UNIX™, AT&T, and take-grant models.

The Bell-LaPadula model is an extension of the access matrix model to include classification of the information and the clearance of the user. Two basic axioms of the Bell-LaPadula model are: (1) "No user may read information classified above his clearance level ("No read up") and (2) "No user may lower the classification of information ("No write down")." Seven rules governing state transitions are given: get access, release access, give access, rescind access, create object, delete object, and change security level. Extensions and applications of the Bell-LaPadula model include integrity and database management systems. The model has been reformulated and altered to accommodate formal proofs of correctness. Other models and concerns addressed include information-flow, integrity, and programs as channels for information transition as filters with strong dependency and constraints.

A table compares the models discussed as to their motivation, view of security, and approach. The paper concludes that "formal models for computer security are needed in order to organize the complexity inherent in both 'computer' and 'security.'. . . Controlling the sharing of information in a computer is in fact a critical problem in operating system design."

In his paper, "Non-Discretionary Controls for Commercial Applications," Steve Lipner ". . .examines some ways in which the lattice model non-discretionary controls might be used in commercial data processing." Lipner concludes that the lattice model may have commercial data processing application; however, the model may have to be different than the model used to represent security requirements in the national security community. The issue is should a commercial system be partitioned by levels and categories? If a commercial organization can use the notion of clearance, then the lattice model has applicability. Some commercial organizations approximate this condition with data categories such as unlimited distribution, sensitive, restricted, restricted-critical. Additional discussion of similarities and differences between military and private sector computer security is found in Chalmers' paper which is discussed in Section 2.1. Lipner agrees with Chalmers that "commercial institutions may be more interested in unauthorized modification of information than its compromise." After discussing the (security) lattice model, Lipner addresses the integrity model, which is "directed toward the control of modification (rather than disclosure) of information." He discusses integration of an integrity policy into commercial processing applications as an addition to the lattice model.

In addition to its stated purpose, Lipner also provides an explanation of the implementation of the lattice model as the Bell-LaPadula model for defense security systems. Written for a commercial audience, it clearly explains classification labels, Defense security rules, and subject processes.

The paper, "A Security Model for Military Message Systems," addresses specialized security needs for military message systems, which are significantly different from programming or database applications. Carl Landwehr, Constance Heitmeyer, and John McLean focus on the goal of multilevel security, which means that the system ". . .protects information of different classifications from users with different clearances; thus some users are not cleared for all of the information that the system processes."

Characterizing the Bell-LaPadula model as an application-independent abstraction, which is often coupled with a class of *trusted subjects* that do not violate security even though they may violate its rules in order to meet operational needs, the authors propose an alternative to "start with the application and derive the constraints that the system must enforce from both the functional and security requirements of the application." The illustrative application selected is a family of military message systems.

After defining the functional and security requirements of military message systems and experiences with several implementations of the Bell-LaPadula model and trusted processes, the military message system security model is defined and described informally from the user and the security viewpoints. A formal model is developed and shown to correspond to the informal model. The most important conclusions concerning an application-based security model are (1) "The model captures the system's security requirements in a way that is understandable to users" and (2) "The model and its formalization provide a basis for certifiers to assess the security of the system as a whole."

Proving a Computer System Secure

A model of a computer system written in a formal notation can be reduced to a collection of theorems in mathematics and logic. The model is proved to be secure by proving these theorems.

W.D. Young (University of Texas);
W.E. Boebert (Honeywell Secure Computing Technology Center);
R.Y. Kain (University of Minnesota)
MN55-7282; HVN 378-6792

*I*s it possible to be as confident that a computer system is secure as that the Pythagorean theorem is true? A right-angle triangle is a mathematical object, but a computer system is an elaborate assemblage of hardware and software interacting in complex ways. How can one construct a rigorous argument about such a machine?

The task is not as hopeless as it might seem. A theorem in geometry can be accepted with confidence because the reasoning behind it has been examined and accepted by generations of mathematicians. Such general agreement is possible in part because the reasoning is expressed in a formal language, one that enforces a more rigorous relation between successive statements than does a natural language such as English. Programming languages are also formal languages; they must be, because a machine cannot follow an open-ended or ambiguous set of instructions. As a result, it is possible to prove to a skeptical audience that a proposition about a program is true. For example, one can formally describe the purpose of a program and then prove that the program is correct, in the sense that it does what it is intended to do. Or, to put it in the vocabulary of computing science, one can specify a program and then verify the program's correctness.

Proving that a computer system is secure is a slightly different problem.

Ultimately one would like to show that no program running on the computer can change the values held in a few hardware registers and areas of memory to values that violate the mathematical relations expressing a security policy. The demonstration will be more convincing if the physical machine — a network of semiconductor chips and the transient electric charges they store — can be represented by a collection of equivalent mathematical objects, like right-angle triangles or, for that matter, a set of computer programs.

The techniques of formal modeling provide the tools to tackle this problem. The system and its working are formally described at a high level of abstraction. The formal description, which is called a design specification, resembles a program, although the operations it specifies are abstract ones and they are carried out on abstract entities. Just as a program can be proved to have a particular property, the design specification can be proved to enforce security controls. Then progressively more concrete machines are specified and these specifications are proved secure. Since the specifications of two different models of the system are both formal, mathematical techniques can be used to show that they are consistent, a process that is also called verification.

Ideally the most abstract specification is analogous to an axiom in Euclidean geometry in that the security of the abstract machine it describes is self-evident. The successive formal specifications and the arguments that show that each specification is consistent with the one before it constitute a proof. The lowest-level specification should follow the working of the physical system so closely that the machine can easily be shown to have the properties the specification exhibits. If it does, the proposition that the physical machine invariably preserves security can be accepted with confidence. This proposition is therefore analogous to the Pythagorean theorem.

This is not to say that the proof that a program is correct or the proof that a computer system is secure is as straightforward as a traditional mathematical proof. A typical computer program consists of thousands of statements whose sequence of execution varies with the input. Proving that such a complex entity is correct is so difficult that it is rarely done. Low-level design specifications may be even more elaborate. It is hardly surprising, therefore, that few computer systems have been formally proved secure. Only some designs have been based on formal modeling, and of those only a few have included specifications more than two levels deep.

The Department of Defense has defined criteria for evaluating the degree of assurance provided by secure computer systems. On the basis of these criteria systems are assigned to classes. The higher classes require that more security mechanisms be provided and that the demonstration that security is indeed maintained be more convincing. The highest class yet defined, called the A1 class, requires that "formal design specification and verification techniques" be used to provide a "high degree of assurance" that the computer system correctly implements security controls. To date only the Honeywell Secure Communications Processor (SCOMP) has been awarded A1 certification. The Secure Ada Target, now being designed at the Honeywell Secure Computing Technology Center, is intended to surpass the requirements for A1 certification.

A description of the modeling and proof of the Secure Ada Target illustrates the application of the techniques of formal reasoning to a computer system. The techniques and tools that are being hammered out in this and other design projects may someday be applied routinely to all computer systems. Although the flaws in most machines do not have consequences as serious as a breach of military security, they are at best irritating and at worst gluttonous consumers of time and money. Any reasonable means of eliminating them would be welcome.

Gypsy

Although formal specifications can be written in familiar programming languages, such as Ada and Pascal, programming languages designed with specification in mind make the task far easier. Among the specification languages are Special, Ina Jo, Affirm and Gypsy, the language we chose to work with. Gypsy, which was designed by Donald I. Good and his associates at the Institute for Computing Science of the University of Texas, is a general-purpose programming language based on Pascal that includes additional constructs particularly suited to specification. Gypsy is integrated into a complete environment for formal verification, which provides auto-

mated assistance for the maintenance and proof of programs. It has been used extensively for the proof of large software systems, among them a secure interface to the Arpanet that consists of more than 7,000 lines of Gypsy code, and for the modeling and proof of computer systems, including portions of SCOMP. The Gypsy system runs on Digital Equipment Corporation's System-20 and the Symbolics 3600 Lisp Machine and is currently being ported to Honeywell's Multics.

We chose Gypsy for its expressive power but also because the Secure Ada Target team had sufficient experience with the language that the modeling and proof could begin early and proceed in parallel with the design effort. This was important because difficulties with a proof can expose design flaws and thus prevent expensive design corrections late in the process.

Modeling Security

The application of formal proof methods to the design of a secure system required that the key ideas be captured in the formal notation we had chosen. In this case the key ideas were the notion of security itself and a proposed system design. Once the properties that would qualify the system as secure and a model of the system were written in Gypsy, it would be possible to prove that the model invariably exhibited the properties.

The security properties were originally specified at a highly abstract level and in a system-independent manner. Here we describe the proof at the level of abstraction where the system is first modeled, called the Abstract Model level. The levels of abstraction in the design of the Secure Ada Target are discussed at length in the companion article (*Secure Computing: The Secure Ada Target Approach*). The argument we present assumes familiarity with the higher levels of abstraction, particularly with the two properties that together make up the mandatory security policy: the Simple

Security Property and the *-Property. Since the model of the machine we will be discussing is actually proved to have several other properties and since the proof of the Secure Ada Target includes the proof of several models, our discussion is illustrative rather than comprehensive.

At the Abstract Model level the security-enforcing hardware can be thought of as a matrix, a two-dimensional array M indexed on rows by subjects and on columns by objects. Each entry $M(s,o)$ in the matrix gives the access rights that one subject s is granted to one object o. The complete matrix describes all possible accesses by subjects to objects. Consequently its state (the contents of all its cells at any given moment) completely characterizes the security state of the system at that moment.

The security properties the system is to satisfy can thus be defined as characteristics of the access matrix. The system satisfies the Simple Security Property provided that each entry $M(s,o)$ in the access matrix contains read access only if the level of subject s dominates the level of object o. The system satisfies the *-Property provided that each entry $M(s,o)$ in the access matrix contains write access only if the level of object o dominates the level of subject s. The system is secure only if its access matrix satisfies both of these properties.

These verbal descriptions must be converted into Gypsy statements, a process that requires that symbols or symbolic expressions be substituted for words. Subjects and objects are represented in Gypsy as data types. Gypsy, like Pascal, requires a programmer to specify the type to which each variable belongs so that automated programming tools can verify that the operations carried out on the variable are ones that are valid for its type. The attributes of subjects and objects, such as their security levels, are handled by functions whose domain is a particular data type. The access matrix is simply a two-dimensional array that is indexed by subjects and objects. The elements in the array are pairs of boolean values (either true or false), which indicate whether read and write access is granted or denied. The security properties are represented as specification functions whose domain is the matrix and which return a boolean value. It is in this representation that the power of Gypsy is particularly apparent; the specification functions can include complex expressions in the logical formalism called predicate calculus.

The formal definition of security that puts all of these pieces together is shown in the illustration on this page. The gist of the definition is that the system is secure if the formal statements of the Simple Security Property and of the *-Property hold for all subjects *s* and for all objects *o*. Note that the definition resembles a program insofar as it is an algorithm, or set of steps, for distinguishing a secure matrix from one that is not secure. It consists of three functions: one function returns a value of true if the Simple Security Property holds; the second returns a value of true if the *-Property holds, and the third function combines the results of the other two. The definition is not a program in the usual sense of the term, since it could not be compiled and executed, but its resemblance to a program is not accidental, as we shall see.

We have now modeled a secure system, but the system is a static one. The access matrix displays the security state of the system and provides a means of determining whether the system is secure or not. Any useful system, however, must allow subjects to alter the security state in order to gain legitimate access to objects. A model of a dynamic system must characterize the operations available to subjects and determine the effects of these operations on the security state. Each operation that could potentially affect the security state is modeled as a Gypsy procedure.

```
function SATISFIES_SIMPLE_SECURITY (M: access_matrix)
                                   : boolean =
begin
   exit (assume result iff
         all s: subject, all o: object,
           ( M (s,o).read
          ->
                 dominates (subject_level (s),
                            object_level (o))));
end; {satisfies_simple_security}

function SATISFIES_STAR_PROPERTY (M: access_matrix)
                                  : boolean =
begin
   exit (assume result iff
         all s: subject, all o: object,
           ( M (s,o).write
          ->
                 dominates (object_level (o),
                            subject_level (s))));
end; {satisfies_star_property}

function SECURE (M: access_matrix) : boolean =

begin
   exit (assume result iff
         ( satisfies_simple_security (M)
         & satisfies_star_property (M)));
end; {secure}
```

DEFINITION OF SECURITY in the specification of an abstract machine consists of definitions of two characteristics of an element of the machine, an access matrix *M*. *M* is an array indexed by subjects and objects. Each entry *M* (*s,o*) in the array designates whether subject *s* is granted read or write access to object *o*. SATISFIES _SIMPLE _SECURITY is a boolean function (one that returns either true or false) that takes the access matrix *M* as its argument. The function returns a value of true only if read access in an entry always implies that the security level of the subject is greater than or equal to (dominates) the security level of the subject. SATISFIES _STAR _PROPERTY is a boolean function that returns true only if write access always implies that the object's level dominates the subject's level. The boolean function SECURE returns true only if both SATISFIES _SIMPLE_ SECURITY and SATISFIES _STAR _PROPERTY return true.

Instantiate Object, the only operation modeled at this level of abstraction, provides an example. Instantiate Object creates an object and fills in the access values in the column of the matrix corresponding to that object. Each subject is granted those access rights not explicitly disallowed by any of the security properties (in our case the Simple Security Property and the *-Property).

Because Instantiate Object alters the access matrix, it is possible that it might grant access rights in violation of security policy and thus

change the system's state from one that is secure to one that is not. The same is true of any operation that causes a change in the access matrix. Moreover, it is possible that some sequence of operations could lead to a state that is not secure even though no one operation could have this effect. To demonstrate that the system is secure one must show that this can never happen or, in other words, that security is an invariant of the system. The demonstration has two steps. The system's initial state is shown to be secure; then it is shown that each operation that could potentially affect the system's

```
     procedure INSTANTIATE_OBJECT (var M: access_matrix;
                                   o: object) =
begin
   exit correct_M_update (M', M, o);
   pending;
end; {update_M}


   function CORRECT_M_UPDATE (M_in, M_out: access_matrix;
                              o: object) : boolean =
begin
   exit (assume result iff
         all s: subject, all o2: object,
           ( M_out (s ,o).read
             = dominates (subject_level(s), object_level (o))
          & M_out (s,o).write
             = dominates (object_level (o), subject_level(s))
          & ( o ne o2
             ->
                M_in (s,o2) = M_out (s,o2))));
   end; {correct_M_update}
```

INSTANTIATE_OBJECT is a Gypsy procedure that models an abstract operation in the abstract machine. The operation adds a column to the access matrix when a new object is created and fills in the appropriate access values. The key word "pending" indicates that the steps by which the matrix will be updated have not yet been defined. Any algorithm that is consistent with the procedure's exit specification, however, will be correct. The exit specification is correct_M_update (M', M, o). (M' is the input value of access matrix M, and o is the new object.) **CORRECT_M_UPDATE is a boolean function that stands in the place of the missing algorithm. The function specifies the result wanted without specifying how to get it: each subject is granted read access to the new object if the subject's level dominates the object's level; write access is granted if the object's level dominates that of the subject, and the access rights to all old objects o2 are unaffected by the operation.**

state can never change a secure state into one that is not secure.

Procedures such as INSTANTIATE_OBJECT are written to facilitate this demonstration. The Gypsy version of this procedure is shown in the illustration on this page. It includes an exit specification, a statement that invariably holds true when the procedure terminates. The obvious exit specification for INSTANTIATE_OBJECT would be that the access matrix will be in a secure state when the procedure terminates. Unfortunately the level of abstraction at which we are working prohibits this straightforward approach.

Note that the body of IN-STANTIATE_OBJECT is missing. It cannot be supplied at this high level of abstraction because the sets of subjects and objects that define the rows and columns of the access matrix are unbounded and the subjects and objects have no visible structure. Thus it is impossible to write an algorithm that would examine each subject in turn and fill in a column of the matrix. A function that describes the relation between the output of such an algorithm and its input can, however, be written. This function, which is called CORRECT_M_UPDATE, is shown below INSTANTIATE_OBJECT.

The exit specification included in INSTANTIATE_OBJECT is that the matrix will have been updated in accordance with CORRECT_M_UPDATE when the procedure terminates. This exit specification allows the Abstract Model specification to be proved secure even though the details of INSTANTIATE_OBJECT are missing; any later implementation of the procedure that is consistent with its exit specification will be a correct one.

It will be correct, that is, provided that CORRECT_M_UPDATE itself preserves security. The proposition that it does is embodied in a lemma, or subsidiary theorem (in the proof of INSTANTIATE_OBJECT). The lemma, which is shown in the illustration on page 22, specifies that if the access matrix is secure and if it is updated in a way that is consistent with CORRECT_M_UPDATE, then the resulting matrix will be secure. At a lower level of abstraction the lemma would not be necessary, and the procedure would be proved secure directly.

The proof that the system's initial state is secure and the proof of the procedures modeled at a given level of abstraction provide an inductive proof that no sequence of operations can cause a system that began in the initial state to enter a state that is not secure. The initial state of the model is assumed to be one in which no access rights are granted. This state is obviously a secure one. The only procedure modeled at this level of abstraction, INSTANTIATE_OBJECT, also clearly preserves security. At lower levels of abstrac-

```
lemma CORRECT_UPDATE_PRESERVES_SECURITY (M_in,
                                         M_out: access_matrix;
                                         o: object) =
       ( secure (M_in)
       & correct_M_update (M_in, M_out, o))
    ->
       secure (M_out);
```

CORRECT_UPDATE_PRESERVES_SECURITY is a lemma that can be proved and whose correctness implies the correctness of the incomplete and therefore unprovable procedure **INSTANTIATE_OBJECT**. The lemma states that if an access matrix is secure (that is, if it meets the definition of security given in the illustration on page 20) and it is updated in a manner satisfying **CORRECT_M_UPDATE**, the resulting matrix will be secure. Since **INSTANTIATE_OBJECT** is constrained to behave in accordance with **CORRECT_M_UPDATE** by its exit specification, the proof of this lemma ensures that the procedure preserves the security of its access-matrix argument.

tion, however, the procedures that model operations are much more detailed, and it can be difficult to see that they preserve security.

We have noted the resemblance between the Gypsy specification of an abstract machine or operation and a program. There is a very practical reason for the resemblance. The restriction of the specification to the grammar of a programming language means that it can be proved by the techniques that have been worked out for the proof of programs. Moreover, it allows the automated tools that have been designed to prove programs to be used in the proof of the specification.

Proving a Program Correct

The first step in proving a program is to write a specification, or independent characterization, of the program. It is worth emphasizing that the claim that a program is correct merely means that it conforms to a specification. A program that has not been specified cannot be incorrect; it can only be surprising.

Specifications of programs are written by annotating the program with assertions. An assertion is a statement of a condition that must be true (if the program is correct) when control reaches the point in the program about which the assertion is made. A specification of a simple program is composed of two such assertions: one assertion holds before the program executes, and the other holds after the program executes. For example, if P and Q are assertions and S is a program, the notation $\{P\}\ S\ \{Q\}$ means that if P is true and S executes, then Q will be true when S terminates. (Curly brackets signify a comment, or non-executable statement; assertions are a special kind of comment.) P is called the entry condition, input assertion or precondition for statement S; Q is called the exit condition, output assertion or post condition.

How is it possible to show that the statements in a program always lead from an input assertion to an exit assertion — no matter what the input to the program happens to be and no matter what path execution takes through the program? The answer is not obvious; indeed the notion that one can prove that a program meets a specification is a relatively new one. The approach adopted is one frequently taken to difficult problems in mathematics, namely to reduce the problem to a set of more tractable problems. We would like to reduce the problem of proving a program to that of proving a collection of theorems in mathematics and logic.

The programming statements themselves are not mathematical or logical expressions, although they may include such expressions. Indeed, insofar as programming statements specify an action to be taken, they resemble imperative sentences in a natural language such as English. But, fortunately for us, programming languages differ from natural languages in that they allow only a few kinds of statements, each of which has a well-defined meaning.

Among the more common kinds of programming statements are assignment statements, *if* statements and *while* statements. In many programming languages an assignment statement contains the assignment operator := which assigns to the symbol on its left the value of the expression on its right. For example, the statement $x := z + 10$ means that the value $z + 10$ should be assigned to the variable x in the program. *If* statements and *while* statements alter the flow of execution through a program, making it possible to skip or repeat statements. A statement beginning with *if* is executed only if a specified condition is met. Thus an *if* statement is one means of achieving conditional execution. A statement beginning with a *while* is repeated as long as a given condition remains true. Thus a *while* statement is one means of achieving iterative execution, or a looping program construct.

By analyzing the meaning of a programming statement, it is possible to formulate an axiom, or proof rule, for that type of statement. The axioms specify what must be proved to guarantee the truth of the statement $\{P\}\ S\ \{Q\ \}$, where P and Q are assertions and S is an assignment statement, *if* statement, *while* state-

Null Rule	$\dfrac{P \rightarrow Q}{\{P\}\ \textbf{null}\ \{Q\}}$
Assignment Rule	$\{P(x/E)\}\ x{:=}E\ \{P\}$
If Rule	$\dfrac{\{P\&B\}\ S\ \{Q\},\ \ (P\&\neg B)\rightarrow Q}{\{P\}\ \textbf{if}\ B\ \textbf{then}\ S\ \{Q\}}$
While Rule	$\dfrac{\{P\&B\}\ S\ \{P\}}{\{P\}\ \textbf{while}\ B\ \textbf{do}\ S\ \{P\&\neg B\}}$
Consequence Rules	$\dfrac{\{P\}\ S\ \{Q\},\ Q\rightarrow R}{\{P\}\ S\ \{R\}}$
	$\dfrac{\{P\}\ S\ \{Q\},\ R\rightarrow P}{\{R\}\ S\ \{Q\}}$
Composition Rule	$\dfrac{\{P\}\ S1\ \{Q\},\ \{Q\}\ S2\ \{R\}}{\{P\}\ S1;S2\ \{R\}}$

PROOF RULES can be defined for most types of programming statements. Examples are the rules for assignment statements, *if* statements and *while* statements. The rules specify what must be proved to guarantee the truth of a statement of the form $\{\,P\,\}\,S\,\{\,Q\,\}$, which means that if an assertion P is true and a programming statement S is executed, an assertion Q will be true. If the rule is in a tabular form, proving the statement above the line is sufficient to prove the statement below the line. The consequence rules make it possible to make use of logical inference in the proofs; the arrow signifies implies. The composition rule allows proofs of individual statements to be combined to form proofs of sequences of statements.

ment or any other programming statement. Proof rules for some common types of programming statements are given in the illustration on this page.

Although the proof rules bristle with brackets, they are relatively easy to understand. Take, for example, the assignment rule: $\{P\,(x/E)\,\}$ $x := E\ \{P\}$. Here P is an arbitrary assertion and $P\,(x/E)$ is the result of substituting E for x in P. The rule asserts that whatever can be said of E before the assignment can be said of x afterward. For example, $\{x = 1\}\ y := x\ \{y = 1\}$ means that if x equals 1 and y is assigned the value of x, then y equals 1.

The tabular form of the other rules means that proving the state-

ment above the line is sufficient to prove the statement below the line. The consequence rules allow logical inferences to be included in the proof. The composition rule is particularly important because it allows the proofs of individual statements to be combined into proofs of sequences of statements.

The if rule and the while rule allow the proof of programs with conditional branching or while loops. In practice, however, these rules are not used. Instead the program is divided by assertions into blocks of statements that are always executed sequentially, called "straight-line code." Each segment of straight-line code and its bracketing assertions is called a path, and

the paths are proved individually. For example, the two branches that are entered from an *if* statement are proved separately. Loops are annotated with assertions that hold true no matter how many times the loop is executed; such assertions are called loop invariants. The loop invariant has the effect of cutting the loop and flattening it out into a straight line; each execution of the loop can be regarded as the execution of the statements leading from one assertion to a second assertion, although both assertions happen to be the loop invariant. Thus the assignment rule, the consequence rules and the composition rule suffice to prove most paths.

A path is proved by proving a verification condition, or theorem, generated from the assertions that bracket the path. Each theorem proposes that the truth of the assertion at the beginning of the path and the execution of the statements along the path suffice to guarantee the truth of the assertion at the end of the path.

The verification conditions for all paths constitute a more detailed formulation of the program's specification, and so the proof of the verification conditions constitutes a proof of the program's specification. In this manner the difficult problem of proving a program correct is reduced to the problem of proving a collection of theorems in mathematics and logic.

Proving a Simple Algorithm

Programs are proved by following a regime consisting of three steps. The first step is to annotate the program with assertions that describe the program state at the point at which the assertion appears. In order to ensure that the program can be divided into a finite number of paths, each loop must contain at least one assertion. The second step is to write the verification conditions for every execution path, or way of getting from one assertion to the next one. Since every loop contains at least one assertion, there will be no statement that is not on a path and no path will contain a loop. The third step is to prove for each path that if the assertion at the beginning of the path is true and the path is executed, then the assertion at the end of the path will be true.

A simple algorithm for computing the product of two integers by means of repeated addition provides an example. In this instance it is evident that the program is correct and the steps taken to prove correctness may seem unnecessarily complicated; indeed, it may seem harder to judge the correctness of the proof than to judge the correctness of the program itself. The more complex the program, however, the more apparent the power of assertions and proof rules becomes.

The multiplication program is given in the top illustration on this page. The two integers are u_0 and v_0; the variable w is the partial sum that ultimately becomes the product. Since the program will return the correct value only if v_0 is non-negative, $v_0 > 0$ can serve as the entry assertion. The obvious exit assertion is $w = u_0 * v_0$. (The asterisk signifies multiplication, a convention most programming languages employ.) The specification of the program is thus:

$$\{v_0 > 0\}$$
multiplication procedure
$$\{w = u_0 * v_0\}.$$

Since the algorithm contains a loop, at least one additional assertion must be written — a loop invariant. The annotated program is shown in the middle illustration on this page. There are three paths, or ways of getting from one assertion to another. The first path begins with an entry assertion, includes the execution of the three assignment statements that follow the assertion, enters the loop and ends with the loop invariant. The second path begins with the loop invariant, executes the *if* statement that serves as a guard on the loop, finds that $v \neq 0$, executes the two assignment statements that comprise the body of the

```
w := 0;
u := u₀;
v := v₀;
loop
    if v=0 then leave;
    w := w+u;
    v := v-1;
endloop;
```

SIMPLE PROGRAM multiplies positive integers by repeated addition. The program begins with three assignment statements. Each substitutes an input parameter for a variable in the program. The variables u and v are assigned the values of the two integers to be multiplied. The variable w, which is the partial sum that eventually becomes the partial product, is initially given the value of zero. The heart of the algorithm is the loop, a Gypsy construct that is roughly equivalent to the *while* statement in other programming languages. Each time the loop is executed w is increased by u and v is decreased by 1. The loop continues to execute as long as v is greater than 0. When v equals 0, control exits the loop and the program terminates.

```
Entry:          {v₀>0}
                w := 0;
                u := u₀;
                v := v₀;
                loop
LI:                 {w+u*v=u₀*v₀ & v₀>0}
                    if v=0 then leave;
                    w := w+u;
                    v := v-1;
                endloop;
Exit:           {w = u₀*v₀}
```

FIRST STEP in proving the multiplication program is to annotate it with assertions. The proof of any program requires at least two assertions: an entry assertion and an exit assertion. Other assertions are added as necessary to break the program into paths — blocks of statements in which the statements are always executed sequentially and each is executed exactly once. Here the assertion for the loop, called a loop invariant, allows the loop to be treated as one such path.

```
Path 1:         {v₀>0}
                    w := 0; u := u₀; v := v₀;
                {w+u*v=u₀*v₀}


Path 2:         {w+u*v=u₀*v₀ & v≠0}
                    w := w+u; v := v-1;
                {w+u*v=u₀*v₀}


Path 3:         {w+u*v=u₀*v₀ & v=0}
                    null;
                {w=u₀*v₀}
```

THREE PATHS through the multiplication procedure are shown here. A path is proved by proving that the assertion at the beginning of the path and the execution of the statements on the path suffice to guarantee the truth of the assertion at the end of the path. Proving all three paths suffices to prove the program.

loop and ends with the loop invariant. The third path also begins with the loop invariant, executes the *if* statement, finds that $v = 0$ and exits the loop immediately, reaching the exit assertion. The paths are shown in the bottom illustration on the previous page.

Next, a verification condition is written for each path, and the proof rules are invoked to prove the verification conditions. The proof of the second path serves as an example. Proving the first path guarantees that the loop invariant will be true the first time control enters the loop. Thus we know (from the first condition in the loop invariant) that before the loop executes the sum of two quantities is equal to the product of the two integers we are multiplying. The two quantities are the partial sum w and the partial product $u * v$. We want to show that the same relation holds after the loop executes. Each time the loop executes, v is decreased by 1 and w is increased by u. Therefore the loop should be executed only if the initial partial sum plus one additional u can be added to the partial product obtained when 1 is subtracted from v without disastrous results (namely a negative partial product). The other condition in the loop invariant ($v > 0$) guarantees that the loop will be executed only if it is safe to do so. Therefore we know that after the loop executes the sum of the partial sum and the partial product will be equal to the product of the integers we are multiplying.

This informal thread of reasoning is duplicated by the following formal reasoning. We know from the assignment rule that an arbitrary assertion that holds for $w + u$ and $v - 1$ must hold for the program variables w and v when they are substituted for $w + u$ and $v - 1$. Or in our formal notation:

$$\{P(w/w + u, v/v - 1)\}$$
$$w := w + u; v := v - 1$$
$$\{P\}$$

By choosing P appropriately, we see that:

$$\{(w + u) + u * (v - 1) = u_o * v_o\}$$
$$w := w + u; v := v - 1$$
$$\{w + u * v = u_o * v_o\}$$

As a matter of simple algebra the assertions at the beginning of the loop imply that P is true. Or in our notation:

$$\{ w + u * v = u_o * v_o \ \& \ v \neq 0\} \rightarrow$$
$$\{(w + u) + u * (v - 1) = u_o * v_o\}$$

where the arrow means that the statement on the left implies the statement on the right. We now have an assertion (R) that implies the first assertion in a statement of the form $\{ P \} S \{ Q \}$. According to the second of the two consequence rules, if R is true and S is executed, then Q will be true. Since R is the assertion at the beginning of the path and Q is the assertion at the end of the path, this suffices to prove the path.

Proving Specifications

Design specifications are proved in the same manner as programs. Because the specifications are large, proving them by hand would be tedious, costly and error-prone. The Gypsy verification system, which performs some of the steps in a proof automatically, greatly facilitates the process.

The programmer still must write the code and supply the assertions. By design, Gypsy includes only programming constructs for which proof rules can be formulated. Applying built-in knowledge of the proof rules, the system automatically generates a verification condition for each path between assertions. The verification conditions are given to an algebraic simplifier, which automatically simplifies many of them to true. Any conditions that cannot be handled in this way can be proved with the aid of another component of the system, an interactive theorem-proving program. The system makes it easier to determine the order in which program fragments and the paths through them should be proved by keeping track of the proof status and proof dependencies

of the fragments and of their verification conditions.

The proof of the INSTANTIATE_OBJECT procedure illustrates the process. The first step is to write a specification of the specification. We would like to prove that if INSTANTIATE_OBJECT is invoked when the system is in a secure state, then the resulting state will be secure. In the formal notation we have adopted the specification of INSTANTIATE_OBJECT is:

$$\{secure \ (M\_in)\}$$
$$INSTANTIATE\_OBJECT$$
$$\{secure \ (M\_out)\}$$

where M_in is the initial state of the access matrix and M_out is its state after the procedure terminates.

Because the body of INSTANTIATE_OBJECT is missing, it is not proved directly. Instead the lemma CORRECT_UPDATE_PRESERVES_SECURITY is proved. The proof of this lemma in turn implies that INSTANTIATE_OBJECT is correct. The proof is too long to give in its entirety; excerpts are given here to convey the flavor of machine-assisted proofs. A command to the Gypsy system causes it to analyze a block of code and to generate a verification condition for the code. The verification condition the system generated for CORRECT_UPDATE_PRESERVES_SECURITY is shown in the top illustration on page 26. Because CORRECT_UPDATE_PRESERVES_SECURITY is already in the form of a theorem, no analysis was required to generate the verification condition; in most cases, the verification condition is less directly related to the code.

Because the algebraic simplifier could not handle the proof of the verification condition, it had to be done with the interactive theorem prover. The proof required expanding some of the terms in the condition and doing a simple case analysis. The bottom illustration on page 26 shows the verification condition after the definitions of SECURE and CORRECT_M_ UPDATE had been expanded. The final proof logs for this verification condition are more than 15 pages long.

Managing Complexity

Even with automated assistance, the proof of a large system such as the Secure Ada Target is a big undertaking. Ideally a formal model of a computer system would include every detail of the system. The available automated tools, however, tend to bog down in details if the model takes on too much of the complexity of the system. As a result, the complexity of a formal model is a compromise between realistic complexity and the complexity the automated proof tools can handle.

More powerful verification systems and the computers to run them are gradually allowing the models to become more detailed. A second difficulty stands in the way of realistic modeling, however, and it is one that cannot be overcome by increasing the speed of the available tools or decreasing the amount of human assistance they require. The proofs of complex systems tend to be extremely long and tediously detailed. Indeed, a long computer-generated proof may not be read even by the person supervising the proof. Consequently claims of correctness are often underlain by confidence in the verification system rather than by confidence in the proof the verification system has generated. Yet, in the end, a proof that cannot be understood proves nothing.

For this reason we carefully limited our use of automated tools during the proof of the Secure Ada Target. Our proof is not the creation of the tools, although the tools assisted in the process. The proof is built on a scaffolding of human-generated arguments, such as that we have given for the security of the Abstract Model specification. The proof tools, by succeeding or failing to prove the arguments we had provided, helped us to clarify our reasoning. The role they played, however, was a supporting rather than a leading one. As the companion paper remarks, it is more accurate to say that the Secure Ada Target proof is machine-checked than to say that it is machine-generated.

Automated proof tools will be limited to this supporting role until they can produce a chain of reasoning that is humanly intelligible. This problem is being attacked by work on "journal-level" theorem-proving programs. The goal is to devise programs that will suppress many of the low-level details of the proof and allow the human member of the team to work at the level of the proofs that appear in mathematical journals.

Given the current state of program verification, what can be done to reduce the complexity of the proof of a large system? One answer is to model only a part of the system. Much of the hardware and software in a computer system is simply not

```
      H1:  CORRECT_M_UPDATE (M_IN, M_OUT, O)
      H2:  SECURE (M_IN)
  ->
      C1:  SECURE (M_OUT)
```

VERIFICATION CONDITION the Gypsy system generated for the lemma in the illustration on page 22 is given here. It consists of two hypotheses and a conclusion. The Gypsy system assents to the truth of this theorem if the automatic theorem prover built into the system can be led by a series of user commands and automatically invoked strategies to reduce the theorem to true. In this case the lemma and its verification condition are almost identical; generally the verification condition is more distantly related to the code to be proved.

```
   H1      DOMINATES (OBJECT_LEVEL (O), SUBJECT_LEVEL (S$#1))
           iff M_OUT[S$#1][O].WRITE .
   H2      DOMINATES (SUBJECT_LEVEL (S$#1), OBJECT_LEVEL (O))
           iff M_OUT[S$#1][O].READ
   H3:  O ne O2$#1 -> M_IN[S$#1][O2$#1] = M_OUT[S$#1][O2$#1]
   H4:  SATISFIES_SIMPLE_SECURITY (M_IN)
   H5:  SATISFIES_STAR_PROPERTY (M_IN)
 ->
   C1:  SATISFIES_SIMPLE_SECURITY (M_OUT)
   C2:  SATISFIES_STAR_PROPERTY (M_OUT)
```

EXPANSION OF THE THEOREM given in the top illustration is shown here. Expanding the reference to CORRECT_ M_UPDATE in the first hypothesis of the original theorem yields the first three hypotheses of this theorem. Expanding the definition of SECURE in both the second hypothesis and the conclusion of the original theorem yields references to SATISFIES_SIMPLE_SECURITY and SATISFIES_ STAR_PROPERTY. The expansion is only the first step in the proof of the theorem; the final proof logs for this theorem are more than 15 pages long.

relevant to the proof of security. If the system is appropriately structured, the amount of code that must be proved can be reduced. The Secure Ada Target, like most modern secure systems, is designed around a reference monitor, a subsystem that mediates every attempt of a subject to access an object. The isolation of the functions relevant to security to this subsystem greatly simplifies the proof.

The proof process is also simplified if the models of the system and the system design are constructed of modules, each of which has a clear function or set of functions and each of which interacts with other modules in limited and well-defined ways. One of the primary benefits is that the effects of a change are isolated to a module. As a result, the proof of the system can proceed incrementally, without the threat that later changes will completely invalidate the work that has already been done. Gypsy enforces this type of programming by various means; for instance, it disallows global variables, ones that can be altered by more than one block of a program.

Finally, the choice of appropriate levels of abstraction during modeling is crucial to managing complexity. The proof of the Secure Ada Target actually consists of four separate, increasingly detailed proofs. The proof of the highest level (the one we have discussed) is relatively easy to follow. The proof logs of the lowest level, however, will probably be several hundred pages long and would be unintelligible if it weren't for the higher levels. To allow a reviewer to carry the clarity gained in examining the higher levels down to the lower levels, we have mapped the structures and properties at each level to those at the next higher level. Although the mapping is informal, it has been carefully done and should increase confidence that the low-level model is actually the same system whose security is so evident at a higher level of abstraction.

By structuring the system around a reference monitor, constructing modular models, devoting some thought to the levels of abstraction at which the models are written and carefully documenting mappings between layers, it is possible to provide a rigorous and yet comprehensible proof even of a system as large and complex as the Secure Ada Target. The proof of the Secure Ada Target will be scrutinized during the evaluation process at the Department of Defense, but it should also be accessible to any interested person with some background in proof techniques and a few hours to spare. As the companion paper remarks, one of the goals of the team was that the proof should be one that could be evaluated by the social process.

Acknowledgements
This effort has been supported by U.S. Government Contracts MDA 904-82-C-0444 and MDA 904-84-C-6011. Our approach to verification was strongly influenced by that of workers at the Institute for Computing Science and Computing Applications of the University of Texas, particularly Don Good, Mike Smith, Bob Boyer and J Moore.

Section 2.3: Standards

Introduction

This section presents standards and guidelines applicable to computer and network security. These are "official" standards in the sense that they are issued by organizations whose business it is to produce standards; they should not be confused with de facto market domination and leadership, sometimes erroneously called standards. They are often formal precise documents, which may make them difficult to read.

There are very few national or international standards and guidelines available for use in defining computer and network security. There are four organizations that produce standards in the area of computer and networks standards. Two are U.S. government agencies, and two are independent standards organizations. The government agencies are

- The National Bureau of Standards (NBS), in the Department of Commerce, publishes Federal Information Processing Standards (FIPS) Publications (PUBS) and various other technical publications.

- The National Computer Security Center (NCSC), in the Department of Defense, publishes technical guidance, which may become Defense standards. Under National Security Decision Directive (NSDD) 145, their responsibility has been broadened to include non-defense security. The interface with NBS is uncertain at the time of publication.

The standards organizations are

- The American National Standards Institute (ANSI), a voluntary organization for developing industrial standards. Participation is open to interested and qualified parties, including government agencies.

- The International Organization for Standardization (ISO), the international umbrella organization of national standards organizations.

The standards and guidelines for computer and network security produced by these organization are naturally interrelated with each other. One example of a relationship is the set of standards applying to electronic funds transfer (EFT). A hypothetical case is developed for large bank B to illustrate some possible relationships. Bank B has five computer centers with IBM MVS environments and remote terminals interacting with each MVS environment. EFT transactions be-

tween each computer center are transmitted through a packet switching network. Some of the possible standards or recommendations involved are (1) *Trusted Computer System Evaluation Criteria—NCSC:* Bank B uses CA's TOP SECRET access control software to ensure proper access of data at each computer center by remote terminimals. TOP SECRET is evaluated by the NCSC at a C2 level of protection; (2) *Financial Institution Message Authentication (Wholesale)—ANSI:* Bank B uses ANSI specified message authentication for EFT transfers from one computer center to another; (3) *Data Encryption Standard—NBS:* The ANSI message authentication standard uses the *Data Encryption Standard* (DES) produced by NBS. (4) *Open Systems Interconnection—OSI:* Bank B uses a commercial computer network to connect each of its 5 centers. The computer network conforms to various ISO network standards.

We shall introduce several important standards and guidelines in the following sections to give a basic foundation in preferred security practice. These sections discuss the *U.S. Department of Defenses's Trusted Computer System Evaluation Criteria and Their Application in Specific Environments,* network evaluation criteria, and password management guideline. We also present the NBS's *Guidance on Computer Security Certification and Accreditation,* and preliminary guidance on the security of personal computer systems. A related area is also introduced concerning a military standard for software quality evaluation, which is followed by a subsection on reprints.

The sections discuss standards and guidelines that are in various stages of acceptance, reflecting the current status of standards development for computer and network security. We are careful to point out in each section whether the discussion pertains to a standard, draft standard, guidance, or preliminary guidance at the time of publication. The interested reader is advised to determine the current status. Each security evaluation should be performed with respect to the critical criteria for organizational objectives. The available security guidance should be considered within the managerial constraints of each organization. For example, a computer standard may be applicable to the banking industry but of limited value to corporate management in the control of a steel mill's production system. The similarities and difference of military and business computer security requirements and approaches are discussed in the paper by

Chalmers reprinted in Section 2.1. We caution that the following sections are only an introduction to the substantial body of knowledge available from standards organizations such as NCSC and NBS.

Computer and network security standards can be very complex because of the need to evaluate total systems or information security. An introduction to the basics for the U.S. Department of Defense *Trusted Computer System Evaluation Criteria* follows to give you a framework or basis to build upon. This discussion is a continuation of the concepts introduced in the section on the Bell-LaPadula Model.

Trusted Computer System Evaluation Criteria

The *Trusted Computer System Evaluation Criteria (TCSEC)*, published in 1983 [CSCS83] (and revised in 1985 [DODS85b]), are the most authoritative criteria for evaluating the security features in a hardware and software system. This section is adapted from discussions in the standard. Because of the fundamental importance of understanding the concepts presented in this standard, an excerpt is also included in the reprints. Where possible, the original wording in the standard is preserved as in the previous section on the Bell-LaPadula model. However, we are highlighting important aspects of the standard, and this discussion does not replace the standard for use in evaluating computer security of hardware and software systems.

The following aspects of the standard are highlighted: six fundamental computer security requirements, evaluation criteria classes, and security features necessary for a C2 evaluation.

Six Fundamental Computer Security Requirements

The security features should be designed to meet, with varying degrees of control, six fundamental computer security requirements. These requirements are derived from the basic statement of the objective for secure systems. The objective is to control access to information so that only properly authorized individuals, or processes operating on their behalf, will have access to read, write, create, or delete information. Four of the requirements address what needs to be provided to control access to information and to address how to obtain credible assurances that control access is being accomplished in a trusted computer system. The other two pertain to assurance that the hardware/software mechanisms can be independently evaluated and are continuously protected against tampering and unauthorized changes.

The objective of controlling access to information has a broader meaning in the computer security business than may be apparent. The meaning is that many of the hardware/software mechanisms used to control access to information can also be of substantial value in maintaining data and applications integrity. Integrity is essential to the orderly conduct

of business. In particular, as major organizations become more dependent upon computer systems, then computer security becomes more critical. For example, the maintenance of continuous integrity is essential to the fulfillment of major objectives such as meeting customer requirements in a timely and accurate manner. In addition, integrity should be interpreted as depending upon the control of accidental errors as well as deliberate attacks. Most of the economic loss associated with computer systems is believed to originate from accidental errors, such as those pertaining to input processing.

When using the standard presented in the TCSEC, the six fundamental computer security requirements should be reviewed first because they are basic to all of the TCSEC evaluation criteria classes. The six requirements are presented in three groups: policy, accountability, and assurance. A brief overview of each requirement follows within the three groups:

Group 1. Policy: Requirement 1—SECURITY POLICY—There must be explicit and well defined security policy enforced by the system. Requirement 2—MARKING—Access control labels must be associated with objects (passive entities that contain or receive information). Access to an object potentially implies access to the information it contains. Examples are records, blocks, pages, segments, files, directories.

Group 2. Accountability: Requirement 3—IDENTIFICATION—Individual subjects must be identified. A subject is an active entity, generally in the form of a person, process, or device that causes information to flow among objects or changes the system state. Each access to information must be mediated on the basis of whom is accessing the information and what classes of information they are authorized to deal with. Requirement 4—ACCOUNTABILITY—Audit information must be selectively kept and protected so that actions affecting security can be traced to the responsible party.

Group 3. Assurance: Requirement 5—ASSURANCE—The computer system must contain hardware/software mechanisms that can be independently evaluated to provide sufficient assurance that the system enforces requirements 1 through 4. Requirement 6—CONTINUOUS PROTECTION—The trusted mechanisms that enforce these basic requirements must be continuously protected against tampering and/or unauthorized changes. Trusted mechanisms employ sufficient hardware and software integrity measures to allow their use for processing simultaneously a range of sensitive or classified information.

Evaluation Criteria Classes

The six fundamental computer security requirements apply to all of the evaluation criteria classes. There are four hierarchical divisions of criteria (i.e., D, C, B, and A). Hierarchical means that provisions of division D are included in division C, the provisions of C in B, and B in A. The seven criteria classes are hierarchical subdivisions of the criteria (i.e., D, C1, C2, B1, B2, B3, and A1).

Important computer security concepts inherent in this structure, include (1) *testing:* Testing is necessary to gain assurance that the security-relevant portions of a computer system have a correct and complete security design and (2) *trusted computing base* (TCB): The hardware/software security-relevant portions of the computer system are referred to as the TCB. A summary of the evaluation criteria classes, derived from Appendix C [CSCS83], illustrates the types of controls necesssary to satisfy the security requirements of each class. In general, the higher classes in division B and A focus on formal assurance of security attributes from their design and implementation structure. The following rules of thumb can be used to assist you in understanding the commercial value and application of these criteria classes:

- *C2 level:* Most access control software that has been evaluated by NCSC is or will be at the C2 level for the near term.
- *B1 level:* The practical limit of NCSC evaluation for access control software on pre-existing mainframe architectures is B1.
- *B2 level:* New security-oriented hardware/software designs or TCB designs are generally required before a B2 or higher evaluation can be given by the NCSC.

Each of the criteria classes is now briefly highlighted by abstracting each class description:

- *Class D: Minimal protection:* This class is used only for those systems that have been evaluated but that fail to meet the requirements for a higher evaluation class.
- *Class C1: Discretionary security protection:* The TCB of a class C1 system nominally satisfies the discretionary security requirements by providing separation of users and data. The class C1 environment is one of cooperating users processing data at the same level(s) of sensitivity.
- *Class C2: Controlled access protection:* Systems in this class enforce a more finely grained discretionary access control than C1 systems. Users are individually accountable for their actions through login procedures, auditing of security-relevant events, and resource isolation.
- *Class B1: Labeled security protection:* In addition to the C2 features, an informal statement of the security policy model, data labeling, and mandatory access control over named subjects and objects must be present. Exported information must be accurately labeled. Flaws identified by testing must be removed.

- *Class B2: Structured protection:* The TCB is based on a formal security policy model and is structured into protection-critical and non-protection-critical elements. Discretionary and mandatory access control applies to all subjects and objects. Covert channels are addressed. Authentication, testing, review, and configuration management are strengthened. A B2 system is considered relatively resistant to penetration.

  The division between B1 and B2 is substantial. The configuration management requirement, among others, makes it necessary for a system to be designed from the start with security in mind. If not impossible, it would be prohibitively expensive for a pre-existing system to be upgraded beyond B1.

- *Class B3: Security domains:* The TCB must satisfy the reference monitor requirements that it mediate all accesses of subjects to objects, be tamperproof, and be small enough to be subjected to analysis and tests. A security administrator is supported; audit mechanisms are expanded; system recovery procedures are required. A B3 system is considered highly resistant to penetration.

- *Class A1: Verified design:* No additional architectural features or policy requirements. Formal design specification and verification are required.

  Note that formal verification of the TCB is the salient characteristic of A1. Future developments beyond A1 may require an extension of formal verification.

  The separation between B3 and A1 is another major discontinuity in the series of evaluated systems. The emphasis on formal proofs for A1 certification implies considerable expense. At the time of writing, it appears that one business decision is to develop a system that could meet A1 requirements, but to seek only B3 certification because of the time and expense of formal proofs.

  An example of the security features necessary for a C2 evaluation follows. The purpose of this example is to introduce the types of features found in certain access control software for the IBM /MVS environment, such as TOP SECRET.

Security Features Necessary for a C2 Evaluation

Seven security features are necessary for a C2 evaluation. In addition, four documentation requirements must be met. These features and requirements are briefly introduced and generally adapted from Appendix D in the TCSEC. The overall category for each security feature is in parentheses.

Feature 1. Discretionary access control (security policy): The enforcement mechanism (e.g., self/group/public controls, access control lists) shall allow users to specify and control sharing of those objects by named individuals, or defined groups of individuals, or by both.

Feature 2. Object reuse (security policy): The initial assignment, allocation, or reallocation by the TCB of a storage object (an object that supports both read and write accesses) to a subject should assure that the object contains no data that should not be read by the subject. Clearing memory after each subject's use effectively meets this requirement.

Feature 3. Identification and authentication (accountability): The TCB shall be able to enforce individual accountability. This is accomplished by uniquely identifying each individual ADP system user. The TCB shall also be able to associate this identity with all auditable actions taken by that individual.

Feature 4. Audit (accountability): An audit trail of accesses to the objects protected by the TCB. This protection applies to the creation, maintenance, modification, or unauthorized access or destruction.

Feature 5. System architecture (assurance): The TCB shall logically isolate the protected resources thereby providing access control and associated auditing capabilities.

Feature 6. System integrity (assurance): The correct operation of the on-site hardware and firmware elements of the TCB must be periodically validated by using the applicable hardware and/or software features.

Feature 7. Security testing (assurance): Obvious flaws that would allow violation of resource isolation, or that would permit unauthorized access to the audit or authentication data should be tested for as well as other flaws. Authentication is establishing the validity of a claimed identity, as in user identification and authentication at a remote terminal.

In addition, the four documentation requirements for a C2 level are (1) *Security Features User's Guide (documentation):* A single summary, chapter, or manual in user documentation shall describe the protection mechanisms provided by the TCB, guidelines on their use, and how they interact with one another. (2) *Trusted Facility Manual (Documentation):* Procedures shall be specified for examining and maintaining the audit files as well as the detailed audit record structure for each type of audit event. (3) *Test documentation (documentation):* The evaluators shall receive from the system developer a document that describes the test plan and results of the functional testing of the security mechanisms. (4) *Design documentation (documentation):* Documentation shall be available providing a description of the manufacturer's philosophy of protection and explaining how this philosophy is incorporated in the TCB. The interface between the TCB modules shall be described, if applicable.

The next subsection presents a suggested set of guidance for using the TCSEC criteria in specific environments. Before we start the section, it is important to realize that there are several uses for the U.S. Department of Defense *Computer System Evaluation Criteria.* First, hardware/software companies can use the criteria as security performance specifications for specific products (e.g., RACF, TOP SECRET, and ACF2). Second, organizational management can use the criteria as a basis for measuring the degree of security controls in an existing computer system or for a system under development. The third way of using the criteria is to suggest the minimum acceptable level of computer security for a particular system operating in a specific personnel environment, as in the next subsection.

Guidance for Applying the Computer System Evaluation Criteria

This section presents the NCSC suggestions for identifying the minimum evaluated class of computer system required for a given risk. As mentioned in Section 2.1 in our discussion of the Landwehr and Lubbes paper, this is not a closed issue. The Chalmers paper in the same section further points out the different security policies in Defense and commercial organizations. Each class is defined in the TCSEC (i.e., C1, C2, and so on). The risk is computed by using an algorithm that results in a risk index. The values of the risk index (e.g., 0, 1, and 2) are associated with minimum criteria classes for a particular system.

The limitations of this method, as presented in *Computer Security Requirements—Guidance for Applying the Department of Defense Trusted Computer System Evaluation Criteria in Specific Environments* [CSCS85] (known as the *Yellow Book*), include

- *Minimum computer security requirements:* This method applies primarily to establishing minimum computer security requirements for Defense processing and/or storage and retrieval of sensitive or classified information.

- *Risk index computation:* The risk index computation applies to a model or representation of the risk, and the index values must be interpreted for each actual environment.

  For example, where there are many categories or groupings of classified, or unclassified but sensitive information to which access is restricted, a higher risk index may be justified than the results obtained from the algorithm.

- *One anomalous value:* There is an inconsistency in the risk index computation that results in one anomalous value that is corrected in the risk index computation.

  This occurs because there are two personal clearances, top secret (TS) with a background investigation (BI) and top secret with a special background investigation (SBI), but only one top secret data classification. In other words, the risk index model had to be adjusted for this imbalance (i.e., two categories for one type of data).

Two aspects of the *Yellow Book* are introduced to demonstrate the methodology. The risk index computation is presented, and this is followed by the computer security requirements, measured in terms of TCSEC criteria classes. Each section is adapted from the *Yellow Book* to introduce the approach. The TCSEC focuses on technical controls; other important security controls to be considered are managerial, physical, administrative, and communications controls.

Risk Index Computation

For simplicity of discussion, we present the risk index computation methodology for sensitive data without categories or groupings, but with labeling. Further, we only present the basic case of a computation where

$$\text{Risk index} = \text{Rmax} - \text{Rmin}$$

Note that Rmax is based on the highest classification of data stored in the system and Rmin is based on the lowest clearance of users who access the system. Rmax is determined for this type of computation from the following rating scale for maximum data sensitivity:

Table 1: Rating Scale for Maximum Data Adapted from Table 2 [CSCG85]

Sensitivity

Maximum Sensitivity Ratings Without Categories	Rating (Rmax)
Unclassified (U)	0
Not classified but sensitive	1
Confidential (C)	2
Secret (S)	3
Top Secret (TS)	5

Table 1 gives you the Rmax value. A Rmin value is derived from the following rating scale:

Table 2: Rating Scale for Minimum Clearance Adapted from Table 1 [CSCG85]

Minimum User Clearance	Rating (Rmin)
Uncleared (U)	0
Not cleared but authorized access to sensitive unclassified information (N)	1
Confidential (C)	2
Secret (S)	3
Top Secret (TS)/Current Background Investigation (BI)	4
Top Secret (TS)/Current Special Background Investigation (SBI)	5

The Rmin value is taken from Table 2 and entered in the Risk Index computation. For example, if you have secret data (Rmax = 3) processed by a computer system that allows users with a confidential clearance (Rmin = 2) to access the system, then the risk index is

$$\begin{aligned} \text{Risk index} &= \text{Rmax} - \text{Rmin} \\ &= 3 - 2 \\ &= 1 \end{aligned}$$

The risk index is used to identify the minimum evaluation class appropriate as discussed next.

Computer Security Requirements

By using the risk index method, the *Yellow Book* enables you to select an appropriate minimum evaluation class from the TCSEC. This method requires case by case interpretation; however, it is a good start to get your computer security requirements defined in the right ball park. Depending on organization policy, the *Yellow Book* methodology can be applied directly to a specific security environment. Alternately, an organization can develop its own environment policy as suggested by Landwehr and Lubbes, Chalmers, and Lipner.

Let us look at how this definition of minimum evaluation class works for TCSEC classes. The security operating mode indicates how much trust may be placed in the technical security by specifying who may use such a system. The modes are briefly identified below; more complete definitions may be found in the glossary:

- *Dedicated:* system exclusively used for one classification.
- *System high:* entire system operated at, and all users cleared to highest sensitivity level of information stored.
- *Limited access:* all users not fully cleared or authorized to all data.
- *Controlled:* limited multilevel.
- *Compartmented:* at least one compartment or category of information requiring special access authorization, to which not all users have been cleared; all users cleared to highest level.
- *Multilevel:* two or more classification levels; some users not cleared for all levels.

Concluding our example, a risk index of 1 would generally equate to a B1 level (Table 3). The security operating mode in this example is limited access, controlled, compartmented, and multilevel. The compartmented mode of operation allows the computer system to isolate and process two or more types of information logically at the same sensitivity level that require special access authorization (compartmented information). A controlled security mode of operation is in the general class of multilevel security operations where a limited trust is placed on the TCB. Therefore, there are restrictions on the classification and clearance levels that can be processed. Multilevel applies to the mode of operation that supports the simultaneous processing of two or more classification levels in one computer system, where some users are not cleared for all levels.

Table 3: Computer Security Requirements Adapted from Table 3 [CSCS85]

Risk Index	Security Operating Mode	Minimum Criteria Class for Open Environments
0	Dedicated	No prescribed minimum
0	System high	C2
1	Limited Access, Controlled, Compartmented, Multilevel	B1
2	Limited Access, Controlled, Compartmented, Multi- level	B2
3	Controlled, Multilevel	B3
4	Multilevel	A1
5	Multilevel	*

The B1 level in this example applies to an open security environment. In general, an open environment exists when there is inadequate configuration control for the system control software and applications or inadequate control over the application developers. If control were maintained and over the configuration and the developers a closed security environment would exist. In certain cases, the minimum criteria class for closed environments may be less than for open environments (e.g., for risk indexes of 3, 4, and 5).

The next section discusses a potential extension and modification of the *Orange Book* criteria, which is based on the Bell-LaPadula model. An introduction is provided to NCSC's draft Department of Defense *Trusted Network Evaluation Criteria (TNEC)* [CSCD85].

---

*There is no current state-of-the-art protection for this particular environment, e.g., may be an A2 requirement where managerial, physical, administrative, and communications controls are required to supplement the technical controls to meet these security requirements in excess of A1.

Reprints

The paper by Sheila Brand, "A Status Report on the Development of Network Criteria," presents an overview of the initial progress made by NCSC in developing trusted network evaluation criteria. A draft *Trusted Network Evaluation Criteria (TNEC)* was published in 1985 [CSCD85], following an invitational workshop on network security. The proceedings of that workshop [CSCW85] are a wealth of some of the best thinking about network security; several papers are reprinted or referenced in this tutorial. Conceptually, the TNEC are an extension and modification of the TCSEC. However, it is not a simple extension and modification of the criteria nor a simple extension and modification of the Bell-LaPadula model.

NCSC is no longer working on the *Draft Trusted Network Evaluation Criteria* document, but instead is developing interpretations of the U.S. Department of Defense *Computer System Evaluation Criteria (TSEC)* to apply to networks. Our discussion of the *Draft Trusted Network Evaluation Criteria* is limited to generic network security issues of historical interest. The telephone number to call for the status/publication date of the replacement draft, which is expected to be available late in 1986/early 1987, is 301-859-4371.

There are several reasons why this is not a simple extension and modification. Three are offered. First, the Bell-LaPadula model does not adequately address each of the key network considerations for security policy: data compromise (violation of secrecy), communications integrity (inaccurate information), and denial of service (for a continuing level of service). Second, networks involve many components (e.g., modems, telecommunications controllers, message switches, technical control devices, hosts, gateways). Third, there are many combinations of communications channels in networks that must be protected.

We shall adapt aspects of Brand's paper in the following discussion and supplement as indicated with selected topics from the TNEC. The following aspects of the draft criteria are highlighted: six draft fundamental network security requirements [CSCD85], draft evaluation criteria divisions [BRAN85], and draft relationship with *Trusted Computer System Evaluation Criteria* [CSCD85].

Six Draft Fundamental Network Security Requirements

As in computer security, there are six fundamental network security requirements in the draft TNEC. They are briefly highlighted below. Our discussion is subject to change, since this is the first draft.

Group 1. Policy: Requirement 1—SECURITY POLICY— the trusted network base (TNB) enforces an explicit and well-defined security policy. The TNB is the totality of the protection mechanisms within a network (hardware, firmware, and software) that are responsible for enforcing a security policy on the network. Conceptually, the TNB is an extension of the TCB over the network. There is a single TNB that may be distributed in host computers, cryptographic devices, front ends, packet switches, etc. The three aspects of security policy are (1) *data compromise* (There must be a set of rules used by the network to determine whether a given network subject can be permitted to gain access to specific network objects. Network subjects are active entities that cause information to flow through the network or change the network state. Network objects are passive entities that contain or receive information. These terms are extensions of the TCSEC subjects and objects for computer systems); (2) *erroneous communications* (A set of mechanisms is required for the network to ensure that information is accurately transmitted from source to destination (regardless of the number of intermittent connecting points)); and (3) *denial of service* (The network uses a set of mechanisms to ensure some continuing level of service). *Requirement 2—MARKING*—Access control labels must be associated with objects and network objects.

Group 2. Accountability: Requirement 3—IDENTIFICATION—Subjects and network subjects must be identified. All accesses to information are mediated based on the subject's identity and the classes of information that subject is authorized to access. This identity must be authenticated. *Requirement 4—ACCOUNTABILITY*—Actions affecting security can be traced to the responsible network subject, because applicable audit information is securely maintained.

Group 3. Assurance: Requirement 5—ASSURANCE—Hardware/software mechanisms can be independently evaluated to provide sufficient assurance that the network enforces the above requirements (1 through 4). *Requirement 6—CONTINUOUS PROTECTION*—The trusted mechanisms must be continuously protected against tampering and/or unauthorized changes to ensure compliance with the basic security requirements.

Since the TNEC are in a draft status at the time of writing, only preliminary information is available concerning the criteria divisions. There is currently no breakout of criteria to the subdivision or class level.

Draft Evaluation Criteria Divisions

Each of the draft network evaluation criteria hierarchical divisions uses the same basic designation as for the equivalent computer system evaluation criteria. An N for network is used to differentiate the network criteria (i.e., ND, NC, NB, and NA). Highlights are developed for the *Draft Trusted Network Criteria* in a manner similar to that used for the

Trusted Computer System Evaluation Criteria. The examples used are for global security features and assurance requirements to be met by the TNB. The draft criteria also have a minimum set of security and assurance requirements that each component must meet in order to ensure that the global TNB requirements can be achieved; however, we only focus on the global requirements in this discussion.

Each of the draft criteria divisions is briefly highlighted, generally adapting the first few sentences of each division description in Part I of the *Brown Book*:

- *Division ND: Minimal protection:* This division provides minimal security. No security features are available to protect against compromise, erroneous communications, and denial of service. Those networks that have been evaluated but fail to meet the requirements for a higher evaluation division are placed in this division.

- *Division NC: Controlled access protection:* Minimal data compromise, erroneous communications, and denial of service protection are provided in this division. Security decisions are based on the classification of objects. Administrative procedures are used for security decisions based on the classification of information.

- *Division NB: Mandatory protection:* The TNB is based on a clearly defined and documented formal security policy model that requires mandatory access control enforcement over all network subjects and network objects. Covert channels are also addressed. A covert channel is a communications channel that allows a process to transfer information in a manner that violates the network's security policy. The TNB must be carefully structured into protection—critical and non-protection—critical elements.

- *Division NA: Verified design:* The reference monitor requirements for a network must be met. These requirements are: mediate all accesses of subjects to objects, be tamperproof, and the distributed portions of the TNB shall be small enough for the required analysis and tests. The distributed TNB does not include code not essential to security policy enforcement. TNB complexity should be minimized by using systems engineering techniques during TNB design and implementation. Networks in this division will be unique because of the high degree of design assurance that the TNB is correctly implemented. Formal design specification and verification techniques will be used to gain the assurance.

As you can see, the ND, NC, NB, and NA criteria are parallel in approach to D, C, B, and A. However, the distributed nature of the TNB and the additional security policy dimensions of data compromise, erroneous communications, and denial of service add considerable complexity to the

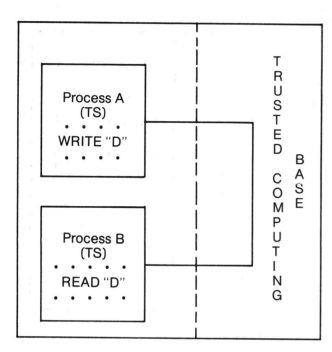

Figure 1: Process to Process Transfer within a Trusted Host

development of a standard for *Trusted Network Evaluation Criteria (TNEC)*.

A third section follows, which relates this discussion of the draft TNEC with the prior TCSEC discussion.

The draft, *Draft Relationship with Trusted Computer System Evaluation Criteria TNEC,* contains a detailed presentation of its relationship with TCSEC. Our purpose is to introduce the relationship. We will focus on highlights from the first three figures in the TNEC. The other figures are 4a, 4b, 5, 6, 7a, 7b, 8a, and 8b. These figures illustrate the role of each TNEC criteria in the overall context of trusted computer systems linked by trusted computer networks. We shall adapt the figure discussions for each of the figures we are focusing on, 1, 2, and 3.

Figure 1. Process to Process Transfer within a Trusted Host: a trusted computer system is shown in Figure 1. Information is transmitted between processes A and B operating at the same security level, which is top secret in this example. Process A attempts to transfer information to Process B and executes a Write D command to transfer the data. In the meantime, Process B executes a Read D command to receive it. The interprocess communications mechanisms will complete the transfer as long as the TCB security policy on security level is complied with. For review, security policy consists of the following two requirements for the TCB, from the *Orange Book:* (1) *Security Policy:* There must be an explicit and well-defined security policy enforced by the sys-

tem. (2) *Marking:* Access control labels must be asociated with objects. These labels can identify security level.

Figure 2: Process to Process Transfer between Two Trusted Hosts: two trusted hosts linked by a single wire or circuit are shown in Figure 2. The TCBs in the figure are distributed across tightly coupled Hosts 1 and 2. Process A on Host 1 attempts to transfer information to Process B on Host 2 by using the same Read-Write synchronization as before. The address of the destination process and the data to be transferred are given by Process A in the Write command. The network driver portion of Host 1's operating system generates a "message unit" of data for transfer to Host 2. The Host 1 TCB will ensure that the security label of the message unit (TS) is that of Process A (TS). The Host 2 TCB receives the message unit and checks the security level (TS) for Process B.

The information is transferred to Process B if the security levels match. The TCB in Host 1 must have prior knowledge of the range of sensitivity levels over which Host 2 is accredited to operate before it can send the message. Host 2 must have similar knowledge of Host 1 sensitivity levels. These accredited ranges are used by the TCB to enforce the interconnect rules that are specified in these criteria for host-to-host interconnection.

Figure 3: Process-to-Process Transfer through a Trusted Packet Switch: Host 1 and Host 2 are now shown in Figure 3 operating with Process A and Process B connected by a trusted packet switch. The information flow within the hosts is the same as Figure 2. The message unit assembled in Host 1 consists of a header, security label (guaranteed by the TCB), and the data to be transmitted. The trusted packet switch receives the unit and performs nonsecurity operations on the header, such as determining its next destination. These operations are performed by untrusted processes, such as the routing process shown in Figure 3. The security label of the incoming message unit that the packet switch transmits to the untrusted routing process operating at the security level of the message unit is determined by the trusted network component base (TNCB) in the packet switch. The TNCB is the totality of the protection mechanisms within a network component, such as the packet switch, which are responsible for enforcing the component security policy. The message unit is reassembled along with the revised header information for the next destination, which is prepared by the packet switch. The TNCB applies the correct security label (TS) to the message unit and transmits the information to the next component or trusted host.

The processing performed by the TCB has been augmented in the examples shown in Figures 2 and 3. Augmentation occurred when the TCB determined if sensitive information could be transmitted to a neighboring component,

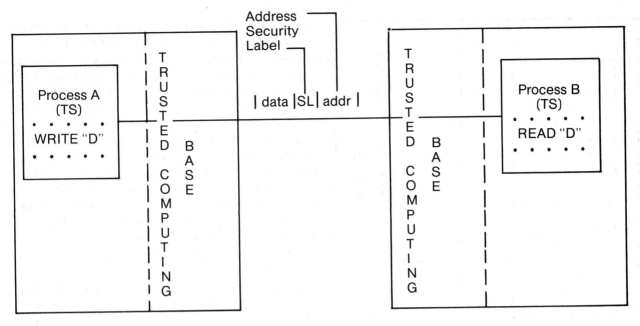

Figure 2: Process to Process Transfer Between Two Trusted Hosts

based on component connection criteria. These criteria state that the security level of information to be transmitted must be within the allowable range of the originating and destination trusted devices.

This is a quick overview of the TNEC as applied to networks. Figure 3 has some specificity at the network component criteria level, which is generally beyond our focus. We have primarily addressed the global network-wide TNEC. However, this introduction to TNEC does provide a basis for the general concept of a TNB, which includes the TNCB's in the network. Again, we must caution the reader that work on applying the TCSEC to networks is underway at the time of writing. The details are subject to change; the TCSEC is a (relatively) unvarying principle. Many of these issues are discussed further in Section 3.

The next section concerns an approach for password management guidance recommended by NCSC.

The U.S. Department of Defense *Password Management Guideline* [CSCG85a] is designed to present acceptable password practices for computer systems processing classified or sensitive data. This guideline, which is referred to as the *Green Book*, is closely related to the NBS, Federal Information Processing Standards Publication (FIPS PUB) 112, *Password Usage Standard* [GUID85]. The focus of this Defense guideline presents managerial and administrative methods to minimize the vulnerability of passwords in a computer system. The key features recommended in the guideline are (1) *user control:* users should be able to change their passwords; (2) *password generation:* passwords should be

machine generated; and (3) *audit reports:* the user should receive from the system selected audit reports (e.g., data and time of last login).

Four aspects of the *Green Book* are adapted to introduce the recommended control mechanisms. These mechanisms should be automated where possible. The four aspects of the guidelines are system security officer (SSO) responsibilities, user responsibilities, authentication mechanism functionality, and password protection.

The SSO is responsible for the computer system security, including security administration. We interpret this responsibility to pertain to all geographic locations of distributed systems. SSO functions include auditing and changing security characteristics of a user.

Briefly, key SSO responsibilities are

- *Initial system passwords:* passwords for all standard user IDs (unique symbols or character strings to identify a user), before the computer system access is made available for use. Examples of standard user ID's are SYSTEM, TEST, MASTER, etc. Several hackers have used these IDs to enter computer systems, because these standard IDs were not changed.

- *Initial Password Assignment:* each user should be assigned the initial password for each user ID, after the password is electronically generated. The key security requirement is to assign the initial password in a controlled manner so that only the user receives the ID. Also, the SSO must have evidence that only the user has

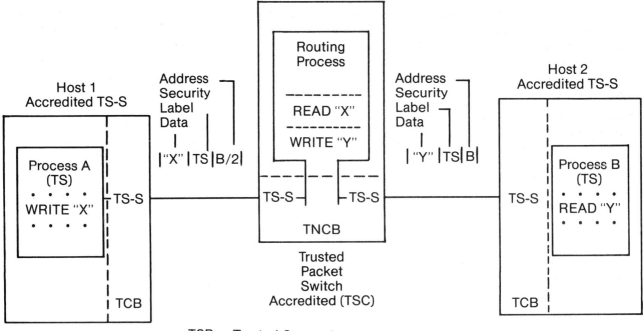

TCB = Trusted Computing Base
TNCB = Trusted Network Component Base

Figure 3: Process to Process Tranfer through a Trusted Packet Switch

received the ID, such as an acknowledgement of receipt.

- *Password change authorization:* to correct problems that may result from lost or compromised passwords, the SSO needs the capability to generate new user passwords. This process should not require SSO knowledge of the user's password, because the process can be performed in an automated manner.

- *Group IDs:* no group ID's should be assigned, except where the second person is the SSO. This requirement generally corresponds to a C2 level of identification and authentication in the *Orange Book,* and conflicts with the practices of organizations that allow several users to share an ID.

- *User ID revalidation:* user IDs should be removed when employees leave or are reassigned and at least annually. The revalidation should include updates of sponsor and phone number and/or mailing address.

User responsibilities: there are basic user responsibilities recommended in the guideline.

- *Security awareness:* Passwords should be kept private, and users should report changes in their status and other security-related events, such as potential security violation.

- *Changing passwords:* passwords should be changed periodically to reduce the risk of compromise. This change should be performed without intervention by the SSO to ensure that the SSO does not know the password. In general, a 1-year life time is recommmended, as mentioned above.

- *Login to a connected system:* identification and authentication should be required of users at login time. This process requires user ID and a password. Computer networks must maintain this identification and authentication control between hosts as users connect to other computer systems in the network.

- *Remembering passwords:* users should memorize their passwords and not write them down. If necessary to write a password, they should be protected according to the nature of the risk.

Authentication mechanism functionality: There are recommended controls to reduce the risk of password compromise in the computer system. However, caution is necessary because there are trusted employees with system programming capability that can override these controls. The recommended controls are

- *Internal storage of passwords:* the recommended practice is to store user IDs and passwords internally in the computer system. The stored passwords should be protected by the system access controls and/or password encryption. These controls should comply with the access control mechanisms from the TCSEC, such as mandatory or discretionary controls. Encryption should be used if the access control mechanisms are insufficient to reduce risk to an acceptable level.

- *Entry:* the two-step entry process of identification and authentication should be followed. After correct authentication, the system should display the date and time of the last login. This display is very useful for alerting users of possible attempts or actual security penetrations. There should be no display of the password on the screen.

- *Transmission:* passwords should be protected during transmission from the user to the system, according to the level of risk. Generally, this does not mean encryption unless the entire message is encrypted.

- *Login attempt rate:* the login attempt rate should be controlled. This helps prevent hackers from guessing passwords. The controls can be a maximum number of attempts for the life of the password and specific limits on attempts per access session at a port. For situations where hackers or other penetrators can switch ports, then the attempt rate should also be controlled for each user ID. The recommended maximum attempt rates should be between one per second to one per minute.

- *Auditing:* the computer system should create an audit trail to track use of the password, including changes. Actual passwords or character strings should not be in the audit trail because they could expose passwords of a legitimate user. Audit trail events should include successful login, unsuccessful login attempts, use of the password changing procedure, and the locking of a user ID when a password is at the end of its authorized lifetime.

The computer system operator or SSO should be notified of each accumulation of five consecutive unsuccessful login attempts from an access port or for a single user ID. In addition, users should be notified of the following after each successful login (1) the date and time of the last login, (2) the user location at the last login, and (3) each unsuccessful login since the last successful login.

Password protection: The final section in the *Green Book* for password guidance reiterates the requirement for using machine-generated passwords. In addition, the guideline recommends that passwords be protected during transmission as well as the associated information.

The next section presents an overview of the NBS guidance for certification and accreditation.

The process of certifying and accrediting should be formalized according to the NBS FIPS PUB 102, *Guideline for Computer Security Certification and Accreditation* [GUID83]. This would require the establishment of a program for certification and accreditation that may be substantially more formal than exists in most non-Defense organizations today. You may question the need for a formal program. We suggest you consider its merits with respect to identifying organizational risks that exist and could be lessened by effective accredited computer and network systems.

There is also companion guidance from NBS providing an overview of computer security certification and accreditation [GUID84]. We will focus on an overview of the basic guideline. Our discussion is an adaptation of the summary guidance provided by NBS in FIPS PUB 102 with cross references to the TCSEC criteria.

Security certification is defined as a technical evaluation of a computer system processing sensitive information using its security requirements as the evaluation criteria. Certification should include a security evaluation of the system's hardware, firmware, and software security design, configuration, and implementation and supporting managerial, physical, administrative, and communications security controls. Our discussion focuses on computer systems; however, the concepts could be generalized for application to networks.

The next step is security accreditation, which is the managerial approval for system operation. Our interpretation of accreditation is that a system may be accredited at a higher level than it is certified for because of the need for organization management to take a risk for business or operational necessity reasons. For example, if an organization (e.g., bank or command) has determined that a B1 computer system is required, management may accredit a system at a B1 level even if it was certified as a C2 system. This can occur by adding managerial, physical, administrative, and/or communications controls. The difference between the protection provided by these additional controls and the level of control specified in a B1 system is an approximation of the organization's level of risk at the B1 operational level. One reason this situation can occur is because there are many requirements for B1 or equivalent security controls but only a limited variety of commercial hardware and software available that is evaluated by NCSC at a B1 or higher level.

NBS divides FIPS PUB 102 guidance into two categories that we shall discuss in the following sections. The categories are (1) establishing a program for certification and accreditation and (2) performing a certification and accreditation.

Establishing a Program for Certification and Accreditation

There are 5 important issues to be addressed when establishing a program for certification and accreditation. These issues are

Issue 1. Policies and procedures: Management should approve a program directive that summarizes the certification and accreditation program. In addition, this directive should establish responsibilities for the program. A technical manager, such as a certification program manager, should issue a program manual defining the processes involved.

Issue 2. Roles and responsibilities: The following key functional roles are defined: (1) The senior executive officer approves the program directive and assigns responsibilities; (2) the certification program manager is responsible for the overall program planning, implementation, and review. He or she assigns an application certification manager; (3) the application certification manager is responsible for the specific program planning, implementation, and review; and (4) security evaluators perform the certification.

Issue 3. Entities requiring certification/accreditation: Application sensitivity determines the need for certification/accreditation. We suggest using the Trusted Computer System Evaluation Criteria defined in the TCSEC as a uniform method of defining sensitivity requirements.

Issue 4. Organization structure concerns: Two rules of thumb are suggested for the organization: (1) The more sensitive or critical the application, the higher the level of the accreditation official and (2) independent evaluations should be performed for certification.

Issue 5. Scheduling: Certification and accreditation should be integrated into the life-cycle management process. NBS recommends using its life-cycle definition for the phases or stages. Further, NBS recommends that certification and accreditation be performed early in the life cycle. The life-cycle phase is listed, and our interpretation of the applicable certification and accreditation efforts is shown in parentheses (1) requirements definition (certification); (2) development (certification/accreditation); (3) operation (recertification); (4) maintenance (recertification/reaccreditation); and (5) staffing, training, and support. Adequate managerial support is necessary to ensure that the required staffing and training are available for the program.

Performing a Certification and Accreditation

Four topics relating to the program are presented: certification, accreditation, recertification and reaccreditation, and evaluation techniques for security certification.

Topic 1. Certification: The certification process consists of a five-step approach to determine how well a sensitive application meets its security requirements. We suggest that this process include consideration of the six fundamental security requirements in the *Orange Book:* security policy, marking,

identification, accountability, asssurance, and continuous protection. The five steps are (1) *planning:* this step focuses on the development of a certification plan; (2) *data collection:* in this step, critical information needs are documented. This includes system or information security requirements, risk analysis data, system flow diagrams and processing steps, and a listing of system controls; (3) *basic evaluation:* this step consists of four tasks including security requirements evaluation, security function evaluation, control implementation determination (managerial, physical, administrative, technical, and communications controls), and methodology review of the acceptability of the implementation method for the computer system; (4) *detailed evaluation:* the quality of the security controls is evaluated as applicable for adequacy of functional operation, performance, and penetration resistance; and (5) *report of findings:* the technical and management security recommendations are presented. This report summarizes the findings and gives a proposed accreditation statement. Information is provided in the report on the applied security standards or policies, implemented controls, major vulnerabilities, corrective actions, operational restrictions, and the certification process used.

Topic 2. Accreditation: Accreditation is a management responsibility. The certification report contains a recommendation; however, the final decision rests with management. As was mentioned before, accreditation does not necessarily have to be at the same security level as certification (e.g., a C2 certification can be used as input to a B1 accreditation). Management may require additional controls on the computer system operations, such as procedural security controls to reduce the risk.

Topic 3. Recertification and reaccreditation: Computer system changes can introduce new hardware/software and/or procedural relationships and resulting vulnerabilities. The greater the magnitude of the change, the more extensive the recertification and reaccreditation requirement. One way to monitor this process is by reviewing the configuration management (i.e., change control) operation to determine the extent of changes. Another way is for management to establish a policy that routinely requires an independent recertification for each major computer system change (e.g., new hardware/software features in the supervisory or control or teleprocessing operations).

Topic 4. Evaluation techniques for security certification: Four groups of techniques are recommended in support of certification. These groups are (1) *risk analysis:* this analytical tool provides an overall systems approach to identifying the existing and potential risk; (2) *verification, validation, and testing (VV&T):* these techniques come from the software engineering discipline. Verification can be viewed in the *Orange Book* sense as a process of comparing two levels of system specification for proper correspondence (e.g., security policy model with the top-level specification or non-procedural description or functional specification or source code with object code). Validation evaluates the system with respect to its requirements. Testing is an empirical method for examining system behavior. A guideline for security testing is provided in the *Orange Book,* which is used by NCSC during the formal product evaluation process; (3) *security safeguard evaluation:* this set of techniques can be useful for those safeguards or controls that require substantial judgment, using tools such as analytical correspondence with specific *Orange Book* criteria, checklists, control matrices, and weighted ratings for levels of security in a computer system; and (4) *EDP audit:* an objective of the EDP audit is to determine if controls meet management's control objectives. An EDP audit may use some of the previously discussed techniques. The audit may focus on an evaluation of security controls with respect to the applicable computer system security criteria.

The next section introduces some of the guidance being considered for microcomputers. This is a relatively new area that is essentially an extension of the basic computer security standards and guidance. However, since the end user has substantial autonomy of operation, there are difficult security concerns to be addressed.

Management Guide for the Security of Personal Computers

Although there are no comprehensive security standards for personal computers, there is preliminary guidance available. The example that we use in this section is *Personal Computer Security Considerations* (NCSC-WA-002-85, December 1985) [NCSC85]—the *Blue Book.* Another example of such guidance from Steinhaur is [GUID85]. This discussion is adapted from the *Blue Book,* which illustrates some of the key issues. Three issues are briefly discussed and related to the *Orange Book* criteria: basic information security concerns, PC security concerns, and management.

The importance of personal computers (PCs) is multidimensional because of their widespread use in the organizational environment. A PC may be a dumb terminal communicating with a host computer, a smart terminal engaging in peer-to-peer communication with other processors (e.g., IBMs LU6.2 and PU2.1 protocols in the systems network architecture), a dedicated word processor, and/or a stand-alone processor. Most importantly, a single PC may perform in any or all of the above functions, thereby giving the end user substantial operational flexibility and freedom. These dimensions of flexibility and freedom raise managerial questions concerning the computer and network security safe-guards or controls associated with computer systems, because the PC is in many respects an autonomous computer system. We are concerned that the requisite security responsibilities and controls are implemented.

Basic Information Security Concerns

The *Blue Book* basic principle of information security is the control of access to information, which is the same principle used in the *Orange Book.* Using this approach, three security objectives are offered: (1) "Confidentiality of personal, proprietary, or otherwise sensitive data handled by the system;" (2) "Integrity and accuracy of data and the processes that handle the data;" and (3) "Availability of systems and the data of services they support."

According to the *Blue Book,* there are four catagories of threats that can affect the successful accomplishment of these objectives: (1) "Lack of awareness or concern for the implication of computer security issues;" (2) "Carelessness, errors, or omissions;" (3) "Equipment and media failure hazards; and (4) "Intentional attacks by disgruntled or dishonest personnel, hackers, or hostile agents."

PC Security Concerns

Three concerns are adapted from the *Blue Book:* hardware, data, and software. These concerns are highlighted to illustrate the nature of the issues involved in PC security.

Hardware concerns: the hardware concerns include physical protection of the equipment against unauthorized access, theft, environmental damage, magnetic media damage, improper media declassification or destruction, unauthorized hardware modification, and hardware attacks.

Two other hardware issues are mentioned: lack of built-in security mechanisms and electomagnetic emanations. Most PCs do not have built-in hardware mechanisms needed to logically isolate PC users from security kernel and related functions. One reason is that the PC is generally a single-state machine and does not support the following security mechanisms found in host systems: (1) "Multiple processor states—enabling separate 'domains' for users and system processes;" (2) "Privileged instructions—limiting access to certain functions (e.g., reading and writing to disk) to trusted system processes" and (3) "Memory protection features—preventing unauthorized access to sensitive parts of the system." Newer PC systems based on multi-state chips, such as the Intel 80286 and 80386, potentially support the preceding security mechanisms.

In addition, controls are required for electromagnetic emanations on sensitive environments. In these cases, security measures are available to combat the radio frequency emissions. The equipment is called "Tempest," and Tempest-certified equipment is available for processing classified data.

Data Concerns: Five data concerns are presented in the *Blue Book*. They are briefly discussed

(1) The nature of the data makes it more vulnerable to attack, because it is generally easily accessed. Also, the data is generally in more final form and easier to use.

(2) Labeling is primarily a physical process except where data encryption is used. "Data encryption provides a partial solution to the problem of labeling as well as providing access control. . . ." The algorithm used in most commercial applications is the *Data Encryption Standard* (DES), adopted in 1977 by the National Bureau of Standards as a Federal standard. DES is not approved for classifed applications." See Section 3.2, for a discussion of encryption.

(3) Securing data media suggestions are provided: lock floppy disks; use removable hard disk systems where feasible; make back-up copies of key software and data files; "clear the PC's memory between users. For some equipment, such as an unmodified IBM PC model 5150, this appears to be achievable by turning the machine off for at least 5 seconds."

(4) Data corruption considerations are provided: data corruption cannot be prevented in PCs, because of the lack of hardware security features. "For example, when editing an unsensitive file on a PC that has been used to process sensitive data, a save command may actually append residual sensitive data from the computer memory after the end of the document file on disk; media exposed to a sensitive environment should always be considered to assume that level of sensitivity;" PCs should go through a power-off, power-on sequence, . . .when changing processing sensitivity levels.

(5) Data transmission should be "carefully controlled and monitored."

Software Concerns: The five software concerns from the *Blue Book* are briefly introduced

(1) *Software vulnerabilities exist:* since there is no hardware security, modifications cannot be prevented. For example, operating system routines can be modified.

(2) *Operating system weaknesses exist:* these systems cannot be trusted. "For example, DOS provides the means to set file status to 'read-only,' 'system,' or 'hidden.' This feature is intended to supply a small measure of discretionary access control. However, the switches that control these states are not protected and can be easily manipulated. Thus, access to files cannot be restricted—a file residing on the system is available to anyone with physical access to the PC;"

(3) *User identification and authentication:* there are three basic aspects to data access control requirements for

personal computers that are closely related to the *Orange Book* evaluation criteria. Before we review these aspects, we introduce the concepts of identification and authentication (accountability); a most complete discussion may be found in Section 3.3. We also review TCB enforcement of individual accountability. The applicable *Orange Book* terms are (a) *identification:* "The TCB requires user to identify themselves before beginning to perform any other actions that the TCB is expected to mediate. . .;" (b) *authentication:* "Furthermore, the TCB shall use a protected mechanism (e.g., passwords) to authenticate the user's identity." Authentication is the process of establishing the validity of a claimed identity; (c) *access control:* access control is the control of "a specific type of interaction between a subject and an object that results in the flow of information from one to the other."

Three types of identification and authentication are offered by the *Blue Book*. First, identification and authentication usually apply to host computer systems (*Orange Book*) but can be required in a PC environment. For example, hardware-based access control systems exist that require the users to enter a password before the PC will boot up. Second, the *Blue Book* offers several suggestions for discretionary access control mechanisms. Login is mentioned by using a password to authenticate the identification. Also, attaching an ID card reader, which will electronically transmit identification information, is offered. Third, "authentication (and, for multiple-user PCs, identification) should occur whenever the system is powered up or rebooted."

(4) *Software attacks include trapdoors, Trojan horses, and viruses:* (a) the "trapdoor attack, involves the insertion of a mechanism that provides the attacker the means to later gain unauthorized access to the system;" (b) "the Trojan horse attack, involves the insertion of unauthorized algorithms into the system. Many times, a trapdoor is used to activate a Trojan horse. A Trojan horse is a body of code that is designed to subvert the person or process that uses it;" and (c) "a 'virus' is a software attack that infects computer systems much the same way as a biological virus infects humans. A computer virus is a small program that searches the computer for a program that is uninfected, or 'germ-free.' When it finds one, it makes a copy of itself and inserts the 'germ' in the beginning of the healthy program." The problem with viruses is that they can spread and cause substantial damage. For example, if a virus is in the PC operating system it may copy itself on each disk inserted in the PC."

(5) Communications attacks involve all the basic issues

that we discuss in Section 3 on network security. These include (a) some of the protections involve dial-back and other port-protection mechanisms to thwart masquerading and (b) "Encryption can be adapted as a means of remote user authentication." (See Section 3.2 for a discussion of encryption.) A user key, entered at the keyboard, authenticates the user. A second encryption key can be stored in encrypted form in the calling system firmware that authenticates the calling system as an approved communication endpoint. When dial-back is used in conjunction with two-key encryption, data access can be restricted to unauthorized users (with the user key) with authorized systems (those whose modems have the correct second key), located at authorized locations (those with phone numbers listed in the answering system's phone directory).

Management

The *Blue Book* suggests three aspects of an approach to implement management's responsibility for PC's. First, user responsibility is recommended along with PC security training in the organization. We interpret the guidelines recommended for PC systems and data access control as essential to extend the basic computer and network standards to the PC. Emphasis should be placed upon managerial, physical, administrative, and communications controls, because there are relatively few effective technical controls available for PCs. However, technical controls should be implemented in the host computers that communicate with the PCs.

Second, the following strategies are recommended for the PC information management security program: "*Prevent* threats from striking, detect *threats that have struck, and recover* from damaging effects."

The third aspect is a plan of action, which we interpret as above (a subset of host computer security policy, risk assessment, control measures, and security monitoring). The host computer system can maintain rigorous data and application software integrity. This integrity can be maintained during system development and operations. However, where key organizational data and applications are electronically available to PCs, management should consider extending and modifying the formal controls over software development testing and data integrity to the PC environment. This should include applications written in traditional languages, such as BASIC, FORTRAN, and COBOL; new languages or packages, such as Ada, LOTUS 1-2-3, and dBase III.

The guidelines recommended for data and applications integrity parallel those for systems and database control. When major computer system applications are implemented by using or involving PCs, formal system development and operational procedures should be applied in a manner similar to that used for systems implementation on a host computer. This includes operational procedures for data preparation and input processing procedures, program operation procedures, storage procedures (on-line and off-line), and output processing procedures.

In addition, provisions for continuity of operations or system backup become critical as more sensitive and important data are being processed on PCs. Once again, managerial control is necessary to identify the requirements for continuity of operations and to provide the procedures and capabilities necessary for startup and recovery after accidental or deliberate disaster.

The next subsection relates our discussion on computer and network security standards to a software engineering approach for computer and network standards for systems design, development, and testing. An example is used to demonstrate the interrelationship.

Software Quality Evaluation

The software engineering principles that apply to software development and quality assurance also apply to computer and network security. We show this relationship by adapting the discussion of *Software Quality Evaluation Standard* from the U.S. Department of Defense [DODS85a]. We shall briefly discuss three aspects of the standard to illustrate the relationship of systems design, development, and testing methods with computer and network security. Software quality evaluation within the system life cycle is presented first. This is followed by evaluation criteria and software quality factors.

Software Quality Evaluation within the System Life Cycle

Software quality evaluation is the evaluation of the degree to which the attributes or features of the software enable it to perform its specified end item use or application. The U.S. Department of Defense four-phased definition of system life cycle for computer systems is highlighted along with an approximate cross reference in parenthesis to the equivalent NBS life-cycle terms:

(1) *Concept exploration (initiation):* evaluate the role of the computer system within a broader perspective of a major system, such as a command and control system, and plan for the application of computer resources within the major system's life.

(2) *Demonstration and validation (development: definition, design, programming, and testing):* define the major system requirements, which include the computer system requirements. Evaluate alternate computer system approaches.

(3) *Full-scale development (development):* contract for the

major system development, including computer system development. Effectively manage the program.

(4) *Production and deployment (operation and maintenance):* deliver major systems that contain computer systems to the selected location(s). Provide computer hardware/software support during the major system's life cycle.

A software quality program is recommended to assure that the desired quality is achieved during the major system design and development activities. This program should provide for the prevention and detection of software errors and their resolution. The general rule of thumb is that it is substantially more effective to identify and correct software errors early in the life cycle.

Evaluation Criteria

During the life cycle, there are evaluation criteria that should be met to maintain software quality. These criteria are adherence to required format and documentation standards; compliance with contractual requirements; internal consistency; understandability; technical adequacy; appropriate degree of completeness; traceability to indicated documents; consistency with indicated documents; feasibility; appropriate requirements analyses, design, coding techniques used; appropriate level of detail; appropriate allocation of sizing, timing resources, adequate test coverage of requirements; adequacy of planned tools, facilities, procedures, methods, and resources; appropriate content for intended audience; adequacy of quality factors, all plans—updated and non-updated—reflect current approaches and plans; testability of requirements; consistency between data definition and data use; adequacy of test cases and test procedures (test inputs, expected results, and evaluation criteria); completeness of testing; and adequacy of retesting.

As you can see, these criteria are directly related to computer system security criteria. For example, in FIPS PUB 102, one of the evaluation techniques for security certification is verification, validation, and testing (V,V,&T). Several of the above quality assurance criteria address aspects of V,V,&T (e.g., adequate test coverage of requirements, testability of requirements, adequacy of test cases, test procedures).

The last section in this discussion pertains to the preceeding evaluation criteria concerning the adequacy of quality factors.

Software Quality Factors

There are ll software quality factors referred to in the U.S. Department of Defense standard that are equally applicable to computer security. These factors are derived from Sorko-

witz [SORK79] and are quoted (1) "*Correctness:* The degree to which the software satisfies its specified requirements;" (2) "*Efficiency:* The degree to which the software performs its intended functions with minimum consumption of computer time and storage resources;" (3) "*Flexibility:* The effort required to enhance the software or to modify it to meet new requirements. (This factor and maintainability make software supportable);" (4) "*Integrity:* The degree to which the software controls unauthorized access to, or modification of, system software and data;" (5) "*Interoperability:* The degree to which the software is able to interface with other systems;" (6) "*Maintainability:* The effort required to locate and correct an error in the software. (This factor and flexibility make software supportable);" (7) "*Portability:* The effort required to transfer the software from one hardware or software environment to another;" (8) "*Reliability:* The degree to which the software consistently performs its intended functions;" (9) "*Reusability:* The degree to which the software can be used in multiple applications;" (10) "*Testability:* The efforts required to ensure that the software performs its intended functions;" and (11) "*Usability:* The effort required to learn the human interface with the software, to prepare input, and to interpret output of the software."

These software quality factors are directly applicable to computer security because one aspect of computer security is to provide for protection against internal failures, human errors, and attacks. Software quality factors are objectives that when satisfied can assist in meeting this type of protection requirement (i.e., protection against internal failures, human errors, and attacks).

The next section discusses the reprints pertaining to standards.

Reprints

We have focused considerable effort on identifying the key aspects of the Department of Defense *Trusted Computer System Evaluation Criteria* (TCSEC) also known as the *Orange Book* (excerpts printed in this tutorial). The key points are as follows:

- *Six fundamental security requirements:* security policy, marking, identification, accountability, assurance, and continuous protection.

- *Seven evaluation criteria classes:* class D: minimal protection, class C1: discretionary security protection, class C2: controlled access protection, class B1: labeled security protection, class B2: structured protection, class B3: security domains, and class A1: verified design.

In the article, "A Status Report on the Development of Network Criteria," Sheila Brand provides the first draft of the trusted network evaluation criteria. This paper relates directly to our discussion of the Draft Department of Defense *Trusted Network Evaluation Criteria* both in this section and in Section 3. Briefly, the eight key issues that require resolution are highlighted from Brand's paper.

(1) *"Policy and models:* Security policies must be stated for protection against compromise, for integrity, and against denial of service."

(2) *Access controls:* There is a ". . . need for standardization of labels within a network."

(3) *Accountability:* ". . . the basic principle of individual user accountability must be supported by the network just as it is in hosts."

(4) *Network architecture:* ". . . the *Orange Book* is not adequate for evaluation of networks and that additional criteria are needed. The new criteria must allow incremental evaluations which would allow an evaluator to examine the parts of a network that are used as building blocks as well as allow for evaluations of network(s) in their entirety."
We interpret this observation to mean that network evaluation is essentially an extension of the *Orange Book* criteria. However, there are certain network features that are not adequately covered by the *Orange Book* (e.g., denial-of-service).

(5) *Configuration management and testing:* configuration management is recommended as early as possible in the network life cycle. "This should be instituted for networks of all evaluation classes from the lowest class on upwards. Support must be a global responsibility."

(6) *Verification and covert channel analysis:* ". . . System-level requirements should be decomposed to yield component-level 'constraints' (read: component security requirements)." Also, ". . . *all* hosts connected to multi-level networks should be subjected to covert channel analysis, not just those at the B2 or above evaluation class."

(7) *Network components:* Components should ". . . be evaluated with respect to system level security requirements. . ." within the context of a specific network environment. "this will allow a network architect the latitude to meet system level security requirements in a variety of ways."

(8) *Denial-of-service:* "Integrity and authenticity of control are of utmost importance in coping with denial-of-service."

Recommended Readings

We have highlighted the computational method used by *Computer Security Requirements: Guidance for Applying the Department of Defense Computer System Evaluation Criteria*

in Specific Environments [CSCG85], also known as the *Yellow Book.* The key steps are listed (1) *Risk index computation:* Rmax—maximum data sensitivity and Rmin—minimum user clearance and (2) *computer security requirements:* risk index and minimum criteria class (i.e., C2, B1, B2, B3, A2), or * (beyond the state-of-the-art).

In addition, the paper by Landwehr and Lubbes in the subsection recommended reading, management issues, presents a methodology for determining computer security requirements. The Landwehr and Lubbes work is based on the *Yellow Book* risk index approach.

In the guideline, *Department of Defense Password Management Guideline* [CSCG85a], known as the *Green Book,* guidance was discussed with respect to the Department of Defense (TCSEC). One of the relationships with the *Orange Book* is defining control objectives in the *Green Book* for password systems that meet the accountability control objectives in the *Orange Book.* This is highlighted for password system control objectives: personal identification, authentication, password privacy, and auditing.

The *Green Book* guidelines are discussed in the following four categories: (1) SSO responsibilities, (2) user responsibilities, (3) authentication mechanism functionality, and (4) password protection.

The NBS *Guideline for Computer Security Certification and Accreditation* [GUID83] was presented. We suggested coordinating this NBS guidance with *Orange Book* technology to utilize that computer security standard (e.g., evaluation criteria classes). This NBS guidance is (1) *certification:* planning, data collection, basic evaluation, detailed evaluation, and report of findings; (2) *accreditation:* management review; and (3) *recertification and reaccreditation.*

In addition, NBS mentions the available techniques for security certification, which are also related to other disciplines such as systems engineering and software engineering. They are risk analysis; verification, validation, and testing; security safeguard evaluation; and EDP audit.

The work, "Overview of Computer Security Certification and Accreditation," by Zella Ruthberg and William Neugent provides ". . . a comprehensive summary and guide to FIPS PUB 102, *Guideline to Computer Security Certification and Accreditation* [GUID84]." The authors suggest that for each life-cycle phase there should be a security concern and a preferred security process. We discussed a similar approach in Fred Tompkins' paper in Section 2.1. The National Bureau of Standards approach to accreditation is to provide guidance for each life-cycle phase. Security concerns are listed and followed by preferred security processes in parentheses:

(1) "Initiation: Understand the security problem: identify security risks, determine their magnitude, identify ar-

eas where safeguards are needed (risk analysis) and define security requirements."

(2) "Development (definition, design, programming, and testing): Validate security requirements (risk analysis, VV&T); assess recommended and implemented safeguards, determine whether they satisfy requirements (certification); and approve for operation (accreditation).

(3) "Operation and maintenance: Reassess security risks (risk analysis, safeguard evaluation, EDP audit); reassess safeguards (recertification); and approve for continued operation (reaccreditation).

The work, "Technology Assessment: Methods for Measuring the Level of Computer Security," by William Neugent, John Gilligan, Lance Hoffman, and Zella Ruthberg provides a supplement to FIPS PUB 102, *Guidelines for Computer Security Certification and Accreditation.* One of the security evaluation methodologies discussed by the authors are the U.S. Department of Defense *Trusted Computer*

System Evaluation Criteria. The authors provide a background for a wide variety of environments, controls, system evaluation methodologies, and risk assessment methodologies. This is followed by a summary of the state-of-the-art, security policy impact, and a document overview.

The viewpoint of Marvin Schaefer and Dave Bell in their paper, "Network Security Assurance," is that network security is an extension of computer security [SCHA85]. For example, they believe the similarities include traditional concepts of subjects, objects, security parameters, and formal design verification. However, they suggest research is needed for network-level data integrity, denial-of-service, and the theory and practice of trusted paths between geographically desparate parts of the TCB [TNB].

This paper is placed in Section 2.3 because of its heavy emphasis on traditional computer security issues such as level of abstraction and scope of security properties. The reader is encouraged to contrast this view with those expressed in Section 3 text and reprints.

**DEPARTMENT OF DEFENSE
COMPUTER SECURITY CENTER
Fort George G. Meade, Maryland 20755**

CSC-STD-001-83
Library No. S225,711

FOREWORD

This publication, "Department of Defense Trusted Computer System Evaluation Criteria," is being issued by the DoD Computer Security Center under the authority of and in accordance with DoD Directive 5215.1, "Computer Security Evaluation Center." The criteria defined in this document constitute a uniform set of basic requirements and evaluation classes for assessing the effectiveness of security controls built into Automatic Data Processing (ADP) systems. These criteria are intended for use in the evaluation and selection of ADP systems being considered for the processing and/or storage and retrieval of sensitive or classified information by the Department of Defense. Point of contact concerning this publication is the Office of Standards and Products, Attention: Chief, Computer Security Standards.

Melville H. Klein

Melville H. Klein
Director
DoD Computer Security Center

15 August 1983

Reprinted from *Department of Defense Trusted Computer System Evaluation
Criteria, CSC-STD-001-83*, 1983, pages 1-5, 91-92, 107. U.S. Government
work not protected by U.S. copyright.

ACKNOWLEDGMENTS

Special recognition is extended to Sheila L. Brand, DoD Computer Security Center (DoDCSC), who integrated theory, policy, and practice into, and directed the production of this document.

Acknowledgment is also given for the contributions of: Grace Hammonds and Peter S. Tasker, the MITRE Corp., Daniel J. Edwards, Col. Roger R. Schell, Marvin Schaefer, DoDCSC, and Theodore M. P. Lee, Sperry UNIVAC, who as original architects formulated and articulated the technical issues and solutions presented in this document; Jeff Makey and Warren F. Shadle, DoDCSC, who assisted in the preparation of this document; James P. Anderson, James P. Anderson & Co., Steven B. Lipner, Digital Equipment Corp., Clark Weissman, System Development Corp., LTC Lawrence A. Noble, formerly U.S. Air Force, Stephen T. Walker, formerly DoD, Eugene V. Epperly, DoD, and James E. Studer, formerly Dept. of the Army, who gave generously of their time and expertise in the review and critique of this document; and finally, thanks are given to the computer industry and others interested in trusted computing for their enthusiastic advice and assistance throughout this effort.

PREFACE

The trusted computer system evaluation criteria defined in this document classify systems into four broad hierarchical divisions of enhanced security protection. They provide a basis for the evaluation of effectiveness of security controls built into automatic data processing system products. The criteria were developed with three objectives in mind: (a) to provide users with a yardstick with which to assess the degree of trust that can be placed in computer systems for the secure processing of classified or other sensitive information; (b) to provide guidance to manufacturers as to what to build into their new, widely-available trusted commercial products in order to satisfy trust requirements for sensitive applications; and (c) to provide a basis for specifying security requirements in acquisition specifications. Two types of requirements are delineated for secure processing: (a) specific security feature requirements and (b) assurance requirements. Some of the latter requirements enable evaluation personnel to determine if the required features are present and functioning as intended. Though the criteria are application-independent, it is recognized that the specific security feature requirements may have to be interpreted when applying the criteria to specific applications or other special processing environments. The underlying assurance requirements can be applied across the entire spectrum of ADP system or application processing environments without special interpretation.

INTRODUCTION

Historical Perspective

In October 1967, a task force was assembled under the auspices of the Defense Science Board to address computer security safeguards that would protect classified information in remote-access, resource-sharing computer systems. The Task Force report, "Security Controls for Computer Systems," published in February 1970, made a number of policy and technical recommendations on actions to be taken to reduce the threat of compromise of classified information processed on remote-access computer systems.[34] Department of Defense Directive 5200.28 and its accompanying manual DoD 5200.28-M, published in 1972 and 1973 respectivley, responded to one of these recommendations by establishing uniform DoD policy, security requirements, administrative controls, and technical measures to protect classified information processed by DoD computer systems.[8;9] Research and development work undertaken by the Air Force, Advanced Research Projects Agency, and other defense agencies in the early and mid 70's developed and demonstrated solution approaches for the technical problems associated with controlling the flow of information in resource and information sharing computer systems.[1] The DoD Computer Security Initiative was started in 1977 under the auspices of the Under Secretary of Defense for Research and Engineering to focus DoD efforts addressing computer security issues.[33]

Concurrent with DoD efforts to address computer security issues, work was begun under the leadership of the National Bureau of Standards (NBS) to define problems and solutions for building, evaluating, and auditing secure computer systems.[17] As part of this work NBS held two invitational workshops on the subject of audit and evaluation of computer security.[20;28] The first was held in March 1977, and the second in November of 1978. One of the products of the second workshop was a definitive paper on the problems related to providing criteria for the evaluation of technical computer security effectiveness.[20] As an outgrowth of recommendations from this report, and in support of the DoD Computer Security Initiative, the MITRE Corporation began work on a set of computer security evaluation criteria that could be used to assess the degree of trust one could place in a computer system to protect classified data.[24;25;31] The preliminary concepts for computer security evaluation were defined and expanded upon at invitational workshops and symposia whose participants represented computer security expertise drawn from industry and academia in addition to the government. Their work has since been subjected to much peer review and constructive technical criticism from the DoD, industrial research and development organizations, universities, and computer manufacturers.

The DoD Computer Security Center (the Center) was formed in January 1981 to staff and expand on the work started by the DoD Computer Security Initiative.[15] A major goal of the Center as given in its DoD Charter is to encourage the widespread availability of trusted computer systems for use by those who process classified or other sensitive information.[10] The criteria presented in this document have evolved from the earlier NBS and MITRE evaluation material.

Scope

The trusted computer system evaluation criteria defined in this document apply to both trusted general-purpose and trusted embedded (e.g., those dedicated to a specific application) automatic data processing (ADP) systems. Included are two distinct sets of requirements: 1) specific security feature requirements; and 2) assurance requirements. The specific feature requirements encompass the capabilities typically found in information processing systems employing general-purpose operating systems that are distinct from the applications programs being supported. The assurance requirements, on the other hand, apply to systems that cover the full range of computing environments from dedicated controllers to full range multilevel secure resource sharing systems.

Purpose

As outlined in the Preface, the criteria have been developed for a number of reasons:

* To provide users with a metric with which to evaluate the degree of trust that can be placed in computer systems for the secure processing of classified and other sensitive information.

* To provide guidance to manufacturers as to what security features to build into their new and planned, commercial products in order to provide widely available systems that satisfy trust requirements for sensitive applications.

* To provide a basis for specifying security requirements in acquisition specifications.

With respect to the first purpose for development of the criteria, i.e., providing users with a security evaluation metric, evaluations can be delineated into two types: (a) an evaluation can be performed on a computer product from a perspective that excludes the application environment; or, (b) it can be done to assess whether appropriate security measures have been taken to permit the system to be used operationally in a specific environment. The former type of evaluation is done by the Computer Security Center through the Commercial Product Evaluation Process. That process is described in Appendix A.

The latter type of evaluation, i.e., those done for the purpose of assessing a system's security attributes with respect to a specific operational mission, is known as a certification evaluation. It must be understood that the completion of a formal product evaluation does not constitute certification or accreditation for the system to be used in any specific application environment. On the contrary, the evaluation report only provides a trusted computer system's evaluation rating along with supporting data describing the product system's strengths and weaknesses from a computer security point of view. The system security certification and the formal approval/accreditation procedure, done in accordance with the applicable policies of the issuing agencies, must still be followed before a system can be approved for use in processing or handling classified information.[8;9]

The trusted computer system evaluation criteria will be used directly and indirectly in the certification process. Along with applicable policy, it will be used directly as the basis for evaluation of the total system and for specifying system security and certification requirements for new acquisitions. Where a system being evaluated for certification employs a product that has undergone a Commercial Product Evaluation, reports from that process will be used as input to the certification evaluation. Technical data will be furnished to designers, evaluators and the Designated Approving Authorities to support their needs for making decisions.

Fundamental Computer Security Requirements

Any discussion of computer security necessarily starts from a statement of requirements, i.e., what it really means to call a computer system "secure." In general, secure systems will control, through use of specific security features, **access to information** such that only properly authorized individuals, or processes operating on their behalf, will have access to read, write, create, or delete information. Six fundamental requirements are derived from this basic statement of objective: four deal with what needs to be provided to control access to information; and two deal with how one can obtain credible assurances that this is accomplished in a trusted computer system.

Policy

Requirement 1 - SECURITY POLICY - There must be an explicit and well-defined security policy enforced by the system. Given identified subjects and objects, there must be a set of rules that are used by the system to determine whether a given subject can be permitted to gain access to a specific object. Computer systems of interest must enforce a mandatory security policy that can effectively implement access rules for handling sensitive (e.g., classified) information.[7] These rules include requirements such as: No person lacking proper personnel security clearance shall obtain access to classified information. In addition, discretionary security controls are required to ensure that only selected users or groups of users may obtain access to data (e.g., based on a need-to-know).

Requirement 2 - MARKING - Access control labels must be associated with objects. In order to control access to information stored in a computer, according to the rules of a mandatory security policy, it must be possible to mark every object with a label that reliably identifies the object's sensitivity level (e.g., classification), and/or the modes of access accorded those subjects who may potentially access the object.

Accountability

Requirement 3 - IDENTIFICATION - Individual subjects must be identified. Each access to information must be mediated based on who is accessing the information and what classes of information they are authorized to deal with. This identification and authorization information must be securely maintained by the computer system and be associated with every active element that performs some security-relevant action in the system.

Requirement 4 - ACCOUNTABILITY - Audit information must be selectively kept and protected so that actions affecting security can be traced to the responsible party. A trusted system must be able to record the occurrences of security-relevant events in an audit log. The capability to select the audit events to be recorded is necessary to minimize the expense of auditing and to allow efficient analysis. Audit data must be protected from modification and unauthorized destruction to permit detection and after-the-fact investigations of security violations.

Assurance

Requirement 5 - ASSURANCE - The computer system must contain hardware/software mechanisms that can be independently evaluated to provide sufficient assurance that the system enforces requirements 1 through 4 above. In order to assure that the four requirements of Security Policy, Marking, Identification, and Accountability are enforced by a computer system, there must be some identified and unified collection of hardware and software controls that perform those functions. These mechanisms are typically embedded in the operating system and are designed to carry out the assigned tasks in a secure manner. The basis for trusting such system mechanisms in their operational setting must be clearly documented such that it is possible to independently examine the evidence to evaluate their sufficiency.

Requirement 6 - CONTINUOUS PROTECTION - The trusted mechanisms that enforce these basic requirements must be continuously protected against tampering and/or unauthorized changes. No computer system can be considered truly secure if the basic hardware and software mechanisms that enforce the security policy are themselves subject to unauthorized modification or subversion. The continuous protection requirement has direct implications throughout the computer system's life-cycle.

These fundamental requirements form the basis for the individual evaluation criteria applicable for each evaluation division and class. The interested reader is referred to Section 5 of this document, "Control Objectives for Trusted Computer Systems," for a more complete discussion and further amplification of these fundamental requirements as they apply to general-purpose information processing systems and to Section 7 for amplification of the relationship between Policy and these requirements.

Structure of the Document

The remainder of this document is divided into two parts, four appendices, and a glossary. Part I (Sections 1 through 4) presents the detailed criteria derived from the fundamental requirements described above and relevant to the rationale and policy excerpts contained in Part II.

Part II (Sections 5 through 10) provides a discussion of basic objectives, rationale, and national policy behind the development of the criteria, and guidelines for developers pertaining to: mandatory access control rules implementation, the covert channel problem, and security testing. It is divided into six sections. Section 5 discusses the use of control objectives in general and presents the three basic control objectives of the criteria. Section 6 provides the theoretical basis behind the criteria. Section 7 gives excerpts from pertinent regulations, directives, OMB Circulars, and Executive Orders which provide the basis for many trust requirements for processing nationally sensitive and classified information with computer systems. Section 8 provides guidance to system developers on expectations in dealing with the covert channel problem. Section 9 provides guidelines dealing with mandatory security. Section 10 provides guidelines for security testing. There are four appendices, including a description of the Trusted Computer System Commercial Products Evaluation Process (Appendix A), summaries of the evaluation divisions (Appendix B) and classes (Appendix C), and finally a directory of requirements ordered alphabetically. In addition, there is a glossary.

Structure of the Criteria

The criteria are divided into four divisions: D, C, B, and A ordered in a hierarchical manner with the highest division (A) being reserved for systems providing the most comprehensive security. Each division represents a major improvement in the overall confidence one can place in the system for the protection of sensitive information. Within divisions C and B there are a number of subdivisions known as classes. The classes are also ordered in a hierarchical manner with systems representative of division C and lower classes of division B being characterized by the set of computer security mechanisms that they possess. Assurance of correct and complete design and implementation for these systems is gained mostly through testing of the security-relevant portions of the system. The security-relevant portions of a system are referred to throughout this document as the *Trusted Computing Base* (TCB). Systems representative of higher classes in division B and division A derive their security attributes more from their design and implementation structure. Increased assurance that the required features are operative, correct, and tamperproof under all circumstances is gained through progressively more rigorous analysis during the design process.

Within each class, four major sets of criteria are addressed. The first three represent features necessary to satisfy the broad control objectives of Security Policy, Accountability, and Assurance that are discussed in Part II, Section 5. The fourth set, Documentation, describes the type of written evidence in the form of user guides, manuals, and the test and design documentation required for each class.

A reader using this publication for the first time may find it helpful to first read Part II, before continuing on with Part I.

APPENDIX C

Summary of Evaluation Criteria Classes

The classes of systems recognized under the trusted computer system evaluation criteria are as follows. They are presented in the order of increasing desirablity from a computer security point of view.

Class (D): Minimal Protection

This class is reserved for those systems that have been evaluated but that fail to meet the requirements for a higher evaluation class.

Class (C1): Discretionary Security Protection

The Trusted Computing Base (TCB) of a class (C1) system nominally satisfies the discretionary security requirements by providing separation of users and data. It incorporates some form of credible controls capable of enforcing access limitations on an individual basis, i.e., ostensibly suitable for allowing users to be able to protect project or private information and to keep other users from accidentally reading or destroying their data. The class (C1) environment is expected to be one of cooperating users processing data at the same level(s) of sensitivity.

Class (C2): Controlled Access Protection

Systems in this class enforce a more finely grained discretionary access control than (C1) systems, making users individually accountable for their actions through login procedures, auditing of security-relevant events, and resource isolation.

Class (B1): Labeled Security Protection

Class (B1) systems require all the features required for class (C2). In addition, an informal statement of the security policy model, data labeling, and mandatory access control over named subjects and objects must be present. The capability must exist for accurately labeling exported information. Any flaws identified by testing must be removed.

Class (B2): Structured Protection

In class (B2) systems, the TCB is based on a clearly defined and documented formal security policy model that requires the discretionary and mandatory access control enforcement found in class (B1) systems be extended to all subjects and objects in the ADP system. In addition, covert channels are addressed. The TCB must be carefully structured into protection-critical and non-protection-critical elements. The TCB interface is well-defined and the TCB design and implementation enable it to be subjected to more thorough testing and more complete review. Authentication mechanisms are strengthened, trusted facility management is provided in the form of support for system administrator and operator functions, and stringent configuration management controls are imposed. The system is relatively resistant to penetration.

Class (B3): Security Domains

The class (B3) TCB must satisfy the reference monitor requirements that it mediate all accesses of subjects to objects, be tamperproof, and be small enough to be subjected to analysis and tests. To this end, the TCB is structured to exclude code not essential to security policy enforcement, with significant system engineering during TCB design and implementation directed toward minimizing its complexity. A security administrator is supported, audit mechanisms are expanded to signal security-relevant events, and system recovery procedures are required. The system is highly resistant to penetration.

Class (A1): Verified Design

Systems in class (A1) are functionally equivalent to those in class (B3) in that no additional architectural features or policy requirements are added. The distinguishing feature of systems in this class is the analysis derived from formal design specification and verification techniques and the resulting high degree of assurance that the TCB is correctly implemented. This assurance is developmental in nature, starting with a formal model of the security policy and a formal top-level specification (FTLS) of the design. In keeping with the extensive design and development analysis of the TCB required of systems in class (A1), more stringent configuration management is required and procedures are established for securely distributing the system to sites. A system security administrator is supported.

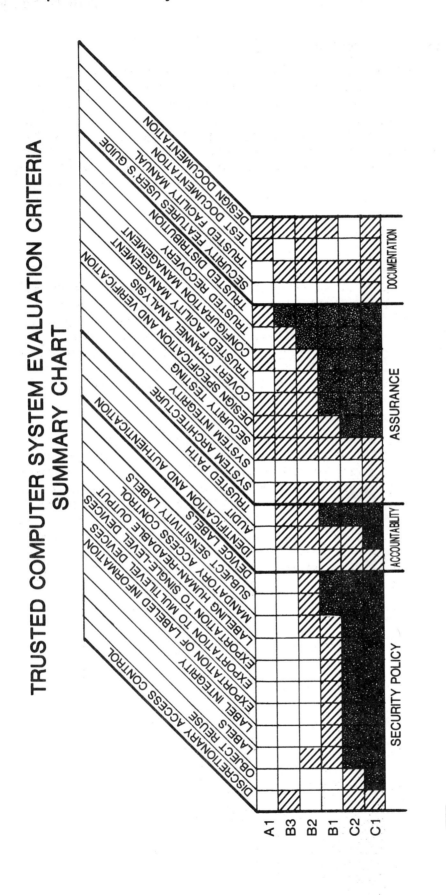

TRUSTED COMPUTER SYSTEM EVALUATION CRITERIA
SUMMARY CHART

Figure 1

A STATUS REPORT ON THE DEVELOPMENT OF NETWORK CRITERIA

by

Sheila Brand

DoD Computer Security Center

Ft. George G. Meade, Maryland 20755-6000

1.0 Introduction

The purpose of this paper is to describe the steps that have been taken by the DoD Computer Security Center (the Center) to develop guidance in the area of security of computer networks. The Center's Invitational Workshop on Network Security will be discussed along with how results of this meeting are being used to prepare draft Trusted Network Evaluation Criteria. The paper will close with a brief overview of the emerging network criteria and the major differences between this document and the DoD Trusted Computer System Evaluation Criteria. (4)

2.0 Background

In August of 1983, the Department of Defense Computer Security Center published the Department of Defense Trusted Computer System Evaluation Criteria, CSC-STD-001-83. (4) (To be referred to as the Orange Book) That document provided a basis for the evaluation of the effectiveness of security controls built into automatic data processing system products. Though the Criteria defined in the Orange Book are application-independent, it was recognized early-on that specific security feature requirements in that document would have to be interpreted when applying them to applications and other special processing environments.

Soon after publication the question arose as to whether or not guidance in the Orange Book was sufficient for the evaluation of computer networks and network components. Debate has raged over this issue for the past two years with both points of view being strongly adhered to. In order to provide definitive guidance on network security it was necessary for the Center to address this

issue head-on. The strategy was to examine security related issues involved in the evaluation of computer networks with the objective of publishing network guidance in one of two ways: (a) by developing a totally new set of criteria, or (b) by extending and/or revising the Orange Book so that it can be used unequivocally for the evaluation of computer networks.

In January of this year the Center's Division of Standards identified a series of issues whose resolution would bring the process one step closer to the development of network security criteria. It was recognized that for these issues to get a fair "airing," pooling of the Nation's scarce resources in this area would be necessary. It was therefore decided to organize a workshop, invite the Country's computer and network security experts to it, and use the Center's issues as the focal point for the workshop.

2.1 The Issues

The issues requiring resolution covered eight areas:

* Policy and Models

* Access Control

* Accountability

* Network Architecture

* Configuration Management and Testing

* Verification and Covert Channel Analysis

* Network Components

* Denial-of-Service

The complete list of issues are presented in the Proceedings of the workshop. (1)

To address the issues in advance of the workshop the Center invited a number of the Nation's network and computer security experts to write issue papers. Twenty-nine papers were written with an approximate distribution of three papers per issue area.

2.2 The Workshop

The DoD Computer Security Center Invitational Workshop on Network Security was held in New Orleans, Louisiana, 19-22 March 1985, with the stated objective of providing the Center with input necessary for the development of Trusted Network Evaluation Criteria. In addition to the issue paper authors approximately 50 more experts in network and computer security representing both the public and private sectors were invited to participate.

Each of the invitees was assigned to one of eight specific working groups organized around the eight issue areas and remained with that group throughout the Workshop. Each group was asked to read and discuss pertinent issue papers and provide criteria recommendations based on group findings. Each Working Group leader was asked to prepare a group report and provide that report to the Workshop organizer before leaving New Orleans.

3.0 Workshop Results

With a few exceptions the overwhelming consensus was that the Orange Book is alive and well and, yes, useful for the evaluation of the effectiveness of security controls in networks. However, extensions, interpretations and some additional criteria are necessary. The prevailing reasoning was that the distributed nature of a network allows it to be analyzed as a special case of a distributed system. As the Orange Book does not preclude, but also does not specifically include, distributed systems much interpretation is needed when applying Orange Book criteria.

Some of the conclusions reached by the working groups (and summarized by issue area) include the following:

3.1 Policy and Models

Security policies must be stated for: protection against compromise, for integrity, and against denial-of-service. Furthermore, these policies must be implemented at both the network level and at the component level. In the area of compromise the network mandatory policy should be enforced by a set of interconnection rules that provide the conditions under which two components can communicate. These rules are expressed in terms of the security level of the information being transmitted and the accreditation range of the sending and receiving network components. (7)

3.2 Access Controls

In this author's opinion one of the most important findings of the access control group was their recognition and emphasis on the need for standardization of labels within a network. They concluded that if a network is expected to make access control decisions based on the sensitivity level of the data for which transmission service is being requested, (i.e., mandatory access control decisions) then all subscribers of the net had better use the same representation for a specific sensitivity level. They went one step further and suggested that not only must internal representations be exactly the same but external label representations also. Their fall back position was that mutually communicating systems be required to maintain a mapping of each other system's labels to the other.

In addition to their recognition that mandatory access control can be implemented in a network, the access control group also suggests that some form of discretionary access control internal to the network is crucial for correct network functioning as well as for security. This is because it is closely tied to the problem of correctness of received identity. (8)

3.3 Accountability

The Accountability group recommends that the basic principle of individual user accountability must be supported by the network just as it is in hosts. They recognize that to accomplish this task networks will require the cooperation of hosts to trace network activity back to individual users.

This group's report also discusses the nature of a network reference monitor. That portion of the network that is responsible for enforcing the network security policy is referred to as the Trusted Network Base (TNB). The TNB, which a network will have only one of, will include a network reference monitor. The TNB will be distributed over the network with parts of it residing in hosts which are attached to the network, other parts may reside in cryptographic devices, front ends, packet switches, etc. (3)

3.4 Network Architecture

This group's consensus was that the Orange Book is not adequate for evaluation of networks and that additional criteria are needed. The new Criteria must allow incremental evaluations which would allow an evaluator to examine the parts of a network that are used as building blocks as well as allow for evaluations of network in their entirety.

Some notion of formal decomposition of a network is necessary. This decomposition would require that when a system is partitioned into subsystems a security policy must be derived for each subsystem. The derived subsystem policy may not be the same as the containing system's security policy or adjacent subsystems policies. However, the security policies of all subsystems within the containing systems must be shown to completely satisfy the system security policy of the containing system. (10)

3.5 Configuration Management and Testing

The group recommended use of configuration management from the onset of network design if possible, but at the earliest stage possible. This should be instituted for networks of all evaluation classes from the lowest class on upwards. Support must be a global responsibility. That is, it is crucial that all security-relevant components of a network be integrated under configuration

management so that a global authority can evaluate how proposed components changes would effect network security. (5)

3.6 Verifications and Covert Channel Analysis

As was the case with the network architecture group this group's findings emphasized decomposition. They viewed the network as a special case of a distributed system. From this perspective system-level requirements should be decomposed to yield component-level "constraints" (read: component security requirements).

The report emphasized the greater potential for exploitation of covert channels in a distributed system and recommends that all hosts connected to multi-level networks should be subjected to covert channel analysis, not just those at the B2 or above evaluation class. This group recommends that the definition for covert storage channel be expanded from that in the Orange Book. (9)

3.7 Network Components

This group believes that only with respect to or in the context of a specific network environment should components be evaluated with respect to system level security requirements. This will allow a network architect the latitude to meet system level security requirements in a varity of ways. A specific security requirement may be satisfied by one component, a homogeneous ensemble of components or by a heterogeneous collection from a variety of vendors. (6)

3.8 Denial-of-Service

Their major findings: (a) Integrity and authenticity of control are of utmost importance in coping with denial-of-servie problems. (b) The Orange Book is of little help in this area. (c) No generic denial-of-service conditions could be identified which were independent of mission objectives. (d) No increasingly comprehensive subsets of denial-of-service were identified but some categorizations in terms of detection, recovery, and resistance was done. (2)

Though the group was unable to recommend generic criteria they did provide mission oriented criteria starting with a general policy which is: "Denial-of-service requirements will be considered for all networks relative to the user mission being supported by that network. Each network provider, in cooperation with the user, will define what conditions constitute network denial-of-service."

4.0 Network Criteria

Following the workshop, the Center asked a number of people to assist in analyzing workshop results. The objective was to identify emerging trends and themes and to provide an assessment of the direct applicability of workshop products to the development of network criteria. As a result of this activity the basic outline for the criteria was laid out. The remainder of this paper will provide an overview of major features of the draft document, titled: Department of Defense Trusted Network Evaluation Criteria. (TNEC)

4.1 Definition

The draft TNEC uses the following definition to describe a network: a network is composed of a communications medium and all components attached to that medium whose responsibility is the transference of information. Such components may include, but are not limited to, hosts, packet switches, telecommunications controllers, key distribution center, access control centers, technical control devices, and other components used by the network.

As the definition implies, though we recognize that networks can be viewed as distributed systems and therefore be evaluated at a high service level of abstraction, we chose not to. Basically we believe that though implementation detail does not belong in a set of criteria, viewing the network at too high a level of abstraction would lead the evaluator to ignoring too many details and security problem areas.

4.2 Structure

The TNEC is divided into two major parts. Part I provides network-wide level criteria and is meant to be used for evaluating the security behavior of the network as a whole. Part II provides network components criteria and is meant to be used to evaluate components in isolation just as the Orange Book is used today to evaluate ADP products in isolation. Both Part I and Part II are closely linked to and derived from the Orange Book.

The TNEC classifies networks into four hierarchical divisions of protection. However, as of this writing, the TNEC does not contain "subdivisions" (i.e., classes) as does the Orange Book. This was done for a number of reasons—none of which are sacred. First, it is simpler to do initial analysis if fewer categories of protection need identification. Second, it is not at all clear that even if simplicity was not an objective we could at the early stages of TNEC development, identify additional significant gradations in network security requirements. The divisions are referred to as:

* ND: Minimal Protection

* NC: Controlled Access Protection

* NB: Mandatory Protection

* NA: Verified Design

4.3 Policy

One of the conclusions reached by many of the groups in New Orleans was that a major deficiency of the Orange Book for network evaluations was the lack of policy requirements for transmission integrity and denial-of-service. Though some individuals have been heard to say that integrity is addressable within the context of an Orange Book evaluation, no explicit requirements are stated for integrity in that document. The overall scope of the TNEC is broader than the Orange Book, as the TNEC not only addresses the compromise problem but also addressed transmission integrity and denial-of-service. However, because we recognize that different parts of the network and even different portions of a component within a network will probably be used to meet the three separate sets of requirements, separate evaluation and separate ratings are suggested for each. It is quite possible that a network may meet the NA requirements for compromise but only achieve an NC for denial-of-service and an ND for integrity. However if these sets of ratings satisy the network design requirements, so be it. The point is, that unlike the Orange Book which only requires one kind of policy implementation, the draft TNEC is meant to meet a number of difference types of security requirements which may and probably will vary in importance to mission objectives.

4.4 The Divisions

As the TNEC is in a state of flux as of this writing, a detailed description of individual criteria may serve only historical purpose. However the following short description of the overall character of each network division may prove useful.

4.4.1 Division ND: Minimal Protection

This devision provides minimal security. There are no security features which are trusted to protect against compromise, integrity, or denial-of-service. This division is reserved for those networks that have been evaluated but that fail to meet the requirements for a higher evaluation division.

4.4.2 Division NC: Controlled Access Protection

This division provides for minimal data compromise, integrity, and denial-of-service protection. Networks within this division are not required to make security decisions based on the level of sensitivity of information being transmitted. Security decisions based on the classification of information are handled administratively.

Instead of the discretionary access control as required in the Orange Book the draft TNEC requires a "Network Discretionary Access Control". At the NC level the network knows nothing about the sensitivity level of data being transmitted, only that hosts and other network components are attempting to communicate with each other or to use functions or services of the network. This criteria requires that the network be able to limit communication between components based on their identity. At the NC level this is the only policy requirement for limiting a subscriber's capabilities on the network.

In the accountability area, the draft TNEC requires all network components to identify themselves to the TNB before service can commence. Identity however will not require authentication for NC networks. There is also a requirement for audit trail maintenance.

4.4.3 Division NB: Mandatory Protection

In this division, the portion of the Trusted Network Base (TNB) that deals with compromise is based on a clearly defined and documented formal security policy model. It requires mandatory access control enforcement over all network resources. This policy is stated in terms of a set of interconnection rules that take into account that all network components must be accredited over some security range, where the range may be as small as a single security level. The rules only allow components to communicate in the range where they share common security levels, and only allows data flow between components communicating at the same security level.

Covert channels are addrressed for NB networks and there are requirements for careful structuring of the TNB into protection-critical and non-protection-critical elements. The TNB interfaces must be well defined and its design and implementation should enable more thorough testing and review. The TNEC at this level also requires Trusted Facility Management and Configuration Management.

4.4.4 Division NA: Verified Design

A network in Division NA must satisfy the reference monitor requirements that it mediate all accesses of subject to objects, be tamperproof, and the distributed portions of the TNB shall be small enough to be subjected to analysis and tests. To this end, the distributed TNB is structured to exclude code not essential to security policy enforcement, with significant systems engineering during TNB design and implementation towards minimizing its complexity. A distinguishing feature of networks in this division is the analysis derived from formal design specification and verification techniques and the resulting high degree of assurance that the TNB is correctly implemented. This assurance is developmental in nature, starting with a formal model of the security policy and formal top-level specification (FTLS) of the design. Independent of the particular specification language or verification system used, there are five important criteria for Division NA design verification:

* A formal model of the security policy must be clearly indentified and documented, including a mathematical proof that the model is consistant with its axioms and is sufficient to support the security policy.

* An FTLS must be produced that includes abstract definitions of the functions the TNB performs and of the hardware and/or firmware mechanisms that are used to support separate execution domains.

* The FTLS of the TNB must be shown to be consistent with the model by formal techniques where possible (i.e., where verification tools exists) and informal ones otherwise.

* The TNB implementation (i.e., in hardware, firmware, and software) must be informally shown to be consistent with the FTLS. The elements of the FTLS must be shown, using informal techniques, to correspond to the elements of the TNB. The FTLS must express the unified protection mechanism required to satisfy the security policy, and it is the elements of this protection mechanism that are mapped to the elements of the TNB.

* Formal analysis techniques must be used to identify and analyze covert channels. Informal techniques may be used to identify covert timing channels. The continued existence of identified covert channels in the system must be justified.

In keeping with the extensive design and development analysis of the TNB required of networks in Division NA, more stringent

configuration management is required and a network security administrator is supported.

5.0 Summary

As of this writing the Center has put a significant effort into the development of Trusted Network Evaluation Criteria. A National forum was organized and held at the DoD Computer Security Center Invitational Workshop on Network Security. Products of that workshop have been used by the Center to formulate draft criteria. The Criteria fall into two types: (a) global criteria, to be used for evaluating the network as a whole; and (b) component criteria to be used for evaluation of individual elements that are to be incorporated in a network and are to play a part in the enforcement of a security policy. In terms of policy this document differs from the Orange Book in that it includes requirements to insure integrity of data transmission as well as requirements to assist in protecting against denial-of-service.

The draft TNEC is about to go out for review by a large divergent group of experts. After receiving their comments we will revise the document and reiterate the process. We expect this process to finally result in the Center's being able to provide guidance in this complex area.

REFERENCES

1. Brand, S. and Arsenault, A. "Network Security Issues " in Proceedings of the Department of Defense Computer Security Center Invitation Workshop on Network Security, DoD Computer Security Center, March 1985.

2. Cerf, V. "Report of the Denial-of-Service Group" in Proceedings of the Department of Defense Computer Security Center Invitational Workshop on Network Security, DoD Computer Security Center, March 1985.

3. Denning, D.E. "Report of the Accountability Group" in Proceedings of the Department of Defense Computer Security Center Invitational Workshop on Network Security, DoD Computer Security Center, March 1985.

4. DoD Computer Security Center, Department of Defense Trusted Computer System Evaluation Criteria, CSC-STD-001-83, 15 August 1983.

5. Downs, D. "Report of the Configuration Management and Testing Group (Assurance II)" in Proceedings of the Department of Defense Computer Security Center Invitational Workshop on Network Security, DoD Computer Security Center, March 1985.

6. Kent, S. "Security for Network Components" in Proceedings of the Department of Defense Computer Security Center Invitational Workshop on Network Security, DoD Computer Security Center, March 1985.

7. Lane, J. "Report of the Policy and Models Group or Plato Agonistes" in Proceedings of the Department of Defense Computer Security Center Invitational Workshop on Network Security, DoD Computer Security Center, March 1985.

8. Lipner, S. And Bailey, D. "Report of the Access Controls Group" in Proceedings of the Department of Defense Computer Security Center Invitational Workshop on Network Security, DoD Computer Security Center, March 1985.

9. Rushby, J. "Report of the Working Group on Verification and Covert Channels (Assurance III)" in Proceedings of the Department of Defense Computer Security Center Invitational Workshop on Network Security, DoD Computer Security Center, March 1985.

10. Snow, B. "Report of the Network Architecture Group of the Invitational Workshop on Computer Security" in Proceedings of the Department of Defense Computer Security Center Invitational Workshop on Network Security, DoD Computer Security Center, March 1985.

Section 2.4: Technology and Methodology

Advances in computer and network security are continually occurring and are related to the advances in the hardware, software, and communications technologies. In this section, we discuss trusted computing base (TCB) issues, concentrating on implementation and verification of the kernel and access control, by reviewing the TCSEC and papers based on practical experience. The theme of this section is review and consolidation, oriented toward advice for the system developer. Perhaps even more than some other subsections, the reprints and suggested readings constitute an integral part of our discussion on these topics.

The Security Kernel

Security kernel concepts are based on the ideas of a reference monitor and several mechanisms of modern multiprogramming operating systems. As discussed in Section 2.2, the security kernel is the hardware and software that implements the reference monitor abstraction.

Security design and implementation are introduced in two subsections: basic principles and implementation considerations.

Basic Principles

Security design starts with a basic statement of objectives, from which security requirements are developed. The TCSEC security objective is to control access to information ". . . such that only properly authorized individuals, or processes operating on their behalf, will have access to read, write, create, or delete information." The TCSEC fundamental security requirements are being used by several computer companies as a basis for their security kernel developments; undoubtedly their products are targeted for National Computer Security Center (NCSC) evaluation. Several of these developments are discussed in Section 2.6. Briefly for review, the six requirements in the *Orange Book* are:

Policy: Requirement 1—SECURITY POLICY; Requirement 2—MARKING

Accountability: Requirement 3—IDENTIFICATION; Requirement 4—ACCOUNTABILITY

Assurance: Requirement 5—ASSURANCE; Requirement 6—CONTINUOUS PROTECTION

The Policy requirements are fundamental to the discussion in this section and are therefore quoted in full:

Requirement 1—SECURITY POLICY—There must be an explicit and well-defined security policy enforced by the system. Given identified subjects and objects, there must be a set of rules that is used by the system to determine whether a given subject can be permitted to gain access to a specific object. Computer systems of interest must enforce a mandatory security policy that can effectively implement access rules for handling sensitive (e.g., classified) information. These rules include requirements such as: No person lacking proper personnel security clearance shall obtain access to classified information. In addition, discretionary security controls are required to ensure that only selected users or groups of users may obtain access to data (e.g., based on a need-to-know).

Requirement 2—MARKING—Access control labels must be associated with objects. In order to control access to information stored in a computer, according to the rules of a mandatory security policy, it must be possible to mark every object with a label that reliably identifies the object's sensitivity level (e.g., classification), and/or the modes of access accorded those subjects who may potentially access the object.

We shall be returning to these requirements as we discuss objectives and mechanisms throughout this section.

The TCSEC defines the security kernel as "the hardware, firmware, and software elements of a Trusted Computing Base (TCB) that implement the reference monitor concept. It must mediate all accesses, be protected from modification, and be verifiable as correct." The reference monitor is an abstraction; the kernel is the implementation. But it is not sufficient to simply assert that the kernel mediates all accesses of subjects to objects; we must consider what rules or policies are followed in this mediation process.

Security Policy

We have separated two ideas: establishment of a policy and enforcement of that policy. Now we turn to the definition of that policy. A security kernel can enforce many different policies; but it will not work at all without some policy. Stanley Ames, Jr. et al. state it well: "In a computer system, a well-formed protection policy should identify all the permissible modes of access between active entities, or subjects, and the passive entities, or objects."

Various operating systems define access modes differently. Sometimes these differences are dependent on the perceived applications for which the systems are designed. In other cases, the (security) architects of different systems may have different opinions of which access modes are important. Another difference occurs in the grouping of modes; often modes are collected in sets, with access privileges being denied or granted for all modes in a set. The following modes occur to us: write, create, destroy, append, modify, and execute. We leave it as an exercise for you to identify and define the modes and sets on the operating systems with which you are familiar.

Next, we turn to two subsets of protection policy: *discretionary* protection policy, and *mandatory* protection policy.

These are complementary policies: either or both may be in effect at any given instant. Using *Orange Book* criteria, discretionary access control is required at C1 and above. However, mandatory access control is only required at B1 and above.

Mandatory access policy: Mandatory access control is based on security rules imposed on all users (subjects). Mandatory, or nondiscretionary, rules take precedence over discretionary rules. Mandatory access policy is inseparably tied to the concept of labels. Every object is labeled with the sensitivity levels and classification it is permitted or authorized to access. The kernel compares the subject's authorization with the object's label to determine if access is permitted. Mandatory access rules do not distinguish among different users with the same authorization. Note that the TCSEC does not require sensitivity labels and mandatory access control until B1.

Labels may be arranged in a hierarchy. Access to level 1 may be easier to obtain and be granted to more people than access to level 2. The data stored in level 2 are considered more sensitive than the data stored in level 1. Access to level n implies access to all levels less sensitive than (below) n. The U.S. Department of Defense hierarchy labels are relatively well known; the following list is ordered from least sensitive to most. Each classification label has a one or two letter abbreviation, given in parenthesis: (U) Unclassified, (N) Not classified but sensitive, (C) Confidential, (S) Secret, and (TS) Top secret. Other organizations may have a different number of levels.

Mandatory access control may also be enforced for non-hierarchical labels. For example, access to salary data in many companies is restricted. The terms *compartment* and *category* have been applied to non-hierarchical seta of objects. Defense only assigns compartmented data at the top secret level, but it is reasonable to do so at lower levels. Consider, for example, at which hierarchical level you might want to classify salary data. The organization's security policy must provide rules for granting access to compartmented data. The most common such rule is is that the individual requires access to the data in order to perform his or her job; this is commonly referred to as *need-to-know*.

Discretionary access policy: Discretionary access to an object may be granted to individual subjects or groups. Access is granted accordingly to the identity of the subject; this can be an individual identity, a group of people sharing an identity, or otherwise belonging to a group. C2 systems "shall be capable of including or excluding access to the granularity of a single user." B3 systems "shall be capable of specifying, for each named object, a list of individuals and a list of groups of named individuals with their respective modes of access to that object." Summarizing, the TCSEC require discretionary access controls at the C1 level,

strengthen them in C2 and again in B3. Mandatory controls begin at the B1 level. Examples of software packages that add discretionary access control capabilities at the C level are RACK, ACF2, and TOP SECRET.

The question of who can grant access is operating system and/or application dependent. In most cases access control is exercised by the person in whose directory the object exists. Colloqually, this person is said to be the "owner" of the object. It is conceivable that this access control could rest elsewhere, say in the system security officer (SSO). Discretionary access may also be transitive. That is, a person who is granted access may be able to grant access to others. Transitivity is dependent on the type of access and on the operating system.

The Bell-LaPadula Model

The next step is to define a formal security policy model. An example of this type of model is the Bell-LaPadula (B-LP) model. We have described the B-LP in Section 2.2 as a formal state transtition model of computer security policy that describes a set of access control rules. There are rigorous requirements for this type of model. Essentially, there must be a mathematically precise statement of a security policy. This model is iterative in the sense that it represents the initial state of the system and the way it moves to each additional state.

TCB requirement for a formal security policy model includes a formal proof that the iterative states of the system are "secure" states. "Secure" means that the accesses of subjects to objects comply with a specific security policy.

Two fundamental mandatory access rules discussed for the B-LP model are briefly reviewed: (1) The simple security condition. This rule is used as the method or rule of the B-LP model to control granting a subject read access to an object only if the security level is equal to or greater than the security level of the object (the security level of the subject dominates that of the object); and (2) The *(star)-property. This rule allows write access to an object only if the security level of the subject is essentially equal to or less than the security level of the object (the security level of the subject is dominated by that of the object).

Ames et al. point out that a model's mandatory access rules ". . . do not provide a protection policy that distinguishes different users within the same access class. Discretionary rules are included in the model to provide that type of protection." They also mention an additional threat called denial of service, which is not specifically addressed in the B-LP model. This condition also applies to network security.

Faithful Implementation

There is one more important aspect of the model for security kernel design and implementation to discuss. This is faithful implementation, which ensures that the functions of the model are implemented in the security kernel. Provision for faithful implementation is provided in the TCSEC by the use of a formal top-level specification (FTLS). The FTLS is written in a formal mathematical language with theorems showing the correspondence of the system specification to its formal requirements. Formal verification is defined as the process of using formal proofs to demonstrate the consistency between the formal specification and security policy level. In addition, formal verification can be used to demonstrate the consistency between the formal specification and its program implementation.

Design verification is the process of using formal proofs to demonstrate the consistency between a formal specification of a system and a formal security policy model. Implementation verification is the demonstration of the consistency between a formal specification of a system and implementation.

In the TCSEC provision is also made for a descriptive top-level specification (DTLS), which is a top-level specification written in a natural language such as English. Also, an informal program design notation could be used instead of or in conjunction with the natural language.

The DTLS of the TCB is necessary for the TCSEC design specification and verification for classes B2 and greater (i.e., B2, B3, and A1). Briefly, B1 requires that an informal or formal model of the security policy that is supported by the TCB shall ". . . be maintained and shown to be consistent with its axioms." At the B2 level, this requirement becomes more rigorous. For example, "a descriptive top-level specification (DTLS) of the TCB shall be maintained that completely and accurately describes the TCB in terms of exceptions, error messages and effects. It shall be shown to be an accurate description of the TCB inferface." At the B3 level, the additional requirement is added to provide ". . . a convincing arguement" that the DTLS is consistent with the model.

A1 security requirements for design specification verification state the FTLS ". . . shall be shown to be an accurate description of the TCB inferface. A convincing argument shall be given that the DTLS is consistent with the model."

This design certification and verification process is rigorous, but achievable. For example, Honeywell SCOMP (secure communications processor) has been evaluated by the NCSC at the A1 level and the Honeywell Multics operating system at the B2 level.

We conclude this part of the technology and methodology discussion with a section on implementation considerations.

Implementation Considerations

The implementation of a security kernel at the B2, B3, and A1 levels must be carefully balanced with performance needs. For example, on-line interactive response time must be fast enough to meet user requirements. The implementation meaning of this performance requirement is the computer system must have an architecture that supports security kernel functions, such as mediating accesses, in a high speed manner. This means that some TCB functions must be hardware implemented or supported.

Briefly, the conceptual levels of implementation functions that are involved are (1) users (at terminals) (trusted and untrusted users/subjects), (2) user interface, (3) applications (trusted and untrusted subjects), (4) operating system interface, (5) supervisor (trusted and untrusted subjects), (6) security kernel interface, and (7) security kernel

Trusted subjects (users) are privileged subjects that may be able to override the kernel access checks. Examples of trusted users are system programmers performing maintenance. Landwehr, in Section 2.1 suggests that the presence of trusted subjects makes it very difficult to determine the security policy, since these trusted subjects bypass the access controls.

Ames et al. suggest that there are four general architectural categories where TCB oriented mechanisms are useful. These are necessary to improve processing speed because many security kernel functions, such as process switches, are computer resource or capability intensive. The suggested categories are:

Explicit processes: These processes or activities of a processor performing a computation specified by a program should provide efficient support for multiple processes (multiprogramming) and interprocess communication. One aspect of the need for simultaneous processes is the requirement of a large number of process switches necessary to support the security kernel mediation function.

Memory protection: Virtual memory is usually used to achieve the mediation required in a security kernal environment. The mediation requirement means that no process can access memory without using a descriptor. In general, this means that ". . . all information within the system must be represented in distinct, identifiable objects. In all but the simplest case, the virtual address space of a process includes more than one object, each with distinct logical attributes such as size, access mode, and access class. This logically distinct memory is commonly called a segment." The segment descriptors are manages by the security kernel with support from the address-mapping hardware.

Execution domains: A minimum of three states or domains is required for effective TCB support, such as isolation and protection of the security kernel. Preferably, these three states would be hardware supported. The states or domains are for: user, supervisor, and kernel processes.

Input/output (I/O mediation): The I/O mediation pertains to the security kernel's control of access to I/O devices, external media, and to memory by I/O processors. The security kernel controls and considers I/O devices as objects. As computer systems become more communications oriented, the I/O processor function becomes more complex. A hardware architecture designed to provide support for execution domains by allowing direct user or supervisor domain access to I/O is preferable. Ames et al. state that "such an architecture would provide some form of descriptor to control access to the devices, in a manner similar to the use of memory descriptors. In addition, for the I/O processor to effectively operate outside the kernel by accessing virtual memory on behalf of the user, we need descriptor-controlled access to memory by the. . ." Honeywell SCOMP, which is discussed in Section 2.6.

Reprints are discussed in the next section, starting with a brief summary of the Ames et al. paper.

Reprints

The paper, "Security Kernel Design and Implementation: An Introduction," by Stanley Ames, Jr., Morrie Gasser, and Roger Schell develops the basic considerations necessary for designing and implementing a security kernel. The authors provide the historical basis for the concept of the reference monitor, which is adapted from the models of Butler Lampson. The security kernel approach limits the protection mechanism to a small part of the operating system. Since the security kernel, which is defined as the hardware and software that implement the reference monitor abstraction, checks every reference to information, only the kernel need be trusted. Actually, there is another trusted code, not mentioned in this paper, which performed security-relevant work beyond the scope, or in support of, the reference monitor. For example, the SSO uses trusted processes to add and delete system users, and to initialize their passwords, to enter thier security clearances for use in mandatory access control and their group clearances for use in discretionary access control.

As was mentioned previously in this section, the kernel enforces a security policy that must identify all modes by which subjects access objects. This policy, expressed in a set of mathematical rules, "must define the information protection behavior of the system as a whole, . . . and must include a 'security theorem' to ensure that the behavior defined by the model always complies with the security requirements of the applicable policy." The Bell-LaPadula model is presented as an example of a security kernel,

providing two mandatory security rules: the simple security condition and the *-property. It neglects denial of service, which is "difficult to formalize in a model."

The formal model does not "specify the design for the applications interface to the kernel," although "the most abstract kernel specification defines all the kernel's interface characteristics." A succession of small steps in a hierarchy of abstract specifications gradually introduces more implementation detail. Three classes of formal verification techniques are discussed, as are the following implementation considerations. "The rules of the policy model help to clearly identify which [operating system] functions are security relevant." The kernel must handle resource management, hiding the locations from untrusted (non-kernel) software. Performance and functionality considerations force a tradeoff causing some non-security-related functions into the kernel. If one starts with a general policy model, such as B-LP, it is often necessary to tailor the policy to the specific application system by permitting trusted subjects to perform actions unchecked by the security kernel.

Acceptable performance can only be achieved with hardware support for kernel functions. Explicit process support requires nonforgeable and unalterable user identification and clearances to be bound to each process. Switching of processor state and address spaces (for multiprogramming) is required, as is reliable memory access, interrupt structure, and process synchronization. Memory protection must force hardware-supported indirection or virtualization on all non-kernel processes; various segment management techniques can help performance. Covert channel problems must be addressed.

Three hierarchical execution domains (address space of a process) are required: kernel, supervisor, and user; this is an extension of the two domains found on many third generation systems. The transfer between domains should be eased and expedited by providing multiple kernel entry points as well as argument validation and stack management. Input/output instructions must be restricted to the kernel, accessed by the user through kernel function cells. External I/O involving single-user devices are distinguished. Trusted labeling for removable media is also required.

The paper concludes with the requirement for a degree of formal verification for security kernel verification. Reference is given to the *Orange Book* criteria, which are now the basis for formal verification by NCSC. At the time of the paper, NCSC was at an early stage of security kernel verification as part of its evaluation of trusted hardware/software products.

In his paper, "A Security Kernel for a Multiprocessor Microcomputer," Roger Schell shares some of his early expcriences with a research and development project to write and test software for selected microcomputer-based systems that require effective computer security. Since the work focused primarily on microprocessors that are not very supportive of the security kernel approach—the Z8000 and the Intel 8086,—Schell focuses on the broader design issues. "The challenge of this project was to identify a viable security kernel structure for a multiprocessor system using a commercially available microcomputer." The Intel iAPX 286 was the processor of choice. Its specifications were available at the time, but not the device itself.

The design structure was based on "three distinct extended machine layers: the security kernel, the supervisor, and the applications." All physical resources are managed within the kernel. Much of the operating system is outside the kernel in the supervisor. "The kernel must provide extended virtual machines that specifically support both asynchronous processes and segmented address spaces." Unlike the design in the Ames paper above, "both the kernel and the supervisor have certain responsibilities for system security. The kernel manages all physical resources." Kernel isolation requires hardware enforcement, avoiding the need for any trusted processes. The kernel enforces mandatory access control and can support any lattice access policy. Discretionary access control is completely outside the kernel.

Schell offers three categories of lessons learned, with respect to the design structure for security kernels:

Microprocessor testbed: Schell supports the need for three state microprocessors to implement the three processor-supported execution domains for the security kernel, supervision, and application (or user) functions.

Programming experiences: An important message from this research is that top-down software design is good software engineering practice and is necessary. This top-down design was coupled with bottom-up implementation. He emphasizes the use of loop-free layer organization, which supports the software engineering concept of "information hiding." The kernel is organized into five layers: gate keeper, segment and event manager, traffic controller, memory manager, and inner traffic controller. As a matter of interest, Ada supports "information hiding" in its package (or module) structure and Ada is the language used for the secure computing work reported by W.E. Boebert, R.Y. Kain, and W.D. Young [BROE85].

Performance issues: Schell presents some of the performance results of the security kernel on the Intel 8086 and the Z8000. Bus contention and process switch were the major issues. However, the focus is on "future" (in 1983) applications such as the Intel iAPX 286 microprocessor because it provides better support for security kernel functions, such as domain swiching. The Intel iAPX 286 microprocessor is

also reported in another paper by Schell as the basis of ". . . a commercial product family of secure, high performance computer systems" offered by Gemini Computers, Inc. The design work for the GEMSOS security kernel is presented in Section 2.6. GEMSOS is Gemini multiprocessing secure operating system.

The very readable paper, "Issues in Discretionary Access Control," by Deborah Downs, Jerzy Rub, Kenneth Kung, and Carole Jordan presents important issues on the often obscure subject of discretionary access control (DAC). A number of operating system implementation examples add credibility. Recall that the TCSEC defines discretionary access control as ". . . a means of restricting access to objects based on the identity of subjects and/or group to which they belong. The controls are discretionary in the sense that a subject with certain access permission is capable of passing that permission (perhaps indirectly) on any other subject."

The authors present 13 topics providing in-depth coverage of DAC issues. The key issues and concepts are discussed here. The paper begins with definitions of terms—discretionary, subject, and object—following which authors observe that "consistency in handling DAC objects leads to less complexity in the DAC implementation and, therefore, to more assurance in its correct operation." Unfortunately, they conclude that "DAC does not have well defined rules as do mandatory access control systems. In fact no formal model of DAC currently exists." Research is called for.

An important myth is clarified. Discretionary access can be granted or denied on whatever criteria the grantor wishes to employ. "Criteria such as 'need to know' and 'whom do I like' are equally possible. Access is based entirely on the subject's identity and the mechanism has no knowledge of, and bases no decisions on, the semantics of the data." The authors note that "if actions can be performed using another person's identity, then DAC can be subverted." We note that if the other person's authentication is compromised so that it is impossible to to detect an imposter, then mandatory access control can be subverted.

Descriptions, pros, and cons of DAC mechanism types in current operating systems are discussed. The authors define all DAC mechanisms as special cases of an access control matrix as having ". . . subjects represented on the rows and protected objects on the columns." Each matrix entry describes the type of access of each subject to each object. Current operating systems use compact variations of the access comtrol matrix for efficiency. Row-based representations attach a list of acceptable objects to the subject; these mechanisms include capabilities, profiles, and passwords. Column-based representations attach a list of subjects to the object; representative mechanisms are protection bits and access control lists.

In capability-based systems, the ability to access an object is ascertained by a subject possessing an unalterable and unforgeable capability or "ticket" to the object. Since capabilities can be transferred, and in some systems, increased or decreased, it is in general impossible to determine for a given subject how many objects have access to it or what their access privileges are.

Profiles are lists of objects and access rights associated with a subject, which are checked when access is attempted. Problems with this mechanism include "restricting the size of profiles, distributing access when an object is created or when the access is changed, and determining all the subjects that have access to an object." Profiles must also be changed securely; "timely revocation of access to an object is very difficult."

Passwords can be associated with objects for access control. Practical considerations including human memory limit passwords to one per object or per object access right. Revoking, or just periodically changing, passwords is extremely difficult. Encryption is equivalent to but stronger than password protection.

Protection bits are an extremely common third-generation operating system subset of the access control matrix column representation. The shortcomings are manifold. An access control list (ACL) is the best way to implement DAC in current technology, and is therefore discussed in considerable detail.

Groups are useful with ACLs for identifying multiple subjects. Group creation, membership control, names, and subject-identifier should all be managed by the SSO or equivalent. To enforce the principle of least privilege, groups should be as small as possible. Objective conflict in some operating systems which also use groups for purposes of accounting and file system. The number of groups in which a subject can have simultaneous privileges has additional ramifications. Wild cards and defaults simplify ACL creation and user friendliness.

It is necessary to distinguish access permissions and access modes. Access permissions define the ability to change and/or transfer the ability to change access modes. One organization of access permission is hierarchical, with the SSO at the root. The tree may only extend to the creator of an object, often called the owner; this "strict ownership policy results in the owner being the only subject that can delete and object." The most primitive system, which exists in (perhaps assumedly) benign, naive, or immature environments is laissez-faire, in which no ownership concept exists.

Access modes define ". . . a specific action that can be applied to the object." DAC is first explained in terms of files, extendable to other similar objects; implementation- or application-dependent objects such as mailboxes and messsage queues, communications channels, forums and bulletin boards, and devices are not discussed. The authors identify three basic access modes: ready-copy, write-delete, and execute. They observe that write-delete access is not readily useful with read-copy; we disagree. There are cases where data aggregation changed the mandatory access level of a set of data, so that while a subject may have mandatory access privilege to a datum, it does not have access to the set of data. Access to directories and the files they contain has three options: on directories but not on files, conversely, or both. Questions of access to the whole (hierarchical) path also arise. Minimal directory access modes are read and write-expand-delete.

Protected subsystems can provide finer access granularity by encapsulating objects. The subsystem manager provides the only route to these objects; it can enforce its own controls. DAC add-ons can be viewed as a limited case in that they "are basing their assurance on the inability of the user to get access to the operating system through another interface or to cause the operating system to retrieve illegal data with a legal request."

Recommended Readings

Several additional recommendations are in order to supplement the specific papers cited below. The computer system application examples in Section 2.6 further illustrate the principles and mechanisms discussed so far. We have also pointed out that the security kernel is an extension to three states of the two state operating systems of the third generation. Familiarity with several of these operating systems would be beneficial. In addition, we suggest consulting the forthcoming *Proceedings of the NCSC Invitational Workshop on Database Security*.

A historical overview of the important technologies for computer security that existed through 1983 is presented by Carl Landwehr, in his paper, "The Best available Technologies for Computer Security." Jargon and U.S. Department of Defense policy are defined. Four of the computer systems that we discussed in the subsection computer system applications are introduced: (1) SCOMP—The secure communications processor (SCOMP) by Honeywell was started in the late 1970's; (2) DEC OS—Digital Equipment corporation (DEC) operating system security projects were started in 1979; (3) PSOS—This provably secure operating system (PSOS) work is using Ada. Honeywell started it in 1980; and (4) GEMSOS security kernel—This is the security kernel work by Gemini Corp., which was reported by Landwehr as GSOS. GEMSOS started in 1982.

Tables list 27 projects, answering questions such as: when development began, sponsor, builder, security goals, approach used, formal specifications, hardware, programming language, performance, certification, evaluated decision, installed, and lessons learned. The paper concludes with advice for the developer, addressing requirements, design, implementation, verification and testing, and operation. An appendix briefly describes the projects listed in the tables.

Four systems for use in automated specification and verification ". . . to aid in producing correct and reliable software" are presented by Maureen Cheheyl, Morrie Gasser, George Huff, and Jonathan Millen [CHEH81]. The paper, "Verifying Security," shows how these four systems can assist in proving security properties of a security kernel functions in the operating system.

Specification and verification systems components described are specification languages and processors, verification condition generators, and theorem provers. Like many of the other concepts we have discussed, "a hierarchical approach makes it possible to carry out a verification in stages," encompassing "three representations of a system, [ranging] from abstract to concrete: security model; formal specification; and implementation. Access control and in-

formation flow models are discussed; a low water mark example is presented.

The four systems that are described in considerable detail are (1) Gypsy—Developed by the University of Texas, Institute for Computing Science and Computer Applications; (2) HDM—Developed by SRI International; (3) FDM (Ina Jo)—Developed by System Development Corporation; and (4) AFFIRM—Developed by the University of Southern California, Information Sciences Institute.

The authors conclude with an overall assessment of the systems and general observation. They point out that although these systems are useful for varying applications, they are difficult to apply. Several reasons are that the syntax is similar to programming languages and certain constructs, such as "state" arguments, are new ideas. Also, they point out that specifications are difficult to test by using these systems because of the need to verify capabilities, such as security properties. Their overall conclusion is that these systems are for very knowledgeable users to use and interpret the results.

*The security kernel approach provides controls
that are effective against most internal attacks—including some
that many designers never consider.*

Reprinted from *Computer*, July 1983, pages 14-22. Copyright © 1983 by
The Institute of Electrical and Electronics Engineers, Inc.

Security Kernel Design and Implementation: An Introduction

Stanley R. Ames, Jr., and Morrie Gasser, The Mitre Corporation

Roger R. Schell, DoD Computer Security Center

Providing highly reliable protection for computerized information has traditionally been a game of wits. No sooner are security controls introduced into systems than are penetrators finding ways to circumvent them. Security kernel technology provides a conceptual base on which to build secure computer systems, thereby replacing this game of wits with a methodical design process. The kernel approach is equally applicable to all types of systems, from general-purpose, multiuser operating systems to special-purpose systems such as communication processors—wherever the protection of shared information is a concern.

Most computer installations rely solely on a physical security perimeter, protecting the computer and its users by guards, dogs, and fences. Communications between the computer and remote devices may be encrypted to geographically extend the security perimeter, but if only physical security is used, all users can potentially access all information in the computer system. Consequently, all users must be trusted to the same degree. When the system contains sensitive information that only certain users should access, we must introduce some additional protection mechanisms. One solution is to give each class of users a separate machine. This solution is becoming increasingly less costly because of declining hardware prices, but it does not address the controlled sharing of information among users. Sharing information within a single computer requires internal controls to isolate sensitive information.

Continual efforts are being made to develop reliable internal security controls solely through tenacity and hard work. Unfortunately, these attempts have been uniformly unsuccessful for a number of reasons. The first is that the operating system and utility software are typically large and complex. The second is that no one has precisely defined the security provided by the internal controls. Finally, little has been done to ensure the correctness of the security controls that have been implemented.

The security kernel approach described here directly addresses the size and complexity problem by limiting the protection mechanism to a small portion of the system. The second and third problems are addressed by clearly defining a security policy and then following a rigorous methodology that includes developing a mathematical model, constructing a precise specification of behavior, and coding in a high-level language.

The security kernel approach is based on the concept of the *reference monitor*, an abstract notion adapted from the models of Butler Lampson.[1] The reference monitor provides an underlying security theory for conceptualizing the idea of protection. In a reference monitor, all active entities such as people or computer processes make reference to passive entities such as documents or segments of memory using a set of current access authorizations (Figure 1). Of particular importance is that *every* reference to information (e.g., by a processor to primary memory) or change of authorization must go through the reference monitor.

The security kernel is defined as the hardware and software that realize the reference monitor abstraction. To successfully implement a security kernel, we must adhere to three engineering principles: (1) *completeness*, in that all access to information must be mediated by the kernel; (2) *isolation*, in that the kernel must be protected from tampering; and (3) *verifiability*, in that some correspondence must be shown between the security policy and the actual implementation of the kernel. The completeness and isolation requirements are best addressed with an adequate hardware foundation. A formal development methodology can be a powerful tool for addressing the verifiability requirement.

Schell first introduced the security kernel concept in 1972 as "a compact security 'kernel' of the operating system and supporting hardware such that an antagonist could provide the remainder of the system without compromising the protection provided." In 1974, Mitre tested the hypothesis that such a security kernel could actually be constructed. The first security kernel consisted of less than 20 primitive subroutines that directly managed the physical resources and enforced protection constraints. The entire security kernel contained fewer than a thousand compilable high-level language statements and ran on a DEC PDP-11/45.

To demonstrate this kernel, Mitre also constructed a simple, experimental operating system along with applications for a practical military example. The operating system had a hierarchical file system, cooperating processes with controlled information sharing, and interfaces to a few interactive terminals. The operating system and applications were outside the kernel and could not impact the information protection provided by the kernel.

Since this initial prototype effort, a number of research efforts have dealt with the issues of security kernel construction and verification. Today, a few security-kernel-based products are being introduced commercially. One such system, the Honeywell Secure Communications Processor (Scomp), is discussed by L. Fraim[2] (see the article in this issue); others are surveyed by C. Landwehr[3] (also in this issue).

Basic principles

The first step in developing a kernel-based system is to identify the specific set of protection policies to be supported. A given system is "secure" only with respect to some specific policy. In a computer system, a well-formed protection policy should identify all the permissible modes of access between the active entities, or subjects, and the passive entities, or objects. The external policy that corresponds to the people, paper, and methods of accessing information in the real world must be interpreted in a way that allows the policy to apply to the internal entities of the computer system.

This requirement—that policy be precisely defined—is a primary distinction between a security-kernel-based system and several other efforts to develop security-relevant operating systems, such as "capability" machines.[4] These other systems tend to strive for general-purpose protection, yet do not have any definitive criteria for what is security relevant. The mechanisms in these systems essentially provide a computer with special security features. By contrast, the security-kernel approach explicitly addresses both policy and mechanism. If general-purpose protection mechanisms are well-defined and augmented to enforce a specific policy, however, they can provide an underlying base for subsequent security kernel construction.

A formally defined security model. We need to define two types of policy: nondiscretionary and discretionary. A *nondiscretionary* policy contains mandatory security rules that are imposed on all users. A *discretionary* policy, on the other hand, contains security rules that can be specified at the option of each user.

The protection policy enforced by a security kernel is encapsulated in a set of mathematical rules that constitute a formal security model. Both discretionary and nondiscretionary policies must be addressed by the rules of the model.

In determining whether the model of a policy is sufficient, we need to consider two key issues, which occasionally have been a source of misunderstanding. First, a model of a policy must define the information protection behavior of the system as a whole. Merely modeling distinct operations with respect to individual assertions about a protection mechanism does not indicate much about overall system security and can, in fact, be misleading. Second, a model of a policy must include a "security theorem" to ensure that the behavior defined by the model always complies with the security requirements of the applicable policy.

The model enforced by most security kernels has been derived from early security kernel work at Mitre[5] and Case Western Reserve University.[6] Commonly referred to as the Bell and LaPadula model, this model provides rules for preventing unauthorized observation and modification of information. By representing the security kernel as a finite state machine, these rules define allowable transitions from one "secure" state to the next.

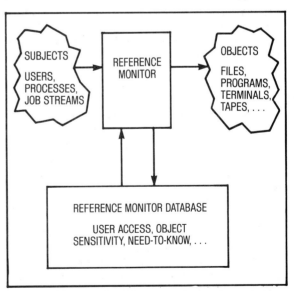

Figure 1. Reference monitor. The security kernel approach is based on the concept of a reference monitor, in which active entities (subjects) make reference to passive entities (objects) using a set of access authorizations (reference monitor database).

Within the model, each subject and object of the reference monitor is given a security identifier termed an *access class*. The access classes of subjects and objects are compared at each state transition to determine whether a subject is allowed to access an object. By organizing the access classes in the form of a mathematical structure called a lattice, a wide range of potential policies can be supported. The lattice defines the relations among access classes, allowing us to determine whether one access class is less than, greater than, equal to, or disjoint from (not comparable to) another. Examples of environments in which access classes form a lattice include the privacy protection compartments of medical data, financial data, criminal records, and the hierarchical government security classifications.

The protection policy enforced by a security kernel is encapsulated in a set of mathematical rules that constitute a formal security model.

Of the model's nondiscretionary rules, two are fundamental. The first, called the *simple security condition*, states that a subject cannot observe the contents of an object unless the access class of the subject is greater than or equal to the access class of the object. This simple security condition prohibits users from directly viewing data that they are not entitled to see.

The second basic nondiscretionary rule, the *-property* (pronounced "star" property) rule, helps to prevent all illicit indirect viewing of objects. It stipulates that a subject may not modify an object unless that object's access class is greater than or equal to the access class of the subject.

The purpose of the *-property is to explicitly address the problem of "Trojan horse" software, which as the name implies is software that appears legitimate but in fact is designed to do something illicit in addition to its normal function. For example, any generally used software utility, such as a text editor or compiler, has the potential for accessing a user's files in a manner the user might not have intended. A Trojan horse implanted in a text editor could make illicit copies of a user's file and store the information in a file belonging to an unauthorized user, all unbeknownst to the original user.

The Trojan horse problem is serious when highly sensitive information is involved, especially on large systems where the programmer responsible for a given utility program cannot always be determined. A person is, of course, charged with the responsibility for maintaining the confidentiality of information, but a computer utility such as a text editor cannot necessarily be given the same trust. The reason is that we may have no practical way to determine whether the utility contains a Trojan horse.

With the *-property, information cannot be compromised through the use of a Trojan horse. Under this rule, the program operating on behalf of one user cannot be used to pass information to any user having a lower or disjoint access class.

The simple security condition and the *-property are primarily to prevent the unauthorized disclosure of information, but the model also includes integrity properties to protect information from improper alteration. Integrity rules prevent subjects with a given integrity class from modifying objects of higher integrity or being affected by objects of lower integrity.

The nondiscretionary rules of the model do not provide a protection policy that distinguishes different users within the same access class. Discretionary rules are included in the model to provide that type of protection policy. The discretionary rules of the Bell and LaPadula model allow authorized users and programs to arbitrarily grant and revoke access to information based on user names or other information. Since discretionary controls are more or less arbitrary, we cannot make very many absolute statements about the movement of the information. In particular, the Trojan horse attack is more difficult to address under these controls than under nondiscretionary controls. Therefore, the latter, being much stricter, always takes precedence.

In addition to the threats of improper disclosure or modification of information, we have a threat known as *denial of service* (e.g., crashing the system or making it unresponsive), which most security models such as the Bell and LaPadula model do not explicitly address. While a kernel-based system is likely to withstand this threat at least as well as any conventional system, rules dealing with denial of service are more difficult to formalize in a model.

Faithful implementation. The mathematical model aids in identifying the types of functions that a kernel should provide. It does not, however, specify the design for the applications interface to the kernel. To bridge the gap between model and implementation, the development process must be broken into small steps. One common technique is to apply a hierarchy of abstract specifications to the design of the security kernel. For each step, it is important to demonstrate security so that we have confidence in the security of the final system.

We can use numerous formal and informal methods to demonstrate security with varying degrees of confidence—the reference monitor concept does not mandate any one approach. However, early in the formulation of the kernel approach, we recognized that formal specification and mathematical verification had the potential for providing real proof that the implementation of the kernel faithfully followed the rules of the model. These formal methods have since been applied to various degrees in demonstrating the correspondence between the model, the hierarchy of specifications, and the high-level language implementation (Figure 2).

As with any operating system design effort, preparing the specifications is a creative activity, molded by the particular design and security goals of the system. The most abstract kernel specification defines all the kernel's interface characteristics. We can use this high-level specification to judge functionality as well as to demonstrate that the interface preserves the rules of the model. Once the interface functionality is specified abstractly and its security properties are precisely established, we can expand the functionality by gradually introducing more implementation detail. This process is done without affecting the validity of the security properties already established. (For examples of systems that use formal specification techniques, see the article by Landwehr in this issue.)

Three classes of formal verification techniques have been applied to different stages of kernel development (Figure 2), and several techniques are available within each class. The first class is used to prove that the kernel's intended behavior, as described in the formal high-level interface specification, is secure with respect to the policy model. One common technique, *security flow analysis,* is a relatively simple way to identify and analyze information flows in a specification.[7] Note that only the security of the interface specification must be demonstrated, not the more difficult problem of its functional ''correctness,'' since functional properties, most of which are not security related, are not addressed by the model.

In the second class of formal verification techniques, we verify the correspondence or correctness of mappings between any intermediate specifications in the hierarchy and the interface specifications. Finally, a third class of verification techniques, the most traditional way to prove correctness, shows that the kernel implementation corresponds to its specification.

Cheheyl et al. have documented a survey of current verification systems covering most of these techniques,

along with their application to Department of Defense security policy.[8] Walker et al. describe an example of a formal specification and verification.[9]

Implementation considerations

To successfully realize a kernel-based system, we must take into account architectural and engineering considerations that may not be encountered in the development of other systems. Although the kernel approach can be applied to all types of systems, these considerations are best illustrated in the context of a general-purpose operating system with online, interactive users (Figure 3). The kernel, as already noted, provides a relatively small and simple subset of the operating system functions. The kernel primitives are the interface of this subset to the rest of the operating system (generally referred to as the supervisor). In turn, the supervisor primitives provide the general-purpose operating system functions used by the applications.

Kernel/supervisor trade-offs. An operating system is usually broken down into functional areas, such as process management, file system management for segments, and I/O control. Within each area, some functions are clearly security relevant and must be in the kernel, while some are not. The rules of the policy model help to clearly identify which functions are security relevant.

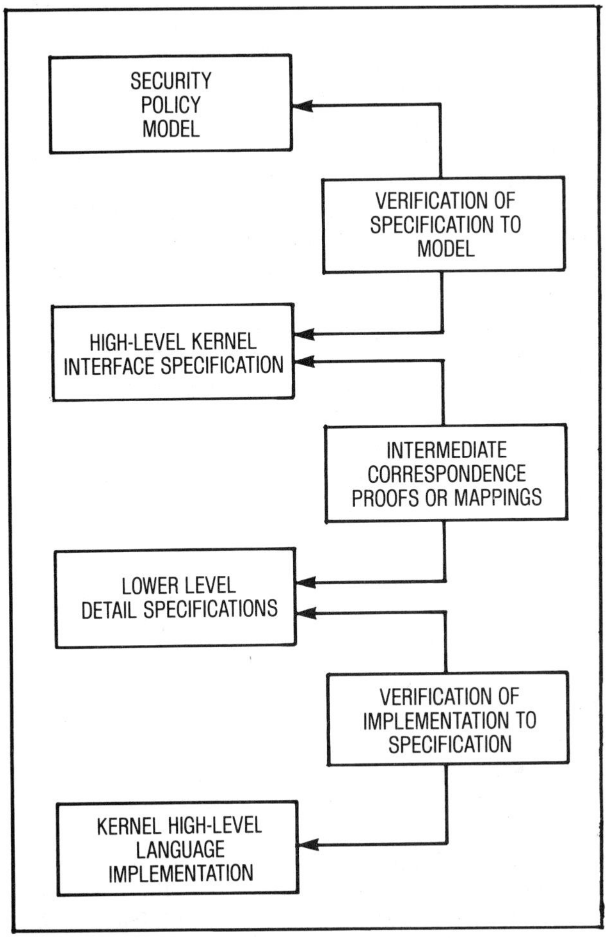

Figure 2. Development and verification hierarchy.

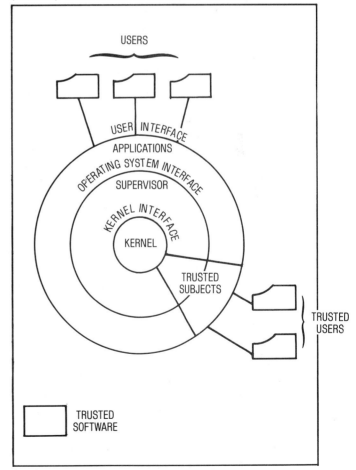

Figure 3. Structure of a kernel-based operation system.

The kernel must handle the parts of an operating system that manage resources, such as memory and disk space, shared by multiple users. These parts are in the kernel because the model requires that these resources be virtual to hide their location from untrusted (nonkernel) software. The functions that provide useful common utilities but do not manage anything shared among users and those that address denial of service are outside the scope of the security policy and can generally be in the supervisor.

In practice, we can usually apply the details of the model and a particular security policy to determine what must be in the kernel and what must be in the supervisor. However, issues such as performance and functionality often force us to consider engineering problems that necessitate putting non-security-related functions in the kernel. We might have trouble, for example, separating the operating system's file-name interpretation mechanism, which may not be security relevant, from the kernel's file management system. We must constantly make trade-offs among performance, functionality, and complexity when designing a kernel-based system. Trade-offs are especially important when the system is emulating a previously existing operating system whose functions may not be easy to reallocate.

The kernel must handle the parts of an operating system that manage resources shared by multiple users.

Trusted subjects. Most systems require a security policy that is more specifically tailored to their needs than that defined by the basic security model. This tailored policy is generally exercised on a limited basis for infrequent operations and may apply only under special circumstances or to a special class of users. A kernel that implements such an extended policy will usually provide a set of interfaces that can be invoked only by certain *trusted subjects* (Figure 3), that is, software it recognizes via some internal identifier, such as a privilege indicator. When a running program has such privileges, it may be able to perform actions not permitted by the access checks built into normal kernel functions.

Trusted subjects usually perform system maintenance and are needed to control the access policy that the kernel enforces for untrusted subjects. For example, a security officer must be given access to maintain the table that the kernel uses to specify access classes of users. Software the security officer uses for this purpose is a trusted subject. Sometimes normal users invoke certain trusted subjects to perform security-sensitive functions. For example, since the basic security model does not allow an untrusted subject to lower the access class of information, the occasional need for downgrading a segment that a user accidentally overclassifies is satisfied by providing a trusted subject for the user.

Trusted subjects are often implemented as asynchronous processes, called trusted processes, or as extensions of the kernel itself, called trusted functions. Regardless of the implementation technique, trusted subjects must adhere to the same engineering principles as the kernel if the security policy is to be correctly implemented. Other than the implementation technique, the only difference is the specific security policy enforced.

Hardware/software features. The kernel approach may need considerable hardware support to achieve adequate performance. The amount of hardware support is bounded by two extremes. At one extreme, the kernel can be built entirely in software on any conventional machine so that the kernel runs as a pure interpreter, executing and checking every user instruction and permitting no direct user execution of hardware instructions. In this case, no particular security demands are placed on the hardware architecture other than the requirement to execute the kernel software correctly. At the other extreme, all the kernel functions can be implemented as hardware instructions; in this case the hardware architecture would be completely responsible for security. As with the supervisor/kernel trade-offs, the specific choices are heavily influenced by the trade-offs among complexity, size, and performance. In this article, we examine only a pragmatic middle ground, one close to a traditional view of the functional division between the hardware and the operating system software.

The hardware features and software mechanisms necessary for a kernel-based operating system to perform adequately are sophisticated but not exotic. The specific hardware features desirable for a kernel-based system are provided in many (but by no means all) modern computer architectures, from microprocessors to mainframes. Several past and ongoing kernel implementations have resulted in significant performance degradation from the lack of adequate hardware. However, with appropriate hardware, we see no reason that a kernel-based operating system should perform any worse than a non-kernel-based system with similar capabilities. R. Schell gives a specific example of the features necessary to implement a microprocessor-based kernel in another article in this issue.[10]

There are four general architectural areas in which specific hardware and software mechanisms have proved useful or necessary to support a kernel-based general-purpose operating system (for special-purpose kernels, some of these mechanisms might be less appropriate):

- explicit processes—efficient support for multiple processes (multiprogramming) and interprocess communication;
- memory protection—large segmented virtual memory, access control to memory, and explicitly identified objects;
- execution domains—minimum of three states or domains (user, supervisor, and kernel) and efficient transfer of control between domains; and
- I/O mediation—control of access to I/O devices, to external media, and to memory by I/O processors.

Although most of these mechanisms are familiar internal components of many current commercial operating systems, their impact is quite hidden from the users, and they are usually of interest only to system designers.

Explicit processes. The reference monitor's notion of a subject is traditionally realized in most operating systems as a process that operates as a surrogate for some user. The user's identification and access class must therefore be represented within the system as nonforgeable (and unalterable) identifiers tied to each process. The identifiers become the basis for making access decisions with respect to discretionary and nondiscretionary policies.

By *process* we mean the activity of a processor carrying out the computation specified by a program, the processor being either a computation or I/O processor. For information protection to be meaningful, an on-line environment must of course include multiple users, so the kernel must support multiple simultaneous processes. This requirement mandates that the kernel save and restore the representation of a process in execution, otherwise known as the state of the processor. Depending on when a process is allowed to be suspended, this state may include the internal state of the CPU, the user-visible processor registers, or merely the instruction counter. In addition, the architecture must provide a means of saving and restoring a definition of the accessible information (i.e., the address space) distinct for each process. The address space is typically defined by a set of descriptors, as we discuss later in the section on memory protection.

Because of the multiplicity of simultaneous processes, a kernel-based operating system typically has a large number of process switches, and an efficient process-switching mechanism is desirable. This mechanism can be supported in a number of ways: we can use high-speed memory instead of explicit processor registers, or we can load and store processor registers as a block or even have several independent sets of registers in the processor. The efficient switching of address spaces can be aided by using a descriptor base or root register instead of copying memory descriptor tables, or by simultaneously retaining several sets of descriptors.

In addition to the multiprogramming support, we need direct support for interprocess communication. Particularly for multiprocessor configurations, we need a race-free communication mechanism (e.g., read-alter-rewrite memory access) as well as a processor-to-processor interrupt capability. Note that an I/O initiation instruction is primarily a mechanism for directing an interrupt to an I/O processor. More sophisticated hardware mechanisms, such as operations to assist process synchronization, can also contribute to kernel simplicity and performance.

Memory protection. The reference monitor abstraction of a storage object is usually realized by memory, and this realization is constrained by the principle of completeness identified earlier. Clearly, some fundamentally interpretive mechanism is needed to completely mediate all access to memory. Virtual memory is commonly used to accomplish the needed mediation. In a virtual memory system, some form of descriptor is used to control the access to memory. There must be no way outside the kernel for a process to access memory without using a descriptor.

With a reference monitor, all information within the system must be represented in distinct, identifiable objects. In all but the simplest case, the virtual address space of a process includes more than one object, each with distinct logical attributes such as size, access mode, and access class. This logically distinct memory is commonly called a *segment*.

With a reference monitor, all information within the system must be represented in distinct, identifiable objects.

Hardware-supported segmentation of virtual memory is the underlying mechanism to support this concept. Each segment is identified by a descriptor that controls the virtual-address-mapping hardware. The descriptor contains some logical attributes as well as a physical base address and a segment size (or bound) to distinguish each segment. Complete access mediation is provided, since for each access to virtual memory the hardware must interpret the relevant descriptor.

Two factors are quite important in supporting an efficient and simple secure system: (1) each process should be able to have a relatively large number of independent segments, and (2) any segment should have a wide range of possible sizes. These requirements tend to result in a large number of segment descriptors for each process. A high-speed associative cache memory can be useful to speed address translations without requiring software to reload descriptors on each process switch.

Architectures in which a process's view of virtual memory is not segmented but is simply a large, linear address space, with no portion shared by other processes, are often compatible upgrades to older systems without virtual memory. Although kernel-based systems can be and have been built on such architectures, considerable flexibility (and resulting performance) can be lost because of the inability to directly address different segments with differing access rights.

To implement typical discretionary and nondiscretionary access policies of the reference monitor, the segment descriptor must support distinct access modes of at least null, read, and read-write for each segment.

Overall system performance can often be enhanced by including a referenced and modified flag for each block of physical memory. This enhancement permits more efficient operating system memory management schemes when information must be moved back and forth between primary memory and secondary storage.

The segment descriptors are, of course, managed by the security kernel software, although much of the actual mediation of the reference monitor is performed by the address-mapping hardware. Since address mapping requires an examination of the descriptors, the hardware can conveniently check access using information in the descriptor at the same time with no additional performance penalty. The security kernel software enforces reference monitor authorizations by controlling the access mode specified in the descriptors for all segments of each process.

Even if all access to segments is fully controlled, the kernel designer may encounter a major pitfall: the possibility that information will be leaked unintentionally through the use of *control information*. Control information consists of items that are not memory objects in the usual sense but are shared repositories of information. They include items maintained within the kernel database, for example, file names and attributes, system variables such as the number of users logged in, and the sizes of message queues. Although these items are not within the hardware-supported virtual address space, they are objects to the reference monitor, and thus the kernel must mediate access to each of them in the same way that it controls access to segments. Access to most of these items is usually done interpretively through explicit kernel calls, rather than through hardware.

Any accidental leakage of information through the use of control information should, of course, be detected by appropriate design and verification techniques. The pitfall is the possibility that some fundamental aspect of the design is based on (and in fact may depend on) this leakage. This issue must be recognized early in the design because at a late stage of system development, the removal of undesired leakage channels can be one of the most difficult tasks a kernel designer can encounter.

Execution domains. Execution domains are essential to the isolation and protection of the security kernel mechanism. The total address space of a process includes the programs and data of the security kernel, since these must clearly be accessible when the security kernel functions are invoked. Yet, the kernel also requires a distinct execution domain so that a process can access some objects (most notably the segment descriptors) only when executing in the kernel itself.

The simplest and most common domain structure is made up of two hierarchical domains implemented by privileged and nonprivileged modes of processor execution. The privileged domain contains only the kernel. Although two domains are sufficient to protect the kernel, the supervisor would have to reside in the same domain as the applications software—a serious limitation. Operating systems traditionally reside in the privileged domain while the user applications do not. Thus, to retain the benefits of separating the operating system from the user, we need a minimum of three hierarchical domains: kernel, supervisor, and user.

More general nonhierarchical domains could be useful in simplifying the design of a kernel-based system. Domain and capability machines fall into this class. Work on using a more general domain structure for kernel development is now in the research stage.

A process typically experiences a large number of calls to the kernel and supervisor, so we want mechanisms that ease the transfer of program control between domains. Entrance into the most privileged domain must, of course, be limited to well-defined entry points. A common means of limiting entrance is by using a system or supervisor fault or trap that transfers control to a known location. However, kernel simplicity and efficiency are improved if the hardware supports multiple entry points in a fashion more like a procedure call, so that each kernel function has a distinct entry point. The hardware should also support some form of argument validation (i.e., checking the validity of arguments passed by the application or supervisor to the kernel) and stack management for cross-domain calls. The Multics system employs a particularly elegant and efficient hierarchical domain architecture with domain-crossing hardware.[11]

Input/output mediation. I/O in most machines can take place in two fundamentally different ways. The simplest way, often called "programmed I/O," requires software to explicitly execute an I/O instruction to transfer each byte or word of information between an I/O device and a register or memory. We must therefore consider I/O devices as objects within the reference monitor framework; thus the kernel must control access to these devices. Typically, we would restrict the use of I/O instructions to the most privileged software domain (i.e., the kernel), and allow user and supervisor software to invoke kernel functions to perform I/O on their behalf.

A more complex architecture for I/O provides independent I/O processors that, once activated by the central processor, asynchronously transfer information between devices and memory. This transfer of information is specified by an explicit I/O program residing in memory or an implicit program (one built into the I/O processor) that is given parameters such as buffer and device addresses. The kernel must consider I/O programs in execution, or *I/O processes,* as subjects, and it must therefore control access to memory by I/O processors in the same manner as it controls access to memory by the CPU. As in programmed I/O, the conventional approach to handling this access control is for hardware to limit initiation of I/O processors (e.g., execution of a start I/O request) to the most privileged domain. I/O requests made by a user are in the form of kernel function calls. These calls cause a check of the I/O program or parameters to ensure that both the I/O devices and memory segments containing the I/O buffers are accessible to the user. The I/O processor itself, usually lacking multiple domains, typically works entirely in the kernel domain and uses physical memory addresses supplied by the kernel. Consequently, the kernel must often translate virtual addresses in the I/O program to physical addresses. Because of the sophisticated capabilities of some I/O processors, kernel checking of user-defined I/O programs can be a complex function.

Because of the complexity of handling I/O, a hardware architecture that allows direct user or supervisor domain access to I/O is desirable. Such an architecture would provide some form of descriptor to control access to the devices, in a manner similar to the use of memory descriptors. In addition, for the I/O processor to effectively operate outside the kernel by accessing virtual memory on behalf of the user, we need descriptor-controlled access to memory by the I/O processor. Such a capability is provided by the Scomp as discussed in the article by Fraim, which appears in this issue.

A careful concept of I/O operation should be part of the kernel development effort. We need to clearly distinguish between two device types: (1) external I/O involving devices such as terminals, local printers, and tape drives, which are effectively accessed by only one user at a time, and (2) internal I/O that includes devices such as disk drives and their storage media, which the kernel must manage because they can access information common to multiple users. For all removable I/O media on external devices capable of accessing information with varying access classes, we need a trusted labeling technique to ensure that the access class of the medium is correctly marked, or that some operator is in control of the access class of information accessible to the device. Labels can include, for example, nonforgeable banner sheets on printer output and operator interaction with the kernel for mounting tapes and removable disks.

Verification. Most kernel developments to date have been accompanied by some degree of formal verification. Some of the early promises of formal verification were overstated—verification has turned out to be more difficult than we expected.[12] Formal verification of a kernel involves problems of program correctness, and we are still quite a long way from being able to prove the correctness of a large computer program. Because formal verification technology has not fully matured, we need to understand its current capabilities before defining requirements for a major kernel development. Unrealistic expectations for verification can turn a practical development effort fully within the bounds of current technology into a research effort that could consume unlimited resources.

Many traditional nonmathematical methods such as structured design and testing can contribute to the overall confidence in the security of the kernel. With realistic goals, formal verification can enhance these traditional techniques and play a major and useful part in the kernel development process. Of the various stages of kernel development to which verification can be applied, the greatest degree of success has been obtained in specification verification. We have several techniques for verifying a formal specification against its model, and some of these, such as the flow analysis method mentioned earlier, have become almost routine. We can also verify correspondence between intermediate levels of specifications. However, even if there is no intent to complete a full mathematical proof, we still have the rigorous review, documentation, and kernel-development guidelines that most verification methodologies enforce. These alone will ensure a more secure and reliable system.

Although total confidence in the security of a system is not yet achievable, we can specify degrees of confidence in the security of different systems. The Department of Defense has recently promulgated a set of *Trusted Computer System Evaluation Criteria*[13] that define several distinct evaluation classes of progressively increasing confidence. These criteria explicitly recognize the value of following most of the security kernel design principles we have identified, yet they have widespread applicability to most types of systems, kernel-based or not.

The security kernel design approach is the most promising methodology currently available that can provide both the internal security and the functional capabilities that many of today's computer systems need. This approach is based on a firm foundation and will support a wide range of commercial and governmental information protection policies. The kernel provides security controls that are effective against most internal attacks—including many that kernel designers never considered. Bugs of malicious software contained in applications, or even in the operating system, cannot cause unauthorized access to information.

The overall trend in hardware and software technology for computer systems is toward greater application of the principles and features applicable to the kernel approach. We have in fact recently seen the emergence of a security kernel in a commercial product (Honeywell Scomp). The required hardware and operating system technology is thus clearly within practical application. ■

References

1. B. W. Lampson, "Protection," *Proc. Fifth Princeton Symp. Information Sciences and Systems,* Mar. 1971, pp. 437-443.

2. L. Fraim, "Scomp: A Solution to the Multilevel Security Problem," *Computer,* Vol. 16, No. 7, July 1983.

3. C. Landwehr, "The Best Technologies for Computer Security," *Computer,* Vol. 16, No. 7, July 1983.

4. R. M. Needham and R. D. H. Walker, "The Cambridge CAP Computer and Its Protection System," *ACM Operating Systems Review,* Vol. II, No. 5; also in *Proc. Sixth Symp. Operating System Principles,* Nov. 1977, pp. 1-10.

5. D. E. Bell and L. J. LaPadula, "Computer Security Model: Unified Exposition and Multics Interpretation," tech. report ESD-TR-75-306, AD A023588, The Mitre Corporation, Bedford, Mass., June 1975.

6. K. G. Walter et al., "Structured Specification of a Security Kernel," *Proc. 1975 Int'l Conf. Reliable Software,* IEEE Cat. No. 75CH0940-7CSR, Los Angeles, Calif., Apr. 1975, pp. 285-293.

7. J. K. Millen, "Operating System Security Verification," *Case Studies in Mathematical Modeling,* W. E. Boyce, ed., Pitmann Publishing, Marshfield, Mass., 1981, pp. 335-386.

8. M. H. Cheheyl et al., "Verifying Security," *ACM Computing Surveys,* Vol. 13, No. 3, Sept. 1981, pp. 279-339.

9. B. J. Walker et al., "Specification and Verification of the UCLA Unix Security Kernel," *Comm. ACM,* Vol. 23, No. 2, Feb. 1980, pp. 118-131.

10. R. R. Schell, "The Structure of a Security Kernel for a Multiprocessor Microcomputer," *Computer,* Vol. 16, No. 7, July 1983.

11. M. D. Schroeder and J. H. Saltzer, "A Hardware Architecture for Implementing Protection Rings," *Comm. ACM,* Vol. 15, No. 3, Mar. 1972, pp. 157-170.

12. "Verification of Secure Software Systems," *Proc. 1980 Symp. Security and Privacy,* IEEE Cat. No. 80CH1522-2, Apr. 1980, pp. 157-166.

13. *Trusted Computer System Evaluation Criteria,* DoD Computer Security Center, Ft. Meade, Md., Jan. 1983.

Stanley R. Ames, Jr., is guest editor of this special issue on computer security technologies. His photo and biography appear on p. 12.

Morrie Gasser is a group leader at The Mitre Corporation in Bedford, Massachusetts. Since 1971, he has been involved in most aspects of computer security including hardware and software design and implementation, formal specification and verification, and computer security applications. His role at Mitre includes both in-house design and development as well as consulting to the Department of Defense on various research and development programs. Gasser received a BA in physics in 1969 from the University of Chicago.

Roger R. Schell is a colonel in the United States Air Force and is currently assigned as the deputy director of the Department of Defense Computer Security Center, Ft. Meade, Maryland. His interests include operating systems, software engineering, and computer security. From 1978 to 1981, he was associate professor of computer science at the Naval Postgraduate School in Monterey, California. Other experience includes serving as program manager and software engineer for several large military software developments, designing and implementing a dynamic reconfiguration for a commercial operating system, and introducing the security kernel technology.

Schell received a BS in electrical engineering from Montana State College, an MS in electrical engineering from Washington State University, and a PhD in computer science from the Massachusetts Institute of Technology.

An operating system with a security kernel, segmented memory, and multiple processors has been designed for the Intel iAPX 286 microprocessor. Initial performance data show it really works.

A Security Kernel for a Multiprocessor Microcomputer

Roger R. Schell, DoD Computer Security Center

Security kernel technology can provide the technical foundation for a highly reliable method of protecting computerized information. However, to implement a kernel-based operating system for a microcomputer, we face two significant challenges: (1) providing adequate computational resources for applications tasks and (2) developing a clean, straightforward structure whose correctness can be easily reviewed. These were the challenges faced by the Computer Science and Electrical Engineering Departments of the Naval Postgraduate School in Monterey, California. As part of a three-year research project, our task was to explore realizations for microcomputer-based systems needing a high degree of security. The target implementation was the Intel iAPX 286 microprocessor, but running hardware was not available in time, and the Zilog Z8000 and Intel 8086 were chosen as interim implementations.

The systems envisioned emphasized shared file system controllers, signal processors, and a relatively static set of application programs, such as those for network processors. The wide range of required computational capacities led us to conclude that a system with multiple microcomputers must be provided. Our experience during this project, which began in late 1978, showed that the strictly hierarchical (loop-free) module structure provides a series of increasingly capable, separately usable operating system subsets. Performance issues evaluated include process switching, domain changing, and multiprocessor bus contention. Overall, the implementation demonstrated the ability of a modern microcomputer to effectively support the security kernel approach.

Project overview

Security kernel technology (discussed in detail earlier in this issue by Ames et al.[1]) was identified as the only viable approach for achieving the required security.

However, the security kernel approach had previously been applied only to medium- or large-scale processors with supportive hardware features, which in some cases (such as the Scomp*) were specifically designed to support a security kernel. Furthermore, a multiprocessor kernel had never been designed and implemented. Thus, the challenge of this project was to identify a viable security kernel structure for a multiprocessor system using a commercially available microcomputer.

The effort began with the design of a rather general family of secure operating systems not tied to any specific microcomputer hardware. After reviewing available and anticipated processors, we determined that the planned Intel iAPX 286 was the best implementation choice.[3] In fact, its hardware directly supports the processor features identified earlier by Ames as important: explicit processes, memory protection, and execution domains. Unfortunately, as mentioned earlier, running hardware was not available in time for project implementation. Therefore, we chose two specific family members using a less supportive hardware base. The results discussed here are from these two implementations, with emphasis on the kernel rather than the particular application.

A secure archival storage system. The first effort has come to be known as the SASS, or Secure Archival Storage System, project.[4] We chose the Zilog Z8000 microprocessor[5] early in the project because of the protection afforded by its two processor states—the "Normal" and "System" modes—and the imminent hardware memory management unit. The Z8000 was primarily an interim choice to provide hardware support for kernel security experiments, pending the availability of the iAPX 286.

---

*The Honeywell Secure Communications Processor, or Scomp, is discussed earlier in the article by L. Fraim (this issue).[2]

Reprinted from *Computer*, July 1983, pages 47-53. Copyright © 1983 by The Institute of Electrical and Electronics Engineers, Inc.

However, at the outset no bus interface hardware was available to permit a multiprocessor Z8000 configuration.

The SASS was our principal testbed for exploring security, implementation, and single-processor performance issues. Although not fully implemented, the SASS supervisor was designed to provide a comprehensive multiuser, multilevel, secure file-storage system. As designed, the SASS has a Z8000-based single-board computer sharing a single bus with storage and I/O devices. The SASS is designed to interface via bidirectional lines to a number of host systems, as illustrated in Figure 1. The SASS provides each host with a hierarchical file system, which can be used to store and retrieve files and share files with other hosts. This design allows the SASS to serve as a central hub for a data-secure network of computers with diverse security authorization for sensitive information. The SASS provides archival, shared storage while ensuring that each interfaced host processor can access only the information appropriate to its security authorizations.

Real-time image processing. The second effort involved the use of a tightly coupled multiprocessor for processing digitized infrared images in real time.[6] We selected the commercial Intel 16-bit 8612 single-board computer, which is based on the Intel 8086 microprocessor, because its instruction set is directly upward compatible with the iAPX 286. In addition, multiprocessor bus hardware was available as part of the 8612 single-board computer. Although the Intel 8086 provides little hardware support for security, the strong compatibility with the iAPX 286 permits confidence in security, once the design is moved to the iAPX 286.

The image-processing applications run directly on the security kernel, with no additional supervisor support required, because the application programs are basically static. A version of this kernel was completed with fully functional image-processing algorithms using actual (prerecorded) digitized infrared sensor data. In exploring alternatives for parallel processing partitioning, more than 20 cooperating processes have been run in various parallel and pipeline combinations on up to six processors. This experimentation has provided the principal testbed for exploring multiprocessor performance issues.

Design structure

Both the Z8000 and the 8086 implementations are but specific instances of the design for the same general family. For this family of operating systems the security kernel technology has been used not only to effect security but also to provide the underlying organizational framework for the operating system. The development experience has highlighted the importance of several features that are key to this family:

- the pervasive and systematizing impact of the security kernel methodology,
- the design simplicity accompanying a loop-free modularization that is highly compatible with the resource sharing and multiprogramming functions, and
- the significance of a high degree of configuration independence, particularly when using diverse microprocessors for testbed implementations.

Independent of security, this particular kernel structure is attractive as a canonical operating system interface. It appears adequate for a wide range of functionalities and capacities. Although specifically targeted for the iAPX 286, it shows a high degree of independence from hardware idiosyncrasies.

Kernel supervisor partitioning. Members of this operating system family are organized with three distinct extended machine layers (Figure 2): the security kernel, the supervisor, and the applications. The concept of a hierarchy of extended machines is, to be sure, not new; however, the security kernel significantly constrains the organization. In particular, for security reasons, all management of physical resources must be within the kernel itself. Furthermore, confidence is increased by keeping the kernel as small and simple as possible. Consequently, much of what is commonly thought of as the operating system is provided outside the kernel in the supervisor layer.

In the basic design for this family of operating systems, the kernel must provide extended virtual machines that specifically support both asynchronous processes and segmented address spaces. The kernel virtualizes processors, all levels of storage, and I/O, as well as creating virtualized objects—processes, segments, and devices. This "pure" virtual interface makes an attractive basis for canonical operating system features. The supervisor is in turn designed to be built on the kernel, using these virtualized objects to provide the usual functions of an operating system, such as a file system.

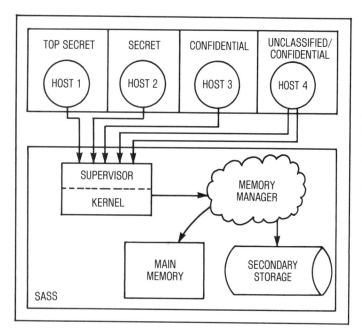

Figure 1. SASS system interfaces.

Both the kernel and the supervisor have certain responsibilities for system security. The kernel manages all physical resources, and the kernel is distributed (included) in the address space of every process. Isolation of the kernel—protection from users and the supervisor—must be provided by hardware-enforced domains. The design of the system is strictly hierarchical (that is, the kernel is more privileged than the supervisor), so the four hierarchical privilege levels provided by the iAPX 286 are an entirely satisfactory domain implementation. In the Z8000 version, the two CPU states are used to provide two domains. By exploiting the available hardware support, this kernel design avoids the need for any trusted processes.

The kernel is responsible for enforcing mandatory access limitations; that is, the kernel provides the mechanism for supporting nondiscretionary security policy. The kernel can support any policy that can be expressed by a lattice of access classes.[7] Every object—process, segment, or device—has a nonforgeable label that denotes its access class. This nondiscretionary security label has been assigned parameters such that exactly one module knows the interpretation of this label in terms of a specific policy. Thus, not only does the kernel support a broad range of security policies but only a single module has to be tailored to support a particular policy.

The design for the SASS supervisor provides the file structure and discretionary security (shared access within the bounds of the kernel's nondiscretionary policy) on the basis of individual user identification provided by the connected host. This discretionary security is completely outside the kernel, in contrast to the Scomp approach.

The SASS supervisor capabilities are achieved by associating two processes with each host link. These processes access the portion of the SASS file structure associated with that host. One of these processes provides I/O transmission and communication link management. The other, a file manager, is responsible for the file system structure for its associated host. Communication between these processes is achieved using shared segments as a mailbox (as is communication among all processes). Synchronization is provided because the kernel includes Reed's advance and await primitives.[8]

The complementary kernel/supervisor approach to security has several advantages for the SASS version. The size and the complexity of the kernel can be minimized, and if we have reliable authentication of the access class for the host, host weaknesses do not impact the reliable enforcement of the nondiscretionary security policy. Furthermore, with this approach, the same security kernel design can be used for the 8086 signal processing version, which needs neither a substantial supervisor nor discretionary security.

The security kernel approach constrains not only the interface but also the detailed design and implementation of internal state variables. One significant problem is preventing indirect information channels between processes with different access classes. This confinement problem can be addressed using essentially the approach detailed by Millen,[9] although without the rigor of a proof. Internal state variables, such as shared resource tables, are assigned an access class, and the design en-

sures that values will not be reflected to processes with an inconsistent access class. The most apparent result is that the success code (returned in response to the invocation of kernel primitives) reflects the state of the per-process virtual resources, not the shared physical resources. The same confinement problem requires a nonexclusionary approach to provide secure synchronization between processes of different access classes. The interprocess communication provided by Reed's event counts and sequencers[6] provides the solution to this "secure reader-writer problem."

Loop-free organization. A principal design property that has helped to keep the security kernel simple and understandable is the loop-free structure of the modules. The loop-free design supports the software engineering concept of "information hiding."[10] As a result, the SASS really does not have any global data structures. The kernel is internally organized into five distinct layers (Figure 3): (1) gate keeper, (2) segment and event managers, (3) traffic controller, (4) memory manager, and (5) inner traffic controller.

In practice we have been quite doctrinaire in enforcing the loop-free structure for the layers of this organization. While many operating systems claim to be modular or well-structured, our experience empirically validates this claim. The upper layers can be literally "peeled off" one at a time by removing the code and data. The remainder can then be loaded and run as a functionally intact, but obviously limited, operating system subset. Since the true substance of the system is in the lower layers, I will describe each layer from the bottom up.

Inner traffic controller. Processor multiplexing has two layers, similar to those proposed for Multics.[11] Each physical processor has a fixed number of "virtual processors" that are multiplexed onto it by the inner traffic controller. Two of these virtual processors are dedicated to system services: an idle process and a memory mana-

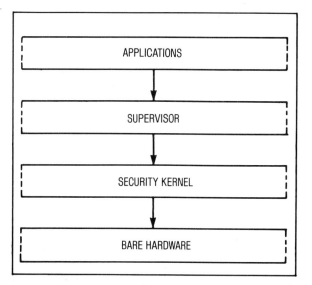

Figure 2: Extended machine layers. The security kernel significantly constrains organization, since for security reasons, all management of physical resources must be within the kernel itself.

ger process to manage the asynchronous access to secondary storage devices. The remaining virtual processors (currently two per physical processor) are available to the traffic controller (layer 3). The inner traffic controller provides primitives for synchronization between virtual processors. In terms of traditional jargon, we mean that the inner traffic controller provides multiprogramming by scheduling virtual processors to run on the CPU they are permanently associated with.

This structure implies that the security kernel is interruptible; that is, it is not a critical section. The inner traffic controller itself, however, is not interruptible. In addition, it provides all the multiprocessing interactions among individual physical processors, using a hardware "preempt" interrupt. An additional benefit of the strict

layering is that the existence of multiple processors is visible only at this lowest level. Thus, the multiprocessing adds no difficulty to the design of the rest of the kernel.

Memory manager. This layer manages the multiplexing of the physical storage resources, such as the disk and core. It also manages the segment descriptors in the iAPX 286 description table for each process. (In the Z8000 design, the memory management unit provides the descriptors.) Most of the functions of this layer are executed by the per-CPU memory manager processes, with synchronization provided by inner traffic controller primitives. The single-board computers have per-processor, local memory that is addressable by only that one processor. Additional global memory is addressable by

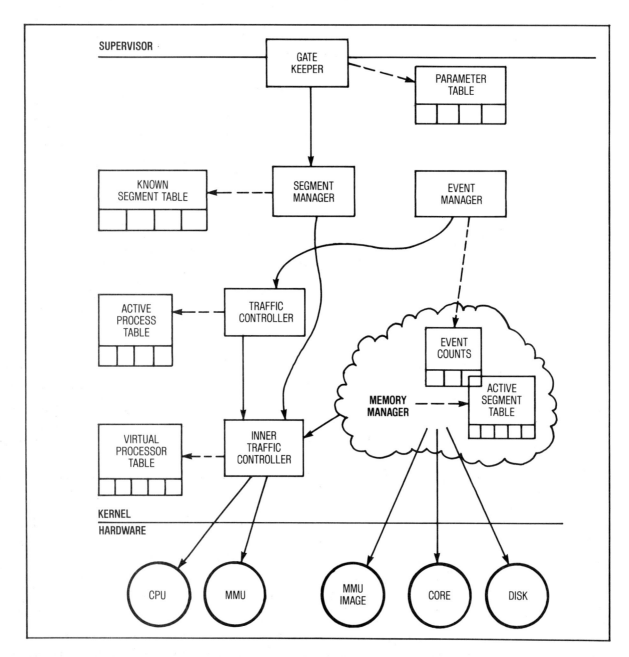

Figure 3. Internal kernel organization. The kernel has five distinct layers. From the top down are the gate keeper, the segment and event managers, the traffic controller, the memory manager, and the inner traffic controller.

all processes. The memory manager ensures that only shared segments (those needed by more than one processor) are in global memory. This policy can require some transfer between local and global memory, but this structure does minimize bus transfer requirements.

Traffic controller. The variable number of processes are multiplexed onto virtual processors defined by the inner traffic controller. Each process has an affinity to the physical processor whose local memory contains a portion of its address space at the time of the process scheduling decision. As indicated earlier, the traffic controller layer uses Reed's advance and await mechanism to provide secure interprocess communication.

Segment and event managers. All entries into the kernel pass through the segment/event manager layer. The explicit nondiscretionary security checks are made at this level by comparing the access class labels of subjects and objects. This layer uses a per-process segment table to convert process local names (segment number) for objects into systemwide names. In this kernel design, each segment has associated with it two event counts and a sequencer; thus, segment numbers also serve as the names used with the advance and await interprocess communication primitives. The segment manager provides for the creation and deletion of segments and their entry into and removal from a process address space.

Gate keeper. A process in the application or supervisor domain invokes a security kernel function using the traditional trap mechanism. A "system call" instruction causes a trap, and a gate keeper handles it. All parameters and return values are "passed by value" to simplify security validation. The instruction of the iAPX 286 for parameter verification provides further assistance in passing a parameter to the kernel. The gate keeper merely calls the particular procedure that corresponds to the requested function.

The implementation experience

The lessons learned up to now fall into three broad categories: the experimental testbed, programming (software engineering) experiences, and performance experiences.

Microprocessor testbed. One important aspect of this research was the actual implementation and testing of the concepts developed. Traditionally, the implementation of multiprocessor structures has been expensive. Today, however, sophisticated microprocessors such as the iAPX 286 are becoming available, which feature multiple domains, advanced segmentation addressing, support of multiprocessor configurations, and a standard bus configuration with peripheral support. With these developments, prototype implementation of advanced operating systems on a microprocessor base is economically feasible. As mentioned earlier, the Z8000 and 8086 processors were used in our testbed as an interim choice in anticipation of the iAPX 286.

In the 8086 kernel design, all the processors share the same bus; each processor is a commercial, single-board computer with on-board RAM. These processors also share a global memory and certain peripheral devices (Figure 4). This multiprocessor configuration was provided using the 8086 processors.

In general, security-kernel-based operating systems find three processor-supported execution domains (operating states) highly desirable—a separate domain for the kernel, supervisor, and applications layers. The Z8000 processor, however, provided only two domains (the "Normal" and "System" processor states).

The Z8000 hardware used for the SASS version was a single-board computer in a standard backplane. This configuration had a significant limitation in that it did not include the hardware memory management unit. Since we had to simulate in software the hardware segmentation, the kernel was not completely protected from the supervisor as the design specified. In spite of these limitations, we found the testbed quite effective as a research vehicle.

Programming experiences. This research effort was highly structured, emphasizing modularity at every opportunity. The software design is strictly "top-down," a matter of good design practice and necessity. Since most of the work was performed by a succession of graduate students, each of whom spent a brief six to nine months in research, the clear definition of distinct software modules has been vital to the success of the effort. We found that this high degree of modularity allowed the students to work on the project with a minimum of startup time, and a maximum of productive effort and learning.

The only access to the functions of the kernel is through the gate keeper. As mentioned before, the SASS supervisor has not been fully implemented. Consequently, the Z8000 kernel is a core-resident implementation that includes a simple external output primitive. To illustrate the nature of the kernel interface, all the kernel calls for the Z8000 kernel are shown in Table 1.

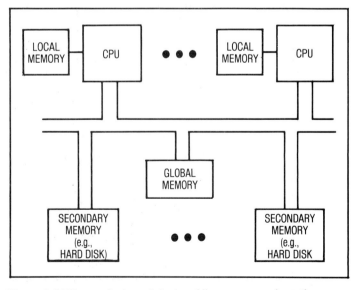

Figure 4. 8086 security kernel design. All processors share the same bus, a global memory, and certain peripheral devices.

The research goals of this project did not include verification methodology. However, we have thought about how the use of formal proof techniques could affect the design. In fact, as an experiment, we prepared a top-level specification of the kernel in a formal specification language, but without the aid of any supporting tools. This experience and the kernel's design to a formal nondiscretionary security model lead us to speculate that the kernel is indeed "verifiable." Verification would not immediately succeed, of course, but any problems discovered by verification would not require major changes to the design.

The actual implementation was essentially a bottom-up procedure, with test harnesses and stubs being written as necessary for testing. The modules were specified in a pseudolanguage resembling current high-level languages. The kernel for the 8086 multiprocessor was coded in PLM-86, a high-level language somewhat similar to PL/I. The high-level language had a definite positive impact on the time required for implementation.

For the Z8000, the modules were coded in PLZ-ASM, the Z8000 structured assembly language. We found that the pseudocode specifications of modules were adequate and that the translation from this code to the structured assembly language was straightforward. The structured assembly language of the Z8000 supported many of the constructs usually thought of as unique to high-level languages, including typed record structures, DO-loops, IF-THEN-ELSE, and CASE. In fact, our programmers thought of this assembly language as a high-level language. Approximately 40 percent of the statements in this implementation are directly equivalent to statements in modern programming languages.

Despite the qualities of the structured assembler, we selected it by default. When the decision was made, the prototype hardware boards were just becoming available and virtually no software support was available. In particular, no high-level language was available. The software environment was by modern standards very primitive, with no tools for operating system development—and it has grown slowly. Yet, this handicap was not significant. The Z8000 kernel was implemented as a core-resident kernel with no secondary storage devices needed to support segmentation. The size of the kernel significantly impacts the difficulty of verifying its correctness. For this implementation, the size of the kernel (Table 2) was considered small.

Performance issues. In programming the kernel, we generally treated performance as a secondary issue, in deference to more basic concerns such as security and modularity. However, we did address performance on a design level where it is strongly related to architectural choices.

Obviously, one basic design choice is the use of multiprocessing as a way to increase processing capacity. However, bus contention is a major performance concern in multiprocessor configurations, since all processors share a single bus. The actual performance for the signal-processing multiprocessor system based on the 8086 is shown in Figure 5 for various percentages of bus use. The figure shows, for example, that if all code and data are located in shared global memory, even two or three processors would saturate the bus. Fortunately, only shared, writable segments need to be in global memory. Our use of a purely virtual, segmented memory permits the kernel to determine exactly which segments are shared and writable. As noted before, the memory mana-

**Table 1.
Z8000 kernel calls.**

NAME	FUNCTION
Segment Manager	
Create _ seg	Create segment
Delete _ seg	Delete segment
Make _ known	Add segment to address space
Terminate	Remove from address space
Sm _ swap _ in	Make addressable in memory
Sm _ swap _ out	Make unaddressable
Event Manager	
Await	Process waits for an event
Advance	Signals occurrence of event
Read	Read value of an event count
Ticket	Obtain next sequencer value
Input/Output	
Sndmsg	Output message on serial link

**Table 2.
Z8000 kernel size.**

MODULE	SIZE (16-bit words) Code	Data
Inner Traffic Controller (includes initialization)	590	268
Memory Manager	742	1289
Traffic Controller	1384	243
Segment and Event Managers	804	---
Gate Keeper	114	---
Total	3634	1800

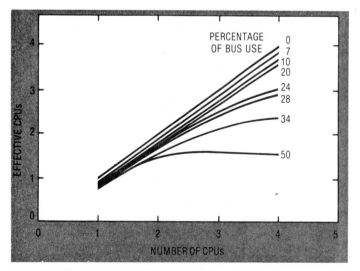

Figure 5. The performance of the multiprocessor system based on the 8086. If all code and data are located in shared global memory, even two processors would saturate the bus.

ger layer totally controls the allocation to local and global memory, and thus markedly controls bus contention by allocating segments to the processor-local memory whenever possible. Our experience with the signal processing applications is quite encouraging in that typically less than 10 percent of processor references are to global memory. Thus, a number of processors can be effectively used.

In the current implementation, we use the "Normal" and "System" modes of the Z8000 hardware, with the "System" mode dedicated to the security kernel. The domain change automatically generates a switch of the stack within the hardware. This automatic switching is particularly important to the efficiency with which we can switch domains while maintaining the integrity of the kernel. The iAPX 286 also provides this support for domain switching.

A process switch is achieved on the Z8000 and 8086 by switching the stack. The kernel saves the process history in the stack, so a process switch requires only the stack exchange. Preempt hardware interrupts between separate physical processors initiate scheduler changes and the associated virtual interrupts to the virtual processors. This sequence is relatively efficient given the hardware architecture. The iAPX 286 provides complete process switching in hardware for even greater efficiency.

The question of process-switching performance is more interesting in the context of processor multiplexing. The multiprogramming time is the interval from the time the inner traffic controller signal primitive is invoked in one virtual processor until a return from a (pending) wait invocation occurs in a different virtual processor. This interval includes both process switching and message passing operations.

For interprocess communication, the read and ticket calls from outside the kernel include a system call through the gate keeper to the kernel, the nondiscretionary security checks, and access to the event-count or sequencer value; however, no process switch is involved. The synchronization time includes the interval from the invocation of the system call for advance in one process until the return from a (blocking) await invocation in a different process. This interval includes the security checks and scheduling of both a virtual and a physical processor.

A set of measurements from the Z8000 implementation is summarized in Table 3. We made no effort to "tune" the system to improve performance, since these results are within our range of expectations for a single-chip microprocessor.

Table 3.
Z8000 performance measurements.

FUNCTION	TIME (milliseconds)
Multiprogramming signal/wait pair	0.5
Synchronization advance/wait pair	2.3
Read (Event count)	0.6
Ticket (Sequencer)	0.6

A modern operating system featuring kernel-based security, segmented memory, and multiple processors has been designed for the Intel iAPX 286 microprocessor. Initial testbed implementations on the Zilog Z8000 and Intel 8086 are finished, and preliminary data on the operating performance of such systems are encouraging. The focus on methodical design has paid off: The implementation of a carefully designed, simple structure using elementary software development tools has proceeded well.

Data gathered suggest that the security kernel is indeed an attractive structure for a modern operating system. A wide range of applications exist where sophisticated operating systems can be implemented on microprocessors, and performance levels are high, particularly when multiple processors are used. ∎

Acknowledgments

I thank Lyle A. Cox for his most helpful participation in the project and his contributions and assistance in the preparation of this paper. The many long hours of creative and dedicated work by the students working on the project is also gratefully acknowledged.

References

1. S. Ames, M. Gasser, and R. Schell, "Security Kernel Design and Implementation: An Introduction," *Computer,* Vol. 16, No. 7, July 1983.

2. L. Fraim, "Scomp: A Solution to the Multilevel Security Problem," *Computer,* Vol. 16, No. 7, July 1983.

3. *Introduction to the iAPX 286,* tech. report 210308, Intel Corporation, Santa Clara, Calif., 1982.

4. R. R. Schell and L. A. Cox, "A Secure Archival Storage System," *Proc. Compcon Fall,* Sept. 1980, pp. 679-682.

5. B. L. Peuto, "Architecture of a New Microprocessor," *Computer,* Vol. 12, No. 2, Feb. 1979, pp. 10-20.

6. R. R. Schell et al., "Processing of Infrared Images by a Multiple Microcomputer System," *Proc. SPIE Symp.,* Vol. 241, 1980, pp. 267-278.

7. D. F. Denning, "A Lattice Model of Secure Information Flow," *Comm. ACM,* Vol. 19, No. 5, May 1976, pp. 236-242.

8. D. P. Reed and R. K. Kanodia, "Synchronization with Eventcounts and Sequencers," *Comm. ACM,* Vol. 22, No. 2, Feb. 1979, pp. 115-124.

9. J. K. Millen, "Security Kernel Validation in Practice," *Comm. ACM,* Vol. 19, No. 5, May 1976, pp. 243-250.

10. D. L. Parnas, "On the Criteria To Be Used in Decomposing Systems into Modules," *Comm. ACM,* Vol. 15, No. 12, Dec. 1972, pp. 1053-1058.

11. M. D. Schroeder, D. D. Clark, and J. H. Saltzer, "The Multics Kernel Design Project," *Proc. Sixth ACM Symp. Operating Systems Principles,* Nov. 1977, pp. 43-56.

Roger R. Schell is a coauthor of an article that appears earlier in this issue. His photo and biography are on p. 22.

ISSUES IN DISCRETIONARY ACCESS CONTROL

Deborah D. Downs, Jerzy R. Rub, Kenneth C. Kung, Carole S. Jordan

Abstract

This paper discusses the types of mechanisms that can be used to implement Discretionary Access Control (DAC). It also covers the access types that can be controlled by a DAC mechanism. and includes a brief discussion of related topics including protected subsystems; administering, auditing, and verifying DAC; and DAC implemented as an add-on to an operating system. Finally this paper discusses how the DAC information presented in this paper will be used by the Department of Defense Computer Security Center in the preparation of a DAC Guideline to aid system designers and developers in their selection of DAC mechanisms.

1. Introduction

One of the features required of a secure operating system is discretionary access control (DAC) which is a means of restricting access to objects based on the identity of subjects and/or groups to which they belong. The controls are discretionary in the sense that a subject with a certain access authorization may, at its discretion, be capable of passing (perhaps indirectly) that access type or a subset on to any other subject. The objective of this paper is to provide information on the various DAC issues that are of concern to computer vendors, system designers and developers.

2. Terminology

Subjects are those entities that initiate activities which cause information to flow between objects. Usually these entities are persons, but processes or devices can also be subjects. Hence, a user who performs any actions on files is a subject; a job, which the user schedules to be run later, is a subject when it is running; and a device such as a power sensing unit which initiates backup routines upon detecting power failures can be a subject. In most interactive systems a user logs on, and a process starts and does work on behalf of the user. The process takes on the attributes of the user, such as access rights, and the process associated with a user is the subject. Generally, subjects are held accountable for the actions that they have initiated, and the audit trail associates with one subject any security relevant action performed on an object.

Objects are those entities that contain or receive information.

Depending on the system, objects may include, but are not limited to, records, blocks, pages, segments, files, directories, directory trees, mailboxes, messages, and programs, as well as bits, bytes, words, fields, processors, communication lines, clocks, and network nodes. Subjects may also be treated as objects. For example, if a process may spawn child processes, those processes may be treated as objects.

In systems where the smallest amount of information that is normally handled as a unit is a file, each file is an object. But if each file can be broken into smaller pieces so that each piece can be individually manipulated (such as segments or pages), then each of these smaller pieces is an object. In addition, if the files are organized into a tree structure, then the directories for these files are also objects. In this guideline, "file" will be used as a generic term for files, segments, etc.

In some systems all the objects are treated logically as files, and DAC is handled by associating the access information with these files. Hence, each of the hardware devices (i.e. disks, terminals, printers) is treated as a file, with access control information associated with it. In order to access any of these devices a subject must have the proper access rights, and the security checking mechanism for the device is the same as the mechanism used for standard files. For example, writing to a terminal involves moving information to the file associated with this terminal. The access control information associated with this file determines which subjects are or are not allowed to write to this terminal. Consistency in handling DAC objects leads to less complexity in the DAC implementation and, therefore, to more assurance in its correct operation.

The number of objects to be protected by the DAC mechanism depends on the environment for which the system is intended. Almost all systems include in their DAC mechanisms files, directories (if the file system is tree structured), communication channels, and devices. General purpose operating systems trying to provide a more complete and user friendly DAC interface also include objects such as mailboxes, messages, and bulletin boards and their entries as objects protected by DAC. Again, the tradeoff is user friendliness and broader security versus the complexity of the DAC mechanism and the difficulty of assuring its correctness.

3. An Inherent Deficiency in Discretionary Access Control

DAC controls restrict a subject's access to a subset of the

Reprinted from *Proceedings of the 1985 Symposium on Security and Privacy,* 1985, pages 208-218. Copyright © 1985 by The Institute of Electrical and Electronics Engineers, Inc.

protected objects on the system. The subject is also restricted to a subset of the possible access types available for those protected objects. The set of objects and access types can change dynamically based on whatever criteria the subject and/or other subjects wish to employ. Criteria such as "need to know" and "who do I like" are equally possible. Access is based entirely on the subject's identity and the mechanism has no knowledge of, and bases no decisions on, the semantics of the data.

Therefore the identity of the subject is crucial, and if actions can be performed using another person's identity, then DAC can be subverted. Thus the basic definition of DAC makes it vulnerable to Trojan Horses[1]. On most systems, any program which runs on behalf of the subject acts with the subject's identity and therefore has all of the DAC access rights of the subject's process.

The software produced by the computer system manufacturer, especially if the system has a high EPL[2] rating, should not contain Trojan Horses. Configuration management, testing, and trusted distribution should assure this. If a trusted user-created source and/or object module has been properly protected by DAC and has not executed in an environment with a Trojan Horse, it will also be free of Trojan Horses. But software written by software houses or by other untrusted users could easily contain Trojan Horses. Software with a Trojan Horse, running on behalf of a subject, not only could access the subject's protected objects, but also could copy the subject's objects (those which have read access) to a data space accessible to the subverter. The Trojan horse could also change the subject's DAC so that the subverter could have continuing access to the subject's protected objects. A Trojan Horse could also append code to all of the subject's executable objects so that, when those objects were executed by another user, the code would give the subverter access to all newly accessible objects and would attach the same code to them. This has been termed a "virus."[3]

The DAC Trojan Horse problem could be restricted in a system that implemented many domains (the set of objects that a subject has the ability to access) or dynamic small domains for each process, such as a capability based system or protected subsystems that supply a domain per process. In most systems today, with only user and supervisor domains, all of a subject's objects are available to a process running on behalf of a subject. If domains were created dynamically for a process, with only the necessary objects available in that domain (implementing the least privilege principle[4]), then a Trojan Horse would be limited to accessing only those objects. In most current general purpose computing environments, DAC cannot protect objects from users who are determined to gain access to them.

4. DAC Mechanisms
In order to implement a complete DAC system the information that is represented by the access control matrix model[5] must be retained in some form. An access control matrix has subjects represented on the rows and protected objects on the columns. The entries in the matrix describe what type of access each subject has to each object. Current operating systems have attempted to retain the access control matrix using either row or column based representations since storing the entire matrix is inefficient because it is sparsely populated. The implementations of row-based representations are, in some form, attaching to the subject a list of accessible objects and include:

- Capabilities

- Profiles

- Passwords.

The column-based representations that in some form attach a list of accessing subjects to the object include:

- Protection Bits

- Access Control Lists.

The following discussion describes each mechanism and presents its pros and cons.

4.1. Capabilities
Capability[6] based systems provide dynamically changeable domains (name spaces) for processes. Ability to access an object is demonstrated when a subject has a capability or "ticket" to the object. This capability contains allowable access rights (e.g., read, write, execute). Capabilities can be added to and deleted from a process during its execution, thereby changing the size of its name space. In some implementations, programs can contain capabilities and capabilities can also be stored in data files. Hardware and software mechanisms or encryption provide protection from alteration. Capabilities can be passed along to other processes and can sometimes be either increased or decreased in scope depending upon the access characteristics they contain. Because capabilities implement dynamic domains, ideally, they can limit the objects accessible to any program to the minimal set necessary for it to accomplish its task. This would limit, to some extent, a Trojan Horse's access to a subject's protected objects and to objects to which the stolen data could be output.

Because the ability to pass capabilities is not controlled by any policy, and because capabilities can be stored in files so that giving access to a file may give access to many other objects, in general one cannot determine for a particular object all the subjects that have access to it. Thus a complete DAC implementation, including revocation and access review, is impossible with capabilities. At this time, few systems have been implemented with capabilities and very few, if any, have attempted to implement a complete DAC mechanism. Some research has been conducted in restricting capabilities by overlaying a DAC mechanism.[7]

4.2. Profiles
Profiles associate a list of protected objects and access rights with each subject. When a subject attempts to access an object, the subject's profile is checked for the required access rights. Three main problems with this mechanism exist: restricting the size of the profiles, distributing access when an object is created or when the access is changed, and determining all the subjects that have access to an object. Since object names are usually not consistent or amenable to grouping, the profile for a subject that has access to many protected objects can get very large and difficult to manage. Also all protected object names must be unique, so fully qualified object names must be used.

Creating, deleting, and changing access to protected objects may require many operations since multiple subjects' profiles may have to be updated. When users create objects and want to give themselves and others access to the object the profiles must be updated in a secure manner. Users cannot be allowed to update their own or other user's profiles directly. CA-Sentinel's DOS/VSE[8] security add-on uses profiles and only allows the security administrator to change the profile. With such an implementation no user, including the creator, would have access to a new object until the security administrator updated the appropriate profiles, since as a general security principle access to an object by a subject must be null unless specific access is granted. Security administrator controlled profiles are extremely restrictive and would not be usable in environments where objects are created and/or access rights are changed frequently.

Timely revocation of access to an object is very difficult unless subjects' profiles are automatically checked on each access to an object. Deleting an object requires some method of determining which subjects have the object in their profile. In general, with profiles as with capabilities, answering the question of who has access to this protected object is very difficult. Since this question is usually important in a secure system and management of profiles is difficult, profiles are deficient as a DAC mechanism.

4.3. Passwords
Password protection of objects attempts to represent the access control matrix by row and involves associating with an object a password that must be presented to the operating system before access is granted. If each subject possesses its own password to each object, then the password is like a ticket to the object, similar to a capability system (except, of course, no dynamic domains exist). Most DAC implementations using passwords allow only one password per object or one password per object per access mode. Passwords on protected objects have been used in IBM's MVS[9] and with other mechanisms in CDC's NOS[10] to implement DAC.

Using a password protected DAC system poses many problems. It is virtually impossible for a user to remember a password for each protected object, especially if they have access to many objects, and when the passwords are stored in programs or files they are vulnerable since no hardware protection is provided. To restrict access to certain access modes requires a password for each combination of access modes. But in most systems that use passwords, access to a protected object is either total or nonexistent. In such implementations revoking a subject's access requires revoking access from all other subjects with similar access and then distributing a new password to those who are to retain access. This procedure becomes almost impossible when passwords are stored in programs or files. To be secure, passwords should be changed periodically, which is very difficult to do in such password protected DAC systems. In systems such as MVS, the default access to a file is unrestricted access. A file is protected only when the password protection is initiated for that file.

If passwords are used as in CDC's NOS to supplement another DAC mechanism they do have one positive aspect. If all objects are protected with different passwords, a Trojan Horse can be restricted to only the objects that are handed to it. An alternative to passwords that has the same problems, but adds extra

protection when a DAC system is not trusted, is the use of encryption to protect objects.

4.4. Protection Bits
Protection bits are an incomplete attempt to represent the access control matrix by column. Implementations include systems such as Unix[11] that use protection bits associated with objects instead of a list of subjects that may access an object. In the Unix case the protection bits indicate a set of access modes for all subjects, a single group and the owner of the protected object. The subject that creates the object is the owner, and ownership can only be changed through superuser privileges. The owner is the only one (besides a superuser) who can change the protection bits. Subjects can belong to more than one group but they can only belong to one group at a time (there is a current active group). The group name (the group in which the owner was active at creation of the object) and the owner name are listed with the protection bits.

The problem with any implementation similar to protection bits is that implementing the access control matrix model is virtually impossible. The system cannot allow or disallow access to a protected object on any single subject basis. Groups set up to specify any needed combination of subjects has been suggested, but the combinatorics of such a solution are impractical. Since groups are controlled by system administrators, such a scheme would certainly require their full time attention. Also, since only one group can be specified per object, different, non-owner subjects cannot be given different access types to an object.

4.5. Access Control Lists
Access Control Lists (ACLs) permit any particular subject to be allowed or disallowed access to a particular protected object. They implement the access control matrix by representing the columns as lists of subjects attached to the protected objects. Each entry in the list is an identification of a subject(s) and its authorized access to the object . The lists do not have to be excessively long if groups and wild cards are used.

Within the current technology, ACLs are the best way to implement a DAC mechanism. ACLs are the only mechanism that allows inclusion and exclusion of an individual subject. Therefore the following discussion of ACLs is more detailed concerning options than the previous sections. Also the discussion of DAC access types will be couched in terms of ACLs.

4.5.1. Groups
Groups are a mechanism for representing sets of subjects. In the ACL, multiple subjects can be identified by a group name. The ACL is sorted so that access identified by specific subject-id is ordered before access identified only by group. If more specific subject identification exists, it is used to compute access. Before implementing a group mechanism, the designers must decide what the groups are to represent. A group can be a shorthand way of referring to a set of subjects, an accounting mechanism, a structuring mechanism for the file system, a method of grouping project work, a means of identifying and restricting the accessible objects (implementing the least privilege principle), or a combination of these and other concepts.

Honeywell's Multics[12] is an example of a system that uses groups to represent projects, for structuring the file system, to implement the least privilege principle and for accounting. Multics implements a group mechanism (called projects) that allows subjects to be active in only one group at a time, although they can be members of many groups. Several reasons exist for this requirement. Since Multics uses a group mechanism for accounting and defining the storage hierarchy, allowing only one active group simplifies the algorithm for determining whom to charge for computer time and where in the storage hierarchy segments are to be searched for and stored. Allowing a subject only one active group also simplifies access decisions. A subject could belong to two groups that have different access rights to the same object. In the worst case, one group could have null access to the object, while the other had full access to the object. If the subject has only one active group at a time, decisions are not required. Changing a subject's active group on Multics requires a log out and a new log on because the process' environment must be reset. Maybe the most important reason to have only one active group is to implement the least privilege principle. When a subject logs on to a particular project, the subject is restricted to only the objects accessible to the user by subject-id or through the project group-id. At best, only the objects necessary to do that project's work are accessible. To work on another project requires essentially a new log on and a change of reference. Unfortunately in Multics, since projects are also associated with the accounting and file system, they may tend to be of larger granularity than desired for least privilege.

If groups are used only as a shorthand way of referring to a set of subjects, an efficient implementation of groups allows subjects to always be active in all groups in which they have membership. In other words, to specify an active group or to default to an active group at log on is not necessary, and if the subject has membership in any group on an ACL, it always has that access right. The decision as to what access should be given when the subject has current membership in multiple groups which have different access rights should be based on the rights available by changing active groups on a Multics-like system. The union of the access from all group memberships, with null access treated as the empty set, should be given to the subject. Therefore if one group has null access and another has read, the subject should be given read access to the object. If the system supports other negative access modes, the decision process becomes more complicated. Implementing groups with this mechanism does result in some access rights being different from a Multics-like system. If a subject is a member of both group A, which has read access to object 1, and group B, which has write access to object 1, under the Multics-like system the subject could never read and write the object at the same time. However the subject could copy the object and then give both groups read and write access to the copy. On the other hand, in a system with multiple groups active for access, the subject would be given read and write access to the object. Using this method also means that after unsuccessfully checking for the subject-id on the ACL, all of the group entries must be compared to the list of groups of which the subject is a member.

In a DAC implementation where subjects can have active membership in many groups at once, the group mechanism could still be used for accounting and/or storage hierarchy management by specifying a specific group for only those purposes. Such a change in a Multics-like mechanism (still restricting a subject to only one active group at a time for the least privilege principle) would allow for a more flexible use of groups with a finer granularity.

The Apollo's Domain[13] system has a multiple, hierarchical group mechanism. The ACL entry has the form "subject-id.project.organization.node." As in Multics, if the ACL specifies access rights for the subject only (subject-id.*.*.*), then all other group access rights are ignored. This allows inclusion and exclusion of any single subject. In the Apollo's Domain system, as with Multics, if a subject is not on the ACL by subject-id, but is a member of a group that is specified on the ACL with no subject-id (*.project-id.*.*), the group rights are used, and organization and node memberships are not examined. But with Domain, if the subject is not identified by subject-id or group-id and the ACL contains an entry that specifies the subject's organization or organization and node (*.*.organization.* or *.*.organization.node), the subject will be allowed the specified access. The same process follows for the node entry in the ACL. Multiple group mechanisms add more complexity that may facilitate administrative control of a system, but do not affect the basic utility of a DAC mechanism.

Controlling the creation of groups is important, since becoming a member of a group can change the ability to access many objects. In many systems, e.g., Multics, a subject must be a member of at least one group. One detriment of any group mechanism is that changing the members of a group results in changing the effective access granted by every ACL containing that group name (usually an unknown set). Creation of groups should be only a Systems Administrator function or be distributed as a Project Administrator type function. Problems result from allowing all subjects to create groups and then be "owner" of that group. Subjects could choose group names that would mislead other subjects that wish to use that group on their ACL (e.g., "Top Secret"). Subjects should not be allowed to list the members of groups because of possible covert channels and privacy; therefore it is difficult to determine which group is the correct one to use. Group names and subject-ids must be controlled to prevent their re-use. Re-use of a subject-id or group name could result in unexpected access to objects.

Performance considerations exist in the design of the group mechanism. If groups proliferate and all groups on the ACL must be searched for the subject's membership, keeping a list of group memberships with the subject will probably be necessary. Otherwise a performance price is paid for searching the ACL for the subject's membership whenever the file is opened.

4.5.2. Wild Cards

A simple wild card mechanism allows the substitution of one or more characters where the wild card is specified. In ACLs wild cards can be used in two basic ways. In the first, the entire subject-id or group is replaced when the wild card is specified. For example in Multics, an ACL entry of "*.DODCSC" gives access to any subject who is a member of the DODCSC group. An ACL entry of "Downs.*" gives Downs access, no matter in what group the subject Downs is currently active . An ACL entry of "*.*" gives access to any subject in any group. The exclusion capability is possible by specifying a subject or group with an access type of "no-access." The group and wild card mechanisms allow the ACL list to be kept to a reasonable size. In fact, studies on the Multics system on the ARPAnet at MIT showed that the average ACL length was about 3-4 entries, and only 2% of the ACLs had over 10 entries, but some of the ACLs had as many as 200 entries. On a system where the use of groups was not restricted by requiring that only one group be active or by accounting and storage system considerations, as it is in Multics, the very large ACLs are not necessary.

The other use of wild cards is to allow the wild card to substitute for a portion of the subject-id or group name. For example, "Dwo*" could allow all subjects access whose subject-id began with Dwo (e.g. Dwons, Dwo, Dwo111111). In some systems, this use of the wild card substitutes for a group mechanism. Effective use of this wild card mechanism requires subject-ids to be chosen so that the group is part of the name. For example, all members of the security project could be given subject-id's that end with "sec" and the ACL could contain "*sec." Obviously choosing subject-ids. allowing membership in multiple groups. and revoking someone's membership from one group become very complicated operations. Sorting the ACL entries to place the most restrictive entries first requires a complicated algorithm and rigid subject-id specification rules. If a group mechanism is available, allowing wild cards to substitute for particular characters does not add functionality and only complicates the use of the DAC mechanism. Therefore, the use of wild cards should be restricted to complete substitution for a subject-id or group name.

4.5.3. Default ACLs
Many side issues exist with regard to the implementation of ACLs. Default ACLs are usually necessary to ensure user friendliness in the DAC mechanism. At the very least, in an owner type system when an object is created by a subject, the subject should be placed on its ACL by default. Some of the other possible default mechanisms include a system-wide default, a subject-associated default, or, if the file structure is a tree, a default associated with the directory.

A system-wide default cannot be tuned to allow access judiciously, but can be used as the default in cases where no other default has been specified. A system-wide default might give access only to the creating subject. A subject-associated default works well on a system with a flat file structure. When a subject is first entered on the system, its default ACL is specified.

For tree-structured file systems, a default(s) associated with the directory is efficient. If the subject organizes its directory structure to represent project work or areas of interest, then the ACLs for all objects in a sub-tree are similar. One default ACL in the directory is for children that are files. For children that are directories, either a separate sub-directory default ACL is specified or the default ACL has to be stated explicitly by the subject. Otherwise, unless care is taken using this mechanism, subjects with access to the root sections of the storage hierarchy receives access by default to all of the storage hierarchy. The overriding principle of least privilege implies that the use of defaults should not inadvertently give away more access than the subject intended. In other words, it is better to err on the conservative side. In all implementations some subject(s) must have permission to change the ACLs after they have been set by default, and a way to change the defaults must exist.

4.5.4. Named ACLs
An implementation of ACLs that is sometimes proposed is "named" ACLs. This mechanism is implemented by attaching to the protected object either the ACL name or a pointer to the named ACL. Thus a separate database of named ACLs is needed. The difficulty with this implementation is that when the named ACL gets changed, access to all of the objects pointing to that ACL also get changed. Determining all of the protected objects affected by the change is very difficult. The named ACLs proliferate since many objects need unique ACLs. Determining whether the correct named ACL already exists may be difficult. and allowing subjects to search named ACLs may divulge sensitive information on access rights and provide covert channels. The named ACLs also have to be protected in the same way as the real ACLs.

5. DAC Access Types
In this section, access permissions and access modes for objects are discussed. In the access control matrix model, access permissions and access modes are the entries that specify what kind of access rights the subject has to the object.

The access permissions define who has the ability to change access modes and/or the ability to pass to another subject that ability. In other words, subjects that have an access permission to an object may change the ACL of that object and, perhaps, pass this ability to other subjects. These two abilities, which should be implemented as separate access permissions, are used to specify the control of the DAC mechanism.

In contrast, access modes indicate a specific action that can be applied to the object. For example, the 'execute' mode allows the object to be executed. Access modes will be discussed in more detail later.

6. Access Permissions
In many current systems the concept of access permissions is not separated from access modes. For example, in Multics, modify access on the directory is actually the ability to change the ACLs of the children of the directory. Access modes and access permissions should be kept conceptually separate on any DAC system. This separation allows control of the object to be separated from access to the object.

Since access permissions allow a subject to change the ACL of the object, they can be used to implement the control model for a DAC system. Three basic models exist for control in a DAC system; hierarchical, owner, and laissez-faire.

6.1. Hierarchical
Permissions to change the ACL of objects can be organized so that control is hierarchical, similar to the way most business organizations are formed. A simple example would have the systems administrator at the root of the hierarchical tree. He/she would have the ability to change the ACL and to pass on that ability. The system administrator (or the company structure) divides everyone else into subsets (e.g., departments). The default ACL for each department gives the department head permission to change the ACL and the permission to pass on the ability to change the ACL. The department heads divide their subordinate subjects into subsets (e.g.,projects) and set the defaults so that for each project, they give the project heads the permission to change the ACL. The subjects at the bottom of the

hierarchy have no access permissions on any object. Notice that in the hierarchy those who have the ability to change the ACL on an object can give themselves any access mode on the object.

The advantages of a hierarchical structure are that control can be placed in the most trusted hands and the control can mimic the organizational environment. The disadvantage of the example hierarchical structure is that multiple subjects have the ability to change the ACL on an object.

Other hierarchical organizations can be imagined and implemented using access permissions. Hierarchical organizations could also be programmed into the DAC system without using access permissions. However, such a restrictive implementation would result in a choice of a specific hierarchical structure which would hinder use of the system by organizations that did not fit that mold.

6.2. Owner

Another control model associates with each object an owner (usually the creator of the object) who is the only subject that has the permission to change the ACL of this object. The owner is always in "full" control of the objects that he/she has created and has no ability to pass control of the original object to any other subject. Hence the owner may change the ACL at any time in order to grant and deny to other subjects the access modes to the objects under their control.

This near absolute control by the owner can be implemented administratively with a DAC mechanism that supports access permissions. The system administrator could set up the system so that each subject would have a "home" directory. The default ACL for files and sub-directories would always give that subject the access permission to change the ACL. and the access permission to pass on the ability to change the ACL would never be used on the system. Of course the system administrator has the ability to alter all of the access control on the system. Owner control can be viewed as a limited hierarchical system of only two levels and could be implemented with a flexible hierarchical control model.

Another way to implement owner control is by programming it into the DAC system without implementing any access permissions. The DAC mechanism stores the identity of the creator of the object as the owner and the only subject that can change the ACL, with no method of passing the capability of changing the ACL to another subject. Such an implementation is restrictive but has been used on many systems. A strict ownership policy results in the owner being the only subject that can delete an object. If the owner leaves the organization or dies, it takes privileges such as Unix's *super user* to delete the subject's objects. Unix is an example of an operating system where only the owner of an object has the ability to change its ACL and no access permissions are implemented.

Another disadvantage of owner control is that for non-owner subjects to change their access modes for an object is difficult (i.e., to share the objects is harder). In order to gain or lose any access to an object, subjects must ask the owner of the object to change its ACL for them. However, in certain operating environments, this disadvantage is actually a desired system characteristic.

6.3. Laissez-faire

In a laissez-faire scheme, the creator of an object may pass to any subject they wish the ability to change the ACL and the ability to pass on that ability, and no ownership concept is present. Once a subject has passed on the permission to pass the ability to change an ACL to still other subjects, they may pass this permission to other subjects without the consent of the creator of the object. Hence, once the access permissions are given away, control of an object is difficult. The ACL will show all the subjects that could change the ACL of an object, but not which subject, if any, is in charge of the final decisions about the object.

Such a control mechanism could work very well on a egalitarian research system, but is not recommended as the only possible control mode on any system.

7. File Structure

Use of access permissions is also related to the structure of the storage system. In operating systems where the storage system is tree structured, two types of objects are involved: directories and files. Access permissions can be applied to both. Permission to change the ACL on a file just changes access to that particular file, but permission to change the ACL on a directory may be implemented as the ability to change not only the directory's ACL but also the ability to change the ACLs of all of the children of the directory (this will be called extended dir ACL change). This implements a hierarchical control structure since permission to change the directory ACL means that the subject can change any access on the whole subtree below that directory.

The hierarchical control scheme described above would use the extended dir ACL change and the permission to pass on the ability to change an ACL. Giving the system administrator, the department heads, and the project leaders extended dir ACL change to the correct directory in the storage structure (with the tree organized to represent the hierarchical structure) would give them control over the correct portion of the file system. A pure owner control policy could be implemented without using the extended dir ACL change. The subject who creates a file or a directory would receive the ability to change the ACL of either. Laissez-faire could use the extended dir ACL change together with the ability to pass on the ability to change an ACL on both the directories and the files. This would only produce a slightly more complicated state of anarchy.

Depending on the situation, one or a combination, of the above schemes could be used to implement the control model of the DAC mechanism. In general, the use of access permissions could allow the organization to structure the DAC mechanism to best fit the particular environment. Of course, the tradeoff for this flexibility is a more complex DAC mechanism and a more difficult training process in learning to set up a DAC that is correct for a particular environment.

8. Access Modes

A fairly wide range of access modes are available on various computer systems implementing DAC mechanisms. This section discusses various modes and describes a minimal set. The discussion begins with the most basic protected objects supported by the system: files.

Read-copy allows an object to be read and copied.

On most, if not all. systems. the "read" mode is actually implemented as read-copy. Conceptually a read mode that allowed only display of the object would be valuable. However. the implementation of a display-only mode as a basic access type would be very difficult since it would involve displaying the file only on media with no storage capacity. Read-copy only restricts the subject to reading or copying the "original" object. If subjects copy the object, they may set any access rights they want to the copy.

· **Write-Delete** allows a subject to modify the contents of an object in any manner they choose including expanding, shrinking or deleting.

Many additional types of write access modes have been used in different systems for controlling what changes can be made to an object. Examples of such write access modes include write-append, delete, and write-modify. These access modes apply only when the system understands something about the characteristics of the object. For example, a hardware and/or operating system may have several more specific write modes that apply to the support of index sequential files. Computer systems that support several different file types with differing write access modes may either map those modes into a single, or minimal, set of modes to be supported by DAC, or all of the possible write modes can be specified and only a subset would apply to a particular file type. The former simplifies the DAC mechanism and the user interface but the latter gives a finer granularity of access control. In contrast, systems with virtual memory file systems like Multics, and, to some extent, stream files like Unix, cannot enforce varieties of write access on the basic file or segment objects.

Of course, the basic write-delete access is not really useful without read-copy access. But giving a subject read-copy access without giving write-delete access will often be useful.

Execute allows a subject to run the object as an executable file.

On many systems execute access requires read access. For example, in Multics, operations involving constants and finding entry points, etc. in the linkage section are seen as reading the object text, and therefore read access is necessary to execute a segment. But more basic problems exist in Multics-like environments where the address space is created for the lifetime of the process and each program is executed in that address space. The subject has the ability to manipulate the address space (change descriptors or registers) before or while a program is running. Almost any program can be manipulated to copy itself if its environment can be manipulated (e.g., find a move-long instruction. change the pointers and execute). So even if the DAC allowed an execute only access. in a Multics-like environment that access cannot be enforced. The solution is to create a new process (and therefore address space) to run each program; for Multics this is too expensive. On any system the execute access should also control where execution can begin and where calls to other programs return; execute access should enforce defined entry points. A correct implementation of execute without read allows proprietary programs to be protected from copying.

· **Null** grants no access permissions and is used to allow exclusion of a particular subject in an ACL.

Often a null access mode does not exist but is implied in the ACL by specifying no access modes for a particular entry.

The minimal set of access modes for an object that is a **file** is the set of access modes used on many existing systems (e.g., Unix, Multics); read-copy, write-delete, and execute, with null implied by no access modes. These access types supply minimal, but sufficient, granularity in limiting the access to a file. With any smaller set a file cannot be controlled independently with respect to read, write, or execute.

Most operating systems apply DAC to objects other than files. Many times these other objects are really structured files, and the system understands the semantics of the object. These objects usually have "extended" access modes which are relevant to the particular structure of the object. They are usually implemented in a manner similar to data abstractions in that the operating system maps the "extended" access modes down to the basic access modes.

8.1. Directories

If the files are organized in a tree structure, then the directories are used to represent the non-leaf nodes of the tree. Directories are usually implemented as structured files or segments. Whether access modes are associated with directories depends on how the tree structure is used to control access.

Three methods can be used to control the access to the directories and their associated files:

1. access control on the directories but not on the files

2. access control on the files but not on the directories

3. access control on both the files and the directories.

If access mode controls are placed only on the directories. then once a subject is given any access to a directory it has that access to all files under the directory. Of course if one of the objects under this directory is another directory (a sub-directory), then the subject needs access mode permission to the sub-directory before it can access the objects under the sub-directory. Placing access control only on directories requires subjects to group files according to access types. This requirement could be too restrictive and could conflict with other reasons for grouping files.

If access mode controls are placed only on files, the controls are more granular. Access to individual files are controlled independently of other files under the same directory. But if no access controls are placed on directories, subjects could browse through the storage structure looking at the names of other subjects' files. Moreover, file placement would be uncontrolled, thereby defeating the main purpose of a tree structure.

The most efficient way to implement DAC with ACLs on a tree structured file system is to control access at both the directory and file levels. However, the designer must then make a decision as to whether the subject must have access to the whole path to access an object, or whether access to only the object itself is sufficient. For example, Multics designers made the decision that if the subject knew the correct pathname to an object, and had non-null access to the object, then non-null access to the intervening directories was not necessary. This decision makes checking for legal access much easier and allows a user to grant another user access to an object by merely changing the ACL on that one object. If the user does not know the correct pathname to an object and does not have access to the intervening directories, no way exists to determine the pathname of the object, and therefore no way exists to access it. Allowing access to an object without access to the parent directories complicates decisions about when access should be given to the other attributes of a file (e.g., length, date contents modified). Such decisions depend on the particular implementation.

In Unix the lack of access to the directory implies that no access is available to the entire sub-tree controlled by that directory. A user cannot give another user access to a file without having given that user access to the parent directories.

The minimal set of access modes for an object that is a <u>directory</u> should include read and write-expand.

- **Read** allows a subject to see the directory entries (i.e., the names, the ACLs, and the associated information about files and sub-directories in this directory).

Read access implies the ability to access the children of the directory. depending on their own ACLs.

- **Write-expand-delete** allows a subject to add new objects to the directory (i.e., to create and delete files and sub-directories under the directory).

Since directory access modes are extended access modes and depend upon how the directory is structured, the actual access modes that would be implemented for a directory are very system dependent. For example, Multics implements three access modes for directories: status allows a subject to see the attributes of the directory and its children; modify allows the subject to modify those same attributes including deletion; and append allows new children to be created.

The tradeoff in determining what objects should be included in the system DAC mechanism and how many access types should be implemented for each object is between the user friendliness of the operating system and the complexity of the DAC mechanism. The DAC mechanism is part of the Trusted Computing Base and therefore must be included in the assurances necessary in the Criteria. At the A1 level, the mechanism to support each new protected object and its access mode will have to be verified. Also, the final implementation of the access modes should not be so complicated that subjects cannot easily remember the implication of each mode. If subjects cannot distinguish the functions of each access mode, they may just grant to other subjects either the full access rights or no access rights to an object.

Other objects that have been protected with a computer system's DAC mechanism include mailboxes (message queues in general), communication channels, forums (a type of bulletin board), and devices. Their access types are dependent on the implementation and will not be discussed here.

9. Protected Subsystems

In order to provide users with access types finer than the standard *read, write, execute,* etc., a rather limited number of systems support protected subsystems. Saltzer and Schroeder[14] refer to the need for "protected subsystems", which they define as user-provided programs which control access to files.

By extending the access control mechanism to allow objects to be accessed in ways specified by subjects (programs as well as users), a system may allow a specific user-written program to be designated "the only subject" allowed any access or a particular type of access to specific files. A protected subsystem can be defined as a collection of procedures and data objects that is encapsulated in a domain of its own so that the internal structure of a data object is accessible only to the procedures of the protected subsystem, and the procedures may be called only at designated domain entry points and only by designated subjects.

The encapsulated data files are the protected objects. Programs in a protected subsystem act as managers for the protected objects and enforce user-written access controls on them. Subjects outside the protected subsystem are allowed to manipulate the protected objects only by invoking the manager programs. Any access constraints that can be specified in an algorithm can be implemented in a protected subsystem. Giving users the ability to construct protected subsystems out of their own program and data files allows users to provide arbitrary controls on sharing.

By allowing programs inside a protected subsystem to invoke programs in another protected subsystem without compromising the security of either, multiple protected subsystems can be used to perform tasks. This limits the extent of damage a malicious or malfunctioning borrowed program might have to objects protected by the subsystem. Likewise, the lending user could also encapsulate the loaned program in a protected subsystem of its own to protect it from the programs of the borrower.

9.1. Domain, MTS, and Others

Apollo's Domain and University of Michigan's Michigan Terminal System (MTS) implement limited protected subsystems. Both systems allow users to write their own subsystems, but they do not provide mechanisms for protected subsystems to interact with each other. The general claim is that implementation of multiple protected subsystems would require additional hardware and/or extensive software assistance.

The two systems use different approaches in implementing protected subsystems. In Domain, a user has to have an ability to add a subsystem name to a system-wide list of subsystems, thereby creating the subsystem. The user then assigns a certain file to be a manager of the subsystem and another file to be an object. The user then removes all other access to the object, making the manager an exclusive accessor. Access to the subsystem is controlled by the ACLs associated with the subsystem manager.

During execution, the system verifies that both the manager and the object are in the same subsystem and that the manager has raised its privilege level allowing it to access its own protected objects. Only then is the subsystem manager allowed to operate on the object. The additional step of raising the manager's privilege level is designed to prevent any unintentional access to the object.

In MTS the connection between the manager and the object is done via user-named "program keys." A user attaches the key to the manager program and sets access on the object to that key. MTS makes each key unique by prefixing it with the user name. The user then removes all other access (if any) to the object and for additional protection sets the access to the manager to *execute-only*. A user does not need special privileges to set up a protected subsystem.

During the association of the program key with the object, the user is also required to specify a basic access mode that the manager will be using. That is, if the manager needs only a *read* access to the object, the object should be made only read-accessible to the manager. This further enhances the protection of the object.

Other operating systems provide features which can be used as limited protected subsystems. In Digital Equipment Corporation's TOPS-10[15] a "file daemon" mechanism allows a user to better fine-tune access to objects. Control Data Corporation's NOS is capable of object protection with access control lists as well as with passwords. If passwords on objects are kept secret from all but the managers, then protected subsystems can be implemented in NOS. Unix has a "setuid" privilege which allows the process running a program to have the access rights of the program's owner. Multics' ring structure can be viewed as a mechanism to support protected subsystems.

9.2. Features of a Good Protected Subsystem

If protected subsystems are to be implemented, the capability should be designed and built into an operating system during the design and implementation of the operating system itself. Adding it on later is difficult.

A good implementation of protected subsystems should provide a straight-forward means for creating the subsystem. The connection between the manager and the object should not be obscured with secret passwords. The operating system should protect the subsystem so nothing is revealed about the object or the manager other than their interface with the user.

Objects should be allowed to have more than one manager so that various groups of users could access the same objects through specific managers. Managers should not be allowed to manage more than one subsystem to avoid making the manager more powerful and difficult to control than originally intended. Managers should be further controlled with the basic access modes provided by the operating system for objects. Managers must be allowed to manage multiple objects in the same subsystem. Not only user-prepared programs, but system programs and utilities, should qualify as potential managers.

Protected subsystems could provide a capability for increasing the integrity of applications by providing the users a means of implementing data abstractions. The mechanism to ensure the ability to set up protected subsystems could be part of the Trusted Computing Base (TCB), but the subsystems themselves would not. The user could be assured that the manager programs were the only object manipulators, but no assurance of their correct

operation, other than the basic access checks supported by the operating system, would be provided.

10. Administering DAC

To set up the DAC mechanism requires a Facilities User's Guide that explains how to properly administer a DAC system, and how to identify the system security administrator and any project administrators and their functions. The correct access must be set on the system administration database, which would include user registry, group definitions, etc. The guide must explain how access must be set to handle fixing system problems, including viewing dumps and repairing file systems, etc. Access must be set correctly to the standard libraries, including the system commands and subroutines, initialization modules, and the operating system source code. ACLs may need to be set on the supervisor entry points and the I/O daemons or device queues.

In general, documentation should describe how to initialize the ACLs to best provide a protected environment. If the DAC mechanism is flexible and provides the ability to set up different control structures, examples should be given for a range of control structures.

11. Auditing DAC

Auditing is an important part of a secure computer system. In general an audit log message should include a time stamp, the subject's identity, the object's identity, the type of action and any other pertinent information. Much of the auditing on any operating system is not specific to the DAC mechanism, but in many instances the DAC mechanism should place an entry in the audit log. Any operation that changes the control structure of the DAC should be audited. Any change in any ACL, including the default ACLs, should be audited. Any attempt to access a DAC protected object should be audited. Any changes to group definitions should be audited.

12. Verifying DAC

Verifying the correctness of the DAC mechanism is difficult. As has been illustrated in this paper, DAC does not have well defined rules as do mandatory access control systems. In fact no formal model of DAC currently exists although some mention is made of the DAC mechanisms in the Bell and LaPadula[16] formal model for mandatory access control. In systems such as SCOMP,[17] whose design has been formally verified for security, the only property that was proven about the DAC mechanism was that it did not violate the mandatory access formal model. Research is needed in developing a formal model for DAC, and verification of systems where DAC is important should prove at least that the DAC mechanism is consistent with its descriptive top level specification.

13. DAC Add-ons

Systems such as IBM's MVS have had DAC mechanisms added on. The DAC checks are made before the operating system gets a request for an object, and the request is not forwarded to the operating system if it requests illegal access. Such add-ons are basing their assurance on the inability of a user to get access to the operating system through another interface or to cause the operating system to retrieve illegal data with a legal request. Most add-on packages are applied to systems that provide little security on their own. Thus the assurance that the operating system could not be subverted is non-existent.

I. PREPARATION OF A DAC GUIDELINE

The Department of Defense Computer Security Center (DoDCSC) was established in 1981 to provide uniform DoD policy for security requirements, controls and measures to reduce the threat of compromise of classified and sensitive information processed in computer systems. The main goal of the DoDCSC is to encourage the widespread availability of trusted computer systems. In support of that goal a metric was created, the DoD Trusted Computer System Evaluation Criteria,[18] against which computer systems could be evaluated for security. Since one of the features required of a secure system is a DAC mechanism, several vendors and system designers have expressed a need for guidance from DoDCSC on how to build and implement effective DAC mechanisms. In response to this need. the DoDCSC is preparing a DAC Guideline.

I.1. PURPOSE OF THE DAC GUIDELINE
The purpose of the DAC Guideline is to:

1. discuss the issues involved in implementing and evaluating various DAC mechanisms.

2. provide information to the evaluator which will aid in assessing the effectiveness of a DAC mechanism in meeting the requirements of a particular evaluation class defined in the Criteria, and

3. provide guidance to systems designers and developers on how to build DAC mechanisms.

I.2. PROPOSED CONTENTS OF THE DAC GUIDELINE
The contents of the DAC Guideline have not been finalized at this time. Most of the information presented in this paper will be included in the Guideline. The following additional topics are proposed and may be changed or added to as the Guideline is being developed.

- DEFINITION OF DISCRETIONARY ACCESS CONTROL. The DAC definition, as it appears in the Criteria, will be included along with a narrative interpretation of the definition.

- DESCRIPTIONS OF DAC MECHANISMS. Currently-used DAC mechanisms, such as Capabilities, Profiles, Passwords, Protection Bits, and ACLs, will be described, including their limitations, strengths, and weaknesses. The Guideline will include recommendations as to which mechanism or DAC features can be used to satisfy the requirements of a particular evaluation class of the Criteria. Emphasis will be placed on 'good practice', not just on the minimum requirements for a particular evaluation class. Good practice means that the DAC mechanism should be designed so that users can easily use the computer to enforce the same information access rules that would be enforced in an all-paper world.

- ENVIRONMENTAL CONTROLS. The Guideline will include information on the environmental security controls (physical, personnel, and administrative) on which various DAC mechanisms depend in order to be effective.

- FACILITIES USER'S GUIDE INFORMATION: DAC mechanisms can be degraded by improper use, therefore, the Guideline will include information on the preparation of a Facilities User's Guide that explains how to properly set up and administer a DAC system.

- MAPPING THE CRITERIA AGAINST DAC MECHANISMS. The Guideline will give an overview and interpretation of the DAC requirements as they appear for each evaluation class in the Criteria.

I.3. SCHEDULE FOR PUBLICATION OF THE DAC GUIDELINE
A first draft of the DAC Guideline will be written and distributed for review by the end of July 1985.

I.4. VENDOR PARTICIPATION IN THE PREPARATION OF THE DAC GUIDELINE
Several computer hardware and software vendors are in the process of installing, or have already installed, DAC mechanisms in their systems which are intended to meet the requirements of the DoD Trusted Computer System Criteria. Much of the technical information presented in this paper was collected at the request of the DoD Computer Security Center by the Aerospace Corporation in response to the need and the interest shown by vendors.

Representatives of the DoD Computer Security Center plan to visit computer hardware and software vendors to discuss the DAC technical paper developed by the Aerospace Corporation. Discussions with each vendor will be aimed at answering the following questions:

- Has the vendor installed any of the DAC mechanisms described? Does the vendor have any experience with the reliability, user-friendliness, or implementation problems of any of the mechanisms that they have installed?

- How difficult would it be for the vendor to change a current DAC mechanism or add a new mechanism if necessary to meet a particular class of the Criteria?

- Does the vendor know of other DAC mechanisms which were not covered in the DAC technical paper?

In order to produce a DAC Guideline that is relevant and helpful to the vendor community, vendor reaction to the DAC technical paper and vendor feedback to draft versions of the DAC Guideline will be solicited by the DoD Computer Security Center.

References

1. Schroeder, M.D., *Cooperation of Mutually Suspicious Subsystems*, PhD dissertation, M.I.T., 1972.

2. DoD Computer Security Center, *Evaluated Products List for Trusted Computer Systems*, DoD, CSC-EPL, 1984.

3. Cohen. F., "Computer Viruses - Theory and Experiments," *7th Security Conference*, DOD/NBS, September 1984, pp. 388-402.

4. Saltzer, Jerome H., "Protection and the Control of Information in Multics," *Communications of the ACM*, Vol. 17, No. 7, July 1974, pp. 388-402.

5. Lampson, B.W., "Protection," *Proc. Fifth Annual Princeton Conference on Information Sciences and Systems*, Princeton University, March 1971.

6. Fabry, R.S., "Capability Based Addressing," *Communications of the ACM*, Vol. 17, No. 7, July 1974, pp. 403-411.

7. Karger,P.A. and A.J. Herbert, "Lattice Security and Traceability of Access," *Symposium on Security and Privacy*, IEEE, April 1984, pp. 13-23.

8. Computer Associates, *CA-SENTINEL Reference Guide*, 1983.

9. IBM, *Access Method Services*, 1983.

10. Control Data Corporation, *NOS Version 2 Reference Set*, 3 ed., 1983.

11. UC Berkeley, *Unix Programmer's Manual*, 7 ed., 1981.

12. Honeywell Informations Systems, Inc., *Multics Programmer's Manual -- Reference Guide*, 7 ed., AG91.

13. APOLLO Computer Inc., *The DOMAIN System Administrator's Guide*, 3 ed., 1983.

14. Saltzer, Jerome H. and Michael D. Schroeder, "The Protection of Information in Computer Systems," *Proceedings of the IEEE*, Vol. 63, No. 9, September 1975, pp. 1278-1308.

15. Digital, *DECSYSTEM10 Users Handbook*, 1983.

16. Bell, D.E. and LaPadula, L.J., "Secure Computer Systems: Unified Exposition and Multics Interpretation," Tech. report MTR-2997 Rev. 1, MITRE Corp., March 1976.

17. Benzel Vickers, T., "Overview of the SCOMP Architecture and Security Mechanisms." Tech. report MTR-9071 MITRE Corp.. September 1983.

18. DoD Computer Security Center, *Department of Defense Trusted Computer System Evaluation Criteria*, DoD, CSC-STD-001-83, 1983.

Section 2.5: Database Security

Database management systems (DBMS) are receiving attention concerning their security-relevance. From a security viewpoint, they may be viewed as applications that require considerable kernel service or as protected subsystems and/or trusted processes. In addition to the more common security concerns of integrity, trusted path, audit, and access control, DBMSs add concerns for journaling, granularity, inference, and aggregation. Some of these toward the end of the list are current research topics. DBMS is a major specialization in computer operations and computer science; the literature is rich. If you wish to become acquainted with it, we suggest consulting the forthcoming *Proceedings of the NCSC Invitational Workshop on Database Security.*

There are critical database management system (DBMS) security and integrity issues that must be addressed. Our first concern focuses on the capability of the DBMS to maintain data integrity, probably because this is the one we know the most about. In addition to technical security issues and not dissimilar from the discussions of the security kernel, performance factors such as response time for inquiries must also be considered. A DBMS is a software application that provides subjects an ability to use or modify data or objects in the database. Conceptually, the DBMS is a filter restricting access of subjects to objects.

Database security and integrity are essential to the successful operation of an organization. Integrity is a current issue; security will grow in importance as the National Computer Security Center progresses on its plan to produce guidelines or criteria for applying the TCSEC to DBMS. Management cannot be expected to support a database that fails to provide integrity. Data integrity is defined in the TCSEC as "the state that exists when computerized data is the same as that in the source documents and has not been exposed to accidental or malicious alternation or destruction." The TCSEC does not go much further in addressing the criteria necessary for trusted databases. Some argue that the existing criteria are sufficient.

We shall discuss selected database security issues pertaining to the *Orange Book* criteria and identify unresolved security issues pertaining to DBMS.

Trusted Process

DBMS functions such as update, extract, insert, and reclassify must be trusted to perform as specified without violation of security policy or to violate security policy within predefined constraints. The former requires kernel mediation; the latter is a definition of a trusted process. Of course non-security-related functions would be implemented by non-trusted processes; but performance considerations might cause these non-trusted processes to be implemented in or close to the kernel.

Trusted Path

The first database security-relevant issue pertaining to the TCSEC criteria introduced to illustrate the interrelationship between the trusted computing base (TCB) and database security is trusted path. The TCSEC defines trusted path as ". . . a mechanism by which a person at a terminal can communicate directly with the trusted computing base [TCB]. This mechanism can only be activated by the person or the trusted computing base and cannot be imitated by untrusted software." Communicating with the TCB can be considered as Step 1 in a DBMS operation. Step 2 is the DBMS interfacing with the user in support of functions such as on-line database retrieval and maintenance. Return of control to the TCB can be referred to as Step 3.

The two TCSEC requirements for trusted path occur at the B2 and B3 levels. They are quoted in order, with security level identifiers in parentheses (1) *trusted path (B2):* "The TCB shall support a trusted communication path between itself and user for initial login and authentication. Communication via this path shall be initiated exclusively by a user and (2) *trusted path (B3):* "The TCB shall support a trusted communication path between itself and users for use when a positive TCB-to-user connection is required (e.g. login, change subject security level). Communications via this trusted path shall be activated exclusively by a user or the TCB and shall be logically isolated and unmistakeably distinguishable from other paths."

The secure operation of a DBMS at a B2 or B3 level would require trusted path capability for DBMS communication, as described above for TCB communication.

Audit Trail, Journaling, and Continuity of Operations

We continue our discussion with an illustration of another pair of DBMS capability that has a much extended DBMS function as well as an analog in the TCSEC criteria. This capability pair is journaling and audit trail, which we shall discuss after introducing the broader considerations for continuity of operations.

The TCSEC definition of audit trail is: "A set of records that collectively provide documentary evidence of processing used to aid in tracing from original transactions forward to related records and reports, and/or backwards from records and reports to their component source transactions." The same functions in the database area are referred to as journaling.

Continuity of operations is a basic management responsibility that is supported in many cases by continuous data integrity. It is mandated in the TCSEC at the B3 level with a requirement for trusted recovery. This requirement is that "Procedures and/or mechanisms shall be provided to assure that, after an ADP system failure or other discontinuity, recovery without a protection compromise is obtained." One way to achieve continuous data integrity is to have redundant on-line facilities so that if a computer system fails, the backup system can continue operations. Some organizations with less critical continuity of operations requirements allow for downtime during prime shift. This allowance can vary from seconds to minutes to hours depending upon the nature of the business. For example, the New York Stock Exchange operations would be severely restricted if electronic support for transactions was unavailable for 10 hours. In another example, if you are purchasing a ticket for a flight that leaves in 20 minutes, you would be disappointed if the airline reservation system was unavailable for one hour.

Another way to achieve trusted recovery for continuity of operations is the restart and recovery process, which includes rebuilding the database to a current status. Effective rebuilding requires that the system know the previous status of the database at time ti before system failure and the details of all database transactions from time t_i up to the point of failure. This knowledge can be obtained by periodically copying the database at t_i, t_j, etc., and by using a journal function. The journal contains a history of all transactions, that change the state of the database. The journal requires mandatory access control protection at the highest level of data stored in the database and perhaps at the finest granularity as well. (See below for a discussion of granularity.) In addition to the journal, related DBMS constructs, such as the data dictionary and directory must also be protected. The data dictionary defines the meaning (semantics) of each field or item, while the directory contains a pointer to its location. In other words, the directory tells you where to find an item and a dictionary tells you what it means.

Audit trail capability is essential for the TCB and for database operations in a DBMS environment. The TCSEC defines audit trail as ". . . a set of records that collectively provide documentary evidence of processing used to aid in tracing from original transactions forward to related records

and reports and/or backwards from records and reports to their component source transactions."

Audit requirements are defined in the TCSEC for the C2, B1, B2, and B3 levels. For example, at C2

> The TCB shall be able to create, maintain, and protect from modification or unauthorized access or destruction an audit trail of accesses to the objects it protects. The audit data shall be protected by the TCB so that read access to it is limited to those who are authorized for audit data. The TCB shall be able to record the following types of events: use of identification and authentication mechanisms, introduction of objects into a user's address space (e.g. file open program initiation), deletion of objects, and actions taken by computer operators and system administrators and/or system security officers. For each recorded event, the audit record shall identify: date and time of the event, user, type of event, and success or failure of the event. For identification/authentication events the origin of request (e.g. terminal ID) shall be included in the audit record. For events that introduce an object into a user's address space and for object deletion events the audit record shall include the name of the objects. The ADP system administrator shall be able to selectively audit the actions of any one or more users based on individual identity.

The TCSEC criteria for audit add specific dimensions for trusted computer systems beyond restart and recovery. In addition, there is a related TCSEC requirement at the B3 for trusted recovery. This states that "procedures and/or mechanisms shall be provided to assure that, after an ADP system failure or other discontinuity, recovery without a protection compromise is obtained."

The TCSEC audit dimensions generally include seven requirements (class levels are noted in parentheses): (1) maintain and protect an audit trail (C2), (2) ADP system administrator audit capability (C2), (3) maintain a record of an object's security level (B1), (4) ADP system administrator audit capability extended to object security level (B1), (5) TCB audit of overrides of output markings (B1), (6) TCB audit of events for covert channel exploitation (B2). (For review, "A covert channel is a communication channel that allows a process to transfer information in a manner that violates the system's security policy."), and (7) TCB monitor events that may indicate imminent violation of security policy (B3).

Discretionary Access Control

As mentioned for trusted path, there is no specific criteria for DBMS audit in the TCSEC; however, the criteria can be used for a DBMS. A third example concludes the discussion. This example pertains to discretionary access control (DAC), which was extensively discussed in the paper by Deborah Downs et al. in Section 2.4.

Discretionary access control (DAC) is a basic requirement for DBMS security and data integrity. Briefly reviewing from the TCSEC, DAC is a means of restricting subjects' ". . . access to objects based on the identity of subjects and/ or groups to which they belong. The controls are discretionary in the sense that a subject with a certain access permission is capable of passing that permission (perhaps indirectly) on to any other subject."

The TCSEC requirements for DAC occur at the C1, C2, and B3 levels. These requirements are similar to TCB DAC for database security. To illustrate, the DAC at the C1 level is "The TCB shall define and control access between named users and named objects (e.g. files and programs) in the ADP system. The enforcement mechanism (e.g. self/group/ public controls, access control lists) shall allow user to specify and control sharing of those objects by named individuals or defined groups or both."

The following DAC requirements generally become more rigorous (class levels are noted in parentheses): The enforcement mechanism includes groups of individuals (C2), DAC provides that objects are protected from unauthorized access (C2), the enforcement mechanism allows controlled sharing of objects (B3), and no access specified for each named object (B3).

The next section presents selected reprints on key aspects of database security.

Other Security-Related Functions

This subsection briefly introduces some of the current research issues in DBMS. Granularity is fundamentally important as a tradeoff among performance, overhead, and operational necessity. One question is the size of a labeled object. Traditionally, the size of objects has been thought of as the order of magnitude of a file, with devices being a special case. In a DBMS, much smaller information units are manipulated. It may be appropriate to apply security labels to records or even items (fields). The pre-DBMS kernel may not be able to support such a fine level of granularity. One alternative is to implement the DBMS as a protected subsystem which encapsulates the database so that the only access is through the DBMS, which enforces fine granularity access control. Another question is auditing granularity. Complete auditing of every DBMS event would probably be counter productive, both from security and from efficiency viewpoints. Selective auditing is indicated.

Filtering is concerned with examining data semantics as it interacts with access control. Both mandatory and discretionary access control are involved. When a database operation attempts access to data for which the subject is not privileged, one approach is to satisfy the operation but to delete the offending data. From an operational viewpoint, this may be preferable to aborting the operations. From a security

viewpoint, aborting the operation may be a security violation in itself.

Aggregation is perhaps the most vexing DBMS issue. The problem is that a collection of data may be classified at a higher mandatory security level than any individual datum. For example, one person's salary may be restricted, but the company's salary database may be much more sensitive. Determining the threshold at which point aggregation should trigger security upgrading is one problem. Extracting or filtering so that the data subset at the lower classification may be extracted is even more difficult.

Reprints

The paper, "On the Logical Extension of the Criteria Principles to the Design of Multilevel Database Management Systems," by Marvin Schaefer evaluates the applicability of the TCSEC methodology to the development of multilevel DBMS (MDBMS) technology. The good news is that the TCSEC is directly applicable to MDBMS; the bad news is that the "MDBMS largely consists of trusted code." Schaefer bases his opinion on "many special-purpose but multilevel database management systems [that] have been designed, implemented, and evaluated in concert with the TCSEC." These MDBMSs are the internal system tables in trusted operating systems; examples are cited.

The results of Schaefer's work suggest ". . . that it is possible to provide adequate definitions and constraints for the trusted subjects needed to implement a MDBMS only if the complete semantic classification requirements are specified for each database under consideration." He feels that "it should be possible to derive a constructive transformational approach to establishing the formal security requirements for each such trusted subject."

He also points out that considerable amounts of trusted code would be required to support a MDBMS for ". . . dynamic databases in which classification is semantically derived . . ." as contrasted with those cases ". . . that are only referenced and wherein the data classification relationships can be derived syntactically." He states that classification should be "on the basis of an association between specific data entries" and that these associations also require classification.

The paper, "Design Overview for Retrofitting Integrity-Lock Architecture onto a Commercial DBMS," by Richard Graubart and Kevin Duffy addresses a simpler problem to provide a measure of security through retrofitting an existing DBMS. The problem addressed is assurance of data integrity. The paper presents integrity lock as a near-term solution that limits the amount of trusted code. A trusted front end is required to act as a reference monitor that mediates all input and output of information to and from the DBMS. An encrypted checksum computation is employed, based on the data content at the tuple (row) and the security level. The checksum is checked on data retrieval and update.

The thrust of this paper is research oriented to demonstrate ". . . that the integrity lock architecture can be supported by a B2 level secure operating system with minimal restrictions upon the user." In their test case, the authors found that "the majority of changes involve removing some functionality from a single process and placing that functionality into multiple processes."

In "Filters for Reducing Inference Threats in Multilevel Database Systems," Dorothy Denning has shown how authorized views and a commutative filter can be used in a DBMS environment to solve the problem of user inference. According to Denning, "the technique allows query selections, some projections, query optimization, and subquery handling to be performed by the database system." An authorized view of the DBMS is provided by the commutative filter, which is similar to the trusted front end described by Graubart and Duffy.

There are, according to Denning, four categories of threats to disclosure of unauthorized data in addition to the need for enforcing multilevel security in a multilevel DBMS (MDBMS): (1) *direct access*—user requests unauthorized data. Disclosure "can be prevented with database access controls that compare the classification of the data with the clearance of the user before releasing the data." (2) *indirect access by inference*—user requests authorized data; however, the output data is a function of unauthorized data d. "The user can infer d from the response." The solution to this problem is the subject of this paper. (3) *Trojan horse direct release*—a Trojan horse causes unauthorized data d to be output but with an incorrect label that makes d appear to be authorized data. This problem can be circumvented with a trusted filter reference monitor front end, such as the TFE discussed in the preceding paper. (4) *Trojan horse leakage*—a Trojan horse causes unauthorized data d to be output ". . . by encoding it in authorized data returned to the user." This problem remains unsolved.

Denning first defines the inference problem and gives two examples. She then solves it, considering classification by record select-project and select-project-join queries. Classification by attribute and by element require consideration of select only, select-project, and select-project-join queries. The processing steps in filtering each type of classification are summarized. Unsolved inference problems are aggregation functions, constraints not reflected in the classification

policy, classification of suppressed data, and low entropy data.

Roger Schell and Dorothy Denning address DBMS integrity in the TCSEC context in "Integrity in Trusted Database Systems." They conclude that further experience is required before mandatory integrity policies, based on integrity classifications and enforced by the reference monitor, can be recommended. Discretionary integrity policy, based on a subject's identity is extremely useful when the definition of objects includes database concepts such as views, elements, records, and subschema. Most interestingly, they suggest that mandatory and discretionary policy may have different security perimeters. Constraints on database integrity rules imposed by mandatory secrecy concerns for covert channels are noted.

Six mandatory integrity policies from the literature are described, but the useful set reduces to the following two: (1) The Strict Integrity Policy assigns a fixed integrity class to subjects and objects. A subject is prohibited from reading down or writing up. Note that this is an exact dual of the Bell-LaPadula secrecy rules where a subject is prohibited from reading up or writing down. The integrity level of a subject is constrained by the integrity of programs executed and the data that control program execution. The Honeywell SCOMP, Gemini GEMSOS, and I.P. Sharp multilevel database model incorporate strict integrity. (2) Domains and Types are being implemented in the Honeywell SAT. This approach is similar to mandatory non-hierarchical compartmentization.

Consistency integrity rules that define the correct states of the database are divided into domain integrity rules, which are context-free specifications of allowable values, and relational integrity rules, which are context-sensitive global constraints. While integrity rules appear essential, their incorporation in (TCSEC rated) B2 systems introduce covert channel problems. Bringing the DBMS inside the mandatory security perimeter (i.e., incorporating its integrity features in the TCB) is considered infeasible and undesirable. This introduces problems of data invisible to a subject because it is of a higher secrecy category. Schell and Denning suggest requirement and properties for integrity rules, concluding that "mandatory secrecy policy affects the interpretation and application of integrity constraints."

Integrity concerns with recovery and concurrency require incorporation of traditional database approaches to transactions with commit and roll-back, serializability, deadlock, and livelock. Covert channel concerns also limit implementation in these areas.

ON THE LOGICAL EXTENSION OF THE CRITERIA PRINCIPLES
TO THE DESIGN OF
MULTILEVEL DATABASE MANAGEMENT SYSTEMS

Marvin Schaefer

DoD Computer Security Evaluation Center
Fort Meade, Maryland

Several researchers have opined that the *Trusted Computer Systems Evaluation Criteria* (TCSEC) cannot be applied to the multilevel database management problem. We do not subscribe to this view, and observe that many special-purpose but multilevel database management systems have been designed, implemented and evaluated in concert with the TCSEC. In this paper we intend to examine the nature of what has been done and, through *gedankenexperiment*, suggest the possibility of generalising on the trusted operating systems work that has been done to date.

A DATABASE INTERPRETATION

We begin by noting that every trusted operating system must necessarily implement and maintain a number of internal system tables that consistently describe the real state of the machine, its processes and its physical resources. These system tables describe and are used to control information at or about all supported sensitivity levels with respect to all of the system's subjects and objects. Those system tables that are within the TCB must be supported by functions that act consistent with the system security policy. While the TCSEC requires it be shown that the system tables are correctly interpreted by the TCB, it is also required that information flow analysis be performed on the functions that maintain or depend on the contents of the tables in order to demonstrate that the TCB does not leak classified information derived from the system tables.

In large systems, the system tables may contain several *millions* of entries. Many of the tables are updated frequently, dynamically, and asynchronously on behalf of processes and requests from all supported security levels. Such tables were characterised as a multilevel relational database in 1976 during DARPA's KVM/370 effort, and similar observations were later made about the KSOS system tables.

Although it may at first appear unreasonable to consider these tables as anything other than a highly-contrived example of a database, examination shows that they have all the characteristics of a multilevel relational database. Even if one were to argue that since the TCB implements the security level abstraction, and hence does not deal directly with classified entities, but rather with the *descriptors* of classified entities, the fact remains that the system tables constitute a database that describes multilevel data and that is used to place classified objects into the domains of untrusted subjects.

RELATIONAL DBMS ANALOGUE

A table can be likened to a relation whose *tuples* correspond to the table's rows, and whose *attributes* or *fields* correspond to the columns. The classification granularity of data in system tables may apply to fields as small as a byte or a bit, or it may be distinctly applied to larger structures, e.g., each row of a table, or in some cases to an entire table. Locating specified data in the rows of a table corresponds to *selection*, and extracting data from specific fields of these rows corresponds to *projection*. In many cases, (e.g., demand page management, I/O scheduling, etc.,) data in one system table must be correlated with data in another system table, where the data associations are given by pointer chains. This latter operation is the equivalent of the *join* operation.

The system tables can also be considered as a subschema from which "secure views" of the physical machine and its resources are derived for the user processes (untrusted subjects) consistent with the operating system's formal security policy model. Under interpretations of [B&L73], e.g., each subject's domain may be built from the space of real pages such that the read-bit is set for a domain page only if its security level is dominated by the subject's security level; and the write-bit is set only if the two security levels are equal. Under this interpretation, the TCB can be viewed as a trusted database management system: a multilevel DBMS (MDBMS) no less general than a multilevel document retrieval system or any other general purpose database management system.

SECURITY REQUIREMENTS

The TCSEC requires that each secure view of real- and virtual machine resources be implemented such that each subject be granted a set of permissible operations on its derived data view, that this data view be consistently maintained, and that the exploitation of certain information flow channels be precluded. At and above the TCSEC's B2 level, forbidden information flow channels include covert storage and, ultimately, covert channels.

It is clear that this MDBMS largely consists of trusted code, much of which should be implemented with least-privilege (B3) as trusted subjects in restricted small domains of the TCB. It should be possible to derive a constructive transformational approach to establishing the formal security requirements for each such trusted subject.

Reprinted from *Proceedings of the 8th National Computer Security Conference*, 1985, pages 28-30. U.S. Government work not protected by U.S. copyright.

We propose to follow a process of "folding": that is, we begin by assuming that there exists an uninterpreted but "sufficiently secure" TCB to satisfy the B2 requirements (i.e., we hypothesize that untrusted subjects can be supported and be granted access to relatively "large" single level objects called *segments*). We recall that a Secure Relational DBMS (SRDBMS) architecture was derived by Hinke and Schaefer [RADC75] in an investigation of the possibility of designing a DBMS application system that could be used to create and maintain authorized views of multilevel databases. The project was constrained by a requirement that no modifications were to be made to any the Multics kernel code or its trusted code, and no new code was to be introduced into the privileged domains of execution (rings 0 or 1).

This leads to the idea that by using the [RADC75] architecture it would be possible to construct a completely untrusted DBMS that implements multilevel secure views of a database partitioned into single level segments and over which all accesses are controlled by the TCB while the SRDBMS implements the semantics of the database. It would then be possible to implement fully untrusted single level [i.e., least privilege] views of a multilevel internal system database of the type described above, each of whose relations is implemented in single level segments. This would of course be illegitimate in both theory and practise, since this database would have to have already been implemented within the TCB in order to support our hypothetical untrusted database implementation.

However, suppose for the moment that this implementation were legitimate. Then once having done it, we could proceed to define the precise semantics and the permissible operations that could be performed on such a database on behalf of an untrusted subject operating at an arbitrary formal security level. Among the defined operations, we most have fully detailed the required procedures and the conditions that must hold in order to update the individual components of a multilevel view, to add or delete a tuple, and to view a tuple.

Operations that Must be Trusted

In some cases the [RADC75] architecture requires that an operation be performed in quanta that are initiated at several distinct security levels. (For example, in order to update (or delete) a multilevel tuple with purely untrusted code, direct application of the Simple Security Condition and the *-Property require that the fields in a tuple be sequentially updated (deleted), each field in turn by a subject that acts at precisely the security level of the field undergoing modification. Such a regimen is not only awkward, but it introduces a number of potential semantic integrity problems in the face of concurrent readers and updaters on the system who could be operating at different security levels.) These cases arise precisely because of the lack of a trusted process and/or a trusted path in the [RADC75] paradigm's use of an underlying security kernel. We conjecture

that such analysis leads directly to the identification of the set of database-specific operations that need to be supported by a trusted implementation: it is the set of operations that cannot be completed under the [RADC75] syndrome at a unique security level.

This makes it possible to produce a precise definition of the data-specific input and output assertions and constraints that would be required to define a trusted process that would perform the same operation as an atomic state transition. Given such a precise characterisation, we would suggest that the untrusted sequential operation could be replaced by a trusted, but suspicious, subject that would be invoked by a kernel call. Assume then, that the kernel call and the trusted subject exist, replacing the untrusted code sequence by the kernel call and its trusted implementation. Continue to proceed along these analytical lines until such time as no remaining non-atomic database operations need be performed as atomic operations.

At this point, we claim, the MDBMS has been partitioned into its trusted and untrusted components, completely along the lines of the TCSEC's architectural and assurance requirements. However, since the databases that were first modeled as partitioned relations were integrated into a heterogeneous classified single database, and since the databases were derived from the hypothesised underlying components of the TCB, we have managed to completely define the internal structure and semantics of the TCB's hypothesised underlying MDBMS schema. We would further observe that by following the method of our *gedankenexperiment* to derive the trusted MDBMS primitives, we obviated the need to store the multilevel database in single level segments. It appears that in this way each of the TCB's required system table implementations can be constructed with the required assurances.

REFLECTIONS

We are sensitive to the fact that the thought process we followed led us to construct a one-of-a-kind trusted database management system. Although we were capable of identifying the primitive trusted DBMS functions needed to support this application, we were not able to come up with a closed-form solution to the general problem. We worked with a database wherein it was possible to define the precise classification of every data *relationship* at the time the database was conceived. While the approach explicitly allows for the dynamic classification of new entries in predefined relations, we further constrained the generality of our result by limiting the set of permissible domains for join operations, thereby not having to address the problem of deriving classifications for dynamically-created relations. However, we harbour no doubts that archetypes of the trusted primitive functions we derived under this process would be present in a wide variety of trusted database management applications.

In reflecting on the simplification we used of the general trusted database management problem we employed in this *gedankenexperiment*, we recall several observations on security policy models that came from the Air Force Summer Study on Multilevel Data Management Security [NAS83]. Some observers have said that the Bell and La Padula Model does not apply to the MDBMS problem. The reasons given have ranged from the misconception that the [B&L73] does not apply to "small" objects where the granularity of classification is "fine", to the identification of a lack of detail on the treatment of classified entities that contain subentities that are distinctly and individually classified.

It is to be observed that classification in a database is rarely *determined* purely on a *syntactic* basis, but rather on the basis of an *association* between specific data entities. Hence, there are contexts in which a specific data value, e.g. 17.3, may be viewed as a TOP SECRET value while 42 would be CONFIDENTIAL, and there are contexts like this paper where both numbers are unclassified. Such *semantic* bases for classification must either be based on a trusted implementation of an approved dynamic algorithm or they must be determined by a trusted path communication with an individual possessing original classification authority.

We are aware of some classification decisions that are so complex that no such algorithm has been produced, while we are aware of simpler cases in which algorithms can be formulated. In either case, it appears evident that a classified record cannot be entered into a database until it and its constituent classified entity classification relationships have been identified and assigned. The wording of the preceding sentence hints at the potential complexity of a complete classification determination and assignment. It is not only the case that the components of a new tuple need to be classified, but it is also necessary to consider the classification of all possible join operations in which the tuple could be involved, including those potential joins between the new tuple and tuples in *different* relations.

If such algorithms can be expressed, we see no reason to prevent their implementation as trusted subjects under the constraints of [B&L73]. If the algorithms cannot be expressed (e.g., in cases where classification is determined intuitively), then a trusted subject would necessarily need to be invoked through a trusted path in order to allow an authorised individual to communicate all of the classification requirements to the MDBMS.

In both cases it would be required that assertions be formulated and proven to demonstrate that the MDBMS preserves the invariance of secure state for the system. This clearly calls for a precise definition of the semantics of each of the MDBMS operations with respect to the domain of each security-relevant operation. Potentially, every modification to the value of any tuple would require a determination of the classification of the tuple and all of the identified classified semantic data interrelationships mentioned above.

It may serve as a useful example to observe that volume III of [B&L73] treats the classification of the relationship between two classified objects. The compatibility requirement for a directory and segment hierarchy requires that all paths from the root node to a directory or segment be monotonically non-decreasing in classification level. Since the hierarchy is represented as a directed graph whose nodes are objects (single level directories or segments), it can be observed that the individual arcs between compatible hierarchy elements are classified. This is the equivalent of assigning a classification to a join operation between pairs of elements in the relation that represents the hierarchy. (A directed graph can be represented by a relation in which a predecessor and a successor field is defined for each element.) Node x is the immediate predecessor of node y just in case there exist domains *pred*, *succ* such that

$$pred(y) = x \text{ and } y \neq succ(x).$$

This is precisely an example of a classified join operation. Every modification to the hierarchy must be shown to preserve compatibility. In the Multics implementation of [B&L73], the operations on upgraded directories and the establishment of links are equivalent to modifying the arcs in the graph of the hierarchy and are necessarily implemented with trusted code.

We believe that the methods used in previous trusted operating system development provide useful insight into the MDBMS problem and to its partial solution. Our investigation suggests that it is possible to provide adequate definitions and constraints for the trusted subjects needed to implement an MDBMS only if the complete semantic classification requirements are specified for each database under consideration.

We recognise that much of the code needed to support a multilevel database management application may need to be trusted, and would observe from the experience of [RADC75] that the preponderance of trusted code would be required for dynamic databases in which classification is semantically derived than in those that are only referenced and wherein the data classification relationships can be derived syntactically.

ACKNOWLEDGMENTS

We would like to thank our colleagues D. Elliott Bell, Earl Boebert, Swen Walker, Brian Hubbard and other researchers in the Center for their helpful and critical comments on our *gedankenexperiment*.

REFERENCES

[B&L73]   D.E. Bell and L.J. La Padula, "Secure Computer Systems: Mathematical Foundations;" "A Mathematical Model; and "A Refinement of the Mathematical Model," MTR-2547, vol. I, II, and III, The MITRE Corporation, Bedford, MA, March, November and December 1973 (also ESD-TR-73-278, vol. 1-3.)

[NAS83]   Marvin Schaefer, chairman, "Multilevel Data Management Security," Committee on Multilevel Data Management Security, Air Force Studies Board, National Academy of Sciences, Washington, DC, 1983.

[RADC75]   T.H. Hinke and Marvin Schaefer, "Secure Data Management System," RADC-TR-75-266, Rome Air Development Center, Air Force Systems Command, Griffiss Air Force Base, New York, November 1975.

Design Overview for Retrofitting Integrity-Lock Architecture onto a Commercial DBMS

Richard D. Graubart   Kevin J. Duffy

The MITRE Corporation

ABSTRACT

This paper is a design overview document, intended to aid in the implementation of an integrity-lock database management system. The authors believe that the paper is a realistic overview of the changes that need to be made to a commercial database management system in order that it may support the integrity-lock architecture. The paper examine the integrity-lock retrofit at a high level of abstraction. In particular it concentrates on changes that need to be made at the process level and in terms of the functionality that needs to reside in the various functions. It is hoped that this high level view will aid in the portability of the integrity-lock architecture to other systems. While the authors' work has involved retrofitting the integrity-lock onto a specific system, we believe that many of the lessons learned in this exercise can be applied to other commercial database management systems.

I. Introduction

This paper is a design overview document, geared to aid in the implementation of the integrity-lock architecture described in "The Integrity-Lock Approach to Secure Database Management" [GRAU84]. The authors of this paper believe that it represents a reasonable overview of the changes that have to be made to an existing DBMS in order to enable it to support the integrity-lock design. The paper will concentrate on changes that have to be made at the process level and in terms of functionality that has to reside in various functions.

Due to size considerations and the proprietary nature of the code, no discussions shall be included regarding the actual routines that need to be changed. The authors of this paper hope that it demonstrates the feasibility of the integrity-lock architecture for enhancing the security of an existing relational database management system. To give the reader some flavor of the work, some of the problems of retrofitting the integrity-lock onto a commercial DBMS are described as well as the methods chosen to circumvent the difficulties. This paper assumes that the reader is generally familiar with the integrity-lock concept. However, a brief synopsis of some of the major points of the integrity-lock is provided below.

SYNOPSIS OF INTEGRITY-LOCK

The integrity-lock architecture is an outgrowth of the 1982 Summer Study On Database Security [AFST83]. It is intended as a near-term solution to the problems of having a **database management system (DBMS)** [1] process data at multiple security levels in an environment where the users of the system are not all cleared to see the same data. The architecture attempts to retrofit security onto an existing DBMS, instead of designing security into the DBMS from the system's creation. The integrity-lock approach attempts to limit the amount of trusted code and makes use of encryption technology.

Essentially the system works in the following manner. As a user inserts a record (tuple) into the database the tuple is first handled by a trusted process known as the Trusted Front End (TFE). The TFE will associate with the tuple a security level supplied by the user and an encrypted checksum. The checksum is based on the data content of the tuple and the security level (the security level may also be encrypted). The tuple, associated checksum, and security level are then passed from the TFE to the DBMS. The DBMS places the tuple and associated components into the database. When information needs to be retrieved from the database, the DBMS will retrieve the information in the same manner that it retrieves any data. However, instead of passing the data directly to the user, the information is passed to the TFE. The TFE first validates that the user requesting the data has a current security level greater than or equal to that of the security level associated with the tuple. Assuming that this test is passed, the TFE then recalculates the checksum and compares the newly calculated checksum with that associated with the tuple. This test is used to ensure that neither the data nor the security level has been modified. If either test fails, the data is not returned and the TFE takes some appropriate action. If both tests are passed then the data is given to the Untrusted Front End (UTFE), which passes it on to the user. The UTFE is an untrusted, but memoryless, process that handles certain functions that are not security critical.

---

[1] Words appearing in boldface are defined in the Glossary.

Reprinted from *Proceedings of the 1985 Symposium on Security and Privacy,* 1985, pages 147-159. Copyright © 1985 by The Institute of Electrical and Electronics Engineers, Inc.

In the case of an update, a similar procedure is followed. The data is retrieved and given to the TFE, which validates it in the manner described above. Assuming that the data passes the validation test, then it is given to the UTFE, which performs the actual update. The updated tuple is then given to the TFE, which recalculates the checksum based on the updated data. The updated tuple and checksums are then given back to the DBMS for processing.

It should be emphasized that the integrity-lock approach is not designed as the ultimate solution to DBMS security concerns. It is merely a method of enhancing the security of currently existing database management systems.

ASSUMPTIONS AND COMPROMISES

As this design is for a prototype and not a fully robust or commercial implementation, certain assumptions and compromises have been made. We are using a commercial relational database management system known as MISTRESS [RHOD83]. It is believed that MISTRESS typifies relational systems and that lessons learned from utilizing MISTRESS can be applied to other relational database management systems. MISTRESS was chosen primarily because of its cost and because it is one of the few relational systems for which one can obtain copies of the source code.

Obviously, this project requires the use of an encryption function. Ideally this encryption should be handled by hardware (e.g., DES encryption chips). Such chips would minimize the time needed to calculate the checksum. However, as we are currently only developing a prototype in order to test the principles of the integrity-lock architecture, all encryption shall be done in software, using the UNIX[2] crypt function.

As mentioned in [GRAU84], the integrity-lock architecture is subject to a potential inference threat. This inference threat is a result of the fact that the integrity-lock achieves its limited amount of trusted code by failing to mediate each access to the data by a trusted mechanism. It is not yet clear how severely this inference threat would impact the security of the DBMS. It is not the intent of this document (or of the actual implementation) to explore the inference threat. The document is designed to aid in the actual implementation of an integrity-lock system. Once an integrity-lock system is implemented, experimentation could be performed on the system to determine the severity of the inference threat.

As noted in [GRAU84], there are multiple variations of the integrity-lock architecture, each with certain advantages and disadvantages. Some of the approaches optimize for projections, and others optimize for use of space. Some of the approaches

---

[2]UNIX is a trade/service mark of the Bell System.

support data element level security, some support field level security, and others support tuple level security. In designing the prototype we examined the strengths and weaknesses of each approach in terms of what made best use of MISTRESS's features.

We have decided that for this prototype tuple level granularity with one checksum per tuple is best. Data element level granularity would be more desirable, but the expense in terms of space is significant. In addition, we have discovered that there is a significant inference problem that arises when data element level granularity and indexed fields are used together. Because of MISTRESS's method of storing and retrieving tuples, it appears that no significant improvement of retrieval efficiency will be achieved by associating checksums with data elements, instead of with tuples.

In the course of this paper, other compromises that we have made in our design will become apparent. These are usually in the form of features that MISTRESS normally supports, but which our security enhanced version of MISTRESS must limit in some form. The reasons why such compromises have been made will become apparent as well.

OPERATING SYSTEM SUPPORT

In order for the integrity-lock approach to be viable it must exist in a secure environment. This means that a secure operating system must support the relational DBMS. Such a secure operating system should be able to authenticate a user's identity and security level and pass this information on to the TFE. In addition, a secure operating system must ensure that the database files are isolated so that a user can access the files only via the relational DBMS (and associated integrity-lock components). The supporting operating system must enforce the isolation of the integrity-lock components from each other and ensure that the UTFE and the DBMS cannot communicate with each other without going through the TFE. In particular, the operating system must somehow enforce the rule that the ability to read data from the database and the ability to output data to the user or to some file cannot reside in the same untrusted process. If this assumption cannot be enforced, then the belief that the TFE is a mediating process is not valid.

While there may be multiple methods of ensuring the above requirements, the authors believe that the most secure method of operation involves associating with each subject (process) and object (file, device) a security level and enforcing a mandatory security policy. Such a mandatory security policy would in general allow processes to read only from objects whose security level is less than or equal to that of the process. The process could, in general, write only to objects whose security level is greater than or equal to that of the object. The above policy statements apply only to untrusted processes. The system must allow for the existence of trusted processes that would be privileged to violate these policies under controlled circumstances.

An operating system that satisfied the above requirements would be consistent with a B2 class system outlined in the "Department of Defense Trusted Computer System Evaluation Criteria" [CRIT83]. An example of such a system is MULTICS.

For this project, what is required is a B2 class system that is UNIX-compatible. UNIX is required since that is the operating system upon which MISTRESS runs. No B2 UNIX-like system currently exists, although theoretical and prototype work on such systems has been done [KRAM84]. The creation of a secure UNIX is beyond the scope of this project. The authors are satisfied that such a system is possible. Therefore, we will assume that such an operating system exists, and that it underlies and supports our integrity-lock system.

II. Architectural Overview

MISTRESS STRUCTURE AND ORGANIZATION

Before detailing the changes that need to be made to the DBMS in order that it can support integrity lock security enhancements, it is necessary to have some general overview of the structure of the unmodified DBMS. To aid in the discussion of this overview, a high-level overview diagram is supplied in Figure 1.

As the diagram shows, MISTRESS is initiated by the execution of the shell script ms. The sole argument to this shell script is the name of the database upon which the user wishes to operate. The ms routine execs what we shall refer to as the control process.

When an ´exec´ is initiated, the calling process is overlaid by the executable file specified in the exec call. In effect, the process that made the ´exec´ call (in this case ms) is destroyed and is replaced by a new process; however, the process id remains the same. There is no return to the calling process after a successful ´exec´. Throughout this paper the word exec´ is used as a verb to describe the act of executing the ´exec´ system call.

The control process takes as an argument the name of the database. Through a series of execs and subroutine calls the control process invokes code that does error checking and some parameter manipulation. Most important of all, the control process invokes code that prompts the user to enter his/her query and then parses the query. Once the query is parsed, the control process is able to discern the nature of the query based on the parse stream and then spawn a process which is responsible for carrying out the query. For example if the user posted the query "select from

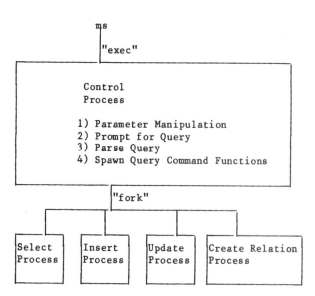

Note, that the query command processes listed above represent only some of the commands and associated processes. There are other commands (e.g., delete). They are not shown above merely to economize on space.

Figure 1. Top Level View of MISTRESS

EMPLOYEE", the control process would spawn a process that would perform the select task.

This brings to light one of the differences between MISTRESS and other DBMSs. The entire DBMS does not reside in one process in MISTRESS. This means it is not possible to invoke a series of routines merely by subroutine calls; instead an entire process must be invoked. As will be shown later, this arrangement is well suited for our purposes, since we are assuming an operating system that provides security protection at the process level.

Although a new process needs to be created to carry out the requested task (select, insert, update, etc.), one still needs to preserve the controlling process. Thus, we cannot exec the new process as this would destroy the existing control process. Instead, in order to assure that control will return to the control process after the appropriate task is finished, the control process executes a **fork** and wait command. The fork command is a UNIX system call which causes the calling process to spawn a child. The child process is given its own process id (pid) and a parent pid is also associated with the process. Otherwise, the child and parent processes are identical. The parent process suspends itself by using the wait command and lets the child continue processing until it receives a signal from the child that the child has died. In this case, the child process will execute a command which in turn execs to a query command program that carries out the task to be performed (select, insert, update, etc.). When the child process terminates it sends a signal to the parent (control) process that it has died and the parent (control) process then resumes execution. The control process then prompts the user for his/her next query, and the procedure continues until the user types "stop", indicating that he/she is done with issuing queries.

Database and Relation Structures

The MISTRESS DBMS is closely tied to the underlying UNIX operating system. A database in MISTRESS is simply a UNIX directory. The name of the directory is the name of the database. This is a reasonable method of organization as a database can be viewed as simply a collection of data relations, with the DBMS imposing organization on the data. One creates a new database in MISTRESS by executing the "msmkdb" shell script. The argument to this shell script is the name of the database that the user wishes to create. The result of this command is the creation of a new directory with some supporting files (see below).

Correspondingly, a **relation** is represented by a UNIX file. The data relation consists of two part: the header and the the data tuples. The header contains information that the DBMS uses to correctly interpret the data tuples. Included in the header is information such as the number of records, the size of the records, the number of attributes, the starting position of each attribute, and the size of each attribute. The data portion of the relation consists of a series of data records. In addition, associated with each record is a field, known as the free list, which indicates whether the record is logically present or whether the record has been logically deleted and therefore can be overwritten.

Supporting Files

Any given database can consist of several relations. Each of the relations contains multiple attributes. To aid MISTRESS in rapidly locating the proper relation and attribute in response to a query, MISTRESS maintains two support files.

One file, **rel.dir**, is an index containing the names of all relations. Associated with each relation name is a pointer to the corresponding data relation. Also associated with the attribute name is a pointer into the second support file, **attr.dir.**

This second file, attr.dir, is a flat file. It contains the names of all of the attributes in the system, the attribute number, the data type of the attribute, a flag indicating whether or not the attribute is indexed, and the name of the index if the attribute is indexed. The pointer into attr.dir allows for the rapid association of relation names with the corresponding attributes.

The rel.dir and attr.dir files allow MISTRESS to authenticate the existence of relation and attribute names prior to opening the actual relation. For this reason, all MISTRESS operators access one or both of these files in some manner.

Index Files

Between the relations, the attr.dir, and the rel.dir file, there is sufficient information for MISTRESS to access the relations in an organized manner and answer user's queries. However, to allow for faster response to some queries, MISTRESS allows for the creation of **indexes**. In MISTRESS, the indexes are organized as B+ trees, and one index is allowed for each field of each relation.

MODIFIED ARCHITECTURE

For the security-enhanced MISTRESS, the current arrangement of files and processes (described above) is not sufficient to support a secure environment. Additional processes are required for the system to function securely. In addition, the notion of security levels associated with processes and files, and the existence of trusted processes necessitate some restructuring of the MISTRESS system.

Modification to the Data Objects

A data relation may consist of tuples of multiple security levels. The best way to protect the tuple in the relation is to store the entire relation at system high. From the point of view of the secure operating system, all of the data in the relation (i.e., all of the tuples) are viewed as system high data, regardless of the actual security level of the data. Only the TFE is able to discern the security markings of the individual tuples. This is examined in more detail later.

By storing the relation at system high, the operating system ensures that only an untrusted process running at system high or a trusted process is able to read and write the data in the relation. By restricting the number of untrusted system high processes and the number of trusted processes we are able to minimize direct assaults upon the data in the data relations.

Similarly, each index is maintained as a file and is stored at the same security level as its corresponding relation. This ensures that the data in the index is protected to the same degree as data in the relation.

The one set of files not maintained at system high are the attr.dir and rel.dir files. These are maintained at system low. The reason for this is given below.

The security level of the database (directory) is dependent upon the policies of the secure operating system. Most secure operating systems that support hierarchical file systems require that the security level of the directory be less than or equal to that of the files contained within. If such is the case with our hypothetical operating system, then the database must be at system low.

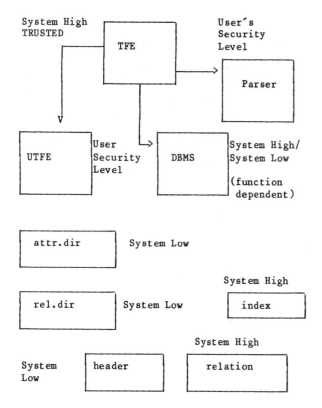

The upper portion of the above diagram represents the control flow of the processes in the system. The lower portion depicts the data objects of the system and their associated security levels.

Figure 2. Components of Modified Architecture

Process Structure in Security Enhanced Mistress

The security enhanced version of MISTRESS will consist of up to four processes. The processes consist of the TFE, which is the parent process, and three child processes, the DBMS, the UTFE, and the Parser. This arrangement is shown in figure 2, the inter-relationship between the parent and child processes depicted by arrows. The remainder of this section gives an overview of the functioning and interaction of these processes.

The Trusted Front End (TFE)

The main function of the TFE is to act as a gate which mediates all information to and output from the DBMS. The DBMS is untrusted and generally runs at system high. As such, it can read data from the database relations. The operating system will only allow the untrusted, system high DBMS to output to a process or file classified at system high. In order for the DBMS to output to a subject or object of a lower classification, the data must go through the TFE. To perform this function, the TFE is invoked to execute various tasks. These tasks include:

1) Booting MISTRESS up

2) Interpreting the output from the parser and invoking the appropriate MISTRESS programs

3) Fork and exec processes at different security levels

4) Calculating security levels and checksums for tuples

5) Encrypting and decrypting data

6) Allowing or disallowing tuple access

7) Signaling to the UTFE to :

  a) print header information

  b) select and print data from a tuple

  c) print error messages

  d) print prompts

8) Downgrading information

9) Logging the user in at a user specified security level

10) Informing the user of the highest classification of data retrieved during a query.

11) Creating a new directory to hold a newly created database

12) Requiring the user to run at system low when issuing a create, create index, rename, drop or delete index operation

13) Prompting the user to verify that the correct data is being inserted into a tuple during an update or insertion operation

A detailed description of each of these tasks follows.

The TFE boots up the system to assure that no Trojan horses are invoked. A user invokes MISTRESS by executing the shell script "ms". The shell script invokes the rest of control process as described above. The ms shell script, and the bulk of the control process functionality must be included in the TFE because it is the TFE that forks and execs the Parser, the DBMS, and the UTFE. The Parser, the DBMS, and the UTFE may be at different security levels than the TFE, depending upon the functionality required (e.g., select, update, etc.). Only a trusted process is able to **spawn** (fork and exec) processes at a security level different than itself. All of the code within the TFE is considered trusted, because privileges are associated with the process as a whole. If any non-trusted code is contained within the TFE, it is possible that a Trojan horse could be placed within the TFE and circumvent the functions of the TFE. Therefore, all of the TFE code must be developed with special care to prevent the inclusion of Trojan horse code that could circumvent the functions of the TFE.

As noted earlier, MISTRESS decides which of the query command programs it should fork and exec by looking at the parse stream returned by the Parser. This functionality has been included in the TFE. Under the original version of MISTRESS, the parser was part of the control process. It was invoked by a subroutine call not a fork or an exec. The parser is written in yacc and lex, a compiler generator and lexical analyzer provided by UNIX. The parser is relatively large and complex and it does not perform any security critical tasks. Therefore, it does not appear either necessary or logical to include the parser functions within the TFE. In this security enhanced version of MISTRESS, the parser has been placed in a separate untrusted process which is spawned by the TFE. The parser process passes the parsed query to the TFE via a UNIX pipe. The TFE then invokes the appropriate function based upon the parse it receives.

The DBMS, UTFE, and Parser must all be spawned at the proper security level. It is the responsibility of the TFE, which spawns these processes, to ensure that they are spawned at the correct security levels. The DBMS (or the query command programs) are all spawned at system high except for create, create index, rename, drop and delete index (see the discussions following for an explanation of why this is true). The UTFE process is spawned at the same security level as the user, as is the parser process. The TFE spawns the UTFE and DBMS processes. The context and security level of the UTFE and the DBMS process is determined by the TFE based on the output of the Parser. It is necessary to re-exec the Parser after each query has been parsed and processed.

The TFE is called to calculate a security level and checksum when a tuple is created or updated. The security level assigned to a tuple is the same as that of the user. This ensures that everything a user creates will be securely classified. A tuple's classification is regarded as system information to be used by the TFE to mediate access. Although this information is stored with the tuple it is not treated as an ordinary attribute. A tuple's classification should not be treated as a legal subject of a query unless the person issuing the query has system programming status. Because of its sensitive nature the security level should be protected from the exploitations of a possible Trojan horse. For these reasons the security level information is encrypted before it is stored in the tuple. The checksum is a line of cipher text obtained by using the tuple as input to the encryption algorithm. When a tuple is created MISTRESS automatically creates a checksum and security level field in addition to the user specified attributes. This action is transparent to the user.

The encryption scheme used by the TFE is a form of the Cipher Block Chaining (CBC) algorithm [DENN82]. This technique is not a simple encryption based on the tuple content. Using the CBC algorithm, the cryptographic checksum is calculated by iteratively applying the encryption algorithm to a fixed portion of the tuple, exclusively or-ing (XOR) the intermediate result to the next portion of the tuple, and then repeating the procedure, until the entire tuple (data and encrypted security level) has been run through the algorithm. Note that the encryption algorithm is merely used to obtain the cryptographic checksum; the actual tuple is left as clear text [AFST83].

The encryption algorithm that the TFE applies to the tuple is complicated enough that neither a user nor a Trojan horse embedded in the database can determine from examining the tuple the specific checksum that the TFE will impose. The "unbreakability" of the algorithm is an inherent underlying assumption upon which the integrity-lock approach is built. In order to ensure such unbreakability, the encryption algorithm used for calculating the checksum, like that used to encrypt the security level, is a DES derivative. The same algorithm that is used for determining the checksum is used for encrypting the security level. The only difference is that for calculating the checksum the encryption algorithm is applied recursively. The algorithm also provides for the decrypting of the cypher text.

Using the checksum associated with each tuple, the TFE can determine if a user is authorized to access the tuple. Each time a user attempts to access a tuple, the TFE will first determine if the user has the clearance to access the tuple. This can be easily done by decrypting the security level stored with the tuple and comparing that to the security level of the user. The user must be at a security level equal to or greater than that of the tuple if the access is to be allowed. The next step in this authorization process is an integrity check. The tuple (data and security level) are run through the recursive encryption algorithm for a second time to determine the checksum of the tuple. The resulting value is then compared to the checksum that was stored with the tuple. If the two values match then this shows that the tuple contents have not been altered. If the values were not the same then the tuple access is disallowed because the tuple has been illegally changed. After this two-step authorization process the TFE can determine if the tuple access is legal. If the access is legal then the tuple will be passed to the UTFE for further processing. If the access is illegal then the TFE will not pass the tuple to the UTFE. This prevents the tuple data from being output to a subject or object running at less than system high.

The TFE decides what data can be released from the DBMS but it is the UTFE that actually outputs data. The TFE passes two types of data to the UTFE when data output is needed. These two types of data are tuples and signals which take the form of numeric codes. See the discussion on the UTFE for an explanation of how the UTFE interprets the data passed to it and what actions it takes.

The TFE is a privileged process that is allowed to communicate with processes running at lower security levels. A major portion of this communication is passing approved tuples from the TFE to the UTFE. None of the tuples passed to the UTFE are of a security level greater than that of the UTFE. The action taken by the TFE is analogous to the people-paper world scenario of taking a Secret document from a TS safe and placing it in a Secret safe. The security level of the document is not changed; it has been placed in a container of a lower security level.

The TFE will also be called to log the user in at a user-specified security level. The TFE will prompt the user to enter the security level at which he wishes to operate. The TFE checks to make sure that the user is not attempting to log in at a level greater than he is cleared for. If the security level entered by the user is equal to or less than his maximum clearance then he can continue with the MISTRESS session. When using a secure operating system the task of determining a user's security clearance can be done with a system call. Just as each user has an associated user id, he would also have a security level assigned to him by the systems personnel. A call such as get_sec_level(userid) would return the user's clearance level.

When data is retrieved after the execution of a 'select' command, it is useful to know its classification. Tagging each data item printed on the screen with its security level may offer more information to the user than would be useful. In addition, ensuring that the correct security level is associated with each data item would require that the output function be trusted. This is not desirable as we wish to limit the amount of trusted code in the system. Instead, after all the tuples to be output have been reviewed by the TFE, the

highest security level read by the TFE will be printed on the screen. This serves as a security tag for the entire output. In order to remind the user of the security level he logged in at, the TFE will also post the security level of the user. This information will always be visible to the user.

The msmkdb shell script and its associated routines are also included in the TFE. As explained above, the execution of this shell script causes the creation of a database. It is essential that the database is created at the proper security level (system low). To ensure this, the creation of a database must be handled by the TFE.

The discussion on tasks 12 and 13 listed above is delayed until after the sections on the DBMS and the UTFE have been given. They are discussed in the sub-section labeled "Potential Security Flaws and Countermeasures."

The DBMS

The DBMS consists of any of the query command programs shown at the bottom of Figure 1. The execution of any one of the programs constitutes the execution of the DBMS. In the security enhanced version of MISTRESS the security level of the DBMS process may differ at each invocation because MISTRESS will not exec all of the query command programs at the same security level. The task that ensures that processes are execed at different security levels is extremely important for the security of the system. The code that performs this task must be trusted. For this reason the DBMS (as well as the UTFE and Parser) must be invoked by the TFE.

In most instances, the DBMS will run at system high. This is because the actual data relations will be maintained in files whose security level is at system high. The DBMS must also be at system high in order to be able to read the relations. By maintaining the data at system high we eliminate the chance that unauthorized users can access the data. Only the encrypted security levels associated with the tuples indicate the true security levels of the data tuples.

Even though the DBMS is untrusted, it is unable to directly pass to the users the data it has obtained from the relation. This is because the DBMS runs at system high and users (with the possible exception of a few trusted security officers) run at lower security levels. Thus, the user is prevented from leaking data illegally to the user. All data transfers must be mediated by the TFE.

As will be explained below, there are some instances when the DBMS will be spawned at system low. This is usually done so that the DBMS can be allowed to modify some system low file. For some of the more complex operations, it is necessary for the TFE to spawn two DBMS processes, one at system high and one at system low.

The Untrusted Front End (UTFE)

The TFE examines the data passed to it by the DBMS and decides what data can be released, but it is the UTFE that actually outputs the data to the user. The UTFE is also responsible for outputting prompts to the user, printing error messages, and performing the built-in MISTRESS functions (sum, average, count, max, min). The UTFE must run at a security level equal to that of the user. This is so that information can be output to the user (the DBMS cannot output to the user because it is usually running at a higher security level than the user). As with the DBMS, the UTFE process will differ depending upon the task to be performed.

If the DBMS is performing a select, then the UTFE is responsible for outputting the fields of the tuples selected. The tuples are chosen by the DBMS, and passed to the TFE for authentication. The authenticated tuples are then passed to the UTFE. Afterwards, the UTFE performs a project operation on the correct fields. In order for the UTFE to know the boundaries of the fields that it needs to perform a project, the UTFE needs access to the header information contained in the relation. However, in our enhanced MISTRESS the relations are stored at system high, and therefore the UTFE will not be able to access the header information. To circumvent this problem we plan to duplicate the header information contained in the data relation, and store it in a separate relation at system low. A separate header file will be required for each relation. Since the header file will be maintained at system low, the UTFE will be able to read it and hence properly interpret the data tuples for projection.

As mentioned earlier, MISTRESS maintains a rel.dir file and a attr.dir file. The information contained in these files is needed by both the DBMS and the UTFE. One example of the UTFE utilizing these files is data projection. The UTFE needs to access these files in order to project the correct fields. In order for the UTFE to utilize the rel.dir and attr.dir files these files must also be maintained at system low.

Information is placed into the rel.dir, attr.dir, and header files by the DBMS when relations are created. In order for the information to be placed into these files the DBMS must run at system low. (This is one of the five instances when the DBMS does not run at system high. The others are Rename, Drop, Create Index and Drop Index. These are described later, where appropriate.) During the create relation phase, the DBMS places the appropriate data in rel.dir and attr.dir. It also creates the data relation and the header file. Note that no data is actually in the relation at this time. The header file and the data relation that are created are created at system low. After performing all of the necessary create functions the DBMS will signal the TFE to upgrade the security level of the data relation to system high. If for some reason the TFE does not perform this task, then there still is no security violation. When data is to be inserted in the relation, the DBMS is spawned at system high. If the relation is not also at system high then the data cannot be inserted, and the attempted security violation is detected by the operating system. Because the attribute names and relation names are stored at system low, users must be careful in their choice of names. Obviously, no names should be used that convey information of sensitivity greater than system low.

For those instances when the DBMS does run at system high, it will be unable to communicate with the user, including transmitting error messages. Therefore, the function of informing the user of errors will be performed by the UTFE. The UTFE will maintain a series of error messages. The determination of which error message (if any) the UTFE will output is based on a signal that the UTFE receives from the TFE. This signal in turn is based on a signal sent from the DBMS to the TFE. Such signaling does pose a possible covert channel threat, but the authors believe that this threat is manageable.

Potential Security Flaws and Countermeasures

The Parser, the DBMS and the UTFE are not trusted, which means that Trojan horses could be present in these processes. There is a threat that a Trojan horse in the Parser, one in the DBMS and one in the UTFE could collaborate in an effort to leak data to an unauthorized user. This could happen if the UTFE, spawned at a certain security level, opens a surreptitious file and stores the data that was passed to it by the TFE. The security level of this file would be the same as the level the UTFE was running at when the file was created. At a later time, the TFE may exec the Parser at the same security level as the surreptitious file. The Parser can read the data from the file, and place it in the parse stream that the TFE passes to the DBMS. In most instances, the DBMS runs at a security level greater than or equal to that of the Parser. However, in the case of the five commands, rename, create, drop, create index and drop index, the DBMS runs at system low. This allows the Trojan horse in the Parser to leak the data read from the clandestine file into the parse stream. The parse stream (including the surreptitious data) is then passed to the system low DBMS as a parameter. Once the data has been passed to the system low DBMS, the DBMS can illegally downgrade the data by placing it in a system low file. To counter this threat, the TFE will require that the user be logged in at system low when issuing a request to perform rename, drop, create or delete index. Since the parser is always run at the security level of the user, the parser will be prevented from reading any files created by the UTFE which are classified higher then system low. If the user is not logged in at system low when issuing these commands, then the DBMS is not spawned and the command is not performed.

It may at first appear that requiring the user to be logged in at system low to issue these commands is overly cumbersome. However, in most instances these commands will only be used by a Data Base Administrator or System Security Officer. Such individuals will be more appreciative of the need to maintain the security of the system, and therefore will understand the need for the restrictions. In any event, the commands impacted tend to be those that are less frequently used in most DBMS environments.

The second threat is that the DBMS could insert into a tuple data which is classified at a higher level than the tuple itself. This is possible because the untrusted update and insert programs which run at system high and have access to the entire database could substitute sensitive data for the user specified data to be used in the update or insert operations. The TFE would have no way of knowing that sensitive data was being inserted in the tuple and the result would be an illegal downgrading of information. To avoid this problem, the TFE echos the data that it has been given to perform the update or insert and then it asks the user to confirm that the correct data is being used. If the user confirms that the correct data has been passed to the TFE then the operation can continue. If the wrong data has been passed then the operation is terminated.

Summation of Architecture

In summary, the general overview of the enhanced MISTRESS architecture is the following. The user initially communicates with TFE, which is trusted and runs at system high. This process spawns an untrusted process for handling the parse. The parse process runs at the user's security level. After this process parses the query the parse stream is passed via a pipe back to the TFE. The TFE then forks and executes the DBMS process and the UTFE process. The UTFE process is always created at a security level equal to the current security level of the user. The DBMS in most instances is created at system high. The exception is when a relation or index needs to be created, renamed, or dropped in which case the DBMS process runs at system low.

All data relations are stored at system high (they are initially created empty at system low and then the TFE raises them to system high). Indices are created and maintained at system high. An associated header file is created with each relation, and is stored at system low. The attr.dir and rel.dir files associated with each database are also maintained at system low.

III. Structure of Commands in Secure MISTRESS

The previous section gave an overview of how the processes and files would be organized and maintained in a secure MISTRESS that supports the integrity-lock. In this section we will examine how individual commands are implemented and which processes are needed to support the various commands in a secure manner. In some instances, the information covered will be the same as mentioned in the previous section. However, in this section, the information is organized so that one can more clearly understand how each of the commands function.

CREATE RELATION

The create relation command will be implemented as three processes. There will be the TFE running at system high, the parser running at system low, and the DBMS running at system low. The DBMS needs to run at system low because creating the relation involves modification to the rel.dir and attr.dir files, both of which are maintained at system low. The DBMS also creates an empty relation (empty in that there is no data in it) and the header file at system low. The relation does contain the relation header. After the create relation process is complete, the TFE raises the security level of the newly created relation to system high.

Because the DBMS and the Parser are running at system low the user creating the relation must also be at system low in order to communicate with these processes. As noted earlier, if the user and Parser were running at a level higher than system low, then it would be possible for classified data to be leaked to the DBMS process (and from there the rel.dir and attr.dir files) via the parse stream.

INSERT

The insert command is represented by four processes: the TFE running at system high, the Parser running at the user's security level, the UTFE running at the user's security level, and the DBMS running at system high. The TFE is the control process that spawns the other processes. The UTFE prompts the user for the data to be placed into each tuple and the security level of the data. After the user has supplied all of the data, the UTFE passes the data tuple to the TFE. The TFE echos the data and security level back to the user, and asks the user to confirm that the information is correct. Once confirmed, the TFE encrypts the security level, associates a checksum with the data tuple (and encrypted security level), and passes it on to the DBMS.

Note that the data that the TFE echoes to the user has no checksum associated with it at the time. The checksum is only supplied after confirmation. Therefore, it is essential that the TFE know that the data it is echoing was supplied by a process running at the user's security level (i.e., the UTFE). Otherwise, a Trojan horse in the untrusted system high DBMS could use this opportunity to pass highly classified data to the TFE (without checksums) in the guise of data that needs to be confirmed.

Once the DBMS receives the data from the TFE, the DBMS places the data into the relation. Note that if the DBMS cannot find the requested relation or if the relation was never raised to system high at create time, no data will be stored and the appropriate individuals will be alerted to an attempted security breach. It is true that a Trojan horse in the untrusted DBMS can hide a duplicate copy of the data in some separate file, but the operating system will ensure that this file is maintained at system high, thus preventing any unauthorized user from accessing it.

SELECT

The select command is implemented by four processes: the TFE at system high, the DBMS at system high, the UTFE at the user's security level, and the Parser at the user's security level. The DBMS accesses the data relations and the indexes, and retrieves the data tuples from the relation. The DBMS performs logical qualification (does it satisfy the condition of the where clause) on each tuple. Those tuples that satisfy the qualification clauses are then passed to the TFE. The TFE examines the checksum and security level, and authenticates that the user is authorized to access the tuples. Those tuples which the user is authorized to view are then passed to the UTFE. The UTFE performs any non-security relevant manipulations (e.g., sum, count, average) and outputting of the data to the user. In order for the UTFE to output the data to the user it must be able to locate the appropriate fields within the tuple. The information needed to do this is found within attr.dir, rel.dir, and the header portion of the relation. To give the UTFE access to all this information, the attr.dir and rel.dir files are maintained at system low, and the header file of each relation must be duplicated and stored at system low.

DROP

The drop function is responsible for deleting an entire relation. It runs as four processes: the TFE at system high, the Parser at the user's security level (which in this case is system low), and two DBMS processes. One DBMS process runs at system low and the other runs at system high. The DBMS process at system low is responsible for deleting the appropriate relation information in rel.dir and the appropriate attribute information in attr.dir. It is also responsible for deleting the duplicate header file associated with the relation. The system high DBMS process is responsible for deleting the actual relation. As with create, a user must be logged in at system low to issue the drop command without risk of data being illegally passed down in the parse stream. Note that because the DBMS processes are untrusted there is no assurance that the correct relation is deleted, or that any relation is deleted. However, this is not considered a security violation, but rather a denial of service problem.

CREATE/DELETE INDEX

The create and delete index commands tend to be mirror images of each other. They require the same number of processes, but in one instance the processes create an index and in another case they delete an index. Both commands require a TFE running at system high, a Parser running at the user's security level (system low in this case), and two DBMS processes. One DBMS runs at system high and the other runs at system low. The DBMS at system high actually creates/deletes the index. The DBMS at system low sets a bit in the attr.dir file indicating that the specified attribute has/hasn't been indexed.

As with create and drop, the user must run at system low to invoke these commands. Again the reason for this is to prevent an illegal data flow via the parse.

UPDATE

The update command is represented by four processes: the TFE at system high, the Parser at user's security level, the DBMS at system high, and the UTFE at the user's security level. An update is essentially a combination of an insert and a select. As such, it is a rather complex operation to perform in a secure manner.

The DBMS which runs at system high is responsible for retrieving the tuple(s) that is to be updated. The tuple is then passed to the TFE which authenticates that the user is authorized to access the tuple and that the tuple has not been tampered with since being entered into the database. The UTFE is responsible for obtaining the new data values that are to be placed into the tuple. If the user is updating interactively, then the UTFE prompts the user for these new values. If the update is non-interactive (the determination of which tuples are to be updated and with which values is based on the query) then the UTFE obtains the value to be inserted from the user's parse.

The new value to be placed into the tuple is passed from the UTFE to the TFE, and the TFE asks the user to confirm the value. As with an insert, the data passed to the TFE to be echoed does not have a checksum associated with it. If this data had come from the system high DBMS instead of the UTFE (which is at the user's security level) this would allow a Trojan horse in the DBMS to illegally pass highly classified data to the user. Thus it is essential, that the TFE authenticate that the data to be echoed has come from the UTFE and not the DBMS.

Once the new data is inserted into a tuple, the security level of the tuple may have to be upgraded. If the newly inserted data does not have a security level associated with it then there is no way of knowing if the tuple's security level should remain the same or be upgraded to the level of the newly inserted data. The tuple could be upgraded to the level the user is running at, but this would lead to over-classification of data. For these reasons, the TFE asks for the security level of each data value used in an update. If the data inserted in a tuple has a lower security level than the tuple, then the security level of tuple will remain the same. If data of a higher classification is inserted into the the tuple then the security level of the tuple will be set to the level of the higher classified data. A user will not be able to assign a security level which is higher than his/her own security level to a data element.

The above policy is acceptable for standard updates. However, there are instances when only the security level, not the data, needs to be changed. The just described methodology is an awkward way of making such changes. Also, there are instances when data must be downgraded by some authorized user. The above policy does not allow for downgrading.

If the user's update request is a downgrading of the security level field, then the TFE must authenticate that the user issuing the request is one of the users authorized to downgrade the data. The TFE can determine if the user is so authorized by comparing the user's logon identification against some system-maintained list of privileged user identities. The TFE must also ensure that the security level of the user is greater than or equal to that of the data. If the user is authorized and of the correct security level, then the TFE will encrypt the new security level supplied by the user and places it into the tuple.

Once the data (and if necessary the security level) has been confirmed, the TFE inserts the new data into the tuple, recalculates the checksum and passes the tuple to the DBMS. It is the DBMS that actually places the tuple into the database.

FINAL OBSERVATIONS ON IMPLEMENTATION OF COMMANDS

There are several commands whose security enhanced, detailed description has not been included in this section (e.g., delete tuple, display attribute name, etc). The reason for not detailing all the commands is simply to economize on space. We believe that the security concerns noted in the commands that have been described tend to typify the concerns involved in retrofitting the integrity-lock design onto an existing DBMS.

Another point that should be noted relates to the untrusted Parser. As noted earlier, the Parser is untrusted because it performs no security relevant function, and would prove difficult to verify. Because the Parser is untrusted, the user has no assurance that the command he/she issues is the command that is performed. Thus if a user issued a select command, a Trojan horse in the Parser could result in a drop command being performed instead. The reason for this is that the command process spawned by the TFE is based on the parse stream that the TFE receives from the Parser. However, whatever command is performed, it will be performed securely.

Finally, no mention has been made in this section regarding error messages. Errors (security relevant and non-security relevant) that occur in the course of performing a command should be reported to the user. If the error occurs in the TFE or in a process running at the user's security level there is no concern. This information may be reported to the user directly. However, if the error occurs in one of the system high DBMS processes then there is a potential for security compromise. The DBMS, which has complete access to the database, could pass highly classified data out to the user (via the TFE) in the guise of error messages. Since the TFE can only determine whether data should be passed to the user from the DBMS based on checksums, the the TFE has no way of authenticating the contents of the error messages, as they lack checksums. As a possible solution to this problem we propose the following.

Whenever the system high DBMS encounters an error it will transmit to the TFE a predetermined coded signal. Effectively, this signal will be of the form "error number N" encountered. The TFE will use the value N to index to a stored list of predefined error messages. The error message corresponding to the error number will be output to the user.

Because the messages are predefined, they tend to be less helpful to the user. However, predefined messages cannot contain data read in from the database. A smart Trojan horse in the DBMS could attempt to signal data to the user by printing a certain predetermined message based on having read a certain value. However, this inference channel does not seem any worse than if a Trojan horse passed back N number of unclassified tuples from a select, having read the value N in some classified tuple.

IV. Conclusion

The intent of this paper has been to show how the integrity-lock architecture could be retrofit upon an existing DBMS. The fact that the processes can be arranged to securely support each of the MISTRESS functions strengthens us in our belief in the correctness of the system.

We believe that this design tends to support the basic premise that the integrity-lock architecture can be retrofit onto an existing DBMS with minimum changes to the DBMS. In the case of MISTRESS, the majority of the changes involve removing some functionality from a single process and placing that functionality into multiple processes (e.g., UTFE and multiple DBMS processes). The remaining changes to the DBMS and UTFE appear to be limited to reserving space for the checksum and security level fields.

The design has also helped to clarify the question of the size and complexity of the TFE. At this juncture, the TFE still appears to be of a manageable size, although its functionality has increased since the original integrity-lock inception.

Certain aspects of the integrity-lock have not been sufficiently addressed in this design and deserve further study. In particular, the question of how vulnerable this system is to covert channel threats and data inference threats in general has not been discussed.

The design has not adequately dealt with the the threat of unauthorized deletions from the database. Because deletion is a denial-of-service problem, it appears to be more of an integrity threat than a security threat. To adequately address this concern would require an operating system that enforces integrity as well as security.

In conclusion, we believe that this document clearly indicates that the integrity-lock architecture can be supported by a B2 level secure operating system with minimal restrictions upon the user. Of course, implementation will be the final arbiter of the correctness of this statement.

V. Glossary

Attr.Dir - A flat file, which contains the names of all of the attributes in the system, the attribute number, the data type of the attribute, a flag indicating whether the attribute is indexed, and name of the index (if it exists).

DBMS [1] (**Database Management System**) - The software that facilitates the use and control of large information files normally maintained on external storage devices. A DBMS permits the insertion, deletion, retrieval, and modification of the data maintained in the files of the database [CLAY83].

DBMS [2] (**DBMS Process**) - In the integrity-lock system, this is the process that handles the insertion, deletion, modification, and logical selection of data from the database. The DBMS runs either at system high or system low. The DBMS process is generally unable to communicate directly with user, and instead communicates with the TFE.

Exec - A UNIX system call that overlays a calling process with a named file. In effect, the process that made the ´exec´ call is destroyed and and is replaced by a new process, but with the same process identifier.

Fork - A UNIX system call that creates a new process (child process) that is an exact duplicate of the calling process (parent process) except that it has its own process identifier (pid).

Index - A file in which each entry consists of a data value together with one or more pointers into a flat file [DATE81]. In MISTRESS, the indices are maintained in ´of´ files [RHOD83].

Relation - A flat file. A two-dimensional array of elements [MART77].

Rel.Dir - In MISTRESS, an index containing the names of all of the relations in the database. Associated with the relation names is a pointer into the attr.dir file, associating the relation name with the attributes contained in that relation.

Spawn - The combination of a fork and exec, resulting in a new process.

TFE (Trusted Front End) - The trusted process of the integrity-lock system. It is responsible for mediating access between the DBMS process and the UTFE process. The TFE handles all data and user authentication. It also spawns the DBMS, UTFE, and Parser processes.

UTFE (Untrusted Front End) - In the integrity-lock system, an untrusted process spawned at the security level of the user, this process handles all outputting of data to the user.

REFERENCES

AFST83   Air Force Studies Board, "Multilevel Data Management Security," National Research Council, National Academy Press, Washington, D. C., 1983.

CLAY83   B. G. Claybrook, _File Management Techniques_, Wiley Press, 1983.

CRIT83   Department of Defense Trusted Computer System Evaluation Criteria. Department of Defense, CSC-STD-001-83, 15 August 1983.

DATE81   C. J. Date, _An Introduction to Database Systems Third Edition_, Addison-Wesley, 1981.

DENN82   D. E., _Cryptography and Data Security_, Addison-Wesley, Reading, MA, 01803, 1982.

GRAU84   R. D. Graubart, "The Integrity-Lock Approach to Secure Database Management," 1984 IEEE Symposium on Security and Privacy, Oakland, California.

KRAM84   S. M. Kramer, "LINUS IV: An Experiment in Computer Security," 1984 IEEE Symposium on Security and Privacy, Oakland, California.

MART77   J. M. Martin, _Computer Data-Base Organization_, Prentice-Hall Inc., Englewood Cliffs, NJ, 1977.

RHOD83   "MISTRESS: Relational Database Management System," Version 2.2 Rhodnius, Incorporated, Toronto, Ontario, Canada M4Y1P9, 1982.

COMMUTATIVE FILTERS FOR REDUCING INFERENCE
THREATS IN MULTILEVEL DATABASE SYSTEMS

Dorothy E. Denning

SRI International
333 Ravenswood Ave.
Menlo Park, CA 94025.

Disclosure of classified data in multilevel database systems is threatened by direct user access, user inference, Trojan Horse release, and Trojan Horse leaks. Earlier work showed how the problems of direct user access and Trojan Horse release can be solved by using a trusted filter and cryptographic checksums, but left the problems of inference and leaks open. We now show how the problem of user inference can be solved with the concept of a commutative filter that ensures that the result returned to a user is equivalent to one that would have been obtained had the query been posed against an authorized view of the database. The technique allows query selections, some projections, query optimization, and subquery handling to be performed by the database system. It does not solve the Trojan Horse leakage problem.

INTRODUCTION

Consider a multilevel relational database system, which handles data of different security classifications and provides shared access to users with different clearances. The *disclosure* requirement of multilevel security states that if cd is the classification of data d (security level plus compartment), and cu the clearance of user u, then disclosure of d to u is authorized only if $cu \geq cd$, where $\geq$ is the usual partial ordering relation on security levels and compartments. We assume that all data is labelled with its security classification, and that labelling is either at the relation, tuple, attribute, or element level.

Ignoring for the moment the problem of enforcing multilevel security, there are four categories of threats to the disclosure of unauthorized data. The first two of these are initiated by a user without assistance from the database system; the other two normally require assistance from a Trojan Horse in the database system, although they could also arise through faults in the system. The first and third represent direct disclosures; the second and fourth indirect disclosures.

1. **Direct Access.** Here the user queries the database system for unauthorized data d, and the system responds with d, correctly labelled with its classification.

2. **Indirect Access by Inference.** Here the query is for authorized data, but the data returned is a function of unauthorized data d in such a way that the user can infer d from the response.

3. **Trojan Horse Direct Release**. Here a Trojan Horse in the database system causes unauthorized data d to be released with an incorrect classification label that effectively makes the data appear to be authorized to the user. This may be achieved either by changing the label on d, by placing d in a record (or field) with the lower classification, or by failing to update the label on d if its classification increases.

4. **Trojan Horse Leakage.** Here the Trojan Horse indirectly leaks unauthorized data d by encoding it in authorized data returned to the user. Whereas the result returned by the database system appears to answer the user's query, it actually answers a different query, namely one for d.

All of the above forms of disclosure could arise from accidental as well as malicious actions on the part of a user. For example, a user could request a set of records, not realizing that some of the records in the set are classified higher than his clearance permits. Although we are primarily concerned with malicious attacks, we must also protect against accidental disclosures.

Reprinted from *Proceedings of the 1985 Symposium on Security and Privacy*, 1985, pages 134-146. Copyright © 1985 by The Institute of Electrical and Electronics Engineers, Inc.

Turning now to the problem of protecting against unauthorized disclosure, we observe that disclosure by direct access (type 1 threat) can be prevented with database access controls that compare the classification of the data with the clearance of the user before releasing the data. Although most commercial database systems do not provide this capability, including this capability in a relational system would be relatively straightforward.

Unfortunately, adding simple access controls to a database system does nothing to prevent the other three types of disclosure. Of particular concern are Trojan Horses in the database system that release classified data improperly labelled (type 3 attacks), thereby circumventing the access checks. If the database system is "untrusted" (i.e., not verified with respect to its security properties), installing such a Trojan Horse in the code would seem to be relatively straightforward.

The seriousness of this Trojan Horse threat combined with the difficulties of designing large verifiable systems led researchers to look for solutions that do not require verification of a complete database system. The solution that emerged uses a trusted (verified) and isolated filter (guard), which interfaces with the untrusted database system as illustrated in Figure 1. The filter is a reference monitor responsible for enforcing the requirements for multilevel security. The filter labels the data at the relation, record, attribute, or field level (or some combination), and binds the data to its classification by computing a cryptographic checksum over the data and its label using a secret key. The cryptographic checksums make it practically impossible for the untrusted database system to change the data or the classification labels. The checksum is recomputed when the data is retrieved in order to authenticate the data and its classification. If the response to a query includes data that the user is not cleared to see, the filter simply removes that data from the response returned to the user.

Figure 1 shows two users, with low and high clearances respectively, with shared access to the database. In practice, any number of users with different clearances could have shared access. Each user (or group of users with identical clearances) is connected to the filter through a private interface process (untrusted front end) that performs pre- and post-processing of queries. These interface processes must be isolated from one another, e.g., on separate machines.

The basic idea, due to Roger Schell, has been applied by Anderson to the RECON bibliographic system, which is essentially a record storage and retrieval system with record level classification[1]. The idea was suggested by Weissman's group at the 1982 Woods Hole Summer Study on Multilevel Data Management Security[2] as a

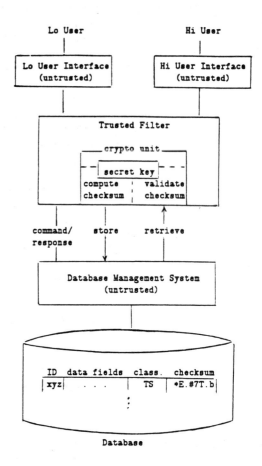

Figure 1. Multilevel Database Protected by Filter and Cryptographic Checksums.

possible method of providing multilevel database security for more general database systems. Since then, we have shown how labels and cryptographic checksums could be securely applied down to the element level[3] and have examined the implementation and security of the approach[4]. The approach has also been studied by Graubart[5].

These studies showed that whereas the approach could effectively eliminate direct disclosure (type 1 and 3 threats), including the return of falsely labelled data by Trojan Horses, it did not eliminate either user inference threats (type 2) or Trojan Horse leaks (type 4). The inference threat was found to be particularly serious because it is often simple to perform and requires no assistance from a Trojan Horse. It appeared that the only secure way of dealing with the threat is for the filter to see all data used to answer a query so that it can remove any element not authorized to the user from the user's view of the database.

Based on this observation, we concluded that the database system cannot perform selections and projections, handle subqueries, do query optimization, or perform statistical computations; these functions must be placed either in the filter or the user interfaces, effectively reducing the database system to a record storage and retrieval system[4]. It thus appeared that the general approach of using a trusted filter with cryptographic checksums is well suited for record storage and retrieval applications such as RECON, but not for general purpose databases.

The objective of this paper is to show how the user inference threat (type 2) can be practically eliminated with a minimal amount of support in the filter. The approach allows the untrusted database system to perform all selections, some projections, subquery handling, and query optimization. Section 2 reviews the nature of the inference threat, showing that attacks can be simple yet devastating. Section 3 presents our solution, which is based on the concepts of authorized views and commutative filters. Section 4 discusses the remaining threat, Trojan Horse leaks. Section 5 concludes.

THE INFERENCE PROBLEM

The inference problem of concern here arises when the classification of the response returned by a query permits the data to be released to the user even though the data used to form the response is not authorized to the user. Under many circumstances, the user can infer the unauthorized data from the authorized response. To make this concrete, we give two examples. We assume that the data is SECRET and TOP-SECRET collateral (not compartmented), and that the user making the queries is cleared only to SECRET.

Example 1. Consider a relation EMPLOYEE with attributes NAME and ID, which are classified SECRET, and attribute PROJ, which is classified TOP-SECRET (thus classification is by attribute). The following query returns SECRET data, but reveals TOP-SECRET data, namely whether there is a project called GEMINI and, if so, which employees are working on the project.

```
RETRIEVE EMPLOYEE.NAME
WHERE EMPLOYEE.PROJ = "GEMINI"
```

One can argue that a SECRET user should not even be aware of the existence of the TOP-SECRET attribute PROJ, whence such a query would never be posed. Indeed, the filter should hide the existence of unauthorized data. The point of the example is that knowing the existence of unauthorized data should not allow a user to obtain the data.

The example shows the problems that can arise when the database system performs selections and projections, and the filter sees only the results of these operations. If the database system instead returns the complete EMPLOYEE records to the filter, without doing the selection on PROJ code or projection onto NAME, the filter could delete the PROJ field, and securely pass the result back to the user interface (where the selection would no longer even be feasible). Alternatively, the filter could observe that the query named an attribute (PROJ) that was unauthorized to the user and abort the query (without passing it to the database system). This latter approach will be an important part of our proposed solution.

It is interesting that if classification is by record rather than by attribute, where records with certain PROJ codes including GEMINI are TOP-SECRET, then the query does not pose an inference problem. This is because the filter will remove all TOP-SECRET records regardless of whether PROJ is GEMINI. Hence, no information in TOP-SECRET records can be inferred from the response. Note, however, that some information may be inferred still since a null response from the filter reveals either that GEMINI is TOP-SECRET, that no employee belongs to the project, or that GEMINI is not in fact a valid code. There is little that can be done to protect against this type of inference short of classifying the entire relation as TOP-SECRET.

Classification by record or relation does not by itself solve the inference problem, however, as illustrated by the next example.

Example 2. Consider a database with two relations: EMPLOYEE, with attributes NAME and ID; and TRIPS, with attributes ID and DEST (destination), where the employee ID field in the two relations can be joined. Suppose classification is by record, where all records in EMPLOYEE are SECRET, and all records in TRIPS are SECRET unless DEST is "RHODESIA", in which case they are TOP-SECRET. The following query returns records from EMPLOYEE, which are SECRET, although it reveals TOP-SECRET information, namely the employees that went to Rhodesia:

```
RETRIEVE EMPLOYEE.NAME
WHERE EMPLOYEE.ID = TRIPS.ID
AND TRIPS.DEST = "RHODESIA"
```

This query is a standard "select-project-join", which would normally be optimized and performed in one step by a database system. If for security the database system must return all the data needed to answer the query to the filter, then the database system could not be allowed to perform the standard optimization trick of selecting on DEST before doing the join to reduce the volume of data to be joined. Our proposed solution will allow the database system to perform the optimized join, but require that it return the record classifications from the joined records in both EMPLOYEE and TRIPS that satisfy the selection formula over DEST.

SOLUTION TO INFERENCE PROBLEM

Observe that if each query is made against a view of the database consisting only of that data authorized to the user (i.e., all unauthorized data is effectively deleted from the database), then unauthorized data cannot be inferred from the response. Observe further that partitioning the data into authorized vs. unauthorized sets for a given user is straightforward since classification is applied to data objects (relations, records, attributes, or elements), and it is a simple test to determine whether an object's classification is less than or equal to a user's clearance.

We can imagine implementing authorized views by inserting a data management filter between the database management system and the stored data on disk. This filter would ensure that all data returned from the disk were authorized to the user making the query; unauthorized records and attributes would be deleted, and unauthorized elements replaced by nils. The data management filter would know the secret key used by the user interface filter to compute checksums so that it could authenticate retrieved records. The approach resembles the two kernel approach proposed by Downs and Popek[6].

Figure 2a illustrates. For a given query q, the result returned to the user is equal to the result of a query $qsec$, which is q applied to the user's *maximal authorized view*, i.e., that subset of the database consisting of all data authorized to the user, but no unauthorized data.

The use of a data management filter was suggested by Tad Taylor and Bret Hartman, who observed that it could solve the Trojan Horse problem as well as the inference problem since the database system would see the maximal authorized view with respect to the user. Unfortunately, the approach assumes that the database system does not mix user views in its internal workspace; if it can mix the data in a TOP-SECRET view with that in a SECRET view, for example, then leaks and inferences may be possible. Such mixing might arise when the database system is simultaneously accessed by users with different clearances, but could also arise with sequential accesses. To ensure that such mixing does not occur would require that some trust be placed in the database system, which is what the filter approach is designed to eliminate.

We propose instead an indirect implementation of the principle, which we call the *authorized view equivalence scheme*, whereby the filter serves to make the result returned from a user's query q equal to what would be obtained had the query been applied to the maximal authorized view, that is, equal to $qsec$. Figure 2b illustrates how the filter obtains a result equal to $qsec$ in two steps: Step 1 poses a query q_1 to the database system; q_1 is the original query q, augmented as necessary

a) Maximal Authorized View Approach.

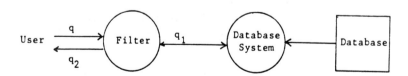

b) Commutative Filter Approach (Authorized View Equivalence).

Figure 2. Preventing User Inferences with Authorized Views and Commutative Filters.

to include classification and checksum fields. Step 2 filters the response from q_1 to obtain a result for a query q_2 that is equivalent to *qsec*; the result of q_2 is returned to the user.

The approach effectively creates a filter that is commutative with the database management system; that is, the operations of removing unauthorized data and computing the response to a query are commutative. We emphasize, however, that this is true only to the extent that the database system does not have a Trojan Horse that leaks data.

We will now show how the scheme can be implemented when data is classified by record, attribute, or data element (or some combination). For clarity, we develop the approach for three types of increasingly complex queries: select only, select-project, and select-project-join. Generalizing the approach to more complex queries over more than two relations, including nested queries, is straightforward. The approach is not described in terms of the elementary relational operators since our objective is for the filter to pass complete queries to the database system for processing. For each type of classification and each type of query, we show the secure version *qsec* for an arbitrary query q, the query q_1 presented to the database system, and the query q_2 corresponding to the result returned to the user.

All queries are expressed in the relational algebra using the relational operators σ (selection), Π (projection), and $\times$ (join). Properties of the relational algebra are used to prove that q_2 is equivalent to *qsec* (e.g., see Ullman[7] for a description of the relational algebra operators and their properties).

Classification by Record

Let R be a relation, and let C denote an attribute that gives the classification of a record (tuple) of R. Let cu be the clearance of the user making the query. The maximal authorized view of R is thus given by

$$AUTH\text{-}VIEW\text{-}R = \sigma_{C \,\leq\, cu}(R) \,.$$

We now consider the three classes of queries.

Select Only Query

Consider the following query

RETRIEVE *R.All* WHERE F ,

where "*All*" denotes all attributes in R, and F is a selection formula over the values of the attributes. This

query is expressed in the relational algebra as

$$q = \sigma_F(R) \,.$$

The secure version of q is thus

$$qsec = \sigma_F(AUTH\text{-}VIEW\text{-}R) = \sigma_F(\sigma_{C \,\leq\, cu}(R)) \,.$$

To obtain a result equivalent to *qsec*, the filter first poses the user's query to the database system, and gets back the response:

$$q_1 = \sigma_F(R) \,.$$

The filter then selects out those records unauthorized to the user, using the checksums to check the integrity of the data and the classification labels, and returns:

$$q_2 = \sigma_{C \,\leq\, cu}(q_1) = \sigma_{C \,\leq\, cu}(\sigma_F(R)) \,,$$

which is equivalent to *qsec* because selections commute. This means that as far as protecting against inference is concerned, the order in which selections are performed does not matter; records can be selected first by their classification and then by other criterion (formula F), or vice-versa. Thus, the database system can use index structures on the database to efficiently perform selections and reduce the volume of data that must be returned to the filter.

Select only queries correspond to the queries handled by the RECON guard; indeed, the RECON guard processes these queries in the same manner described here, returning q_2. Because q_2 is equivalent to *qsec*, the RECON guard is secure against user directed inference attacks. Of course, this does not mean that it is free from Trojan Horse leaks (see Section 4).

Select-Project Query

Consider now a select-project query on R:

RETRIEVE *R.A* WHERE F ,

where A is a subset of the attributes in R. Expressed in the relational algebra, this query becomes:

$$q = \Pi_A(\sigma_F(R)) \,,$$

and its secure version is given by:

$$qsec = \Pi_A(\sigma_F(\sigma_{C \,\leq\, cu}(R))) \,.$$

To obtain a result equivalent to *qsec*, the filter can again let the database system perform the selection using F, and then take the result and select by the classification C. If the checksums are at the record level, the filter cannot, however, let the database system perform the projection onto A since complete records are needed for authentication; the projection must be done in either the filter or user interface. If the checksums are at the element level, the database system can project out data attributes, but must not project out the classification label C^*. Because we are interested in knowing the minimal amount of data that must be returned to the filter for processing, we will pursue the case of element level checksums. Then the query sent to the database is[**]

$$q_1 = \Pi_{A,\,C}(\sigma_F(R)) \;.$$

The filter then selects out the records authorized to the user and projects onto A, thereby returning

$$\begin{aligned}
q_2 &= \Pi_A(\sigma_{C \,\leq\, cu}(q_1)) \\
&= \Pi_A(\sigma_{C \,\leq\, cu}(\Pi_{A,\,C}(\sigma_F(R)))) \\
&= \Pi_A(\sigma_{C \,\leq\, cu}(\sigma_F(R)) \\
&= qsec \;.
\end{aligned}$$

This shows that the database system can perform projections securely, thereby reducing the volume of data returned to the filter. This would be important in applications where the communication link between the filter and the database system is a potential bottleneck.

Select-Project-Join Query

Finally, we consider a query which involves the joining of two relations:

RETRIEVE $R.A$, $S.B$ WHERE F ,

where A is a subset of the attributes in relation R, B is a subset of the attributes in S, and F is an arbitrary selection formula over the attributes of the two relations, which would include clauses for joining pairs of attributes in R and S by equality (for equijoin, including natural join) or by some other relational operator. Either of the projected subsets, A or B, may be null. In the relational algebra, the query is given by

$$q = \Pi_{R.A,\,S.B}(\sigma_F(R \times S)) \;.$$

Since the secure view for this query is obtained by selecting the authorized records from R and S independently before performing the join, we have

$$\begin{aligned}
qsec = \\
\Pi_{R.A,\,S.B}(\sigma_F(\sigma_{R.C \,\leq\, cu}(R) \times \sigma_{S.C \,\leq\, cu}(S))) \;.
\end{aligned}$$

To obtain a result equivalent to $qsec$, we follow the same strategy as for select-project queries, namely, of obtaining the classification attributes from both relations along with the other requested attributes. The queries q_1 and q_2 are thus:

$$q_1 = \Pi_{R.A,\,R.C,\,S.B,\,S.C}(\sigma_F(R \times S))$$

$$\begin{aligned}
q_2 &= \Pi_{R.A,\,R.B}(\sigma_{R.C \,\leq\, cu \,\wedge\, S.C \,\leq\, cu}(q_1)) \\
&= \Pi_{R.A,\,R.B}(\sigma_{R.C \,\leq\, cu \,\wedge\, S.C \,\leq\, cu} \\
&\qquad (\Pi_{R.A,\,R.C,\,S.B,\,S.C}(\sigma_F(R \times S)))) \\
&= \Pi_{R.A,\,R.B}(\sigma_{R.C \,\leq\, cu \,\wedge\, S.C \,\leq\, cu}(\sigma_F(R \times S))) \\
&= \Pi_{R.A,\,R.B}(\sigma_F(\sigma_{R.C \,\leq\, cu}(R) \times \sigma_{S.C \,\leq\, cu}(S))) \\
&= qsec \;.
\end{aligned}$$

Note that the filter must examine the classification fields from both relations, even if all attributes are projected out of one of the relations. This is necessary to prevent the type of inference illustrated by Example 2 in Section 2, where the records in the returned relation were classified lower than the records in the relation joined to it.

Classification by Attribute

Let $c(A_i)$ denote the classification of attribute A_i in relation R. The set of attributes authorized to a user u with clearance cu is defined by

$$R.AUTH = \{A_i \in R \mid c(A_i) \leq cu\} \;.$$

Thus, the maximal authorized view of R is

$$AUTH\text{-}VIEW\text{-}R = \Pi_{R.AUTH}(R) \;.$$

Again, we examine the three classes of increasingly complex queries:

Select Only Query

Consider again the query

$$\begin{aligned}
q &= \text{RETRIEVE } R.All \text{ WHERE } F \\
&= \sigma_F(R) \;.
\end{aligned}$$

With attribute level classification, the secure version of q becomes

---

[*] In addition, the checksum fields are needed to authenticate the data, and the record identifier is needed to compute the cryptographic keys (using the field authentication technique we proposed in[3]); these fields are not shown in the augmented queries since they are not relevant to the inference problem.

[**] Strictly speaking, we should write "$A \cup \{C\}$" instead of "A, C" since C could be in the set A; we will use "," since it is notationally simpler.

$$qsec = \sigma_F(\Pi_{R.AUTH}(R)) .$$

If we adopt a strategy similar to the one taken for record level classification, the filter would obtain a result equivalent to $qsec$ by first presenting the user's query to the database system:

$$q_1 = \sigma_F(R) ,$$

and then filtering out the unauthorized attributes by computing:

$$q_2 = \Pi_{R.AUTH}(q_1) = \Pi_{R.AUTH}(\sigma_F(R)) .$$

But in this case q_2 is equivalent to $qsec$ if and only if the formula F names only attributes in $R.AUTH$; otherwise, the projection onto $R.AUTH$ does not commute with the selection on F. Thus, to achieve equivalence, the filter must check the attributes named in F to determine whether they are in $R.AUTH$, disallowing the query if they are not. This requires more processing in the filter than for record level classification since the filter must obtain the attributes named in a query explicitly or implicitly (through $R.All$) and their classifications. The attribute classifications could be stored in the database system (e.g., in a relation ATTRIBUTES that gives the type and classification of each attribute in the database), and checksums used to guarantee their integrity.

Classification by attribute may also require additional processing in the user interface if the attributes returned do not include all of the ones expected (i.e., because they are not authorized to the user). The interface must be able to receive shorter records with fewer fields and know which fields have been deleted.

Select-Project Query

For a query

$$q = \text{RETRIEVE } R.A \text{ WHERE } F$$
$$= \Pi_A(\sigma_F(R)) ,$$

the secure version is

$$qsec = \Pi_A(\sigma_F(\Pi_{R.AUTH}(R))) .$$

The query from the filter to the database is again $q_1 = q$, and the response from the filter to the user

$$q_2 = \Pi_{R.AUTH}(q_1) = \Pi_{R.AUTH}(\Pi_A(\sigma_F(R))) .$$

As before, q_2 is equivalent to $qsec$ if and only if the formula F names only attributes in $R.AUTH$; the filter must check this property.

Select-Project-Join Query

For a join query over relations R and S:

$$q = \text{RETRIEVE } R.A, R.S \text{ WHERE } F$$
$$= \Pi_{R.A, S.B}(\sigma_F(R \times S)) ,$$

the secure version is

$$qsec =$$
$$\Pi_{R.A, S.B}(\sigma_F(\Pi_{R.AUTH}(R) \times \Pi_{S.AUTH}(S))) .$$

Again the query from the filter to the database system is $q_1 = q$, and the result returned to the user is

$$q_2 = \Pi_{R.AUTH, S.AUTH}(q_1)$$
$$= \Pi_{R.AUTH, S.AUTH}(\Pi_{R.A, S.B}(\sigma_F(R \times S))) ,$$

which is equivalent to $qsec$ if and only if the formula F names only attributes in $R.AUTH$ and $S.AUTH$. This implies that the join itself, which is expressed by one or more clauses in F, must be over authorized attributes.

Classification by Element

For each data attribute A_i in a relation R, we assume there is a corresponding classification attribute C_i that gives the classification of the data element stored in the field for A_i in the records of the relation.

The maximal authorized view of R consists of all data elements whose classification is less than or equal to the user's clearance cu; unauthorized data elements and their classifications are effectively replaced by a "nil" value (meaning "undefined"), which itself must be unclassified. Since this is difficult to express formally in the relational algebra, but simple to grasp intuitively, we will not give a formal definition here.

Of course, the presence of a "nil" value signals the user that the missing data is either undefined or unauthorized. If undefined is considered less likely than unauthorized, the user can thus deduce something about the classification of the suppressed data. For example, if classification is not compartmented, then a SECRET user can deduce that suppressed data is at least TOP-SECRET. Moreover, the domain of values may be such that the data itself can be deduced (e.g., if there is only one TOP-SECRET value possible for a given attribute). In general, the presence of a nil can reveal up to one bit of information about the data suppressed.

Now, if the filter applies this definition of maximal authorized view by replacing unauthorized values with nils, security is achieved only if selections are performed by the filter instead of by the database system. To see why, consider again the EMPLOYEE relation of Example 1, but now suppose that the data is classified by element. Suppose also that all NAMEs are SECRET, but that PROJ is either SECRET or TOP-SECRET, depending on its value; in particular, the PROJ code GEMINI is TOP-SECRET and the code APOLLO is SECRET. Consider the query

> RETRIEVE EMPLOYEE.NAME,
> EMPLOYEE.PROJ
> WHERE EMPLOYEE.PROJ="GEMINI"
> OR EMPLOYEE.PROJ="APOLLO"

If the database system performs the selection on PROJ, it will return something such as:

NAME, CLASS	PROJ, CLASS
Baker, SECRET	GEMINI, TOP-SECRET
Jones, SECRET	APOLLO, SECRET
Smith, SECRET	GEMINI,TOP-SECRET

The filter will then delete the TOP-SECRET data, and return

NAME, CLASS	PROJ, CLASS
Baker, SECRET	nil, nil
Jones, SECRET	APOLLO, SECRET
Smith, SECRET	nil, nil

The user, however, can deduce that the nil code is GEMINI, that GEMINI is TOP-SECRET (in case this was not known), and that employees Baker and Smith have these codes. This inference could be prevented by moving all selections from the database system to the filter, which would disallow selections over unauthorized data. However, since we are interested in minimizing the amount of query processing in the filter, we seek an approach that allows the database system to perform selections.

The example illustrates an important principle about classification of data: data is classified by its context, that is, by its association with other data, and not by its inherent value. The name GEMINI by itself is certainly not classified. It becomes classified only by its association with a particular attribute (in this case PROJ), and possibly also by its association with a particular record (employee). Two policies that would lead to element level classification of PROJ codes are :

1. **Single Attribute Association**. The domain of PROJ codes is partitioned into TOP-SECRET values, SECRET values, etc; thus, the value in a particular record is classified according to the block to which it belongs.

2. **Multiple Attribute Association**. The classification of a PROJ code is determined by the employee having that code; note that this is equivalent to partitioning the domain of NAME into those with TOP-SECRET codes, those with SECRET codes, etc. The names themselves, however, may all be at the SECRET level so that users cleared only at the SECRET level can access them. More complex classification policies can also be envisaged - for example, where classification is determined by attributes in other relations that are associated with an employee (through joins).

Note that classification by attribute is a special case of single attribute association where all values belong to the same block; classification by record is a special case of multiple attribute association where all fields in a record are uniformly classified by their association with the record.

Now, because of these associations, the database system can be allowed to perform selections only if the filter does not return nils for unauthorized data. This means that the filter must either suppress complete attributes (columns) or records (rows) so that the relation returned does not have "holes".

With the suppressed attribute approach, the filter would remove any attribute that has an unauthorized value in some record selected by the query. This requires a two-pass algorithm over the records: the first pass to authenticate the records and determine which (if any) fields have unauthorized data; the second to delete those fields. In the preceding example, the attribute PROJ would be deleted since it is referenced by the query and some of the records selected contain TOP-SECRET codes.

With the suppressed record approach, the filter would delete those records containing an unauthorized value in one of the requested fields. This can be implemented with a one-pass algorithm over the records where the decision to keep or delete a record is made as each record is authenticated. In the preceding example, the records for Baker and Smith would be deleted; thus, the user would be unable to deduce anything about their PROJ codes.

Suppressing records is more efficient and sensible to implement than suppressing attributes since the data is returned from the database system by record. Moreover, we would expect users to prefer this approach since they will get data for requested attributes. But there is another important reason for adopting record suppression: attribute suppression does not prevent inference with multiple attribute associations; that is, when data associated with one attribute (e.g., PROJ) is classified by its association with another attribute (e.g., NAME). In the preceding example, suppressing the PROJ field would not prevent inference of a TOP-SECRET PROJ code if the query selected only on the basis of a single TOP-SECRET value (e.g., the WHERE clause were simply "PROJ="GEMINI"). The filter would return the NAME field of all employees assigned to GEMINI, and deleting the PROJ field would not prevent a user from inferring the deleted value. Record suppression, by comparison, thwarts this inference because the user is not even aware of the existence of records containing the PROJ code GEMINI, let alone which employees have this value.[***] Attribute suppression can prevent inferences with single attribute classification since the filter could know that GEMINI is a TOP-SECRET value of PROJ and disallow the selection. This could be done with record suppression as well, but is unnecessary since selections over unauthorized data have no effect (since they commute with the filter's selection to remove records with unauthorized data).

We therefore adopt record suppression and define an authorized view to be one whose records contain only authorized data. Applying this definition to a complete relation, however, will restrict much more data than necessary, since any record containing even one unauthorized field would be deleted, even if the query does not include that field. For example, if the user's query is simply

RETRIEVE EMPLOYEE.NAME ,

then all employee names can be returned securely, even if their PROJ codes are unauthorized to the user. Thus, we shall instead apply the definition of authorized view to a projection of a relation onto the set of attributes named either explicitly or implicitly (through *All*) in a query; as before, this includes any attributes named in a selection formula.

[***] There is an exception. If GEMINI is the only TOP-SECRET code, then a user can deduce which employees have this code by requesting the set of all employee NAMEs and the set of all (NAME, PROJ) pairs and then computing the set difference over the names.

For a subset A of the data attributes of a relation R, let C denote the corresponding classification attributes. We shall write $C \le cu$ as shorthand for the "and" over all terms $C_i \le cu$ for C_i in C:

$$\wedge \{ C_i \le cu \mid C_i \in C \} .$$

The authorized view of relation R projected onto data attributes A with classification attributes C is thus:

$$AUTH\text{-}VIEW\text{-}R\text{-}A = \sigma_{C \le cu}(\Pi_{A,C}(R)) .$$

Now, this definition of authorized view admits exactly the same set of data admitted by the original definition with the nils. This is because the set of all projections onto all possible subsets of attributes of R gives exactly the set of authorized data. In particular, for each record, there is exactly one subset A of attributes for which a projection onto A will return all authorized data in that record; every superset of A will result in that record being deleted, allowing the user to deduce which fields are unauthorized (i.e., nil). Thus, the new definition gives the maximal authorized view.

But unlike the original definition, the definition here leads directly to authorized view equivalence. We now show how this is done.

Select Only Query

The query

$$q = \text{RETRIEVE } R.All \text{ WHERE } F$$
$$= \sigma_F(R)$$

has no projections, so its secure version is given by

$$qsec = \sigma_F(AUTH\text{-}VIEW\text{-}R\text{-}All)$$
$$= \sigma_F(\sigma_{C\text{-}All \le cu}(R)) ,$$

where $C\text{-}All$ denotes all classification attributes.

The query from the filter to the database is the user's query, $q_1 = q = \sigma_F(R)$, and the result returned by the filter is:

$$q_2 = \sigma_{C\text{-}All \le cu}(q_1)$$
$$= \sigma_{C\text{-}All \le cu}(\sigma_F(R))$$
$$= qsec .$$

Select-Project Query

Consider now the query

$$q = \text{RETRIEVE } R.A \text{ WHERE } F$$
$$= \Pi_A(\sigma_F(R)) .$$

Letting A' denote the attributes A plus those named in F, and C' the corresponding classification attributes, the secure version of q is

$$qsec = \sigma_F(AUTH\text{-}VIEW\text{-}R\text{-}A')$$
$$= \sigma_F(\sigma_{C' \leq cu}(\Pi_{A',C'}(R))) .$$

The query presented by the filter to the database system is

$$q_1 = \Pi_{A',C'}(\sigma_F(R)) ,$$

and the result returned to the user is

$$q_2 = \Pi_A(\sigma_{C' \leq cu}(q_1))$$
$$= \Pi_A(\sigma_{C' \leq cu}(\Pi_{A',C'}(\sigma_F(R))))$$
$$= qsec .$$

Select-Project-Join Query

This case is a straightforward extension of select-project queries.

Summary of Filter Requirements

The following summarizes the processing steps in the filter for each type of classification.

Classification by Record

1. Filter must augment a query to include the classification, checksum, and possibly ID fields in each relation specified, even if all other attributes in that relation are removed (as in a join query where the requested attributes are all from one relation); this query is then presented to the database system.

2. Filter must check the classification fields in every record returned, suppressing unauthorized records and records that fail the authentication check.

Classification by Attribute

1. Filter must obtain the classification of each attribute named in a query either explicitly or implicitly; these could be obtained from the database system.

2. Filter must check the classifications of all attributes named in a selection (WHERE clause) to determine if the attributes are authorized to the user. If all attributes are authorized, the user's query is sent to the database system, augmented to include checksum fields and other fields needed for authenticating the data; otherwise, the query is disallowed.

3. Filter must delete all fields corresponding to unauthorized attributes from the records returned by the database system, and delete all that fails the authentication check.

Classification by Element

1. Filter must augment a query to include the data and classification field associated with every attribute named explicitly or implicitly in a query, plus the fields needed to authenticate the data; this query is then presented to the database system.

2. Filter must check the classification of every element in every record returned, suppressing those records that contain elements that are unauthorized or that fail the authentication check.

For all types of classification, the bulk of query execution can thus be handled by the database system. In particular, selections, joins, query optimization, subquery handling (for nested queries), and some projections can be managed by the database system. The main role of the filter is to augment the user's query to the database system to ensure that all relevant classification fields (and checksums) are returned (for record and element classification), and that all named attributes are either authorized (for attribute classification) or returned (for element classification). Of course, this requires that the filter have access to the record structures of the relations stored in the database, and that it know the query structure passed from the user interface so that it can access and manipulate it. The latter can be simplified if the interface parses the query first, and passes a parse tree (or equivalent structure) to the filter.

Unsolved Inference Problems

The authorized view equivalence scheme does not address all types of inference. These fall into four general classes:

1. **Aggregate Functions.** The filter cannot pass queries for sums, averages, counts, and other statistical (numerical, etc.) functions over aggregates of data to the database system for evaluation. This is because the filter would not know the classification of the data used to compute the query, and there would be no guarantee that unauthorized data could not be inferred from the computational results returned. Instead, the user interface must ask for the raw data and perform the computation itself. This means that the filter cannot, for example, release aggregate statistics with a security classification lower than that of the raw data; to do so, would require complex inference controls in the filter of the type used by census agencies (e.g., see[8] for a survey).

2. **Constraints.** Inferences may arise from constraints on the data imposed by integrity conditions or external factors if these constraints are not reflected in the classification policy. For example, consider a system where classification is by attribute. If an attribute B can be derived from a lower classified attribute A, then unauthorized data associated with B may be inferred from authorized data associated with A. To prevent this type of inference, data that derives other data stored in the database must be classified at least as high as the derived data. Since the rules for deriving data are often not explicit in the database, preventing this type of inference can be extremely difficult.

3. **Classification.** As noted earlier, a user can infer something about the classification of suppressed data if the user knows that the data exists in the system. Moreover, if there is only one possible classification code for the suppressed data, then the user can infer its exact classification. Of course, in general we would expect that users would not have enough information about data that is unauthorized to them to realize that it has been suppressed, or even to ask for it in the first place.

4. **Low Entropy Data.** Also noted earler, if unauthorized data has low entropy, inference may be possible by taking the set difference of a set of records and the same set constrained by a selection over unauthorized data, allowing the contents of the records in the difference to be deduced.

The last two categories of inference in particular point out the desirability to restrict a user's knowledge about the database to authorized data. If a user does not know about unauthorized data, including the names of unauthorized attributes or unauthorized values associated with multilevel attributes (i.e., where the data associated with the attribute is classified by element), these types of inference are less likely. Obviously, the filter should not provide this information to users in response to queries about the database schema. Assuming such "meta queries" are simply queries on the system relations of the database, then the techniques described in Section 3 will also protect the system data.

TROJAN HORSE LEAKS

The authorized view equivalence scheme thwarts user inferences where the database system is not party to the attempted subversion. Subversive attempts on the part of the database system to return unauthorized data directly (by modifying classification labels or by stuffing the data into authorized records) are prevented by the filter's checksums.

This leaves the threat of a Trojan Horse (TH) in the database system leaking unauthorized data by encoding it in authorized data. The threat is present with all three types of classification: record, attribute, and element.

It is difficult to assess the seriousness of this threat in a general way since the difficulty of performing such encodings depends on the structure and contents of the database. We observe, however, that to leak data, the following conditions must be satisfied:

1. There must be a conspiracy between the TH and the user receiving the data. This means that the person planting the TH in the database system must either be the user or else collaborate with the user.

2. Either the TH must regularly return unauthorized data, which the cognoscente recognize and know how to decipher, or else the user must have some way of signalling the TH to return unauthorized data. If the database system is not informed of the user originating a query, then the signal would have to be through some agreed upon query.

3. There must be a way of encoding the unauthorized data in the response to an agreed upon query for authorized data, and the user must know the encoding scheme. In particular, the TH must return a response that looks like the response to the user's query (i.e.,

consists of same set of attributes from the same relations), but which in fact answers a different (hypothetical) query (namely, one for the leaked data). In addition, either the user must know exactly what data elements are being returned and how to locate them in the response, or else the encoding must include enough information to identify the unauthorized data elements in the response.

4. Since the encoding will depend on the presence of authorized data satisfying certain constraints (e.g., having the same value as the unauthorized data), leakage will fail in the absence of such data. Thus, there should be a low signal (leaked data) to noise (authorized data) ratio.

5. There must be a way of recognizing unauthorized data in the database. If the classification labels are stored in the clear, then this is trivial. But if the labels are encrypted[3, 4], the TH would have to deduce classification by access patterns to the database, or else would require assistance from the user. Encrypting the labels, however, has the disadvantage of making it impossible for the database system to perform selections based on classification (to reduce the volume of data returned to the filter).

The following scenario illustrates how these conditions might be satisfied. The leaked data are integers between 1 and 1000.

1. The penetrator creates an unclassified relation VALS with an integer attribute, and inserts 1000 records into VALS covering the domain 1 to 1000.

2. The penetrator plants a TH in the database system by modifying the query processor to respond to the query "RETRIEVE VALS.All" by translating and executing a query which is encoded in the relation LEAK. The amount of code required for the TH will depend on the capabilities provided by the database system for dynamic query interpretation.

3. The penetrator creates a relation LEAK with the format used by the TH.

4. The penetrator inserts records for a query into LEAK that, when translated, leak classified data in the range 1 to 1000 by returning the

records from VALS having the identical values. Thus, the data returned looks like a legitimate response to the penetrator's original query.

The TH used in this scenario is particularly devastating because it is not bound to any particular leakage. The penetrator has only to update the relation LEAK to obtain other unauthorized data. Thus, the TH behaves like a "universal Trojan Horse" which executes user-programmable leakage queries.

SUMMARY AND CONCLUSIONS

Disclosure of classified data in multilevel database systems is threatened by direct user access, user inference, Trojan Horse release, and Trojan Horse leaks. Earlier work showed how the problems of direct user access and Trojan Horse release can be solved by using a trusted filter and cryptographic checksums, but left the problems of inference and leaks open. The inference threat was found to be particularly troublesome because it did not require a Trojan Horse in the database system, and seemed to suggest that most query processing, including selections, could not be performed securely in the database system.

This paper has shown how the problem of user inference can be solved using authorized views and a commutative filter, which ensures that the result returned to a user is equivalent to one that would have been obtained had the query been posed against an authorized view of the database. The technique allows query selections, some projections, query optimization, and subquery handling to be performed by the database system.

We have not solved the Trojan Horse leakage problem. Whether this a serious shortcoming, or whether an acceptable solution might be found, is not known and requires further study.

Acknowledgments

The idea for this paper came while I was preparing my slides for the 1984 Symposium on Security and Privacy and realized that not all of the conclusions in my paper were justified; in particular, the inference problem could be managed without moving all selections and projections into the filter. A provocative discussion with Bret Hartman, Tad Taylor, and Kim Wilson at SRI following the symposium helped me clarify my ideas. A later discussion on Trojan Horses with Peter Denning and

Steve Lipner at the University of Newcastle upon Tyne led Peter to propose the universal Trojan Horse. Peter, Jim Anderson, and Richard Graubart provided many helpful comments on earlier versions of this paper. I am deeply grateful to the NSF for supporting this research through Grant MCS83-13650.

References

1. Anderson, J. P., "On the Feasibility of Connecting RECON to an External Network", Tech. report, James P. Anderson Co., March 1981.

2. Committee on Multilevel Data Management Security, "Multilevel Data Managment Security", Tech. report, Air Force Studies Board, National Research Council, 1982.

3. Denning, D. E., "Field Encryption and Authentication", *Proc. of CRYPTO 83*, Plenum Press, 1983.

4. Denning, D. E., "Cryptographic Checksums for Multilevel Data Security", *Proc. of the 1984 Symp. on Security and Privacy*, IEEE Computer Society, 1984, pp. 52-61.

5. Graubart, R. D., "The Integrity-Lock Approach to Secure Database Management", *Proc. 1984 Symp. on Security and Privacy*, IEEE Computer Society, 1984, pp. 62-74.

6. Downs, D. and Popek, G. J., "A Kernel Design for a Secure Data Base Management System", *Proc. 3rd Conf. Very Large Data Bases*, IEEE and ACM, New York, 1977, pp. 507-514.

7. Ullman, J. D., *Principles of Database Systems*, Computer Science Press, 1982.

8. Denning, D. E. and Schlorer, J., "Inference Controls for Statistical Database Security", *IEEE Computer*, Vol. 16, No. 7, July 1983, pp. 69-82.

INTEGRITY IN TRUSTED DATABASE SYSTEMS

Roger R. Schell
Gemini Computers, Inc.
P.O. Box 222417
Carmel, CA 93922

Dorothy E. Denning
SRI International
333 Ravenswood Ave.
Menlo Park, CA 94025

INTRODUCTION

A trusted computer system is designed to be 'secure' with respect to some well-defined security policy. There are two major classes of information security policy: (1) secrecy policies, which govern the disclosure of information and (2) integrity policies, which govern its modification. Although much of the literature on computer security emphasizes secrecy, for many systems integrity is of equal or greater importance. The DoD Trusted Computer System Evaluation Criteria[1] is careful to encompass (although not require) security policies that include integrity. A trusted computer system is designed to protect 'sensitive information,' which is defined in the Criteria as information that must be protected from "unauthorized disclosure, alteration, loss or destruction."

In databases, the term 'integrity' is interpreted broadly, as illustrated by the following definition taken from Date[2]:

> "The term *integrity* is used in database contexts with the meaning of *accuracy, correctness,* or *validity.* The problem of integrity is the problem of ensuring that the data in the database is accurate -- that is, the problem of guarding the database against invalid updates. Invalid updates may be caused by errors in data entry, by mistakes on the part of the operator or the application programmer, by system failures, even by deliberate falsification. The last of these, however is not so much a matter of integrity as it is of *security* ... The term 'integrity' is also very commonly used to refer just to the special situation ... in which it is possible that two concurrently executing transactions, each correct in itself, may interfere with each other in such a manner as to produce incorrect results."

In this paper, we address all aspects of integrity in that all are essential to the operation of secure database systems.

Classes of Integrity Policies

There are two distinguishable aspects of integrity policies: whether a given modification of information is *authorized*, and whether the modification results in information that is in some sense *consistent* or *correct*. Authorization is subdivided into two categories: (1)

mandatory integrity authorization, which is based on integrity classifications, reflecting importance of data, and clearances, reflecting user trustworthiness, and (2) *discretionary integrity authorization*, which is based on users' needs to modify information. Both mandatory and discretionary integrity controls can protect data from malicious tampering and destruction as well as from accidental modification and destruction through operator errors (e.g., an operator may inadvertently attempt to delete the wrong relation) or faulty software.

Consistency is subdivided into three categories: (1) *database integrity rules*, which define correct states of a database in terms of relationships among the data, (2) *recovery management*, which returns the database to a consistent state after failure, and (3) *concurrency controls*, which ensure that concurrent transactions do not interfere, thereby creating inconsistent states of the database.

We shall discuss each aspect of integrity in more depth after first discussing assurance for these different aspects.

Assurance

The notion of a security perimeter is essential to obtaining assurance that a security policy is actually enforced by the Trusted Computing Base (TCB) of a system. As stated in the Criteria "the bounds of the TCB equate to the 'security perimeter' " and "includes all those portions ... essential to the support of the policy." That is, the security perimeter is with respect to the security policy being enforced. Thus, the two categories of policy, viz., mandatory and discretionary, may well have two distinct security perimeters. This, of course, only applies to systems of Class B1 or above, because Class C systems do not support a mandatory policy.

The mandatory policy, for both secrecy and integrity, can be enforced with a very high degree of assurance against concerted attacks, including Trojan horses. As the evaluation classes move from B1 to B2, B3, and finally A1, the primary distinctions relate to the use of improved architecture, specification, verification, and testing to increase the assurance in the mandatory access controls enforced by the TCB. It is expected that the higher evaluation classes will be used to protect against users with a wider range of authorizations.

Reprinted from *Proceedings of the 9th National Computer Security Conference,* 1986, pages 30-36. U.S. Government work not protected by U.S. copyright.

In contrast, because of their richer policies, discretionary access controls have inherent limitations (known as the 'safety problem'[3]) and more complex mechanisms than mandatory controls. This is especially true for database systems that protect data at the granularity of individual elements and have powerful access mechanisms, such as views, which rely on much of the database system for their support. Because of the inherent as well as technological limitations, little meaningful assurance of discretionary controls can be obtained beyond that of Class C2; in particular, one cannot obtain high assurance against Trojan horses. Fortunately, this matches well the real-world need for discretionary controls for need-to-know and corresponding integrity enforcement. Moreover, because discretionary controls operate within the confines of mandatory controls, the damage that can result from their failure is limited.

Because of the sharp distinction in the possible assurance for mandatory versus discretionary controls in a database system, the following discussion presumes that there may be two distinct security perimeters for systems at Class B2 and above: an inner perimeter (the 'reference monitor') for mandatory controls, and an outer perimeter (or perimeters) for discretionary and consistency controls. The maximum assurance that seems required, and the maximum practical, for the portion of the TCB outside the mandatory perimeter appears to be that prescribed for Class C2.

As discussed later, the assurance requirements for Class B2 and above, in particular the need to control covert channels, affects the meaning of consistency and the functionality of other aspects of a database system. However, having separate security perimeters makes it possible to more meaningfully address these problems.

AUTHORIZATION INTEGRITY

Mandatory Integrity Authorization

Mandatory security policies are particularly important because they describe global and persistent properties that are required for authorizations in a secure system. As defined in the Criteria[1], mandatory policies employ a reliable label to reflect the degree of protection required for information and to reflect the authorization of a subject to access information. When considering integrity, these labels reflect what the Criteria refers to as the 'sensitivity designation of the information,' or what is commonly termed the *integrity access class*, or simply *integrity class*, of the information objects. There is a comparable label that reflects an individual's 'authorization for the information;' this label is assigned to corresponding subjects. The primary systems of interest are those that can be represented by a Formal Security Policy Model, as defined in the Criteria. For such a system it is shown that if the initial state of the system is secure with respect to the policy, then all future states of the system will be secure.

For mandatory secrecy policies, the secrecy access classes must form a lattice. This requirement may be appropriate for mandatory integrity policies as well, although nonlattice mandatory integrity policies have been proposed[4].

For lattice-based policies, the integrity classes could correspond to integrity levels (analogous to secrecy levels such as SECRET), category sets of disjoint integrity compartments (analogous to secrecy compartments such as CRYPTO), or both.

Six mandatory security policies have been variously proposed to deal with integrity. In the context of the above concept of mandatory policy, each of these is examined as a possible integrity policy for databases:

1. Strict integrity
2. Low-water mark
3. Ring policy
4. Multilevel security with no write-up
5. Program integrity
6. Domains and types

The first three policies were introduced by Biba[5] as possible policies for multilevel-secure systems.

Strict Integrity Policy. This policy is an exact dual of multilevel secrecy as defined in the Bell and LaPadula model[6]. Each subject and object is assigned a fixed integrity class taken from the lattice of integrity classes, and strict integrity is preserved by prohibiting a subject from reading down or writing up in integrity.

There are two distinct considerations in assigning integrity classes to objects and subjects. First, the integrity class of the object to be protected from unauthorized modification must reflect the sensitivity of the information, viz., the potential damage that could result. Second, the integrity class of the subject must reflect its trustworthiness for making modifications. However, it is essential to note that the modifications by a subject are effected by the programs it executes and the data that control the execution of these programs. Thus, if a high integrity class is assigned to objects (files or segments) containing programs and program data, this assignment must reflect a determination that the resulting execution will produce only acceptable modifications.

The strict integrity model was initially introduced to deal with the threat of deliberate falsification or contamination of very sensitive information. One such application in which high integrity is of great importance is the preparation of targeting data that are used to control ballistic missiles. The practical threat is not so much that an unauthorized individual will be allowed to use such a system, but rather that a program and/or data maliciously prepared will be incorporated into a Trojan horse to retarget the weapons towards inconsequential or even friendly targets. This kind of Trojan horse could be implanted in what has become popularly known as a 'virus,' and strict integrity has been recognized as one of the few effective defenses.

There is a growing body of experience with the implementation and use of strict integrity in highly trusted operating systems. For example, in the Honeywell SCOMP, the first Class A1 system on the Evaluated Products List, strict integrity is included as part of the protection for segments. This mechanism is used for the protection for security related information such as audit data. In addition, the Gemini GEMSOS[7] has incorporated strict integrity as part of the sensitivity label for all subjects, objects, and devices; this approach has been found useful when designing the integrity protection both of sensitive application information and of system information used to support the security controls themselves. Although there has been little comparable experience in database systems, the I.P. Sharp multilevel database model[8] incorporates strict integrity along with multilevel secrecy.

Low-Water Mark Policy.

This policy is analogous to the high-water mark security policy of the ADEPT-50 system[9]. A subject's integrity class is dynamic and decreases as the subject reads data of lower integrity. If the integrity classes of objects are static (as in the strict integrity policy), a subject will be unable to write into an object with a higher integrity class than it has read; if the object classes are dynamic, then their integrity classes are possibly lowered if the subject writes into the object. As summarized by Biba[5], "This policy, in practice, has rather disagreeable behavior. . . . In a sense, a subject can sabotage (inadvertently) its own processing by making objects necessary for its function inaccessible (for modification). The problem is serious since there is no recovery short of reinitializing the subject." To the best of our knowledge, this policy has not been included in any system design.

Ring Policy.

By prohibiting read-downs in integrity class, it seems the strict integrity policy and the low-water mark policy could prove to be quite restrictive for most systems, especially database systems. Because database processes must have both read and write access to user data, system tables, index files, logs, and other structures to answer queries and update the database, it would appear that the only workable assignment of integrity classes is system low. Because of the restrictiveness of the two preceding policies, Biba also introduced a more flexible policy called the ring policy. Each subject and object has a fixed integrity class, and a subject is only allowed to write into objects whose integrity classes are dominated by the subject's class. No restrictions are placed on reading, so a subject can write high integrity data even if it has read data of a lower integrity. Unfortunately, the relaxation of this policy makes the integrity class of the subject essentially meaningless, because there are no restrictions on even what programs the subject can execute. Thus, what would appear to be a high integrity subject can, without restriction, be executing erroneous or malicious programs that destroy the high integrity information to which the subject has access. In reality, this policy fails to meet the requirements for a mandatory policy. Moreover, there is no real experience using this policy as a basis for mandatory integrity.

Multilevel Security with No Write-Up.

Extending the Bell and LaPadula model to prohibit 'writing-up' in secrecy class provides a limited form of mandatory integrity. In particular, this extended policy model addresses the 'write-up' problem of the mandatory secrecy policy, which allows a subject to write up in secrecy class. The extended model would prevent a SECRET subject, for example, from inserting data labeled as TOP-SECRET into a multilevel relation or from overwriting a TOP-SECRET element (which

it cannot observe). This approach appears to protect subjects from lower-level subjects. Closer examination makes it clear that this approach is a case of the ring policy just addressed in which the secrecy labels, such as SECRET, are also used as the integrity labels; the difference is thus only syntactic with no difference in the results of the policy. Of course, this policy also has the same weaknesses as the ring policy.

Program Integrity Policy.

The restrictions of the strict integrity policy remain a concern, so it seems important to try to identify a more flexible but useful policy. The real world supports some notion of integrity class through job levels and chain of command. However, the flows between different levels (usually adjacent) are bidirectional, so information flows both up and down in integrity class. Moreover, the trust placed on the information provided by any individual is often more a function of the individual than position. The key to the effective protection in this context is that the individuals are trusted to make only the desired modifications of high integrity information, even though they have been exposed to information of lower integrity classes.

This same concept can be applied to software by imposing more stringent requirements on assigning an object containing executable code a high integrity class. It seems unreasonable to assume that once a program has observed data of low integrity that it is incapable of writing data of higher integrity, or because data are entered by a user of low integrity into a database, that indexes and other structures on the database must be treated of low integrity also -- there is little relationship between the quality of the data that go into a database and the quality of the system structures that represent it.

This problem has been approached by distinguishing read access from execute access (which are treated identically in the preceding policies). Based on this distinction, Shirley and Schell[10] have defined a program integrity policy in which a subject is only allowed to write into objects of less than or equal integrity class and only allowed to execute objects of greater than or equal integrity. As with the ring policy, there are no restrictions on reading. This policy appears to be better suited for databases because the database processes could operate with a high integrity class, where they would be able to read and update the entire database. Users and application processes would be assigned integrity classes reflecting their 'trustworthiness'. Furthermore, Shirley has shown not only that this is a mandatory policy but also that it is the identical policy implemented by the hardware protection ring mechanism of Multics and several other systems (no connection with Biba's use of the term 'ring'). Thus there is a substantial body of experience with this policy, and it has indeed been shown to be quite useful in operating systems. There is no comparable body of direct experience with database systems.

An even closer look at the program integrity policy reveals the somewhat unexpected result that it is just a special case of the strict integrity policy. To understand this, it should be recalled that in the Bell and LaPadula model there is the notion of a 'trusted subject.' When interpreted for integrity, as in the case of the strict integrity policy, a trusted subject is trusted exactly to be able to read low integrity information without damaging the integrity of high integrity data. This notion of trusted subject is too coarse for the problem at hand because a trusted subject can read any integrity class. However, the notion has been refined in the Gemini GEMSOS[7] to identify a 'multilevel subject' that has both a minimum and maximum class. Now, if the subject in each protection ring is regarded as multilevel (with respect to integrity classes) with a maximum integrity equal to the ring of execution and a minimum integrity equal to the least trusted ring, the strict integrity policy in this case becomes the program integrity policy if the multilevel subject is trusted not to execute any program with a lower integrity class than its maximum.

Domains and Types. Domains and types have been proposed as a means to specify a mandatory integrity policy, as illustrated by the Honeywell SAT system[4]. Here, each object is typed, and each domain has a list of types that it can observe and modify plus a list of domains that it can call. Although this policy model is similar to discretionary policies based on the access matrix model, the set of types, domains, and rights cannot be altered. Because it is a relatively new approach, its properties are not yet completely clear. So far, there is no experience applying this type of policy to a database system, although Honeywell is working on it.

Discretionary Integrity Authorization

Discretionary integrity authorization policies control access to data at the user or user group level. The usual approach to controlling access in database systems includes *authorization lists*, which specify what operations a user (or group) is authorized to perform on some set of data. For integrity, the operations of interest include update, insert, and delete.

The authorization lists of database systems are included in the data model at different layers of abstraction. At the lowest layer, they are associated with files, records, or elements. At the highest layer, they are associated with *views* or *subschema* on the data. The high-level approach has the advantage of specifying a context for access. The context -- i.e., exact set of elements that fall within the target of a view -- is dynamic, changing as the underlying database is updated. Because it is easier and more natural for users, the high-level approach has proven to be far more useful than the low-level approach, and is embodied in many systems including SQL/DS, DB2, ORACLE, and INGRES (though in a somewhat different form).

The discretionary security policy contained in the Trusted Computer System Evaluation Criteria[1] is appropriate for database systems as long as the concept of object is interpreted to mean views (actually view specifications or subschema) rather than just physical elements, records, or files. Note that this does not mean that discretionary controls cannot be associated with individual records and elements; such controls are easily defined as views on the database.

The Criteria specify that discretionary controls are to be applied to 'each named object.' There is no requirement that the named objects be disjoint in memory, and in some operating systems a file may be accessed via different path names through different directories with different discretionary authorizations placed on the different names. Similarly, applying discretionary controls to views is consistent with the Criteria because views are just a way of naming objects. Also, there is no requirement that the 'named objects' of the discretionary policy be the same objects or even at the same layer of abstraction as the 'storage objects' of the mandatory policy.

CONSISTENCY INTEGRITY

Database Integrity Rules

Database integrity rules protect a database from data entry errors as well as from other errors made by the operator or by software. They define the correct states of the database and may specify actions to take if an update would cause the database to enter an incorrect state. They are similar to exception conditions built into programs, except that the conditions are represented in the database (as metadata) rather than in the application programs so that they can be automatically applied to all transactions updating the database.

In a relational system, there are two common types of database integrity rules: domain integrity rules and relational integrity rules. *Domain integrity rules* are context-free rules specifying the allowable set of values (i.e., domain) for an attribute, e.g., DRIVER.AGE is greater than 16 but less than 100. *Relational integrity rules* are context-sensitive rules specifying more global constraints on individual tuples or sets of related tuples, e.g., that every tuple in a PROGRAMMER relation has a corresponding tuple in an EMPLOYEE relation (this is a form of 'referential integrity'). Many relational systems, e.g., INGRES, provide mechanisms whereby users can define rather complex integrity rules.

Integrity rules play a vital part in ensuring the integrity of a database. Indeed, they are a very important part of access controls because most systems are vulnerable to errors as well as to sabotage. It is probably fair to say that a database system would not be regarded as a useful trusted system if it does not support integrity rules.

There are, however, intrinsic problems associated with integrity rules in a multilevel system that is rated at the evaluation level of B2 or higher, arising from the requirement to protect against covert channels. Because the implementation of integrity rules is outside the mandatory security perimeter, the database subjects that enforce the integrity rules must be denied access to data that is classified higher than the subject level. Thus, if the subjects are processing a transaction on behalf of a user, the only data visible to those subjects will be data that is classified at a level dominated by the user's level. If the database system were given access to data not dominated by the user's level, then a Trojan Horse in the database system could leak the unauthorized data -- that is, unless the database system (or a large portion thereof) were part of the mandatory security perimeter. Because the latter is neither feasible nor desirable, in multilevel systems rated at the level of B2 or higher, we are forced to consider integrity constraints as constraints on the subset of the database dominated by the user's clearance.

To see how this revised interpretation of integrity constraints affects the enforcement of integrity rules, consider the relational model, which requires each tuple in a relation to have a unique primary key. Suppose the tuples in a multilevel relation are classified SECRET or TOP-SECRET, and suppose the relation contains a TOP-SECRET tuple with primary key FOO. This tuple will be invisible to subjects operating on behalf of SECRET users. Thus, if a SECRET user attempts to insert a new tuple, also with key FOO, the system will accept the tuple. Because the access class becomes the only means of distinguishing the tuples, the class must then be considered to be part of the primary key. We refer to the coexistence of multiple tuples with the same primary key except for access class as *polyinstantiated* tuples[11].

Problems also arise with respect to referential integrity. For example, suppose a TOP-SECRET user creates a TOP-SECRET tuple in a relation T(ID, A), which is associated with a SECRET tuple in a relation S(ID, B) through the join attribute ID. The relation S represents the entities named by the primary key ID. If a SECRET user deletes the referenced tuple in S, referential integrity will be violated. But because the SECRET user, as well as all subjects that run on that user's behalf, cannot know of the existence of the TOP-SECRET tuple, this cannot be avoided.

As a third example of the problems that arise from invisible data, consider a relation that contains the weights of items on board various flights. Suppose there is maximum weight restriction of 5000 for any given flight and that some of the items on board a flight are classified SECRET while others are TOP-SECRET. If the integrity constraint is specified simply as an upper bound of 5000 for the total of all weights for a flight, a flight could be overloaded because the TOP-SECRET weights would be invisible when the constraint is applied at the SECRET level to determine whether an additional SECRET item can be placed on board. A possible solution is to have separate constraints for SECRET and TOP-SECRET weights.

Thus, in B2 or higher systems, the consistency defined by integrity constraints must be interpreted with respect to the secrecy class of the subject applying the constraint. However, whether there should be some notion of inter-level consistency, or how this might be specified, is unclear. It is also unclear how triggers fit into this notion since a trigger activated by an operation on behalf of a user having one secrecy class cannot read up or write down in secrecy class. Finally, we note that if the database is polyinstantiated at the tuple or element level, problems arise in applying the integrity constraints because more than one tuple or element with different values may be selected by the constraint, each with different outcomes. Thus, the integrity rules must specify which values to select among polyinstantiated values.

In a multilevel system, the concept of integrity constraints should also be extended to include constraints on the classifications assigned to data. For relational systems, we have found that several properties should hold:

- The complete definition (schema) for a relation, including the names of all attributes, should have a single access class that is dominated by the access classes of all data that is to go into the relation. Integrity rules that constrain the data going into the relation should also be assigned this access class.

- The attributes representing the primary key in a relation should be uniformly classified -- that is, within any given tuple, the elements forming the primary key should have the same access class.

- The classification of the primary key should be dominated by the classifications of all other elements within a tuple.

In that integrity rules enforce constraints on the relationships among data in the database, they can be associated with inference problems. For example, if an integrity constraint states that C = A + B for attributes A, B, and C, where A and B are SECRET but C is TOP-SECRET, then a SECRET user with access to A, B, and the integrity constraint can infer C. In this particular case, the best strategy for dealing with the problem may be to use the integrity constraint to force classifications on the data to prevent the inference -- e.g., classify A or B, or both, as TOP-SECRET. In cases where the rule of inference is complex and unknown, it may be more appropriate to classify the integrity constraint (which can be viewed as an inference rule).

In summary, although a multilevel secure database system should provide database integrity rules, the mandatory secrecy policy affects the interpretation and application of integrity constraints.

Recovery Management

Another vital aspect of database integrity is protecting the database from operator or software errors, including system crashes. The accepted method of dealing with such errors and faults is based on the concept of a *transaction*, which is a sequence of operations that behaves atomically -- that is, it either successfully completes (*commits*) all updates or else it has no effect on the state of the database (*rolls back*). The overall integrity policy for trusted systems should include the concept of transactions with commit and roll-back.

Multilevel updates raise some difficult issues regarding transaction management. For example, if a trusted user can simultaneously insert or update multilevel data (within the user's range of trust), it may be desirable to decompose these updates into single-level updates represented as single-level transactions and performed by single-level database subjects. However, the unit itself must also be treated as a transaction, so the concept of a multilevel transaction with single-level nested transactions appears to be very useful. The problem is rolling back the low portions of the transaction if the high portions fail.

Assuming recovery management is outside of the mandatory security perimeter, it is not clear how the database recovery log should be managed and processed in systems that are rated at the level of B2 or higher. However, some of the techniques used for general-purpose operating systems to ensure the consistency of file systems during backup and recovery may be useful.

Concurrency Controls

An important aspect of database integrity is ensuring that concurrent transactions do not interfere with each other, giving rise to inconsistent states of the database. *Serializability*, which states that any transaction schedule must be equivalent to one in which the transactions execute serially, has been shown to be a necessary and sufficient condition for global consistency[12], although there are systems that enforce somewhat weaker policies. Some notion of global consistency, however, is an essential aspect of the overall integrity policy for trusted database management systems. The concurrency policy should also address the problems of *deadlock*, where multiple transactions cannot proceed because they are waiting on each other, and *livelock*, where a transaction never exits from a wait state, both of which create denial-of-service problems.

In B2 or higher systems, the concurrency mechanisms must use techniques other than simple locks because read-write locks on multilevel data provide a signalling channel. Event counters[13] are not vulnerable to covert channels, but require that higher-level transactions roll back when a lower-level one causes an update that could interfere with its behavior.

CONCLUSIONS

We do not know enough about the application of mandatory integrity policies to databases to recommend any one in particular or even state that one be mandated at all. While the strict integrity policy without trusted subjects may be appropriate for some threat environments, the more flexible program integrity policy, which uses restricted trusted subjects to manage a database, may be appropriate for most environments. It would be premature to adapt a particular mandatory policy in criteria for trusted database systems until such a policy has been experimentally tried in at least one operational environment and has been demonstrably successful. On the other hand, a discretionary policy along the lines of that given in the criteria is extremely useful provided it is interpreted to apply to views rather than just elements, records, or files.

Database integrity rules should be included in an overall integrity policy because they provide users with considerable assurance that the data is protected against many errors. This is one of the best ways in which the users themselves can greatly enhance the integrity of their data. However, the interpretation and application of integrity rules is constrained by the requirements for mandatory security. Similarly, any trusted system should support the concepts of atomic transactions, recovery, and noninterference, though again the features are constrained by the mandatory security requirements.

Although we believe it is vital for trusted systems to support these different integrity policies, it is neither necessary nor possible to have the same degree of assurance in the enforcement of them all. Whereas Classes A and B are appropriate for mandatory access controls, Class C2 is appropriate for discretionary controls and consistency

controls, which are considerably more complex than mandatory controls and require much of the database system for their support.

To provide a high degree of assurance, the mandatory integrity policy must be enforced by the reference monitor. In addition to enforcing the mandatory secrecy policy, the reference monitor ensures the integrity of all data in the system, including the labels that represent the secrecy and integrity access classes. If the data are vulnerable to tampering during storage or transmission to and from the reference monitor, cryptographic checksums may be used to ensure the integrity of the data and its labels. For cryptographic checksums to be meaningful, it is essential that the processes that compute and validate the checksums and manage the key be under the strict control of a reference monitor.

ACKNOWLEDGMENTS

An earlier version of this paper was prepared for the National Computer Security Center's Invitational Workshop on Database Security, where both authors participated in a working group on integrity and inference. The current version has benefited greatly from the group discussions, and we would like to thank the other group members, namely A. Arsenault, W. E. Boebert, D. Bonyun, D. Downs, K. Jacobs, R. Miller, G. Raudnbaugh, J. Spain, and S. Walker. We also thank T. Lunt, M. Heckman, and P. Neumann for their comments on this paper. This research was supported by the U.S. Air Force, RADC under contract F30602-85-C-0243.

REFERENCES

1. Dept. of Defense, Computer Security Center, *Department of Defense Trusted Computer System Evaluation Criteria*, 1983, CSC-STD-001-83

2. Date, C. J., *An Introduction to Database Systems*, Addison-Wesley, Vol. II, 1983.

3. Harrison, M. A., Ruzzo, W. L. and Ullman, J. D., "Protection in Operating Systems", *Comm. ACM*, Vol. 19, No. 8, Aug. 1976, pp. 461-471.

4. Boebert, W. E. and Kain, R. Y., "A Practical Alternative to Hierarchical Integrity Policies", *Proc. of the 8th DOD/NBS Computer Security Conf.*, 1985, pp. 18-27.

5. Biba, K. J., "Integrity Considerations for Secure Computer Systems", Tech. report ESD-TR-76-372, USAF Electronic Systems Division, Bedford, Mass., April 1977.

6. Bell, D. E. and LaPadula, L. J., "Secure Computer Systems: Mathematical Foundations and Model", Tech. report M74-244, The MITRE Corp., Bedford, Mass., May 1973.

7. Schell, R. R., Tao, T. F., and Heckman, M., "Designing the GEMSOS Security Kernel for Security and Performance", *Proc. 8th Dod/NBS Computer Security Conf.*, 1985, pp. 108-119.

8. Grohn, M. J., "A Model of a Protected Data Management System", Tech. report ESD-TR-76-289, I. P. Sharp Assoc. Ltd., June 1976.

9. Weissman, C., "Security Controls in the ADEPT-50 Time-Sharing System", *Proc. Fall Jt. Computer Conf.*, Vol. 351969, pp. 119-133.

10. Shirley, L. J. and Schell, R. R., "Mechanism Sufficiency Validation by Assignment", *Proc. of the 1981 Symp. on Security and Privacy*, Apr. 1981, pp. 26-32.

11. Lunt, T. F., Denning, D. E., Schell, R. R., Heckman, M., "Polyinstantiation in a Secure Relational Database System", Tech. report, SRI International, May 1986.

12. Rosenkrantz, D. J., Stearns, R. E., and Lewis, P. M., "Consistency and Serializability in Concurrent Database Systems", *SIAM J. Comp.*, Vol. 13, No. 3, Aug. 1984, pp. 508-530.

13. Reed, D. P. and Kanodia, R. K., "Synchronization with Eventcounts and Sequencers", *Comm. ACM*, Vol. 22, No. 2, Feb. 1979, pp. 115-123.

Section 2.6: Computer Systems Applications

This section constitutes a review of computer security concepts and a set of examples of application of these concepts in commercially available computer systems. The availability of these systems reflects increasing concern in the commercial market and the government's investment in encouraging the development of more secure computers. Government investment in research has helped advance the state-of-the-art. Government demand and increased commercial recognition of computer security risks have stimulated established vendors to enhance the security capabilities of existing systems and to encourage new firms to enter this specialized market.

Our previous discussions that referenced add-on access control software for existing operating systems, such as RACF, TOP SECRET, and ACF2, were addressing a part of the growing hardware and software industry investment in *Orange Book* trusted computer system technology. The existence of the *Trusted Computer System Evaluation Criteria* (TCSEC) provides a uniform metric for comparing computer systems' security. The National Computer Security Center (NCSC) publishes an *Evaluated Products List* and individual product evaluation reports. As more hardware and software products are evaluated by NCSC, a wider variety of security-oriented products with know attributes will become commercially available. The important factor is that each evaluation is against the same criteria; therefore, users know what type of security capability they are purchasing (e.g., C1, C2, B1, B2, and so on).

A sample of NCSC's activity as of October 1985, with limited updates, is presented in Table 1 to illustrate the extent of computer system applications of the TCSEC.

We present several papers that report on the security kernel and related developments in the above list. These papers should be easy reading. In many cases, they have introductory sections, which present the fundamental TCSEC concepts in slightly different words and from slightly different terms of reference. These multiple viewpoints should help reinforce understanding. In fact, you may find yourself disagreeing with some authors or finding others much clearer, a sure sign that you are developing an appreciation for the important issues.

To set the stage for the product discussions, we mentioned two rules of thumb for security features of computer sys-

Table 1: Computer System Application of *Orange Book* Technology

Status Evaluated (Source NCSC Announcements)	Level
Honeywell SCOMP	A1
Honeywell Multics	B2
IBM RACF	C1
SKK Inc. ACF2	C2
Computer Assoc., Intl., Inc. CA–TOP SECRET	C2
Control Data Corp. (CDC) NOS (Aug. 1986)	C2
Digital Equipment Corp. (DEC) VAX/VMS Aug. 1986	C2

Development	
Honeywell SAT [BOEB85]	> A1
Sperry 1100 Operating System (Unofficial C1 on an older Executive (1983). Not going for C2 evaluation). [ASHL85]	B1
Gemini Computers, Inc. GEMSOS [SCHE85]	B3
Digital Equipment Corp. VAX/VMS (B range, possibly B1) [LIPN85]	B

tems: C1 to B1: C1 to B1 levels are generally achievable without OS redesign. B2 to A1, B2, B3, and A1 levels generally require OS redesign.

Reprints

The first two papers discuss the Honeywell SCOMP, the first computer system to achieve an A1 evaluation. The next two papers are concerned with a system under development, the secure Ada target (SAT). The final two papers each discuss different systems and perspectives. The Digital VAX/VMS, emphasize compatibility, while a newly developed operating system, GEMSOS, is discussed in terms of TCSEC concepts.

An overview of data vulnerability and data security technology is presented in the monograph, Data Security: A Growing Concern, by Paul Roberts who points out that network and operating system security are becoming management concerns, in addition to the more traditional physical and administrative security. This changed concern is due to the growth of office automation, increased reliance of business and government on computers, and the publicity given to incidents of computer security violation. Under these stimuli responsible management is adapting the use of trusted multilevel security—or privacy—systems.

His example of a reference monitor implementation is the Honeywell SCOMP (secure communications processor), which is one of the early computer security programs. Credibility is increased by his comment that "The reference monitor concept seemed simple and elegant in theory. Its implementation was not. It was, in fact, fraught with obstacles." An interesting point is that SCOMP was verified by the hierarchical development methodology (HDM), developed by SRI International. HDM is one of the four systems discussed in Carl Landwehr's paper in Section 2.4, recommended readings. Another interesting point is that the SCOMP is a modified Honeywell DPS 6 minicomputer.

SCOMP is an A1 commercial hardware product offered by Honeywell. In this second SCOMP paper, "SCOMP: A Solution to the Multilevel Security Problem," Lester Fraim reports on SCOMP's development. He points out that ". . .hardware functions support the software functions." For example, in mediation, the following two steps occur

(1) Initial mediation of an access request is provided by the software, using the kernel's internal data structures. The request is validated for the subject and object involved for process (e.g., read or write). A descriptor-based data element is constructed for use by the hardware. "The descriptor consists of four words of information including access permission (i.e., read, write, or execute) and the location of the object."

(2) Continued mediation of an access request. SCOMP hardware computer system applications uses the descriptor-based data element for continued mediation of an access.

"Because the mediation mechanism is in hardware, I/O instructions do not require privilege. . . . the device drivers can be outside the security kernel." Mediation involves additional processing that can degrade performance; building these capabilities in hardware enhances the performance.

Fraim provides some additional insight into the verification methodology. HDM was used with a FTLS (formal top level specification) that was written in Special, a nonprocedural language. The FTLS was verified, using tools developed by SRI, with respect to a meta policy, including the Bell-LaPadula model. The Meta Policy is briefly described in John Mchugh's paper, "An EMACS-Based Downgrader for the SAT." In addition, a second verification occurred for trusted software.

Trusted software is ". . . security-relevant software outside the security kernel that can selectively bypass the kernel's mandatory control." Trusted user services include setting password and default security and integrity level. Trusted operation services include secure startup and operator command processor. Trusted maintenance services allow manipulation of system data. The trusted software was verified by using Gypsy, developed at the University of Texas. HDM is one of the four systems discussed in Maureen Cheheyl's paper in recommended readings [CHEH81].

A development effort focusing on the secure Ada target (SAT) machine is reported on by W.E. Boebert, R.Y. Kain, and W.D. Young in their paper, "Secure Computing: The Secure Ada Target Approach." According to the authors, "the machine is called an Ada target in recognition of its intended first use an an environment for the execution of programs written in the Ada language." This development effort appears to be directed to an A1 or greater level of security.

Three categories of threat to a computer system are mentioned: accidental flaws, deliberate flaws, and design flaws. Trojan horses are explained, followed by a discussion of the fundamental principles of computer security and the SAT. A homely touch is the explanation that the name "*-property" was more or less an accident because no one could think of a better name.

There are three state spaces or collections of stored information in SAT, extending the work of John Rusby at SRI International. They are (1) The value state ". . . Consists of all objects that can possibly be made visible to subjects," and is outside the reference monitor. (2) The protection state: ". . . The information that the reference monitor keeps internal to itself and uses in making access decisions . . ." The protection state is a matrix consisting of subjects in rows, objects in columns, and access modes in cell entries. (3) Underlying abstractions: The underlying abstractions are in tables giving the attributes of subjects and objects, such as security levels. "These values are used to decide what value should appear in a particular cell of the protection state."

The paper concludes with an informal proof of the SAT security. Responding to criticism of incomprehensibility of machine-generated proofs, the SAT proofs are machine checked but not machine generated so that others can trace the steps with a different set of tools. Their bottom line is that ". . .each and every instruction executed on the secure Ada target machine is constrained by the mandatory and the discretionary security policies." Mathematical induction in a progression from abstraction to engineering reality are described. Tamperproof hardware mechanisms are employed. Segment addressing is extended to implement security access policy.

Since trusted subjects are exempted from the *-property, they must be independently proved secure in that they "can never be made to violate the mandatory security policy." An effort was made to reduce the number and privileges of trusted subjects.

A kernel extension for the SAT called an EMACS-based downgrader is described in John Mchugh's paper, "An EMACS-Based Downgrader for the SAT." Kernel extensions extend the functionality of the base hardware to produce a more full-featured reference monitor. Kernel extensions fall into three classes: (1) neither trusted nor verified (e.g., run-time support library); (2) verified but not trusted (e.g., labelers); and (3) both trusted and verified (e.g., software that supports downgrading of information).

The downgrader, which selectively supports the downgrading of information, is discussed in detail. While the downgrader violates the *-property, it does not violate the Meta Policy, which states that "information may not be disclosed to any individual without the necessary authorization." The Bell-LaPadula model is thus seen to be more restrictive than absolutely necessary; a violation of Bell-LaPadula is not a violation of the underlying security policy.

The downgrader works by forcing its user to work reasonably slowly, observing each sentence in context. "Trust in the downgrader resides primarily in the human user who makes the judgements. . . . satisfying the Meta Policy requires extending the notion of the trusted computing base to encompass trusted individuals. . . an implementation probably requires trusted hardware for the display."

A report on the major design choices for the Gemini multiprocessing secure operating system (GEMSOS) security kernel and initial system performance measurements for Version O GEMSOS are presented by Roger Schell, Tien Tao, and Mark Heckman in "Designing the GEMSOS Security Kernel for Security and Performance." The Gemini computer systems discussed in this paper are based on the Intel iAPX 286 (80286) microprocessor and are designed to meet the Class B3 requirements. This paper reports on major design choices and performance measurements.

It is no surprise that a paper from one of the leaders of TCSEC development contains an excellent review of basic concepts. We note, however, that as mentioned in the paper by Deborah Downs et al. reprinted in Section 2.4, discretionary access control enforced need-to-know policy only to the extent that the owners of data objects understand and execute that policy.

GEMSOS implementation details are described, including access classes reflecting classification and clearance, secrecy protection, integrity policy and its hardware implementation, and security kernel features such as labels, segments, volumes, processes, devices, and their interactions.

An interesting approach of GEMINI is its focus to provide a secure ". . . multiprocessor computer specifically intended for incorporation as a component of embedded systems." The authors state that performance can be increased by using multiprocessors. Bus contention, a potential bottleneck, is avoided by reducing global (on the bus) memory references to less than 10%, with most memory being local to one processor only. Another feature is designing the kernel so that it does not constitute an uninterruptable single thread critical section so that "multiple processors can execute simultaneously in the kernel." Some preliminary performance is reported showing effective multiprocessor operation up to seven processors.

"SE/VMS: Implementing Mandatory Security in VAX/VMS" is the 1986 update on the development of a trusted computer system at Digital Equipment Corporation. The 1985 version included in the recommended reading is "Secure System Development at Digital Equipment: Targetting the Needs of a Commercial and Government Customer Base." In this 1986 paper, Blotcky, Lynch, and Lipner describe the multiple steps required to bring VAX/VMS up to a B1 evaluation. These steps are incomplete; VAX/VMS has received a C2 evaluation. This paper, like the other papers in this section, provides operating system specific information as well as insight into the process of implementing security.

Security Enhanced VMS (SE/VMS) is a set of replacement and additional software components and data structures to VAX Version 4.2 that provide the capability to support mandatory labeled protection. The 4.2 features that justified the C2 evaluation are described, including account management, password management, dialup line controls, access control lists, security auditing features, prevention of disk scavenging, secure server key implementation, and supporting documentation.

Mandatory security based on the Bell-LaPadula model is supported for both secrecy and integrity models of 256 hierarchical levels and 64 nonhierarchical categories through the use of a 160 bit block incorporated into the data structure for each subject and object. Volumes and devices may be multilevel which files and directories are single level. Since labeling of certain system internal objects and fine granularity auditing is absent, the mandatory controls are described as "latent." No effort was made to add support for mandatory controls to any object that did not already have space reserved in its associated data structure.

After describing the features added to SE/VMS that support names for access classes, user registration and login, device and volume management, file creation and access, operations on files and directories, and the labeling of printed output, the paper concludes with a discussion of the engineering required to make complex applications, such as mail, operate in a trusted system.

Recommended Readings

The paper, "B1 Security for Sperry 1100 Operating System," by R.E. Ashland reports on Sperry's evolutionary work toward meeting a B1 level for the 1100 operating system [ASHL85]. The Sperry implementation requirements are given which essentially ensure that the current user base will have full compatibility if they wish to use the future B1 capabilities. In addition, performance will be maintained to the extent feasible.

The Sperry executive was evaluated for C1 in an earlier release. It now has C2 capabilities but will not be resubmitted until it meets B1 requirements. Sperry is adding six features to the 1100 OS in order to achieve B1. These B1 features are: (1) common sign-on for all users, (2) password controls, (3) compartment labeling of all objects, (4) transaction file and program security, (5) device security, and (6) output labeling.

A progress report of secure system development directions at Digital Equipment is provided by Steven Lipner in "Secure System Development at Digital Equipment: Targetting the Needs of a Commercial and Government Customer Base" [LIPN 85], Reminiscent of Courtney's classification of risks, Lipner defines three classes of threats (1) user irresponsibility, including disloyal or criminal conduct abusing the trust placed in the individual. (He observes that in this behavior pattern the computer is incidental); (2) probing, where an individual takes advantage of poorly managed or inadequate computer security; and (3) penetration, involving deliberate malevolent behavior. The paper focuses on compatible security enhancements for the VAX/VMS operating system, which has been submitted to the National Computer Security Center for evaluation at the C2 level.

Examples of the Version 4.0 security capabilities include four features (1) login and password management, (2) discretionary access control, (3) auditing, and (4) integrity improvements. Lipner also presents an initial report on the security kernel for the VAX, observing that "formal verification of any secure system poses a fearsome challenge—especially to an organization whose experience runs to operating system development rather than verification research." A prototype kernel has been completed and tested.

Other interesting observations are that it is unusual to sell a computer system without networking, that compatibility constraints are fairly high, that lead times for product development are relatively long and that it is possible for government security requirements to change faster than products can be built, that formal security assurance has been introduced while still "research" or "advanced development," that export controls work against security product implementation, and that a classified system development requirement would be impractical.

> **If data security clearly was not perceived as a major problem by most data processing managers, why should it be a concern of senior management?**

Data Security: A Growing Concern

Paul M. Roberts
Honeywell Information Systems

Senior management in the private and public sectors now finds itself addressing critical issues with regard to computer security. For almost two decades, most electronic data processing managers and senior management saw "computer security" as comprising the physical security of the computer installation and administrative security logically controlling access to the actual system.

Physical security of the installation seemed easy to achieve. Chain link fences were installed, guards were placed at entrances to the plant or office, and badge systems were introduced to control physical access to both the plant and the actual computer facilities.

Some administrative security was usually provided with the system, in the form of user IDs and passwords to control electronic access to data.

Data Vulnerability

Two facets of computer security were given relatively little attention through the early 1970s, especially by the private sector: network security and operating system security.

Rapid expansion of telecommunications in the 1970s increased awareness of the vulnerability of data networks. Numerous financial and commercial organizations, as well as government agencies, began to encrypt data for transmission. However, the security of the operating system, of the data in the system, was still not perceived as a critical issue. When *Computerworld,* in April 1983, asked data processing managers to identify their most pressing problems, data security was not among the five most frequently cited![1] If data security clearly was not perceived as a major problem by most data processing managers, why should it be a concern of senior management? Several recent developments suggest an answer.

The first is the growth of office automation. Computer manufacturers have been developing smaller, more powerful systems to be placed almost anywhere. At the same time, they've been making the systems "user friendly," providing greater and easier access to the computing power of the system. These developments have had serious consequences with regard to data security. More people than ever before are using computers in the workplace and could have access to the company's data base.

The likelihood of inadvertent and covert computer abuse has grown exponentially.

The distribution of computing power throughout the factory and office has made private and public sectors alike increasingly dependent on computer systems for the day-to-day conduct of their business. From billing to accounts payable. From computer design and testing to computer-assisted manufacturing. From word processing and electronic mail to activity monitoring in nuclear power plants.

The growing popularity of fault-tolerant and redundant systems indicates the extent to which business and government recognize their increasing reliance on the computer. As that dependence has grown, the development of the personal computer has also placed millions of individuals only a phone call away from access – authorized or unauthorized – to many private and government computer networks.

A rash of highly publicized incidents in 1982 and 1983 attracted public attention to the issue of computer security. Unauthorized individuals, popularly identified as hackers, were reported to have accessed data bases of such organizations as The Pacific Telephone and Telegraph Company, Digital Equipment Corporation, the Rand Corporation, Stanford University, Cornell University, the Southern California Credit Bureau, the Los Alamos National Laboratory, and the Memorial Sloan-Kettering Cancer Research Institute.[2] Meanwhile, the movie *War Games* drew public attention to the national security implications of data security.

> **Data processing managers and their superiors had clearly underestimated the real value and vulnerability of their data.**

The hackers, some of whom became almost folk heroes, had accessed data bases through various combinations of skill, persistence, and luck. Actual consequences of their unauthorized intrusions were rarely reported, and those reports were often considered suspect. Perhaps the hackers had merely broken through the lowest levels of administrative security on these systems. Even so, it was clear that many current administrative security measures were inadequate, and that data processing managers and their superiors had clearly under-estimated the real value and vulnerability of their data.

Data Security: A Changing Perspective

While public attention focused on hackers who maliciously accessed and abused data bases, security experts emphasized to management that threats to data security were greater from within the organization than from without.[3] An unintentional keyboard error; deliberate, even malicious altering of financial and research reports; stealing funds; stealing data for sale to competitors or agents of foreign governments; or "merely" using the system for the conduct of personal business. All are internal threats to data security.

Data security was clearly developing into a critical concern for the private sector. This perception had long been held by the Department of Defense, which had helped sponsor research on the subject. However, the National Security Decision Directive issued by the White House on September 17, 1984 indicated that the federal government's concern about data security was not limited to the Defense Department.

> Telecommunications and automated information processing systems are highly susceptible to interception, unauthorized electronic access, and related forms of technical exploitation, as well as other dimensions of the hostile intelligence threat. The technology to exploit these electronic systems is widespread and is used extensively by foreign nations and can be employed, as well, by terrorist groups and criminal elements. Government systems as well as those which process the private or proprietary information of US persons and businesses can become targets for foreign exploitation.[4]

The President therefore directed that

> a. Systems which generate, store, process, transfer or communicate classified information in electrical form shall be secured by such means as are necessary to prevent compromise or exploitation.
> b. Systems handling other sensitive, but unclassified, government or government-derived information, the loss of which could adversely affect the national security interest, shall be protected in proportion to the threat of exploitation and the associated potential damage to the national security.
> c. The government shall encourage, advise, and where appropriate, assist the private sector to: identify systems which handle sensitive non-government information, the loss of which could adversely affect the national security; determine the threat to, and vulnerability of, these systems; and formulate strategies and measures for providing protection in proportion to the threat of exploitation and the associated potential damage. Information and advice from the perspective of the private sector will be sought with respect to implementation of this policy. In cases where implementation of security measures to non-governmental systems would be in the national security interest, the private sector shall be encouraged, advised, and where appropriate, assisted in undertaking the application of such measures.[5]

The ramifications of this directive are still subject to much discussion. Clearly, however, data security is no longer primarily the concern of the Defense Department. It is a matter of utmost concern to the entire federal government. The former Department of Defense Computer Security Center, established in 1981 to address computer security issues, has been transformed into the National Telecommunications and Automated Information Systems Security Center. The *Department of Defense Trusted Computer System Evaluation Criteria*, published by the Center in 1983 to establish "a uniform set of basic requirements and evaluation classes for assessing the effectiveness of security controls built into Automatic Data Processing (ADP) systems," now applies to data security standards throughout the federal government and its prime contractors.[6] These evaluation criteria will likely become the accepted commercial standard for data security as prime contractors are required to comply with federal standards.

These stringent government standards should also heighten commercial sensitivity to privacy and confidentiality issues. For example, most computer systems today offer limited administrative security, so most data is available to most users. How, then, does senior management "protect" its business plan and trade secrets? How does a hospital protect the confidentiality of a patient's medical records, or a school preserve the integrity of an academic transcript? Or a lawyer preserve the confidentiality of briefs and memoranda prepared on a word processing system? Or a manager reduce the likelihood of inadvertent loss of data because an employee accidentally accesses data and erases it?

There is also speculation that the potential legal consequences of computer security violations will compel many private organizations to implement greater data security. As Robert Campbell noted in *Computerworld,* "stockholders might sue a corporation that had to devalue its assets and stock because of computer fraud-related losses. Another scenario might find stockholders filing suit because loss of highly sensitive trade secrets seriously hurt the corporate balance sheet. Liability of the corporation and its officers to protect its assets and resources, such as imposed by the Foreign Corrupt Practices Act, will similarly be tested."[7]

Organizations clearly need to improve data security. But how do they respect the integrity of employees while identifying a source of computer abuse? How can they prevent that abuse? The answer? By using a trusted multilevel security – or privacy – system.

DATA SECURITY TECHNOLOGY

Data security is clearly not a new issue. What's new is the public and commercial interest in it – and the commercially available technology that can provide significantly greater security than ever before.

Various agencies of the Department of Defense have long been aware of the shortcomings of data security technology. In 1970, a security-conscious Air Force designated special "Tiger" teams of computer experts who were challenged to gain unauthorized access to the computer systems then used by the Air Force. The teams were far too successful, penetrating every operating system in use. The Air Force therefore commissioned the "Anderson Report," looking for ways to make computer systems more secure.

Operating systems and utilities are so large and complex and have been patched so many times that no one can precisely define the level of security provided by their internal controls.

The Anderson Report, issued in 1972, suggested it was not possible to establish secure systems by adding administrative security measures to old operating systems.[8] The systems in use then – and most of them are still widely used today – were not designed with security in mind. Further, operating systems and utilities are so large and complex and have been patched so many times that no one can precisely define the level of security provided by their internal controls. Consequently, little can be done to verify their effectiveness.

The report suggested, however, that the easiest and fastest way to establish a secure computer system was to implement the reference monitor concept, which is based on the work of Butler Lampson.[9]

The Reference Monitor Concept

The reference monitor concept requires that every active entity (or subject), such as a user or program, be given a security level; and every passive entity (or object), such as data, be given a clearance level. All communications would be required to pass through the reference monitor, which would enforce the given access authorizations. (See Figure 1.)

The reference monitor concept is striking in both its simplicity and its scope. First, currently used operating systems and hardware can be retained. All security-relevant mechanisms in the operating system reside in the monitor, in a single, protected entity called a security kernel that is added to the system. The kernel, technically, comprises the hardware and software that "realize the reference monitor abstraction."[10] The kernel contains

and enforces the lattice of authorized relationships between subjects and objects.

Three basic requirements must be met to implement the reference monitor concept successfully:

- Complete Mediation – security policy rules must be enforced on every access.
- Isolation – the security kernel and its data base must be protected from unauthorized alteration; they must be tamper-proof.
- Verification – formal security verification methods must be applied to ensure that system security controls are effective.

To facilitate verification, the security policy must be "encapsulated in a set of mathematical rules that constitute a formal security model."[11] Further, that model should be verifiable mathematically, and strictly adhered to at all times.

The reference monitor concept seemed simple and elegant in theory. Its implementation was not. It was, in fact, fraught with obstacles.

It was necessary to first articulate a security policy to be enforced by the monitor, then state and verify that policy in a mathematical model and incorporate it into the system. Further, because the demand for such security measures came from agencies of the Defense Department, that model had to accommodate the complex military security system that had developed in a hardcopy environment. Finite-state machine, lattice, access matrix, information flow, and other security models were the subject of extensive research.[12]

In addition, a recognized standard set of criteria for evaluating security had to be developed. Various agencies of the Defense Department attacked the problem during the 1970s, as did the National Bureau of Standards and the MITRE Corporation. The Department of Defense Computer Security Center was formally established in 1981 and 2½ years later, that Center promulgated the *Department of Defense Trusted Computer System Evaluation Criteria*.

The Center established four divisions: "D, C, B, and A ordered in a hierarchical manner with the highest divi-

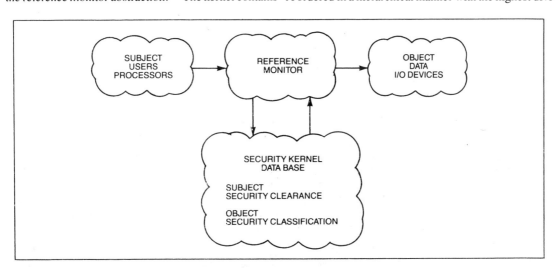

Figure 1. The Reference Monitor Concept

215

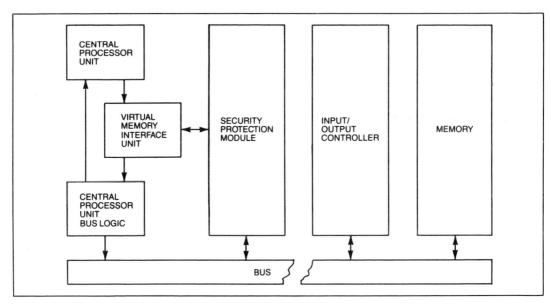

Figure 2. The SCOMP Hardware Configuration

sion (A) being reserved for systems providing the most comprehensive security."[13] Within each division, the lowest class is designated 1. Division D offers minimal security; the two classes of C provide discretionary protection and audit capabilities. Division B's three classes require a trusted computing base that preserves the integrity of sensitivity levels and uses them to enforce mandatory access controls. A formal security model must be provided, along with a specification of the Trusted Computing Base (TCB) – the security-relevant portions of the system.

Division A, "Verified Protection," has only one class: A1. It requires formal security verification methods to assure that the system's mandatory and discretionary security controls can effectively protect its classified and sensitive information. Further, "extensive documentation is required to demonstrate that the TCB meets security requirements in all aspects of design, development, and implementation."[14]

To date, only one system has been approved as meeting these A1 criteria: SCOMP, designed and manufactured by Honeywell.

SCOMP

SCOMP, for Secure Communications Processor, is essentially a standard commercial product – a Honeywell DPS 6 16-bit minicomputer – enhanced with a patented hardware security protection module (SPM).[15] The SPM replaces the standard commercial instruction processor and includes an enhanced mother board, a Virtual Memory Interface Unit (replacing the memory management unit), and a MEGABUS interface and description store (cache memory). The module sits on the bus (see Figure 2) mediating all system requests at hardware rather than software speeds. SCOMP's SPM is the *only* hardware/software implementation of the reference monitor concept commercially available today.

SCOMP's unique architecture embodies the benefits of a long history of data security research at Honeywell.

In 1972, the Anderson Report suggested that Honeywell's Multics operating system was the best platform for implementing the reference monitor concept. That recommendation was not surprising. Multics, a large, multi-user, general-purpose, time-sharing operating system, was already generally recognized as providing the best data security available. The system was well-known for its ring isolation mechanism, which provided hardware-enforced security without significant impairment of system performance.[16]

Honeywell, with support from the Air Force, therefore initiated research to develop a reference monitor for Multics. That project was halted 1976 because of budgetary and other limitations. However, Honeywell was able to significantly enhance Multics security through the addition of an Access Control List (ACL), which defines access rights for each segment and directory, and an Access Isolation Mechanism (AIM), which allows system administrators to define several levels of privilege enforced by the system. AIM supports 8 clearance levels and 18 need-to-know categories within each level and provides security auditing capabilities. In 1975, the Pentagon began to use this enhanced Multics in a controlled multilevel security mode.

In 1977, supported by several government agencies, Honeywell concentrated its efforts on developing a secure front-end processor. Originally, government sponsors requested that this processor incorporate a Unix emulator. Most secure computer research projects then underway were attempting to lay an operating system emulator over the security kernel. Honeywell dropped that approach in 1981 because, although the concept worked technically in several projects, system degradation was clearly unacceptable.[17] SCOMP was designed to provide any operating system with an interface to a secure environment.

To establish verifiable security, it was necessary to build a completely new operating system incorporating security as a fundamental and verifiable design element.

The Secure Trusted Operating Program (STOP), written in high-level languages, is that new operating system. It consists of a Trusted Computing Base, which provides the actual security mechanisms, and an applications interface for the user. SCOMP's security system resides in the security kernel, contained in the security protection module.

The security kernel provides basic resource management, process scheduling, memory management, trap and interrupt management, and auditing. The kernel is intentionally kept small, to facilitate analysis, testing, and verification. Its design adheres to a formal top-level specification that defines the system from the view of a user process. This specification is written in a nonprocedural language called SPECIAL and has been verified by the Hierarchical Development Methodology (HDM) developed by SRI International.[18]

The Bell and LaPadula security model implemented is the access-matrix model used to enhance Multics. The model provides mathematically verifiable rules to prevent the unauthorized reading or modification of information. The model requires that each subject and object be given a security identifier known as an access class. The system then enforces two mandatory rules. The first, known as the simple security condition, allows a subject at a given level to read objects only at the same or lower security level. A user cannot "read up." The second rule, the *- (pronounced star) property, prohibits users from writing down to lower security levels. The *- property is specifically designed to prevent "Trojan horses," whereby programs operating for one user could be used to pass information to a user in a lower or disjoint access class.[19]

The user, system administrator, and operator interact with the system through trusted software, which ensures that all user requests to execute at a particular security level are authorized for that user. The software is "trusted" because it can violate either a security or integrity property enforced by the kernel. The trusted software, written in C, has been verified using the Gypsy methodology.

SCOMP's interface to applications is provided by the SCOMP Kernel Interface Package (SKIP).

SCOMP's security is enhanced by use of four Multics-like rings of hardware-enforced protection (see Figure 3). The security kernel resides in rings 0 and 1, the most protected rings; the trusted software and SKIP reside in ring 2, and users reside in ring 3. This unique hardware/software implementation of the reference monitor concept provides verifiable security while maintaining high standards of system performance.

It is noteworthy that this high level of security can be attained by modifying a standard DPS 6. Thus, most standard DPS 6 systems in use today can easily be converted to secure systems, and all standard DPS 6 peripherals can be used with the system. Large hardware and software investments can therefore be preserved while implementing an A1 level of security.

Technology Tomorrow

The Computer Security Center's evaluation criteria recognize that most security enhancements beyond that provided by A1 systems are not yet technically feasible. Therefore, no specific evaluation criteria are yet defined for security beyond the A1 level.

The direction of Honeywell's research is clear. The next generation of secure computers will be 32-bit, and it will see hardware strictly enforce software-established security policy, providing greater verifiability, greater security, and improved system performance. SCOMP clearly demonstrates the advantages of hardware enforcement of security.

That new generation will include a Honeywell system currently identified as SAT (for Secure Ada Target). SAT will perform security-related functions in a coprocessor known as the tagged object processor (TOP), which will enforce a matrix-access security policy. The design will be processor-independent.

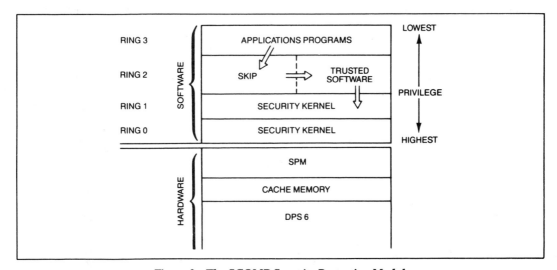

Figure 3. The SCOMP Security Protection Module

For more detailed information on SCOMP, call (703) 827-3227 or write:

Dick Kane
Honeywell Information Systems
Federal Systems Division
7900 West Park Drive
McLean, VA 22102

For more detailed information on advanced secure computing technologies, call (612) 378-6780 or write:

Gordon Aumann
Honeywell Secure Computing Technology Center
2855 Anthony Lane South
Suite 130
St. Anthony, MN 55418

References

1. Marguerite Zientara, 'DPers' No. 1 Headache? Applications Backlog," *Computerworld,* April 11, 1983, p. 8.

2. See article by Jeffry Beeler, *Computerworld,* August 22, 1983, p. 1. See also "The 414 Gang Strikes Again," *Time,* August 29, 1983, p. 75; Katherine Hafner, "Felony Charges Filed Against Alleged Hacker," *Computerworld,* November 14, 1983, p. 15; "Pranksters Gain Access, Destroy Programs," *Computerworld,* February 8, 1982, p. 49; and Jeffry Beeler, "Recent Security Breach at Stanford Has University Officials Worried," *Computerworld,* February 8, 1982, p. 13.

3. See Bill Laberis, "Consultant: Execs Need Help Against DP Crime," *Computerworld,* October 12, 1981, p. 24; Ted Singer, "DP Hackers Not Our Greatest Threat," *Computerworld,* November 14, 1983, p. 84; Brad Schult, "Expert Gives Strong Advice to Halt DP Abuse," *Computerworld,* September 28, 1981, p. 14. For broader perspectives of computer security issues, see Martin Buss and Lynn Salerno, "Common sense and computer security," *Harvard Business Review,* March-April 1984, pp. 112-121; and Donn B. Parker, *Computer Security Management,* Reston Publishing Company, 1981.

4. "National Policy on Telecommunications and Automated Information Sytems Security," *National Security Decision Directive 145 (Unclassified Version),* September 17, 1984, p. 1.

5. *Ibid.,* pp. 2-3.

6. *Department of Defense Trusted Computer System Evaluation Criteria,* Department of Defense Computer Security Center, Ft. Meade, Md., August 15, 1983, Foreword. For a succinct description of the criteria for the four hierarchical divisions of computer system security and the status of various security research projects, see Carl Landwehr, "The Best Available Technologies for Computer Security," *Computer,* July 1983, pp. 86-100. This issue of *Computer,* devoted to computer security technology, is outstanding.

7. Robert P. Campbell, "Locking Up the Mainframe, Part Two" *Computerworld,* October 17, 1983, "In Depth," p. 7. See also Robert P. Campbell, "Locking Up the Mainframe, Part One," *Computerworld,* October 10, 1983, "In Depth." The two articles combined are an excellent introduction to the issues involved in computer security. Campbell's interpretation of the obligations of a corporation and its officers under the terms of the Foreign Corrupt Practices Act is subject to question.

8. See J.P. Anderson, "Computer Security Technology Planning Study," ESD-TR-73-51, vol. 1, ESD/AFSC, Hanscom AFB, Bedford, Mass., Oct. 1972 (NTIS AD-758-206)). See also Richard W. Kane, "Multi-level Security Today," in *National Computer Security and Privacy Symposium Proceedings, April 27-28, 1982,* Honeywell Information Systems, 1982, p.25.

9. See Stanley Ames, Morrie Gasser, and Roger Schell, "Security Kernel Design and Implementation: An Introduction," *Computer,* July 1983, p. 14.

10. *Ibid.*

11. *Ibid.,* p. 15.

12. See Carl Landwehr, "Formal Models for Computer Security," *Computing Surveys,* September 1981, pp. 247-278.

13. *Department of Defense Trusted Computer System Evaluation Criteria,* p.5.

14. *Ibid.,* p. 41.

15. SCOMP is 16-bit rather than 32-bit only because few 32-bit machines were readily available when SCOMP development started a decade ago. For a technical overview of SCOMP, see Lester Fraim, "Scomp: A Solution to the Multilevel Security Problem," *Computer,* July 1983, pp. 26-34.

16. A more detailed description of Multics data security technology can be found in "Multics Data Security," Honeywell Information Systems, 1983, GA01-01.

17. See Landwehr, "Best Available Technologies," pp. 87, 97, and 98. See also Richard W. Kane, personal communication, February 13, 1985.

18. For a detailed discussion of SPECIAL, HDM, and Gypsy, see Maureen Cheheyl, Morrie Gasser, George Huff, and Jonathan Miller, "Verifying Security," *Computing Surveys,* September, 1981, pp. 279-339.

19. Ames, Gasser, and Schell, *op. cit.,* p. 16.

While many multilevel security systems exist on paper and in the laboratory, the Honeywell Secure Communications Processor is the first of its kind to be offered commercially.

Scomp: A Solution to the Multilevel Security Problem

Lester J. Fraim, Honeywell Information Systems

Reprinted from *Computer*, July 1983, pages 26-34. Copyright © 1983 by The Institute of Electrical and Electronics Engineers, Inc.

The Honeywell Secure Communications Processor supports a variety of specialized applications that require the processing of information with multilevel security attributes. A commercial hardware product, the Scomp system is a unique implementation of a hardware/software general-purpose operating system based on the security kernel concept. Scomp hardware supports a Multics-like, hardware-enforced ring mechanism, virtual memory, virtual I/O processing, page-fault recovery support, and performance mechanisms to aid in the implementation of an efficient operating system. The Scomp trusted operating program, or STOP, is a security-kernel-based, general-purpose operating system that provides a multilevel hierarchical file system, interprocess communication, security administrator functions, and operator commands.

The idea for the Scomp system originated in a joint Honeywell-Air Force program called Project Guardian, which was an attempt to further enhance the security of Honeywell's Multics system.[1] A secure front-end processor was needed that would use the security kernel approach to control communications access to Multics.

Multics was designed to provide program and data sharing while simultaneously protecting against both program and data misuse. The system emphasizes information availability, applications implementation, database facilities, decentralized administrative control, simplified system operation, productivity, and growth. The Multics system uses the combination of hardware and software mechanisms to provide a dynamic multiuser environment.

The Multics security mechanisms, considered far more advanced than those available in most large commercial systems, use access control lists, a hardware-enforced ring structure supporting eight rings, and the Access Isolation Mechanism that allows the definition of privilege independent of other controls. Access control provided by these mechanisms is interpreted by software but enforced by hardware on each reference to information. The hardware implementation includes a demand-paged virtual memory capability that is invisible to the user programs.

Although Project Guardian was never completed, the use of Multics features to provide multilevel security was pursued in a revised Scomp effort, a joint project of Honeywell Information Systems and the Department of Defense (specifically, the Naval Electronics Systems Command, or Navelex). In this implementation, the Scomp is a trusted minicomputer operating system using software verification techniques.*

Originally the plan was to use the traditional approach to building a trusted operating system: Namely, to build a security kernel and an emulator of an existing operating system to run on top of the kernel. This approach was taken by UCLA[2] and Mitre in their early development programs and by Ford for KSOS-11.[3] One conclusion drawn from these efforts was that an operating system emulator was many times slower than the emulated system.[4] This performance reduction can be attributed to a variety of factors, including the incompatibility of the security kernel with the emulated system, the hardware capabilities of the system, and the code generated by the implementation language.

*In August 1982, Honeywell requested that the newly formed Department of Defense Computer Evaluation Center formally evaluate the Scomp. This evaluation, which still is continuing, is using the "Draft Trusted Computer System Evaluation Criteria" (dated January 27, 1983) to determine whether the Scomp is a Class A1 system. The evaluation is expected to be complete in late summer 1983.

The planned interface for the Scomp system was a Bell Labs Unix emulator, the same type of emulator used by KSOS-11. The goal was to provide a compatible interface on both systems, thereby using the vast amount of software that exists on current Unix implementations. However, KSOS-11 and other attempts to build Unix emulators on secure systems have shown that certain Unix features (e.g., process family sharing of open-file seek pointers) are incompatible with the requirements of secure systems. Furthermore, the Unix notion of doing I/O by copying data into a process address space is incompatible with the Scomp demand-paging system. Rather than trying to achieve a full Unix compatibility, Honeywell has taken a new approach to building an interface for the Scomp. The SKIP, or Scomp kernel interface package, does not try to emulate a specific system. Instead, it takes advantage of the underlying hardware and security kernel architecture to provide an efficient applications interface.

The Scomp system, a solution to many multilevel security problems, contains the mechanisms necessary to allow controlled processing of different levels of classified information. Implementing MLS applications on the Scomp system can provide greater flexibility and efficiency than the current use of procedural and administrative controls to protect information resources. Many systems today overclassify both people and information because the computer cannot maintain the separation of information with different classifications. Most systems operate in a "system high" mode, in which the level of the system and all its users is cleared to the highest level of any information in the system. Procedural and physical controls are applied to protect the information in the system.

The Scomp system provides for the processing of information at its classification level, and it enforces the separation of users with different security characteristics. In addition, the Scomp system can provide specialized interfaces between systems of different classifications to provide more efficient management of information. Such MLS applications, referred to as guard systems,[5] provide the timely flow of information from resources

with different security levels. These resources can be two networks, two systems, or a system with users at a level lower than that of the systems.

The Scomp's basic security mechanism

The Scomp system is a unique implementation of the security kernel approach because of the way in which the hardware functions support the software capabilities. The Scomp system satisfies the requirements of the reference monitor by providing complete mediation, isolation, and verification of the system design.

Mediation is provided through the interaction of the Scomp hardware and software. The software provides the initial mediation of a request for access using the kernel's internal data structures. It validates the request for both the subject and the object of the requested action (e.g., read or write). The software then builds a data element, in the form of a descriptor, for use by the hardware in the continued mediation of the access. The descriptor consists of four words of information including access permission (i.e., read, write, or execute) and the location of the object. This cooperative mediation of hardware and software is shown in Figure 1. The hardware implementation provides performance advantages over a mechanism implemented strictly in software.

Isolation is provided by the hardware implementation of a Multics-like four-ring mechanism,[6] with ring 0 containing the security kernel. This implementation, which was developed from the Multics architecture to meet the needs of a Level 6/DPS 6 operating system, includes controlled ring-crossing to allow less privileged software to access an inner ring for a service function. A ring-bracket mechanism controls operations of read, write, and execute using the ring of execution.

The Scomp security-relevant software (the security kernel and trusted software) is verified with two technologies. The first is the SRI International Hierarchical Development Methodology.[7] This method of verification requires the development of a formal top-level specification, which defines the system from the view of

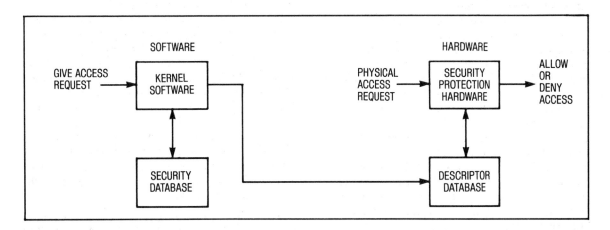

Figure 1. Mediation implemented through a combination of hardware and software. The software establishes the descriptor, deriving physical permissions on the basis of subject/object security attributes. The hardware controls physical access on the basis of descriptors.

a user process. The FTLS, written in a nonprocedural language called Special, is then verified using tools developed by SRI. The Scomp security kernel FTLS has been verified, using this methodology, against a model of DoD security policy.[8]

The second verification technology involves trusted software, which is security-relevant software outside the security kernel that can selectively bypass the kernel's mandatory control. Trusted software must be verified to ensure that it enforces the policy for which it was designed. The Scomp trusted software will be verified using the Gypsy methodology developed at the University of Texas.[7] Gypsy was selected because of its procedural nature and its ability to specify arbitrary enforcement policies—two capabilities needed to adequately specify the trusted functions. Verification of the Scomp trusted functions is expected to be complete in September 1983.

In addition to the formal verification mechanism, other assurance techniques must be applied to system development to demonstrate the completeness of the design and implementation. Scomp development has been tightly controlled to ensure that the implemented code corresponds to the verified design. Control has been possible only because of the clarity and consistency of the documentation developed during product implementation. The formal review by the DoD Computer Security Evaluation Center was augmented by Navelex reviews during development. This comprehensive technical review process has provided invaluable support to the quality and completeness of the security mechanisms in the Scomp system.

Scomp hardware implementation

Scomp hardware is implemented on the Honeywell Level 6/DPS 6, a bus-structured 16-bit minicomputer.

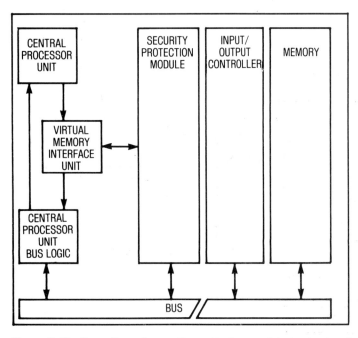

Figure 2. Configuration of security protection module in the Level 6/DPS 6, a bus-structured 16-bit minicomputer.

All system components connect to the Level 6/DPS 6 bus, allowing access to I/O controllers, processors, and memory. The Scomp hardware design uses all standard peripherals and provides the security mechanisms totally through the special hardware. Consequently, we can easily convert a standard Level 6/DPS 6 to a Scomp—the standard processor is simply replaced with a modified processor and the Security Protection Module.

The SPM, which enforces the complete mediation and isolation properties of the reference monitor, resides on the Level 6/DPS 6 bus between the modified processor and all other system elements. This structure enables the SPM to capture all processor requests and perform the required mediation before accessing memory or I/O devices. Figure 2 shows the placement of the SPM on the bus.

Mediation mechanisms. The SPM mediates access to objects using virtual addresses and a process identifier called the descriptor base root. The DBR points to the memory and I/O descriptors for the resources available to the process. If the process requests that an action be performed, the SPM mediates it using the information in the appropriate descriptor. If the request is valid, the SPM maps the virtual request to a physical request and allows the action to take place. If the action is not allowed, the SPM generates a trap, which is processed by the security kernel.

The virtual memory for a process is established by assigning a DBR to each process. Each memory descriptor, pointed to by the DBR, contains a pointer to physical memory, access permissions, and memory management data. Each process can address a 1M-word virtual address space (512 segments). A segment is treated as an object, and its size varies from 0 to 2K words. Segments can be subdivided into pages of 128 words each.

Addressing within the processes' virtual memory space is done using a generalized two-dimensional address. Here, memory is addressed via the ordered pair (segment number, offset), in which segment number identifies the memory segment and offset is the word number within the segment. In the simplest form of addressing, the DBR for the process is used to find the descriptor segment, and the segment number from the virtual address is used to find the specific descriptor. The descriptor is then used to find the data segment, and the offset is used to find the specific memory word. The SPM searches for the descriptor and generates the physical address. This form of address generation is shown in Figure 3. By using indirect descriptors and pages for descriptor storage, more sophisticated descriptor structures are possible. Figure 4 shows a three-level descriptor structure used for memory management.

To mediate I/O, the Scomp uses a virtual I/O mechanism with descriptors similar to those used for memory mediation. This method provides several advantages over the typical implementation of I/O capabilities. Because the mediation mechanism is in hardware, I/O instructions do not require privilege (i.e., execution in ring 0). Consequently, the device drivers can be outside the security kernel, making it smaller and simpler be-

COMPUTER

cause it does not have to support many different device types. Also, I/O capabilities can be added without modifying the security kernel, a complex process that would mean reverifying the kernel's design. The reduced overhead in the kernel and the reduction in kernel calls provide performance advantages over kernels that must perform all I/O functions themselves. The virtual I/O processing implemented in the Scomp hardware has thus made the implementation of a general-purpose operating system more practical.

In the virtual I/O mechanism, all I/O requests are captured by the SPM. The SPM maps the virtual name to a physical device and provides for two types of DMA transfers. To support premapped I/O, the SPM mediates the device and memory resources and then initiates the transfer using an absolute address. Subsequent requests by the device to memory are made with no SPM intervention. Mapped I/O is similar, except that the device controller is provided with a virtual memory address, and each request by the device for memory is captured and mediated by the SPM. The mapped I/O mechanism requires more overhead; however, it reduces the risk of error created by an I/O device hardware failure and reduces verification requirements on controllers.

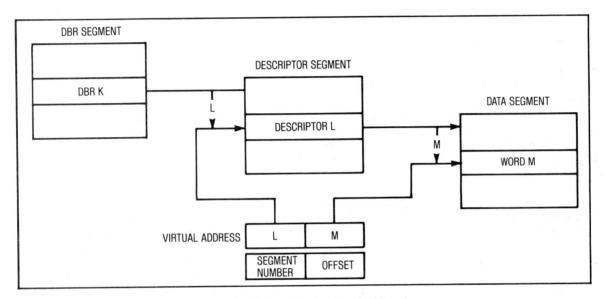

Figure 3. Two-dimensional address generation independent of physical location.

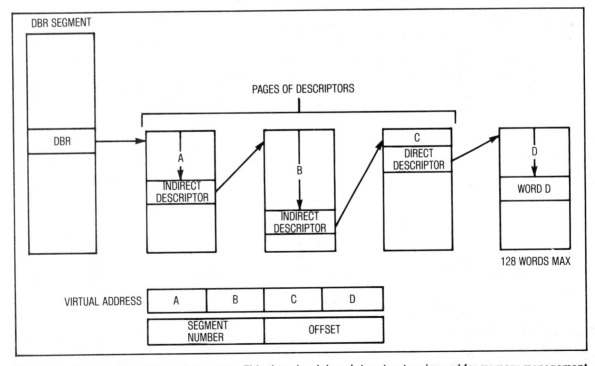

Figure 4. Addressing in a fully paged system. This three-level descriptor structure is used for memory management.

Isolation mechanism. In the Multics-like, four-ring structure of the Scomp hardware, ring 0, the kernel ring, is the most privileged ring, and ring 3, the user ring, is the least privileged. The hardware supports a call/return mechanism that allows a less privileged procedure to request a service from a more privileged procedure. The hardware also supports a mechanism that allows a called procedure to access caller-supplied arguments at the caller's privilege level. This mode, called the argument-addressing mode, prevents the kernel from accessing data that the caller could not access. Thus the hardware validates the access for the kernel with the same checks used to validate access for the user. The AAM eliminates the need for duplicate software checks in the kernel.

Performance mechanisms. The performance of trusted systems has always been a major concern. Many early attempts to provide reference monitor functions in software have shown that these functions result in a slower execution. The performance of both the KVM370[9] and the Ford KSOS-11 systems did not meet design expectations.

The major reason for implementing the SPM was to enhance the performance of a trusted system by building mediation capabilities in hardware. Of course, the hardware and software needed to enforce security can degrade performance, but the degree of degradation is significantly lower.

The SPM has several capabilities specifically designed to reduce the overhead of the security mechanism. One of these is the use of the DBR to define a process descriptor tree in memory. With this approach, the SPM can load descriptors from memory as needed; no descriptors need to be preloaded at dispatch time. The hardware loads only descriptors required for mediation, and there is no requirement to save or restore descriptor memory in the mediation mechanism. Consequently, the overhead associated with process switching and dispatching is kept to a minimum. The initial overhead of a process switch is reduced, and the overhead associated with descriptor loading is distributed over the entire execution of the process. Many other hardware architectures produce a larger

amount of overhead at process initiation by requiring the loading of registers or descriptors to begin execution.

The Scomp system also takes advantage of a descriptor cache to save the most recently used memory descriptors. This cache is the part of the SPM called the virtual memory interface unit. The VMIU mediates memory requests and saves the descriptors in its cache. If another request is received for the same page, the VMIU can mediate it without performance penalty since no descriptor fetch is required. The overall system degradation caused by the mediation process is a function of the hit ratio, that is, the number of times the descriptor is in the cache when it is requested. If the hit ratio is 95 to 98 percent, the performance degradation from hardware will be between 5 and 15 percent. Hit ratios in this range do not appear to be difficult to maintain if good programming techniques are used.

The Scomp trusted operating program

The Scomp trusted operating program, or STOP, consists of three major components. The security kernel enforces the security mechanisms and controls all access in the system. The trusted software provides the administrator, operator, and user services necessary to interface with the security kernel, and the Scomp kernel interface package provides a file system mechanism, process control, and device I/O. These elements of the Scomp operating system provide the user with an efficient interface for the development of applications. Figure 5 shows how these software capabilities are structured, using the Scomp ring mechanism to provide a layered operating system.

Security kernel. The security kernel is the basic operating system that performs all resource management, process scheduling, memory management, trap and interrupt management, and auditing. The security kernel also functions as the software portion of the reference monitor implementation. As such, it controls access to objects in accordance with its embedded securi-

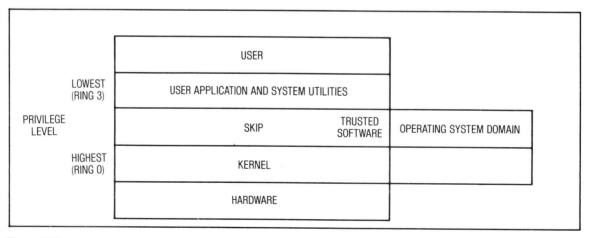

Figure 5. Scomp software architecture using hardware ring mechanism.

ty policy. The kernel supports segments, devices, and processes (processes can also be subjects, according to reference monitor nomenclature). Each of these objects is distinguished by a 64-bit identifier that never changes for the life of the object in the system. The kernel also maintains two types of data on each object in the system—access information and status data. The access information consists of the security level and category set and the integrity level and category set. The levels are hierarchical, and the category sets are 32 separate compartments for both security and integrity. Also contained in the access information is the discretionary information, which includes read, write, and execute permissions for the owner of the object, the group of the owner, and all others. Additionally, the kernel maintains ring brackets for owner, group, and "other," which limit the ring of privilege required for access to an object. Subtypes are also provided to allow user control of objects. The status information varies depending on the object type.

The security kernel provides 38 functions, called gates, that can be used by a process. These kernel gates allow for creating and deleting objects, mapping (including in-process address space) and unmapping a segment or device, wiring (keeping in main memory) or unwiring segments, getting or setting status, interprocess communicating, and reading and setting the system clock.

The Scomp security kernel, written in UCLA Pascal,[10] consists of approximately 10K lines of code. It requires approximately 46K words of text and 9K words of global data. Dynamic tables are required to manage the Scomp demand-paging virtual memory. The amount of space needed depends on the number and size of the system processes.

Trusted software. The user, system administrator, and operator interact with the Scomp system through trusted software, which uses the security kernel for service and for special privileges to perform the trusted functions. This software is called "trusted" because (1) it can violate one of the security or integrity properties enforced by the kernel (e.g., simple integrity or the security *-property, pronounced "star" property) or (2) it uses functions that must be correct because the system's enforcement of security policy relies on their processing. An example of the second type of trusted software is the database editor, which builds the user access database. If it does not properly construct the database for the login process, the login actions cannot be assured.

The trusted software for the Scomp system has been implemented in the C language. The trusted functions are implemented in 23 processes, which consist of 11.1K lines of C language code. The software is divided into three functional areas according to the type of trusted service provided. *Trusted user services* provide the interface to the Scomp system for the user, *trusted operation services* provide the system operator with the capabilities necessary to run the system, and *trusted maintenance services* allow the system administrator to build and maintain the Scomp system.

The user accesses the trusted software through a trusted communications path that is implemented in software and hardware. This path provides protection against Trojan horse attacks caused by users responding to requests from application software that is acting like the operating system. The user knows that he is indeed communicating with the system and not with a bogus user program because he must strike the "secure attention" key to initiate the dialog with the operating system. The secure attention key generates a unique interrupt to the security kernel that causes the kernel to connect the device to a known trusted program. When the user requesting a service strikes the secure attention key, he accesses the operating system.

Trusted user services allow the user to establish a processing environment in which applications can be run. The easiest way to understand these functions is to step through the process of logging a user on and establishing his working environment. To initiate the login sequence, the user depresses the break key, which acts as a secure attention key, on the terminal connected to the Scomp system. The kernel recognizes this condition and notifies the secure initiator process. The secure initiator controls all terminals and creates a secure command processor, called the secure server, for his terminal. The secure server then prompts the user for the function to be performed. If this login is the user's first, the login function is invoked by the server. The login function then validates the user through his identification and password. If the user had already logged in, he would have been prompted for his next request. Services available to the user are log in, change group, modify password, set access level, set default access, log out, file access modifier (the only means of changing a file's access), run, process status, kill, and reattach.

Trusted user services allow the user to establish a processing environment in which applications can be run.

These functions provide the user with the ability to establish an application environment at a given security level. The login command validates the user's access to the system and establishes his security and integrity level at the defaults defined in the access authentication database. If the user wishes to run at a level other than his default, the "set access level" command provides the mechanism for changing security and integrity levels. If the user wishes to change the group designation for the session, the "change group" command is executed. The run command is used to initiate the execution of an application program. To communicate with the system, the user hits the secure attention key, which transfers the terminal to trusted software. If the user desires the status of his application programs, he requests the "process status" service. If the user wishes to terminate the execution of his application, he invokes the kill command. With the reattach command, the terminal can be reconnected to an existing application that was suspended via the secure attention key.

The user also has trusted services that modify the information in his entry of the access authentication database. These features include setting the user's password (modify password) and setting the user's default security and integrity level (set default access). The file access modifier provides the controlled upgrading or downgrading of individual files. The system administrator determines whether a user is allowed to downgrade files. If the user has this capability, he may be required to review data before downgrading. A user can upgrade files to any security level he has permission to access.

Trusted operation services consist of the functions necessary to start the system and to ensure that normal operation continues. These functions include secure startup, audit collection, secure loader, and operator commands.

Trusted maintenance services allow the system administrator or operator to manipulate system data.

Secure startup is the process that receives control at the end of security kernel initialization. It is responsible for intializing all devices on the system and creating the audit collection process, which receives audit records from both the kernel and trusted software and builds audit files. The secure loader, which loads a secure process, is known to the kernel and is used for all requests to load trusted software.

The operator commands process is called by the secure server after the operator has established a connection to the system. The operator commands include setting the system clock, shutting down the system, switching audit files, changing device attributes, and obtaining device status.

Trusted maintenance services allow the system administrator or operator to manipulate system data. All maintenance services fall into the second class of trusted software because they ensure the validity of the overall system. These functions include the ability to initialize a kernel file system, perform consistency checks on kernel file systems, repair inconsistencies in the file system, and dump or restore the file system content. A database editor is also provided so that the system administrator can modify system databases. The databases maintained include the access authentication database, the group access authentication database, the terminal configuration database, the security map, and the mountable file system database.

SKIP—the Scomp kernel interface package. The basic requirements defined for the SKIP are to

- provide a hierarchical multilevel file system,
- provide the ability to create child processes,
- contain an event mechanism for process synchronization,
- use the Scomp hardware and kernel capabilities to provide an efficient interface, and
- provide a low-level interface that can be used for multiple purposes or systems.

This interface was designed with the help of a government-provided steering group of experts in computer security and operating systems. Honeywell has worked with this group to design and implement the SKIP. The SKIP is not an operating system but rather an interface to the secure environment—it enables the users to effectively interface applications and systems with the security mechanisms of the Scomp system.

The SKIP comprises two sets of routines. The major portion of the SKIP resides in ring 2 and is activated through SKIP gate calls. These routines are always mapped into the user's address space to alleviate the overhead associated with loading these functions. The other part of the SKIP is a library of routines that execute in the user ring (ring 3). The SKIP provides three basic user capabilities, a hierarchical file system, a process control mechanism, and support for device I/O.

The SKIP file system is a hierarchical structure composed of directories, files, and links. It is an entry-naming system in that the SKIP gates do not interpret path names. Instead a SKIP subroutine interprets them, and the subroutine can be modified if the user desires a different path-name interpretation from that provided. The file system is protected through the use of the Scomp ring mechanism and subtypes. Only ring 2 software is allowed to modify the file system structure. The security level of the file system must be monotonically nondecreasing from the file system root. The directories, files, and links are identified by names of up to 24 printable characters. Directories are entries that contain information about other file system entries. A file is a collection of segments with a maximum size of 4951 segments (18,804,736 bytes), the contents of which can be directly modified by the user. All segments in a file must be at the same security and integrity level. The third file system entry is a link that points to a directory, to a file, or to another link. The SKIP link mechanism is the Multics implementation of a link, in which the entry pointed to is defined by the path name in the link entry.

The SKIP allows the user to manipulate non-file-system segments by performing certain functions similar to those provided by the kernel. To protect the integrity of the file system, only a limited number of kernel functions can be called directly from the user ring.

The SKIP also allows the user to create and delete processes, set priority, and send and receive events. Events are messages indicating the occurrence of something meaningful to a process. These capabilities provide communication to build and manage processes in an application environment. The SKIP event mechanism is interrupt driven, which allows for immediate processing when notification of an event occurs. The user can provide handlers for different events as required. A process can wait on multiple events and selectively wait on specific events or events from a specific process. Events are queued by the SKIP to allow the user to receive them in the order they occur. The event mechanism relays interrupt information to a process owning a device, enabling the user to process I/O using SKIP subroutines. This capability is required because the security kernel does not support the I/O service function.

The user-device I/O routines are contained in a subroutine library. They provide support to asynchronous terminals, mass storage devices, tape devices, printers, and the 1822 communications line adapter. The I/O functions provide the capability to perform data transfers or issue commands to the devices. The user is required to link only the routines necessary for the particular program, thereby reducing the overhead associated with linking unused support software.

Two types of guards are being implemented on the Scomp system.[11] The Navy is implementing the Advanced Command and Control Architectural Testbed guard to allow two networks at different security levels to communicate with each other. This configuration will provide more timely information without the delays that now exist because the networks cannot be physically connected with the current controls.

The Army is implementing the Forscom security monitor on the Scomp.[11] This guard implementation will allow users at a low level to access a host at a higher security level by providing two primary functions. First, it will filter the input from the user and validate that the requested service is authorized for this user. Second, the guard will screen the information returned from the host to ensure that it reasonably accommodates the request. The assurance built into the Scomp system allows for a high level of trust that these applications will not allow unauthorized information to flow to a user.

In addition to its potential guard applications, the Scomp system is being evaluated and considered as a base for a variety of applications that require its security features. Some of these applications are database management, office automation, message processors, and general-purpose systems.

The technology of MLS applications is moving forward. The efficient use of the Scomp system in many of these applications will demonstrate the improved processing capabilities that can be provided in a multilevel security environment.

The Scomp system meets the security needs of both the DoD and industry. Scomp hardware efficiently controls information in an operating system. The operating system, in turn, provides the user with the control necessary to process information with different security attributes. The operating system design is being verified using the most current methods of program verification. The assurance techniques applied to the Scomp make it the first candidate for the DoD Computer Security Evaluation Center's Class A1 system. The Scomp is the first of many systems developed by Honeywell and other manufacturers that will provide solutions to the problems associated with processing sensitive information. ∎

References

1. *Honeywell Multics Distributed Processing System, Summary Overview*, tech. report DL92, Honeywell Information Systems, Waltham, Mass., 1982.

2. G. J. Popek, "UCLA Secure UNIX," *AFIPS Conf. Proc.*, Vol. 48, 1979 NCC, AFIPS Press, Montvale, N.J., 1979, pp. 355-364.

3. E. J. McCauley and P. J. Drongo ski, "KSOS—The Design of a Secure Operating System," *AFIPS Conf. Proc.*, Vol. 48, 1979 NCC, AFIPS Press, Montvale, N.J., 1979, pp. 345-353.

4. "Panel Session—Kernel Performance Issues," *Proc. Symp. Security and Privacy*, IEEE Cat. No. 81CH1629-5, Oakland, Calif., 1981, pp. 162-178.

5. J. P. L. Woodward, "Applications for Multilevel Secure Operating Systems," *AFIPS Conf. Proc.,* Vol. 48, 1979 NCC, AFIPS Press, Montvale, N.J., 1979, pp. 319-328.

6. M. D. Schroeder and J. H. Saltzer, "A Hardware Architecture for Implementing Protection Rings," *Comm. ACM*, Vol. 15, No. 3, Mar. 1972, pp. 157-170.

7. M. H. Cheheyl et al., "Verifying Security," *ACM Computing Surveys*, Vol. 13, No. 3, Sept. 1981, pp. 279-339.

8. D. E. Bell and L. J. Lapadula, *Secure Computer Systems: Mathematical Foundations and Model,* tech. report M74-224, The Mitre Corporation, Bedford, Mass., Oct. 1974.

9. D. B. Gold et al., "A Security Retrofit of VM/370," *AFIPS Conf. Proc.,* Vol. 48, 1979 NCC, AFIPS Press, Montvale, N.J., 1979, pp. 335-344.

10. E. Walton, *The UCLA Pascal Translation System*, tech. report, UCLA Computer Science Department, Jan. 1976.

11. *Proc. Fourth Seminar DoD Computer Security Initiative Program*, National Bureau of Standards, Gaithersburg, Md., Aug. 1981, Section U.

Lester J. Fraim is the manager, Trusted Computer Base Development for Honeywell Information Systems, Federal Systems Division, in McLean, Virginia. His current responsibilities include the development of the Honeywell Secure Communications Processor. He has also held positions as manager, WWMCCS Site Support and manager, Communications System. He received a BS in mathematics from California State Polytechnic College in San Luis Obispo in 1970, and an MS degree from the American University in 1973.

An EMACS Based Downgrader For the SAT

John McHugh*
Center for Digital Systems Research
Research Triangle Institute
P.O. Box 12194
Research Triangle Park
North Carolina 27709

July 2, 1986

1 Abstract

This paper describes the design and verification of a downgrader to be supplied as a kernal extension for the Honeywell SAT. The downgrader implements a restrictive protocol based on traditional, paper document, downgrader procedures. specification and proofs techniques are described for both the security and functional aspects of the downgrader.

2 Introduction

The Honeywell SAT[1] (Secure Ada[1] Target) is a processor designed to meet or surpass the A1 level requirements of the Department of Defense (DoD) Trusted Computer System Evaluation Criteria[2] (TCSEC). It differs from previous systems which attempt to meet the criteria in a number of respects. The most important of these is the use of extensive, specialized hardware to provide the mechanisms for enforcing security policy while allowing the policy itself to remain in software to the greatest extent possible. The SAT is not intended to support a specific application, but rather to provide a vehicle for the construction of a diverse set of applications, military and

---

*This work was supported by Honeywell under U.S. Government Contract MDA904-84-C-6011.

[1]Ada is a registered trademark of the Department of Defense.

Reprinted from *Proceedings of the 8th National Computer Security Conference*, 1985, pages 1-10. U.S. Government work not protected by U.S. copyright.

228

otherwise, which have in common their need for a security policy and rigorous enforcement thereof. The downgrader discussed in this paper represents the first of a series of verified and trusted kernel extensions to be built for the SAT.

In this paper, we will briefly describe the philosophy behind techniques used to build a system on top of the basic SAT and show how this philosophy and guides construction of an extension such as the downgrader. With this background, we will describe the downgrader in terms of its functionality and operational interface. The process through which the downgrader is specified, designed, and verified is then described, followed by a discussion of the ways in which it fits into the overall SAT based system organization. Finally, it will be argued that incorporation of such verified trusted extensions in the SAT framework results in a system which can be shown to comply with an appropriate security policy in all of its operations.

3   Software and the SAT

The SAT is intended to support systems consisting of a number of user programs written in Ada. The hardware of the SAT provides the mechanisms for the enforcement of a security policy, but the policy is largely defined in software. The mechanisms provide support for a very general Meta Policy[3] of which the Bell and La Padula[4] policy is an instance. In providing a formal framework to support verified applications on the SAT, the Meta Policy is mapped to an abstract model level which is in turn mapped to an interpretation and ultimately to a formal top level specification (FTLS) which provides definitions of the actual machine instructions used to manipulate the security state of the SAT. Below the FTLS is a detailed design specification which defines the internal representations of the security state and the mechanization of the security relevant operations.

As noted in the SAT description, [1] complete verifications are performed at each of these levels and convincing arguments are made about the mappings between levels. These constitute the base proof for a SAT system. Addenda, which are proofs of software extensions to the SAT kernel, are combined with the base proof to produce a completely verified application.

The proof strategy of the SAT has been discussed in detail because the SAT design philosophy has been governed by provability considerations. These considerations continue to govern the construction of much of the user software to be run on the SAT to support a given application.

There are two major classes of software in an SAT system: applications software, whose operation is mediated by the reference monitor, and kernel extensions, which extend the functionality of the base hardware to produce a reference monitor that meets the full and detailed DoD requirements.

The first set of kernel extensions, and hence the first reference monitor to be built on the SAT hardware, will be those required for operation as an Ada Target. The initial et of users for SAT will then be system developers who wish to produce secure applications and more elaborate reference monitors in the Ada language. This choice of initial reference monitor characteristics was made in order to provide a secure, Ada-based capability to the development community as rapidly as possible.

Consistent with this goal of timeliness, the first set of kernel extensions will be extremely simple. In general, kernel extension software is subdivided into three classes, based on the degree of trust and verification. (It should be recalled that "trust," in the sense used here, is the privilege to selectively violate the *-property, e.g., "write information down" in security level.) The three classes are:

1. Software that is neither trusted nor verified. Such software performs common resource management tasks, and its behavior is mediated in the same fashion as applications software. An example of this class of software is the Ada Run-Time Support Library (RSL), which provides a virtual machine congenial to the semantics of the Ada language.

2. Software that is verified but not trusted. Certain kernel extensions must be verified to exhibit security-relevant properties, but these properties may not involve the benign violation of the *-property. Examples of this class of software are labelers, which must be shown to properly format exported labels, and login responders, which must be shown to properly consult a table of passwords before assigning a user name and a security level to a subject. Both modules perform functions that are security-critical yet do not involve information flows between security levels.

3. Software that is both trusted and verified. An example of such software are the tools that support the downgrad-

ing of information. Such tools must selectively violate the *-property and be verified to do so only in ways that are visible to and cleared by an authorized user. A secure downgrader, with an Emacs-like user interface, will be developed for SAT as a proof of principle that the basic SAT functionality simplifies the development and verification of such software[1].

The downgrader discussed above is typical of kernel extensions which must be provided in order to produce a useful system for some application. It is patently obvious that such a facility violates the *-property of Bell and La Padula. It does not, however, violate the Meta Policy[3].

In its broadest sense, the Meta Policy captures our intuitive motion of security. The policy can be simply stated as "information may not be disclosed to any individual without the necessary authorization[3]." It is important to note that, in this context, information is a semantic concept rather than a syntactic one and that the notion of authorization may involve the exercise of judgements based on semantics as well as syntactic constructs such as classification labels. This allows us to prove the security of the resulting system in a broader sense.

There are three sets of properties which must be included in a proof addenda for an extension such as the downgrader. The first of these is its functionality. The downgrader must be shown to enforce a protocol which is satisfactory for accomplishing the declassification of information when exercised by a trusted individual. It must then be shown that, as integrated into the SAT framework, the downgrader can only be invoked by such trusted individuals and, even then, only under suitably audited circumstances. Finally, it must be argued that this usage is consistent with our broader notion of security as represented by the Meta Policy.

4 The Downgrader

The downgrader is designed to force its user, a trusted individual, to follow a protocol which mimics the pencil and paper world. A primary objective is to ensure that the production of a draft document for downgrading takes place at human rather than electronic speeds. There are three phases in the operation of the downgrader. In the first phase, the user transfers information from a file representing a document at a high level of classification, H to a draft document, also classified at level H but ultimately intended for downgrading to a lower level L. This transfer is done a sentence at a time. During this transfer, limited changes can be made to the information being transferred. Following the transfer phase is a review phase in which both documents are reviewed in parallel with the context of each sentence displayed in both versions. During review, sentences in the draft may be accepted or rejected. Once review is complete, the draft document is copied down from classification H to classification L using the privileged TOPOP TWO (Trusted Write Override). The operations during each phase are discussed below in more detail.

Several aspects of the process are worth discussion. The most important is the fact that trust in the downgrader resides primarily in the human user who makes the judgments as to what information can be downgraded. The protocol serves to raise the level of assurance associated with the downgrading process by ensuring that the user has transferred information in relatively small chunks and under conditions requiring at least two inspections of each chunk. The process is also audited. Initiation of the downgrading process can create an audit record containing the identities of the user and the object being downgraded. Because the process operates on syntactic entities in the source object, the exact transformation of the source required to produce the downgraded object may be recorded for audit purposes. The actual downgrading of the draft may be made a System Security Officer (SSO) function.

The discretion implied above is deliberate. The downgrader design provides for capture of the transformations and for separating the transfer and review phases from the TWO. The SAT base provides the ability to restrict use of the downgrader and to preserve audit detail. The question of how much to restrict use of the downgrader is one of administrative policy and is ultimately a question of interpretation of the security Meta Policy.

The downgrader appears to its user as a two window screen editor which executes a set of commands which are a very restricted subset of those provided by EMACS[5]. In the transfer mode, the user may scroll through the source document at will, but may not change it. This assures a constant basis for the transformation history. The display is labeled with the classification of the object being downgraded as required by the TCSEC[2]. The user selects sentences to be transferred to the draft. In order to assure that the user is presented with a context containing the selected sentence, sentences are limited to approximately four lines. Limiting sentence length prevents simple subversions of the protocol such as converting a document to a single "sentence" prior to invoking the downgrader and downgrading it in a single operation. Restricting a sentence to a maximum of four lines ensures at least three lines of context on either side of the sentence in each window (plus the security labeling required by the TCSEC[2] assuming a standard 24 line CRT display.

When a sentence is selected for transfer, it is highlighted or displayed in reverse video. The user then positions the cursor in the draft window which is labeled with the level of the source object and an annotation of the target level of the draft. The draft is displayed as individual sentences in cannonical form, separated by blank lines. New sentences can only be inserted at the beginning or end of the draft or between existing sentences. The user may scroll through the draft to determine an appropriate location to insert the transferred sentence. When the user issues the transfer command, the selected sentence is inserted in the draft window in cannonical form.

The cannonicalization process left justifies the sentence on the screen, converts all nonprinting characters to blanks and replaces all multiple blanks by single blanks. Line breaks are inserted as necessary. The purpose of the cannonical form is to prevent the covert passing of information to the draft document in the form of invisible data encodings such as sequences of nulls, backspace/blank pairs, etc. The user is left to deal with visible encodings although some of these could be included in the cannonicalization if desired.

At this point, the "whiteout" sub mode is entered. In this mode, the user can delete any word or sequence of words or can replace any word or sequence of words in the sentence with a cannonical marker. The words and phrases thus removed are saved for use during the review phase. Once the "whiteout" phase is finished, the sentence is considered as part of the draft. The user may delete sentences from the draft at any time or may re-enter the "whiteout' sub mode for any sentence in the draft at any time, but no other modifications are possible.

When the user has constructed the desired draft, the review phase is entered. At the beginning of this phase, the user reviews the list of deleted and replaced words and phrases. Unless the user explicitly eliminates a word or phrase from the list, it will be used as a review pattern, and all sentences in the draft containing the word or phrase will be singled out for special review in "whiteout" mode. During this part of the review, the user will be required to take an affirmative action to retain the word or phrase. These actions are subject to audit.

The general review causes the system to display the draft document in order while displaying the source document and context for each sentence in the draft. The user retains or rejects each sentence in the draft based on this review.

When the review is complete, the protocol has been satisfied and the actual downgrading of the draft may take place. The downgrading process may be suspended and resumed at will. Only the downgrader has access to the draft, ensuring its integrity. It is possible to revert to the transfer phase from the review phase, but the review must begin anew if this is done. It is also possible to abandon the downgrading as well.

5   Specification Issues

There are two issues to be addressed concerning with the specification and verification of the downgrader. The first of these deals with its security aspect. The downgrader must be trusted because it invokes a privileged SAT instruction, TWO when it creates the downgraded object from the draft. The power of the SAT's type and domain mechanisms allow us to define a lemma, AuthorizedDowngrader (In, Out), which captures the security aspects of the proof. This lemma is formulated and proved as an extension to the SAT base proof and states that any downgraded object, Out, can only be produced by the downgrader, operating on the object, In, and executed on behalf of a user who is specifically authorized to have access to both In and the downgrader. The proof of this aspect of the downgrader's operation depends entirely on SAT properties and is independent of the functional aspects of the downgrader. Because of the use of the TWO operation to perform the actual downgrading operation, AuthorizedDowngrader is shown to be secure with respect to the Meta Policy.

Proofs of the addenda described above should be sufficient to show that the system with the downgrader incorporated still satisfies the security Meta Policy and is thus secure. One could, in fact, envision a much simpler downgrader which would merely do TWO on its input object and leave an audit trail. This too could be shown to satisfy the Meta Policy under the proper circumstances. Why then the elaborate protocol?

The answer to this question leads to the second issue which involves the specification and verification of the downgrader's functionality. Basically, although we trust the users who are allowed to downgrade, we do not expect them to be infallible. The trivial downgrader mentioned above provides no protection against such human errors as specifying the wrong object as input or overlooking a line or two during a review. The protocol does not completely obviate mistakes of this sort, but it makes them less likely and causes the downgrade process to be spread over a longer time, increasing the chances of catching an error before a policy violation occurs.

At the present time, the functional specification for the downgrader is under development. Like the SAT, the downgrader is being specified in Gypsy[6]. The functional specification presents a number of interesting issues. We want to show that the output of the downgrader bears a certain relationship to its input. This relationship say `ProperlyDowngraded (In, Out)` provides the desired traceability between the objects. This is not a sufficient condition for our purposes however, since `ProperlyDowngraded (In, In)` is necessarily true if only the document contents are considered. Thus, we need some way to link the procedural aspects of the downgrading process to the functional relationship between its input and output. This is further complicated by the interactive nature of the process and the use of a screen display to present the user with a window into the current state of the draft.

To support this notion, we start by considering the source as a sequence of characters. We map onto this, a syntactic index structure which creates a sequence of sentences of limited length as discussed above. This is a sequence of indices into the source identifying each sentence. The draft is a similar syntactic structure containing references to the source index and recording the modifications made in the downgrading process.

The user commands are obtained from a Gypsy buffer and are screened for illegal commands by a simple finite state recognizer. The display is described as an abstract type with a set of appropriate operations and "Hold" specifications. An implementation probably requires trusted hardware for the display to ensure that the user and software "see" the same thing.

Given this model, the transfer phase is specified in terms of a finite state machine which as operations to select from the source, mark a source sentence for transfer, position the draft, move the marked sentence to the draft in whiteout mode, and exit whiteout mode.

It will be proven that every sentence in the draft is there as the result of applying this series of operations. Similar specifications and proofs will be supplied for other phases of the operation. The successful completion of a phase is recorded in the draft structure so that the definition of proper downgrading can be expanded to include the notion of the proper application of the sequence of operations required by the protocol.

6 The Downgrader and the SAT

Kernel extensions such as the downgrader play an important role in the construction of secure, useful systems on the SAT base. Such extensions may require verification either because they involve an element of trust as part of the TCSEC required reference monitor or because they enforce non-policy requirements, such as labeling imposed by the criteria. Verification may also be indicated when a high level of functional assurance is required due to nonsecurity aspects of the intended use of the system.

The SAT base proof provides support for all aspects of kernel extension verification for both trusted and untrusted processes by providing the formalisms necessary for the specification of processes calling on the SAT operations. In the case of the downgrader, a mixture of base addenda proofs and external, purely operational proofs will be performed. The net result will be to provide assurance that a SAT based system incorporating a downgrader enforcing an elaborate protocol to ensure that a downgrading procedure similar to that used in the pen and paper world conforms to an acceptable security Meta Policy.

It is important to note that satisfying the Meta Policy requires extending the notion of the trusted computing base to encompass trusted individuals, the authorized users in the case of the downgrader. Because the Meta Policy is expressed in terms of semantic rather than syntactic information, information flows such as those occurring during a downgrade do not, per se, violate the policy. Ultimately, it is the responsibility of the systems owner to define the level of assurance required (and the limitations on the trust to be placed in individuals) to show conformance with a given Meta Policy. The strength of the SAT approach is that it permits an owner to build on a proven base to extend the capabilities of the system in arbitrary directions while providing mechanisms to control these new capabilities and contain them within the TCB as necessary.

7 Conclusions

The Honeywell SAT and its use as a base for building secure systems has been discussed. A downgrader, functionally similar to the EMACS editor, has been described and its place in a secure system based on the SAT discussed. It has been demonstrated that this process, combining proofs of security and functionality, leads to a technique for implementing useful and trustworthy systems which meet or exceed the TCSEC criteria for A1 systems.

8 Acknowledgements

The notion to attempt design of the downgrader came from Earl Boebert of Honeywell. Marv Schaefer of the DoD Computer Security Center provided the idea of a Meta Policy and many of the details of the protocol in the guise of reviewing the initial proposal. Discussions with Earl Boebert, Marv Schaefer, Bill Young of the University of Texas and Scott Hansohn of Honeywell have been extremely useful in refining the ideas presented here. Any omissions and errors are, of course, my own.

References

[1] W. E. Boebert, W. D. Young, R. Y. Kain, and S. A. Hansohn, "Secure Ada Target: Issues, System Design, and Verification," in *Proceedings of the 1985 IEEE Symposium on Security and Privacy*, 1985.

[2] The National Computer Security Center, "Trusted Computer Systems Evaluation Criteria," Tech. Rep. CSC-STD-001-83, Department of Defense, August 1983.

[3] W. D. Young, "Security in an Abstract Setting," Tech. Rep. Internal Note 186, Institute for Computing Science, University of Texas, Austin, Texas, July 1985.

[4] D. E. Bell and L. J. LaPadula, "Secure Computer System: Unified Exposition and Multics Interpretations," Tech. Rep. MTR-2997, MITRE Corporation, Bedford, MA, July 1975.

[5] R. E. Stallman, "EMACS Manual for Twenex Users," Tech. Rep. AI Memo 556, MIT Artificial Intelligence Laboratory, August 1980.

[6] D. I. Good, R. M. Cohen, C. G. Hosch, L. W. Hunter, and D. F. Hare, "Report on the Language Gypsy, Version 2.0," Tech. Rep. ICSCA-CMP-10, Institute for Computing Science, University of Texas, Austin, Texas, September 1978.

Secure Computing: The Secure Ada Target Approach

A small, trustworthy subsystem in the hardware of a computer enforces strict rules that protect data from hostile users. The subsystem can be proved trustworthy in a more rigorous sense than can earlier mechanisms.

W.E. Boebert (Honeywell Secure Computing Technology Center);
R.Y. Kain (University of Minnesota); W.D. Young (University of Texas)
MN55-7282; HVN 378-6792

Put those things that naturally go on a high place onto a high place, and those that would be most stable on a low place onto a low place; things that naturally belong on a high place settle best on a high place, while those which belong on a low place find their greatest stability there.

--Dōgen Zenji
Instructions for the Zen Cook

Most computer systems are secure only in the sense that they have not yet been compromised or in the sense that the methods by which they can be compromised are known to only a small and select group of individuals. Honeywell has long been involved in efforts to improve the security of computer systems; both the Multics and the SCOMP machines were significantly more secure than contemporary machines. The Secure Ada Target machine, currently under development at Honeywell's new Secure Computing Technology Center, is the next step toward a truly secure system: it is secure in a precisely defined sense and its security can be proved with mathematical rigor.

The machine is called an Ada target in recognition of its intended first use as an environment for the execution of programs written in the Ada language. Ada, which was developed under Honeywell's leadership, has been adopted by the Department of Defense as its standard high-level programming language. In this paper we give an overview of the general computer-security problem, describe the technical themes of which the Secure Ada Target is a variation and explain the sense in which our machine is secure.

The Threat

There are, broadly speaking, three classes of risks to information in a computer system: there may be accidental flaws an exploiter can attack; flaws may have been deliberately introduced, or the design may be fundamentally flawed. We can make an analogy with aircraft safety: an aircraft can be unsafe because of faulty workmanship or maintenance; it could have been sabotaged, or its design could be inherently unsafe — for instance, its center of gravity might be improperly placed.

In both airplanes and computers the first two classes of flaws are rich in detail and relatively barren of principle; they can be counteracted by diligently applying various quality-assurance techniques. And in both fields no degree of diligence in workmanship and inspection can overcome an inherent flaw in design.

Inherent flaws in aircraft design tend to fall into general categories, such as structural weakness or aerodynamic instability. In the case of computer systems the richest category of design flaws leaves the system open to what are called Trojan Horse attacks.

To understand the workings of a Trojan Horse attack it is first necessary to note that all knowledge one gains about a computer system is gained indirectly; there is no directly observable physical reality whatever. The relation between man and machine has been characterized as "computer-enhanced hallucination" because responses in human minds are triggered by events inside the machine that are not themselves directly observable.

Consider the difference between a mechanical typewriter and a computerized word processor, two machines that accept keystrokes and convert them into visible text. In the typewriter there is a direct and observable mechanical connection between a given keystroke and the appearance of the corresponding letter. In the word processor no such observable link exists. An intermediary, or agent, in the form of a computer program performs the transformation; the actions of this agent cannot be directly observed by the user of the machine. Indeed, the reliability of the agent is established only by experience; every keypress so far has displayed the corresponding letter. Experience may convince the user that the machine is correctly performing its intended function. There is, however, no assurance whatever that the program inside the word processor is not performing extra tasks inimical to the interests of the user: making clandestine copies, corrupting stored text or scanning input for indications that a critical document is being prepared and then destroying the document when it is completed.

This is the first element of a Trojan Horse attack: agents in the form of computer programs whose actions are visible indirectly, if at all. The second element is a computer organization in which several such agents operate on data simultaneously. This organization, variously called resource-sharing, time-sharing or the multiuser approach, was originally used for only the largest hardware sets. The rapid decline in hardware costs has now allowed it to be applied to computer hardware costing as little as $5,000. Spreading the benefits of multiuser computing (such as lower computational cost, flexible access and the ease with which data can be shared) has also meant expanding the domain in which Trojan Horse attacks are possible and increasing the threat they pose.

The designers of even the earliest multiuser systems recognized the need to control the sharing of data, if only to limit the damage faulty programs could cause. The standard mechanism for such control has been the access control list, or acl. There are two parts to this mechanism. First, users are required to identify themselves by name (and, generally, by secret password) before they can invoke a program; the system therefore knows at all times on whose behalf a program is executing. Second, every unit of data, such as a file, has an associated list of paired attributes of the form *name, access*. A set of such pairs forms the acl for the unit of data.

The name portion of an acl entry is the name of a user and the access portion defines the modes of

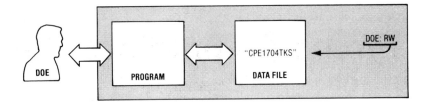

ACCESS-CONTROL LIST is the means by which most computer systems attempt to protect sensitive data. Associated with each data file is an access-control list, or acl, that pairs a user or a group of users and allowed modes of access. In this case, Doe, attempting to protect the critically sensitive character string "CPE1704TKS," has set the acl for the file to allow read and write access to programs executing on his behalf and no access to programs executing on behalf of other users. One possible attack on acl-protected files is shown in the illustrations below.

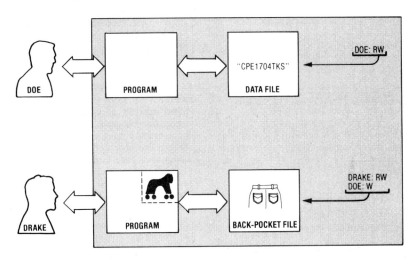

HOSTILE USER (Drake) prepares a raid on Doe's data by installing a Trojan Horse program and a private file. The Trojan Horse program has two functions. One of the functions is innocent and is visible to the user who invokes the program. The other is hostile and is invisible. The private file is intended to serve as the "back pocket" during the attack. Drake sets the acl on this file to allow programs executing on his behalf read and write access and programs executing on Doe's behalf write access only.

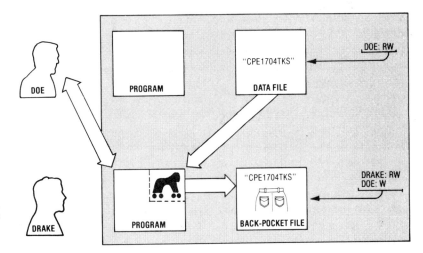

TROJAN HORSE program is designed to detect that it is being executed by user Doe. When Doe unwittingly invokes the program, it acquires read and write access to his files and write access to Drake's back-pocket file. The Trojan Horse code within the program surreptitiously reads Doe's files and writes their contents to Drake's back-pocket file. Drake has then only to read his file at some later time to learn the value of the critically sensitive character string.

access to the data permitted programs executing on behalf of that user. For the sake of illustration we shall assume that the possible modes are *read*, which means that a program can examine data in the file, *write*, which means that a program can alter data, *read/write*, which means that it can do both and *null*, which means that it can do neither. Before permitting a program to access data the system searches the acl associated with that data for an entry containing the name of the user on whose behalf the program is running. If such an entry is found, the system allows only those modes of access granted by the access portion of the acl entry. If no such entry is found, all access is denied.

This arrangement has appeared intuitively secure to many observers. Unfortunately, the computer-security field is rich in results that are counterintuitive and dismaying to system designers; in this case a description of the workings of a Trojan Horse attack shows that the acl mechanism is fundamentally and fatally flawed.

Consider first the situation depicted in the top illustration on page two. A user named Doe interacts through a program with a data file containing the critically sensitive character string "*CPE1704TKS.*" (A small prize of no intrinsic value will be awarded the first reader who identifies the significance of this string.) User Doe has diligently applied the acl mechanism to ensure that only programs executing on his own behalf can gain access to the sensitive file.

The Trojan Horse attack begins when a hostile user, whom we shall call Drake, gains legitimate access to the system and installs both a Trojan Horse program and a private file to be used in the attack as a "back pocket." Drake sets the acl of this private file to allow programs executing on his behalf full access and to allow programs executing on Doe's behalf to write into the file. Drake is careful not to notify Doe of

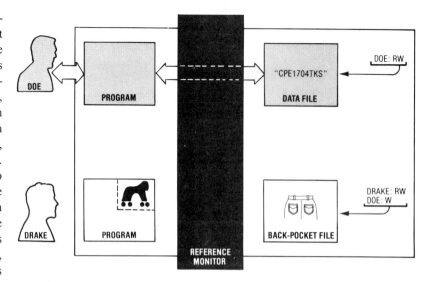

SECURE COMPUTER includes a subsystem called a reference monitor whose function is to check the legitimacy of every attempt to access data. The reference monitor makes access decisions on the basis of security levels. Every subject, such as an executing program, and every object, such as a file, is assigned a security level. In this illustration there are two security levels: sensitive (*gray*) and public (*white*). The reference monitor enforces two rules. A program cannot read a file at a higher security level (the Simple Security Property). Nor can it write to a file at a lower security level (the *-Property). Here the program executing on behalf of Doe is allowed access to the file containing the important character string because the program and the file have the same security level.

this fact. This situation is shown in the middle illustration on page two.

Drake now induces Doe to invoke the Trojan Horse. The inducement can take any one of a number of forms. He might, for example, implant the Trojan Horse code in a useful utility program or an entertaining game. When the Trojan Horse detects that the program in which it is embedded is being executed on Doe's behalf, it copies the critically sensitive character string from Doe's file to Drake's. This copying, which is depicted in the bottom illustration on page two, takes place completely within the constraints imposed by the acl mechanism; that is, it happens even if the mechanism is flawlessly implemented and correctly used. Drake then has only to access his file at some later time to learn the value of the string.

This example should make clear the principle, and the effectiveness, of Trojan Horse attacks: they represent the improper use of properly granted rights by a subverted agent whose actions cannot be

directly observed. A particularly dangerous form of Trojan Horse is the so-called virus program, which embeds a copy of itself in other programs, thereby propagating throughout a system and even over a computer network. A virus has to be invoked only once to infect the other programs commonly invoked by the target user; thus one invocation allows it to obtain frequent invocation and frequent opportunity to create havoc.

Fundamental Principles of Computer Security

Work began in the late 1960's to develop system principles that would prevent Trojan Horse attacks. This work, which was performed largely at the System Development Corporation, Case Western Reserve University, the Mitre Corporation and the Air Force Electronic Systems Division, resulted in the concept of a reference monitor, the definition of a mandatory security policy and the formulation of the Bell and La Padula Model of Security. We shall describe each of

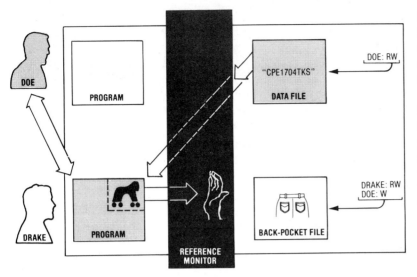

REFERENCE MONITOR blocks the Trojan Horse. When Doe unwittingly invokes the Trojan Horse program, the program acquires his security level. Since it is running at sensitive, it has the same security level as Doe's file. Because the security levels are the same, the Simple Security Property is preserved, and the reference monitor allows the program to read Doe's file. The program running at sensitive, however, has a higher security level than the back-pocket file. Because a write from the higher to the lower level would violate the ∗-Property, the reference monitor blocks this action. Note that the reference monitor blocks actions the acl's would permit; the reference monitor blocks the write even though the acl for the back-pocket file allows it.

these in turn and then return to our example to show how they frustrate Trojan Horse attacks.

The reference monitor, or security kernel as it is sometimes called, is a subsystem whose task is to check the legitimacy of a program's attempt to access data. A reference monitor was defined to have the following attributes: it must be tamperproof; it must be constructed so that it cannot be bypassed, and it must be small enough and simple enough that it can be thoroughly tested. More recently, it has become practical to make the third requirement stronger; the requirement is now that there be an *a priori* proof that the reference monitor works properly. Both versions of the requirement reflect the recognition that security is critical; the fact that a system has not exhibited vulnerability so far cannot be considered sufficient evidence that it is secure.

The next element, the mandatory security policy, is a statement of the restrictions on information transfer that a reference monitor is to enforce. The term mandatory

emphasizes that the policy is one that cannot be selectively invoked.

The mandatory security policy characterizes access restrictions in terms of the actions of subjects. A subject is an active agent, such as a running program, that operates on behalf of a user. Each subject is assigned an immutable security level. The security level takes the form of a value belonging to a partially ordered set of values. (A value in a partially ordered set may be greater than, less than, equal to or noncomparable to any other value in the set. In a fully ordered set the values must be comparable.) The security level of a subject reflects the degree of trust placed in the user on whose behalf the subject operates.

The general statement of the mandatory security policy is that a subject at a high level may not convey information to a subject at a lower or noncomparable level unless that "flow" accurately reflects the will of an authorized user. (Here and elsewhere "authorized" means authorized to cause such downward flows.) The movement of informa-

tion from a higher to a lower security level is called downgrading; movement to the lowest level, where open access is permitted, is called declassification.

The final element, the model devised by D. Elliot Bell and Leonard J. La Padula of the Mitre Corporation, translates the intent of the mandatory security policy into rules that a reference monitor must follow. To state such rules two additional concepts are necessary: objects and accesses. Objects are passive, information-holding entities such as files. Every object must be assigned a security level — one of the same set of values that may be assigned to subjects. Accesses are operations such as those described in the discussion of acl's: read, write and so on.

The Bell and La Padula model describes the mandatory security policy in terms of operations (such as decisions to grant or deny access) rather than in terms of abstractions (such as information flow). In the simplified form we shall use for exposition, the model states that a reference monitor is secure in the sense described in the discussion of mandatory policy only if it exhibits two properties. These properties are called the Simple Security Property and the ∗-Property (pronounced *star property*). The "∗" in ∗-Property does not stand for anything. No one could think of an appropriate name for the property during the writing of the first report on the model. The asterisk was a dummy character entered in the draft so that a text editor could rapidly find and replace all instances of its use once the property was named. No name was ever devised, and so the report was published with the "∗" intact.

The Simple Security Property states that a reference monitor shall grant a subject read access to an object only when the security level of the subject is greater than or equal to (dominates) the security level of the object. The ∗-Property states that write accesses shall be granted only when the security level of the object being written to is greater than or equal to the security level of the subject doing the writing. Together the two properties restrict the access of subjects to objects to reading down or writing up. Since the only way to obtain the information stored in a computer system is to access an intermediary object, the combined effect of the two properties is to ensure that information can only flow up.

We shall now return to our example, interpose a reference monitor, assign security levels to subjects and objects and show how the system organization that results is secure against Trojan Horse attacks.

Security levels are typically assigned to subjects at log-on, on the basis of criteria such as the terminal from which the machine is being accessed and the user associated with the subject. The identity of the user is generally confirmed by his knowledge of a secret password. The mechanisms described here are not proof against lost or stolen passwords, just as no lock is proof against a purloined key.

The system organization is illustrated on page three. There are two security levels, sensitive and public, ordered so that sensitive is greater than public. Subjects executing on Doe's behalf and the file containing the important character string are assigned the security level sensitive. Drake's file and subjects executing on Drake's behalf are (for good reason) restricted to the security level public.

The illustration on page four shows what happens when Doe unwittingly invokes the Trojan Horse program. As before, the program acquires the privileges associated with Doe and runs at a security level of sensitive. It is therefore able, under the Simple Security Property, to observe the character string "CPEI704TKS." When the program attempts to store the string in a public file, however, the *-Property is violated, and the

attempt is disallowed by the reference monitor. Thus one link of the Trojan Horse copy-and-observe-later chain is broken. The reader can easily verify that the rules frustrate the other two possibilities: Drake logging on and attempting to read the string directly and Drake assigning a security level of sensitive to the back-pocket file.

Note that the illustrated system, like most real systems, retains the acl mechanism. The enforcement of the mandatory security policy as interpreted by the Bell and La Padula model takes precedence over the acl mechanism. For example, the attempt to copy into the back-pocket file is denied even though the acl permits it. The acl mechanism, which is also called the discretionary access policy, is retained primarily as an administrative convenience; it allows a user to restrict access to an object to a subgroup of the subjects that would be granted access under the mandatory security policy alone.

Proofs of Security
As we have mentioned, a reference monitor must exhibit three attributes to be secure: it must be tamper-proof; it must be impossible to bypass, and it must be proved correct. Of these three requirements the last is by far the most difficult to meet.

Early attempts to prove a reference monitor correct relied on automated proof tools. A description of the reference monitor was written in a special-purpose notation called a specification language. The description, called a Formal Top-Level Specification, was scanned by a computer program that generated logical statements about the security state of the described system. The set of rules governing the generation of the logical statements was supposed to ensure that if all of the statements were true, the specified system would be secure in the sense defined by the Bell and La Padula model. The logical statements were then proved true, with the aid of another computer program.

Richard A. DeMillo of the Georgia Institute of Technology and Richard J. Lipton and Alan J. Perlis of Yale University have severely criticized the resulting proofs on the grounds that they are complex and incomprehensible, that there is no assurance that the universe of discourse covered by a proof covers the system actually implemented and that the proof process relies on tools whose reliability is no greater (and in many cases is substantially less) than the system being reasoned about.

We considered these criticisms of early work and resolved from the beginning of the Secure Ada Target effort that our proofs would be machine-checked but not machine-generated. In particular, we were determined that we would present a traditional, informal argument stating why and in what sense our system was secure and that this argument would be comprehensible to our technical peers. Such a proof could be submitted to the "social process," that is, it could be subjected to the same critical examination to which a traditional mathematical proof is exposed. In order to encourage examination we have used computer tools based on commonly accepted principles; as a result, referees can trace our steps with a different set of tools, thereby reducing the risk that our seemingly correct system has been fallaciously validated by a faulty tool.

We shall now sketch the informal thread of reasoning upon which our proofs are based. To do so we need to introduce three concepts: levels of abstraction, properties and mappings. We will describe them by returning to our aircraft analogy.

Consider a project to produce a commercial aircraft. The most general statement that can be made about such an aircraft is that it should be safe and useful. These are properties, and their degree of generality is their level of abstraction. At this high level of abstraction one can have recourse only to intuition and basic principles. It is inhumane to produce an unsafe aircraft. The property of usefulness is required to avoid absurdity since an aircraft that never moves can clearly be made safe.

Now we have, at this level of abstraction, two properties (safe and useful) and a description (airplane). In order to proceed we must become more specific, or drop down a level of abstraction, and write the description traditionally called the engineering specification: a statement of the range, the payload and similar characteristics of the airplane. As our description of the airplane becomes more detailed, so must our definitions of safe and useful. Thus we may insist that the aircraft be able to fly from New York to Los Angeles nonstop and that it have enough fuel in reserve to reach to San Francisco in case of bad weather. Next we verify that the entity described by the engineering specification exhibits the defined properties — by means of inspection, review and mathematical reasoning or, in other words, the social process.

Now we have two descriptions at two levels of abstraction, and we must map between them; that is, we must show that the more detailed one is a proper interpretation of the more general one. So we examine our specification and determine whether it actually describes an entity that is commonly agreed to be an airplane. Similarly we must map the properties. We examine our definitions and determine whether the ability to fly from New York to Los Angeles is a suitable refinement of useful and whether the requirement that the plane be able to reach to San Francisco is a suitable refinement of safe.

Following the same process, we work our way down through several levels of abstraction. Finally, we arrive at the lowest level of abstraction: a real airplane used to transport real people at velocities which are, in the words of the aviation writer Ernest K. Gann, "capable of terminating the human life span

instantly." At this point the interpretation of "airplane" involves thousands of assembled pieces and the interpretation of "safe and useful" involves thousands of procedures and specifications. Both are complex to the point of incomprehensibility, yet we fly with confidence because we have methodically mapped down to this point, one level of abstraction at a time, in comprehensible increments.

Our proofs of security adopt precisely this paradigm; indeed, it can be seen to be at work in our earlier discussion of security. At the highest level of abstraction we have a general description (multiuser computer) and a general property (secure). We then mapped down to the level of the mandatory security policy, where the multiuser computer became an interacting set of subjects and their associated security levels, and secure became a rule about information flow between levels. We presented an argument that the system as described was secure as so defined, and then we mapped down to the level of the Bell and La Padula model. At that level the concepts of objects and access modes were introduced into the description, and the rule restricting information flow was mapped down to the Simple Security Property and the *-Property. Two arguments were then produced: one, essentially a tautology at this level, was that the reference monitor exhibits the properties. The other, by no means a tautology, was that the two properties were a proper interpretation of the rule at the higher level.

We shall follow this paradigm in the rest of our discussion of the Secure Ada Target machine, dropping down in levels of abstraction and describing the associated mappings. In the project as currently constituted there are four more levels, called (from the top down) the Abstract Model, the Interpretation, the Formal Top-Level Specification and the Design Specification. (The number of levels and their names are

legacies of earlier projects; there is nothing sacrosanct about either.) Before we discuss the more detailed levels of our design, however, we must introduce one of the stickiest problems in computer security, that of trusted subjects.

Bell and La Padula recognized that the Simple Security Property and the *-Property were an incomplete interpretation of the mandatory security policy. The two properties ensure that information does not flow down in security level, but they do not permit authorized downward flow. Jonathan K. Millen of the Mitre Corporation has shown that a practical system must permit such flows; it is not, in general, possible to construct a computer system in which information flows exclusively upward in security level and still have a computer system that performs useful work. An exception to the properties in the form of trusted subjects was accordingly incorporated into the model.

A trusted subject is a subject that is exempted from the *-Property, or one that may selectively write information down. Each such subject must independently be proved secure. It must be shown that the programs executed by the trusted subject are tamperproof and can never be made to violate the mandatory security policy. The latter step requires a mapping between the programs invoked by the subject and the mandatory security policy. The mapping usually involves arguments that downward flows are identified, well understood and reliably reflect the intentions of an authorized user. Trusted subjects can therefore be thought of as special-purpose extensions of the reference monitor.

Like any exception to a set of rules, trusted subjects can be abused — becoming what Roger R. Schell, then of the DoD Computer Security Center, once called the "rug under which everything is swept." An important goal of the Secure Ada Target effort was to radically reduce the number of trusted subjects

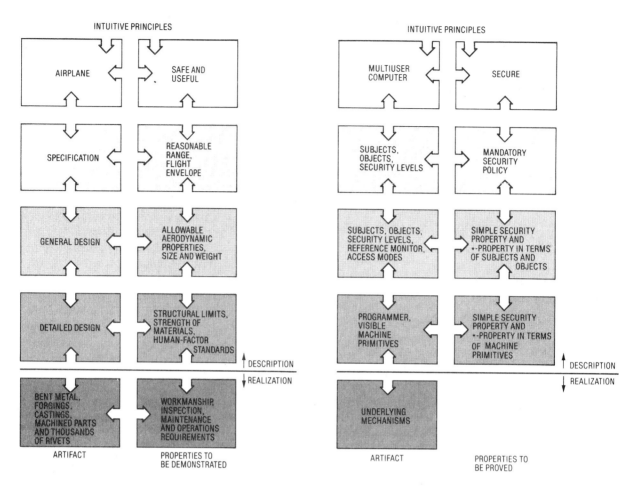

INTUITIVE PRINCIPLES

AIRPLANE

SAFE AND USEFUL

SPECIFICATION

REASONABLE RANGE, FLIGHT ENVELOPE

GENERAL DESIGN

ALLOWABLE AERODYNAMIC PROPERTIES, SIZE AND WEIGHT

DETAILED DESIGN

STRUCTURAL LIMITS, STRENGTH OF MATERIALS, HUMAN-FACTOR STANDARDS

↑ DESCRIPTION
↓ REALIZATION

BENT METAL, FORGINGS, CASTINGS, MACHINED PARTS AND THOUSANDS OF RIVETS

WORKMANSHIP INSPECTION, MAINTENANCE AND OPERATIONS REQUIREMENTS

ARTIFACT

PROPERTIES TO BE DEMONSTRATED

INTUITIVE PRINCIPLES

MULTIUSER COMPUTER

SECURE

SUBJECTS, OBJECTS, SECURITY LEVELS

MANDATORY SECURITY POLICY

SUBJECTS, OBJECTS, SECURITY LEVELS, REFERENCE MONITOR, ACCESS MODES

SIMPLE SECURITY PROPERTY AND *-PROPERTY IN TERMS OF SUBJECTS AND OBJECTS

PROGRAMMER, VISIBLE MACHINE PRIMITIVES

SIMPLE SECURITY PROPERTY AND *-PROPERTY IN TERMS OF MACHINE PRIMITIVES

↑ DESCRIPTION
↓ REALIZATION

UNDERLYING MECHANISMS

ARTIFACT

PROPERTIES TO BE PROVED

STEPS IN THE DESIGN of a secure computer can be compared to those in the design of a safe airplane. The final design is the end result of a series of progressively more detailed and progressively less ambiguous descriptions of the notion of an airplane (*left column*). Each of these engineering artifacts is demonstrated to have a different set of properties (*right column*). The properties are progressively more refined definitions of the notions safe and useful. The artifact and the properties at each level of abstraction are demonstrated to correspond to those at the next higher level. At some point a shift in the media occurs, and metal parts replace abstractions. The constructed airplane is complex to the point of incomprehensibility, but we fly with confidence because the final design is derived from first principles in comprehensible increments.

PROOF OF SECURITY of the Secure Ada Target is constructed on a framework similar to the one used in designing an airplane. The framework is a series of progressively more detailed representations of the notion of a multiuser computer (*left column*), each of which is paired with a similarly detailed definition of the notion of security (*right column*). The security proof involves two arguments for each level. First, the description of the system must be shown to exhibit the security property formulated for that level (*horizontal arrows*). Second, the security property must be shown to be a proper interpretation of the property at the next highest level (*vertical arrows in right column*). The final mapping, which demonstrates that the physical machine corresponds to the most detailed description, is done by inspection and testing.

required to do useful work, restrict the privileges they have (and thereby reduce what must be proved about them) and ensure that if they perform functions critical to security, they cannot be bypassed.

Fundamental Principles of the Secure Ada Target
We shall now begin discussing the levels of abstraction at which enough detail is introduced that our design decisions become visible. We begin with what we call the Abstract Model level, the level at which the

reference monitor is given a general internal structure.

At this level the overall system consists of three state spaces, or collections of stored information. (This characterization of the system is an extension of the work of John M. Rushby of SRI International.) The state spaces are called the value state, the protection state and the underlying abstractions. The value state consists of all objects that can possibly be made visible to subjects; it is therefore outside the reference monitor. The protection state and

the underlying abstractions are the information that the reference monitor keeps internal to itself and uses in making access decisions. At this level the protection state is represented as a matrix and the underlying abstractions are represented as tables.

The protection state is a matrix whose rows are subjects, whose columns are objects and whose entries specify the access modes to each object currently allowed each subject. The underlying abstractions, at this level, are tables that

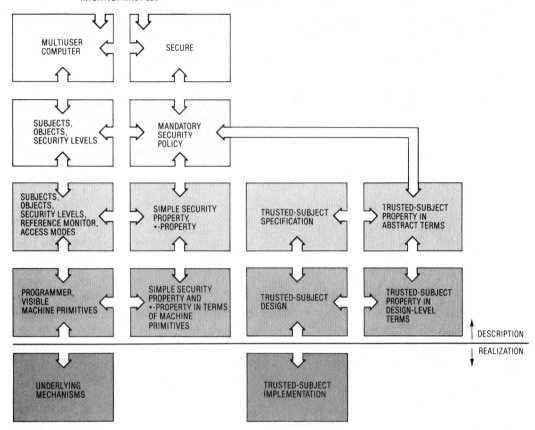

INTUITIVE PRINCIPLES

MULTIUSER COMPUTER

SECURE

SUBJECTS, OBJECTS, SECURITY LEVELS

MANDATORY SECURITY POLICY

SUBJECTS, OBJECTS, SECURITY LEVELS, REFERENCE MONITOR, ACCESS MODES

SIMPLE SECURITY PROPERTY, *-PROPERTY

TRUSTED-SUBJECT SPECIFICATION

TRUSTED-SUBJECT PROPERTY IN ABSTRACT TERMS

PROGRAMMER, VISIBLE MACHINE PRIMITIVES

SIMPLE SECURITY PROPERTY AND *-PROPERTY IN TERMS OF MACHINE PRIMITIVES

TRUSTED-SUBJECT DESIGN

TRUSTED-SUBJECT PROPERTY IN DESIGN-LEVEL TERMS

DESCRIPTION

REALIZATION

UNDERLYING MECHANISMS

TRUSTED-SUBJECT IMPLEMENTATION

TRUSTED SUBJECTS require an extension to the proof that a computer system is secure. The mandatory security policy allows information to flow down in security level *if* the flow accurately reflects the intent of an authorized user. The Simple Security Property and the ∗-Star Property prevent *any* downward flow of information. A practical system must allow authorized users to downgrade information, but it must be proved that the subjects acting on behalf of these users cannot violate the intent of the mandatory security policy.

give the attributes of subjects and objects, such as their security levels and acl entries. These attributes are used to decide what value should appear in a particular cell of the protection state.

Finally, we introduce the concept of an operation invoked by a subject and performed by the reference monitor. This operation consults the underlying abstractions and updates the protection state accordingly. Together the new definitions begin to give the system some structure: we have a reference monitor with an interface to subjects, information to be protected by it and information it uses to make protection decisions.

Next we map the Bell and La Padula model of security down to three properties. The two properties

we call the Mandatory Security Property and the Discretionary Security Property are discussed here. The third property, called Type Enforcement, is the means whereby we restrict trusted subjects, facilitate the implementation of complex security policies based on aggregation and inference and ensure that critical subsystems (such as those that mark output with the proper security level) cannot be bypassed. A description of the type-enforcement mechanism is beyond the scope of an introductory paper.

The Mandatory Security Property states that the protection state is secure in the Bell and La Padula sense at all times; that is, the protection state always conforms to the Simple Security Property and the ∗-Property. The Discretionary

Security Property guarantees that a subject executing on behalf of a given user cannot access an object unless the name of that user appears on the acl of the object at the time that the subject declares its intention to access the object.

Our proof method, at this and all levels of abstraction, involves two steps. First, a given level of abstraction must be verified: the description at the level in question must be shown to exhibit the security properties formulated for that level. Second, the properties must be mapped up: it must be shown that the statement of security at the level in question is a proper interpretation of the statement of security at the next higher level.

We verify using mathematical induction. First we show that the

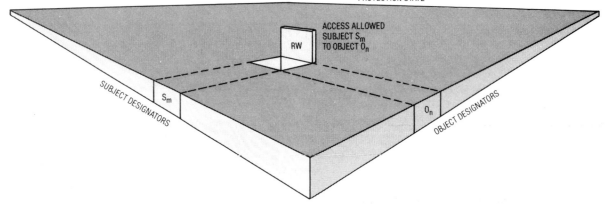

MODEL OF COMPUTER SYSTEM consists (at an intermediate level of abstraction) of three collections of information, or state spaces, which are called the value state, the protection state and the underlying abstractions. The value state, which consists of all of the objects in the system that can be made visible to subjects, is outside of the reference monitor. Shown here is the protection state, represented as a matrix. The rows of the matrix are indexed by subjects and the columns are indexed by objects. At the intersection of a row and a column is the access mode or modes currently allowed a subject to an object. The underlying abstractions are shown in the illustration on the facing page.

initial value of the protection state is secure. Then we demonstrate that each operation described at a given level is security-preserving: if it is invoked when the protection state is secure, then the protection state will be secure after the invocation. We have thereby demonstrated that the protection state is secure throughout all possible sequences of operations. This use of mathematical induction gives us the benefit of theoretically exhaustive testing without the unbounded time and effort such testing would require.

The second part of the proof, the mapping between our properties and the Bell and La Padula model, is trivial at this level of abstraction but becomes more complex as the amount of detail grows. In general, mappings are based on the representations of particular entities at the different levels of abstraction. At this level of abstraction, for example, the security levels are stored in a table and are designated as table elements; at the next lower level they may be collected in two files (a subject file and an object file) for efficient access. The statement of the Simple Security Property at this level includes a clause: level [subject] $\geq$ level [object]. At the lower level the same clause may be stated:

file subject_levels, entry subject [n] $\geq$ file object_levels, entry object [m]. The mapping must be accompanied by an argument that the file organization is the equivalent of a table.

The Engineering Approach of the Secure Ada Target

At the lower levels of abstraction we begin to confront engineering reality. Obviously no practical or economical machine is going to refer to a large matrix upon every access to data; we must arrive at a realization of the protection state that is both practical and secure. Our realization must also enable us to show something that was omitted from the discussion of mappings and verifications: that the operations by subjects on objects are indeed restricted by the protection state. Finally, we must determine how the reference-monitor operations are to be realized. All of these decisions involve complex engineering tradeoffs. Dominating every tradeoff is the requirement for provability —no feature, no matter how attractive for other reasons, can be included if it precludes proof in the sense we have defined.

In the design of secure computers, as in the design of any computer, most of these tradeoffs revolve around what are called binding-time

decisions. Such decisions involve selecting when in a chain of events a particular association between two values is to be made. In general the later one binds, the more flexible the system will be and the more costly; the earlier one binds, the more hardware one can save and the more rigid the system will be. These issues and the workings of the Secure Ada Target hardware can be made clear by considering the general problem of fetching and storing data.

At a suitably low level of abstraction a simple computer architecture can be thought of as consisting of a working register, in which temporary results are stored, and a linear array of cells, or memory, in which more permanent results are stored. An element in the array of cells is selected by giving its position in the array, which is called its address. The instructions in a program have two parts: an operation code, which defines the operation to be performed, and an address, which designates an element of stored data in the memory. One such instruction, *LDA*, is shown in context in the top illustration on page 11. (*LDA* stands for Load Accumulator; for historical reasons, the primary working register is often called the accumulator.) The instruction can be considered the atomic ele-

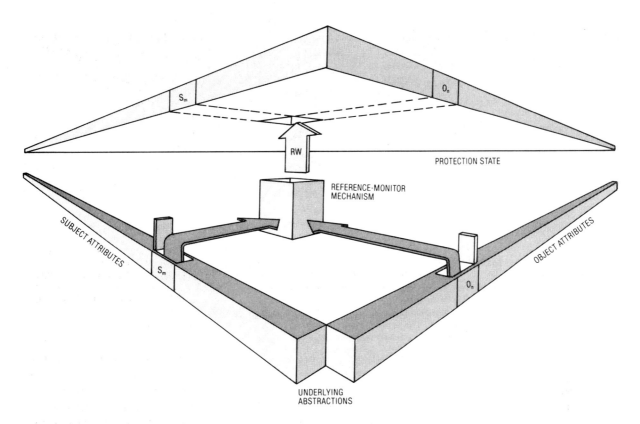

Labels in figure:
S_m ... O_n ... PROTECTION STATE ... RW ... REFERENCE-MONITOR MECHANISM ... SUBJECT ATTRIBUTES ... S_m ... O_n ... OBJECT ATTRIBUTES ... UNDERLYING ABSTRACTIONS

UNDERLYING ABSTRACTIONS are tables that give the attributes of subjects and objects. The attributes include ones that are relevant to security, such as security levels and acl's. The tables are consulted by that portion of the reference monitor whose duty it is to insert values in the protection state.

ment of a subject; it is the smallest subdivision of a subject considered during security studies. In this case the instruction *LDA* is requesting a memory read on behalf of its subject.

The illustrated design is an example of a very early binding. The assignment of the data of interest to location *1069* is made at the time the program is written, and the assignment is embedded in the program stored in the machine. If we wish to move our item of data, we must find all references to its address in the program and change them, a costly and error-prone process.

Once the limitations of this binding-time decision were understood, hardware designers invented the technique called two-dimensional, or segmented, addressing. An intermediary table translates the address given in an instruction into a memory address. The address in the instruction is divided into two parts. The first part selects an entry in the

intermediary table. The entry gives the memory address of the base, or lowest, element in the segment. The second part selects a cell inside the segment. The first part of the address in the instruction is usually called the segment number, and the second is called the offset. This arrangement is shown in the bottom illustration on page 11. Address *1069* has been divided into two parts. The *10* selects a value from the intermediary table (*4835*) and the *69* is treated as the offset from that base value. Therefore the memory address of the cell designated by instruction address *1069* is *4904*.

The delayed binding between an item of data and a memory address has several advantages. Instead of assigning the memory address at the time the program is written, we can assign it at any time up to the instant when the instruction is executed, simply by entering the appropriate value in the intermediary table. Moreover, the inter-

mediary table lowers the cost of moving a data segment within the memory. If we do not change the locations of the data items relative to the start of the segment, the addresses given in the instructions need not be changed. The address of the segment can be changed simply by changing the tenth entry in the intermediary table. The increased flexibility is achieved at some cost in hardware complexity and performance, since the act of fetching data now involves an intermediate fetch and an arithmetic operation, but the cost is reasonable.

Segmented addressing was developed in response to the software requirements of early multiuser systems. In these systems unanticipated events, such as the logging on of a new user, caused programs and data to move frequently. As we have seen, the designers of multiuser machines were also faced with the problem of controlling the sharing of data between programs. Their

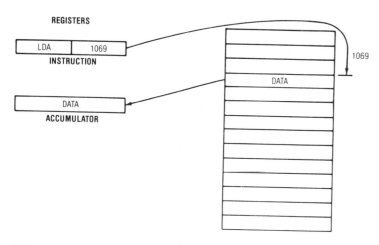

SIMPLE ADDRESSING MECHANISM is shown here. The address of the data an instruction requires is included in the instruction. The instruction has two parts: the code that specifies the operation to be performed (*LDA* or *Load Accumulator*) and the address of the data to be loaded into the accumulator (*1069*). The accumulator is the subject's primary working register; the data the instruction transfers there will be manipulated by the succeeding instructions. The problem with this mode of addressing is that every instruction referencing a given data element must be found and changed when the data is moved.

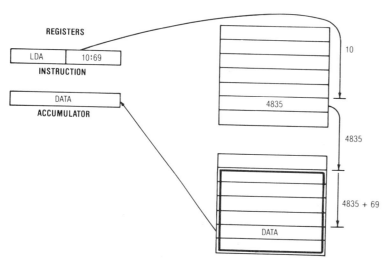

SEGMENTED ADDRESSING is an addressing technique that allows data to be moved more easily. The memory address of the data is stored in an intermediary table. The address given in the instruction is an indirect address. The first part of the indirect address is a segment number (*10*) that selects an entry in the intermediary table. The entry (*4835*) gives the address of the lowest element in a block of memory called a segment. The second element of the address is an offset that specifies the location of the data of interest relative to the lowest element of the segment. If the memory address of the segment is changed, the value stored in the tenth location in the intermediary table must be changed, but no changes need be made to the instructions.

answer was to add a field to the intermediary table and to list the allowed access modes in that field. Each operation code now designates the mode of access to be exercised by the operation as well as the operation itself. Prior to executing each instruction the hardware checks the access mode required by that instruction against the access modes allowed by the appropriate entry in the intermediary table. If the required access mode is not allowed, the instruction is not permitted to execute.

This mechanism has several attributes that are consistent with the requirements of a reference mon- itor. It is a hardware mechanism and is therefore tamperproof. It cannot be bypassed, since an instruction cannot obtain an address without going through the intermediary table and encountering the access checker. The problem with the mechanism lies in the area of proof.

If we return to our considera- tion of mappings and levels of abstraction, we can see that the intermediary table corresponds to one row of the protection state. The table is associated with a subject (the executing program of which the instruction using the table is a part) and contains object designations (segment addresses) and allowed accesses. This mapping is shown in the bottom illustration on page 12.

We now have a mechanism that guarantees that a value of the pro- tection state, once established, is enforced. What we do not have is a mechanism that guarantees that the value of the protection state is secure. We know that an attacker cannot execute a read access unless an *r* appears in the appropriate place in the table. We do not know, with any assurance, where that *r* came from; in particular, we do not know whether an attacker placed it there. Similarly the subject is not explic- itly identified anywhere in this mechanism. Since instructions exe- cute anonymously from the point of view of the hardware, another line of attack is possible: a flaw in the implementation of the operating- system software may allow a subject with a low security level to capture an intermediary table that was filled in for a subject with a higher security level. This type of attack is called a reused-parameter attack; the access values are the reused parameters. Such an attack requires that a criti- cal value (such as a security level) be changed between the time access is granted and the time access is exer- cised. The attack would be blocked if the access values were changed whenever the attributes of subjects or objects changed.

Early secure systems are vulnerable to this line of attack

because the reference monitor is constructed in the form of software. Segmented addressing is implemented in hardware. In our terms this means that the underlying abstractions are in software and the protection state straddles the interface between the software and the hardware; its values are set by software and used by hardware. As a result, updating the protection state involves a complicated set of interactions between software-maintained tables and hardware. In practice, the complexity of the interactions virtually precludes a humanly intelligible proof that the reference monitor enforces security.

Implementing a reference monitor in software has another disadvantage as well. A software reference monitor must share hardware

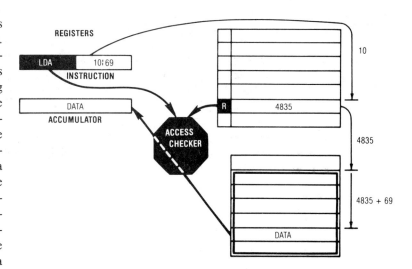

ADDITIONAL ENTRY in the intermediary table that lists the memory addresses of data segments allows the table to be employed to check the access rights of the executing instruction. The operation code in the instruction specifies (indirectly) the mode of access the operation requires. The additional field in the intermediary table specifies the mode of access allowed the subject in whose context the instruction is executing. In this case the intermediary table allows the required mode of access (read) and the instruction is therefore permitted to execute.

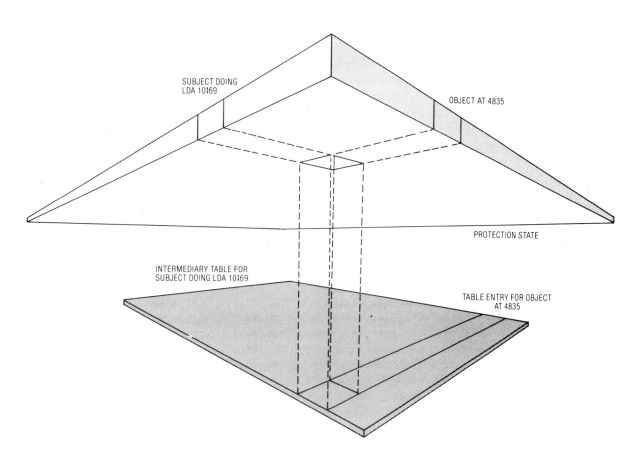

MAPPING between the intermediary table in a machine with segmented addressing and the protection-state matrix is shown here. The table corresponds to a row of the protection-state matrix. It is associated with a subject and contains designations of objects (segment addresses) and the allowed modes of access. The intermediary table ensures that access will be granted according to the values in the protection state. It is difficult to demonstrate, however, that the values in the table reflect the attributes of the subjects and objects they relate, that is, that the protection state reflects the underlying abstractions in the manner shown in the illustration on page 10.

REGISTERS
USER NAME

SECURITY LEVEL
SUBJECT-DEFINITION REGISTERS

WORKING REGISTER

UID	ADDRESS	ACCESS

NAME SPACE TABLE

SECURITY LEVEL
ADDRESS
ACL

ENTRY
ASSOCIATED
WITH A
GIVEN UID

GLOBAL OBJECT TABLE

EXTENSION OF THE STRUCTURE of segmented addressing ensures that subjects and objects are explicitly identified and that the protection state properly reflects their attributes. A subject is identified by two registers that give it a compound name composed of the user on whose behalf it is executing and the security level at which it is executing. Objects are identified by UID's (Universal Identifiers). The Universal Identifiers are values contained in tagged objects, which name units of storage called containers. Container attributes are listed in the Global Object Table, which is indexed by a UID. Among the attributes are the security level, acl and current memory location of the container. Objects accessible to a subject are identified by UID's stored in an intermediary table belonging to the subject, which is called a Name Space Table. This structure makes it possible to construct a security mechanism that checks the attributes of both a subject and an object before altering an entry in the intermediary table.

resources with untrusted and presumably hostile programs. This circumstance reduces the level of assurance that the reference monitor is tamperproof and increases the likelihood that hostile programs will use the reference monitor itself to signal information in ways that violate the mandatory security policy. Such signalling paths, called covert channels, permit what Butler W. Lampson of Xerox PARC has called "pounding on the walls." A Trojan Horse program can send a message to a confederate program by performing operations that tie up the reference monitor for greater or lesser periods of time. By agreement a greater period of time indicates a *1* and a lesser period a *0*. The confederate decodes the message by observing at regular intervals whether the reference monitor is using the hardware that all of the programs share. Thus information can be downgraded even if the reference monitor successfully blocks attempts to copy it directly.

Our approach to these problems has been to move the reference monitor, the protection state and the underlying abstractions completely within the hardware. In so doing we have been able to radically simplify the mappings between the higher and lower levels of abstraction in our proof structure. We have also been able to provide more concrete and convincing arguments that the reference monitor cannot be bypassed and that it is tamperproof. In the next section we shall describe the resulting hardware architecture.

Architecture of the
Secure Ada Target

The Secure Ada Target hardware enforces access rights by means of segmented addressing and access-mode fields. In this it resembles any number of contemporary machines. Where it differs is in the steps by which the intermediary table is modified. To permit modifications of the table to be completely controlled by the hardware, the Secure Ada Target architecture introduces a new form of stored information.

Conventional architectures leave the interpretation of a particular item of stored information to the software. The hardware does not recognize that one string of *1*'s and *0*'s encodes a numerical value and another encodes the name of a data file. Our hardware (in the simplified form discussed here) recognizes two forms of stored data, which we call containers and tagged objects.

A container is a unit of storage in the traditional sense: an array of data items to be interpreted by the software as it sees fit. Our containers therefore correspond to the segments in the discussion of segmented addressing.

A tagged object is the hardware-recognized name of a container. The distinguishing characteristic is an extra bit, or tag, associated with the object in its stored form — hence the name tagged object. The use of tagged objects by software is severely restricted by the hardware: once it is created, a tagged object can be neither examined nor modified. It can, however, be freely stored in a container. Subjects communicate with the reference monitor primarily through tagged objects.

In the current design a tagged object is 128 bits long. The bits give a protected value called the UID (Universal Identifier) of the container the tagged object names. Each container has a different UID value and is therefore uniquely named. The hardware creates a tagged object naming a container when memory is allocated for the container.

Consider, for a moment, the mapping of this hardware-level representation of the system to the representation at the next higher level of abstraction. We have now defined objects (as containers) and given a trustworthy means for designating them (opaque tagged objects that cannot be forged). Next, we need some way of representing the underlying abstractions. These are the attributes of containers, such as their size, their current location in memory, their security levels and their acl's.

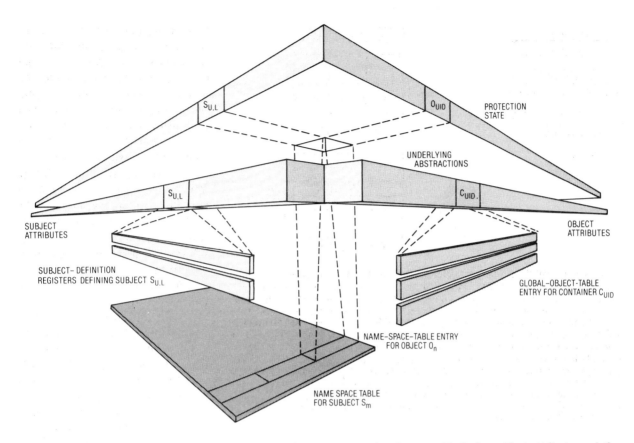

MAPPING between the state spaces of a reference monitor and the elements of the Secure Ada Target architecture (shown the previous illustration) is sketched here. The Name Space Table maps to the protection state and the remaining elements map to the underlying abstractions: the subject-definition registers to the abstract table listing subject attributes and the Global Object Table to the abstract table listing object attributes. The clarity of the proof of the Secure Ada Target is due largely to the extreme simplicity of the mappings between design levels.

The reference monitor of the Secure Ada Target maintains underlying abstractions in a private file indexed by the UID's. The file is called the Global Object Table, or GOT, because it tells you what you've got. The GOT can be visualized as a large file containing attributes for all of the containers in the system. The GOT entry for a container (in the simplified form of the architecture we are discussing) specifies the security level, acl and current location of the container.

We have now established the architectural characteristics of the value state: a set of containers, each uniquely named and associated with physical attributes (used in normal processing), a security level and an acl (used by the reference monitor).

The next problem we face is that of the hardware-level representation of a subject. This representation must support efficient processing, must lend itself to straightforward mappings to the higher levels of abstraction in our proof structure and must give assurance that the restrictions defined by the protection state are uniformly imposed on operations on the value state.

In general terms, we take the well-understood structure of segmented addressing and extend it. For every executed instruction the reference monitor has available the name of the user on whose behalf the instruction is executing (so that discretionary-access-policy decisions can be made), the security level at which the subject is running (so that mandatory-access-policy decisions can be made) and the relevant portions of the security state (so that decisions, once made, can be enforced). Enforcement of the secu-

rity policies therefore extends down to the level of the individual machine instruction.

The first element in the representation of a subject is two hardware registers that name a subject and define its attributes. The registers carry a user's name and security level. The intermediary table associated with the subject is extended to include, for each entry, the UID of the container the entry refers to. The extended table is called the Name Space Table, or NST, because it defines the set of objects that can be named (referenced) by the subject. The representation of a subject is completed by the inclusion of the working registers used by the atomic elements of the subject — the instructions. These registers can be thought of as containing the subject's private information.

The mapping between this

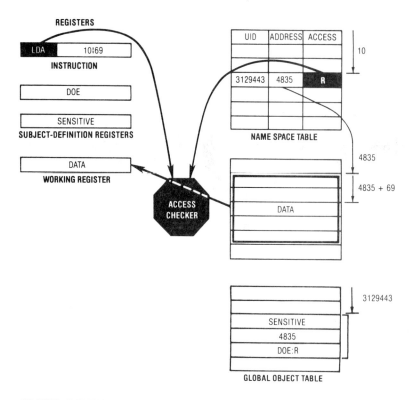

ORDINARY INSTRUCTIONS undergo the access check shown above. The diagram shows a container whose UID is *3129443* and whose current memory location is *4835* being accessed by a subject executing on behalf of user Doe at a security level of sensitive. In this access check the Name Space Table plays the role of the intermediary table shown in the top illustration on page 12; in both cases the address given in the instruction serves as an index to the table. The extensions to the segmented-addressing mechanism play no role in the execution of ordinary instructions.

hardware-level representation and the matrix representation of the protection state is sketched in the illustration on page 14. In the Secure Ada Target, a subject is designated by a compound name of the form *user, level*. The parts of its name are the values of the attributes given in the subject-definition registers. Thus the subject-definition registers map both to an index on the subject axis of the protection-state matrix and to the abstract table that gives subject attributes. The NST maps to a row of the protection-state matrix, although this mapping is not shown in the illustration.

Objects are more complicated. They cannot be given a compound name composed of their attributes because they have too many attributes. Instead, they are named by a UID. The UID maps to an index on the object axis of the protection-state matrix. The GOT entry for the object maps to the abstract table that gives object attributes. (Note that the GOT entry includes information, such as the current address of the object, that does not map up; this is typical of the relation between two levels of abstraction.) Finally, an NST entry for the object maps to an intersection of a row and a column in the protection-state matrix.

The NST puts operations on the value state under the control of values of the protection state exactly as does the cruder and less secure intermediary table employed in segmented addressing. An address in an instruction is interpreted as an NST index and an offset. The NST index selects an entry in the NST belonging to the subject of which the instruction is a part, and the hardware constructs the address of the item of data from the NST entry (which gives the base address of the

container) and the offset in the instruction. At the same time the access-mode value in the NST entry is checked against the access mode required by the instruction. If the required access mode is permitted, the hardware then permits the memory access to proceed; on the other hand, if the required access mode is not permitted, the instruction is suspended and an alarm is raised. This process is diagrammed in the illustration on this page.

The use of a well-established technique for checking the access rights of ordinary instructions gives us an efficient and inexpensive system, since we can draw on the hardware and software technology that has been developed in the last 20 years. As the diagram suggests, however, the access check does not make use of any of the extensions we have incorporated in the hardware-level representation of the protection state to pin down the identities of subjects and objects.

These extensions are employed by a second class of operations, which are also performed by the reference monitor. The most basic of these operations, and the one we will use to illustrate the class, is the *Load NST*, or *LNST*, instruction. Its execution is normally preceded by the execution of the *Create GOT Entry*, or *CGEN*, instruction.

The subject executes the *CGEN* operation to create an object. Assume user Doe, running at a security level of sensitive, wants to create a memory object. The *CGEN* operation creates a new object and allocates memory space to hold its contents. The new GOT entry is assigned a security level conforming to the security level of Doe's subject. The acl of the new object is set to allow access to Doe and no access to other users. After the execution of *CGEN* has been completed, the reference monitor returns a tagged object to a memory location the subject specified in invoking the *CGEN* operation.

After the *CGEN* operation has been completed, there is a new GOT entry and a new tagged object, but the executing subject cannot access the new object. Before it can do so, it must execute the *LNST* operation, which adds the new object to its name space. The reference monitor, while executing *LNST*, examines the state space we have called the underlying abstractions to ensure that the access rights it transfers to the Name Space Table enforce the mandatory and the discretionary security policies.

The operation of the *LNST* instruction is shown in the illustration on this page. User Doe, still running at the security level of sensitive, invokes the *LNST* command. The reference monitor requires that such an invocation include the tagged object that designates the container to be added to the name space and the NST index (or segment number) by which the subject will later refer to the container.

Once the tagged object is inside the reference monitor, the UID value inside the tagged object (*3129443* in this example) becomes visible and is used to locate an entry in the GOT. The attributes of the container listed in the GOT include a security level (sensitive), an address (*4385*) and an acl (containing a single entry that restricts user Doe's access to the mode read).

The first operation performed by the reference monitor is the computation of the maximum access rights that the subject (*Doe, Sensitive*) could ever exercise on object *3129443*. This requires two steps: a check against the mandatory policy and a check against the discretionary policy. The mandatory check involves a comparison of the security level of the subject (contained in the subject-definition registers) with the security level of the object (contained in the GOT). In this case both are equal to sensitive, and so an intermediate result consisting of the maximum possible access (read/ write) is produced. The discretionary check involves comparing the name of the user for which the subject is executing (contained in the

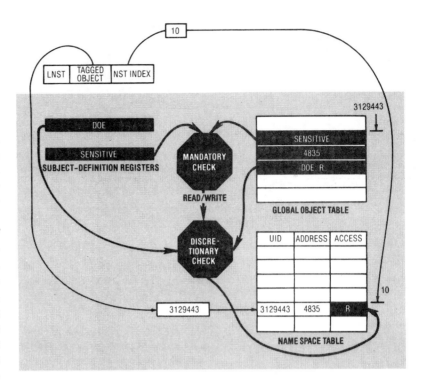

EXTENSIONS TO THE STRUCTURE come into play only when a subject adds a container to its Name Space Table. A subject adds a container by means of the *LNST* instruction. The instruction gives the location of a tagged object that contains a Universal Identifier. The value of the Universal Identifier becomes visible within the reference monitor and serves as an index to the Global Object Table. The reference monitor retrieves the object attributes stored in the Global Object Table, including the security level of the container, its address and its acl. The reference monitor compares the container's security level to the subject's security level to determine whether the requested access conforms to the mandatory security policy. It compares the user's name to the container's acl to determine whether the requested access conforms to the discretionary security policy. The access mode both checks allow is entered in the Name Space Table, together with the address of the container. Because the values in the Name Space Table are derived from attributes stored in hardware under the control of the reference monitor, they are more reliable than the values in the intermediary table used to check access in a system with segmented addressing.

subject-definition registers) with the acl of the object (in the GOT). In this example the user's name matches an acl entry, and this entry further restricts access to read only. The resulting access mode (read) is moved into the appropriate NST field. The rest of the operation of the instruction is a simple data movement from the GOT and the tagged object, as shown in the diagram.

Given the mapping shown on page 14, the proof that the *LNST* command preserves security is straightforward. The Simple Security Property and the *-Property were originally defined as functions that expressed the proper relation between protection-state values and

the values in the underlying matrices. Analogous functions govern the relation between NST access-mode entries and the values in the subject-definition registers and the GOT. Since the mapped statements of the Simple Security Property and the *-Property are incorporated in the algorithm for the *LNST* instruction, the proof that the instruction preserves security becomes a tautology.

There are, of course, many other engineering issues in the design of the Secure Ada Target, such as the location of the reference-monitor hardware, the details of the operations it performs and its interaction with software. For a discussion of these issues the interested reader is referred to "Secure Ada Target: Issues, System Design, and Verification," a copy of which can be obtained by writing to MN55-7282.

Proof of Security of the Secure Ada Target

We should like to conclude by giving the informal proof of the system's security that was a goal of our project:

1. All visible data are collected into containers, and every container has a security level.

2. In order to access an element of data, an instruction (subject) must obtain the address of the container (object) containing that data.

3. In the course of obtaining that address, the subject unavoidably encounters reference-monitor hardware that checks the requested mode of access against the allowed modes of access.

4. In order for an address to be obtainable, the subject must have previously added the object to its name space.

5. In the course of adding an object to its name space, the subject unavoidably encounters reference-monitor hardware that computes a maximum allowed access mode based on the mandatory and the discretionary security policies.

6. Therefore each and every instruction executed on the Secure Ada Target machine is constrained by the mandatory and the discretionary security policies.

Acknowledgements

This effort has been supported by U.S. Government Contracts MDA904-82-C-0444 and MDA904-84-C-6011. We have drawn heavily on the work of our predecessors, notably the Multics and SCOMP projects within Honeywell and the work done on the Provably Secure Operating System by SRI International. Our work has benefited from the scrutiny of many able and dedicated reviewers; we are particularly indebted in this regard to Morrie Gasser of the Mitre Corporation. We have also benefited from our conversations with the staff of the Department of Defense Computer Security Center.

Bibliography

J. P. Anderson, "Computer Security Technology Planning Study," ESD-TR-73-51, FSD/AFSC, Hanson AFB, Massachusetts, October 1972.

D.E. Bell and L.J. La Padula, "Secure Computer Systems: Unified Exposition and Multics Interpretations," Technical Report MTR-2997, Mitre Corporation, Bedford, Massachusetts, July 1975.

H.K. Berg, W.E. Boebert, W.R. Franta and T.G. Moher, *Formal Methods of Program Verification and Specification*, Prentice-Hall Inc., 1982.

W.E. Boebert, R.Y. Kain, W.D. Young and S.A. Hansohn, "Secure Ada Target: Issues, Systems Design, and Verification," *Proceedings of the 1985 Symposium on Security and Privacy*, IEEE Computer Society, April, 1985.

DESIGNING THE GEMSOS SECURITY KERNEL
FOR SECURITY AND PERFORMANCE

Dr. Roger R. Schell
Dr. Tien F. Tao
Mark Heckman

Gemini Computers, Incorporated
P. O. Box 222417
Carmel, California 93922

INTRODUCTION

Gemini Computers, Inc., offers as a commercial product a family of secure, high-performance computer systems based on the Intel iAPX 286 microprocessor. These systems are designed to meet the Class B3 requirements of the DoD Trusted Computer Computer System Evaluation Criteria,[1] and a developmental evaluation by the DoD Computer Security Center is ongoing. An earlier paper[2] of about a year ago discussed the major concepts underlying the design and the functionality of the Gemini Multiprocessing Secure Operating System (GEMSOS). The security kernel as discussed in that paper is structured into eleven distinct layers, and as of that time only the lower five layers were implemented. All of the layers described have now been implemented and delivered as a Version 0 kernel, and a production Version 1 is currently being implemented. The purpose of this paper is to report on the major design choices for security functionality and to report the results of initial system performance measurements on the Version 0 GEMSOS commercial product.

BACKGROUND

The GEMSOS security kernel design is based on the trusted computer system technology that has emerged over the past decade. This technology provides a high degree of assurance that a system developed in accordance with the principles underlying the DoD Trusted Computer System Evaluation Criteria can be objectively evaluated to determine its ability to protect sensitive information from unauthorized viewing or modification. The primary experience with this technology is with general purpose operating systems for single processor computers.

The Gemini design extends this security technology into the realm of a multiprocessor computer specifically intended for incorporation as a component of embedded systems. The question is often raised whether secure computers can be expected to deliver high performance. In the design of the GEMSOS security kernel, a good deal of attention has been given to supporting throughput and response time without adverse impact on security assurance. Of particular importance are the operating system techniques provided to ensure that the multiple processors can indeed be used effectively to increase overall system performance in concurrent computing applications.

The Reference Monitor Foundation

The reference monitor is the primary abstraction for dealing with a system that is designed to be "evaluable" with respect to

security, i.e., a system for which we want to have a high degree of assurance of its correct security behavior. In this abstraction a system is considered as a set of active entities called "subjects" and a set of passive entities called "objects". The reference monitor is the abstraction for the control over the relationships between subjects and objects and for the manager of the physical resources of a system. To be effective in providing security, the implementation of a reference monitor must be: (1) tamper-proof, (2) always invoked, and (3) simple enough for analysis. The hardware and software that implement a reference monitor that meets these principles is defined as a security kernel.[3]

Security Policy Model

For a specific set of applications, e.g., for DoD systems, there will be a particularization of the reference monitor abstraction that incorporates the "security policy" (the desired security behavior) of the system. This particularization is formally defined in a "security policy model." The choice of a model will be influenced by a desire to have an intuitive tie to the engineering properties of the target system. Thus, in selecting a model for a trusted computer, it is desirable that the model's objects can easily represent the security-relevant information repositories of the contemplated applications. By far, the most widely used formal security policy model is the Bell-LaPadula model.[4] This model has a level of abstraction that is high enough to permit application to a wide variety of specific designs and is also deliberately designed to be extended to support system-specific policy refinements. This model has been used as the basis of the GEMSOS security kernel design.

An Extensible TCB

A pivotal concept in developing a system that is secure in a practical sense is the identification of a Trusted Computing Base (TCB). A security policy model is expected to model a broad range of actual systems. However, if the system is of a practical size it is expected that it will be too complex to systematically evaluate for security. However, the reference monitor concept provides a basis for identifying a small and simple subset of the system that is responsible for and able to assure the security of the total system. This subset is called the TCB. The TCB includes both (1) the security kernel that implements the reference monitor and manages the physical resources, and (2) the "trusted subjects" that support refinements to the fundamental policy supported by the security kernel.

As noted in a recent paper by Marvin Schaefer of the DoD Computer Security Center,[5] if the TCB has a strict hierarchical layering it is possible to extend a mandatory policy security kernel to support a richer set of security properties, such as those desired for a discretionary security policy of a particular application. The GEMSOS security kernel has the kind of strict layering that was postulated. The Intel iAPX 286 processor that is used in the Gemini computer provides four strictly hierarchical, hardware enforced protection rings that enforce the strict layering. In particular, the most privileged ring (Ring 0) is devoted to the mandatory policy security kernel. Typically, Ring 1 would be similarly devoted to the particular discretionary policy of an application.

The key to the evaluation of the security of a TCB is the Descriptive Top Level Specification (DTLS) and for the Class A1 a corresponding Formal Top Level Specification (FTLS) for the interface to the TCB. For the GEMSOS security kernel the approach is to have specifications that are themselves layered so that there is a DTLS of the mandatory security kernel as well as a DTLS for the refinements, such as that for discretionary security policy; the latter specification includes references to the underlying mandatory DTLS. Thus the GEMSOS security kernel provides an ideal foundation for a truly extensible TCB for support to a wide range of extended policies, such as those frequently encountered in military embedded systems.

MAJOR SECURITY CONCEPTS

A reference monitor implementation such as the GEMSOS security kernel must mediate all access by active entities (called "subjects") to passive entities (called "objects"). The GEMSOS kernel permits or prevents each access by a subject to an object based on relationships between the subject's authorization and the objects sensitivity. This set of relationships is called a security policy. The GEMSOS mandatory policy security kernel can enforce any of the various policies that are represented by the lattice of security labels used in the Bell and LaPadula mathematical security model.[4] This model provides a set of rules for controlling the dissemination and modification of information in a secure system. Kernel calls map into the rules of the model, and internal data structures represent the model's mathematical sets. The GEMSOS security kernel is secure because it is a valid interpretation of this security model. In the sections that follow, we define and introduce the major security system concepts and then use those concepts to describe the specific GEMSOS security kernel features.

Subjects and Objects

Rules in the Bell and LaPadula model are concerned with controlling the access of subjects to objects. Subjects are "active" entities that observe or modify objects. Objects are "passive" entities that are observed or modified. A subject is defined as a process executing in a specific domain and may be thought of as a (process, domain) pair. Objects are distinct, logical entities that contain information and possess security attributes called access classes.

Domains

A domain is a set of objects to which a subject has a given type of access, e.g., the "observe domain." Domains in the GEMSOS security kernel are determined by the hardware-enforced ring mechanism. The rings define a set of hierarchically ordered domains (see the section on ring integrity).

Security Policy

The permission of "authorized" access and the prevention of "unauthorized" access by subjects to objects constitutes the security enforced by a system. A security policy is the set of relations between subjects' authorizations and objects' sensitivities that determines permissible access. A system that enforces a particular security policy may be said to be secure only with respect to that policy.[3]

Nondiscretionary Security. A security policy based on externally defined constraints enforced by a secure system is called a "mandatory" or nondiscretionary security policy. A nondiscretionary policy controls all accesses by subjects to objects and may never be modified or bypassed within the system. The military classification and compartment policy is an example of a nondiscretionary policy.

Discretionary Security. Within the limits of mandatory controls, authorized subjects in the system may place additional constraints on other subjects' access to objects. This internally modifiable set of constraints is called a discretionary security policy. The military "need-to-know" policy is an example of a discretionary policy. The complete security of a system may include both mandatory and discretionary controls, but while discretionary controls provide finer access "granularity," in no case may they override mandatory controls. The GEMSOS mandatory policy security kernel (viz., Ring 0) enforces a nondiscretionary security policy and provides a base to which a discretionary policy may be added (e.g., in the Ring 1 "supervisor" domain, as noted above).

Access Classes

Every entity in the GEMSOS security kernel possesses an access class. The access class of an object reflects the object's sensitivity, viz., its "classification." The access class of a subject reflects the subject's authorizations to observe and modify objects, viz., its "clearance." The complete nondiscretionary (mandatory) security attributes of any subject or object in the GEMSOS security kernel are defined by its access class.

Security Labels. Security labels are attached to every entity (subject and object) in the system. A security label is a representation of an entity's access class.

Access Components. An access component is a way of describing separately the secrecy and integrity security attributes that constitute an access class. Discussion of access components simplifies the description of relations between subjects and objects based on access classes (i.e., the non-discretionary security policy). In the GEMSOS security kernel, an access component is defined similarly to a Bell and LaPadula "security level." Both the secrecy and integrity access components consists of two parts: a hierarchical classification level and a set of compartments (induced by disjoint "categories").

Access Component Dominance. One access component (A1) is said to dominate another access component (A2) if the hierarchical level of A1 is greater than or equal to that of A2, and A1's compartments are a superset of A2's compartments. The symbol ")=" is used in following sections to indicate dominance (e.g., "A1 dominates A2" is depicted as "A1)= A2")

Dissemination and Modification of Information

The nondiscretionary security policy enforced by the GEMSOS security kernel addresses both the secure dissemination and secure modification of information. The access class of every subject and object in the GEMSOS security kernel contains an access component to control dissemination and another access component to control modification. These two access components are referred to as "secrecy" and "integrity," respectively.

Secrecy Protection

Secrecy protection in the GEMSOS security kernel is similar to the usual interpretations of "security" in the Bell and LaPadula model.[4] The notion of secrecy is concerned with the secure distribution of information. Although the exact statement of security in the model is considerably more complex, the rules for enforcing secrecy protection in the GEMSOS security kernel can be simply described by two properties:

1) If a subject has "observe" access to an object, the secrecy access component of the subject must dominate the secrecy access component of the object.

2) If a subject has "modify" access to an object, the secrecy access component of the object must dominate the secrecy access component of the subject.

Property 1 is called the "no-read-up" or "simple security" property. Its effect is to keep low-secrecy subjects from observing information of higher secrecy. Property 2 is called the "no-write-down" property or "*-property" (read "star-property"). Its purpose is to keep high-secrecy subjects from improperly transmitting sensitive information to low-secrecy subjects (e.g., with a Trojan Horse). Thus, a low-secrecy subject can never directly or indirectly observe high-secrecy information.

Integrity

The concept of integrity is concerned with the secure modification of information. The GEMSOS security kernel provides two complementary mechanisms for enforcing integrity:

one in software and one in hardware. The software mechanism enforces an integrity policy equivalent to the strict integrity policy described by Biba.[6] The hardware mechanism supports Multics-like hierarchical protection rings[7]. The integrity enforced by the ring mechanism is equivalent to the notion of "program integrity"[8] and is a subset of the strict integrity policy.

The two mechanisms for enforcing integrity are provided for efficiency reasons. Were no ring mechanism available, the complete strict integrity policy could still be enforced by separate processes (rather than separate rings) using the software mechanism, but the hardware ring switching mechanism is considerably faster than process switching.

Strict Integrity. Like secrecy protection, the rules for enforcing strict integrity protection in the GEMSOS security kernel can be described by two properties:

1) If a subject has "modify" access to an object then the integrity access component of the subject dominates the integrity access component of the object.

2) If a subject has "observe" access to an object then the integrity access component of the object dominates the integrity access component of the subject.

Property 1 is called the "simple integrity" property. Its purpose is to prevent subjects of low integrity from modifying objects of higher integrity. Property 2 is called the "integrity *-property." It prevents high-integrity subjects from observing and relying on information that a low-integrity subject might have modified. If high-integrity subjects could observe low integrity information then their behavior might be improperly influenced ("spoofed") by a low-integrity subject. The two integrity properties prevent low-integrity subjects from directly and indirectly modifying high-integrity information.

Ring Integrity. Under the GEMSOS ring integrity mechanism, each subject and object possesses a hierarchical ring level ranging from 1 (most privileged) to 3 (least privileged). Subjects are only permitted access (observe, modify, or both) to objects with equal or greater ring numbers (equal or less privileged rings). No access to objects with a lower ring number is permitted.

For example, only the GEMSOS security kernel supervisor is allowed to have ring level 1. No application program, therefore, can access any part of the supervisor, but the supervisor can access any object in rings 1 thru 3. Ring 0 of a Gemini system is reserved for the isolation and protection of the security kernel.

Trusted Subjects

In general, the properties of secrecy and integrity are strictly enforced by the GEMSOS security kernel. Rigid adherence to these properties, however, can complicate the use of a system by forcing extremely fine "granularity" of security on objects. For example, imagine a system where storage objects are large files, and which has an incoming stream of messages at different access classes. One logical method of distributing messages would be to have all incoming messages put in the same file, and to have a single process distribute the messages to the proper recipients.

The secrecy and integrity properties described above, however, force a secure system to create a different file for each access class in which to store messages. In addition, a different process of the appropriate class must be used to distribute messages out of each file. Distributing messages, a relatively simple operation on most systems, could become a needlessly complicated, resource-consuming procedure in a secure system.

Imagine instead that the secrecy and integrity *-properties were relaxed just for this application. All incoming messages could be temporarily put in the same file and a single process could distribute messages of any access class. What would be the security characteristics of the file and process? The file would have the most sensitive access class possible, since it could conceivably contain messages of that class. Messages in the file, however, could be of lower classes. The distributing process would need authorization to observe objects of the highest class in order to read the file, and be able to modify objects from the most sensitive class down to the least sensitive in order to distribute the messages at their appropriate class. Since the process would be operating at many different access classes simultaneously, it must be trusted not to improperly pass sensitive messages to subjects with insufficient authorizations.

In order to support this type of application, the Bell and LaPadula model includes a "trusted subject" as part of the model. Trusted subjects in the model are subjects unconstrained by the *-property. Trusted subjects in the GEMSOS security kernel, unlike Bell and LaPadula's definition, are trusted (the *-property is relaxed) only within a given range, and are therefore "multilevel" subjects instead of general trusted subjects. Even with this additional security constraint the GEMSOS security kernel is still a valid interpretation of the Bell and LaPadula model for, as Bell and LaPadula write, "... restrictions of the concept of security will not require reproof of the properties already established because additional restrictions can only reduce the set of reachable states."[4]

GEMSOS SECURITY KERNEL FEATURES

Each of the structures and concepts described above is embodied in some way in the GEMSOS security kernel. The GEMSOS security kernel organization for implementation has been described previously,[2] and the reader interested in the specific primitives and kernel calls identified in the following discussions is encouraged to review this description. The following sections describe the major security features. The basic abstraction used in the GEMSOS design are segments, processes and devices. The segments are instances of "objects" of the model. The processes and devices are "subjects" of the model.

Security Labels

Security labels are representations of the sensitivity of objects and the authorizations of subjects. A security label is attached to every subject and object in the GEMSOS security kernel. Security labels are called "access classes" since they symbolize the complete set of security attributes possessed by each entity. The GEMSOS security kernel access classes (security labels) are records with two fields, representing secrecy and integrity access components. For secrecy the default label has eight (8) hierarchical classifications and twenty-nine (29) non-hierarchical categories. For strict integrity the default label has eight (8) hierarchical classifications and sixteen (16) non-hierarchical categories.

Some entities in the GEMSOS security kernel have two access classes: a maximum and a minimum. The secrecy and integrity access components of the maximum access class always dominate the secrecy and integrity access components of the minimum access class. The maximum and minimum classes together describe a range of permissible access classes.

Segments

All information in a Gemini system is contained in discreet, logical objects called segments. Each segment has an access class that reflects the sensitivity of information contained in the segment. Segments may be simultaneously and independently shared by multiple subjects but access to the segment (observe, modify, or both) on the part of each subject is controlled by the relationship between the segment's access class and each subject's access class, in accordance with the security properties of the model.

Every segment in the GEMSOS security kernel has a unique identifier. This identifier is effectively different for every segment ever created in any Gemini system. Unique identifiers are used internal to the kernel to prevent "spoofing" of the system by substituting one segment for another and are not visible at the kernel interface.

Eventcounts and Sequencers. The GEMSOS security kernel uses abstract data objects called "eventcounts" and "sequencers" for process synchronization and communication. These objects may be observed and modified by subjects so, to preserve security, the GEMSOS security kernel must control access to them. In order to identify eventcounts and sequencers, one eventcount and one sequencer are associated with the name of each segment. Each segment name, therefore, is used to identify an eventcount and a sequencer as well as a segment (see the section below on segment aliasing for more information on segment names). The eventcount and sequencer associated with a segment name have the same access class as the segment whose name they share. Process synchronization and communication are thus subject to the same rules of security as observing and modifying segments.

In order to modify an eventcount (using the primitive "advance") a process must be permitted modify access to the segment. Similarly, in order to observe an eventcount (using the primitives "read" or "await") a process must be permitted observe access to the segment. The primitive "ticket" for sequencers requires the potential for both observe and modify access to the segment. See the description by Reed[9] for more information on eventcounts and sequencers.

Volumes. Secondary storage in Gemini systems is divided into distinct logical volumes. Each segment is associated with only one volume, determined when the segment is created. Each volume may be considered to be a collection of segments. Volumes have two access classes, a maximum and a minimum, assigned when the volume is formatted. The secrecy and integrity components of the maximum access class must dominate the secrecy and integrity of the minimum class. The maximum and minimum volume access classes are upper and lower limits on the security of information contained on the volume (see the section below on the use of volumes).

Processes

A subject in the GEMSOS security kernel is a (process, domain) pair, where the domain is determined by the current hierarchical ring level at which the process is executing. The ring level determines the set of objects to which, within security constraints, the process potentially has access. Processes may change their ring levels, but the same process executing in a different ring is a different subject. The primary application of rings envisioned under the GEMSOS security kernel is for the creation of distinct domains so that a process can have up to three (rings 1, 2, and 3) "subjects." Each subject has a minimum and a maximum access class (security label) that is typically uniform for a process, no matter which ring it executes in. The secrecy and integrity access components of the maximum access class dominate those of the minimum access class. If the maximum and minimum access classes are equal then the subject is a "single-level" subject. If the two classes are unequal then the subject is a "multilevel" subject.

Single-level Subjects. Subjects that have equal maximum and minimum access classes are single-level subjects. Single-level subjects may only have the access to objects permitted by the simple and "*" secrecy and integrity properties (see the sections on secrecy and integrity).

Multilevel Subjects. Multilevel subjects have unequal maximum and minimum access classes. This property of multilevel subjects gives them the ability to have both observe and modify access to objects whose access classes fall between the subject's minimum and maximum. Multilevel subjects are the the GEMSOS security kernel implementation of "trusted subjects" (see the section on trusted subjects). Unlike general trusted subjects, however, multilevel subjects are only trusted within a range demarcated by their maximum and minimum access classes. Within this range, multilevel subjects are not constrained by the *-properties of secrecy and integrity (but they are still subject to ring integrity).

Only subjects guaranteed not to improperly downgrade or modify information should be created as multilevel subjects.

I/O Devices

I/O devices are viewed by processes as system processes. Processes communicate with I/O devices using shared segments and may also use eventcounts. Like other processes, I/O devices have both maximum and minimum access classes. These limits are intended to reflect the security constraints imposed by the physical environments in which devices are located and are critical to the employment of a secure computer in a multilevel environment.

Devices may be either single-level or multilevel. Unlike processes, which are classified single-level or multilevel based on their minimum and maximum access classes, the Criteria[1] categorizes I/O devices as "single-level" or "multilevel" based on the access classes of the data they manipulate. Data transmitted or received by a single-level device has no attached security label. Single-level devices thus consider all data to have a single access class. Data transmitted or received by a multilevel device has a security label attached to or stored with the data in the same form as the data. Multilevel devices therefore may handle data with a range of access classes.

Single-level Devices. A single-level device handles data to which no explicit security label is attached. In many environments the minimum and maximum access classes for a single-level device will be the same. A single-level device at a given time treats all input data as having a single access class, which is determined by the security of the physical environment at that time. Output data must have an access class that falls within the range of the device's maximum and minimum access classes.

In order to establish communication between a process and a single-level device in the GEMSOS security kernel (called "attaching" the device), the range of the subject must "intersect" the range of the device. Specifically, the following relationships between the process's access classes and the device's access classes must hold to ensure that the process will be able to receive or send data through the device.

1) To receive ("read") information:

   Process maximum secrecy)=
       Device minimum secrecy

   Device maximum integrity)=
       Process minimum integrity

2) To send ("write") information:

   Device maximum secrecy)=
       Process minimum secrecy

   Process maximum integrity)=
       Device minimum integrity

An example of a single-level device with different minimum and maximum access classes is a log-on terminal in a room to which users with authorizations ranging from the highest possible (system-high) access class down to the lowest possible (system-low) access class have access. In this example, the maximum and minimum access classes of the device would be system-high and system-low respectively, although narrower ranges are possible in other situations. There is only the single terminal in the room and only one person is allowed in the room at a time. Users log on to the system through a "trusted path"[1] which allows the GEMSOS security kernel to directly and securely determine their access class; it then creates a process of the same access class to represent the user in the system.

After a user has logged on using the trusted path, and the user's process has attached the device, the GEMSOS security kernel considers the security of the terminal device environment to be the same as the security of the user's process. Different users will have different access classes, but at a given time there is only one user so the data has only a single access class.

When a single-level device receives data, an access class (security label) must be established for the data. If the current security of the device has been reliably transmitted to the GEMSOS security kernel (e.g., through a trusted path) then the attached process will have an access class that represents the current security of the device. The received data is usually assigned the maximum secrecy and minimum integrity of the process that attached the device. A single-level device with a range of access classes, as can be seen from this example, must have a trusted path of some sort in order to be used in a secure manner. If not, then the minimum and maximum access classes of the single-level device should be identical.

Multi-level Devices. Any data input or output through a multilevel device must have an access class that falls within the range defined by the device's maximum and minimum access classes. Multilevel devices may handle data with a range of access classes. All data transmitted or received by a multilevel device has a security label attached or stored along with the data.

In order for a process to attach (establish communication with) a multilevel I/O device, the following relationships between the process's access classes and the device's access classes must hold to ensure that the process can send and receive information through the device without violating security.

1) To receive ("read") information:

Process maximum secrecy)=
    Device maximum secrecy

Device minimum integrity)=
    Process minimum integrity

2) To send ("write") information:

Device minimum secrecy)=
    Process minimum secrecy

Process maximum integrity)=
    Device maximum Integrity

Process and Segment Interaction

This section explains how the GEMSOS security kernel controls the ability of subjects, viz., (process, domain) pairs, to access objects (segments). A process may create and destroy segments, may add segments to and delete segments from the process's address space, and may move segments between main and secondary storage.

The total set of objects to which a subject potentially has access is the subject's access domain. A subject's access domain is determined by the subject's hierarchical ring level. The subset of the access domain that includes all objects to which, at a given time, a subject actually has access is called the subject's address space. Segments are brought into a subject's address space using the kernel call "makeknown_segment".

Access Modes. The GEMSOS security kernel allows processes to have execute only, read-execute, read only, and read-write access mode combinations to segments. Of these access mode combinations, all but read-write are considered to be "observe" type access modes. Read-write is both an "observe" type and a "modify" type access mode. The GEMSOS security kernel has no write only (modify only type) access mode for segments.

A process may have only one access mode combination to a segment at a time, but may simultaneously have different access modes to different segments. The access mode a process has to a segment is selected by the process at the time the segment is brought into the subject's address space. The actual type of access selected need only be a subset of the potential types of access allowed by the security policy. For example, if a process may potentially have both observe and modify type access to a segment based on the relationship between the process's and segment's access classes, it need not select the read-write access mode (observe and modify) to the segment, but can instead select any of the observe type access modes, since "observe" is a subset of its potential access types.

In order to have any of the observe access mode combinations to a segment, a process's maximum secrecy access component must dominate the segment's secrecy and the segment's integrity access component must dominate the process's minimum integrity. These requirements enforce the simple security and integrity "*" properties. In order to have modify access to a segment, the segment's secrecy access component must dominate the process's minimum secrecy and the process's maximum integrity access component must dominate the segment's integrity. These requirements enforce the secrecy "*" and simple integrity properties. In order to have both observe and modify access to a segment all four of these requirements must be met. Multilevel processes thus potentially have both observe and modify access to any segment whose access class falls within the process's range, while single-level processes are only permitted both observe and modify access to segments with the same access class as the process.

Segment Naming (Aliasing). In order to create or delete a segment, or to add a segment to its address space, a process must tell the GEMSOS security kernel the process-local name of the segment. The method of naming segments is called aliasing. Aliasing allows processes to uniquely identify shared segments in the system while still maintaining security.

A segment name consists of a system-wide component and a process-local component. The system-wide component is an index called an "entry number." A segment's entry number is the same for all processes, can be stored for future reference to the segment, and can be passed to and used by other processes. Were it not for the danger of covert information channels, the totally "flat" (non-hierarchical) entry number naming scheme would itself be sufficient for naming all segments.

Due to the danger of covert channels however, the system-wide entry number of a segment is always relative to a "mentor" segment. The mentor segment is identified by a process-local number that is not unique across processes, that cannot meaningfully be passed to another process, and that cannot be saved for future use (although the mentor itself also has a system-wide name, as described below). The paired process-local mentor segment number and system-wide entry number constitute a process-local segment alias used by a process for identifying the segment to the kernel.

A segment's alias is different from its ("invisible") unique identifier (described in the section on segments). Only one segment can have a particular (mentor, entry) pair as its name at a time, but if that segment is deleted then another segment can be created with the same name. The unique identifier of the new segment, however, will be different from the old segment.

A mentor segment may not be deleted until all segments named with that mentor have been deleted. This restriction prevents the problem of "zombie" segments that, although they exist in storage, cannot be accessed or deleted since they cannot be named.

Segment Naming Hierarchy. The process-local segment alias, viz., (mentor, entry) pair, of a segment can be used to add the segment to a process's address space. When a segment is entered into a process's address space, the process assigns the segment its own process-local segment number. The segment may then itself be used as a mentor segment if its process-local segment number is used as the mentor in the alias of another segment. Recursive application of this naming scheme results in a "hierarchy" of segment aliases.

Compatibility Property. The hierarchical segment naming scheme, using segment aliases, allows the GEMSOS security kernel to preserve system security by preventing the creation of covert channels through the use of segment names. Were processes able to name and thereby sense the presence or absence of any segment in the system (as they would in a flat naming scheme), this would constitute a source of covert channels. High secrecy level pro-

cesses could signal low secrecy level processes, and low integrity level processes could signal high integrity level processes, just by creating and deleting segments.

The GEMSOS security kernel alias hierarchy, however, allows processes to name segments only where that naming will not cause a covert channel. The hierarchy prevents covert channels by strictly ordering the security relationship between segments and their mentors:

Segment Secrecy)= Mentor Secrecy
Mentor Integrity)= Segment Integrity

These properties of the hierarchy have been called the Compatibility Property[4] (for secrecy) and the Inverse Compatibility Property (for integrity).[6]

The compatibility and inverse compatibility properties are maintained because of the way segments are named. A segment name consists of a (mentor, entry) pair. The entry number is relative to that particular mentor and is considered to be information associated with the mentor segment. A segment's entry number, as a result, is considered to have the same access class as the segment's mentor segment.

Whenever a process tries to create or delete a segment, or to add a segment to its address space, the process must "observe" the segment's entry number to see if, in fact, the segment exists. Since entry numbers are information associated with a mentor, a process must potentially have observe access to the segment's mentor in order to name the segment.

A mentor's alias consists of another (mentor, entry) pair, its mentor is named in the same fashion, and so on recursively back to the "root" of the naming hierarchy. Each segment's alias can thus be thought of as a vector consisting of a series of entry numbers that together uniquely describe a "path" to the segment. Clearly, in order to name a segment, a process must be able to name every mentor segment in the segment's path and it must therefore potentially have observe access to each of the mentor segments.

If the compatibility property was not maintained and a segment's compromise did not necessarily dominate the secrecy of its mentor, a situation might arise where a process that should have access to the segment based on the relationships between their access classes cannot have it, since the process cannot get observe access to the mentor. Every segment's secrecy, therefore, must dominate the secrecy of its mentor. Applying this rule recursively back to the root gives the result that secrecy is monotonically non-decreasing following a name path from the root to any segment.

Every segment has a unique path. This is achieved by requiring all segments with the same mentor to have unique entry numbers. Whenever a process creates or deletes a segment it specifies the name of the segment (conceptually "modifying" the segment's entry number to indicate the entry is in use or free). Since entry numbers are information associated with a mentor, a process must potentially have modify access to the mentor in order to create or delete a segment's name.

Because a segment name is a vector consisting of a series of entry numbers, changing any of the constituent entries would change the segment's name. A segment's name, therefore, must have at least the integrity of the segment (i.e., must dominate the segment's integrity). Since a segment's name consists of a (mentor, entry) pair, and since the entry number has the same access class as the mentor segment, the integrity of the mentor segment must dominate the integrity of the segment. Applying this rule recursively back to the root gives the result that integrity is monotonically non-increasing following a name path from the root to any segment.

To create a segment, a process requires the potential for both observe and modify access to the segment's mentor segment. Creating a segment affects only the segment's name, which is associated with the mentor, and does not affect the contents of, or information associated with, the segment being created. A process that creates a segment, therefore, does not need to be able to access the segment it creates.

To delete a segment a process requires the potential for both observe and modify access to the segment's mentor and, in addition, requires the potential for observe access to the segment being deleted. This additional restriction is necessary because mentor segments may not be deleted. A process deleting a segment must therefore know if the segment it is trying to delete is a mentor segment, requiring the process to "observe" if any other segments are named using the segment as a mentor. Those segments names, as stated above, are information associated with the mentor and possess the same access class.

The Use of Volumes. Volumes are collections of segments useful for physically organizing and protecting information of similar access classes. Volumes are brought into the GEMSOS security kernel using the kernel call "mount_volume." The first time a volume is mounted, it is uniquely associated for the life of that volume with a segment that will serve as the "root" mentor to segments on the volume. The segment used as a volume mentor may serve as a volume mentor to that volume only, and must not ever have been a mentor to other segments before the initial mounting of the volume. In this way all segments on the volume are guaranteed to have unique pathnames, distinct from the pathnames of segments on other volumes. Were pathnames indistinct, the system could be spoofed by substituting one segment for another of the same name.

Volumes may be unmounted and mounted repeatedly, but, to ensure unique pathnames, if its mentor is deleted a volume may never be remounted. A volume whose mentor is deleted must be reformatted to be reused -- a process that destroys whatever information the volume might contain. A volume mentor segment may not be deleted while the volume is mounted. A volume may not be unmounted if any of the segments on the volume are currently "known" in any process's address space. These pre-cautions prevent the problem of "zombie" volumes (mounted volumes that cannot be unmounted because they are not addressable) and "orphan" segments (segments addressable but not able to be swapped-out to disk).

The names of all segments on a volume must have access classes that fall within the volume limits. Since some segments on the volume will have the volume mentor segment as their mentor, the volume mentor segment's access class must also fall within the maximum and minimum access classes of the volume. According to the compatibility property, secrecy is monotonically nondecreasing and integrity is monotonically nonincreasing. When a volume is first mounted, therefore, the maximum potential secrecy access component of segments on the volume is the volume maximum, but the effective minimum compromise access component becomes the mentor's secrecy. Similarly, the minimum possible integrity access component of segments on the volume is the volume minimum, but the effective maximum possible integrity becomes the the mentor's integrity.

In order to satisfy the compatibility property, the secrecy access component of any segment created on a volume must dominate the secrecy access component of the volume mentor and be dominated by the maximum compromise of the volume. The integrity access component of any segment created on the volume must dominate the minimum integrity of the volume and be dominated by the mentor's integrity. These relationships are summarized below (where S indicates Secrecy, and I indicates Integrity):

$$S(\text{volume max}) \}= \\ \quad S(\text{segment}) \}= \\ \quad\quad S(\text{volume mentor segment})$$

$$I(\text{volume mentor segment}) \}= \\ \quad I(\text{segment}) \}= \\ \quad\quad I(\text{volume min})$$

To prevent a covert channel caused by the mounting and unmounting of volumes, a process that mounts or unmounts a volume must have a minimum secrecy access component dominated by the secrecy of the volume mentor and a maximum secrecy access component that dominates the maximum compromise of the volume. The minimum integrity access component of the process must be dominated by the minimum integrity of the volume and the maximum integrity access component of the process must dominate the integrity of the volume mentor segment. That is:

$$S(\text{process max}) \}= \\ \quad S(\text{volume max}) \}= \\ \quad\quad S(\text{volume mentor segment}) \}= \\ \quad\quad\quad S(\text{process min})$$

$$I(\text{process max}) \}= \\ \quad I(\text{volume mentor segment}) \}= \\ \quad\quad I(\text{volume min}) \}= \\ \quad\quad\quad I(\text{process min})$$

An example of the use of volumes is a floppy diskette environment. Each floppy diskette is a different volume with its own maximum and minimum access classes. Disks are labeled with these classes at the time they are formatted. The first time a diskette is used, the process that represents the diskette user in the system creates a mentor segment for the diskette volume and mounts the volume. Other users' processes may share the volume if the security policy allows them to "make known" the volume mentor segment in their address spaces. After the volume is unmounted and the diskette put away, the diskette may be reused so long as its mentor segment is not deleted. If the diskette volume's mentor is deleted, the diskette must be reformatted to be reused, destroying any information contained on the diskette.

SYSTEM PERFORMANCE MEASUREMENTS

The security-kernel approach to the design of a multilevel secure computer system offers a solution to the size and complexity problems that have dogged other approaches. However, some previous implementations of security kernels have resulted in systems with discouraging performance, reportedly as much as 75 to 90 percent below that of equivalent non-trusted systems.

Design Factors

After about a decade of work in the area of trusted systems, substantial information is available on factors that relate to some of the disappointing performance that has been experienced. Several of these factors are discussed below.

Language Efficiency. For verification purposes, security kernels are written in high-level languages which are chosen for features such as strong typing of data. Some of these languages tend to produce inefficient code. In the case of the GEMSOS security kernel, the PASCAL language has been chosen because of its support for evaluation. The compiler used is not particularly efficient, but is considered typical for microcomputer compilers. Thus there is some performance impact from choosing to use a higher-order language, but no significant additional impact from the choice to support security.

Hardware Support. The different security classes of users and information must be distinguished and where incompatible, kept separate; when hardware support is inadequate, the supporting overhead restricts the bandwidth of information that a secure computer system can process. Previous work has identified[3] four general architectural areas where hardware features are particularly useful or necessary: process management and switching, memory segmentation, Input/Output mediation, and execution domains. The Intel iAPX 286 processor used for the Gemini computers provides a high level of hardware support in all these areas.

System Architecture. The implementation choices for organizing the internal structure and the environment for applications have a major impact on the performance of any operating system. Generally the approach in the GEMSOS security kernel has been to take advantage of the techniques found effective in the industry as long as these do not adversely impact security. For example the choice of system computational model, e.g., process oriented or capability based, can directly affect system response time. We have chosen the proven process oriented approach, as reflected in the security discussion above. Two other choices of particular importance relate to the how multiprocessing is implemented, viz., techniques for avoiding bus contention and for preventing the kernel from being a critical section bottleneck. These are discussed below.

Bus contention is a potential performance concern in the Gemini multiprocessor configuration, since all processors share a single bus. In reality however, only shared, writable segments need be in a global memory on the shared bus. All other segments can be in processor-local memory. Our use of a purely virtual, segmented memory permits the kernel to determine exactly which are the shared, writable segments. The memory manager layer internal to the kernel totally controls the allocation to global memory to insure that only the required segments are in global memory. This policy can require some transfer between local and global memory but this structure markedly controls bus contention by allocating segments to the processor-local memory whenever possible. Our experience with sample applications is encouraging in that typically much less than 10% of the references of a processor are to a global memory. Thus, a number of processors can be effectively used on a single, shared bus.

In most, if not all, previous security kernel implementations, the kernel is a single critical section. This means that the kernel can be executed by only a single process at a time, and in addition cannot be interrupted. For a single processor, the adverse impact of this choice is somewhat contained in that there are no other processors that can be forced to wait. However, even in the single processor case real time response may be affected because there will be no response to an interrupt from an external device until any call to the kernel, that has begun before the interrupt, is completed. The GEMSOS security kernel is designed to be close to interruptible throughout its entire execution.

The impact of the critical section design choice is much more severe in the multiprocessor case. With a critical section, if one processor is executing in the kernel when another processor wants to invoke the kernel, the second processor must wait in essentially an "idle" condition until the first processor completes its execution of the kernel call. The degradation is clearly a function of the amount of service, viz., the number and type of calls, that the application demands of the kernel. In addition, the degradation increases as the number of processors increase. In the GEMSOS security kernel there are limited critical sections internal to the kernel itself that can result in contention, but the kernel itself is not a critical section so that multiple processors can execute simultaneously in the kernel.

Performance Results

Although the design approach to provide good performance is of interest, the real proof of any system is the actual measured performance. We have taken some preliminary measurements that focus on demonstrating (1) the throughput performance for multiprocessor configurations and (2) the response to real-time inputs. It is emphasized that these measurements were taken on Version 0, and that several performance enhancements have been designed for Version 1 that have not yet been implemented. Although we believe the results illustrate the general behavior, these early measurements should not be considered a definitive characterization of the Gemini product.

Multiprocessing Throughput. We have prepared a message processing emulation that runs on the multiprocessor environment. The emulation is reminiscent of a military communications processing application. The processing consists of a "front end processor" servicing multiple communication lines, and interfacing to an additional single communication line. The demonstration is not connected to physical communication lines, but emulates receiving messages from an input buffer segment and putting output messages in an output buffer segment.

The details of the demonstration are not very important to the measurements, but will be briefly summarized. Messages are treated as a series of line blocks of 84 bytes each. Each message requires some amount of processing and then a resulting message is placed in the message queue segment for "transmission" through the output buffer segment. A message processing process is created for each pair of input communication lines; this process does all the message processing and places the message, a line block at a time, in the message queue. In addition there is a single output process that takes messages, a line block at a time, and puts them in the output buffer. The kernel synchronization primitives for eventcounts are used to ensure that each message processing process waits for room in the message queue and to ensure that the output process takes the messages from the queue when they are available.

All the processes and buffer segments are actually created and used. The only actual Input/Output is to a screen for interface to the test operator. A display is generated for each message line block, and at the end of the "test run" timing information based on the internal real-time clock is displayed. The demonstration is intended to show the additional capacity that can be provided by additional processors. A distinct "test run" is used for each processor configuration of from one to seven processors, emulating service for from two to fourteen input lines, with each processor servicing two lines. The test operator selects a parameter that controls the amount of processing for each message. This parameter determines the amount of processing that is in the demonstration application versus the amount of processing in the kernel. The processing is simulated by repeated execution of a mix of instructions taken from a communication processing application.

An estimate is made of the percentage of the total processing time spent in the application for various choices for the parameter that controls the amount of processing for each message. The measurements taken on a single processor are used to normalize the results for additional processors, so that the number of "effective processors" can be determined. The number of effective processors becomes the primary figure of merit for the true effectiveness of the multiprocessing. Because of the multiprocessor contention within the kernel, this will be reduced if the application requires extensive services from the kernel, viz., as the percentage of application processing is reduced.

The results of a series of actual measurements as described above are summarized in Figure 1. This shows that for substantial application processing, there is a nearly linear increase in system throughput as the number of processors is increased. This clearly reflects that there is very little contention between processors for the shared bus. Futhermore, even when only 85% of the processing is in the application, there is still effectively six processors worth of throughput for a seven processor configuration.

Real Time Response. We have prepared a set of tests that require real-time response to external input. For this test we process communications input in a way that requires character-at-a-time processing. For each character there is an interrupt and the system must respond before two additional characters are received, or else with the hardware used for the interface, the communication will be broken. This is not necessarily the preferred implementation for such communication, but serves as a useful test implementation. Thus if the interrupts occur frequently (i.e., for a high transmission rate), it is essential that the kernel be interruptible. The specific test is an implementation of the HDLC support for the X.25 protocol that is used for the Defense Data Network interface to a computer host. The test has no higher level "flow control" protocol, so the input data must be received in real time.

The communication is synchronous, so that the actual amount of time available to respond to the interrupt depends on the transmission rate used. The other primary parameter for the test is the size of the HDLC frame used. Each HDLC frame includes about three bytes of overhead in addition to the frame size, so that the effective throughput will be inherently reduced for small frame sizes. The test uses a kernel call for each HDLC frame. Thus the choice of frame size affects both the probability that the interrupts will occur while the kernel is executing and the amount of kernel processing required for each frame.

The test is conducted using two Gemini computers connected with an HDLC link. The application programs in one computer makes a series of kernel calls to transmit a sequence of frames and the other makes a series of kernel calls to receive the sequence of calls. Figure 2 shows the results of the series of tests. For all the tests there were no communications errors, demonstrating that the kernel was able to support the real-time response at all the transmission rates tested -- up to 64 kilobits per second. The amount of application and kernel processing per frame was constant for all the data points. For purposes of this test, unrealistically small frame sizes are included to illustrate that even when the throughput is being limited by this processing, the character-by-character real-time response is still maintained.

SUMMARY AND CONCLUSIONS

The design of the GEMSOS security kernel for the Gemini commercial product has been influenced first by the Class B3 security requirements and second by the objective of high performance. We have described the major security design choices and believe that these provide an implementation that is particularly attractive for application in embedded systems. We have also reported the results of preliminary throughput and real-time performance measurements. These show effective real-time capability and nearly linear increase in throughput as the number of processors is increased up through seven processors. Although these are on an early version of the kernel that will be improved, we believe that these results already demonstrate that a secure system can also have high performance.

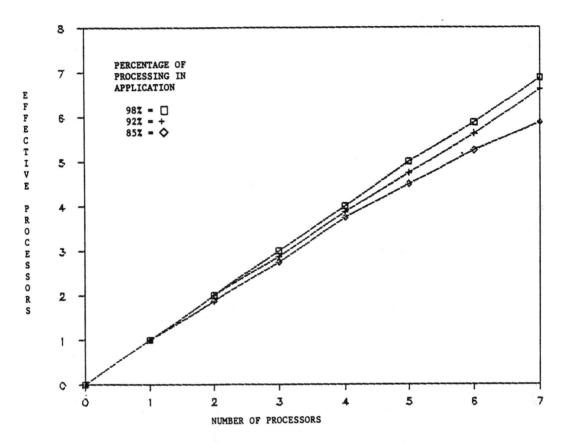

Figure 1. Gemini Multiprocessor Enhancement

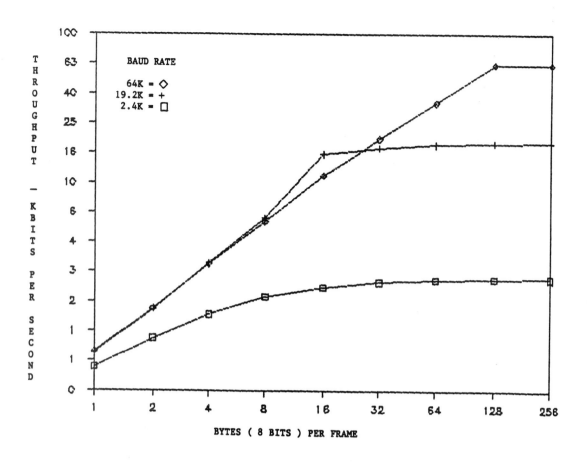

Figure 2. Gemini Real-Time Processing

REFERENCES

1. DoD Trusted Computer System Evaluation Criteria, CSC-STD-001-83, 15 August 1983, DoD Computer Security Center, Ft. Meade, Md.

2. Schell, R. R., and Tao, T. F., Microcomputer-Based Trusted Systems for Communication and Workstation Applications, Proceedings of the 7th DoD/NBS Computer Security Initiative Conference, NBS, Gaithersburg, MD, 24-26 September 1984, pp. 277-290.

3. S.R. Ames, M. Gasser, and R.R. Schell, "An Introduction to the Principles of Security Kernel Design and Implementation," Computer, Vol. 16, No. 7, July 1983, pp. 14-22.

4. D.E. Bell and L.J. LaPadula, "Computer Security Model: Unified Exposition and Multics Interpretation," Tech. report ESD-TR-75-306, AD A023588, The Mitre Corporation, Bedford, Mass., June 1975.

5. M. Schaefer and R.R. Schell, "Towards an Understanding of Extensible Architectures for Evaluated Trusted Computer System Products," Proceedings of the 1984 Symposium on Security and Privacy, April 1984, pp. 42-49.

6. K.J. Biba, "Integrity Considerations for Secure Computer Systems," Tech. Report ESD-TR-76-372, The Mitre Corporation, April 1977.

7. M.D. Schroeder and J.H. Saltzer, "A Hardware Architecture for Implementing Protection Rings," Communications of the ACM Vol. 15, No. 3, March 1972, pp. 115-124.

8. L.J. Shirley and R.R. Schell, "Mechanism Sufficiency Validation by Assignment," Proc. 1981 Symp. Security and Privacy, IEEE Cat. No. 81CH1629-5, April 1981.

9. D.P. Reed, and R.K. Kanodia, "Synchronization with Eventcounts and Sequencers," Communications of the ACM, Vol. 22, No. 2, February 1979, pp. 115-124.

SE/VMS: IMPLEMENTING MANDATORY SECURITY IN VAX/VMS

Steven Blotcky, Kevin Lynch, Steven Lipner
Digital Equipment Corporation
Nashua, NH and Littleton, MA

ABSTRACT

Since the late seventies, Digital Equipment Corporation has been pursuing a development program aimed at improving the security of its computer system and network products. The most visible product of this program to date has been Version 4.2 of the VAX/VMS operating system, which is under evaluation as a candidate for Class C2 of the Trusted Computer System Evaluation Criteria. In addition to implementing discretionary access controls, VAX/VMS Version 4.2 incorporates latent support for mandatory security controls at the level of internal operating system routines and data structures. This paper describes SE/VMS (Security Enhanced VMS), a set of modifications that allow VAX/VMS users to exploit the latent support for mandatory security. The modifications provide facilities that allow a system manager to set up and administer the mandatory security environment, and that allow users to operate on labeled objects. The paper describes the functions of SE/VMS that support user registration and login, device and volume management, file creation and access, and the production of labeled printed output. Discussions are provided of the techniques that were used to implement SE/VMS, of the system's limitations, and of plans to gain user experience with SE/VMS. SE/VMS is viewed as providing an interim mandatory security capability for VAX/VMS users, and will not be submitted for evaluation at Class B1 of the Criteria.

1 INTRODUCTION

Since the late seventies, Digital Equipment Corporation has been pursuing an active development program aimed at improving the security of our computer system and network products. The primary focus of this program has been a series of enhancements to the security of the VAX/VMS operating system. The most visible product of the program to date has been VAX/VMS Version 4.2, which has been submitted for evaluation at Class C2 of the Trusted Computer System Evaluation Criteria[1] (TCSEC).

This paper describes SE/VMS (Security Enhanced VMS), modifications that have been developed to provide an initial mandatory security capability for VAX/VMS. These modifications were developed by Digital's Software Services organization to provide labeled security protection for VAX/VMS. This work is intended to meet most of the requirements for Class B1 of the TCSEC. Because SE/VMS does not meet all requirements and is intended to provide only an interim capability, it would not be a candidate for submission for formal product evaluation at Class B1.

SE/VMS is not an "add-on" security package in the sense of some of the products on the National Computer Security Center's Evaluated Products List. Instead it combines latent capabilities of VAX/VMS, replacements for some VAX/VMS components, and additional components to achieve the overall objective of providing labeled protection.

This paper begins with a review of the security features of VAX/VMS Version 4.2. It then summarizes the support for mandatory security that was included in Version 4.2. Next, the paper presents an overview of the features of SE/VMS along with a sketch of the techniques that were used to implement them. Finally, we conclude with a discussion of areas for future development in providing mandatory security for VAX/VMS.

2 SECURITY IN VAX/VMS

VAX/VMS was initially developed in the mid seventies along with the VAX-11/780 32-bit superminicomputer. The VAX-11/780 was developed as an upward-compatible extension to the PDP-11 minicomputer family and executes PDP-11 code directly. As the VAX family grew out of the PDP-11, so VAX/VMS grew out of the RSX-11/M operating system for the PDP-11.

Initial releases of VAX/VMS actually included a significant number of PDP-11 utility programs that were transported unmodified from RSX. Thus the initial VAX/VMS security design was an extended "minicomputer" model and encompassed passwords at login and "system/owner/group/world" protection on files, directories and a few other objects. VAX/VMS has always supported one-way encryption of user passwords, and over the years a number of security auditing functions were incorporated with the system's accounting features.

In the late seventies and early eighties, a major project was started with the aim of upgrading the security of VAX/VMS. The first product of this project was VAX/VMS

Version 4.0, and some additional enhancements were incorporated in Version 4.2. When this paper discusses the features of SE/VMS, it describes changes or enhancements to Version 4.2. Because the initial implementation of mandatory controls was incorporated in Version 4.0, the paragraphs below will refer to Version 4.0 in some cases. (Odd-numbered versions since 4.0 have been dedicated to "bug fixes" rather than significant feature enhancements.) As it currently exists, VAX/VMS Version 4.2 incorporates the following security enhancements:

o A number of "account management" features including account expiration, restrictions on days and times of login, and restrictions on access to accounts (no dialup, no network, etc.).

o A number of password management features including required change of initial passwords for privileged accounts, password expiration, minimum password length, dual-password accounts, and a random pronounceable password generator.

o Features directed toward systems that support dialup lines or networks including automatic hangup and limits on unsuccessful login attempts directed to an account.

o Access control list and identifier features allow the system manager to define arbitrary groups of users, and allow users to grant or deny access to files by individual users or defined groups.

o Selective security auditing features produce an audit trial of successful and/or failed attempts at such operations as user login, access to files, and use of certain privileges. The audit trail is directed both to a terminal and a log file, and can be analyzed by a reduction procedure included in the system.

o Features introduced in VAX/VMS Version 4.0 prevent "disk scavenging" by insuring that disk files are erased on deletion, or that blocks newly allocated to files are pre-erased. VAX/VMS systems have always erased primary memory pages before making them addressable to a process, so the enhancement to disk storage allocation eliminates the last possibility for disclosure of information by object reuse.

o A "secure server" key prevents users from implementing "password grabbers" by guaranteeing that a user of a hardwired terminal who presses the break key will always receive a login prompt from the operating system. Equivalent features are provided for users whose terminals are attached to terminal concentrators or VAX network hosts.

o A "Guide to VAX/VMS System Security"[2] was developed along with VAX/VMS Version 4.0, and updated for Version 4.2. The guide provides detailed information for both users and system managers.

The development of VAX/VMS Version 4.0 was started before the completion of the final version of the TCSEC. Nonetheless, the developers were aware of the Criteria development process, and tracked the content of each draft of the TCSEC. A specific goal of VAX/VMS Version 4.2 was that it meet the requirements of Class C2, Controlled Access Protection. VAX/VMS Version 4.2 has been under formal evaluation as a candidate for Class C2 since late 1985.[3]

3 MANDATORY CONTROLS FOR VAX/VMS

While the primary security evaluation goal for VAX/VMS Version 4.0 was to meet the requirements of Class C2 of the TCSEC, it was understood during the development process that incorporation of mandatory security controls was both a feasible and desirable objective. Resource limitations and time-to-market constraints prevented the completion of the mandatory security features. However, a good deal of work was completed, and "latent support" for mandatory security has been present in every release of VAX/VMS since Version 4.0.

Early in the development of VAX/VMS Version 4.0, a decision was made that the system would support both the lattice security and integrity[4] models, with fields allocated to support 256 levels and 64 categories for each of the security and integrity models. The fields were encoded in a conventional way - a byte each for security and integrity levels, and a 64-bit quadword for security and integrity category masks. These fields, plus an additional 16-bit word used as a filler, form a five longword structure known as an "access classification block", or CLS block. Thus, the total storage required to represent a security "access class" (levels and categories for security and integrity) is 160 bits. As part of the development of VAX/VMS Version 4.0, CLS blocks were added to the data structures for the system's subjects and objects.

The security properties of a subject are recorded in a CLS block within an "Agent's Rights Block", or ARB, that includes the subject's current access class as well as identity, group and privilege information that is used for the other protection checks performed by Version 4.0. The only subjects on a VMS system are processes.

The security properties of most objects (files, "mailboxes", logical name tables, devices, and global sections) that are active (accessible or "opened") in the system are stored in "Object's Rights Blocks" or ORBs. An ORB contains two CLS blocks, specifying minimum and maximum access classes for the object, as well as discretionary access control information. Other objects (e.g. mounted disk volumes) have CLS blocks as part of their control structure. While the major storage objects are labeled with CLS blocks, a few (less critical) interprocess communication objects are not labeled.

The ORB and ARB are data structures that apply to active subjects and objects in a VAX/VMS system -- processes that are logged in (ARB), and open files, logical name tables, and so on (ORB's). For mandatory security controls to be effective they must also, of course, apply to permanent subjects and objects - registered users, files, directories and volumes. Thus the system's permanent data structures were enhanced to record access class information. The User Authorization File (UAF) entry for a user records that user's minimum and maximum access class. The "volume home block" for a disk volume records the minimum and maximum access class for the volume, while the "file header" for each file records the file's access class. In all cases the standard VAX/VMS 160-bit CLS block is used to store the access class.

Volumes and devices may be multilevel (minimum and maximum access class may differ for each object, as set by the system manager) while a file always has a single access class. Directories are files with special properties and also have a single access class. Additional process control and communication objects (i.e. logical name tables, global sections, "mailboxes") are potentially multilevel objects.

In addition to adding access class information for subjects and objects, the VAX/VMS Version 4.0 development project also completed the code required to implement mandatory controls for files, and extended the executive's central protection checking routine to reflect the access class of subject and object in its decision to grant or deny access. Access checks and propagation of access classes were based directly on the requirements of the Bell-LaPadula model[5]. A subject may only read an object if the subject's access class dominates the object's access class (simple security condition). A subject may only write an object if the object's access class dominates the subject's access class (*-property or confinement property).

While the code that checks access was part of VAX/VMS Version 4.0, no provision was made to allow a subject to have a non-zero access class. Only in the case of files was a subject's access class propagated to objects it created as required by the Bell-LaPadula model's rules for creation of objects. Thus, there was no operational ability to label objects, only a latent one.

A pair of privileges -- downgrade and upgrade -- may be granted to a process to exempt it from the security and integrity *-properties respectively. The execution of the mandatory security access check in VAX/VMS Version 4.0 is conditioned on a global "sysgen" parameter: when the parameter is 1, checking is enabled. The sense of the encoding of access classes is such that, as long as the entire access class

is zero, access is always granted. Thus a user who sets the sysgen parameter inadvertently will lose some processor time to access checks but will not find his system "broken".

The implementation of mandatory controls in VAX/VMS Version 4.0 provides a relatively complete set of structures and support in the operating system kernel for labeled security protection. However, no user (or system manager) interface to the mandatory access controls is provided, access class is only propagated for files, and mandatory access checks are not made during some operations (e.g. mounting disks). In addition, even though file access failures caused by a violation of mandatory security will appear in the system's audit trail, the reason for such failures (i.e. the incompatible access classes) will not.

If an installation is to make use of the mandatory security support in VAX/VMS, it must have a way to associate character-string names with levels and categories, to assign "clearances" to users, to allow users to select an access class at login, and to display access class information on printed output, in directory listings, and so on. In addition, a system manager must have facilities to set up a system, for example defining the access class ranges of drives, volumes, and terminals, and must have access to access class-related information in the system's audit trail.

A number of Digital's users have "discovered" the mandatory security features in VAX/VMS and written their own software to exploit them[6]. The experience of these users seems to show both the viability of the implementation of mandatory security controls in VAX/VMS Version 4.2 and the critical need of some users for these features.

4 SUPPORTING MANDATORY SECURITY IN VAX/VMS

This section describes the features and implementation of SE/VMS. In the following paragraphs, emphasis has been placed on the SE/VMS features that support mandatory security controls. As was mentioned above, integrity labeling is also present and supported in SE/VMS, but most mention of the integrity model has been omitted from the paragraphs below in an attempt to shorten and simplify the presentation.

4.1 Objectives

The discussion above has described the support for mandatory security controls that is present in VAX/VMS Version 4.2, as well as the support that has not yet been completed. The objective of the SE/VMS development was to provide near-term support for mandatory security. The ground rule of the development effort was to provide a complete and usable system, but to defer where necessary support for features or facilities that would unduly complicate or delay the provision of basic support. Specifically, it was decided not to modify any of the existing system data structures. No effort was made to add mandatory controls to any object that did not already have a CLS block in its associated data structures.

4.2 Approach

The technical approach to the development of SE/VMS was, as might be expected, to build on the support for mandatory security in VAX/VMS Version 4.2, and to add those components that were missing or incomplete in Version 4.2. In practice, this effort required a few changes to the basic Version 4.2 executive, the replacement of some Version 4.2 modules with enhanced ones, and the development of some entirely new modules. Because the VMS development group enhanced the latent support for mandatory security that had been present in Version 4.2 by adding system service routines to the executive for VAX/VMS Version 4.4, it was then decided that SE/VMS would be developed as a set of enhancements to Version 4.4.

The following sections describe the features that were added by SE/VMS and the general approaches to implementing those features. An overview of the implementation of SE/VMS is provided at the end of this section.

4.3 Names For Access Classes

VAX/VMS stores an access class (in a CLS block) as a purely numeric value. Therefore a mapping between the alphanumeric name of a security or integrity level or category and the corresponding encoded value is needed both for input (user registration, login, etc.) and output (directory listing, printed output).

The VAX/VMS rights database supports mapping between numeric values and alphanumeric identifiers (names) as part of the user group identifier mechanism mentioned above. A range of binary identifier values was reserved to hold the names of security and integrity levels and categories. A simple arithmetic conversion allows the VMS executive to transform the value corresponding to a level or the bit position corresponding to a category into a binary identifier value. Pre-existing mechanisms for processing the rights database implement the mapping between identifier value and alphanumeric name. VAX/VMS already provides a utility to maintain the rights database, as well as the User Authorization File (Authorize); commands were added to this utility that allow the system manager to specify the names of security and integrity levels and categories.

4.4 System Service Support

A uniform syntax was developed for the specification of access classes by users (Figure 1). This syntax allowed for the specification of classification information by an alphanumeric string (as described above), or by numeric value. The VMS development group provided two new system services in Version 4.4, one to parse ASCII access class strings and translate them into binary CLS blocks and a second to create an ASCII access class string from a CLS block.

```
(LEVEL=SECRET)
(CATEGORY=27)
(LEVEL=TOP_SECRET,
    CATEGORY=(BLUE,RED))
(LEVEL=(MINIMUM:SECRET,
    MAXIMUM:TOP_SECRET), CATEGORY=RED)
(LEVEL=(MINIMUM:UNCLASSIFIED,
    MAXIMUM:255), CATEGORIES=(1,3))
```

Figure 1. Examples of Valid Access Class Strings

A third system service was provided to set and get the access classes of those objects that have associated ORBs. These are the services that became available with VAX/VMS Version 4.4, and motivated the decision to implement SE/VMS under that version rather than Version 4.2.

4.5 Authorizing Users

The system manager who wishes to add a user to an SE/VMS system must be able to specify a "clearance" for that user. The VAX/VMS Authorize utility is normally used to register users and specify their security attributes. Authorize was modified for SE/VMS to accept user access class information. A syntax for entering such information was devised that is consistent with normal usage in VAX/VMS and Authorize (Figure 2). Because VAX/VMS already uses the "/SECURITY" command qualifier for other purposes, "/SECRECY" is used to specify the mandatory security clearance property.

```
UAF>ADD MODEEN/SECRECY=
    (LEVEL:(MINIMUM:UNCLASSIFIED,
    MAXIMUM:TOP_SECRET),
    CATEGORY:(MAXIMUM:(APPLE,BANANA)))
```

Figure 2. Specifying User Clearance

A user can be allowed a single classification, or a range of classifications.

4.6 Logging In

The VAX/VMS LOGINOUT utility was modified to assign an access class to the user's process, and to validate that access class. When a user logs in interactively, an access class for his or her process can be specified using the standard syntax (Figure 3). If none is specified, the process will default to the user's maximum authorized access class.

```
USERNAME: LIPNER/SEC=(LEVEL:SECRET,
              CATEGORY:(BANANA,GRAPE))
```

Figure 3. Login With Classification Specified

The LOGINOUT utility then validates that the access class is between the user's minimum and maximum (as well as validating the login against the other information in the UAF). It also validates the requested access class for the login against the range of access classes authorized for the terminal (See below). LOGINOUT then stores the access class in the process' ARB. In the case of a non-interactive login, such as a submitted batch job, the process is assigned the user's maximum access class and validation is performed against the command, error and log files specified by the user.

4.7 Volumes And Devices

The system manager of a SE/VMS system will normally wish to specify the ranges of access classes for mass storage devices and volumes and for user terminals. A new command and associated utility program allow the system manager to specify the necessary parameters for objects with ORBs (Figure 4).

```
SET CLASS/OBJECT_TYPE=DEVICE/SECRECY=
      (LEVEL:(MINIMUM:SECRET,
       MAXIMUM:TOP_SECRET),
       CATEGORY:(MAXIMUM:(APPLE,BANANA)))
       DUA1:
```

Figure 4. Setting Device Access Class.

New switches (/SECRECY and /INTEGRITY) have been added to the INITIALIZE command (Figure 5) to allow a volume to be initialized so that only files within a specified range of access classes can be written to it. The INITIALIZE command operates on a disk volume that is physically mounted on the VAX system but not yet logically accessible to application programs. The access class is stored in the home block of the disk.

```
INITIALIZE/SECRECY=(LEVEL:(MINIMUM:SECRET,
      MAXIMUM:TOP_SECRET)) USERDISK02
```

Figure 5. Setting Volume Access Class.

The SET CLASS commands may only be used by the system manager or a privileged user to change the classification of objects owned by the system. Their effect is to set the minimum and maximum access class values in the ORB for the specified object. Because the ORB is a transitory data structure, these commands must be repeated each time the system is rebooted. They will normally be included in a command procedure that is executed at system startup time before users may log in. This use of a command procedure is consistent with normal VAX/VMS practice.

When files on a volume are to be made accessible to SE/VMS users and programs, an option of the the SE/VMS MOUNT command compares the access class ranges of device and volume and, if the range of the volume is "within" that for the device, allows the mount to proceed. In this case, the MOUNT command copies the access class range for the volume into the device's ORB, saving the old device access class information so that it may be restored when the volume is dismounted. The MOUNT and SET CLASS commands allow the system manager to mount a foreign disk or tape volume at the access class of the device where the volume is to be mounted.

4.8 Operations On Files And Directories

As was mentioned in the discussion of mandatory controls in Version 4.0, the operations of object creation and initial access (file open) built into VAX/VMS implement the requirements of the Bell-LaPadula model in a straightforward fashion. A newly created file or directory inherits the access class of the creating process. Opens for reading and writing are subject to the constraints of the simple security condition and *-property.

As with any system that implements the lattice model and a hierarchical file system, SE/VMS enforces a "compatible" hierarchy in which the security classes of files and directories are monotonically non-decreasing (and integrity classes non-increasing) as one proceeds away from a volume's root directory. Any user can create an "upgraded" directory via the SET CLASS command, but will then be unable to gain access to the new directory without logging in at a higher access class. The files within a given directory will normally be at a uniform access class and only directories will be upgraded.

Any user who owns or uses files at multiple access classes will require a way to discover what files and directories are present at various access classes. The VMS DIRECTORY/FULL and DIRECTORY/SECURITY commands (requiring read access to the directory) have been modified for SE/VMS to produce a listing of file and directory names and access classes for user review.

The VAX/VMS BACKUP utility was modified to preserve the classifications of files and directories when they are backed up to tape or disk. Access checks are made during both backup and restore operations.

4.9 Additional Objects

Because of the structure of VAX/VMS, any object that has an associated ORB will be protected by the system's mandatory controls.

Logical name tables (used to translate names used by programs and the VAX/VMS command language), global sections (used to map files into shareable areas of main memory), and "mailboxes" (used for interprocess communication like Unix(tm) pipes) have associated ORB's and thus are protected by the system's mandatory controls.

These additional objects are created dynamically by processes in execution. The VMS executive was modified to set the access class of a newly created object of any of these types to the access class of the creating process, except in the case of a global section "backed" by a disk file; in that case the global section is given the access class of the file. The access classes of objects of these types may be altered by the SET CLASS command (given sufficient user privilege) and displayed by the corresponding SHOW CLASS command.

4.10 Labeling Output

For many users, the "bottom line" of a system that implements mandatory controls is the ability to produce properly labeled printed output. As part of the SE/VMS development, a print symbiont was developed that verifies the requesting user's mandatory access to a file, then produces a listing with labeled header and trailer pages and optional top and bottom labels on each page. The layout of the header, trailer, top and bottom labels are customizeable. A SE/VMS utility allows the format to be defined for each unique combination of security level and categories.

4.11 Auditing

The VAX/VMS security auditing facilities seemed to audit the "right things" for SE/VMS, but were insensitive to mandatory security access classes. For SE/VMS, the existing facilities were enhanced to record access class information where appropriate (login, file access).

To allow a reasonable level of audit selectivity at audit trail collection time and avoid flooding the system's audit log file, the VAX/VMS executive was modified to allow system manager selection of auditing of all file access at or above a selected security class. A command, SAUDIT, was implemented as part of SE/VMS to allow a system manager to select the access class threshold for auditing (Figure 6).

```
SAUDIT/ENABLE/SECRECY=(LEVEL:SECRET,
         CATEGORIES:(APPLE,GRAPE))
```

Figure 6. Selecting the Audit Threshold Access
Class

4.12 Mail

The VAX/VMS MAIL utility is used to send messages between users. As distributed with Version 4.2, it would only be possible to send mail between users at the unclassified level. The SE/VMS development project modified MAIL so that a message can be sent from a process to any user who could read a file at the sending process' access class. In some cases, the receiver's copy of the message may have its access class raised to the receiver's minimum access class. The receiving process can only respond with a message built into the mail program that says "user HAS READ YOUR MESSAGE".

4.13 Implementation Considerations

The implementation of SE/VMS was simplified by the level of support for mandatory security already present in Versions 4.2 and 4.4 of VAX/VMS, and by the structure of VAX/VMS. The normal functions of an operating system kernel are performed by the VAX/VMS executive. The executive performs such functions as opening files and checking access. Support functions are performed by programs (images) that are part of the operating system, but run in the context of the process that invokes them. In some cases, these operating system images may have privileges of their own; more often they inherit any special privileges of the user on whose behalf they operate.

SE/VMS implements mandatory security controls in VAX/VMS by first enabling the mandatory control support features that are always present in the VAX/VMS executive. In a few cases, the executive has been modified (patched) to add features not yet supported by VAX/VMS. For example, selective auditing by security access class, and filling in ORBs with classification information are implemented by patches to the executive.

A number of the user and system manager support functions in SE/VMS are implemented by images that are present, but do not support mandatory controls, in the standard VMS product. In these cases, SE/VMS simply modifies the source programs for the images, then replaces these images at SE/VMS installation time. This is the case for the Authorize, LOGINOUT, and Directory utilities. In each case, the required modifications are localized to small segments of the image in question.

Finally, some of the components of SE/VMS required the development of entirely new programs (though perhaps based on existing VAX/VMS software). For example, the labeling print symbiont of SE/VMS and the SAUDIT command are in this category. In this case, too, SE/VMS simply installs the new program in a directory where it will be available to the system manager.

5 LIMITATIONS, EXPERIENCE AND FUTURE DIRECTIONS

5.1 Limitations And Support

The sections above should have made clear the fact that SE/VMS is intended to provide an initial mandatory control facility for VAX/VMS. This section considers what is "not provided" with SE/VMS.

The combination of VAX/VMS Version 4.4 with SE/VMS provides a fairly complete set of mandatory control facilities at the operating system level. Users' processes can create, delete, read, and write objects at the operating system level, and those operations will be constrained by and consistent with the requirements of the mandatory security controls.

Two major system objects - event flag clusters and lock blocks - are not labeled. Event flag clusters are sets of 32 bits, normally used for posting events, that can be used for interprocess communications. A process can access two shared event flag clusters at a time. Lock blocks are structures used to control access to shared resources. They can optionally be associated with a 16-byte value block that can be used to communicate information among processes sharing the resource. Both lock blocks and and event flag clusters are allocated dynamically by the system.

There are a few feature shortfalls that might be expected to be resolved in a full-fledged system. For example:

o Terminals associated with terminal servers (such as DECserver-100s) can not be assigned access classes individually; all such terminals must be given the same access class as a group.

o Some of the auditing facilities are relatively coarse and not well-tuned for the mandatory controls. For example, one cannot tell from the error coding in the audit trail whether a file access attempt was rejected because of the mandatory controls or the discretionary controls.

These and other equivalent shortcomings demonstrate that SE/VMS is still an evolving system at the operating system level, rather than a completely finished one.

The area where SE/VMS will present the greatest challenge to its users is not in the domain of operating system features, but in application structure. It is clear that an ordinary unprivileged VAX/VMS application program that does not attempt to cross access class boundaries will function correctly under SE/VMS. It is equally clear that a complex application that operates on multiple files, perhaps of different access classes, may find itself broken by SE/VMS.

Some complex applications must be installed "with privilege" in a VAX/VMS system. Those applications may have sufficient power to defeat SE/VMS, eliminating part of the benefit of the mandatory controls. On the other hand, some privileged applications (MAIL is an example) may not have enough power to overcome the mandatory controls. The key point is that there is a significant amount of engineering required to make complex applications operate correctly in an environment where mandatory security controls are being enforced, and that engineering has not yet been done for the applications that may be asked to operate under SE/VMS.

SE/VMS may interact in unexpected ways with VAX/VMS applications. A pool of specialists has been trained in mandatory controls in general and in SE/VMS in particular so they might understand their effects on applications. Such training can provide specialists with the skills necessary to provide support for mandatory controls in the future. This support, in addition to basic installation of the SE/VMS software, could include defining initial security policy, setting up device and directory structures, and analyzing the impact of SE/VMS on applications.

On hearing a description of the features of SE/VMS, a listener might naturally be expected to ask "has it been submitted for evaluation?" Digital believes that SE/VMS meets many of the TCSEC requirements for Class B1, Labeled Security Protection. However, absent a full developmental evaluation, it seems likely that there are specific features that fall short of the requirements of Class B1. In addition, the documentation for SE/VMS is not structured in accordance with the requirements of the TCSEC, and the requirements for complete functional testing of the security features have not been met. Digital has requested that NCSC initiate a developmental evaluation of SE/VMS. The intention of requesting this evaluation is primarily to provide better insight into what might be required to make a future release of VAX/VMS meet the requirements of Class B1.

5.2 Experience With SE/VMS

As part of its evaluation of the impact of mandatory controls on VMS and its users, Digital has provided copies of SE/VMS to a selected set of VAX/VMS users. Because this paper was prepared shortly after the evaluation copies of SE/VMS were distributed, there is no experience to report. It is anticipated that some comments on user experience with SE/VMS will be included in the presentation of the paper at the Ninth National Computer Security Conference.

5.3 Directions For The Future

The discussion above clearly points the way toward a possible future release of VAX/VMS meeting the TCSEC requirements for

Class B1. In addition, Digital is continuing
advanced development projects aimed at
evaluating the feasibility of developing a
Class A1 security kernel that would be
compatible with VAX/VMS. Advanced
development and architecture studies are also
continuing to examine the impact of mandatory
controls on VAX/VMS layered software
products. An additional focus of advanced
development work is the need for enhanced
security in Digital's DECnet wide-area
network and Ethernet local-area network
products. As these advanced development
projects reach maturity, they are likely to
form the basis for future papers like this
one.

REFERENCES

1. Department of Defense Trusted
    Computer System Evaluation Criteria,
    CSC-STD-001-83, Department of Defense
    Computer Security Center, Fort George
    G. Meade, MD 20755, August 1983
2. Guide to VAX/VMS System Security,
    AA-Y510A-TE, AA-Y510A-T1, Digital
    Equipment Corp., Maynard, MA 01754, July
    1985
3. Product Evaluation Bulletin, VAX/VMS
    Operating System, Version 4.2,
    Report Number CSC-PB-01-85, National
    Computer Security Center, Fort
    George G. Meade, MD 20755, October 1985
4. Biba, K.J., Integrity Considerations for
    Secure Computer Systems, ESD-TR-76-372,
    Electronic Systems Division, AFSC, Hanscom
    AFB, MA, April 1977
5. Bell, D.E. and LaPadula, L.J.,Secure
    Computer Systems: Unified Exposition and
    Multics Interpretation, MTR-2997, MITRE
    Corp., Bedford, MA, March 1976
6. Technical Description of the VAX/VMS
    Version 4 Non-Discretionary Security
    Implementation, SAIC Comsystems,
    Chesapeake, Virginia, 1985

CAVEATS

Section 3
Network Security

3.1: Network Security Overview

Introduction

Network security interfaces with computer security, because many computer systems communicate with end users via networks. The sum of computer and network security is referred to as information security. The differences between computer and network security are becoming less apparent as the differences disappear between computer and network systems. The reason for this conversion is that new investments in computer systems are including substantial provisions for communication capabilities. For example, an investment in a local area network (LAN) may involve computers, modems, communication switches, and communication links. From the end user's viewpoint, the LAN may be accessed from a personal computer (PC). The resulting automated information system is integrated with a combination of computer and network capabilities.

We shall discuss the different views of network security in the next subsection. This is followed by subsections on network architecture, security services, and architectural issues.

What Is a Network

There is no little dispute concerning the boundaries of computer networks and the level of abstraction necessary and proper for discussion of security. At different times and for different purposes, different definitions and levels of abstraction are appropriate. The concept of levels of abstraction is commonly employed in the engineering of large systems. Sometimes it is appropriate to take a high-level or abstract view, considering the subsystems as closed black boxes. At other times we want to look into these subsystems to see how they function. This decomposition process can be repeated until exhaustion.

The arguments about the nature and definition of networks are really a shifting among different levels of abstraction. Unfortunately, it is rarely so clearly identified. This is not uncommon for the engineering of complex systems; you should be alert to these factors for each article read. This discussion assumes a background knowledge in computer networks, such as might be gained from reading [ABRA84].

All views of computer networks consider them to be interconnections of systems; the differences seem to concentrate on the degree of coupling among these systems and their relative independence. One philososphy, exemplified by ARPANET (now known as the Defense Data Network) is of independent heterogenous systems that exchange information according to well-defined protocols. The communication sub-net (as it is sometimes called) connects sources and destinations of information, providing message services according to these protocols. In particular, there is no single point of control or failure; survivability and adaptability are necessary design objectives in a military network.

Another philosophy is that a network is an extension of an operating system. Modern computer design employs multiple processors; some are general purpose, some special purpose. All of these processors are controlled by the operating system. When there is only a single copy of the operating system, the system is termed tightly coupled; when there are multiple copies, it is called loosely coupled. When the physical distance between these processors is a few meters, we speak of the connections as a bus, or even as individual wires. But when the distance grows, the connection becomes a network. It is most certainly a network if there are active devices such as switches, amplifiers, repeaters, and so on, which participate in the communication. The network operating system philosophy puts this entire network under the control of a single program. IBM's system network architecture (SNA) has evolved into a network operating system.

Network Architecture

The design for interoperation among component systems and subsystems is known as the Network Architecture. It includes overall plans and policy. Ideally, the network architecture should be formulated prior to implementation and periodically reviewed and updated to reflect changing conditions. In practice, network architecture documentation often lags implementation.

In the following subsections, we shall discuss the protocol reference model (PRM), network security architecture, and open system interconnection (OSI) PRM.

Protocol Reference Model

Protocols are sets of standards for data communications and component interoperation. A brief introduction is necessary here; further information is in Section 3.4. The descrip-

EH0255-0/87/0000/0277$01.00 © 1987 IEEE

tion and specification of objectives and means of interaction among the standards is known as a PRM. The PRM is not an implementation specification; it defines the function to be performed but does not prescribe how it should be accomplished.

The PRM is implemented in a set of protocols, sometimes called a protocol suite. It is possible to have a protocol suite without a PRM. In this case, the protocol suite defines the PRM at that point in time. It is generally felt that such an ad hoc definition might lack global perspective or long-term growth plans.

Network Security Architecture

Like the network architecture, the network security architecture constitutes an overall plan and policy for the security of the system. The NSA contains an enumeration of the security services and their inter-relationships. A network security architecture is much more complex than a single-system security architecture because of the number of security services that must be addressed.

The NSA relates to the network architecture by identifying how the security services map onto the layers of the architecture. The NSA is the fundamental statement of the ways in which the network is secure. The placement of a security service within the layered architecture is complex and controversial. It should be subject to the most careful intellectual scrutiny.

A network security model (NSM) is a more precise statement of the NSA. The NSM might be written in very carefully phrased natural language, perhaps even in a legal format. For greater precision, it would more likely be written in a programming language or a specification language. There may even be a formal security model, which is a provably correct program implementation of the NSM. The interested reader is referred to [LAND81a and b] for further information.

Open System Interconnection PRM

The OSI model is an international standard PRM [OSI84]. It is widely published, is well known, and has received considerable professional attention. It defines a seven layer architecture, including the functionally of each layer. Most public data networks are implemented according to its precepts.

Long after the development and widespread acceptance of the OSI PRM, the cognizant ISO committee has drafted an addendum containing a security architecture [OSI85]. This is the best known work extending a PRM to include security provisions.

This addendum "provides a general description of security services and related mechanisms, which may be provided by layers of the reference model; and defines the position within the reference model where the services and mechanisms may be provided." Being based on concepts of peer-level communication, the OSI-SA addresses peer entities as a natural abstraction. The descriptions of security services below are derived from [OSI85].

Security Services

The first step in developing a network security architecture is to identify the constituent parts. The OSI terms *entity, user-data,* and *protocol-data-unit (PDU)* are employed. Loosely paraphrased from OSI definitions, an entity is a logical or physical end-point participating in a data exchange. We are concerned with entities at various layers of the OSI model. A host computer is a network layer (4) entity and a process is a session layer (5) entity. User-data is the data transferred between peer entities on behalf of entities at the next higher protocol layer for which the peer entities are providing service. A PDU is a unit of data specified in the protocol for a specific layer consisting of protocol information and possibly user-data.

Several of the terms presented in this section are similar to the terms introduced in Section 2.3 because of the interrelationships mentioned between computer and network security.

Eight aspects of security services are presented in the following sections: identification, peer entity authentication, access control, data confidentiality, communications integrity, service availability, accountability, and non-repudiation.

Identification: Peer entities must be identified. Each access to a PDU must be mediated based on the entity's identity and what classes of information that entity is authorized to deal with.

Peer entity authentication: The network must ensure that a data exchange is established with the addressed peer entity (and not with an entity attempting a masquerade or a replay of a previous establishment). The network must assure that the data source is the one claimed.

Authentication generally follows identification, establishing the validity of the claimed identity providing protection against fraudulent transactions. Identification, authentication, and authorization information must be securely maintained by the network.

Access control: There must be a set of rules that are used by the network to determine whether a given entity can be permitted to gain access to specific network resources.

These rules may specify both *mandatory* and *discretionary access control* to effectively protect sensitive or classified information. No network entity shall be able to communicate classified information to any other network entity without each being accredited and authorized for information of that classification level. The network must provide protection against unauthorized use of resources accessible through the network.

Access control *labels* must be associated with PDUs and network entities. To control access to information transmitted and/or processed by the network, according to rules of mandatory security policy, it must be possible to mark every PDU with a label that reliably identifies its sensitivity level (e.g., classification).

The concepts of mandatory and discretionary access control relate to the similar terms in the *Orange Book*. Also, the term label relates to mandatory access control, which is first provided at the B1 level.

Data confidentiality: The network must provide protection of data from unauthorized disclosure. Confidentiality can have the following features: (1) *specific protocol layer* (Confidentiality of all user-data on a specific protocol layer connection. Note: depending on use and layer, it may not be appropriate to protect all data (e.g., expedited data or data in a connection request); (2) *datagram* (Confidentiality of all user-data in a single connectionless datagram); (3) *fields* (Confidentiality of selected fields within the user-data of a PDU); and (4) *traffic flow security* (Protection of the information that might be derived from observation of traffic flows).

Communications integrity: The network must ensure that information is accurately transmitted from source to destination (regardless of the number of intermittent connecting points). The network must be able to counter both equipment failure as well as actions by persons and processes not authorized to alter the data. Protocols that perform code or format conversion shall preserve the integrity of data and control information.

Communications integrity service must detect integrity violations and may take one of the following forms:

(1) Integrity of a single connectionless PDU. This takes the form of determination of whether a received PDU has been modified.
(2) Integrity of selected fields within a connectionless PDU. This takes the form of determination of whether the selected fields have been modified.
(3) Integrity of selected fields transferred over a connection. This takes the form of determination of whether the selected fields have been modified, inserted, deleted, or replayed.
(4) Integrity of all user-data on a protocol layer connection. This service detects any modification, insertion, deletion, or replay of any PDU of an entire PDU sequence (with no recovery attempted).
(5) The same as (4), but with recovery.

Service availability: The network must ensure some minimum specified continuing level of service. Availability services may include:

(1) The network shall detect conditions, which would degrade service below a pre-specified minimum, and would report such degradation to its operators.
(2) The network shall possess sufficient resiliency to provide continuing service in the event of equipment failure as well as actions by persons and processes not authorized to alter the data. The resiliency may be provided by redundancy, alternate facilities, or other means. The service provided may be degraded and/or may invoke priorities of service.
(3) The same as (1), but with automatic adaptation.

Accountability: Audit information must be selectively kept and protected so that actions affecting security can be traced to the responsible entity. The network must be able to record the occurrence of security relevant events in an audit log. Audit data must be protected from modification and unauthorized destruction to permit detection and after-the-fact investigations of security violations.

Non-Repudiation: In both commercial and military command and control environments, it is sometimes necessary to prove the validity of orders. The ability to prove to impartial third parties that a specific PDU was actually sent and received is necessary for the conduct of the organization's business. The network must provide either or both of the two following forms: (1) Proof of Origin of Data (The recipient of data is provided with proof or origin of data which will protect against any attempt by the sender to falsely deny sending the data or its contents) and (2) Proof of Delivery of Data (The sender is provided with proof of delivery of data such that the recipient cannot later deny receiving the data or its contents).

Architectural Issues

Service Selection, Placement, and Implementation

The network architect selects which security services to include in the network design. The preceding enumeration of services may be pared for a specific network application. Generally, however, this list should be considered a minimum. The architect must also decide how the services are to be provided within the layered architecture. Placement of a particular service within a specific layer has far reaching implications concerning the nature and extent of the service implementation. Since the services at one layer employ services at a lower layer, the exact nature of the functions provided in each layer affects the total service provided by the network.

Mechanisms

Security services may be implemented by a number of alternative mechanisms. Selection and specification of mechanisms are architectural issues to be specified following selection of service. The process must be iterative or combine top-down and bottom-up approaches. It is not very useful to specify services that cannot be delivered (absolutely or cost-effectively). The invention and perfection of new mechanisms may make it possible to offer new security services previously thought unavailable. The following representative list of implementation mechanisms is extracted from the OSI-SA:

- *Encipherment (encryption):* link encryption, end-to-end encryption, symmetric (secret key) encryption, asymmetric (public key) encryption, cryptographic check function, and key management

- *Digital signature*

- *Access control:* access control lists, passwords, capabilities lists, credentials, and labels

- *Data integrity:* checksums and sequencing and/or timestamping

- *Entity authentication:* passwords and cryptographic means

- *Traffic padding*

- *Routing control*

- *Notarization*

Reprints

Several papers are reprinted to provide specific information on data security in computer networks, network security overview, networks are systems, and observations on local area network security.

In his introduction, "Data Security in Computer Networks," to a special issue of *Computer* magazine, Subhash C. Kak touches all the bases of networks and security. Proprietary and public standard network architectures are mentioned. Encryption, the ubiquitous method for providing communications secrecy, is introduced next and put into the OSI layered architecture concept. The thought that encryption can be done in any of the several layers is introduced, but the more common link encryption in physical layer 1 and link layer 2 and host-to-host (or end-to-end) encryption in transport layer 4 is emphasized. Protection to the user increases along with the encryption layer; user-specific encryption in a higher layer is not neglected.

The combined design of encryption and protocols introduces protocol design as one of the differences between networks and centralized stand-alone computers; the physical

distribution of network components is the other major difference. A discussion of the design and application of the two major competitors in encryption. Private and public key follows. Private-key cryptosystems, also called symmetric and single-key, is the older technique. As the name indicates, private key employs a single key used as an input along with the plaintext data to produce cyphertext and as input with the *cyphertext* to produce *plaintext*. The key must be kept secret! Conversely, the public-key cryptosystem, also called asymmetric, employs two different keys, one of which is used in the first transformation and the other in the second. The public-key system is designed so that the order in which the keys are used in immaterial. One of the keys can be made public; the other must remain secret.

In his paper, "Network Security Overview," Stephen Walker provides an exhaustive analysis of the security implications of networking computers. His approach is to present a series of examples of increasing sophistication, which expose assumptions and required trust in the mechanisms involved. His target is to identify extensions required in the TCSEC and the implications of end-to-end encryption and to identify requirements for network security policy.

The context is an overall system view of networks. The focus is on how the various ways to protect data in networks affect how much and which portions of the network must be trusted. Since the treatment of networks is still evolving, some of the conclusions may bear further examination. For example, it is not universally agreed that "A complex system such as the defense data network, suitable protected with end-to-end encryption measures, needs no reference monitor, enforces no security policy relative to the hosts attached by E3 devices, and requires no criteria evaluation."

The first level model, untrusted hosts on an untrusted network, sets the baseline. The second level model, trusted hosts on an untrusted network, establishes that processes on different hosts operate at equal security levels, trusted hosts on untrusted networks must have the identical network system highest level, and untrusted hosts must operate at system high. The third level model, trusted hosts on trusted networks, requires that the network authenticate each host-to-host connection. In conjunction with this level, the role of cryptography is discussed, with several practical examples being presented. The fourth level model, process access control on a trusted network, discusses alternatives involving labels, E3, the extent of trust required in network components, and overhead.

In his thought-provoking paper, "Networks Are Systems, A Discussion Paper," John Rushby concentrates on system concepts, viewing networks as systems and suppressing implementation issues and details. This level of abstraction is most valuable in conceptualizing a network security architecture. The opening question, "Just what is a network, and what does it mean for a network to be 'secure'?" is closely followed by the the main theme that "The most significant development in modern system design is the trend towards *distributed* systems. . . ." His objective is to exploit the insights that will unify the issues of system and network security by integrating networking, inter-process communications, and operating system services. He argues that networks are systems implemented for the delivery of services such as data transmission and subscriber directory; security is a property of systems, and the security of a network cannot be considered in isolation from the overall system of which it is a component.

Rushby attributes the security implications of systems composed from sub-system to the facts that the components systems are active autonomous entities. Hence, the design objective in monolithic (stand-alone) computer systems of localizing a security kernel cannot be achieved; the assumptions of the Bell-LaPadula security model are invalid and its properties do not apply to distributed systems. State transition models are rejected because the state of the distributed system is not deterministic. An input/output security model is presented as an alternative.

Verification is a second theme of the paper. For our purposes, the goal of verification is to increase confidence that a running system is a correct implementation of its specifications, and that the specifications are correct! The validity of the specifications can only be established by extensive scrutiny and peer review. The implementation can be checked for conformance with these specifications by manual examination peer review (known as informal means) or by mathematical proofs of correctness (known as formal proofs). If the specifications and implementation are written in a language system which supports it, the formal proof can be conducted automatically. Note, however, that formal mathematical proofs are correct only to the extent that they survive peer review. The properties in the specification concerned with security issues are termed the *security model*. In the implementation the security model is contained in the *kernel* or *security-relevant* code. Formal verification cannot presently be carried all the way to running code. At some point formal verification gives way to informal.

Rushby sees two components of a security model. First, the system component contains assumptions about the system in which the implementation will be conducted. Second, the security component contains an interpretation of what security services are appropriate. Comparison of networked systems to monoliths indicates that both components require change.

He advocates a security model based on input/output behavior rather than states and postulates "domain isolation" and interface services as prime candidates for verification.

Marshall D. Abrams, in "Observations on Local Area Network Security," brings into focus whether local area networks (LANs), be they self-contained or interconnected with other local and long-distance networks, represent important security concerns. LANs are characterized by distributed access and control, which enhance some security services, such as availability, while presenting problems for others, such as confidentiality.

LAN technology makes all data available throughout the network. Network protocols, designed to deliver data to addressees, are not security mechanisms; passive acquisition and active modification of the data are possible. Access control between two sets of peer entities is discussed. At the network layer (3), control may be exercised between network interface units (data circuit-terminating equipment). In Data Terminal Equipment control may exist at any higher layer, starting with Transport in layer 4.

LAN media can be protected physically; messages can be separated into security groups by physical circuits, logical or physical channels, and encryption. This security protection decreases interoperability and requires increased trust requirements on the Network Interface Units. Encryption can be used to create logical channels and to protect sessions between peer entities. Encryption involves overhead for key distribution and management.

Data Security in Computer Networks

Guest Editor's Introduction

Subhash C. Kak
Louisiana State University

Reprinted from *Computer*, February 1983, pages 8-10. Copyright © 1983 by The Institute of Electrical and Electronics Engineers, Inc.

Data security in computer networks is becoming increasingly important owing to the expanding role of distributed computation, distributed databases, and telecommunication applications such as electronic mail and electronic funds transfer. There are several proprietary network architectures, including Arpanet, IBM's Systems Network Architecture, and Digital Equipment Corporation's Digital Network Architecture, as well as architectures for specialized applications. The International Standards Organization has proposed an architecture with the capability of universal networking as a first step toward protocol standardization. This model is called the reference model of open systems interconnection, or OSI (Figure 1).

In an OSI-based network, encryption can be done in any of the seven layers. The communication subnet consists of switches, multiplexers, or concentrators connect-ing transmission links. Since these links can be easily accessed, there might be a need for encryption on each data link. One can also choose to encrypt data above the network layer, i.e., the host-host layer, which constitutes an example of end-to-end encryption. The higher the layer at which encryption is performed, the greater security it provides to the user. However, data link encryption can mask traffic characteristics, and that by itself may be of interest to an unauthorized party; therefore, a combination of data link and end-to-end encryption techniques appears desirable.

When designing a computer network, several sources of data insecurity need to be considered. Prominent among these are spurious message injection, message reception by unauthorized receivers, transmission disruption, and rerouting data to fake nodes. To maintain security against these hazards, a combination of encryption algorithms on the data and appropriate protocols for message exchanges is utilized. These techniques also facilitate the handling of other problems in computer communication networks, such as key distribution, authentication, privacy, digital signatures, network mail, and transaction verification.

There are two approaches to encryption. The first requires use of a secret transformation (key) to encrypt data that is then sent over a public channel. At the receiving station, the same key is used to convert the enciphered data back into the original form (Figure 2). The transformation key is sent to the authorized receiver over a secure channel and is therefore unavailable to other parties. This method constitutes a private-key cryptosystem.

The second approach is based on the use of separate keys at the transmitting and receiving stations—keys that cannot, in practice, be obtained from each other. Each user keeps one of these two transformations secret and publishes the other, which can then be used to transform data intended for the user. Systems employing this approach are called public-key cryptosystems.

The Data Encryption Standard of the National Bureau of Standards was adopted for use in the US in 1977. This private-key cryptosystem is the dominant system in use today and has been implemented in hardware as well. The major reason for the popularity of the DES is its speed; it takes about 100 milliseconds to implement on an 8-bit microprocessor, and the time can be brought down to about 5 microseconds on a custom-built LSI device.[1] This should be compared with Rivest-Shamir-Adleman, or RSA, the most promising public-key system, where encryption of 500-bit numbers (a block size necessary for security) using available technology takes about a half second. This speed is unacceptable for many applications. Faster implementations of the RSA cipher are being developed, however. Implementation speed is not of critical importance in some applications, such as a key-management system, and public-key algorithms are already being used for this purpose.

Public-key systems have some intrinsic advantages over private-key systems. For example, the public-key method provides solutions to problems such as key distribution, secure communication over an insecure channel without exchanging keys, digital signatures, transaction verification, and key exchange. Solving these problems with private-key methods is either more cumbersome or impossible. To exploit the advantages of public-key systems, more efficient implementations are necessary so that encryption time can be brought down to acceptable levels. At the same time, better cryptanalytic algorithms may force the use of greater block sizes for a specified level of security. Significant progress on public-key systems in recent years has led to new encryption and protection algorithms and results in cryptanalysis, such as a subexponential algorithm to obtain discrete logarithms; new algorithms to distinguish prime numbers from composite numbers; and a polynomial time algorithm to break knapsack ciphers. Important new results have also been obtained in applications to digital signatures, design of secure protocols, and implementation schemes for electronic mail.

Security in networks differs in several aspects from security in a centralized computer system. This is because (1) the switching nodes and concentrators are distributed physically and cannot be considered secure, and (2) the network protocols, if not properly designed, can be used by an intruder to gain access to the network data or have it misrouted.

This special issue of *Computer* describes many developments in the above-mentioned aspects of data security in networks. In the first article, Selim G. Akl surveys digital signatures. A digital signature is a message-dependent quantity that can be computed only by the sender using private information, and it can be used for

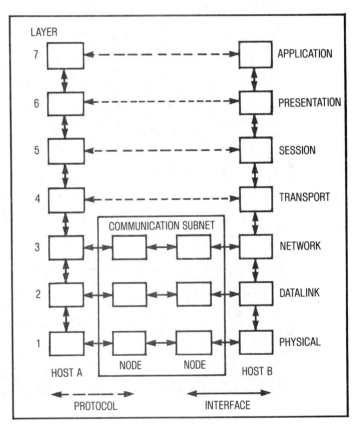

Figure 1. The International Standards Organization's open systems interconnection model for a network connection.

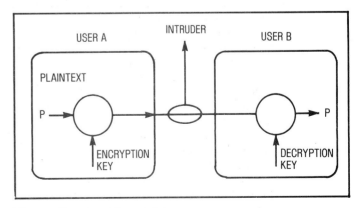

Figure 2. The encryption model.

certifying both the message and its sender. Signature schemes are of two types: those that do not need arbitrators to validate the signed message, and those that do. Both private-key and public-key encryption techniques can be used to generate digital signatures.

Since an unauthorized party can counterfeit public keys or use private keys that have been compromised, the use of public-key encryption alone does not ensure secrecy or a correct digital signature. The article by Dorothy E. Denning discusses the protection of public keys and signature keys. She shows that by using write-once devices such as optical disks, many security requirements for keys can be met.

A protocol is a set of rules to be followed by users to ensure orderly communication. Richard DeMillo and Michael Merritt describe several issues in protocol design and implementation. They argue that new cryptographic tools make it possible to design protocols for new kinds of transactions. The importance of arbitrators in the design of secure protocols is explained and some implementations are described.

An application of the RSA digital signature to electronic mail is described in the article by D. W. Davies. He suggests using a one-way function such as the Data Encryption Standard on the message followed by an RSA signature. He also considers encryption standards issues that will have to be resolved for electronic mail to flow across national borders. ■

Acknowledgments

I am grateful to Dennis Fife for providing considerable help in editing this issue. I would also like to thank the various reviewers who responded promptly and provided valuable feedback to the authors.

Reference

1. D. W. Davies, *Tutorial: The Security of Data in Networks*, IEEE Computer Society Press, Los Angeles, 1981.

Subhash C. Kak has been on the faculty of the Department of Electrical and Computer Engineering at Louisiana State University, Baton Rouge, since 1979. His research interests include data security, computer communication, information structures, and signal processing. In 1977, he was awarded a Science Academy Medal by the Indian National Science Academy. He holds one US patent, has authored more than 50 research papers, and was the convenor of the 1974 National Systems Conference held in New Delhi. Kak received his PhD in electrical engineering from the Indian Institute of Technology, Delhi, in 1970.

NETWORK SECURITY OVERVIEW

Stephen T. Walker

Trusted Information Systems, Inc.
P.O. Box 45, Glenwood, MD 21738

ABSTRACT

Much attention has recently been focused on developing trusted computer network evaluation criteria. Before attempting this however, a better understanding of the relationship between individual trusted computers and networks that link them is required. This paper provides an overall system view of the network and trusted and untrusted computers attached to it, and how various ways of protecting data on networks affect which portions of the network must be trusted and what security policy must be enforced. By examining several network models, it will become apparent where new or additional criteria need to be developed.

I. OVERVIEW

Following the successful introduction of DOD Trusted Computer System Evaluation Criteria (CSC-STD-001-83 [the Orange Book]), much attention has been focused on developing new guidelines for computer networks. The tendency has been, however, to commence developing criteria for various network components without comprehending their role in the Trusted Network Base (the equivalent of the Trusted Computing Base in the Evaluation Criteria). A preferred approach is to establish an overall system's view of the network and any trusted and untrusted computers attached to it, thereby determining which portions of the overall system are to be trusted and which security policy is to be enforced.

This paper provides a framework for understanding network security enforcement measures based upon enlargement of our understanding of individual trusted computers. It will examine how to extend access control mechanisms to stand-alone computers with network connections, and how the various ways to protect data in networks affect how much and which portions of the network must be trusted. Each approach and its implications on network security policy, access control mechanisms, and trusted components will be examined. Out of this will come the basis for network extensions to present Trusted Computer System Evaluation Criteria

and, where necessary, additional specfic trusted network criteria. A systematic identification of where new or additional criteria are needed will be presented, rather than the criteria themselves.

II. DEFINITIONS

Before beginning, definitions are provided for several terms used as common reference points, as follows:

SYSTEM - A collection of two or more COMPUTERS linked by a NETWORK.

COMPUTER - Any device capable of storing and processing information and, if linked by a NETWORK, of communicating with other COMPUTERS. Computers used in this manner are commonly referred to as HOSTS, as contrasted with those used in communications applications, called SWITCHES).

NETWORK - An entity composed of any of a number of communications media (e.g., wire, packet switched network) used to link COMPUTERS and transfer information.

(According to these definitions, computers perform information processing tasks; networks only transmit information between computers. Even networks containing computers for switching purposes do not process or store information, except as needed to perform their intended functions. The simplest model of a network is a set of individual wires; the most complex network model should be able to be described at some level of abstraction in terms of this simple model.)

TRUSTED SYSTEM (COMPUTER or NETWORK) - One which employs sufficient hardware and software integrity measures to allow its use for processing simultaneously a range of sensitivity or classified information from CSC-STD-001-83.

SECURITY POLICY - The set of laws, rules, and practices regulating how an organization manages, protects, and distributes sensitive information.

Reprinted from *Proceedings of the 1985 Symposium on Security and Privacy*, 1985, pages 62-76. Copyright © 1985 by The Institute of Electrical and Electronics Engineers, Inc.

TRUSTED COMPUTING BASE - All the protection mechanisms within a computer system (hardware, firmware, and software) which enforce a security policy on that computer.

TRUSTED NETWORK BASE - All the protection mechanisms within a network which enforce a security policy on that network.

DEDICATED SECURITY MODE - All system (Computer or Network) equipment used exclusively by that system, and all users cleared for and having a need-to-know for all information processed by the system.

SYSTEM HIGH - All equipment (Computer or Network) protected in accordance with requirements for the most classified information processed by the system. All users cleared to that level, but some not having a need-to-know for some of the information.

CONTROLLED - Some users having neither a security clearance nor a need-to-know for some information processed by the system, but separation of users and classified material not essentially under operating system control.

MULTILEVEL - Some users having neither a security clearance nor a need-to-know for some information processed by the system; separation of personnel and material accomplished by the operating system and associated system software.

III. BACKGROUND

Given a collection of trusted computers that meet some level of the Orange Book specifications, it is logical to want to connect them via some form of network to form a trusted system. When must this network be trusted? What portions of it form the trusted network base? What are the criteria against which this TNB must be evaluated? What role does encryption play in trusted networks? This paper will establish a context in which to answer to these questions.

Networks take many forms, from simple wires to complete packet switching systems, but increased complexity does not necessarily involve increased security requirements. A suitably protected wire, for example, the simplest trusted network, needs no reference monitor, enforces no security policy, and does not require evaluation against some form of Trusted Network Evaluation Criteria. A complex system such as the Defense Data Network (DDN), suitably protected with end- to-end encryption measures, also needs no reference monitor, enforces no security policy relative to the hosts attached by E3 devices, and requires no criteria evaluation.

When, then, do we need to be concerned about trusted network bases and network evaluation criteria?

To answer these questions we must explore a series of network security models, ranging from the simplest, untrusted networks linking untrusted hosts, to complex trusted networks making security policy decisions from process control information supplied by the hosts on the network. The following network security models will be considered:

Model 1. The familiar situation of untrusted hosts on an untrusted network.

Model 2. Trusted hosts on an untrusted network network.

Model 3. Trusted hosts on trusted networks, showing the use of various forms of encryption, trusted packet switches, and trusted local area networks (LANs).

Model 4. Sophisticated trusted networks employing detailed detailed process-to-process access control measures.

After this review, the relationship between trusted components of various network configurations will become evident, as well as when and how such components should be employed. To begin, though, we must review the basic elements of process-to-process communications in a trusted computer system and what happens to them when they include communications between hosts over a network.

We will first explore how such hosts communicate over a simple network consisting of individual wires between computers. Such a network has practical value, since many vendor-specific network products are basically implemented on host computers linked by individual communications lines.

In this analysis it is assumed that all resources of the hosts and communications lines are protected to a system high level (i.e., hosts are physically protected and communications lines link-encrypted). It is also assumed that network support software for the host operating systems are part of the Trusted Computing Base of that system, an important area of the Orange Book criteria that needs to be developed.

The next section describes the trusted operating system security model, as applied to several network security situations, citing requisite physical and procedural controls.

A. Trusted Operating System Security Policy Model

Figure 1 depicts a single trusted computer with two processes operating on behalf of specific users. All communication between processes is controlled by the (TCB), enforcing the Bell-LaPadula security model. In trusted computer

Figure 1. Process-to-Process Communications within a Trusted Computer System

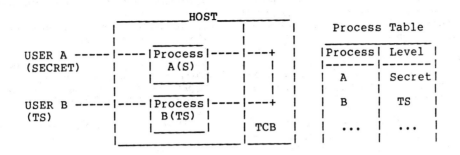

systems, each process has a security level (SL) equal to the present session level of the user (e.g., SL[A] = the present security clearance level of User A). For two processes to communicate, the following conditions, enforced by the (TCB), must be true:

Process A can read information from Process B only if:

$$L(A) \geq SL(B) \quad \text{(simple security rule)};$$

Process A can write information to Process B only if:

$$SL(A) \leq SL(B) \quad (* \text{ property}).$$

In a trusted system of at least B2 on the Trusted Computer System Evaluation Criteria, specific mechanisms provide security level labels for all active processes and objects. The TCB controls the access of all subjects to all objects, ensuring that the above rules are enforced. Within the TCB, a Process Table lists the security levels at which all active processes may operate. When one process attempts to connect with another, the TCB enforces these security rules.

B. Role of Reliable Communications

Process-to-process communication normally utilizes a two-way handshake protocol whereby the receiver acknowledges successful receipt of the information. In the case of a trusted host where security levels of the two processes are not equivalent, the acknowledgment could create an illegal path, allowing the potential transfer of sensitive information from a higher to a lower level. If Process A operates at the Secret level, and Process B at Top Secret, A can send information to B, but, according to the security rules stated above, Process B cannot respond without violating the * property.

Within a single host this is not particularly difficult to overcome. Process A can write information to Process B without explicit acknowledgment because the process-to-process mechanism is highly reliable. Once Process A has initiated the transfer it can proceed, confident that the transfer has occured even without acknowledgment. This

highly useful simplification is not possible, however when two processes are separated by a network with an inherently unreliable communications path.

In a network environment, if Process A on Host 1 (operating at Secret) were to attempt to send information to Process B on Host 2 (at Top Secret), Process A could not assume the transfer would be successful, given the unreliable nature of the network link. Sophisticated protocols employed between between processes on hosts ensure reliable transfer of information over inherently unreliable communications media, but require that acknowledgment of successful transfers be sent to the originator. Such an acknowledgment in the above case would constitute a violation of the * property. The implications of this restriction on trusted computers communicating over a network will be explored in the next section.

IV. Network Security Models

With these concepts in mind, it is now possible to examine a variety of network security models.

A. Level 1 Model - Untrusted Hosts on an Untrusted Network

The simplest model, Level 1, involves untrusted hosts operating in Dedicated or System High Mode on an untrusted network. While typical of systems in use today and accepted in some contexts, its inability to handle multiple levels of classified or sensitive data severely limits its utility. Since there are no trusted components anywhere in the system, there is no need for a trusted network base or for evaluation criteria.

B. Level 2 Model - Trusted Hosts on an Untrusted Network

When a trusted computer system, as discussed in Figure 1, is introduced to our simple wire link network, it becomes a Level 2 model (Figure 2). The essential feature of this is that normal access control mechanisms in a B2 or higher trusted computer system are extended beyond protecting local process-to-process communications to handle process-to-process links across the network.

Figure 2. Level 2 Network Security Model
(Both hosts have a TCB evaluated at B2 or greater)

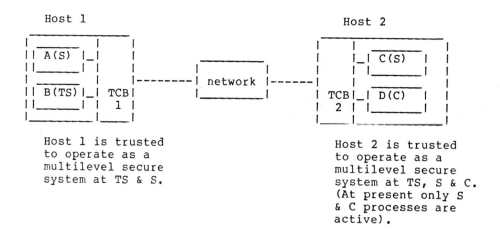

Host 1 is trusted
to operate as a
multilevel secure
system at TS & S.

Host 2 is trusted
to operate as a
multilevel secure
system at TS, S & C.
(At present only S
& C processes are
active).

Operating System Process Tables:

Host 1

Processes	Hosts
A at level S	2 at levels TS-C
B at level TS	...
...	

Host 2

Processes	Hosts
C at level S	1 at TS & S
D at level C	...
...	

Note 1: TCB1 and TCB2 must have individual
authentication codes to ensure against
spoofing from other hosts on the network.

Note 2: Processes on different hosts (or oper-
ting systems that support them) may employ
cryptographic checksums on data messages
before sending them to the host. These
checksums are used to ensure against data
modification during transit.

In addition to the processes which it directly
controls, the TCB within each computer now must be
aware of other hosts on the network and their
security levels. The active process table in each
computer is augmented with a list of hosts on the
network. Because host-security level information
is very stable, updates of this host security table
are easily accomplished by periodic manual table
updates by the Security Officer.

A number of examples illustrate the basic
access control checking flow of this model. When
Process A, operating at SECRET level, attempts to
communicate with Process C, also at Secret, TCB1
receives the request and checks to be sure that A
is within the range level of Host 2. If not, the
request is denied. If within, TCB1 passes the
identity and security level of A to TCB2, which
determines if the level of A equals that of C. If
it does, the connection is extended to the two
processes. If not, TCB2 informs TCB1 that the
connection is invalid.

As illustrated, TCB2 determines whether the
security level of Process A equals that of Process
C. This restriction of the Bell-LaPadula policy
used on a single operating system is critical
because the network is unreliable (subject to
outages, partitioning, lost messages, etc.).
Information sent from Process A to Process C must
be acknowledged by Process C to assure A that it
was received. If the Bell-LaPadula policy model
governed such connections, acknowledgments from
higher levels would constitute security violations.
It is imperative that the two processes on different hosts operate at equal security levels.

The above restriction is not a serious limitation, for if a process operating at Secret wished
to contact one at Top Secret on a separate host, it
could connect across the network to a Secret
process on the remote host, transmitting the information with full acknowledgments. Once received,
the Secret process could pass the information to
the Top Secret process without acknowledgment, as
described in Figure 1.

In a second case, Process B operating at Top Secret attempts to connect with C at Secret. TCB1 determines whether or not the level of Process B is within the range of Host 2. Since it is not, TCB1 immediately rejects the request.

In the third case, when Process A operating at Secret attempts to connect with D at Confidential, TCB1 once again checks to see if the level of Process A is within the range of Host 2. If so, TCB1 passes the identity of Process A and its security level to TCB2, which checks to determine whether the level of A equals the level of D. It is not, so TCB2 informs TCB1 that the connection is invalid.

The Level 2 model represents the simplest structure involving trusted computers, patterned after the process-to-process communications model presently in use on many networks. This simplicity does not require (or permit) host operating systems to be aware of other processes using the network. A more complex model would list foreign processes (existing on remote hosts) in a local host's processor table, allowing the local host to base its access decisions on local information, and eliminating the need to query the remote host. Difficult problems remain, however, in maintaining trusted databases for such processes, because in contrast to the stability of host security levels, individual process security levels change dynami-

Figure 3. Level 2 Network Security Model with an Untrusted Host

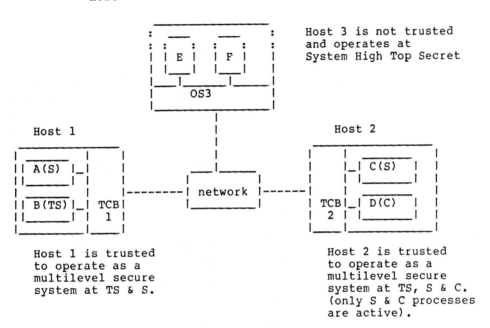

Host 3 is not trusted and operates at System High Top Secret

Host 1 is trusted to operate as a multilevel secure system at TS & S.

Host 2 is trusted to operate as a multilevel secure system at TS, S & C. (only S & C processes are active).

Operating System Process Tables:

Host 1

Processes	Hosts
A at level S	2 at levels TS&C
B at level TS	3 at level TS
...	...

Host 2

Processes	Hosts
C at level S	1 at TS & S
D at level C	3 at TS
...	...

Host 3 (Since this host is not trusted, its process table does not contain any security level information.)

Processes	Hosts
E	1
F	2
...	...

289

cally. Even if these techniques were employed, the remote host must make the final security level check.

Figure 2 assumes that both operating systems are of the same TCB class, and can trust each other's access control mechanisms. The real world will always contain systems that either are not trusted or have different TCB class operating systems. Any network security model must deal with this situation.

Figure 3, an augmented version of Figure 2, shows an untrusted host operating at a System High Top Secret level attached to the network (with the operating system labeled OS3 rather than TCB3). The same caveats associated with Figure 2 apply here. (Note the addition of Host 3 at a single security level to the host tables in 1 and 2. The Process Table in Host 3 knows about Hosts 1 and 2, communicating with them at the Top Secret level; however, it contains no security label information, because such information cannot be trusted to be accurate or reliable.) As shown below, Hosts 1 and 2 accept connections from 3, recognizing its operation in a System High Top Secret mode; all process-to-process communications must therefore be at the Top Secret level.

A number of additional cases are illustrated by the configuration in Figure 3. The first is when Process E, operating at Top Secret, requests a connection with Process B, also operating at Top Secret. OS3 (not trusted and without a security level in its Process-Host tables) establishes the connection with TCB, which checks to determine whether the security level of Process B equals the System High level of Host 3. If it is, the connection is made to B; if not, the TCB rejects the connection.

In the next case, Process A, at Secret level, requests a connection with Process F on Host 3. TCB1 determines whether the level of Process A equals the System High level of Host 3. As it does not, the TCB rejects the connection.

A last case involves Process E on Host 3 attempting to connect with Process D on Host 2. OS3 initiates a connection with the TCB, checking to determine if the security level of D equals the System High level of Host 3. It does not. and the TCB rejects the connection.

At this point we have described a network of trusted and untrusted computers communicating in useful, practical ways, with the network having no trusted components and enforcing no security policy or access control mechanisms. The next step is to understand the limitations of such a network. Figures 2 and 3 consist of host computers physically protected to a system high level (Top Secret is assumed in both cases). Processes for Host 2 currently run at the Secret and Confidential levels, but the computer itself must be operated in a Top Secret system high environment. Host 3 in Figure 3, an untrusted host, also operates at Top Secret System High.

The relationship between the security levels at which hosts can operate on this simple network is shown in Figure 4. The network itself and all computers attached to it must be physically protected to the same system high level. Untrusted

Figure 4. Trusted and Untrusted Computers on an Untrusted System High Network

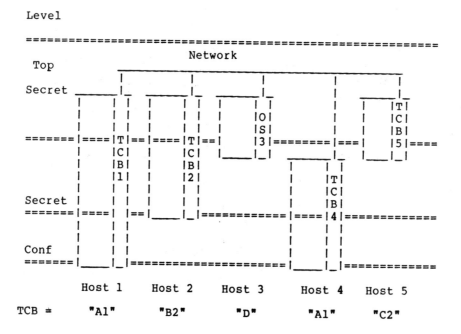

hosts can only operate at that level, but trusted computers may operate over a range with a maximum at the network system high, depending upon the degree of trust in the system. In Figure 4, for example, Host 1 is trusted to the "A1" level, and processes operate over the range Top Secret to Confidential.

Host 2 is trusted to the "B2" level, operating with processes at either Top Secret or Secret. Host 3 is untrusted and processes operate only at Top Secret. Host 4 operates processes over the range Secret and Confidential over the Top Secret System High Network. Since it may receive a Top Secret message from an untrusted host, 4 must operate over the full range, Top Secret to Confidential, and be trusted to the A1 level. Host 5 must operate only at Top Secret because it is trusted only to the C2 level, providing only discretionary access controls and no mandatory labeling.

Trusted hosts in an untrusted network must have the highest point of their operating ranges at the same network system high level, since they can receive system high messages from untrusted hosts. Similarly, since untrusted hosts cannot protect security labels of information, they must operate only at system high.

Note: The operating ranges shown in Figure 4 are arbitrary selections. In an actual systems, the Designated Approving Authority or System Security Officer designates the degree of trust for each situation.

C. Level 3 Model - Trusted Hosts on Trusted Networks

The network depicted in Figure 4 is still a simple wire connecting trusted and untrusted computers. As long as it is physically protected from external attack, it need not be trusted. Local area networks (LAN) and wide area networks (such as DDN), however, involve more sophistication.

Figure 5 depicts a Level 3 network model derived from Figure 3. The Operating System Process Table and all the TCB checks of the Level 2 Model are unchanged, but a Network Access Control Table has been added.

In the Level 2 Model, the untrusted network (our simple wire) established any connection requested by the hosts. In Level 3, the network authenticates each connection prior to establishing it. These checks can be performed on a host-by-host basis (the Level 3 model), or on a process-by-process basis (Level 4, discussed later).

Before proceeding, however, it is necessary to understand various methods of protecting information on a communications network and performing the network access control measures shown in Figure 5.

Figure 5. Network Access Checking - A Level 3 Model

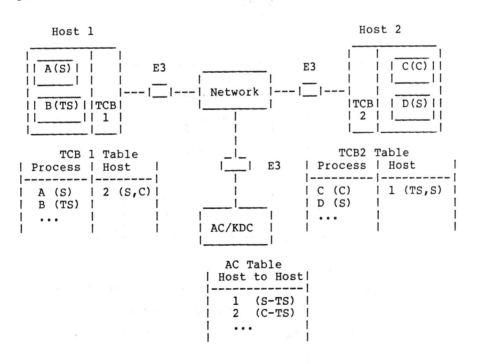

291

1. Role of Cryptography

The principle means of protecting data from compromise or modification in a communications network such as DDN, is by end-to-end encryption (E3). With E3, the data portion of the message is encrypted prior to transmission and remains encrypted until delivered, while the address portion of the message remains in the clear. E3 usually provides a means of operating multiple communities of interest, separated cryptographically from each other, and in some cases operating at a higher security level than the network itself.

a. IPLI

The simplest form of E3, the Internet Private Line Interface (IPLI), is illustrated in Figure 6. The IPLI and its associated cryptographic device are positioned between the host computer and the network. Groups of IPLIs form communities of interest in which all cryptographic devices share a common key.

IPLIs come in two sections: a Red or plaintext side, connected to the host computer and cryptographic device, and a Black or ciphertext side, connected between the cryptographic device and the network. When the host requests a connection across the network, the Red side first determines the validity of the destination by checking the address in its host table. (This is the host-to-host access control mechanism required in the Level 3 Model.) If valid, the Red side passes the data portion to the KG and passes the table index number for the destination host over a special low bandwidth channel which bypasses the cryptographic device.

The Black side then constructs a new message header, using the index entry listed in its host table. When the encrypted data is received from the cryptographic device, the Black side assembles a message from the new header and the encrypted text, and sends it to the network. At the destination, the process is reversed. It should be noted that

encryption provides data protection at all times, except during a brief period in the Red side of the IPLI. The address portion of the original message remains in the clear within the network switches, ensuring proper message routing.

The IPLI provides a means of isolating communities of interest at a specific sensitivity level, even though the network itself may operate at a lower level (even unclassified). Untrusted hosts connected via commonly keyed IPLIs must operate at a specific system high security level.

b. E3 with Access Control and Remote Key Distribution.

IPLIs provide a valuable means of connecting communities to a common network. Their disadvantages, however, are that assignments to communities of interest are static and cryptographic keys must be manually distributed and loaded at each site. In addition, hosts in a particular community cannot communicate with hosts outside that community. In effect, each has its own virtual network operating in System High or Dedicated Mode.

To overcome these drawbacks, efforts have been underway for some time to build E3 systems with remote key distribution techniques. These would allow host-to-host, process-to-process, or per connection individualized keying. A separate Access Controller and Key Distribution Center (KDC) with redundant backup would be attached to the network, as shown in Figure 7. The E3 boxes contain large numbers of separate keys for use on a host or process pair basis.

In the case of the host pair, when A attempts to connect with B, the first E3 box checks its tables to see if a key for such a connection exists. If so, the connection proceeds as in the IPLI case. If not, the E3 box establishes a connection with the Access Controller, and identifies the source and destination hosts for the requested connection. The Access Controller

Figure 6. Internet Private Line Interface (IPLI)

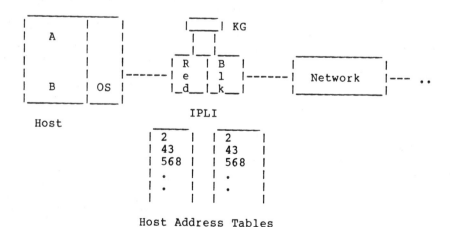

Host Address Tables

Figure 7. E3 with Remote Key Distribution

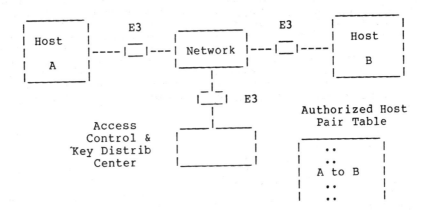

mediates a decision based upon security-relevant authorization data in its Authorized Host Pair Table. If authorized, the KDC generates a new unique key for use by these hosts in their communications. This is passed to both hosts' E3 boxes, encrypted in their individual master keys. Once this host pair key is in place, communication between hosts can proceed as before.

This version of E3 protection has many advantages over the IPLI, for it can operate dynamically, creating new host pair authorizations merely by making or changing an entry in the Authorized Host Pair Table. This works equally well with trusted or untrusted hosts. The latter, operating at the same system high security level, will have appropriate entries in the Authorized Host Pair Table; untrusted hosts at different security levels, not authorized to communicate, will be effectively prohibited by the E3 mechanisms. Authorized trusted hosts will be listed in the Table, and control the security levels of their individual links by utilizing access control mechanisms, as in the examples which follow.

c. More Complex E3 Mechanisms

Host pair connectivity thus described provides dynamic authorization of communities of interest consistent with trusted system access control mechanisms. Nevertheless, a need frequently arises for more sophisticated E3 mechanisms allowing process-to-process or per connection access control. The basic structure remains as in Figure 5, but when A attempts to connect with B, it must identify the source and destination of its message. The access control checking mechanism is now much more complex because the Authorized Host Pair Table at this point becomes an "Authorized Process Pair Table." Update and synchronization problems associated with identifying remote processes are inherent with this type of access checking. These and other factors associated with such mechanisms will be examined in detail later.

d. Message Authentication Checks

End-to-end encryption provides protection against data disclosure and modification while in transit over an untrusted network. If the network is installed in a physically protected environment, as LANS frequently are, data disclosure is not a problem and simpler forms of protection against modification are possible. The Message Authentication Check (MAC) involves the application of an unforgable tag to a block of information.

In such a network, the originator calculates the tag based on the contents of the information, and appends the tag to the information before sending it through an untrusted, but protected, communications medium. The recipient then repeats the tag calculation and compares it with the originator's tag. If the two are equivalent, the recipient can have a high degree of confidence that the information was not modified during transmission. The tag calculation is usually based on a cryptographic function, with a secret key known only to the originator and recipient. Typically, the information is passed through the encryption algorithm and after the block of information has been processed, the residual value is usually appended to the information being sent. Note: this technique is an integrity check; it does not protect information from being read while in transit.

This procedure is being used on a number of systems to ensure the integrity of sensitive information. The SACDIN program will employ the National Bureau of Standards Data Encryption Standard (DES) algorithm to calculate integrity checks on its messages before transmission to the IPLI devices on the DDN. The Intelligence Community is using a similar technique to protect data stored on a large mainframe computer in the RECON system.

The American National Standards Committee on Financial Services, X9, has published a Financial Institution Message Authentication Standard, X9.9, dated April 13, 1982, defining a process for the computation, transmission, and validation of a Message Authentication Code (MAC) using DES. The standard describes the message authentication process and issues related to key management. This standard is being widely adopted in the financial community and implementations of it on the input side of LAN interfaces may provide reasonable means of ensuring the integrity of messages passing through a LAN.

2. End-to-End Encryption Examples in an Internet Environment

The WWMCCS Information System (WIS) is an example of end-to-end encryption in an internetwork environment (Figure 8). LANs will be installed at each WIS site to connect existing Honeywell 6000 computers, other functional module computers, and workstations. Each LAN will have a gateway connection to other LANs via the WWMCCS Intercomputer Network (WIN). As presently configured, the WIN is a System High net with only WWMCCS H6000 hosts attached. In the future, some functional module computers will be trusted, allowing limited multi-level security. Gradually the untrusted hosts will be phased out and full multi-level secure use will be possible.

Figure 8 shows Message Authentication Checks applied at the Internet Protocol layer at each interface to the WIS LAN. A MAC must be calculated for each message entering the LAN, either in trusted host software or in a special interface box on the host or LAN. The Interface with the WIN gateway must be a special back-to-back MAC (probably using different encryption keys) to authenticate messages as they leave the LAN. A new MAC will be applied as the message enters the gateway and WIN. At the receiving site, a similar back-to-back MAC authenticates incoming messages and applies a new local MAC as it enters Site B's LAN.

Figure 8. WIS LANs and WIN with Message Authentication Checks.

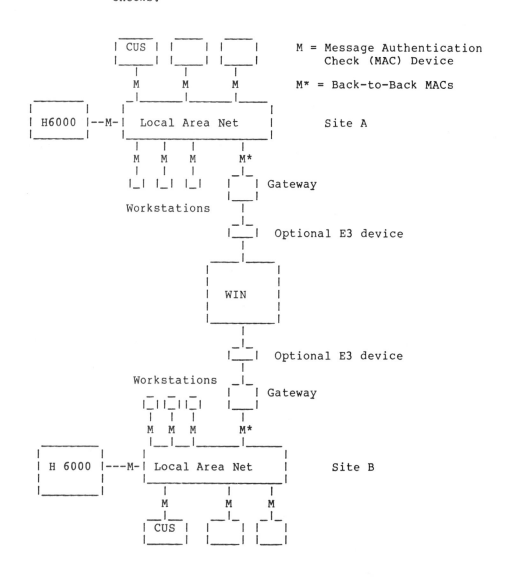

a. WIS LANs Operating at Different Security Levels

In the above discussion, all the LANs operated at the same System High security level. This configuration does not require any special trusted network components; neither the LANs nor WIN enforce a network security policy.

Not all WWMCCS sites, however, will want to operate at the same security level. As systems grow in complexity and take on new functions, some will want to operate at different compartment levels. Once this happens, the system high level of the LANs will change and the simple model shown in Figure 4 (as extended through the use of MACs) will no longer apply. Processes operating at a Secret level on a trusted host connected to a Top Secret Compartment A LAN will still wish to to communicate with processes running at the same Secret level on a Top Secret Compartment B LAN.

The Level 2 network model did not require any explicit network security policy nor enforcement mechanisms. Now, however, we need a network access control mechanism, a defined network security policy, and policy enforcement mechanisms. This new situation, with System High networks and trusted and untrusted hosts at different levels, is depicted in Figure 9.

For the sake of simplicity, the two LANs are shown with only two hosts each, one running at both TS Compartmented and Secret and the other only at Secret. (It should be recalled that the host running at Secret must be capable of running at both Top Secret Compartmented and Secret, so that conditions described in Figure 4 may apply.) Processes at the TS Compartmented levels on the two LAN's may not communicate, as that would violate the separation of compartments. It should be possible (and will be expected), however, that processes running only at Secret on Hosts 2 and 3 should be able to communicate.

To achieve this level of operation, some form of network access control will be necessary to determine which processes on specific hosts may communicate. The IPLI, with its static host connection tables, is not sufficient, but the dynamic access checking system should provide the needed control. Figure 10 depicts the two LANs in Figure 9 connected over the WIN with such E3 devices. The access controller/key distribution center function provides the crucial network access control mechanism, enforcing connections across LANs operating at different Network System High Levels.

Assuming that Hosts 2 and 3 are operating only at the Secret level and that this is known to the access controller, an attempt by a process on Host 2 to connect to a process on Host 3 will be allowed, since both are limited to the same level. If the access controller could communicate with Host 1 in a trusted manner, this same procedure would allow a process running at Secret in Host 1 to communicate with a similar Secret process on Host 3. Processes running at each network system high, however, could not communicate, since the network system high levels are not equivalent.

b. Hosts at Different Security Levels on the Same LAN

The first WIS example (Figure 8) is a set of LANs with trusted and untrusted hosts operating at the same Network System High level. Trusted hosts can operate over a range from Network System High down to some lower level of sensitivity, depending upon their level of trust. Hosts trusted to "A1", for example, might range from Top Secret to Confidential; hosts trusted to "B2", from Top Secret to Secret. This network model has the significant advantage of having no explicit network security policy and, therefore, no Network Reference Monitor or Trusted Network Base. The only requirement is a trusted path across the physically protected LAN, provided by Message Authentication Checks. All security policy enforcement is performed by the hosts themselves.

Figure 9. Two LANs at Different System High Levels

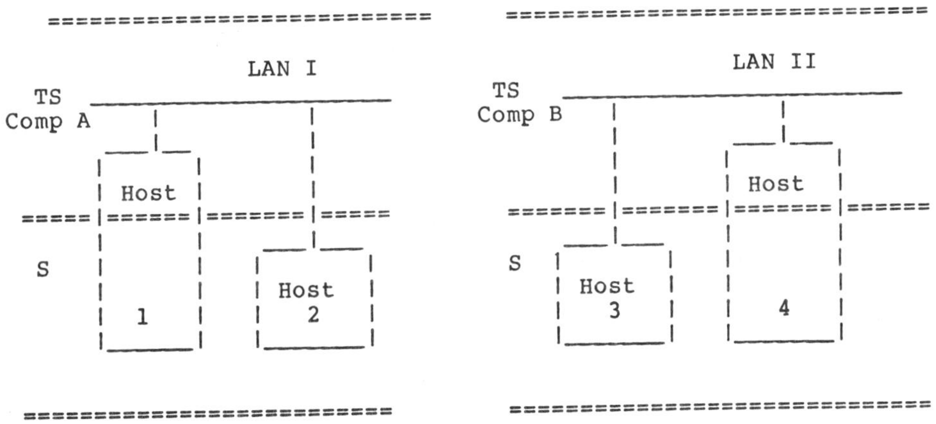

295

Figure 10. Two WIS LANs at Different System High Levels
Connected with End-to-End Encryption Devices.

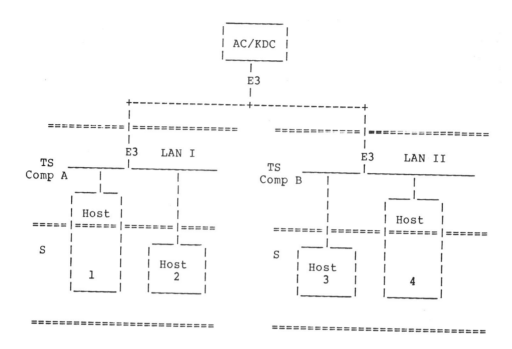

The second example, Figure 10, shows two or more such LAN environments operating at different Network System High levels, connected via a wide area network such as the WIN. In this case, a network security policy is required to determine if the processes wishing to communicate are on equivalent levels. Mediation at the network level is required because the two Network System High levels are not comparable. A network policy enforcement mechanism is required to mediate requests between these LANs. The E3 Access Control mechanism performs the mediation between processes on LANs operating at different Network System High levels. The E3 system thus becomes the Network Reference Monitor or Trusted Network Base.

Other situations will arise, however, for which neither of these network models will be sufficient. In both previous cases, all untrusted hosts were required to operate at the Network System High level. To allow untrusted hosts to operate at less than the network system high, some form of trusted access control mechanism will be necessary within the LAN itself. The LAN must mediate access between security levels of the computers on the network, since they can no longer reliably determine the level at which other computers are operating.

One way this can be achieved is by installing E3 devices on the LAN. Under these circumstances, trusted and untrusted hosts operating at any security level can be attached to the LAN. The level(s) at which hosts operate is known to the E3 Access Controller which constitutes th Trusted Network Base (TNB). Attempts to communicate between processes on different hosts must be

mediated by the TNB. When a process requests a connection with a process on another host, the Access Controller checks to be sure the levels of the two are equivalent. If they are, the AC distributes the key to each E3 device, allowing the connection to be established.

Depending upon the sophistication of the AC, this check can be used to enforce discretionary (need-to-know) access controls, as well as mandatory controls. The former, however, using access control lists, will be difficult to maintain on a process-by-process basis across the network. A distinct advantage of this approach is that no portion of the LAN itself need be trusted.

c. Inter Service/Agency AMPE

Another example of a Level 3 system is the Inter Service/Agency AMPE, which can use either the IPLI (Figure 11) or the more sophisticated E3 capability (Figure 7). The hosts in AMPE have A1 class TCBs, and must be able to trust the integrity of security labels sent over the network; therefore, the portion of the E3 device handling data in the clear must also be developed to the same A1 level standard.

As the IPLI is currently not built to that level, an IPLI-based solution would require re-implementation of the Red side of the IPLI to the A1 level, use of a separate IPLI for each level, or use of a MAC integrity check by the trusted host prior to transmission to the IPLI. Note that if the MAC integrity measures were in place, AMPE could utilize a dedicated DDN segment without requiring IPLIs.

Using the IPLI solution, process-to-process access control mechanisms within the AMPE hosts provide the primary check of information flow between AMPE's. The host-to-host access tables of the IPLI ensure that the AMPE's have their own private subnetwork on the DDN. These tables are static in that they do not change more than on a day-to-day basis. This solution, with the red side integrity check, is a possible networking architecture for AMPE on the DDN.

Use of the more sophisticated E3 capability with AMPR is shown in Figure 7. The method by which this configuration operates has already been described. In this case, host-to-host access control is dynamic, as opposed to utilizing the static tables contained in the IPLI.

Figure 11. I S/A AMPE System with IPLIs - Example of Level 2 Model

AMPE Hosts are trusted to the A1 level.

AMPE Hosts must place integrity check on messages before passing to the IPLIs.

IPLIs have built-in static host access tables.

d. Level 4 Model - Process Access Control on a Trusted Network

In the Level 1 model, there was essentially no host or network access control. In Level 2, host access control was provided by the trusted computting base within the hosts, on a process-by-process basis. Network access control was still not required.

In the Level 3 model, network access control could be provided by several means. In the IPLI case, it was confined to the IPLI static host access tables. The more sophisticated E3 access checking in Figure 7 provides additional flexibility in host-to-host communication control by providing a dynamic host-to-host access control table.

Both the Level 2 or Level 3 network models require that labels associated with data being transferred across the network be protected from modification. This imposes additional restraints on the type of network structure suitable for this model. In each case, either critical components of the network must be trusted not to modify label information, or some form of integrity check must be applied to the information before it enters the network.

If E3 is not used on the network, all portions of the network must be trusted (easily achieved with our simple wires in the Level 3 case, requiring a trusted packet switch or equivalent in the Level 3 case). If an IPLI or more sophisticated E3 structure is used, the portions of these devices able to access data in the clear (up to the point of encryption and after decryption) must be trusted not to modify the text data stream. If the network components cannot be trusted (definitely the case with today's dedicated and system high networks, and also with present versions of the IPLI), the trusted host may apply a MAC to the message before entrusting it to the network or IPLI. The destination host would recalculate this checksum upon receipt and verify that the contents were not modified.

One further network model (Level 4) will be explored, involving even more extensive access checking within the network itself. Here the network is involved in actual process-to-process access control checking, as shown in Figure 12.

When Process A wishes to establish a connection with Process D, A notifies TCB1, which checks to see if it allowed, and then attempts to establish a connection with TCB2, just as in Figure 4. The E3 device intercepts this connection request and, recognizing that no such connection exists, establishes an interim connection with the AC/KDC. AC then refers to its process-to-process table, which lists individual processes and the levels at which they operate on individual hosts.

Figure 12.   Process-to-Process Network Access Checking - An
Example of a Level 4 Model

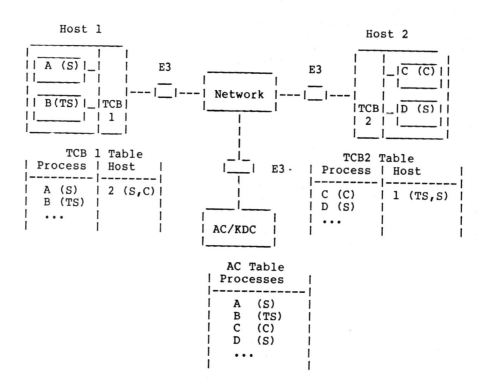

Assuming that the connection is valid, the AC instructs the KDC to issue a key to the E3 devices involved, and the connection from TCB1 to TCB2 proceeds. TCB2 must now perform its own check to ensure that Process D is actually operating at the proper security level to allow the connection. Upon successful completion of this final check, the actual connection from Process A to Process D is completed.

As described above, Level 4 systems involve process-to-process access control within host systems themselves and also within the network. Considerable duplication of effort exists as these hosts and networks perform the checking required to allow specific processes to communicate. A process-to-process check by the network E3 device is not a complete check in itself. The process-to-process access control tables in the AC cannot be as accurate as those within the individua' hosts. TCB2 is still required to check the leve. at which Process D currently operates. It is entirely possible that even though Process D may log in at the Secret level (and does so 90% of the time), in a particular instance that process may operate only at Confidential, in which case the connection cannot be allowed.

V. CONCLUSIONS

This paper has presented a series of network models with increasing levels of sophistication and demands for trusted network components. The analysis used here is vital to understanding when network components must be trusted and the type of security policy the trusted components must enforce, and leads to a number of important conclusions.

A. Orange Book Extensions

The discussion of the Level 2 model indicated that even when no network components require trust, that portion of the host operating system controlling process-to-process communications across the network must be included in the Trusted Computing Base. Today's version of the Orange Book does not explicitly deal with network-related software. These additions must be made before serious consideration is given to developing trusted network evaluation criteria; indeed, as the Level 2 model shows, if host TCBs are extended to include network drivers, many valuable network configurations can be achieved without requiring any further trusted components.

B. Implications of E3

In regard to the Level 3 model, it was indicated that if E3 is used (in either the IPLI or more sophisticated version), trusted network configurations can be achieved without requiring any additional trusted network components. The E3 capability provides the network access control mechanisms (static in the IPLI case; dynamic in the E3). These mechanisms can enforce access control to untrusted hosts operating at a single level and to trusted hosts, as long as the extensions to their TCBs discussed above have been implemented.

C. Network Security Policy

As opposed to the relatively complex security policy enforced on trusted computer systems, (allowing read-down and write-up), the analysis of networks from the process-to-process communications view indicates that the policy which must be enforced across the network is one where only processes operating at equivalent sensitivity levels can communicate. This simplification is forced by the need for two-way communication with acknowledgments across an unreliable medium. As a result of this simplification, the policy enforcement carried out by IPLIs, E3 devices, or trusted packet switches is inherently much simpler than that of a trusted computer system.

Networks are Systems

A Discussion Paper

John Rushby
Computer Science Laboratory
SRI International

26 June 1986

1. Preamble

The DoD Computer Security Center's Invitational Workshop on Computer Network Security is concerned with extension of the Criteria in the Center's "Orange Book" [4] to cover the case of computer networks. My assignment was to prepare a position paper on the role of (Formal) Verification in ensuring network security – but before I could address the issue of verification, I found I had first to consider the notion of "network": just what *is* a network, and what does it mean for a network to be "secure"?

2. Networks

2.1. What Sort of Networks should be considered?

First, we must decide how general a notion of "network" we wish to consider. The letter of invitation indicates that the goal is the production of "Trusted Network Evaluation Criteria for long-haul, packet switched networks similar to the Arpanet or DDN". This restricted focus is, in my view, shortsighted, undesirable, and unnecessary.

The most significant development in modern systems design is the trend towards *distributed* systems; that is, systems composed of smaller systems which communicate over some medium in order to cooperate towards the achievement of a common goal. This trend is especially true in the case of military systems, where C^3I and message systems – which are nothing if not distributed systems – play such a significant, and growing, role. But quite aside from systems whose very function involves communications and networking, modern hardware developments make it inevitable that

Reprinted from *Proceedings of the Department of Defense Computer Security Center Invitational Workshop on Network Security*, 1985, pages 7-24–7-38.

many general and special purpose systems – even systems that fit in a single box – will be structured internally as multi-processor systems communicating over a private bus or LAN.

To ignore these developments in our consideration of network security is to risk the production of Network Evaluation Criteria whose application is restricted to a limited, and declining, section of the market. More importantly, by failing to comprehend these new developments in systems design, we will fail to influence their course and will have to struggle, belatedly, for a proper consideration of their security implications.

Orthogonal to the use of *physical* networks to build distributed systems has been the development of system *concepts* based on the idea of communicating processes. This approach, which regards systems as composed of self-contained, autonomous processes connected by ideal communications channels, seems likely to dominate future language and system design – its influence can already be seen in languages such as CSP, Gypsy, and NIL [8] (and even, to a limited extent, in Ada) and in operating systems such as Thoth [3] and Accent [10]. Using this approach, the decision whether the processes constituting a design should be supported on separate machines connected by physical communications lines, or should be time-shared on a single processor, is relegated to an implementation issue.

Thus, a second reason for considering a broad interpretation of the notion of "network" is the need for Security Evaluation Criteria not only to remain abreast of the best modern approaches to system design, but to exploit the insights which they confer. One of the great merits of the approach based on communicating processes, and a reason for its popularity, lies in the opportunity it provides for integrating networking, inter-process communication, and operating system services. Thus, issues which had formerly seemed quite dissimilar have now been unified. I believe we could expect a similar benefit in the case of security: a unification of the issues of system and network security. Conversely, if we follow the narrow approach, there is a danger that systems based on communicating processes and implemented on a network will fall outside the scope of the Network Evaluation Criteria, while those implemented on a single processor will likewise fall outside the rather narrow scope of the Orange Book!

2.2. What *is* a Network?

If we decide to take a broad view of the sort of networks that should be considered for security evaluation, then we need to agree on what constitutes a network. The definition proposed in letter of invitation states:

> "A network is an entity composed of a communications medium and those parts of all devices attached to that medium whose responsibility is facilitating, controlling, monitoring, or otherwise participating in the transfer of information across the medium. Such devices may include, but are not limited to, packet switches, host front ends, access controllers, monitoring centers, and hosts."

This definition concentrates on the physical characteristics of networks and views them primarily as agents for data transmission. This view is entirely appropriate for networks such as the Arpanet or the X25 networks maintained by PTTs, where the services provided by the network amount to little more than the ability to connect to a remote host or to transfer files from one host to another. In these cases, the user is left in no doubt that the network is simply a data transmission medium and that all services are provided by the host machines attached to the network.

More recently, however, networks themselves have come to provide services or resources – file servers, name servers etc. – while some of the services provided by host machines have become so integrated with those of the network that they give the appearance of a single network-system-wide service – electronic mail, for example. The most recent stage of development is exemplified by systems such as Unix United [2] and Locus [9], and by the products of Apollo, Sun and certain other manufacturers which, to a greater or lesser extent, present their users with a single coherent system interface that hides the fact that their implementation involves separate machines and network communications. In the best of these systems, copying a file from one machine to another is no different than copying it from one directory to another.

If we consider the special issue of access control, a similar evolution may be perceived. In the beginning, access control was exclusively the responsibility of the hosts attached to the network; later, networks themselves came to provide some form of access control; most recently, there have emerged systems in which access control is fully distributed throughout the host systems and the network. In the limit, this last approach can be used to synthesize a multilevel secure system out of largely untrusted components [12].

What we are witnessing in all these cases is the eclipse of the idea that networks are "special" in some way, and its replacement by an integrated, systems-level view that regards networks as simply an implementation mechanism used in certain types of system. There can be few today who would dispute that this is, indeed, the correct view. If I send mail to someone, it is a matter of indifference to me whether his mailbox is on the same machine as mine, or is on a machine of an entirely different sort at the other side of the world: the mechanisms by which our mail is exchanged are an implementation detail, it is the *service* – the ability to exchange mail – that is of interest. Similarly, in the case of security, the properties (and even the existence!) of networks are an implementation issue; the significant matter is the security of the services provided by the total *system*.

I submit, therefore, that security is a property of systems; networks are an implementation mechanism used in certain systems and the security of a network cannot be considered in isolation from that of the overall system of which it is a component. It is therefore unnecessary, and undesirable, to generate Security Evaluation Criteria specifically for networks. Instead, revisions to the Orange Book are needed in order to establish Security Evaluation Criteria for *systems* that will admit implementations using networks. This is not to deny that the security characteristics of network implemetations are important; it is simply to recognise that they should not be treated in isolation.

The significant property of networking technology is that it makes it possible to put systems together to produce bigger systems, or, looked at from the other direction, it makes it possible to build systems out of smaller systems. Thus, the novel problems raised by networks are those concerning systems built from systems. Thus, I claim that *networks are systems*, and the issue we should be concerned with is one of *putting systems together*.

2.3. What is different about Systems built from Systems?

As far as security is concerned, systems made up of other systems differ from monolithic systems in two important respects. The first of these concerns the fact that the component systems are *active* entities; the second is due to the fact that they are *autonomous* entities. These two properties undermine the application of certain cherished principles of secure systems design and modelling.

2.3.1. The Simple-Security Condition doesn't apply

The principle known as the "simple security condition" asserts that security is preserved if an untrusted subject at one security level reads from an object at a lower level.[1] This is sound because, by definition, objects are *passive* entities: they can make no clandestine use of "read requests" received from higher level subjects – a memory doesn't "know" when it has been read by a high level subject.[2]

The situation is different when the participants are active systems. In order for one system to read information from another, the first must send a "read request" message to the second – which must decode the request, obtain the information requested, and return it in a message to the first system. Thus, the reading of information can only be accomplished with the knowledge and active participation of the system being read from, and therefore it is *not* secure for a high level system[3] to read information from a lower level one – since the untrusted high level system may choose to encode high level information in the read requests which it sends to the low level system and the latter can decode this information and record it at a lower level of classification. Thus, an untrusted system may not read information (and, in general, may not request a service) from another such system operating at a lower level.

---

[1]For ease of expression, I am using inexact terminology here. I should, of course, speak of security classifications drawn from a poset with "dominates" as the ordering relation.

[2]In modern paged-memory systems this may not be so, since the "use" bit indicates whether a memory page has been read. If this bit can be read by user processes, then it provides a covert channel; even if it cannot be read, it may still provide a timing channel, since a used page is less likely to be removed from main memory and is therefore more likely to provide rapid access.

[3]By which I mean a system with access to highly classified information.

2.3.2. The *-property doesn't apply

The dual situation arises when information is written from one system to another. The "*-property" asserts that security is preserved when an untrusted subject writes into an object at a higher level. But this rule, too, is inadequate when independent systems are concerned. The problem this time is due to the *autonomy* of the participants. When information is sent from one system to another, it is necessary to receive an acknowledgement that the recipient has received *and acted upon* the information that was sent. It is impossible to build a usefully reliable distributed system in the absence of such acknowledgments. And it is important to recognize that the need for acknowledgements is not merely due to unreliability in the underlying communication mechanism: the problem remains even when the communications channels are perfect – as when when the parties to the transaction are not remote systems, but are independent processes sharing the same hardware.

The root cause of the problem is that if one system sends a file to another, then it needs to know that the receiving system has been able to write the file satisfactorily – which the receiver may be unable to do for any number of reasons quite independent of transmission errors. It may, for example, be out of disk space, or temporarily busy on some other, more urgent task. In fact, since the receiver is an autonomous system, it may choose to reject the "write request" for any reason of its own choosing. Thus *end-to-end* acknowledgements are required and it is these that render it unsecure for a low level system to write information to (or, in general, to request a service from) an untrusted system at a higher level – since the latter can choose modulate its acknowledgements to the former in a manner that encodes high level information.

I should stress that I am not claiming that the Bell and La Padula model of security [1] is wrong; that model is very careful to distinguish (active) subjects from (passive) objects. Rather, it is the case that the assumptions of that model (developed for monolithic systems) do not accord with the different reality of distributed systems.

2.3.3. Reference Monitors must be Application-Specific

The requirement for end-to-end acknowledgements also undermines another tenet of secure systems design: the idea that it is possible to localize most, if not all, security issues, in a small and application independent "security kernel". Because the acknowledgments must come from the remote *application process* (since it alone knows whether it has performed the requested service correctly), a trusted, application-specific reference monitor is required if the application is to service requests from lower level systems.[4] It is difficult to overstate the importance of this last point; it is also the one least appreciated by those unfamiliar with distributed systems.

In fact, this problem is not unique to distributed systems; it arises also with "conventional" multilevel secure systems. Consider, for example, an MLS system that maintains a SECRET file containing structured information (such as a database or message file). There must be some "guardian" process that ensures the structural integrity of that information. Since this process must be able to both read and write the file containing the information, it must operate at the SECRET level. If an UNCLASSIFIED user wishes to update the information in the file, he must send his proposed update to the guardian, which will perform the update on his behalf only if it accords with its integrity criterion. But what if the update does not meet this criterion? It is unsecure for the guardian (a SECRET level process) to communicate this (or any other) fact back to its UNCLASSIFIED client – and the MLS system will ensure that it does not do so, since its reference monitor will prevent the "write-down" that would be required were it to attempt it. Now in a conventional MLS system in which the guardian's clients are human users, this lack of feedback may be acceptable, or it may be feasible to interpose some (human mediated) guard function that lowers the risk of clandestine use of the feedback channel to some acceptable level.[5] In a distributed system, on the other hand,

---

[4]It is because each multilevel service requires its own reference monitor that my DSS system provides only one such service -- namely, file storage and retrieval [12]. Notice that an application-independent reference monitor will suffice if applications are only allowed to service requests from clients at their own level.

[5]Alternatively, the guardian may be made a "trusted process" – which is simply a euphemism for an application-specific reference monitor.

where the client may be another process, and where communications may be expected to operate at high bandwidth, these solutions are likely to be less acceptable. The moral seems to be not so much that distributed systems are intrinsically different than conventional ones, but rather that expectations are greater and that more ambitious functionality may be desired. The single reference monitor of a conventional MLS system (providing secure access only to unstructured files) may not be sufficient to support future applications.

2.4. A Simple Security Model

Fortunately, it seems possible to deduce some fairly straightforward principles for secure operation in distributed systems. I will describe these principles in the context of a simple security model for distributed systems.

A *system* is composed of interconnected *domains*. A *domain* is a self-contained computational entity provided with *sockets*. No information may enter or leave a domain except through one of its sockets. A domain may either be *atomic*, meaning that it has no internal structure (visible at this level of abstraction), or it may be composed, recursively, of a set of interconnected smaller domains (i.e. a system). Domains are interconnected by linking their sockets. Within this model, a conventional monolithic system is an example of an atomic domain; a (simple Arpanet-type) network can be regarded as a domain that provides lots of sockets but rather limited computational power.

In order to talk about security, we associate a *security label* with each socket. For simplicity, I will ignore compartments and speak as if the levels TS, S, C, and U were the only labels – the extension to compartments is obvious.[6] A domain is *secure* if the information *leaving* the domain through a socket tagged with level l is entirely unaffected by any information that may have entered the domain through sockets at

---

[6]At this level of abstraction, sockets are single-level. In practice, sockets of different levels may be multiplexed onto a single physical socket – but this is an implementation-level issue which may be ignored here.

levels *higher* than l.[7] Notice that any domain can be rendered secure by causing all its sockets to have the same level. Consequently, I will talk about *single-level* domains (those whose sockets all have the same level) and *multilevel* domains (those whose sockets may have different levels). An atomic multilevel domain is simply a conventional MLS system – one that could be certified using the criteria in the Orange Book. The question of interest here is: what are the rules for interconnecting domains securely? Because of the problems discussed earlier, the rules are Draconian and, therefore, quite simple.

The basic rule is: sockets may be connected if they have exactly the same security label. Thus, if we have a network that provides no security at all,[8] then it can be used as a single-level domain at, say, the S level, and may interconnect other single-level S domains, and the S level sockets of multilevel domains. Notice that the resulting system is also a domain and may partake in further interconnections.

The simplicity of the scheme described above must be compromised somewhat in order to accommodate domains that are "not quite" multilevel. Such domains are typified by (monolithic) systems cleared to operate in "system high" mode. In this mode of operation, a system may be allowed to operate as multilevel (say, S and TS), but all its users are required to be cleared to the level of the most sensitive information held by the system (TS in this case) and no information may be released at less than the highest level without manual review. This mode of operation is intended for those systems that are believed to do a "good job" of correctly labelling information and of enforcing policy, but which are not trusted absolutely. We can accommodate such systems within our model by labelling their sockets with the entire set of security labels associated with the information they process (e.g. {S, TS}).

It should be clear that it is unsecure to connect a {S, TS} socket with one labelled

---

[7]This is an informal re-statement of the "standard" SRI security model [5, 6, 7, 13, 14].

[8]By which I mean that it cannot reliably associate security labels with its sockets. Remember, it is an axiom that information cannot enter or leave a domain except through its sockets – thus, even an unsecure network is required to be protected against both active and passive wiretapping.

{C, S}, or one labelled simply S. On the other hand, it is secure to connect it to sockets labelled {S, TS} or TS. It is not obvious to me whether it would be secure to allow a connection to a socket labelled {C, S, TS}, but I will assume that it is. With this assumption, the rule seems to be: sockets may be connected if their associated label sets share the same least upper bound. It seems clear that similar rules can be developed to deal with the "controlled" and "compartmented" modes of operation.

Another extension to the simple model is desirable in order to admit certain types of systems (typically, networks) that do provide a fairly strong form of security, but which do not enforce DoD policy. The motivation is as follows: if it is secure to interconnect two sockets, then the length and nature of the interconnecting "wire" is unimportant (provided it is secure against active and passive wiretapping). Thus we should also allow sockets to be interconnected by a "network" domain that provides "pure channels" that are functionally identical to a dedicated wire, even if the network is ignorant of DoD policy.

Simple extensions to the model accommodate this situation. Instead of (or as well as) a security label, a socket may be marked as a *pure channel* connection and labeled with an identifier. At most two sockets may share the same identifier.[9] The requirement is that any information *leaving* the domain through a pure channel socket with identifier i must be entirely unaffected by any information that may have *entered* the domain though sockets bearing any other label or identifier. Notice that this is entirely in accord with the policy on conventionally labelled sockets: the label [pure channel, identifier i] can be regarded as a new security level that neither dominates, nor is dominated by, any other. This requirement ensures that two pure channel sockets bearing the same identifier can be regarded as "collapsed" to a single point. Thus one pure channel socket with identifier i may be connected to a socket of label X and another to one of label Y exactly if sockets X and Y may be directly interconnected.

---

[9]Actually, I think this requirement can be relaxed to allow broadcast systems.

2.5. Certification Criteria

Very little of the security model developed in the previous section is specific to networks, yet it seems to address many of the relevant issues. I believe that with a little rewording, many of the criteria in the Orange Book can be similarly generalized to cover network, as well as monolithic, implementations. To take a single example, the system architecture requirement for B2 systems states, in part: "the TCB shall maintain process isolation through the provision of distinct address spaces." Now the real requirement here is to ensure that no information enters or leaves a domain except through its sockets. The use of distinct address spaces for each domain is an implementation mechanism suitable for achieving this requirement on a single processor. In a distributed system, the appropriate implementation mechanisms include the use of separate processors for each domain and end-to-end encryption to protect their intercommunications. If the Orange book were to say more about underlying requirements and less about specific implementation techniques, networks and distributed systems could be accommodated along with conventional systems.

3. Verification

Just as it is necessary to understand what we mean by "networks", so we need to be clear what "verification" is about before we can consider its role in the evaluation of trusted systems.

3.1. What does Verification Accomplish?

Verification is the demonstration of consistency between two (or more) descriptions the same system. The exact meaning of "consistency" depends on the type of verification being performed. *Formal Verification* operates on system descriptions called *specifications* which are *theories* expressed in some *logic*; in this case, "consistency" means that one specification (the more "concrete" one) is a valid *interpretation* of the other (the more "abstract" one) – i.e., any *model* of the more concrete theory will also be a model of the more abstract one. This form of consistency is demonstrated by showing that the *axioms* of the more abstract theory are *theorems* of the more concrete one.

If two *independent* specifications are verified to be consistent, then one's confidence that both are "correct" is surely increased. If the two specifications are not independent, however, (e.g., if the more concrete one is consciously derived from the other) then all that can be said is that one's confidence in the correctness of the derived specification is raised near to that of one's confidence in the abstract specification. The ultimate goal – confidence in the correctness of an actual running system – can be achieved through a chain of consistency demonstrations running all the way from a highly abstract specification, through possibly many levels of intermediate specifications, to the running code. The starting point for such a verification chain is a highly abstract specification whose correctness is accepted on the basis of extensive scrutiny and peer review. It is not necessary that this most abstract of specifications should describe *all* the properties desired of the system: some properties may be deemed more important than others and it will be these that are included in the most abstract specification and subject to the rigor of verification. In the case of security verification, the properties present in the most abstract specification are concerned exclusively with security issues and the specification is usually called a *security model*.[10]

In practice, it is generally too tedious and too expensive to perform a chain of formal verification all the way from the most abstract specification right down to the running code. Instead, the formal verification is generally broken off at some level and informal techniques are used to carry assurance from there down to the code level. The reason that *formal* verification is used at all is that (especially when machine-checked) it is more complete and reliable than informal verification. This being the case, it is important to choose the right point in the verification chain at which to turn from formal to informal verification: in particular, formal verification should not be broken off too early – the major design decisions affecting security should certainly be subject to the rigor of formal verification, as should any particularly subtle issues (such as covert channels). On the other hand, formal verification should not be pursued too far; in my view (which is by no means universal) the vast cost of code proof yields a poor return in terms of increased confidence in the security of the overall system.

---

[10]Confusingly, this sense of the word "model" is different from that used in logic.

Just as the decision where to *break off* the formal verification chain is an important one, so is the choice of the point at which the chain should *start* – i.e., in the case of security verification, the choice of security model. If the security model is so highly abstract that it can apply to almost any system design, then a number of intermediate specifications and verification steps will be needed to reach a reasonably detailed description of the actual system of interest. Far fewer steps will be needed if one starts with a more concrete and detailed security model, but that model will already embody system details and design decisions that restrict the class of systems to which it can be applied, and there is also the non-trivial problem of establishing the correctness of such a detailed model in the first place.

The choice of security model is therefore a delicate and important matter. A security model comprises two components (termed the *system* and the *security* component, respectively):

- Assumptions about the sort of systems to be verified, and

- An interpretation of "security" that is appropriate to that class of systems.

Since most existing security models were developed with monolithic systems in mind, their system components may not accord with the different reality of distributed systems (recall Sections 2.3.1 and 2.3.2). It therefore seems necessary to consider how the modelling of distributed systems should differ from that of conventional ones.

3.2. What is different about Systems built from Systems? (Revisited)

Most modeling and verification techniques for monolithic systems depend on the notion of "state": at each instant the system is "in" some state, and progress is represented by the transition from one state to the next. This state-based approach is viable because the monolithic systems can be regarded as *sequential* processes. This is not the case with distributed systems: the components of such a system proceed in parallel and, in general, asynchronously. Although the instantaneous state of a distributed system can be defined as the product of the states of its sequential components, the evolution of that composite state will not be deterministic – since its components may proceed at different rates. For this reason, attempts to describe the behavior of distributed systems in terms of their composite state have not been altogether satisfactory. Most current work attempts to describe distributed systems in terms of the communications in which their components participate (i.e. their input/output behavior – sometimes known as "trace semantics"). The benefit of this approach is that it permits the specification of system behavior without excessive placing constraints on system implementation: unlike the case with state semantics, the designer is free to choose either a distributed or a sequential implementation.

The arguments that have led those concerned with general system properties to prefer trace to state semantics apply no less forcefully in the case of security properties. I believe that a formal security model for "putting systems together" is more likely to develop from a security model expressed in terms of input/output behavior (e.g. the SRI model [5, 6, 7, 13, 14]) than one expressed in terms of states. The informal model described in Section 2.4 can easily be formalized using the techniques of the SRI model and seems to provide a step in the right direction.

3.3. What should be Verified?

The model of Section 2.4 is built on two key assumptions, which become *requirements* on the next lower level of modelling:

- No information can enter or leave a domain, except through its sockets, and

- Information leaving a domain through a socket labelled at level l must be independent of any information that entered the domain through sockets labelled at levels not dominated by l.

The first of these requirements is sometimes referred to as "domain isolation" or "separation". It is clearly fundamental to everything else and, in my view, is definitely a candidate for formal verification. For the case of multiple domains supported on a single processor, I have proposed a technique for verifying this property which I call "Proof of Separability" [11]. In the case of networks, the requirement may be achieved in many different ways (e.g. link, node, or end-to-end encryption, or physically protected cableways) and the the appropriate verification techniques will be different also. It is likely that verification of domain isolation in networks will have to consider a "distributed reference monitor" (e.g., crypto boxes and KDC in the case of end-to-end encryption) and this will present an interesting challenge.

The second requirement is to ensure that the services provided at the interface to each domain are secure. This also seems a prime candidate for verification and is one for which several techniques are available. Those based on information flow analysis have the special merit that they identify covert channels as well as the more gross forms of insecurity. The question of covert channels, and whether they (or rather, their absence) should be a target for formal verification, was one that we were specifically asked to consider. It seems to me that if an *overt* channel is a conduit for information that is provided deliberately, then a *covert* channel is simply one that is provided accidentally! It is significant that there is no distinction between overt and covert (storage) channels in the mathematical security model of information flows [5, 6, 7, 13, 14].

Since distributed systems are only feasible in the presence of high-bandwidth communications, it is very dangerous to assume that any covert channels will be of sufficiently low bandwidth that they will not pose a serious threat. Also, because distributed systems are composed of active entities and generally require explicit acknowledgements to messages, the opportunities for covert channels are much greater than in monolithic systems (recall the channels described in Sections 2.3.1 and 2.3.2). Furthermore, since covert channels are provided "accidentally" it is also dangerous to assume that they can be discovered by casual examination. Rather, I believe that the systematic detection of covert channels is one of the main contributions of formal verification to the evaluation of secure distributed systems.

4. Suggested Verification Criteria

The following is a sketch of Verification Criteria that are suggested for Class A1. The bulk of the existing A1 criteria can be retained, with slight rewording. For Class B3, replace the term "formal" by "descriptive" and the phrase "mathematical proof" by "careful argument".

A formal model shall be maintained of the security policy supported of *the complete system* of which the evaluated product is to form a component, and of the evaluated product itself. Formal statements shall be provided of the assumptions made about allsystem components and a mathematical proof shall be provided to demonstrate that these assumptions, in conjunction with the policy supported by the evaluated product, are sufficient to support the policy of the overall system. A FTLS of the evaluated product TCB shall be maintained and verified with respect to the security model established for the product. The formal models employed shall address the issue of covert channels and the techniques used to substantiate the security policy of the evaluated product and to verify its FTLS shall be ones that identify covert channels.

References

1. D.E. Bell and L.J. La Padula, "Secure Computer System: Unified Exposition and Multics Interpretation," Technical Report ESD-TR-75-306, Mitre Corporation, Bedford, MA., March 1976.

2. D.R. Brownbridge, L.F. Marshall and B. Randell, "The Newcastle Connection, or UNIXes of the World Unite!," *Software - Practice and Experience*, Vol. 12, No. 12, pp. 1147-1162, December 1982.

3. D.R. Cheriton, *The Thoth System: Multi-process Structuring and Portability*, North-Holland, Operating and Programming Systems Series, 1982.

4. Department of Defense, Computer Security Center, *Department of Defense Trusted Computer System Evaluation Criteria*, 1983, CSC-STD-001-83.

5. R.J. Feiertag, K.N. Levitt and L. Robinson, "Proving Multilevel Security of a System Design," *Proc. 6th ACM Symposium on Operating System Principles*, pp. 57-65, November 1977.

6. R.J. Feiertag, "A Technique for Proving Specifications are Multilevel Secure," Technical Report CSL109, Computer Science Laboratory, SRI International, Menlo Park, CA., January 1980.

7. J.A. Goguen and J. Meseguer, "Security Policies and Security Models," *Proc. 1982 Symposium on Security and Privacy,* Oakland, CA., pp. 11-20, IEEE Computer Society, April 1982.

8. F.N. Parr and R.E. Strom, "NIL: A High-Level Language for Distributed Systems Programing," *IBM Systems Journal,* Vol. 22, No. 1/2, pp. 111-127, 1983.

9. G. Popek at al., "Locus: A Network Transparent, High Reliability, Distributed System," *Proc. ACM 8th Symposium on Operating System Principles,* Asilomar, CA., pp. 169-177, December 1981, (ACM Operating Systems Review, Vol. 15, No. 5).

10. R. Rashid and G. Robertson, "Accent: A Communications Oriented Network Operating System Kernel," *Proc. ACM 8th Symposium on Operating System Principles,* Asilomar, CA., pp. 64-75, December 1981, (ACM Operating Systems Review, Vol. 15, No. 5).

11. J.M. Rushby, "Proof of Separability - a Verification Technique for a Class of Security Kernels," *Proc. 5th International Symposium on Programming,* Turin, Italy, pp. 352-367, M. Dezani-Cianaglini and U. Montanari, eds., Springer-Verlag Lecture Notes in Computer Science, Vol. 137, April 1982.

12. J.M. Rushby and B. Randell, "A Distributed Secure System," *IEEE Computer,* Vol. 16, No. 7, pp. 55-67, July 1983.

13. J.M. Rushby, "The Security Model of Enhanced HDM," *Proceedings 7th DoD/NBS Computer Security Initiative Conference,* Gaithersburg, MD., pp. 120-136, September 1984.

14. J.M. Rushby, "The SRI Security Model," Draft Report, Computer Science Laboratory, SRI International, Menlo Park, CA., February 1986.

Observations on Local Area Network Security

Marshall D. Abrams

The MITRE Corporation
1820 Dolley Madison Boulevard
McLean, VA 22102

Abstract

This paper addresses Local Area Network security issues. Problems discussed include wiretapping, end-to-end access control, and security groups. Protective mechanisms include physical protection, and separation by physical, logical, and encryption methods. Trusted Network Interface Units, encryption, and key distribution are also discussed.

Introduction

The issues discussed in this paper are germane to many aerospace applications and air-to-ground communications links. Most currently, [9] has included the following statements:

- The Space Station command and data handling system shall be capable of secure communications as required for normal and emergency operating conditions.

- Payloads requiring secure command and data handling shall be responsible for command and data encryption within the payload and on the ground.

- Security considerations will be incorporated into the Space Station Program in a manner consistent with the threat, vulnerabilities and countermeasures that may exist in the 1990's.

- Consideration will be given to the overall security of the ground space station support facilities, communications in general and the various space station related activities, platforms, vehicles, maneuvering systems and satellites.

- In anticipation of DOD utilization of Space Station, potential system requirements will be developed.

This paper discusses security issues in Local Area Networks. To make sure that everyone gets off on the same footing, we start by briefly summarizing the salient features of Local Area Networks. Readers requiring additional information should consult [10].

Local Area Network Technology/Topology Overview

A set of commonly popular technologies for providing data communications between computers go under the name of Local Area Networks (LANs). There are several alternative LAN technologies which need not be differentiated for the purposes of this paper. All provide a shared data communications path interconnecting all attached data terminal equipment (DTE). This DTE may be terminals or may be computers. It makes no difference to the LAN.

In the bus and ring topologies which we are considering, all data traffic is available to every node on the network. There is no routing or switching in the conventional sense, rather there is selection. The equipment at the node which provides the access for the DTE performs this selection. This equipment goes by many names; in this paper, we shall call it "Network Interface Unit" (NIU). Every NIU has an address. When messages are inserted on the network, the address of the destination NIU is part of the message header. As messages flow through an NIU the destination address is examined. If and only if the destination address matches the NIU doing the examining, is the message transmitted to the attached DTE. By this very simple filtering mechanism, NIUs provide for pairwise communication between any two DTE attached to the network. It is also easy to provide broadcast communication to all NIUs by employing a special address.

There are many reasons why LANs have become popular, the most salient being flexibility and cost. LAN flexibility derives from their inherent distributed control. That is, all of the active decision making takes place in individual NIUs. New NIUs may be added to the net or activated, or

Reprinted from *Proceedings of the Aerospace Computer Security Conference: Protecting Intellectual Property in Space*, 1985, pages 77-82. Copyright © 1985 by The Institute of Electrical and Electronics Engineers, Inc.

NIUs may be removed or deactivated without making significant change to the overall intelligence controlling the network. This dynamic flexibility is quite valuable in environments where new DTE may be added to the network at any time or where DTE may be removed accidentally or purposefully without notification and coordination with a central authority. Since every DTE may be either a terminal or a computer, (and sometimes its difficult to distinguish between the two), the LAN provides universal access between and among devices. In particular, the LAN may be compared with the point-to-point wiring between terminals and computers that was prevalent in previous computer communications architectures. The lack of flexibility, the cost of installing point-to-point wiring, and the saturation of the physical space available for such wiring have all led to the replacement of this technology.

It is undoubtedly obvious that many of the operational advantages of LANs are also security liabilities. These liabilities will be discussed in some detail below.

The advent of mini and micro computers has supported the evolution of distributed computing. Instead of a single large computer having to share its time among a large number of applications, multiple computers can be employed, each devoted to a single or at least a few applications. Some applications may indeed require, or at least benefit from, the attention of multiple computers.

It may be possible to work on different parts of the application in parallel. In general, these multiple processors function as part of a coordinated system under the control of an operating system. The terms Distributed Computing and Distributed Operating System are applied to these configurations. Sometimes the processors comprising a distributed system are all housed in the same cabinet or are otherwise located less than a meter apart. In this case, communications among them proceeds over high speed busses which are often extensions of the computers' architecture.

The architecture that we are addressing in in this paper, however, has these distributed computers separated distances the order of tens to a few thousand meters so that the LAN provides the communication path among the processors. Commonly, the data rate requirements for such interprocessor communications is much higher than that of terminal-to-computer communications. Even when not cooperating in the solution of an application, multiple distributed computers may find it necessary to exchange information. For example, when the computer controlling a scientific experiment has finished acquiring, analyzing, reducing, summarizing its data, it may then pass this output data to the communications control computer which handles the air-to-ground communications so that this specialized processor may deliver the data toward its ultimate destination.

LAN Security Problems

LANs share many security problems and approaches for their solutions with point-to-point conventional communications systems. In addition, they have some unique problems of their own. This section surveys these problems and leads into the section which discusses the approaches for solution. The reader seeking further information is referred to [8].

Universal Data Availability

The ready access to data anywhere along the LAN is one of its greatest security problems. Data is made available to any party whether they should have the data or not. LANs make all traffic available at or near every NIU. Covert activity is very difficult to detect. Every NIU has direct immediate access to all of the data on the network. A normal NIU is expected to ignore all data which is not addressed to itself. However, malfunctioning or maliciously designed NIUs can be as acquisitive as they wish.

Passive and Active Wire Tap Threats

The interception of information transmission by an adverse party has been traditionally referred to as wire-tapping. In this paper, we will retain this terminology even though it may not be strictly descriptive of the technology employed. The network media can be tapped. Some media are inherently more tap resistant, or at least give indication when they are tapped. The media may also radiate information. Electromagnetic media are notorious for this weakness. Optical media are orders of magnitude better.

Wire tapping is conventionally subdivided into passive and active categories. In passive wire tapping, the message traffic is observed but not modified. The most obvious objective of passive wiretapping is to learn the contents of messages, but traffic analysis may provide the adverse party with information when message content is not available. Traffic analysis could include steady state and transient analysis of quantities of messages between parties and the lengths of these messages.

In active wiretapping, there are a number of different ways in which the adverse party can modify the communications stream. Messages can be completely deleted, can be inserted, or their contents can be modified. Delay, reordering, duplication and retransmission are also possible. Denial of service by temporary or permanent incapacitation of the LAN is yet another form of active wiretapping.

End-To-End Access Control

"End-To-End" is one of the more overworked and less precise terms that one encounters in data communications. The problem is that one observer's end is another observer's mid-point. To communicate properly in writing, it is necessary to identify exactly the end points being discussed. The communications engineer traditionally thinks of the end point as being the data-circuit terminating equipment (DCE) or at least the interface between the DCE and the DTE. In the LAN context, this means that the data communication end-to-end is from NIU to NIU.

NIU-to-NIU Access Control Access control encompasses a subset of correct operation of the LAN protocol. Access control, like flow control and error control, can occur at multiple levels in the open system interconnection (OSI) architecture. (There are a large number of articles which describe OSI architecture. The author recommends [12].) In fact, one of the criticisms of OSI implementations is the overhead of performing the same or similar functions more than once. But given the Balkinization of the computer communications universe, with LANs covering only the lower three layers of the OSI model, we must accept this duplication. In order for the LAN to function, it must provide addressing and delivery services. These services require that data transmission be delivered undamaged to its destination. For security considerations, mis-delivery and non-delivery are problems associated with damage to the data communications, or at least to the address part thereof. The NIUs play an important part in the delivery mechanism. They must correctly place destination address on each transmission and must likewise correctly identify the addresses of those messages, and only those messages, which they are to pass through to the attached DTE.

DTE-to-DTE Access Control The first extension to end-to-end is to identify the person or process embodied in the DTE. This is the personnel identification problem. (The interested reader should consult [1] and [11] for further information.) Identification of a person can be accomplished by some information which the person knows, such as a password or key string, something the person has such as a machine readable badge or card, or some physical characteristic of the person such as hand writing or fingerprint analysis. Identification of a process appears to be limited to the first of these alternatives. The identification may be shared between the NIU and the DTE. A number of alternative physical designs exist whereby various kinds of readers may be attached to the DTE or to the NIU. Keys or passwords may be passed over primary or secondary data channels between DTE and NIU for the purpose of identifying the person or process.

NIUs typically support two or more attached DTE. For access control it would be simplest to restrict that number to one. Otherwise, we will have to increase our trust in the NIU, as discussed below. Given that the definition of end-to-end has been extended to include person or process, then a mechanism must be built to enforce this decision. Logically, this mechanism may be installed either in the DTE or in the NIU. In practice, since the local area network is a more recent development and is procured separately, it is more reasonable to expect the access control mechanisms to reside in the NIU.

Security Group Control

In many communication systems, the users are subdivided into multiple security groups. National defense classifications have coarse granularities of CONFIDENTIAL, SECRET, and TOP SECRET, and finer granularities based on a need to know. Civilian groupings might be based on membership in a particular organization. In the latter case, it would be entirely reasonable for individuals to belong to more than one security group. We can increase the workload being supported by the NIU and the convenience of its users if we make the NIU responsible for the enforcement of these security group rules. The most obvious function we would like the NIU to perform is to restrict communication to those people and processes which belong to the same security group.

It is possible that there would be an ordering relationship among the security groups. The well-known national defense classifications of CONFIDENTIAL, SECRET, and TOP SECRET are such an example. In this case, it might be permissible for messages to travel up hill, i.e., a source of lower classification could send a message to a destination of more restrictive classification, however, no message could flow in the reverse direction, even acknowledgement of receipt of the original message.

Security Approaches

The problems of security in computer networks are very well discussed in [4], to which the interested reader is referred.

Physical Protection

Physical protection is the most obvious form of security. It is applicable to almost any valuable resource. A local area network is only one example. Physical protection is not discussed in this paper. This section will go on to address alternative schemes for providing security groups. Protection of messages between pairs of communicants will be discussed under Encryption in a subsequent section.

Separation

There are a number of different schemes for separating the security groups using a LAN. The most obvious and straight forward is to provide separate LANs for each security group. Simply providing multiple cables may not be sufficient; some mechanism may be required to make sure that an unauthorized NIU does not get plugged into the wrong LAN.

On a single LAN, there are a number of ways of providing separate channels for each security group. One very common medium for Local Area Networks is coaxial cable which is modulated in frequency channels. These channels are very similar to and in many cases identical with the channels used for commercial television broadcast distribution. In addition to the broadcast channels, there are a large number of additional channels used by the cable television industry (CATV). Assigning separate channels to each security group is an obvious separation mechanism; in technical terms this is frequency division multiplexing (FDM).

An alternative is to provide separate logical channels on baseband and fiber optic cables, each of which employs the entire bandwidth of the medium. While necessary on these media which do not support frequency modulation, such logical channels can be used in addition to FDM. One way to provide logical channels would be to include a channel identification in the header of each data communication packet. The NIU would be required to enforce the channel separation in the same way that it enforces address filtering by recognizing the logical channel and passing messages from it only to authorized DTE.

Another way to achieve logically separate channels is to employ encryption. Assuming for the moment that the security group encompasses the NIU and that an NIU belongs to one and only one security group, then encryption between NIUs is analogous to link encryption in conventional communications systems. Only those NIUs sharing the same encryption key (or pairs of keys) would be able to communicate thereby creating separate logical channels for their security groups. A message may be encrypted more than once, if the encryption algorithms permit. This serial encryption is sometimes called super-encryption. Some algorithms require decryption to be performed in the inverse sequence as encryption; other algorithms are insensitive to sequence of operations. We shall assume multiple encryptions thereby making it possible to form subgroups as many times as necessary and to encrypt specific messages between two parties both of whom belong to the same security group.

Implications and Side Effects

Security comes at a price. Part of this price is fiscal. There are additional components, additional mechanisms which must be implemented and paid for. Another part of the price is decreased convenience of usage. Introduction of security measures make a LAN less convenient to use. Some of the burden may be borne by technology (implemented in the NIUs) but part of the burden must be borne by the parties attempting to communicate.

Interoperability

Let us assume that some recognition exists for separating security groups. Now what happens if parties belonging to different security groups need to communicate? The devices which provide interconnection between separate channels in a LAN, between separate LANs, or between a LAN and a long distance network are variously known as the repeaters, bridges and gateways. This sequence of names reflects the amount of work which must be done in providing this interconnection. Outside of the security arena, there are problems of different protocols and address spaces which have to be solved. To a large extent the solution to such problems are known; there are a large number of commercial devices available to provide such services. When security is an issue, we might add the name filter to the collection implying the function of enforcing security rules and allowing only some messages through.

Trusted NIU

In any local area network, the NIU must be trusted. However, when we add security concerns, it must be trusted a little bit more.

For a commercial LAN NIU, the trust is based on commercial practices. This should not make us exceptionally confident, for our experience probably indicates that many commercial products are released with the implicit decision that the customer will detect some latent errors. In the security environment this approach is clearly unsatisfactory. The problem has been addressed for some time, resulting in the issuance of Department of Defense trusted computer system evaluation criteria. This program is discussed in some detail in [7] in this volume. Work is presently underway to extend these concepts to communication's networks as well. Responsibilities have been assigned under [5]. A standard [3] exists for equipment that is going to be used for implementing the data encryption standard, and procedures exist for endorsing such equipment [6].

Should these NIUs be trusted, and what is it we're going to trust them to do? Briefly, we will trust these NIUs because their hardware and software have been demonstrated to properly implement a set of security rules. There is undoubtedly a hierarchy of trust based on the confidence which we have in the implementation, and the degree of testing or verification which a particular implementation has been subjected to.

At the high end of trust we would find hardware and software which has been demonstrated to be correct using the best software verification tools available. At some intermediate level, we would find software which had been written using all of the rules and tools of structured programming. Somewhat lower, we would find software which has been known to work correctly for some extended period of time and has been subjected to various types of test designed to expose its weaknesses.

What it is we should trust these NIUs to do is also a hierarchical process. At the lowest level, we are asking them to correctly implement the LAN protocols, in particular the affixing of destination addresses and the filtering of received messages according to these addresses. At a somewhat higher level we give the LAN NIU the responsibility of affixing security levels to messages, knowing the security level of the attached DTE, and enforcing the security rules for transferring these messages.

Encryption

Encryption is probably the best available technique for providing security protection in data communications. The current view of encryption is to take the universally readable plaintext and to perform some mathematical operations on it to produce cyphertext. The mathematical operations may or may not be secret. But the protection of the encipherment is based not, or at least not solely, on the secrecy of the algorithm, but rather on the difficulty of inverting it. That is to say, a certain amount of work is required in order to determine the plaintext given the cyphertext. The algorithm takes a key as input as well as the text. The key consists of a finite length string of bits. For the convenience of human users, keys are usually expressed as decimal, hexadecimal, or alphanumeric strings.

From the user's viewpoint, a key is very much like a password; it is a string which must be presented to the computer communication system in order to gain access to the resource and services. The mechanism of using and testing passwords and key have some differences however. Passwords are generally used by comparing the information presented by the user with information which has been stored. The comparison may be direct or may pass through an algorithm such as encryption. The encryption key does not serve as a basis of comparison but rather serves as one of the inputs of the encryption or decryption algorithm, the other input being the message stream.

That is to say, the key directly effects the results of the transformation formed by the encryption/decryption algorithm. The only way to verify that the correct key or pair of keys is being used is to attempt to decrypt a message which has been encrypted. If the matching key or keys were used for the encryption and decryption process, then meaningful plaintext will be recovered.

With the appropriate key, decypherment is trivial. Without this key, breaking the code algorithm should require considerable work. This amount of work should be prohibitively expensive as compared to the value of the information being protected. An example of a algorithm which is well known is the Federal Data Encryption Standard [2]. The DES and its modes of use are discussed in [4].

Channel Separation

Encryption can be used in a rather straight forward way to establish logical channels. Each logical channel is assigned an encryption key (or pair of keys). When an NIU is going to operate on a given logical channel, it need only load the appropriate key. A pair of keys thus establishes a logical channel between NIUs. If an NIU is to be trusted to operate on multiple logical channels, then it need apply a key for each of those channels to every message which passes through it. This seems to be an unnecessarily complex procedure; it would not be unreasonable to restrict a NIU to operating on a single logical channel. If the attached person or process had access to multiple logical channels, then the encryption key could be changed appropriately under the control of that person or process.

Encryption between DTEs would require another pair of keys. Messages between DTEs would then be doubly encrypted. Without this second DTE-to-DTE key, any DTE attached to an NIU possessing the key for the logical channel could eavesdrop on all communication on that logical channel.

Key Distribution and Management

As mentioned above, a key is used in modern encryption systems to control the encryption and decryption algorithms which transform between plaintext and cyphertext. All keys and passwords must have a finite lifetime. There are many reasons for this; among them are loss of a key, employee turnover, and potential key breaking by crypto-analysis. This last problem derives from the property that allows a skilled adverse party to analyze encrypted messages to deduce the key used to encrypt them. The more messages which are available, the better the analysis.

Given that keys must have a finite lifetime, we have the problem of distributing keys and maintaining a historical data base. The historical data base is necessary so that it is possible to ascertain what a particular user's or user group's key, was at a given point in time. Various combinations of manual and automated methods exist for distribution of keys. One common scheme limits the lifetime of a key for communication between pairs of parties to a single session; a session key is generated every time a connection is made. A special master key is used to encrypt the messages used to distribute the session key. The distribution of the master key is usually outside the automated system. It would seem that the operation of key distribution center requires a great deal of trust, and the computer implementing this function requires a significant degree of physical protection.

Summary

This paper has reviewed Local Area Networks with special attention paid to security issues. While the LAN offers many advantages in terms of data access and flexibility, the other side of the coin is increased vulnerability to wiretapping. The problems of end-to-end access control and security groups are also discussed. The mechanisms for providing security are physical protection and separation of security groups by physical, logical, or encryption methods; all of which adversely effect interoperability. Most protection schemes require that Network Interface Units be trusted; the reasons and trusted functions are discussed. Encryption is used for creating logical channels as well as protecting sessions between two persons or processes; the distribution of encryption keys is outlined.

Acknowledgements

The author appreciates the technical advice of Sheila Craig, William Mason, and Fred Tompkins and the secretarial assistance of Jessie Chambers.

BIBLIOGRAPHY

1. Cotton, Ira W. and Paul Meissner, "Approaches to Controlling Personal Access to Computer Terminals," Proceedings of the Computer Networking Symposium, IEEE Computer Society Press, 1975.

2. Data Encryption Standard, Federal Information Processing Standard 46, January 15, 1977.

3. Federal Standard 1027, General Security Requirements for Equipment Using the Data Encryption Standard, General Services Administration, National Communications System, April 14, 1982.

4. Kent, Stephen T., "Security in Computer Networks," in Protocols and Techniques for Data Communication Networks, Franklin F. Kuo, ed., Prentice-Hall, 1981.

5. National Policy on Telecommunications and Automated Information Systems Security, National Security Decision Directive 145, The White House, September 17, 1984.

6. Procedures For Endorsement of Commercial Data Encryption Standard (DES) Equipment for U.S. Government Applications, National Security Agency, Communications Protection Special Projects Office, Oct. 18, 1982.

7. Schell, Roger R. "The Future of Trusted Computer Systems", Proceedings of the Aerospace Computer Security Conference, IEEE Computer Society Press, 1985.

8. Shirey, Robert W. "Security in Local Area Networks," Proceedings of the Computer Networking Symposium, Dec. 1982, pages 28-44, IEEE Computer Society Press, 1982.

9. Space Station Program Description Document, National Aeronautics and Space Administration, TM-86652, March 1984.

10. Stallings, William, Tutorial: Local Network Technology, IEEE Computer Society Press, 1983.

11. Wood, Helen M., "On-Line Password Techniques," Proceedings of the Computer Security and Integrity Symposium, IEEE Computer Society Press, 1977.

12. Zimmerman, Hubert "OSI Reference Model-The ISO model of Architecture for Open System Interconnection," IEEE Transactions On Communications, Volume Com-28, No. 4, April 1980, pages 425-432

Section 3.2: Encryption

Introduction

Computer and network security are components of information security, and the security issues for each application should be viewed with respect to this framework. For example, when reviewing a specific security application for a computer system, it is useful to, first, place the system in the broader framework of information security. This means considering the system and security objectives before focusing on specific security controls. Our point is that there are a wide variety of security controls to choose from, and the selected controls must relate to system performance and security specifications. If this process is followed and a need is established for commercial-level encryption, then the following sections on encryption provide a foundation for evaluating available encryption options. These sections are primarily directed to publically available encryption technology; however, a recommended reading reprint is suggested to introduce you to the commercial COMSEC (communications security) program (CCEP), which offers non-public encryption technology to commercial producers of encryption systems [ROSE86].

The encryption sections discuss encryption, cryptography, link and end-to-end encryption, and function secrecy and standardization. A subsection on reprints completes the encryption discussion.

Encryption: A Fundamental Tool

Encryption is a fundamental tool for security in data communication. Victor L. Voydock and Stephen T. Kent [VOYD-83,VOYD85] go so far as to say it "is the fundamental technique on which all communications security measures are based." Although its primary purpose is to provide secrecy as a countermeasure preventing disclosure under passive attacks, it can detect the active attacks of message-stream modification, denial of service, and fraudulent initial connection. Encryption is a methodology, a means for achieving an end. The end is one or more of the security services described in Section 3.1. This section explores the technology, policy, and application of encryption in computer and network security. Subsequent sections will describe the security service applications in detail.

A Cryptography Overview

Cryptography, hidden writing, dates back at least to ancient Egypt. It is a methodology for transforming the repre-

sentation or appearance of information without changing its information content. One representation, expressed in some natural language, is intelligible to everyone who can read that language; this is referred to as *plaintext* or *cleartext*. The other representation is designed to conceal the information from unauthorized persons; this is refered to as *ciphertext*. The transformation between these representations is called *encryption* or *encipherment;* more precisely, this term refers to the transformation from cleartext to ciphertext; the reverse is called *decryption* or *decipherment.*

Certainly any technology with so long a history is rich with interesting and quaint artifacts; the interested reader is referred to [KAHN67]. The modern view is that encryption is a mapping between cleartext and ciphertext. The function which accomplishes this mapping may have multiple independent variables as input. While the encryption function may be multi-valued, the decryption function must be single-valued if the identical cleartext is to be regained. In order for the encryption process to be useful, it must be very difficult to deduce the cleartext from the ciphertext without certain secret information. The difficulty is measured as a *work factor.* The function and/or one or more of the inputs is kept secret (this is discussed in more detail below). The work factor is often expressed in time units on a specific computer performing *cryptanalysis.* In general, the encryption function may be a discontinuous algorithm.

Keys

Modern encryption functions take at least two inputs. One is the plaintext; the other is called a key. This is named after the similarity of function with a physical lock and key. The encryption key is a set of information that affects the results

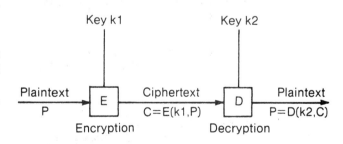

Figure 3.1: Simple Encryption and Decryption Process

of the encryption transformation. The key is often represented as a string in the language's written representation; in computer applications this string is often restricted to printable members of the character set. The size, or length, of the key may be of the same order of magnitude as the cleartext, but is usually much smaller for practical reasons; eight characters is a common length.

The encryption process can be represented pictorially and with mathematical notation. A simple representation of the process is shown in Figure 3-1. Mathematically, let

$$P = \text{Plaintext}$$
$$C = \text{Cyphertext}$$
$$K = \text{Key}$$
$$E = \text{Encryption function}$$
$$D = \text{Decryption function}$$

Then

$$C = E(k1,P)$$
$$P = D(k2,C)$$

Simplifications and variations on this theme are possible; some are discussed below.

Although used very differently internally, keys and passwords have some similar characteristics to users. Both need to be remembered and presented to an automated system in order to gain service from it. Not all applications of encryption require the user to remember a key; the key may be issued or generated at the time of use after identification and authentication has been accomplished.

Conventional Single-Key Cryptosystems

Conventional cryptosystems are designed to operate with a single key and an encryption function which does not change the length of the text. In this case,

$$P = D[k,E(k,P)]$$

and

$$P = E[k,D(k,P)]$$

The order of encryption and decryption is interchangeable. A further refinement is possible by selecting E and D as identical functions

$$E = D$$

satisfying the relations

$$E[k,E(k,P)] = P$$

and

$$D[k,D(k,C)] = C$$

With these selections, the cryptosystem is termed symmetric. The advantages of selecting this class of functions is that only one function needs to be implemented, only one key needs to be employed, and the order of encryption and decryption becomes moot. The key, k, is conventionally kept secret. Furthermore, since cryptanalysis can benefit from multiple samples of P,C pairs, the use of the key may be restricted. For example, as discussed by [VOYD85] and reprinted in Section 3.4, one master key may be used only to distribute other working keys. The working keys will themselves have a limited lifetime such as one message or one connection.

"Public" Two-Key Cryptosystems

Public key cryptosystems are designed to work with two keys; one is used to encrypt the cleartext, the other to decrypt it. We denote these keys as follows

$$ke = \text{Encryption key}$$
$$kd = \text{Decryption key}$$

(Note that notation varies from author to author. Ours is based on [DAVI81], an excellent reference.) The functions are then

$$C = E(ke,P)$$
$$P = D(kd,C)$$
$$P = D[kd,E(ke,P)]$$

Several systems have been proposed for these two key cryptosystems. Like the conventional single key systems, there is one where $D = E$; but for generality we will retain the functional distinction.

Two key systems are called "public" because of the way in which they are used. Each pair of keys is associated with an individual who keeps kd secret. The other key, ke, can be published or otherwise distributed on request. Anyone can send a secret message to the holder of the secret decryption key by employing the public encryption key. If the functions commute, then

$$P = E[ke,D(kd,P)]$$

and the holder of the secret key can send a secret message by encrypting it by using kd. The recipient must know which public key to use for decryption; that is, the sender must be identified. Note that encryption and decryption are inverse functions; under the conditions postulated, it makes no difference which is performed first.

Block and Stream Ciphers

There are two approaches to the size of message unit encrypted in each operation. Block ciphers map an N-bit block

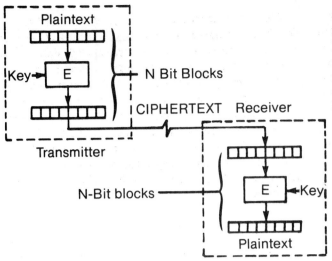

Figure 3.2: Electronic Code Book

onto another N-bit block. If the block size is one character, this reduces to a simple substitution. Much stronger ciphers are possible if the block size is increased and the permutations become complex. Since messages generally do not come in n-bit blocks, in practice it is necessary to fragment the message into blocks, padding the final block as necessary.

An example of a block cipher is the *electronic code book* illustrated in Figure 3-2. Analogous to conventional code book encryption, each block is independently encrypted. An alteration (error or otherwise) in one bit of key or plaintext will affect the entire block of ciphertext, but will not affect other blocks.

Stream ciphers operate on small blocks, typically one and eight bits long, in real time as the blocks arrive. By matching the size of the key stream to the length of the message, padding can be eliminated. An example of a stream cipher is *cipher block chaining*, illustrated in Figure 3-3, in which each block of ciphertext is exclusive-ored with the subsequent block of plaintext. Since there is no block of ciphertext to combine with the first block of plaintext, an *initialization vector* is employed. An alteration in one block will propagate throughout that block and part of the following block, but no further.

Link and End-to-End Encryption

Link Encryption

A simple view of data communications starts with two pieces of equipment closely colocated and interconnected by a perfect circuit which is protected, error-free, and of unlimited bandwidth. When idealization gives way to reality and separation increases, components must be added to provide real services employing physical components. At the top of Figure 3-4, we see *data circuit-terminating equipment* adapting a physical circuit to carry data communications and interfacing the circuit to *data terminal equipment*. In the lower part of the figure, encryption equipment has been added for the reasons discussed in this text.

This *link encryption* is entirely appropriate for point-to-point circuits. It functions at the physical level on the bit stream being transmitted. Although link encryption pre-dates the OSI model, it is easily placed in that context. If the entire bit stream is encrypted, link encryption is functioning at the physical layer (1). If the encryption is sensitive to the protocol used to transmit data, passing some fields in the clear while encrypting others, it is functioning at the data link layer (2).

Even this simple link encryption is not immune to technological changes. To prevent traffic analysis, the message stream is padded so that the volume of traffic is uniform. As long as the link was implemented as a dedicated physical circuit with copper wire or fiberglass, this padding incurred no additional expense. However, when logical circuits were provided by multiplexing physical circuits or radio transmission (as in microwave and satellite communications), this full-time traffic was recognized to be consuming resources that could be otherwise employed. There is a cost associated with this usage; if billing is usage-dependant, the cost is very quickly recognized.

The simple model described above is relatively obsolete. Data communications networks are universally employed for reasons of economy, flexibility, reliability, adaptability, and survivability, to name a few. A schematic representation of a fragment of such a switched network is shown in Figure 3-5. For our purposes there is no need to identify the switching mechanism employed. It is sufficient to recognize that some of the protocol information must be available to the switch in order that it can perform its function. Thus we require a link encryption device between every switch and the circuits connected to it. All of the information is available in the switch in the clear. Even if there were some form of double encryption to protect user-data, there are significant vulnerabilities in the switches such as traffic analysis, mis-routing, and other attacks described in the Voydock and Kent paper reprinted in Section 3.4. To prevent these problems, the switches must be physically protected.

End-to-End Encryption

The simple network view described above falls apart when applied to OSI or any other layered protocol switched network. It must be generalized to protect Protocol Data Units in each layer between communicating protocol entities. The

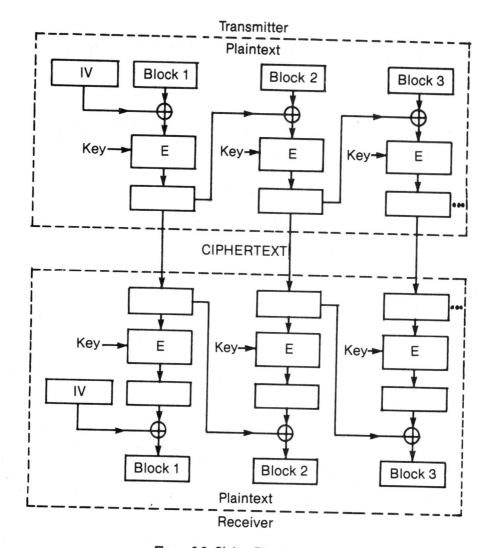

Figure 3.3: Cipher Block Chaining

totality of encryption above the link layer is called *end-to-end* encryption, sometime abbreviated E3.

Extending encryption into higher protocol layers obviously increases the number of entities protected at the cost of infacing and overhead with additional hardware and/or software. While link encryption, like most layer 1 and 2 functions, can be almost completely invisible to network users at the top applications layer (7), higher layer encryption and the accompanying protocols can be intrusive if not actually annoying.

Function Secrecy and Standardization

The functions E and D are sometimes kept secret and sometimes published as standards. This section explores why both paths are followed. The choice involves questions of work factor and open or closed network architecture and user community.

The cryptanalyst has a harder job if the function E and D are kept secret. In general, this is the approach taken for protecting national security related data. Maintaining E and D secret has involved physical protection. If the *cryptographic device* came into an intruder's hands this secret might be broken by reverse engineering; that is, by examining the device to determine how it works. Physical protection can include denial of access to the cryptographic device and automatic destruction of the device if unauthorized access was achieved. Advances in Very Large Scale Integration make it possible to implement the cryptographic function on a single chip that is highly resistant to reverse engineering, even to the extent of self-destruction. Such chips can be put into service with considerably less physical protection than prior technology.

Proprietary considerations may also favor encryption function secrecy. Link encryption devices, illustrated in Fig-

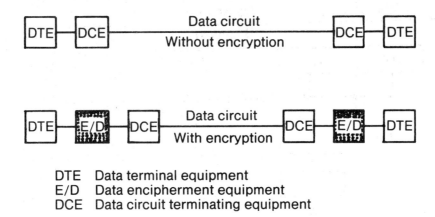

DTE   Data terminal equipment
E/D   Data encipherment equipment
DCE   Data circuit terminating equipment

Figure 3.4: Link Encryption

ure 3-4, are designed to function at OSI layer 1, the physical layer; their interaction with the other parts of the system is minimal. In fact, their presence may be invisible (non-detectable) to users; this requires that all signals be delivered from source to destination unaltered by the presence of the cryptographic device. Proprietary devices certainly can find their place in higher layers of network architecture.

Interoperability—the ability for independently manufactured systems and subsystems to work together—is a major driving force for standardization. (Market share competition is another driving force.) Given the advent of OSI networking standards, it is natural to develop encryption (and other network) security standards. Not only will such standards protect information from intruders, but they will permit mutually suspicious parties (such as competitive banks engaged in electronic funds transfer) to work with each other.

The Data Encryption Standard

Interestingly enough, the public standard for data encryption was initially developed by IBM and was first standardized by a U.S. government agency, the National Bureau of Standards, as the *Data Encryption Standard* (DES), Federal Information Processing Standard Publication (FIPS PUB) 46. It has since also been adapted as an ANSI standard under the name *Data Encryption Algorithm*. We used the electronic funds transfer (EFT) application in our previous discussion of a bank example in Section 2.3. The DES is designated for non-national security applications such as EFT. You will find a detailed treatment in [DAVI84].

The design of encryption functions E and D is a highly specialized activity beyond the scope of this tutorial. Specialists will debate the merits of various alternatives; since the DES is public, the debate concerning it has also been public. We feel, however, that most users will obtain their encryption devices as "black box" closed systems. Government agencies will follow policy directives and official guidance in selecting the function appropriate to the information being protected. Private organizations will generally have to choose among alternative products, except in certain situations where government-specified or furnished equipment is required. If the requirements for open system interoperability are not compelling, they can choose among public and proprietary functions. Expert advice would be appropriate for such a selection.

Reprints

The brief excerpt from a corporate marketing piece, *Everything You Wanted to Know about DES Security But Did Not Know Who to Ask,* provides a very easy to read introduction to cryptographic techniques. Passive attacks result in unauthorized disclosure of information, while active attacks result in alteration or injection of information. Encryption protects against such attacks; when one data terminal equipment is a computer, it also provides computer access control.

If privacy is not required, encryption can still be used to *authenticate* a message. Encryption is performed, but cleartext is transmitted followed by a *message authentication code (MAC)* derived from the ciphertext. The receiver can compute its own MAC and compare it with the one transmitted; a match guarantees that the sender possessed the proper encryption key and that the message was undamaged.

Key management procedures for generation, distribution, storage, and destruction are crucial to encryption security. Manual key distribution must occur at least once, after which automated distribution can occur. The manually distributed keys are used only to encrypt other keys; they are termed *master keys* or *key-encrypting keys (KEK)*. The keys disseminated under the KEKs are terms *session keys, working keys,* or *data-encrypting keys.*

ANSI standard X9.17, Financial Institution Key Management (Wholesale), defines three environments for key management. In a point-to-point environment, two parties share a master key that is used for distribution of working keys that

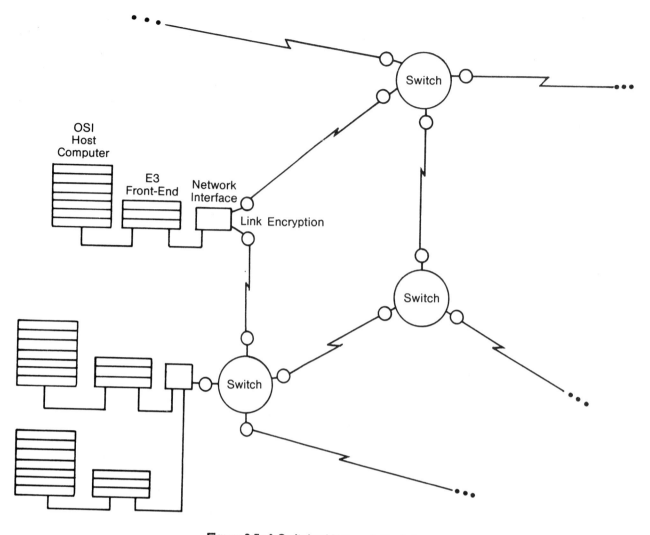

Figure 3.5: A Switched Network Model

one of them must generate. In a key distribution center environment, the master keys are shared between each party and the centralized server that generates the working key. The key translation center environment is a minor variation in which one party originates the working key.

Link encryption is described as providing protection for a line with no intermediate devices, a process that may be repeated many times as a series of isolated transmissions as a message transverses a complex network. *End-to-end encryption* is described as encrypting only user-data; network-data must remain unaltered for intermediate network nodes. Link and end-to-end encryption are compared.

As you may have noticed, it is very difficult to identify in which section of this tutorial a particular reprint should be placed. Almost every paper begins with an overview of security threats. In this case, we have decided to discuss a paper, "Security in High-Level Network Protocols by Voydock and Kent," in two different sections (this one and Section 3.4).

Victor Voydock and Stephen Kent have succeeded in condensing a lengthy report originally written for the National Bureau of Standards into a highly readable paper that still provides an in-depth look at providing security through the use of network protocols; an intermediate length version is also available. The first part of the paper, which addresses encryption, will be discussed here. Most of the paper is concerned with the network protocols necessary to use and support encryption; it is discussed in Section 3.4, where the reprint is also located.

The first contribution of Voydock and Kent is to place the discussion in the context of the ISO Reference Model of Open Systems Interconnection. (If you require further background, we suggest consulting [ABRA84].) Exactly as anticipated, the OSI model provides a framework for organizing a previously ad hoc situation. The lower two layers (the physical and data link), which predate network architecture, were the original locus of encryption activity.

Passive attacks consist of observation of information passing on a connection. *Release of message content* is the fundamental compromise. Even if encryption is used to protect message contents, analysis of message length, frequency, and protocol components such as addresses results in *traffic analysis*. *Active attacks* involve modification, delay, reordering, duplication, and synthesis of transmitted information; these attacks are now categorized and discussed. *Message-stream modification*, the first category of active attack, offers three opportunities. An *authenticity* attack causes doubt that the information actually came from the proported source and was delivered to the intended destination. An *integrity* attack modifies information content, while an *ordering* attack changes the sequence in which information arrives at the destination. Communication protocols offer some minimal protection against these threats as part of their reliability features; but they were not designed to counter a hostile attack.

Denial of message service may be viewed as an extreme case of message-stream modification in which information transfer is either blocked or drastically delayed. *Masquerading*, or spurious initiation, is an attack where an intruder attempts to establish a communications session by falsifying his identity.

Encryption is presented as the fundamental tool for countering these attacks. Through its use, release of message content and traffic analysis can be prevented; message stream modification, denial of message service, and masquerading can be detected.

The most straightforward application of encryption is to the communications link. Stream ciphers are generally employed. By definition, information is not processed as it passes on a link. Therefore, all of the information on the link can be encrypted to prevent release of message contents. If continuous traffic is maintained by padding, traffic analysis can also be prevented. Note that padding entails no additional cost if dedicated links are employed; the converse is true on shared links. Again by definition, link encryption only provides protection on the communications link. Whenever the information enters an intermediate node, such as a switch, it reverts to plaintext. Protection of this plaintext involves physical protection of the node hardware and trust (in the TCSEC sense) of the node software; there is a cost associated with this protection and trust. There is also a cost associated with the operation of the encrypted links, mostly in key management and distribution; this cost can be considerable.

Deferring the discussion of *end-to-end* protection to Section 3.4, we now turn to the discussion of data encryption. Basic concepts are introduced, including the concepts of plaintext and ciphertext, conventional and public key ciphers, block ciphers, and stream ciphers. *Data Encryption Standard* examples of block cipher, the *Electronic Code Book,* and stream cipher, *Cipher Block Chaining,* are given. The use of an *initialization vector (IV) in* cipher block chaining is introduced. Additional mode of Data Encryption Standard operation are discussed in [VOYD83].

In his reprint, "Requirements for Key Management Protocols in the Wholesale Financial Services Industry," Blake Greenlee presents two standards designed specifically for inter-bank EFTs, but more generally applicable to many commercial transactions which require authentication. Generalizations will not be belabored. The two standards are ANSI X9.9-1982, *Financial Institution Message Authentication (Wholesale)* [ANSI82] and X9.17-1985, *Financial Institution Key Management (Wholesale)* [ANSI85].

The paper begins motivating the reader by describing wholesale financial transactions among banks, businesses, and governments; describing volume, liability, management goals of timeliness and accuracy, prior technology (which is unlikely to disappear any time soon), and a sobering tale of an attempt to distribute keys by post. Several points are noteworthy: The goals addressed are authentication rather than secrecy; encryption is used as the basis for both. When both authentication and secrecy are desired, a separate key is used. Separation of duties ensures "that collusion is required in order to perpetrate a fraud." "Use of an encryption algorithm other than DEA [Data Encryption Algorithm] (DES) could be considered imprudent business practice."

Message Authentication Code (MAC): The MAC is a cryptographic checksum appended to a message. It seals the message against modification; all fields such as time, date, and sources included in the checksum are rendered unalterable. "In using the DEA for authentication, either the entire message or selected fields are processed through the algorithm using the cipher block chaining mode. The only output of the process used is that of the last block. Thirty-two bits of that block are converted to hexadecimal and expressed in ASCII to form the MAC."

Two cases form an example of MAC authentication. The first case using TELEX applies a MAC on a hop-by-hop basis. Each transfer of liability for the transaction is authenticated by using a unique key. The second case employs a single key (which should be KD5, not KD4 as incorrectly printed) for source to destination financial institution authentication. A separate key authenticates the message between commercial organization and financial institution; if the commercial organizations had a key relationship between them they could authenticate messages completely end-to-end. (Again we note the ambiguity of end-to-end.)

Greenlee explains why a MAC also requires a key management protocol, listing 14 requirements very clearly expressed. You are encouraged to study them carefully. Applicability to a variety of industries and with other encryption algorithms is noted. Implementations by the U.S. Department of Treasury and BANKWIRE are mentioned. Administrative problems remaining include a need for national and international key translation centers, key generation, and government roles.

Recommended Readings

In his paper, "Cryptology Goes Public," David Kahn discusses public policy issues of cryptology starting with World War II cryptanalysis and ending with a question of the determination of appropriate regulations. In between, he presents issues of formal intergovernmental agreement, microwave eavesdropping and other intelligence gathering, protection of personal information and business transactions, and the counterpotentials between unrestricted inquiry into cryptology versus national security. He observes that "what has happened to other technologies, such as atomic energy, is happening to cryptology. It is becoming a public matter, raising a whole new set of public issues." The readers of this tutorial need to form an educated opinion on the policy trade-offs.

In his paper, "Cryptology in Transition," Abraham Lempel provides a survey of private and public key cryptosystems that begins with the observation that cryptology has "evolved from a government monopoly dealing with military and diplomatic communications to a major concern of business in general, the banking industry in particular." He emphasizes the (then) new concept of public-key cryptosystems, discusses the problematic concept of cryptocomplexity, and notes the need for fundamental research rather than the proliferation of implementations. His comment that "all references to 'known' or 'existing' methods and schemes are with respect to unclassified and nonproprietary knowledge" is universally applicable to the public literature, including this tutorial reprint collection.

A brief survey of classical cryptology introduces the concepts of *encryption, decryption,* and *cryptanalysis.* The security of modern ciphers is based on the amount of work required to break them employing *ciphertext-only* attacks, *known-plaintext* attacks, and *chosen-plaintext* attacks. Stream ciphers, block ciphers, and the *Data Encryption Standard* (DES) are discussed.

Public-key cryptosystems constitute the main focus of the paper. Digital signatures are described as both message and signer dependent. One-way, trapdoor one-way, and puzzle methods are illustrated by the Rivest-Shamir-Adleman, Merkle-Hellman, McEliece, and Fraham-Shamir schemes. Lempel's observation that there is a lack of proof that any of these schemes is hard to break is reinforced by some cases of public-key algorithms being broken. However, we caution that this does not mean a specific algorithm can readily be broken.

Observing that it is only a matter of time before the DES becomes vulnerable to attack, Lempel asserts that "the real task and challenge are to come up with appropriate criteria for cryptosecurity and corresponding measures of crypto-complexity that will serve to replace the current reliance on vague notions of cipher 'certification' by more rigorous assertions of unbreakability."

In his paper, "DES Revisited," Tom Athanasiou reviews the DES debate 8 years after its adaption. He concludes that DES was weakened by reducing its key size from 128 to 56 bits. Other weaknesses in the substitution boxes probably exist, according to Atheanasiou, and may be impossible to disprove. He asserts that the DES is still probably adequate protection, but not for long. This last point is important; he quotes an authority (Gus Simmons of Sandia National Laboratories), "it'll [DES] be a place where people will be unwilling to hide sufficiently valuable information behind it." He notes that international adaption of DES is known as DEA-1 (Data Encrypting Algorithm 1), implying that DEA-2 and DEA-3 cannot be far behind. Athanasiou also summerizes the use of a public key to distribute working keys for conventional DES sessions.

The paper, "Slamming the Door on Data Thieves," by Robert Rosenberg introduces several key security programs offered by the National Security Agency (NSA) under National Security Decision Directive (NSDD) 145. We discussed NSDD 145 in Section 1.2. Rosenberg believes that NSDD 145 ". . . gives the NSA the green light to develop new encryption standards for unclassified government systems and to promote the new standards in the private sector." He interprets the impact of NSDD 145 with respect to the DES is that the directive ". . . effectively puts the lid on new applications using the Data Encryption Standard—the only public-sector standard for encryption implemented in silicon. The NSA says it will no longer approve the DES algorithm when it comes up for review as a federal standard in 1988. Even though it says the algorithm remains 'cryptographically sound,' the agency intends to withdraw support because the algorithm's 10 years as a published standard and the cipher's widespread use in nonclassified (and some classified) systems 'make it an increasingly attractive potential target for our adversaries.'"

Rosenberg does explain that the DES-based applications are likely to have a wide-based market way into the 1990s. Also, he mentions the fact that EFTs will be unaffected. He is probably referring to the ANSI Standards X9.9, 9.17, which have a commercial following in the banking community.

An important new development in commercial encryption systems is introduced by Rosenberg. This is the Commercial COMSEC (Communications Security) Endorsement Program. Essentially, NSA is offering a transfer of non-public encryption technology to commercial producers of encryption systems. At the time of his article, 11 companies had been qualified by NSA for the manufacture of COMSEC devices, using non-public encryption technology. Rosenberg states that the 11 companies ". . . can provide unclassified information about chips and modules; [however,] they may provide application information and sample parts only with NSA approval." The 11 companies are AT&T, GTE, Harris, Honeywell, Hughes, IBM, Intel, Motorola, RCA (GE), Rockwell, and Xerox.

A second NSA program is introduced by Rosenberg. He describes another area where non-public encryption technology is being offered to industry. This second program, which we briefly discuss in Section 1.2, is for secure voice and has an objective of enabling manufacturers to offer secure phones at "about $2,000 apiece," which is a substantial cost reduction from previous equipment. Rosenberg states: "The telephone contract—awarded in April 1985 to AT&T, Motorola, and RCA [GE]—is the first of many expected as part of the commercial COMSEC development effort. One source, knowledgeable about security affairs, speculates that a whole family of integrated circuit chips is likely to evolve because the encryption of voice, high-speed data, and graphics would require different optimization schemes."

Several security provisions are described by Rosenberg. For example, he states that security will be maintained even ". . .if the chips are lost to an adversary," because of the key-management approach. The NSA will, according to Rosenberg, "assign keys to all government and government-contractor encryption systems. It will transmit new keys for each system, probably as often as several times a minute."

3. CRYPTOGRAPHY: ENCRYPTION AND AUTHENTICATION

Today, telecommunication networks are routinely used by banks, industrial, commercial, and government organizations to convey highly sensitive and privileged information. Unauthorized access to this information is easy and cheap to obtain and difficult to detect. The result is an "explosion" in computer crime and other computer-related abuses. This unauthorized access can take the form of either an active or passive attack against the communications channels conveying the information. A passive attack consists of merely eavesdropping on the channel and recording the transmitted information. If proprietary information was in transit over that channel, then an unauthorized copy of this information is now in unauthorized hands. An active attack, often referred to as spoofing, consists of either intercepting and altering the text of a legitimate message in transit or of interjecting a message into the data channel with the intent of making the message appear to the recipient that it originated from an authorized party. In either active or passive attacks, it is difficult, if not impossible, to find electronic tracks leading to the perpetrator. Obviously, as the dependency on telecommunications systems increases, so do the concurrent vulnerabilities of unauthorized access to proprietary information and the spoofing of communicating systems. The SHERLOCK products, via different firmware implementations, can either encrypt or authenticate, thus guaranteeing privacy as well as the integrity of the transmitted data. ISMs offer a high degree of protection against both active and passive attacks.

3.1   HOW ENCRYPTION PROTECTS

When encrypting, the original message (called plain text) is transformed into an unreadable form (called cipher text). The resulting cipher
text is then transmitted over the communications channel. The intended recipient — and only the intended recipient — is equipped to reconvert the
received cipher text back into the original plain text — a process called
decryption. Protection against the passive attack of eavesdropping is
obtained because the eavesdropper has access only to the transmitted cipher
text — a completely unintelligible form. Protection against the active
attack of spoofing is obtained because an attacker cannot generate a cipher
text stream that, when injected into the data channel, will reconvert into
intelligible plain text at the receiving end of the channel. It should be
emphasized that the intended recipient (or the receiving end of the channel)
can be either another network terminal or a computer. When it is a computer,
the aforementioned spoofing protection provided by the ISM translates to computer access control. No unauthorized, non-system terminal or user can access
any computer within the network by virtue of the fact that the unauthorized
terminal is not equipped to either encrypt or decrypt.

3.2   HOW AUTHENTICATION PROTECTS

ISMs also offer a high degree of protection against active attacks
(only) when used in an authentication mode. When authenticating, the original
message is transformed into cipher text just as it was when encrypting. However, rather then transmit this cipher text, the cipher text is accumulated
within the ISM into a 4-byte entity called the Message Authentication Code
(MAC). The original plain text is then transmitted but with the MAC appended
to the end of the message. At the receiving end of the channel, the same process is repeated, i.e., the received plain text is transformed and the
resulting cipher text accumulated to form a second MAC. If the second MAC
just calculated is identical to the transmitted MAC, the recipient is assured
of the integrity of the received data. Note, that in this authentication

mode, privacy of the data cannot be assured. The plain text is transmitted and is therefore vulnerable to the passive attack of eavesdropping.

3.3   THE CRYPTOGRAPHIC TRANSFORMATION

Cryptography has always been a preferred way of securing information being relayed from one location to another. All cryptographic techniques involve a transformation from intelligible text to unintelligible text. In theory, there are an infinite number of transformations into which the original text can be translated. In order to recover the original message (i.e., when encrypted) or to reproduce the authentication code (i.e., when authenticated), a recipient must be able to identify the transformation that was used; having done that, the recipient can then perform the appropriate inverse transformation on the received data.

Practical cryptographic algorithms cannot allow selection between an infinite number of transformations, but if properly designed, they can allow a choice from a set so large that it becomes extremely impractical (computationally infeasible) for an attacker to exhaustively try each possible transformation until the correct one is found. As stated earlier, the cryptographic algorithm used in SHERLOCK products is called the Data Encryption Standard (DES) and has been certified by the U.S. National Bureau of Standards. There is nothing secret about the DES algorithm itself. It is in the public domain and any security evaluation of this algorithm would assume that an attacker knows the details of the algorithm and has a DES device to process messages and data. The DES, which allows for $2^{56} = 10^{17}$ different transformations, has been designed so that there is no known way, through examination of cipher text, of determining which transformation was used in producing that cipher text. The security of DES depends upon the choice of which possible transformation is to be used to encrypt or authenticate a particular message

or group of messages. The transformation chosen, which is called the cryptographic key, must be shared by all parties authorized to receive that particular message or group of messages. An unauthorized receiver may have a DES
device similar to that used by the intended recipient(s), but unless the
unauthorized party has access to the cryptographic key, the message cannot be
decrypted or re-authenticated.

3.4   OTHER USEFUL CRYPTOGRAPHIC TERMS AND CONCEPTS
The following paragraphs of this subsection address and define a few
other cryptographic terms and concepts that may be valuable to the reader who
is not familiar with the science of cryptography.

3.4.1   Key Management
The security of cryptographically secured data is strictly dependent
upon the key in use and if that key is in any way compromised, the security of
the data can no longer be guaranteed. Furthermore, all authorized recipients
of the data must have access to the key in order to decrypt and/or authenticate received data; obviously, this key must be disseminated to all such
recipients, and the dissemination itself must be done securely. Thus, key
management refers to the procedures and methods that must be in place to
generate, distribute, store, and ultimately destroy keys in such a manner that
security is maintained.

Key management can be broken down into two major categories or
methods of implementation; that is, manual and automated. Manual key management generally refers to distributing the keying material to the locations
where it is needed by using some manual procedure such as registered mail or
bonded courier as opposed to automated key management wherein the keying
material is electronically transmitted over some secure communications channel
to the appropriate locations. Often the same network which the new keying
material will subsequently secure provides the circuits for this automated

distribution, and when this is the case, that distribution itself must be secured. Since a secure transport protocol must use existing secure connections to establish a new secure connection, there is a "bootstrap" problem of establishing the first and most basic secure connection. That is, security can only be built on a foundation of trusted mechanisms. Therefore, it becomes obvious that a subset of automated key management is manual key management in that manual key management procedures must be in place to initially instigate a subsequent secure automated method.

The usual way in which the "bootstrap" problem is solved is to define a two-tiered hierarchy of keys. In other words, the keys to be disseminated are treated as though they were normal message data and are encrypted with a higher-level key before they are disseminated. The keys that are to be disseminated are generally referred to as session keys (or data encrypting keys — DEKs). The keys used to encrypt the session keys prior to dissemination and to decrypt the encrypted session keys after dissemination has occurred are termed master keys (or key encrypting keys — KEKs). Master keys obviously must be disseminated also, but this dissemination is normally accomplished through manual means, even in an automated key management environment.

Some key management schemes also define a third level to the keying hierarchy in that they make use of keys for securing information other than transmitted message data or transmitted keys. For example, in a key management facility, master keys and/or session keys may very well be stored in on-line computerized files for rapid retrieval when their use is required. Such storage is, of course, vulnerable to ADP personnel, contractors, and/or consultants working with the system or system components either through accidental or intentional means. In order to protect against such compromises, files of this nature should be encrypted which adds the third level to the keying hierarchy. Such a key is generally referred to as a facility key.

The American National Standards Institute (ANSI) has developed a standard for key management entitled Financial Institution Key Management (Wholesale) and known as ANSI X9.17. Although ANSI X9.17 is directed at financial institutions, many non-financial organizations are intending to adopt the majority of methods and procedures that X9.17 recommends; X9.17 may very well become the "ad hoc" standard for large network applications of security whether financially oriented or not. ANSI X9.17 defines three possible automated environments for key management. These environments are point-to-point, the Key Distribution Center (CKD), and the Key Translation Center (CKT). The conditions applicable to these three environments are:

- A Point-to-Point Environment. A point-to-point environment exists when two parties share a master key in common so that further cryptographic keys may be exchanged. At least one of the two parties must have the capability to generate or otherwise acquire keys.

- A Key Distribution Center Environment. A CKD exists for the purpose of distributing keys to two parties who wish to securely communicate with each other but who do not currently share master keys. However, the two parties do share different master keys with the CKD. Further, the two parties may not have the capability of generating keys.

- A Key Translation Center Environment. A CKT exists for the purpose of distributing keys to two parties who wish to securely communicate with each other but who do not currently share master keys. As before, the two parties do share different master keys with the CKT, but in this case, the party to originate the message does have key generation capability.

3.4.2   End-to-End Versus Link-by-Link Implementations
The terms end-to-end and link-by-link generally refer only to implementations of encryption and not to authentication. However, the concepts can certainly be extrapolated to include authentication implementations as well. A communications link is defined as consisting of a transmission line and a

pair of communicating devices or points such as nodes, switches, user terminals, or the like. The devices are line terminators and there are, by definition, no intermediate devices on the line. Link-by-link security implies that the cryptographic devices are physically located adjacent to line terminators. Exchanges between terminators consist of user data (messages) and network data (routing and protocol information). Cryptographic devices are placed "on" the line such that user data (and possibly network data) are secured. Network data assure the proper synchronization of the transmission, control the flow of user data, and verify the accuracy of the transmission. The network data exists only to support the transmission across the link and is transparent to all but those terminator components directly involved in communications support. Network data is exchanged freely (both ways) between terminators. For any given transmission, however, the data effectively flows in only one direction. The terminator from which the flow is outbound is the sending point on the link and the terminator for which the flow is inbound is the receiving point on the link.

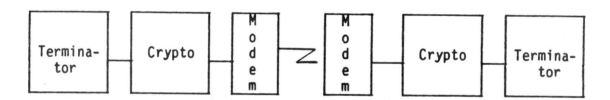

In the link depicted above, a user generates a message at the work station (terminator); it is passed to the cryptographic device and either encrypted, authenticated, or both; it is then passed to the modem and modulated (converted to analog). After crossing the link, it is demodulated (converted to digital), decrypted or reauthenticated, and eventually passed to the receiving terminator. On the next link, the previous receiving terminator becomes the sending point and a device on the other end becomes the receiving point. This process is repeated many times, as a series of isolated transmissions, until such time as the receiving point is the message addressee.

The exact number of links required to carry any given message from originator to ultimate destination is a function of network complexity and the specific routing selected by network components.

Given the prior definition of a communications link, the classes of data in communications exchanges, and the sequence of devices and processes through which the data passes, end-to-end security implementations at the rudimentary level can be viewed a depicted below.

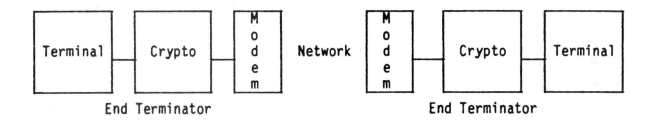

With end-to-end security, cryptographic devices are provided only at points of origin and ultimate destination. Each message is encrypted and/or authenticated at the originating terminator and is decrypted and/or reauthenticated only at the destination terminator. Messages pass through the entire network of links, local computers, nodes, switches, etc. in encrypted and/or authenticated form. Obviously, with this type of security implementation only the user data is cryptographically processed. Network data must remain unaltered to be processable by the network nodes.

In the majority of network applications, end-to-end security is undoubtedly the preferred implementation in that a higher decree of security is attainable because trusted-intermediate network nodes are not necessary. Furthermore, if the network services are purchased by the end users from value-added carriers (i.e., Telenet, Tymnet, etc.) cryptographic equipment cannot be implemented at the link level without permission of the network. Table 3-1 delineates some of the advantages and disadvantages of the two types of implementations.

Table 3-1

Advantages/Disadvantages of
Link-by-Link/End-to-End Implementations

	Link-by-Link	End-to-End
A D V A N T A G E S	1. The "world" as known to any given terminator, consists only of those links to which it has direct access, plus the terminators on the other end of those links. Thus, key management is simplified through the need to share common keys only with physically accessible terminators on these adjacent links. 2. Installation of security may be "grown," link-by-link, in an evolutionary fashion. 3. Those countries which prohibit the transmission of encrypted data may be accommodated by simply not installing devices on affected links.	1. Messages pass through the entire network in a secured form. 2. Fewer cryptographic devices are required. 3. Key distribution is made to terminators only. 4. System overhead is lower because the security function is not required at each link.
D I S A V A N T A G E S	1. A greater quantity of cryptographic equipment is required. 2. Network overhead is higher in that complete security functions are required on each link. 3. Trusted network nodes are required.	1. Flexibility in configuring network security is lower. 2. The cryptographic devices required must be technically sophisticated.

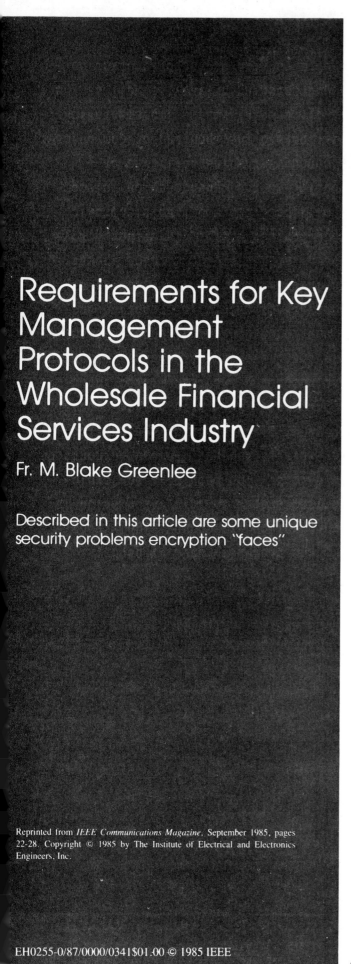

Requirements for Key Management Protocols in the Wholesale Financial Services Industry

Fr. M. Blake Greenlee

Described in this article are some unique security problems encryption "faces"

Reprinted from *IEEE Communications Magazine*, September 1985, pages 22-28. Copyright © 1985 by The Institute of Electrical and Electronics Engineers, Inc.

Discussions of the operations of financial organizations tend to center on two differing types of systems, products, and requirements which are lumped under the terms, "wholesale" and "retail." Retail financial services are characterized by low average transaction size (typically about $50), and high transaction volumes. It's the kind of banking that most of us do. Individual or family checking accounts, savings accounts, credit cards, and auto loans come to mind.

In contrast, wholesale financial transactions tend to average $3,000,000 in value and have much lower volumes—in the thousands or tens of thousands per day—even for very large, "money center" banks. Customers include other (generally smaller) banks, businesses, and governments.

As the activities of these customers have decentralized, there has been an accelerating need for the efficient, secure, and error-free movement of funds and other types of assets to support their needs. From an operational view, the system that is used to mobilize these funds has grown from the use of structured telephone data gathering and the semi-automated production of paper documents using paper tape driven typewriters (in 1969), to on-line computer terminals in the office of the present corporate or government treasurer.

In a make-believe world with no crime, there are two major risks that banks and their customers face when making electronic payments: the interest cost of loss of availability of funds (or other assets) and the cost to the business of not having the assets where they should be when needed. These exposures can result in losses to the institution in "penalty interest" (about $300 per one million dollars per day) and the requirement to pay "consequential damages."

Consequential damages may range from many thousands of dollars lost because a ship load of strawberries spoiled in Hong Kong when the money to pay the crew arrived too late (leading them to turn off the refrigeration and go ashore to enjoy the pleasures of the port) to millions of dollars when a late money transfer results in the failure of a business.

In each case, the financial institution responsible for the error must compensate those that incur the loss. Firms rarely go to court. Under the Uniform Commercial Code, keeping funds or the interest on those funds when they do not belong to your corporation is called "unlawful enrichment." The result is that when money is sent to the wrong customer, it comes back—and with the interest!

The primary management goals are the timeliness and accuracy of the transactions. These goals cause managers to emphasize the use of authentication techniques (which protect against deliberate as well as accidental message alterations) rather than encryption. After all, if there are problems with equipment or the communications path, an encrypted message may not be able to be processed—resulting in penalty interest or a suit for consequential damages. An authenticated message sent in plaintext can be processed even if it fails to authenticate.

Yes, there may be some risk in accepting an unauthenticated order, but if the customer is known, that risk is minimal (amounting to the interest lost on the interest). However, even when transactions that have gone astray are reversed and the correct beneficiary is paid, there is some loss of the customer's good will.

Obviously, if there is a need for protection of confidentiality, then encryption is the only solution other than registered mail—which slows the velocity of decision making and the movement of funds, and has some unique security problems of its own (described below).

Older Protection Techniques

The traditional technique used to protect high dollar value funds transfers is a family of authentication methods called "Testwords" or "Test Keys." A typical "Testword" system creates an authentication code using as input the transaction value (in thousands), the date, a sequence number (not used by all institutions), and a random number. In more complex Testword systems, a single random number may be assigned to each customer of a bank (and rarely changed), or the numbers may be taken from a random number table (100 numbers, used cyclicly, year after year). Old-fashioned bankers call these "Testword Tables." We would call them "keys."

Testword systems provide a redundancy check on the amount field and, when a sequence number is used, provide information on missing or duplicate payments. Note that no protection is provided for the other fields of the message—payee name and account number, method of payment, value date, currency type, and so forth.

Throughout the world, the Testword algorithms presently in use are all amenable to hand calculation. They were designed long before the advent of computers. A few minutes spent with pencil and paper are more than sufficient to compute the most complex Testword. Obviously, the inverse process, that of breaking down the algorithm to determine the "random number" takes just as little time and effort.

Virtually every major bank in the world has its own Testword system. Some banks have several—and use them for different purposes. There is little standardization, although the algorithms tend to be similar. A typical, large, U.S. money center bank has automated its Testword Department—for the algorithms of its major customers and for the algorithms that make up the majority of its "Tested Message" traffic. Operationally, this means that about one hundred algorithms (with their associated tables) are computerized. Perhaps as many as a thousand additional systems are still implemented manually; the business volume does not justify their automation.

Such security systems were perfectly adequate for the earlier funds transfer (wholesale EFT) activity. They look much less adequate in the current environment where there is an absence of voice recognition, most of the assets flow with no human intervention and there is a widespread availability of microcomputers as tools for potential criminals or terrorists.

Manual Distribution of Keying Material and the Concept of "Trust" in Banking

To many outsiders, banks seem to be oblivious to concepts such as "trusted systems" and "trusted channels." In reality, the concept of trust is defined around a set of procedures and controls embedded within the financial systems of the world. We will illustrate this with a brief discussion of how Testword keying material is distributed.

1) In advance of distribution of the keying material, a signed contract must be in place—detailing the responsibilities of each of the parties, control requirements, and allocating financial liability in the event of failure to observe the procedures.
2) Dual control procedures are used in distributing and using the Testword algorithm and the keying material. The intent is to provide sufficient separation of the information required to compute a Testword that collusion is required in order to perpetrate a fraud.

   Typically, at least two separate mailings are used. Within the operations departments of the sending bank, two separate individuals are designated, one to distribute the algorithm and the other to distribute the key. Similarly, two individuals are designated by the receiving bank to receive the algorithm and the keys, respectively. By prior agreement, each individual at the sending bank mails the algorithm or key to the properly designated employee of the receiving bank. It is not uncommon for these individuals to be named in the contract.

   On receipt of the material, it is inventoried. An acknowledgment (receipt) is returned to the sending bank.

   Dual control systems, like the process used to distribute Testword algorithms and two key systems did not originate with the advent of command-control systems. Look at your safe deposit box. Two keys are required to open it. Look at the door of the vault enclosing the box—again, you will see two combination locks. This use of dual control entry is required by regulation, but has long been considered the basis of sound banking control practice.
3) No Testword system or keying material is ever used unless a valid, signed receipt is received by the sending institution. The signature(s) are compared against those on the contracts.

4) Auditors verify that the intended controls are in place and operative.
5) Risk is further limited by the use of "blanket bond" policies to insure against the wrongful acts of employees.

If it is assumed that the postal system used to distribute the keying material is secure (registered mail), then external risks are negligible, and internal risks are covered by the bond and procedures.

Development of the ANSI X9.9 Authentication Standard

In the late 1970s, the financial community realized that Testword systems would neither provide the requisite security nor transaction processing growth potential for the future. A working group formed under the Financial Services Committee (X9) of ANSI began development of a message authentication standard. This standard, X9.9-1982, *Financial Institution Message Authentication (Wholesale)*, utilizes the Data Encryption Algorithm developed by IBM (called DEA in the ANSI standard; DES in Federal Information Processing Standard 46) and a secret key to compute a cryptographically derived check sum called a Message Authentication Code (MAC) from the financial message.

DEA was chosen initially as the algorithm because there was no public key algorithm available; work on the standard began before the publication of techniques such as RSA and "knapsack." DEA continues to be the algorithm of choice for authentication, encryption, and key management for several reasons, including:

1) There is no national or international standard public key algorithm. Use of an algorithm other than DEA could be considered imprudent business practice. It is the only algorithm that is both a government and private sector standard. The very fact that it is a Federal Information Processing Standard puts the credibility of the U.S. Government behind it. Implicitly, by the publication of DES as FIPS-46, the United States government is liable for any cryptologic problems that may occur. "Goodness" is guaranteed in a way that would be obvious to any judge in any court, worldwide.
2) All available public key algorithms require a secure, initial distribution of variables. The public key directory must be authenticated and such authentication would seem to require either its delivery by bonded courier or the use of a secret key algorithm such as DEA for key directory authentication. Also, since banking networks are always expanding in some countries and contracting in others (because of geopolitical problems), the directory contents is dynamic. A single distribution is not sufficient; relationships which are defined by

a Testword or data key for authentication change daily.

3) At present, there are a variety of DEA chips available—at varying speeds and with differing operational characteristics. There are some very fine high-speed software implementation strategies such as those developed by Yvo Desmedt at the Catholic University of Louvain. There are no LSI components available for the public key algorithms. Whether in hardware or software, most public key systems would seem to be much slower than DEA.

In using the DEA for authentication, either the entire message or selected fields are processed through the algorithm using the Cipher Block Chaining Mode. The only output of the process used is that of the last block. Thirty-two bits of that block are converted to hexadecimal and expressed in ASCII to form the MAC.

An authenticated message may also be encrypted. However, the standard requires that different keys be used for encryption and authentication to prevent undetected block transpositions when n-bit Cipher Feedback is used for encryption. Provision is also made to name the key used to compute the MAC so that the receiving financial institution can select the key from a previously distributed key table or list (if more than one key is used in the relationship).

Authentication is designed to be an end-to-end process, in the sense that a new MAC must be computed using a unique key by any parties to the transaction that modifies the message. Such modification carries with it the assumption of financial liability for the changed transaction. Perhaps an example would help in showing the typical way in which a financial message could be authenticated—both using publicly available networks such as TELEX and a banking network such as BANKWIRE or the Federal Reserve Wire System (Fedwire).

Let Company A be a manufacturer located in New York that is a customer of Citibank. Company B is a parts supplier to Company A and is located in Peoria, Illinois. Company B's bank is First National Bank of Peoria (First Peoria). Company A wishes to send $1000 to Company B as a payment for parts received.

Because the companies are customers of two different banks, either those two banks must have a mutual account relationship or have a relationship with a third bank—say, First Chicago (for the TELEX example; the Federal Reserve for the network example). Such banks are termed, "mutual correspondents." Lists of mutual correspondents are maintained by all financial institutions doing funds transfers. These banks tend to be either major money center banks or large regional banks. Data Keys to be used in the MAC computation have been previously distributed, as follows:

Data Key Name	Account Relationship
KD1	Company A-to-Citibank
KD2	Citibank-to-First Chicago
KD3	First Chicago-to-First Peoria
KD4	First Peoria-to-Company B
KD5	Citibank-to-First Peoria

Case 1: a Funds Transfer using TELEX

The steps in sending the $1000 from Company A to Company B via TELEX are:

1) Company A sends a message to Citibank, authenticated using KD1. The message requests that Citibank transfer $1000 to Company B in Peoria, advise Company B when the funds are available, and advise Company A when the transaction is complete.

2) Citibank receives and processes the message, computes a MAC on the message using KD1, and verifies that the computed MAC equals the one received with the message.

3) Citibank determines that First Peoria is Company B's bank and that First Chicago is a mutual correspondent.

4) Citibank debits Company A's account, credits First Chicago's account, and sends a message to First Chicago telling the bank that their account has been credited, requesting that First Chicago transfer the $1000 to First Peoria for the account of Company B, and requesting that all parties be advised when the transaction has been completed. KD2 is used to authenticate the message.

5) First Chicago receives the message, authenticates it using KD2, debits its account with Citibank, credits its account with First Peoria, and sends a message to First Peoria telling them that their account has been credited for the $1000, and asking them to credit the account of company B with the $1000 and advise all parties when the transaction completes. The message to First Peoria is authenticated using KD3.

6) First Peoria receives the message, authenticates it using KD3, credits the account of Company B with the $1000, notifies Company B that the funds have arrived in a message authenticated using KD4, and advises all other parties that the transaction has completed.

Each transfer of liability for the transaction is authenticated with a unique key on an end-to-end basis. Intervening communications network nodes, store and forward switches, and so on, are completely transparent to the authentication process.

Case 2: a Funds Transfer Using the Federal Reserve Wire System (Fedwire)

The steps in sending the $1000 from Company A to Company B via Fedwire are:

1) Company A sends a message to Citibank, authenticated using KD1. The message requests that Citibank transfer $1000 to Company B in Peoria, advise Company B when the funds are available, and advise Company A when the transaction is complete.

2) Citibank receives and processes the message, computes a MAC on the message using KD1, and verifies that the computed MAC equals the one received with the message.

3) Citibank determines that First Peoria is Company B's bank and is a member of the Fedwire network (that is, the Federal Reserve System constitutes a mutual correspondent).

4) Citibank debits Company A's account, credits the account of the Federal Reserve Bank of New York, and sends a third party funds transfer message to the New York Fed, naming First Peoria as the destination bank and Company B as the ultimate beneficiary. KD4 is used to authenticate the message. The message may be link-encrypted between Citibank and the New York Fed.

5) The New York Fed receives the message, decrypts it, debits its account with Citibank, credits its account with the Chicago Fed, and sends the message (unchanged, with the MAC in its proper position) on to the Chicago Fed telling them that their account has been credited for the $1000, and asking them to credit the account of First Peoria with the $1000 for the account of Company B. The message to the Chicago Fed is link encrypted and might be authenticated as well, using a different key.

6) The Chicago Fed receives the message, decrypts it, debits its account with the New York Fed, credits its account with the First Peoria, and sends the message (unchanged, with the MAC in its proper position) on to First Peoria telling them that their account has been credited for the $1000, and asking them to credit the account of Company B with the $1000. The message to First Peoria is link encrypted.

7) First Peoria receives the message, decrypts it, credits the account of Company B with the $1000, and notifies Company B that the funds have arrived in a message authenticated using KD4.

The transfer of liability from Citibank to First Peoria for the transaction is authenticated with a unique key on an end-to-end basis. The communications with the customers are also authenticated. Links to the Federal Reserve Banks are link-encrypted (and could be authenticated, as well). From the standpoint of MAC calculation, the Fedwire system, and intervening Federal Reserve Banks are transparent to the process.

To confuse matters even further, Company A might also have a keying relationship with Company B. In this case, Company A could send a message (such as a reference to an order, or instructions for shipment) to

Company B in a free format field of the funds transfer, authenticate the message using the shared data key, and thus provide end-to-end protection for the message that would be transparent to the intermediate parties.

The working group knew that an automated means of distributing keys was needed, but deferred that effort until the authentication standard was complete.

The Need for an Automated Key Management Protocol

Even though financial institutions now have a method to authenticate messages that is far superior to Testword systems, there will be many years before those insecure systems are replaced in the 10,000 banks that send funds transfers worldwide. Given the experience in trying to change key-like information in the current environment, it is unlikely that authentication will be placed in wide spread use unless an automated means of managing keys is provided. Since control procedures now used for Testkey material would be used in manually distributing keys for authentication, it is instructive to examine them.

Each distribution requires *three letters*. The material is sent out in two separate mailings (both registered). Receipt by the intended recipient is authenticated by the signed receipt. The keying material is not put into use until that receipt is received.

This sounds simple, but the experience of major banks when they attempt to change keys is sobering indeed.

First, most larger banks have thousands of keying relationships, and these relationships are constantly changing—as our customer base changes.

Yet, direct mail advertising campaigns send out hundreds of thousands of letters. That my mailbox is overstuffed, almost daily, with them seems to say that there is no problem. But there is a difference in the consequence of key not arriving and the loss in the mail of an ad for a new toothpaste.

Let's start with the numbers. For convenience, let $n \times (n-1)$ be approximated by n^2.

The private EFT network used by the largest banks in the U.S. is called BANKWIRE. The network is owned by its members and utilizes store and forward message switches, fully backed up. The BANKWIRE network has about 200 members. To distribute key requires:

$$(2 \text{ letters to send key} + 1 \text{ letter receipt}) \times (200)^2$$
$$= 120,000 \text{ letters}$$

That doesn't seem too bad in terms of a load on the operations management—only 300 letters per bank, and this can be regarded as a lower bound for financial institutions of regional bank size or larger. The extreme example is for the 10,000 (or so) banks, worldwide, that send and receive funds transfers. Our approximation yields:

$$(2 + 1) \times (10000)^2 = 300,000,000 \text{ letters}$$

Now, this is an absolute upper bound (at present), but it is enough mail to swamp the postal system if you try to change key more often than once every ten or twenty years!

But, other problems occur. Letters must be addressed to someone. In the case of keying material, they must be addressed to someone in authority, and they must arrive in a timely manner.

A major U.S. bank's recent experience is sobering. They tried to send out 2000 new keys. The mailing was preceded with almost a year of planning—gathering addresses, checking names, preparing control procedures. Yet the result was a disaster. First of all, very few letters were answered by the enclosed receipt. Domestically, the keys apparently arrived. But the addressee— good old Sam in the Podunk Bank Testword Department—had died or retired, and the material was lost or discarded.

Internationally, the result was very interesting. Almost universally, the words on the cover of the letters, "REGISTERED MAIL" were translated into "I'M VALUABLE, STEAL ME" in the language of the country. The key never arrived. It took over two years to sort the mess out. Keys were hand delivered. Keys were re-mailed and the telephone used to verify arrival. In light of this experience, it is no wonder that most banks view the distribution of new keys as being a greater security hazard than not changing keys.

General Requirements for a Key Management Protocol

The requirements for key management for wholesale financial applications include the traditional ones of protecting the keying material from:

1) disclosure
2) modification
3) substitution, insertion, and deletion

The ANSI key management standard contains a detailed list of other requirements, defined in technical terminology. In order to provide background on the operational requirements underlying them, the following general requirements have been listed, along with the rational for their inclusion in the development of the protocol:

4) In order to assure that equipment built by different vendors is interoperable, all equipment must have the capability for entry of manually distributed key in a standardized format (assumes a paper-based distribution).
5) In order to alleviate the operational problems associated with the manual distribution of key, two compatible architectures for automated key distribution are provided:
   a) Two layer—data keys may be automatically exchanged and the exchange is protected by key

345

encrypting keys that have been previously manually distributed. Provision of a two-layer architecture is a minimum requirement of the standard.

b) Three layer—key encrypting keys may be automatically exchanged and the exchange is protected by key encrypting keys that have been previously manually distributed. Data keys may be then be automatically exchanged and the exchange is protected by key encrypting keys that have been previously automatically distributed. A three layer architecture is needed in order to allow key distribution and key translation centers.

Key encrypting keys may be single DEA keys or DEA key pairs. The use of DEA key pairs is required when a key distribution or key translation center is used because of the difficulty of replacing manually distributed keys.

Automatic key exchange is implemented using "Cryptographic Service Messages." Service message fields requiring confidentiality protection are protected by encryption. Protection against modification is provided by authentication.

Protection against substitution, deletion, and replay is provided by the inclusion of a counter field in the service message. The counters are binary counters. They count the uses of the key encrypting key used to protect the highest level key in the service message. They are transmitted in hexadecimal, expressed in ASCII.

There is a legal requirement that a financial institution keep the records needed to prove that a transaction was executed correctly and in accordance with valid instructions for *seven* years. If the actions of the bank are challenged, the keying material used to authenticate it may have to be revealed in open court. Given the difficulty in changing keys manually, and the chance that the other holder of the key may fail to discontinue the use of the underlying key encrypting key adds the following requirement:

6) Data keys transmitted under a key encrypting key must be protected from substitution, insertion, and deletion even if prior data keys sent under that key encrypting key are compromised. To prevent such attacks, the key encrypting key used to encrypt the highest level key in the service message is "offset" by the current value of the counter (the counter value is exclusive-ored with the key).

Because of the difficulty of manual transmission of keys and the high error rates experienced in data communications with some nations:

7) Keys may be sent for immediate or future use.

Customers of financial institutions, while "trusted," are frequently competitors, hence:

8) Valid users must be protected against other valid users—at equivalent or different privilege levels. This prohibits the use of "broadcast" keys. Key notarization is used to protect users of key translation (and distribution) centers from one valid user posing (masquerading) as another valid user. From a cryptographic control standpoint, each and every customer-institution (and sometimes application) pair must be compartmented from every other such pair.

The financial liability of PTT's and International Record Carriers (IRC's) is limited to $500. Vendors will not accept liability for the use of their products. Therefore:

9) The key management protocol must be under the complete control of the using financial institution. In a modern data processing system, the protocol must then be implemented and operate at layer 7 of the OSI model. Where more primitive communications and information processing systems are available, the protocol must be implemented as an independent, secure application.

A large proportion of financial transactions are communicated over networks and via equipment that does not conform to the emerging Open System Interconnect model standards. Therefore:

10) Control characters (for example, ASCII) and control strings (for example, Baudot) must not appear in ciphertext.

Investigation of wayward transactions requires that cryptographic service messages be human readable, therefore:

11) The protocol must utilize coded character sets.

Financial relationships may be terminated, keys may be compromised, and the postal system is an inadequate means of communications. Hence:

12) The protocol must provide for the secure termination of individual keys or a keying relationship. The party requesting termination must receive an authenticated acknowledgment that the action requested has been taken.

Management control and accountability requirements dictate that:

13) Every cryptographic service message must be responded to by either an authenticated acknowledgment or an error message (with the exception of error messages).

These last two requirements are for closure. It's not an academic exercise, closure is a management requirement!

Over time, cryptographic algorithms must be expected to change. Therefore:

14) The protocol must be algorithm independent.

Concluding Remarks

The key management standard, ANSI X9.17-1985, *Financial Institution Key Management (Wholesale)*, was approved in early April of this year. Details of the standard and its initial implementation are described elsewhere in this report. It provides procedures for manual key distribution and a protocol for automated key distribution in point-to-point and center environments.

While the working group developed the protocol based on the requirements of the wholesale financial services industry, it is useable in a variety of industries and with algorithms other than DEA.

Implementations are in process at several large financial institutions. The U.S. Treasury Department requires the use of the standard in their certification criteria for EFT security services. BANKWIRE, a network owned by the 200 largest U.S. banks is implementing the standard and will provide a key translation center for its member institutions.

Major problems remaining to be resolved are primarily administrative. There is a need for a national key translation center. Many banks feel that it should be operated by the Department of the Treasury rather than the Federal Reserve, since the Federal Reserve system is a competitor of private sector financial institutions. From an international standpoint, there will be a need for regional or national key translation centers. How are these to be managed? How is liability to be allocated? Who certifies equipment?

The generation of key is another major issue. It is a non-trivial process. Keys must also be packaged, accounted for, and distributed manually—even when centers are used. This may be another function that can only be performed by a governmental department—who else can provide the guarantee of "goodness" of the keys

and is financially able to provide insurance for the process.

The emergence of privately held, profit-making key translation centers may open the way for national, secure electronic mail. The Congress may have to address the tradeoff between personal and corporate privacy rights and the need to deny such rights in selected cases to organized criminal activities.

Blake Greenlee is a Vice President in the International Technology Security group at Citibank, and is an Episcopal priest (Assistant at St. Thomas Episcopal Church, Bethel, Connecticut; spiritual director in Cursillo in the diocese).

At Citibank, he has staff responsibility for computer and communications security, including authentication and key distribution for the bank's worldwide funds transfer network. Blake chairs the ANSI X9.E Subcommittee (Telecommunications Services, Electronic Services and Operations), and the working group that developed the ANSI authentication and key management standards (ANSI X9.9-1982, *Financial Institution Message Authentication (wholesale)*, and ANSI X9.17-1985, *Financial Institution Key Management (wholesale)*). He is a U.S. technical expert on these subjects and on International Standards Organization working groups.

Previous assignments at Citibank included development of long-range plans for distributed processing; development of corporate standards for *Operations Risk Assessment* and *Protection of Telecommunications;* responsibility for the privacy law/transborder information flow issue and for audit software.

Prior to joining Citibank, he was Technical Director of TTI (East)—a subsidiary of Citibank; with MITRE where he served as a consultant to Joint Chiefs of Staff, USIA, and the IRS; and John Hopkins Applied Physics Lab where as Program Manager he had responsibility for a variety of programs including the Polaris satellite navigation system and the production procurement of Navy Navigation Satellites.

Mr. Greenlee has a B.S. in Physics and Mathematics from Purdue University, has done advanced work in Physics at Purdue and the University of Maryland, received his MBA from George Washington University, and completed a three-year program at the General Theological Seminary. He has written three books and holds three patents.

Section 3.3: Access Control and Authentication

Introduction

Access control and authentication have already been introduced in prior sections as pertaining to computer security. Since computer and network security are integral components of information security, many concepts overlap. An example is access control and authentication, which are discussed in the current sections relating to network security.

Introductory concepts are presented in the first subsection. This discussion is followed by subsections on reprints and recommended readings.

Introductory Concepts

The fundamental issues involved in access control are simple: Access to valuable resources must be restricted to authorized people and processes. The authorization process is accepted as outside the scope of our discussion. In general, access control is based on an authenticated identification. It is not sufficient for a user to claim an identity; there must be some way of proving that identity. In manual systems the most common proof is a credential bearing the photograph and signature of the individual. Other mechanisms are required in automated digital systems; these are discussed below.

A closely related concept is the authentication of objects such as messages. When the content of a message is important, the receiver may find it necessary to be sure of its source and integrity. Similarly, the sender may desire positive proof of delivery. Digital systems provide these necessary authentication mechanisms; in some ways, they are better than non-automated methods.

Access to a resource covers a wide range such as physical presence, reading, writing, altering, appending, and copying. We shall restrict our attention to computer resources such as information and services; the individual to be identified may be a human or may be a process operating on behalf of a person.

User Identification and Authentication

The first step in access control is for the individual, or user, to present identification and authentication of that identification. Passwords are the most common form of authentication; this is an example of information that the user knows.

Other approaches, exemplified in the reprints, utilize a user possession such as a physical key or card and a user physical characteristic such as a handwritten signature. Authentication based on these approaches requires a suitable device to produce an information data stream that the computer can process to perform authentication.

The authentication information must be validated before the user identification is accepted. Validation may be accomplished by comparison of known and presented information; some of this information may have been processed and protected by encryption or some other similar process. Passwords presented by users are compared with stored information associated with the user identification; a match results in acceptance of the identification. The stored information is commonly the user's password encrypted using a one-way non-invertible algorithm. This encryption protects the utility of the authentication information even if disclosed. When a password is presented for authentication, it is encrypted and the result compared with the previously stored information.

A variation that eliminates stored information but depends on modern VLSI technology is a challenge and response exchange reminiscent of an exchange with a sentry: "Halt and be recognized! Give the password of the day." A challenge message is issued by the computer; the user processes that response, perhaps using a credit card size encryption calculator, and enters the response; the response is compared with expectation and the identification is accepted (or rejected, as the case may be). This identification and authentication process has many interesting and ingenious alternatives, some of which are discussed in the reprints.

Message Authentication

Another form of authentication applies to messages sent between users on the same or different computers. In this case, authentication provides assurance that the message came from the claimed source and that it was delivered unchanged. A similarly strong receipt bound to the message may also be desired. The functional similarity to a handwritten signature on a paper document has caused message authentication to be known as *digital signature*. The distinction from a handwritten signature presented as identification au-

349

thentication is clear, but the use of "signature" in two different security contexts is potentially confusing.

The digital signature is able to authenticate all parts of a message including source and destination labels, time and date, and message contents because it is algorithmically derived from this information. In some respects, this is stronger than the authentication provided by a physical signature where detection of alterations to the document is completely separate from determination of the validity of the signature.

Like other cryptographic applications, message authentication is vulnerable to key compromise; various schemes developed for limiting this vulnerability are presented in the reprints. Message authentication provides the ability to convince a third party, such as a judge or arbitrator, that an electronic message is valid and binding according to some rule. Commercial transactions must be substantiated in a court of law, if necessary. Such a substantiation requirement imposes many requirements on message authentication. Not all of them are satisfied by existing systems. Both technical practice and law are continuing to evolve.

Reprints

Robert Juneman, Stephan Matyas, and Carl Meyer in their paper, "Message Authentication," present procedures that allow each party to a message to verify that it is genuine to the extent of authenticating the received message to be identical to the one sent; issues of authorization, message origin, destination, timeliness, and sequence are excluded. Their general approach is to append a check quantity to the message; recalculation and comparison of the check quantity serves to authenticate the message.

Two approaches are for calculating the check quantity. The first is the "conventional" message authentication code (MAC), as discussed in Greenlee's paper in Section 3.2, based on a cryptographic remainder. The second is suggested when the message is going to be encrypted for secrecy; it is called a manipulation detection code (MDC) and is not based on cryptographic processing. Avoidance of cryptography reduces processing overhead and problems of distributing two keys for each message.

Several MDC algorithms are proposed and analyzed for weaknesses. The paper concludes that "the search for an MDC technique that is both independent of the encryption method and strictly a complicated function of the plaintext itself is almost surely doomed to fail under specified attacks."

Details of the MAC standard are discussed in Blake Greenlee's paper, "Requirements for Key Management Protocols in the Wholesale Financial Services Industry," in Section 3.2. Now that this standard is in place, message authentication should be a straightforward routine application wherever needed. Perhaps the encryption algorithm may change, but the basic approach is now specified.

Recommended Readings

One of the guidelines discussed in Section 2.3 is the *Department of Defense Password Management Guideline*. Since passwords are the most common user authentication mechanism, it is appropriate to summarize and comment on them here. Passwords are an example of authentication based on something the user knows. The keys used in encryption fall into the same category.

Although passwords have been used to authenticate identification in computers for a very long time, the guidelines are relatively new. Therefore, we are not surprised to find that not all computer systems are able to meet these requirements. In addition, we find that some system administrators do not activate all of the available protective features. The most positive view of this situation is that the administrator has assessed the risks and determined that the cost of the protection is not justified.

The paper, "Protecting Public Keys and Signature Keys," by Dorothy E. Denning discusses the uses and protection of keys, emphasizing two-key (public-key) applications. She concludes that application of two-key cryptosystems requires mechanisms for detecting and recovering from key compromises. A key server providing logged time-stamped signature certificates is discussed extensively; its potential as a bottleneck is recognized.

The principles of two-key cryptosystems, both for secrecy and for authentification, are briefly reviewed. The use of two-key cryptography for both functions is emphasized, but combined use of single-key and two-key approaches to provide both functions is also discussed. Separate key-pairs are required for secrecy and authentication; a single-key may substitute for the secrecy function. Since the authentication, or "signature," is obtained by using the private key it cannot provide secrecy. The need for communication of encryption and decryption restricts the public key algorithm to Rivest-Shamir-Adleman.

Secrecy and authentication can be combined (composed) by doubly encrypting a message with the recipient's public key and the sender's private key. Proving the signature to a third party requires retaining the encrypted message; if the cleartext is also retained, storage requirement are doubled. Alternatively, a checksum of the message can be encrypted by the sender's private key as a signature, with the advantage that secrecy and authentication are separated, even to the extent of using a different algorithm (such as single-key) for secrecy or omitting it entirely. Signature storage requirements are reduced, and certain other problems are overcome. Note that in the two-key (public-key) community, the entire encrypted message is referred to as the digital signature, while in the one-key community the MAC is often referred to as the digital signature. This non-standardization of terminology can cause confusion.

Key compromise, including disclosure and active wiretaping, could lead to violations of secrecy, forging of signatures, and, in two-key systems, disavowal of previous signed messages. The technique discussed to overcome these vulnerabilities, called a "certificate," involves a network key server to authenticate the operative validity of keys and signatures at a point in time; similarities with a human notary public are obvious. The certificate contains a time stamp, message sender identification, sender's public key, and the signature based on the message checksum, all encrypted under the server's private key. The signature certificate must be retained to resolve future disputes. To limit the exposure that could result from compromise of the server's private key, an unalterable sequential log must retain all public keys, signature certificates, and notifications of key compromise.

The handwritten signature is an example of a physical characteristic (something the user is) employed to authenticate identification. Hewitt W. Crane, Daniel E. Wolf, and John S. Ostrem in the paper, "The SRI Pen System for Automatic Signature Verification," describe a system that analyzes the dynamics of writing employing a pen that decomposes writing motion into three components. A specific signature specimen is compared with stored data derived from five to ten true signatures, using a "rubbery" correlation method developed to accommodate stretch and contraction of the components. True-signature rejection and forger acceptance error rates are presented. Sources of experimental error are discussed; experimental design and equipment improvements are suggested.

Although this paper may be a bit dated, it contains a very clear presentation of the concepts of employing writing dynamics for personal identification. A handwritten signature is a classic method for personal identification which has proven relatively difficult or unreliable for computer implementation. Confusion with the digital signatures based on encryption techniques must be avoided.

Commercial products are now available supporting a number of security mechanisms. It is not the purpose of this tutorial to endorse any product. Mention of a product should not be interpreted as an endorsement. These are simply product descriptions that have come to our attention. Undoubtly

by the time you read these notes, some of these products will no longer be available and new ones will be available.

End-to-end data encryption is available for X.25 packet-switched networks [MCCA86]. This device is placed between the X.25 DTE and modem; it encrypts only the user data. Based on a key database, "a single encryption key may be used to encrypt all virtual circuits, or each virtual circuit may use a different key." Session keys may be transmitted by using a database key as a key-encrypting-key. Based on *Data Encryption Standards,* this device has received endorsement under Federal Standard 1027.

PC-oriented protection devices including a physical or magnetic key for power-on, file and PC-to-PC communications (link) encryption, and dial-in/call back for all sized computers are mentioned in one survey [COLB85]. Biometrics, in the form of retinal eye pattern registration is also available [DATA85]. A product survey [JOHN86] tabulates 17 IBM mainframe security products, 20 for dial-up lines, and 16 for personal computers. Mentioned concerns include user identification and authentication, effective password management, point of origin, control of simultaneous sign-ons, terminal control, dataset/file name control, volume control, transaction/command limitations, program control, map control, field control, time of day, day of week, on-line monitoring, violation and activity reporting, on-line controls modification, capability to decentralize administration, ease of installation, lack of complexity, auditability, adaptability to organizational structures, compatibility with existing applications, and documentation. Product selection should also take into account the following vendor factors: reputation, experience, financial stability, technical resources, and customer support.

The paper, "Personal Authentication System for Access Control to the Defense Data Network," presents an example of a physical device (something the user has) used to authenticate identification. Stephen T. Kent, Peter J. Sevcik, and James G. Herman present the design of a system to authenticate terminal users, especially those connecting through dialup lines. The design provides for retrofit and, through redundant distributed processing, can accommodate large numbers of users. Although the specific design has not been implemented, it is quite instructive in that it addresses many of the problems of personal authentication. Commercial products resembling some of the ideas in this paper are being marketed.

The context of their design is the defense data network (DDN), but there is little specific to that network. After analyzing general approaches for user identification, they propose a challenge-response scheme employing both a cryptographic key and a password. The key could be recorded on a magnetic stripe card that would be read by a desktop unit or terminal, which would encrypt the challenge based on that key, a password entered at the keyboard, and the encryption algorithm. Alternately, a calculator-like device could hold the key and perform the encryption.

Three additional network components must cooperate to verify the response. The user deals directly with an access gate. This gate requests service from a network authentication server. There are several such servers, providing distributed, and possibly partitioned, databases. Provision is made for database update and service outage, including possible denial of service threats. The security of the authentication servers is enhanced by the use of an algorithm of one-way encryption. A central large computer with secondary storage and a database manager is required for management of the authentication system, but is not critical for instantaneous operation.

Since several of the papers discussed above have been concerned with digital signatures, we will focus here on Selim Akl's paper, "Digital Signatures: A Tutorial Survey," which further contributes to our understanding of digital signatures. Akl distinguishes between true, or directly transmitted, digital signatures and arbitrated, or relayed, digital signatures. Private (one-key) or public (two-key) cryptosystems may be used for either category. Examples, advantages, and disadvantages of each category and cryptographic scheme are given. In particular, sender disavowal and arbitrator trustworthiness are addressed.

The paper, "Security without Identification: Transaction Systems to Make Big Brother Obsolete," by David Chaum is very concerned with the social consequences of technology. It starts by asserting that computerization is "robbing individuals of the ability to monitor and control the ways information about them is used" and ends by observing that "advances in information technology have always been accompanied by major changes in society." Along the way Chaum presents a system architecture for the use of public key (two-key) cryptosystems, which would give organization and individuals the ability to authenticate various interactions without threats to privacy.

The technological basis of this proposed architecture is a credit-card-sized calculator that would be used as the individual's transaction device. Protocols for communication, payment, and credential transactions are developed first for paper-based systems and then for digital transactions (the former serving as intuitive analogies for the latter).

While the need for "substantial agreement, outlay, and commitment to design" are required "before widespread use can begin," the implication of applying authentication technology in a broad social context is both refreshing and stimulating. Even if this particular system does not receive accept-

ance, consideration of the issues raised in the context of a proposed engineering solution is praiseworthy.

Another suggested reading, "Dial-Up Security Update" by Eugene Troy, is concerned with authenticating a class of users in order to protect computer resources. The fundamental concern is to prevent access by unauthorized remote (dial-up) intruders. As Troy summarizes, additional protection "devices should be considered if the system manager is unwilling to trust the computer's operating system security capability, when fully utilized, to keep dial-up intruders out of the system."

Security is a management tradeoff. Costs and benefits must be evaluated, risks must be assessed, and decision must be made as to which risks to reduce and which to accept. Among the risk factors are sensitivity to disclosure, availability, and integrity; drawbacks include (legitimate) user resistance, costs, and technical weaknesses of the protection methods.

The paper provides considerable generic information as well as specific product information. Devices are categorized as to whether they operate at one end of the communication circuit (and which end), or both ends; whether they operate in the analog or digital domain, or both; the technology employed; and costs. The reader is guided toward appropriate decision-making.

Our final suggested reading, "Using Encryption for Authentication in Large Networks of Computers," by Roger Needham and Michael Schroeder addresses the use of encryption to achieve authenticated communication in computer networks [NEED78]. The paper presents examples of protocols to show the establishment of authenticated connection, which apply to the management of authenticated mail, signature verification, and document integrity guarantee. The basis for protocols is presented as conventional and public-key encryption algorithms.

This paper discusses the following three functions: (1) *authenticated interactive communication* ("Establishment of authenticated interactive communication between two principals on different machines. By interactive communication we mean a series of messages in either direction, typically each in response to a previous one"); (2) *authenticated one-way communication* ("Authenticated one-way communication, such as is found in mail systems, where it is impossible to require protocol exchanges between the sender and the recipient while sending an item, since there can be no guarantee that sender and recipient are simultaneously available"); and (3) *signed communication* ("Signed communication, in which the origin of communication and the integrity of the content can be authenticated to a third party").

To illustrate the message developed in this paper, we quote, from the paper's commentary: "We conclude from this study that protocols using public-key cryptosystems and using conventional encryption algorithms are strinkingly similar. The number of protocol messages exchanged is very comparable, the public-key system having a noticeable advantage only in the case of signed communications. As in many network applications of computers, caching is important to reduce transactions with lookup servers; this is particularly so with the public-key system. In that system we noticed also that there was a requirement for encryption of public data (the authentication server's database) in order to ensure its integrity. A consequence of the similarity of protocols is that any helpful tricks for the conventional system have analogs in the public-key system, though they may not be needed. Because of this, there may be scope for hybrid systems in which a public-key method may be used to establish an authenticated connection to be used conventionally. The intrinsic security requirements of a public-key authentication server are easier to meet than those of a conventional one, but a complete evaluation of the system problems in implementing such a server in a real system and the need to retain a secure record of old public key to guarantee future correct arbitration of old signatures may minimize this advantage. We conclude that the choice of technique should be based on the economy and cryptographic strength of the encryption techniques themselves, rather than for their effects on protocol complexity.

Finally, protocols such as those developed here are prone to extremely subtle errors that are unlikely to be detected in normal operation. The need for techniques to verify the correctness of such protocols is great, and we encourage those interested in such problems to consider this area.

ELECTRONIC DOCUMENT AUTHENTICATION

Robert R. Jueneman
Computer Sciences Corp.
3160 Fairview Park Drive
Falls Church, VA 22042
(703) 876-1076

1 Introduction

The increasing use of electronic transmission and storage of documents has given rise to new requirements for document security and authentication. In particular, it is necessary to consider schemes that provide at least the authenticity provided by traditional paper documents and written signatures, in order to extend these new techniques beyond the bounds of one individual and into the world of commerce.

Message Authentication Codes (MACs) have been suggested as a means of providing confirmation of the authenticity of a document between two or more cooperating and mutually trusting correspondents, and the ANSI X9.9-1986 message authentication standard[1] represents one such technique. Message Authentication codes make use of traditional cryptographic algorithms such as the Data Encryption Standard (DES), and rely on a secret authentication key to ensure that only authorized personnel could generate a message with the appropriate MAC.

Digital signature techniques such as the Rivest-Shamir-Adleman (RSA) scheme[2] can be used to establish both the authenticity of a document and the identity of its originator, but because of the computationally-intensive nature of the RSA algorithm most digital signature schemes make use of a checksum technique to summarize or represent the document, and then digitally sign the checksum. A DES-based MAC approach is often used for this purpose.

However, several technical difficulties have been identified with the MAC approach, both in the case of the ANSI X9.9-1986 standard and some of the DES-based checksum approaches used to implement digital signatures. In particular, it will be shown that cryptographic checksums that are intended to detect fraudulent messages must be on the order of 128 bits in length, and the ANSI X9.9-1986 standard is criticized on that basis.

---

1. Financial Institution Message Authentication (Wholesale) X9.9-1986 (Approved August 15, 1986), published by the X9 Secretariat, American Bankers Association, 1120 Connecticut Avenue, Washington, D.C. 20036.

2. R. L. Rivest, A. Shamir and L. Adleman, "A Method of Obtaining Digital Signatures and Public Key Cryptosystems" **Communications of the ACM**, vol. 21, no. 2, pp 120-126, Feb 1978.

This is a preliminary version of an article that will be submitted to *IEEE Communications Magazine*, 1987. Copyright © 1987 by The Institute of Electrical and Electronics Engineers, Inc.

In addition, architectural arguments will be advanced to illustrate the advantages of a checksum algorithm which is *not* based on the use of cryptography, and in particular does not require the use of a secret key.

Manipulation Detection Codes (MDC) are defined as a class of checksum algorithms which can detect both accidental and malicious modifications of an electronic message or document, *without* requiring the use of a cryptographic key. Although the MDC result must be protected by encryption to prevent an attacker from succeeding in substituting his own Manipulation Detection Code (MDC) along with the modified text, it is sufficient to append the MDC to the message text and encrypt the entire string. Such techniques are therefore highly useful in allowing encryption and message authentication to be implemented in different protocol layers in a communication system without key management difficulties, as well as in implementing digital signature schemes.

An efficient 128-bit MDC algorithm will be presented which makes use of the Intel 8087/80287 Numeric Data Processor coprocessor chip for the IBM PC/XT/AT and similar microcomputers.

2 Architectural Considerations

A common theme throughout this series of papers[3,4,5,6] has been the desirability of separating the function of encryption from that of authentication, so that the two functions could operate at different architectural layers or levels in an communications system. In the context of the ISO Open System Interconnect reference model, for example, it was suggested that link encryption might be applied to all of the communications from a host, using a stand-alone link encryption device operating at ISO OSI layer 1, the data link layer. In this case the appropriate place for authentication would probably be in the Presentation or Application layers (layer 6 or 7), implemented in an application program inside the host. (It is assumed in this case that the network has already made a best effort to correct any obvious data errors. If the message text has been modified in such a way as to pass the normal network error-detection mechanisms but be caught by the authentication function, then it would appear that a deliberate spoofing attack has been carried out. In that case it is appropriate that the user be informed. Placing the authentication function

3. R. R. Jueneman, "Analysis of Certain Aspects of Output Feedback Mode", **Advances in Cryptology: Proceedings of Crypto82**, Plenum Press, New York, 1983, pp 99-127.

4. R. R. Jueneman, C. H. Meyer, and S. M. Matyas, "Message Authentication With Manipulation Detection Codes", **Proceedings of the 1983 IEEE Symposium on Security and Privacy**, IEEE Computer Society Press, 1984, pp 33-54.

5. R. R. Jueneman, C. H. Meyer, and S. M. Matyas, "Message Authentication", **IEEE Communications Magazine**, Sept. 1985 - Vol. 23, No. 9, pp 29-40.

6. R. R. Jueneman, "A High Speed Manipulation Detection Code", **Advances in Cryptology: Proceedings of Crypto86**, to be published in 1987 by Springer-Verlag, Berlin, from which much of this paper is abstracted.

at any layer lower than the Presentation layer might cause the network administrator to be notified, but it would not necessarily inform the user.)

We have also suggested that since the mode of encryption might change depending on the physical medium involved, it would be desirable if the method of authentication were independent of the encryption scheme used. The recently announced decision of the National Security Agency not to endorse new DES equipment for certification in accordance with Federal Standard 1027 after 1988, and in general to move on to a new family of encryption algorithms for both Unclassified, National-Security Related traffic as well as classified data, should serve to underscore the advisability of such a separation of function, and the desirability of "keyless" Manipulation Detection Code algorithms.

In the earlier papers in this series, the primary concern was to define an authentication algorithm that would be more efficient than a MAC (especially when implemented in software), and/or would not require a traditional encryption operation. Only secondarily did we focus on what this author now believes to be the fundamental distinction between an MDC and a MAC, *i.e.*, that whereas a MAC involves one or more secret keys, *an MDC makes use of only publicly known quantities*, and is therefore considerably more convenient from the standpoint of key management.

It should be observed that there is a fundamental difference between encryption and authentication with respect to the need to change algorithms, for in the case of encryption it is very difficult to know whether the traffic is being broken surreptitiously. In the case of authentication, however, it usually becomes obvious sooner or later if you have been spoofed (*i.e.*, when the books are balanced, or when further conversation reveals the error). The objective of the authentication process is to minimize the amount of time required to detect the spoofing. It would therefore seem that authentication algorithms would not have to be changed nearly as often as encryption algorithms, and that there is perhaps less need for secrecy in their design.

2.1 Cryptographic Checksum Requirements

With that architectural guidance as background, let us assume that we wish to apply a cryptographic seal in the form of an MDC checksum to some electronic message or document, and that we will either use a digital signature approach or else use link or end-to-end encryption to protect the MDC result from anything other than a random attack. We would prefer that the checksum algorithm not require the use of any secret information, in order to eliminate the necessity for a separate and often cumbersome key distribution and management system. We would also hope that the algorithm would execute efficiently, without requiring special-purpose cryptographic hardware.

But the most important of the criteria is that the set of all checksums must be very nearly one to one with respect to the set of all message texts, so that we can easily digitally sign and/or check the checksum in lieu of processing all of the text through the digital signature algorithm. That is, given two messages A and B with checksums, we desire that checksum (A) and checksum (B) be identical if and only if the messages A and B are themselves identical. More specifically, the algorithm should have the following properties:

1. The checksum algorithm should not require any secret information in its operation; although either the text or the checksum result, or both, must be kept secret from the attacker.

2. The algorithm should execute efficiently on both main-frame computers and microcomputers, without depending on any special-purpose cryptographic hardware.

3. The checksum must be sensitive to all possible permutations and rearrangements, as well as the addition, deletion, and insertion of text, so that the message ABC will produce a different value than ACB, etc.

4. If two different texts (of arbitrary lengths) are checksummed, the probability that the two checksums will be equal when the two texts are not identical should be a uniformly distributed random variable that is independent of the text, with an average value over all possible texts of 2^{-k} where k is the number of bits in the checksum.

5. As will be seen, the resulting checksum must be on the order of 128 bits in length, in order to resist a so-called "birthday attack" against the text itself.

6. Finally, as will be discussed below, the checksum function must not be invertible, nor subject to decomposition into separate and independent elements.

Finally, we must point out that although a DES-based Message Authentication Code or MAC could be used to authenticate either an encrypted or unencrypted text without further encryption because it makes use of a secret key, that is not true of a Manipulation Detection Code[7]. Although the text itself does not need to be encrypted, the MDC must be, so that the attacker cannot substitute his own MDC with any significant probability of success. In most cases, the MDC can simply be appended to the message, and if the entire message is encrypted together with the MDC, that will provide adequate protection.

---

7. The use of an unencrypted MAC is not recommended, however, because an unencrypted MAC reveals something about the message itself and may form the basis for a dictionary attack.

3 Attacks Against Checksum Techniques

The papers in this series have presented a number of different attacks against checksum techniques, and the reader is directed to the 1983 paper by Jueneman, Matyas, and Meyer for further details. However, there is one very important attack against the text of a message or document itself which has not received sufficient attention, an attack which we have called the "Birthday Attack".

3.1 The Fundamental Birthday Attack.

Let us assume that user "Alice" is attempting to defraud user "Bob" by devising a version of a bogus or unfavorable contract or agreement which would have an identical checksum as a legitimate one, and have Bob digitally "sign" the legitimate version. At some later time Alice will produce the bogus version of the contract and claim that Bob has defaulted on his obligations, as evidenced by his digital signature.

1. Assume for the sake of argument that a 32-bit checksum of some form is used, and that if necessary the attacker can exercise the authentication system *ad infinitum* to generate the checksum.

2. Alice must secretly prepare a number of subtle variations of the legitimate text in advance, and calculate (or have the system calculate) the checksum for each one. In the case of an electronic mail message or document, for example, suppose that a number of lines contain the ASCII character sequence "space-space-backspace" between selected words[8]. The attacker might prepare a set of variations of the message in which the sequence in selected lines would be "space-backspace-space". The length of the text would not be altered thereby, and all of the variations of the document would appear to be identical, both when printed and when displayed on the normal video display, unless "dumped" in hexadecimal format. Other, more consequential changes to the text could also be made, of course. By systematically altering or not altering the text in only 16 different lines, 2^{16} or 65536 variations could be generated. A file of records consisting of the checksum plus a 16-bit permutation index could be used to summarize what lines were altered by a given variation, and what checksum resulted.

3. Alice would then prepare an equal number of variations on the bogus text which she would like to substitute for the legitimate text, and would calculate (or have the system calculate) the checksum for each one of those variations as well, producing another file of checksum and permutation indices.

---

8. Other combinations, such as null-character, or carriage return - line feed would also work, as well as less subtle variations such as changing "the" to "an", or inserting or deleting commas or spaces in a numeric field.

4. Alice must then compare the two files, searching for a pair of identical MACs or MDCs and noting the corresponding permutation indices. (If no match were found, she could simply generate a few more random variations of the legitimate and the bogus texts until a match is found.) She would then recreate the full text of both the acceptable and the unacceptable documents with the specific modifications necessary to produce the matching checksums, based on the permutation indices.

5. Finally, Alice would offer the appropriate variation of the legitimate contract to Bob, and both would digitally sign it. Since the checksums for the two documents are identical, the digital signatures would be identical also, so Alice could at any time substitute the unfavorable contract for the favorable one, and try to convince the judge that the digital signature "proves" it was that version that was signed by both parties.

This is Yuval's[9] classic "How to Swindle Rabin" form of a so-called "Birthday Problem" attack. According to the famous birthday paradox problem in statistics (*i.e.*, how many people must there be in a room in order to have a good chance that at least two people in the room will have the same birthday), this kind of an attack has about a 50% probability of succeeding if the number of variations of each document that are generated and compared approaches the square root of the total number of possible checksum. That is, if a 32-bit checksum were used, the probability of a successful attack would be about 50% after two files of 2^{16} or 65536 variations each were computed, and would increase rapidly after that point. If a 64-bit MAC or MDC were used, then the 8.6 billion iterations produced by systematically varying 32 lines of text in each of the two document versions would be likely to suffice[10].

3.2 Other Opportunities For Birthday Attacks.

It is not necessary that an attacker be the originating party in order to carry out a Birthday Attack against a message. Similar attacks, even by a "hacker", could potentially succeed against command and control systems, especially if the attacker is able to send bogus commands and random variables over a channel such as a satellite channel that cannot be shut down without denying service to the legitimate users as well. The use of encryption on such links doesn't necessarily help, for unless a sufficiently long checksum is used, random data together with a random checksum will eventually result in a random command being accepted.

Another instance could arise in a multilevel-secure system, where a cryptographic "seal" is applied to an "object", in order to prevent classified information from being disclosed or modified without proper authorization. For example, if the security classification associated with the object could be manipulated by a Trojan Horse program, a classified object's label could be changed to "unclassified", and the information released. Similarly, the contents of a properly marked, unclassified

---

9. G. Yuval, "How to Swindle Rabin", **Cryptologia**, Vol 3., No. 3, July 1979, pp 187-190.

10. The sorting and comparison of this much data is non-trivial, but feasible. C.f. the author's CRYPTO86 paper.

object could be changed and classified information inserted. Because the sensitivity label must be very closely associated with the contents of the object (to prevent a simple cut-and-paste attack), the security seal of the object typically includes both the sensitivity label and the contents of the object as well. In this case, the Trojan Horse program could conceivably manipulate the label together with some innocuous portion of the data, and repeatedly present the information to the cryptographic seal mechanism until two versions, one good and one bad, happened to produce the same cryptographic checksum. The substitution would then be prepared.

As a result, and contrary to the author's previous advice, *the use of the 64-bit Message Authentication Code technique of FIPS PUB 46 and ANSI X9.9-1986 cannot be considered sufficiently strong*, and is not recommended if there is any possibility that the originator may attempt to defraud the message recipient, or if a Trojan Horse could circumvent security controls through such a mechanism. In addition, the use of a MAC in certain command and control situations where the attacker may attempt to spoof computer-controlled equipment or processes is also not recommended.

3.3 Recommended Length For Cryptographic Checksums.

Based on the Birthday Attack, it is apparent that any cryptographic checksum should be on the order of 128 bits in length. Although there may be instances where the design of a system is such that neither the attacker nor the originator could systematically change both the text and the checksum until a combination is found that works, it would be necessary to examine such systems with exceeding care to ensure that some remote possibility was not overlooked. In this case, playing the ace of trump is much more certain than relying on a finesse, and using a few more bits will make such troublesome problems go away completely.

A 128-bit checksum is felt to be sufficient, because in addition to the sorting and searching problem rapidly becoming insurmountable (after about 80 bits), the 2^{65} calculations that would be required by a Birthday Problem attack against a 128-bit checksum would not be computationally feasible even if they were to take only 1 nanosecond apiece. It must be stressed that this attack has nothing to do with the cryptographic strength of the particular checksum algorithm, or whether conventional keys, public keys, or no keys at all are used, but only whether the length of the result is sufficient to withstand any computationally feasible number of random trials.

3.4 The Coppersmith Triple-Birthday Attack

The papers in this series have presented a succession of slightly different schemes for a Manipulation Detection Code that would satisfy the architectural criteria previously presented and be computationally efficient as well. The previous versions made use of a 31-bit hash code of the form $Z_i = (Z_{i-1} + X_i)^2$ modulo N, where N was 2^{31}-1. This basic function was then iterated four times and the results concatenated to form a 124-bit MDC.

Ironically, one week before the publication of the third paper in the IEEE Communications Magazine last year, Dr. Don Coppersmith[11] pointed out a weakness in a double-iteration DES signature scheme by Davies and Price which also applies (to a somewhat lesser degree) to the quadruple-iteration MDC scheme we had proposed, as follows:

- Assuming the use of an arbitrary *invertible* function $F(X,H)$ as a checksum function operating over the message $M = (M_1, M_2, \dots M_n)$, intermediate results $H_1, H_2, \dots H_n$ are produced from the relation $H_i = F(M_i, H_{i-1})$, or alternately from the inverse of F, $H_{i-1} = F^{-1}(M_i, H_i)$.

- During a precomputation phase, select some arbitrary n-bit quantity Z, which is going to be the value of $H_2, H_4, H_6, \dots, H_{18}$. Then randomly select approximately 2^{36} values X, compute the values $F(X,Z)$, and store these values. Then randomly select 2^{36} values Y, compute the inverse function $F^{-1}(Y,Z)$, and store those values as well. Then compare all of the Y values to all of the X values searching for a matching pair, using a sort and compare technique as required. This constitutes the first birthday problem. We expect to find 256 such matching pairs, and if not, we will examine a few more values of X or Y or both. Note that each such pair (X_i, Y_i) can be used as a message pair (M_3, M_4), (M_5, M_6), ..., or (M_{17}, M_{18}) such that if $H_2 = Z$, $M_3 = X_i$, $M_4 = Y_i$ then $H_4 = Z$, etc.

- Given a message $M^* = (M_{19}, M_{20}, \dots, M_n)$, the chosen value of Z, and the 256 pairs (X_i, Y_i) obtained during the precomputation, our task is to select values of $M_1, M_2, \dots, M_n$ which will make H_{2n} a valid hash of $M = (M_1, M_2, \dots, M_n)$. We therefore find values of M_1 and M_2 such that $F(M_1, Z) = F^{-1}(M_2, Z)$ to put ourselves in a standardized position. This takes on the order of 2^{33} hashing operations and 2^{32} storage. This is the second birthday problem.

- Working backwards from H_{2n} (note that this requires the checksum function to be invertible), using the values $M_n, M_{n-1}, \dots, M_{19}$, we find the value of H_{n+18}, the value of the hash function on the *second* iteration. Finally, we make use of the precomputed pairs (X_i, Y_i). For each of the $256^4 = 2^{32}$ choices of the four pairs (X_i, Y_i) to be the values of (M_3, M_4), (M_5, M_6), (M_7, M_8), and (M_9, M_{10}), we compute the value of H_{n+10} that would result then do the same thing with the values of (M_{11}, M_{12}), (M_{13}, M_{14}), (M_{15}, M_{16}), (M_{17}, M_{18}), computing backwards from H_{18} to get a value for H_{10}. We again sort and compare these values as the third birthday problem. We expect one match, and the corresponding values of M_3 through M_{18} finish our task for a two-pass checksum process.

The process could be extended to attack many kinds of checksum algorithms that use multiple iterations by constructing eight "super-pairs" consisting of M_{19} through M_{35} plus M_{36} through M_{52}, etc., up to M_{258}. Each super-pair would be manipulated during the precomputed phase to continue to produce the value of Z, even on the third pass. Only slightly more computation would be required, but obviously 258 blocks of the

---

11. Don Coppersmith, "Another Birthday Attack", **Advances in Cryptology - CRYPTO '85 Proceedings, Lecture Notes in Computer Science**, Vol. 218, Springer-Verlag, Berlin, 1986, pp 14-17.

message M would be constrained, limiting the messages that could be attacked to fairly long ones. Finally, this process could be extended even further to attack a quadruple-pass hash algorithm by computing eight "super-dooper" pairs consisting of 512 blocks each, or a total of 4098 blocks.

The Coppersmith multiple birthday attack therefore serves to reduce the number of variations of both a legitimate and a bogus message that are necessary to defeat an N-pass checksum scheme from an apparent $2^{N*k/2}$ to an almost trivial $N*2^{k/2}$.

It is worth mentioning that Coppersmith's attack also applies to attempts to extend the MAC of FIPS PUB 46 or ANSI X9.9 to 128 bits (in order to try to overcome Yuval's attack against the plaintext) by simply concatenating two MACs using two different authentication keys. The reason is that the MAC function, *i.e.*, DES Cipher Feedback mode encryption, is invertible, and in addition the components are separable and individually too small to resist a birthday attack. This is not to say that a suitable 128-bit checksum could not be constructed using DES or some other 64-bit block cipher, but only to caution that the task is not as trivial as it may appear at first glance.

It should therefore be observed that Coppersmith's triple-birthday attack will succeed against a multiple-iteration checksum routine if two conditions are true:

1. If the checksum function is *invertible*, so that it is possible to work both forwards and backwards to produce matching values in a birthday-problem attack.

2. If the checksum function is subject to *decomposition* into separate and independent elements, each of which is sufficiently small that the birthday-problem attack is feasible from the standpoint of computation time and storage. If the checksum function were to involve a 128-bit result that could not be broken down into something smaller, then the birthday attack would be infeasible because it would involve generating, storing, and comparing on the order of 2^{64} 128-bit checksums and 64-bit permutation indices, or about $8.8*10^{20}$ bytes of storage, or 5 quadrillion reels of 6250 bpi magnetic tape.

This suggests a variation of the previously described routines that would involve XOR(s) or some other non-linear combining function that would not be invertible. If in addition the routine involved all 128 bits of the text and all 128 bits of the MDC of the previous block, then neither of the two conditions would be true and the triple-birthday attack would therefore be defeated.

In order to make the MDC function non-invertible it is necessary to introduce a history function, *i.e.*, some value that would not yet be known when working in the backwards direction, calculated in a non-linear manner so that a modular square root attack would not work. In addition, it appears necessary to incorporate multiple references to both the text to be authenticated and to the previous MDC result, so that the only value that would satisfy the forward relationship is the proper one. Not only must each bit of the checksum function be a function of all of the bits in the full 128-bit text block together with all of the bits in the MDC of the previous block, but additional dependencies should be introduced to ensure that the function is not just minimally dependent on those bits but is over-constrained instead.

Finally, as stated previously, the MDC function must produce a value on the order of 128 bits in length in order to defeat the various birthday attacks against the text itself.

4 The New, Improved Quadratic Congruential MDC Algorithm

The following algorithm, dubbed the Quadratic Congruential Manipulation Detection Code, Version 4 (QCMDCV4), is proposed to satisfy the requirements that have been defined:

Consider a 128-bit (16 byte) block of text, divided into four 32-bit words, $T_1, ... ,T_4$. For reasons that will be explained later, we will be operating on a 31-bit subset of each of those 32-bit words which consists of the sign bit and the low-order 30 bits, *i.e.*, $T^*_i = T_i$ AND BFFFFFFF. In addition, we will define a 30-bit fifth component, T^{**}, consisting of the 6 high-order bits of T_1 (with the 6 bits shifted right two bits and 2 leading zero bits introduced on the left or most-significant-bit position), concatenated with the high order 8 bits of T_2, T_3, and T_4, to make a 32 bit word with two high order zero bits.

Let the 128 bits of the MDC result (obtained from the previous block of text) also be divided into four 32-bit integer components M_1, M_2, M_3, M_4; and let the 32-bit components of the new MDC result be designated as M^*_i.

Finally, define a set of moduli $N_1... N_4$, consisting of the four largest prime numbers less than the maximum 32-bit integer, namely 2147483629 (2^{31}-19), 2147483587 (2^{31}-61), 2147483579 (2^{31}-69), and 2147483563 (2^{31}-85).

Then calculate:

$$M^*_1 = [\ (M_1 \oplus T^*_1) - (M_2 \oplus T^*_2) + (M_3 \oplus T^*_3) - (M_4 \oplus T^*_4) + T^{**} \ ]^2 \bmod N_1$$

$$M^*_2 = [\ (M_2 \oplus T^*_1) - (M_3 \oplus T^*_2) + (M_4 \oplus T^*_3) - (M^*_1 \oplus T^*_4) - T^{**} \ ]^2 \bmod N_2$$

$$M^*_3 = [\ (M_3 \oplus T^*_1) - (M_4 \oplus T^*_2) + (M^*_1 \oplus T^*_3) - (M^*_2 \oplus T^*_4) + T^{**} \ ]^2 \bmod N_3$$

$$M^*_4 = [\ (M_4 \oplus T^*_1) - (M^*_1 \oplus T^*_2) + (M^*_2 \oplus T^*_3) - (M^*_3 \oplus T^*_4) - T^{**} \ ]^2 \bmod N_4$$

Several features of this algorithm should be noted. First, each of the 16 different XOR combinations is unique. Second, even if a significant amount of the text contains all zeroes (with the result that the XOR does nothing), the alternating signs for the M_i and T^{**} components operate in such a manner that the contribution of the various terms will be different in each case. Finally, the M^*_i values are introduced into the computation of the subsequent components as soon as they are available, so that there is a great deal of inter-dependency and mixing. As a result, each 32-bit component of the MDC result is an over-constrained function of all of the text and all of the prior MDC.

The previous papers had proposed a constant value for the modulus, N, equal to the Mersenne prime 2^{31}-1 (2147483647), for all four of the 32-bit M^*_i results. But as Don Coppersmith pointed out when reviewing a draft of the current procedure, because 2^{31}-1 is the largest number that can be contained in a four byte integer in two's complement form, XORing the hexadecimal bit-string 80000001 has the effect of inverting the sign and the low order bit, which can be the equivalent of adding or subtracting the modulus. As a result, even when the intermediate sum is squared, the division by the 2^{31}-1 modulus frequently produces no change in the result, depending on the sign of the T_i and whether a carry would be required, and a modification to the text could thereby escape detection.

Coppersmith proposed picking up the text only 24 bits at a time to avoid this problem, using additional iterations to get back to around 128 bits. In an attempt to overcome this problem without the overhead of an additional iteration, the four different primes for the moduli N_i were introduced, all of them different and less than 2^{31}. However, it was found that if the text consisted of one 32-bit word of random bits and three words of zeroes, then in about 10% of the cases it was possible to either add or subtract the value of the first modulus and have the change go undetected in the corresponding 32-bit word (only) of the MDC result. Although the use of four different values for the moduli means that the substitution does affect the remaining 3 words, or at least 96 bits, it was felt that the full 128-bit strength should be preserved.

For this reason, only 30 bits plus the sign bit of each 32-bit word of text is used in forming the intermediate sum. Since the moduli are all greater than 2^{30}, it is impossible to add or subtract the modulus from the text without detection. The final addition or subtraction of T^{**} ensures that all of the bits in the text affect all of the bits of the result.

One further improvement is possible. Because of the squaring operation, each 32-bit MDC component will be positive, producing a 124-bit result. But we can calculate the parity of the intermediate MDC result, just prior to the multiplication, and then change the sign of the 32-bit result if the parity is even.

Finally, because the algorithm operates on 16-byte blocks, it is necessary to somehow differentiate between a text string that is say 1 byte long and one that consists of the same byte extended with 15 bytes of zeroes. For that reason the last N bytes of text (0 < N < 16) are moved to a 16-byte buffer, the rest of the buffer zeroed, and the MDC algorithm executed N+1 times on that same buffer. N+1 is used instead of N, because a block that is 16 bytes long has to be processed at least once, and therefore a 1 byte block has to be processed twice in order to distinguish it from the previous case. If improved performance is needed, the length code of the text can be prefixed to the text, and the size of the buffer extended to be an exact multiple of

16 bytes. The explicit length code technique *must* be used if it is necessary to deal with text strings that are not multiples of 8 bits in length[12].

In order to avoid a strong correlation between the text and the MDC result in the case where the text is very sparse (contains mostly zero bits), it is desirable to use different values for the starting values of M_i. For purposes of standardization the values 141421356, 271828182, 314159265, and 57721566 are suggested[13].

5 Implementation Considerations

The QCMDCV4 algorithm has been implemented and tested on the IBM PC and AT microcomputers and the Compaq 286 Portable, and should run correctly on any similar machine which uses the Intel 8088, 8086, 80188, or 80286 CPU chip in combination with the 8087 or 80287 Numeric Data Processor chip. The 8087/80287 is used to significantly speed up the calculation of the various arithmetic operations, in particular the division modulo the large primes. During the calculations the results are kept in IEEE Binary Floating Point 80-bit Temporary Real format with a 64-bit mantissa, and T_i and M_i are in the standard Intel 32-bit integer format, low-order byte first. (The text bytes are therefore processed in the order 4, 3, 2, 1, 8, 7, 6, 5, etc.)

The 8087/80287 FPREM instruction computes an exact remainder by successive subtractions the way division is done by hand, instead of using the more usual technique of dividing, rounding, multiplying, and subtracting from the original. The FPREM instruction is as fast as a divide, and is guaranteed to be accurate, without any roundoff.

In order to produce the fastest possible implementation, the XORs and other CPU instructions are executed in parallel with the coprocessor addition, subtraction, multiplication, and FPREM operations whenever possible. The FWAIT instructions necessary to ensure that the coprocessor has finished with its computations before the CPU reads the results are delayed as long as possible to permit the maximum possible overlap. Although the original version was coded using a macro that was invoked four times for the four different iterations within one block, in the final version the code was "unwound" and hand-optimized to permit maximum overlap.

On an IBM-PC with an 8088 & 8087 and a 4.77 MHz clock, the time to MDC check 1,000 512-byte blocks is 43.5 seconds, or 1359.5 microseconds per 16 bytes. This corresponds to 94.2 kilobits per second. By comparison, the time for the fastest

---

12. It should be mentioned here that neither the ANSI X9.9-1986 authentication standard nor the definition of the MAC in FIPS PUB 46 take this problem into account, and therefore they do not differentiate between a short message (one that is not a multiple of 8 bytes in length) that must be padded with zeroes, and one that is a multiple of 8 bytes in length and happens to contain zeroes at the end. Although binary zeroes would be interpreted as ASCII null characters and would not be confused with the ASCII "0" (hexadecimal 30) character in ASCII coded text, formatted binary information could contain binary fields which could be confused. The above technique is suggested as a solution to that problem.

13. C.f. the CRYPTO86 paper for a Pascal test program and other minor details of the algorithm.

known software implementation of DES for the PC is 2801 microseconds per 8 bytes for the PC (22.8 Kbps, or 171K bytes per minute). With an 80287 speedup kit (consisting of an 8 MHz 80287 with its own clock crystal on a plug-in daughter-board) installed in an IBM AT with the standard 6 MHz 80286, the same test took 813.6 microseconds for 16 bytes (157.3 Kbps), or 1.18 megabytes per minute, compared to the DES time of 933 microseconds per 8 bytes.

Depending on the clock speeds of the processors involved, then, the 128-bit MDC technique is anywhere from 4.6 to 8.1 times faster than computing two independent 64-bit Message Authentication Codes in software using the fastest known software DES implementation for the IBM PC or AT. In addition, two independent 64-bit MACs are not believed to be nearly as secure as a single 128-bit MDC. From a human factors standpoint, this performance means that the entire contents of a floppy disk (362K bytes) can be authenticated to the most stringent standards in less than 15 to 30 seconds on current microprocessors, without benefit of any special cryptographic hardware.

6 Summary and Conclusions

Architectural justification has been presented for an authentication algorithm which does not require a traditional crypto "black box" approach using secret cryptographic keys, with all of the key management difficulties that entails. In particular, the relatively common practice of using link encryption for secrecy at the OSI Data Link layer and implementing end-to-end authentication at the Presentation Layer would profit from "keyless", non-cryptographic means of authentication that could be easily implemented in both PCs and general-purpose main-frame computers.

The need for a checksum on the order of 128 bits in length was reaffirmed, both in the case of two mutually suspicious, potentially deceitful users where one may attempt to defraud the other, and in the command and control case where the attacker may have an almost unlimited ability to attempt to spoof the system.

The MAC checksum technique used by ANSI X9.9-1986 is viewed as particularly unfortunate, both because of the inadequate 32-bit length and because no provision was made to distinguish between short block that was padded and a block that is a multiple of 8 bytes that happens to end with the same characters.

The QCMDCV4 algorithm was described, which uses XORs plus a history function to ensure that the function is not invertible. The function computes a 128-bit result that is an over-determined function of 128 bits of the text and the 128-bit MDC result of the previous text block that cannot be decomposed.

The QCMDCV4 algorithm is recommended for use in microcomputer and main-frame applications where encryption will be provided separately and it is desirable not to have to replicate the encryption function for authentication. It is also suitable for use in combination with a public-key algorithm when implementing a digital signature function to protect against fraud.

Section 3.4: Protocols

Introduction

The basic reference model for open systems interconnection (OSI) established the international framework for the development of communication standards for the interconnection of computer systems. Since the objective of OSI is to ". . .permit the interconnection of heterogeneous computer systems so that useful communication between application processes may be achieved" [OSI85], then an extension of the OSI model would be to provide useful and secure communication. An addendum provides a first draft extension to OSI for security [OSI85]. We use this addendum for our presentation of protocols for network security.

Our discussion in the following sections focuses on the OSI protocol reference model (PRM) and on network protocol characteristics. We conclude the presentation on protocols with subsections on reprint and recommended readings.

Protocol Reference Model (PRM)

Protocols are sets of rules that govern the exchange of information in computer communications. The description and specification of the principles of protocol design that serves as a framework for the development of standard protocols is known as a PRM. The PRM is not an implementation specification; it defines the function to be performed but does not prescribe how it should be accomplished.

Open Systems Interconnection (OSI) Protocol Reference Model

The OSI model is an international standard PRM. The supplementary reading by William Stallings is recommended for further background. The OSI PRM is widely published, is well known, and has received considerable professional attention. It defines a seven-layer architecture, specifying the functionality of each layer. The OSI model provides a framework for organizing a previously ad hoc situation. The lower two layers (the physical and data link), which predate network architecture, were the original focus of encryption activity.

OSI networks may be thought of as a collection of nodes connected by communication links. Link encryption concentrates on individually protecting the links. A more abstract view is that information must be protected within this network as it moves between peer entities. As mentioned in Section 3.1, in OSI a protocol-data-unit is a unit of data specified in the protocol for a specific layer consisting of protocol information and possibly user-data, which must be protected as it carries the information.

For historical reasons, when the peer entities are above the second layer, the encryption process is termed end-to-end. The integration of encryption protocols with the protocol suits involves standardization; as it gets applied to higher layers of protocol, encryption standardization and protocol standardization get inseparably intertwined.

Secure Protocol Reference Model (SPRM)

Long after the development and widespread acceptance of the OSI PRM, the cognizant ISO committee has drafted an addendum to address security protections in the PRM. This is the best known work extending a PRM to include security provisions.

The introduction states

> This addendum defines the general security-related architectural elements which can be applied appropriately in the circumstances for which the protection of communication between open systems is required. The addendum establishes, within the framework of the Reference Model, guidelines and constraints to improve existing standards or to develop new standards in the context of OSI in order to allow secure communications.
>
> OSI security functions are concerned only with those visible aspects of a communications path which permit end systems to achieve secure transfer of information between them. OSI Security is not concerned with security measures needed in end systems, installations and organizations except where these have implications on the choice and position of security services visible in OSI. These latter aspects of security may be standardized but not within the scope of OSI standards.

This addendum "provides a general description of security services and related mechanisms, which may be provided by layers of the Reference Model; and defines the position within the Reference Model where the services and mechanisms may be provided." Being based on concepts of peer-level communication, the OSI-SPRM addresses peer entities as a natural abstraction.

Network Protocol Characteristics

A protocol is a description and specification of network properties that can not be ignored in network security analysis. Network protocols are generally designed to be robust in the face of normal operating conditions and perhaps even some malfunction, but they are not designed to withstand malevolent attack. Additional protocols and special attention are required to assure network security. The ability to rigorously establish the security properties of the protocol is essential to achieving the security assurance of the network design.

In a stand-alone computer system, both the users and the computer provided services are physically located in the same system; thus, the services are invoked and served either by procedure calls or by reliable intra-computer process-to-process communications. However, in computer networks, remote services are invoked through remote procedure calls, which are carried out by the lower level message-passing primitives and the message exchange communication protocols. In addition to the security problems common in the centralized computer, there are inter-processes communication threats that can take place during the services provided by the communication protocols.

A protocol may be considered to be a distributed algorithm over the network components. As protocols become more complex, their security properties become more difficult to establish. It is difficult to design and implement secure protocols and to analyze the security properties of protocols as well. It is natural and important to bind network security requirements into protocol layers of the ISO/OSI PRM.

Binding Security Requirements into Protocol Layers

The binding of a security policy requirement to a protocol layer will make the interpretation of the security policy requirements as well as the structuring of the evaluation process much easier. The tangible benefits can include the following: (1) *Protocol layer concept:* to avoid defining a network by its physical boundary. A network can be viewed now as a global service provided by the user interface to its outermost protocol layers. The restriction of the definition of a "network" to mean "a protocol layer interface" has profound implications for how to define what a network is, and how to identify and evaluate its components for the purpose of trusted network evaluation; (2) *security policy requirements:* to allow network security policy requirements to be stated in terms of concepts supported by a particular protocol layer or more than one layer; (3) *evaluation criteria:* to assure that evaluation criteria are meaningful to the kind of networks they are referring to; and (4) *compatible:* to be compatible with the way networks are designed.

Reprint

We continue the discussion of the V.L. Voydock and S.L. Kent paper, "Security in High-Level Network Protocols,"

that was begun in Section 3.1; directing our attention to its in-depth look at providing security through the inter-relationship between encryption and network protocols. One of the major contributions of this paper is to place the discussion of the use of encryption to provide network security in the context of the *ISO Reference Model of Open Systems Interconnection.*

In the OSI model, information may be exchanged between persons or processes operating at the same layer (or level of abstraction) termed *peer entities* by using a *peer-to-peer protocol;* this exchange is termed an *association.* To accomplish this, the information is enclosed in a *protocol data unit (PDU)* (a.k.a. packet) by each layer that it passes through. A very useful analogy is to think of the information as the contents of a letter, and the first PDU as the envelope in which it is placed. Destination and return addresses are written on the envelope, along with other information. Successive PDUs place the preceding PDU in a larger enclosure for forwarding toward the destination. The largest PDU physically moves the information, after which the process is reversed with PDUs (envelopes) being removed from their containers until the information is delivered to the destination entity.

One major contribution of this model is the generalization of many protection concepts and methodologies to protocols between peer entities. This abstraction can help clarify thinking!

Link encryption, which was discussed in Section 3.1, occurs at the first and second layers. In the first layer, the peer entities are involved with transforming the representation of information between forms useful for digital logic and forms useful for communication transfer. Encryption devices operating on the bit level are functioning in this layer. In the second layer, we have protocol standards for encoding characters, message fields such as source address, destination address, priority, and integrity check. Encryption devices that are cognizant of these protocol elements are functioning in this layer.

OSI networks may be thought of as a collection of nodes connected by communication links. These nodes may contain a wide variety of data terminal equipment, which may be providing data communications services or may be providing end-user computational and information processing services. Link encryption concentrates on individually protecting the links. A more abstract view is that information must be protected within this network as it moves between peer entities; PDUs must be protected as they carry the information. For historical reasons, when the peer entities are above the second layer, the encryption process is termed *end-to-end.* In our opinion, the OSI peer entity concept has overtaken end-to-end (sometimes written E3) as a useful descriptor. Any use of encryption involves standardization. As it gets applied to higher layers of protocol, encryption standardization and protocol standardization get inseparably intertwined.

Prevention of release of message contents: This is the first goal of applying encryption. More information is protected the higher the layer in which encryption is done. The transport layer (4) is the lowest layer in which additional protection is gained over link encryption. The granularity of key distribution is a trade-off between convenience and protection. The finest granularity employs a unique key for each association; the coarsest granularity employs the same key for all associations during a time period. There are requirements on the initialization vector (IV) that hold even if a unique key is used for each association. First, a different IV must be used for each association and second, IVs must be pseudorandomly chosen. Finally, IVs must either be protected from disclosure or be different for each PDU of an association.

Prevention of traffic analysis: Traffic analysis countermeasures are concerned with masking the frequency, length, and origin-destination patterns of communications between protocol entities. Encryption can effectively and efficiently restrict disclosure above the transport layer (4); that is, it can conceal the process and application but not the host computer node.

Detection of message stream modification (MSM): The hierarchy of MSM detection measures is integrity, ordering, and authenticity. Independent PDU encryption is assumed. Integrity countermeasures strengthen protocol error detection measures by cryptographically binding an error detection code to each PDU so that changes made to an encrypted PDU will be detected upon decryption, and decryption with the wrong key will be detected. Authenticity countermeasures are based on uniquely identifying an association and its PDUs. Selection of a unique key for each association, proper selection of IVs, and addition of protocol fields all are employed. Message-ordering countermeasures require a unique sequence number and association identification protocol field. Voydock and Kent argue that a transport layer (4) protocol is best suited to MSM countermeasures based on the combination of protocol and protection mechanisms.

Detection of denial of message service: Quiescence is antithetical to detection of this threat. The required active countermeasure is a protocol for active verification that a message path is not under attack.

Detection of masquerade: Countermeasures to attempts to create an association under a false identity or playing back a previous legitimate association initiation sequence require further enhancement of MSM countermeasures. Fine key granularity implies authentication; protocols and hardware implementations for key distribution and management are required. Playback attacks can be discovered by verifying that an association initiation is being attempted in real time. A challenge-response mechanism can be incorporated in the key distribution protocol to discover these attacks.

Key management: The five security goals have led up to a requirement for key management in the form of key distribution protocols and key distribution centers. *Pairwise disjoint key distribution* involves an exchange of a *working key* or *data-encrypting key* between peer entities, possibly protected by a *master key* or *key-distribution key.* To counter the practical problem that N entities would require N-squared master keys, a *key distribution center (KDC)* is introduced as a trusted intermediary. KDCs also can solve the dynamic key requirements, overcoming vulnerability caused by over use or exposure. The initial key distribution requires a "face-to-face" meeting, which may be outside the automated system. Further key distribution depends on a special protocol or a secure trusted connection between the entity and the KDC.

Recommended Readings

A cute example of a protocol to play poker by telephone winds its way through this very readable and valuable paper, "Protocols for Data Security," by Richard DeMillo and Michael Merritt. They agree with Voydock and Kent that cryptography is the basis for secure systems, identifying two "not always disjoint tracks" of development. "The first is the continuing design and analysis of cryptosystems, and the second is the continuing design and analysis of complex communications algorithms that use an underlying cryptosystem as a basic utility." While security undoubtedly has its cost, "since users must communicate in any event (i.e., they must use *some* communication protocol), the incremental cost of executing a secure protocol is often quite reasonable." However, the cost of *developing* a proveably secure protocol may be another matter.

Observing that many systems "operate by a series of message exchanges, and the possibility always exists that one or more of the participants in the exchanges will cheat to gain some advantage, or that some external agent will interfere with normal communications, [they define] security in this context [to] refer to the ability of such a system to withstand attacks by determined cheaters or enemies. . . . The security of a communications system lies in its ability to meet specific operating requirements despite the actions of a knowledgeable and determined attacker. . . . Modern communication systems consist of collections of relatively secure, autonomous processing and storage resources (or nodes) interconnected by communications channels."

"A protocol is a communication algorithm implementing a class of transactions [on these channels among these nodes]. If in doing so it meets the security requirements of the transactions, then it is secure. Protocols . . . involve a complex layering. . ... The principal technique for implementing [secure communications] is cryptographic concealment of the message . . . but the logic of the protocols or even the implementation of the cryptosystem may be flawed. Such flaws, when undetected, are as damaging to overall security as a compromised cryptosystem. . . . Advances in cryptography have led to cryptosystems whose secure implementation require the design of complex protocols . . . point[ing] toward significant problems in protocol design."

One technique is to introduce an arbitrator, "a trusted system component that acts as an intermediary between mutually suspicious users." Arbitrators introduce extra communications and protocol and may create bottlenecks. "Adjudicators" are identified as a special class of arbitrator. After discussing integrity, authentication, signatures, reliability, secrecy, and receipts, the authors conclude that "nonarbitrated adjudicable reception protocols are particularly difficult to design."

Issues relevant to both classic private-key as well as public-key cryptosystems are discussed, including key-distribution channel bandwidth, time stamping, signatures, and the conflict between protection and reliability concerning key replication and distribution. Several apparently secure protocols are described along with their vulnerabilities, leading to the observation: "Not only is it difficult to design and implement secure protocols, it is evidently difficult to analyze the properties of protocols. . . . Secrecy and other security properties of modern cryptographic systems rest on an attacker's practical limitations. . . . Unfortunately, proofs of the difficulty . . . have eluded researchers." To the contrary, advances in computer technology and mathematical theory have continued to reduce the assumed difficulties.

A two-step verification of protocol security is proposed: "(1) Identify explicit cryptographic assumptions (e.g., '200-digit products of 100-digit primes cannot be factored' or 'DES is immune to chosen plaintext attacks') and (2) determine that any successful attack on the protocol requires the violation of at least one assumption made in step (1)."

A generalized concept for examination of security protocols is described. "The key to this approach is the creation of an abstract, axiomatically secure system of cryptographic transformations and predicates that reflects the general properties of the actual cryptosystems utilized by the protocol. . . . Nevertheless, a protocol that has been proved secure using this technique still must be implemented with a real cryptosystem."

Given the difficulties in proving security and correctness, and in modeling physical cryptosystems, proveably correct protocols may not be available for some time.

William Stallings' tutorial text, *Tutorial: Computer Communications: Architectures, Protocols, and Standards,* is a companion to this present one, being published by the IEEE Computer Society. It is designed to present "motivations for, and design principles of, a communications architecture. Considerable attention is devoted to the open system interconnection (OSI) model." The U.S. Department of Defense networking experience is also well represented. The tutorial presents a broad view of communications protocols, exploring principles, services and mechanisms, and standards. While it does not discuss security, it does provide a firm foundation in protocol concepts. In understanding network security, you must grasp the need for protocols to work correctly before they can be secure!

The book begins with protocols, computer-communications architecture, and standards. It then moves on to address the seven layers of the OSI model, with the Defense Advanced Research Projects Agency concept of internetworking interpolated. Thirty-one reprints provide reinforcement of the principles addressed.

Security in High-Level Network Protocols

Victor L. Voydock
Stephen T. Kent

An in-depth look at providing security in high-level network protocols

Reprinted from *IEEE Communications Magazine*, July 1985, pages 12-24.
Copyright © 1985 by The Institute of Electrical and Electronics Engineers, Inc.

There are several trends, which the widespread adoption of standard high-level network protocols will intensify, that emphasize the need to develop network security mechanisms. First, the increased use of networks to provide remote access to computer facilities makes attacking networks more attractive to an intruder. Second, the growing quantity and value of information made vulnerable by the breaching of network security makes networks tempting targets. Third, computer systems connected by networks are likely to cooperate in various ways to provide resource sharing for a user community. As a result of this sharing, the security of information on a given host may become dependent on the security measures employed by the network and by other hosts. Finally, the development of new network technologies facilitates certain kinds of attacks on communication systems; for example, it is easy for an intruder to monitor the transmissions of satellite and radio networks.

Potential security violations can be divided into three distinct categories:

- unauthorized release of information.
- unauthorized modification of information.
- unauthorized denial of resource use.

The term *unauthorized*, used to describe the three categories of attacks, implies that the release, modification, or denial takes place contrary to some security policy. The *intruder* may be either a wiretapper outside of the user community, or an otherwise legitimate user of the network. Communication security techniques have traditionally been employed to counter attacks by the former type of intruder, while authentication and access-control techniques provide the finer granularity of protection required in the latter case. Both techniques must be used in conjunction with traditional physical, electromagnetic-emanation, procedural, and personnel security controls.

The paper begins by describing the threats to security that arise in an open-system environment, and goes on to establish a set of goals for communication security measures. This is followed by a brief description of the two basic approaches to communication security, link-oriented measures, and end-to-end measures, with the conclusion that end-to-end measures are more appropriate in an open-system environment. It goes on to discuss relevant properties of data encryption (the fundamental technique on which all communication security measures are based). The remainder of the paper describes how end-to-end measures can be used to achieve each of the security goals previously established.

Original Production of the information in this paper was supported by the National Bureau of Standards.

Threats to Network Security

Our discussion of security takes place within the context of the ISO Reference Model of Open-System Interconnection [International Organization for Standardization 1980]. In this model, the data communication path is logically composed of an ordered set of subsystems, called *layers*, through which application programs (entities at the highest layer) communicate. Figure 1 depicts the seven layers of the model, and the following paragraphs introduce some terminology from the model that is used throughout this paper.

Each of the seven layers of the model is composed of *protocol entities*. Entities that exist at the same layer are termed *peer entities*. Peer entities communicate with each other using a peer-to-peer protocol. They receive data from the next higher layer, attach the appropriate protocol control information to those data, and then pass the result to the next lower layer. For example, to communicate with a peer entity, a session entity (layer 5) passes its control information and data to a transport entity (layer 4). The transport entity adds its own control information to the session data and passes this new construct as data to a network entity (layer 3). At the destination system, a transport entity will receive these data from its network entity, remove its own control information, and forward the remaining data to the receiving session peer entity.

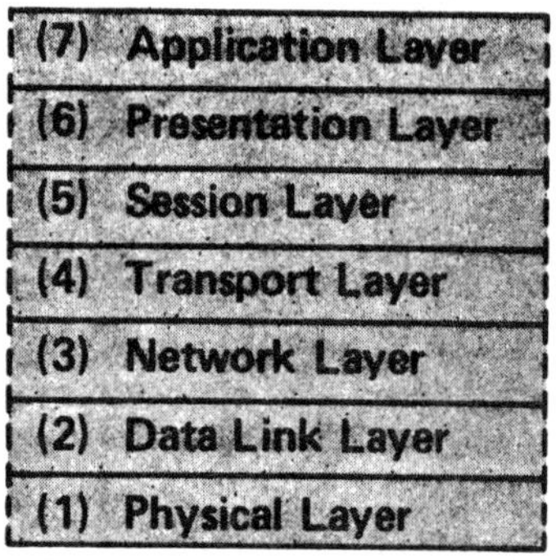

(7)	Application Layer
(6)	Presentation Layer
(5)	Session Layer
(4)	Transport Layer
(3)	Network Layer
(2)	Data Link Layer
(1)	Physical Layer

Fig. 1.   The ISO reference model.

Even if the data are not intelligible to him, the intruder can observe the protocol control information portion of the PDU and thus learn the location and identities of the communicating protocol entities. Finally, the intruder can examine the lengths of PDU's and their frequency of transmission to learn the nature of the data being exchanged. These latter two types of passive attacks are usually referred to as *traffic analysis* or *violations of transmission security*.

Active Attacks

The intruder can also mount active attacks, performing a variety of processing on PDU's passing on the association. These PDU's can be selectively modified, deleted, delayed, reordered, duplicated, and inserted into the association at a later point in time, or be allowed to pass through unaffected. Bogus PDU's can be synthesized and inserted into the association.

While all active attacks involve some combination of the methods listed in the previous paragraph, the countermeasures employed against them vary with the form of the attack. For this reason, it is useful to subdivide active attacks into the following three categories [1]:

- message-stream modification.
- denial of message service.
- spurious association initiation.

Classification of Attacks

As mentioned before, potential security violations can be divided into three distinct categories:

- unauthorized release of information.
- unauthorized modification of information.
- unauthorized denial of use of resources.

Attacks that cause information release are known as *passive attacks*, while those that cause information modification, or denial of resource use are known as *active attacks*. We assume that the intruder can position himself at a point in the network through which all information of interest to him must pass. We also assume that he can mount both active and passive attacks.

Passive Attacks

In a passive attack, the intruder merely observes Protocol Data Units (PDU's) passing on an association (a connection between peer entities), without interfering with their flow. Such intruder observation data in a PDU is termed *release of message contents* and constitutes the most fundamental type of passive attack.

These categories are separately discussed in the paragraphs below.

Message-stream modification includes attacks on the *authenticity*, *integrity*, and *ordering* of the PDU's passing on the association. In the context of the model, authenticity means that the source of a PDU can be reliably determined (that is, that a received PDU was transmitted by the protocol entity at the other end of the association). Integrity means that a PDU has not been modified en route, and ordering means that a PDU can be properly located in the stream of information being transmitted.

Attacks on authenticity can be made by modifying the protocol control information in PDU's, so that they are sent to the wrong destination, or by inserting bogus PDU's (either synthesized or saved from a previous association) into an association. Attacks on integrity, in turn, can be effected by modifying the data portion of PDU's, whereas attacks on ordering can be effected by deleting PDU's or modifying sequencing information in the protocol control portion of PDU's. Although protection against message-stream-modification attacks is often provided by communication protocols for reliability purposes, in this context it must be provided to thwart malicious attacks rather than simply to protect against benign component failures.

Denial of message service, the second category of active attacks, comprises attacks in which the intruder either discards all PDU's passing on an association or, in a less drastic action, delays all PDU's going in one or both directions. The subtle difference between message-stream-modification attacks and denial-of-message-service attacks is a function both of the degree of the attack and of the state of the association.

Spurious association initiation, the third category of active attacks, comprises attacks in which the intruder either "plays back" a recording of a previous legitimate association initiation sequence or attempts to establish an association under a false identity. To counteract the "play-back" kind of attack, association initiation must include a mechanism that verifies the time integrity of the association (that is, determines that the association initiation attempt is being made in real time).

Communication Security Goals

Active and passive attacks are in some sense duals. That is, although message-stream modification, denial of message service, and spurious association initiation attacks cannot be prevented, they can be reliably detected. Conversely, release of message contents and traffic analysis attacks usually cannot be detected, but they can be effectively prevented.

Mindful of these limitations, we have established the following five goals for designing mechanisms to provide communications security:

- prevention of release of message contents.
- prevention of traffic analysis.
- detection of message-stream modification.
- detection of denial of message service.
- detection of spurious association initiation.

In the remaining sections of this paper, we discuss measures for achieving these communication security goals.

Approaches to Communication Security

There are two basic approaches to communication security: *link-oriented* security measures and *end-to-end* security measures. The former provides security by protecting message traffic independently on each communication link, while the latter provides uniform protection for each message all the way from its source to its destination. These two approaches differ not only in their internal implementation characteristics, but also in the nature of the security they provide. In the following sections, we discuss the characteristics of each of these approaches and the implications of using them.

Link-Oriented Measures

Link-oriented protection measures provide security for information passing over an individual communication link between two nodes, regardless of the ultimate source and destination of that information. Each link corresponds to a Data Link Layer association in the ISO Reference Model. Links may be telephone lines, microwave links, or satellite channels. In many cases, the links will be physically unprotected and thus subject to attack.

In a network employing link-oriented measures, encryption is performed independently on each communication link. A different encryption key is often used for each link, so that subversion of one link need not necessarily result in release of information transmitted on other links. To encrypt the information, stream ciphers are generally employed. Since information is not processed as it passes on a link, both the protocol control information and the data in PDU's can be enciphered. This masks origin–destination patterns. If a continuous stream of ciphertext bits is maintained between nodes, PDU frequency and length patterns can be masked as well. In this case, all forms of traffic analysis are completely prevented. Using this technique does not degrade the effective bandwidth of the network because it does not usually require transmission of any additional data; it does, however, entail continuous keystream generation at each node.

Since information is enciphered only on the links and not within the nodes they connect, the nodes themselves must be secure. Although the origin and destination nodes of the network (that is, the hosts) are assumed to be physically secure, link encryption requires that all intermediate nodes (packet switches and gateways) be physically secure as well. Not only must they be physically secure, but their hardware and software components must be certified to isolate the information on each of the associations passing through them.

Subverting one of the intermediate nodes exposes all of the message traffic passing through that node, despite any physical security precautions still in effect at the source and destination nodes.

Another serious problem is the cost of maintaining the security of the nodes. In addition to the one-time expense of providing encryption hardware and a secure physical environment for each node, there are a number of ongoing expenses whose total cost may well exceed the one-time outlays. These include the cost of the employees to protect the physical security of the nodes and the cost of the key distribution process— keys need to be changed frequently; this can be expensive in a network with a large number of nodes.

End-to-End Measures

Link-oriented measures model a network as a collection of nodes joined by communication links, each of which can be independently protected. End-to-end measures, on the other hand, model a network as a medium for transporting PDU's in a secure fashion from source to destination. In keeping with this perspective, end-to-end security measures protect PDU's in transit between source and destination nodes in such a way that subversion of any of their communication links does not violate security.

There is some flexibility in defining the points at which end-to-end security measures are implemented: from host to host, from terminal to service host or process, and from process to process. By extending the domain of end-to-end security measures, one can protect more of the path between communicating protocol entities. However, as their domain is extended, the range of hardware and software that must interface with them increases.

Link-oriented security measures can be implemented so that they are almost completely invisible to network users. End-to-end security measures usually extend beyond the communication subnet and thus require a greater degree of standardization in the protocols employed by those users. Since protocol standardization is already coming about for technical, economic, and political reasons, this is not a serious impediment to the adoption of end-to-end security measures in an open-system environment.

A major advantage of end-to-end security measures is that an individual user or host can elect to employ them without affecting other users and hosts; thus, the cost of employing such measures can be more accurately apportioned. Moreover, these measures can be employed not only in packet-switched networks, but in packet-broadcast networks where link-oriented measures are often not applicable. Finally, end-to-end measures are more naturally suited to users' perceptions of their security requirements. This stems from the fact that they rely on the security of equipment only at the source and destination of an association, while link-oriented measures require that all nodes (packet switches and gateways) in the entire open-system environment also be secure.

Having shown the superiority of end-to-end over link-oriented measures for the open-system environment, we concentrate in the remainder of this paper on end-to-end measures, especially association-oriented measures, for achieving the five security goals:

- prevention of release of message contents.
- prevention of traffic analysis.
- detection of message-stream modification.
- detection of denial of message service.
- detection of spurious association initiation.

We present these measures without regard for the detailed properties of any particular protocol layer. Our discussion centers on conventional cryptosystems as exemplified by the Data Encryption Standard (DES) of the National Bureau of Standards [2–4]. As a Federal Information Processing Standard, the DES forms the basis for cryptographic communication security measures applied to unclassified government information; it appears that it is becoming a de facto industry standard as well.

Data Encryption

Historically, encryption has been extensively employed as a countermeasure to passive attacks [5]. It can also serve as a foundation on which to construct countermeasures to active attacks [1,6–8]. The design and analysis of encryption algorithms are beyond the scope of this paper, but a familiarity with some characteristics of such algorithms is essential to understanding the countermeasures discussed.

Basic Concepts

A *cipher* is an algorithmic transformation performed on a symbol-by-symbol basis on any data. The terms *encipherment* and *encryption* refer synonymously to the application of a cipher to data. An *encryption algorithm* is any algorithm that implements a cipher. The input to an encryption algorithm is referred to as a *cleartext* or *plaintext*, while the output from the algorithm is called *ciphertext*. The transformation performed on the cleartext to encipher it is controlled by a key. For use in the communication context, the encryption algorithm must be *invertible;* that is, there must be a matching decryption algorithm that reverses the encryption transformation when presented with the appropriate key.

In *conventional ciphers,* the key used to decipher a message is the same as that used to encipher it. Such a key must be kept secret, known only to authorized users. Authorized users can use the key both to encrypt their own messages, and to decrypt messages that others have encrypted using it. Figure 2 illustrates these aspects of a conventional cipher.

In contrast, in a *public-key cipher,* the ability to encipher messages under a given key is separated from

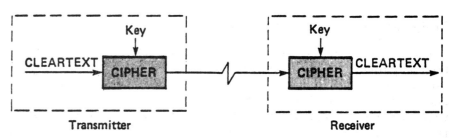

Fig. 2. *A conventional cipher.*

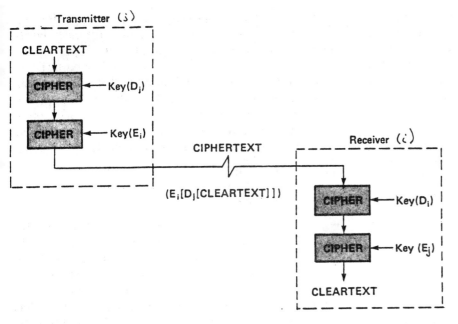

CLEARTEXT

CIPHER ← Key(D$_j$)

CIPHER ← Key(E$_i$)

CIPHERTEXT

Receiver (*i*)

(E$_i$[D$_j$[CLEARTEXT]])

CIPHER ← Key(D$_i$)

CIPHER ← Key (E$_j$)

CLEARTEXT

Fig. 3. A public-key cipher.

the ability to decipher those messages. This is accomplished by using pairs of keys *E, D*. These keys define a pair of transformations, each of which is the inverse of the other, and neither of which is derivable from the other. Each user possesses such a key pair. One key *E* is made public, for use in enciphering messages for that user, while the corresponding key *D* is kept secret, for use in deciphering messages sent to the user under the public key.

Since anyone can transmit a message to a user *i* under that user's public key *E$_i$*, some additional mechanism is needed to securely identify the sender. Identification is accomplished by having the sender *j* encrypt the message under his secret key *D$_j$*, then under the public key of the intended receiver *E$_i$*. The receiver can then strip off the outer layer of encryption using his secret key *D$_i$*, and complete the deciphering using the public key of the sender *E$_j$*. This is illustrated in Fig. 3.

One of the supposed advantages of a public-key cryptosystem is that public keys may be freely distributed without concern for secrecy. But, the need for authentication in the distribution of public keys in an open-system environment results in there being few differences between public-key and conventional-key distribution mechanisms.

Major Encryption Techniques

Two major classes of encryption techniques have been employed in modern non-voice telecommunications and digital computer applications: *block ciphers* and *stream ciphers*. The former method enciphers fixed-sized blocks of bits under the control of a key that is often approximately the same size as the blocks being encrypted. The latter method performs bit-by-bit transformations on cleartext under the control of a stream of key bits, usually using some easily reversible operation, such as addition modulo 2.

Block Ciphers

Block ciphers transform entire blocks of bits under the control of a key. A block cipher maps the space of cleartext blocks into the space of ciphertext blocks. If the block size is *N* bits, then the size of the cleartext space (the range of cleartext block values) and the size of the ciphertext space (the range of ciphertext block values) are both 2^N. Since each ciphertext block must be unambiguously decipherable, the mapping must be one to one; since the sizes of the spaces are equal, this means it will also be onto. Thus, a block cipher defines a collection of permutations on the set of *N*-bit blocks; the key chosen determines which permutation is used.

Stream Ciphers

Stream ciphers can operate on the stream of cleartext in real time, enciphering each quantum of cleartext as it is generated by combining it with a quantum from the key stream. The size of the quanta processed varies with the particular cipher employed; common sizes are 1 and 8 bits. Some cryptosystems allow the user to specify the quantum size. If the quantum size is chosen appropriately, stream ciphers can provide a key stream that is matched exactly to the length of the message, thus avoiding the problems associated with padding cleartext to match block sizes.

The Data Encryption Standard (DES)

The DES has several modes of operation, allowing it to be used as either a block or a stream cipher [3].

ECB Mode

In its most fundamental mode the DES is a block cipher operating on 64-bit blocks, using a 56-bit key. This mode is known as the *electronic code book* (ECB) mode in an analogy to conventional code books. Each key parameterizes the cipher, defining a permutation on the space of 64-bit blocks. In the ECB mode, a message is fragmented into block-sized pieces and padded to occupy an integral number of blocks, if necessary. Each block is then independently enciphered.

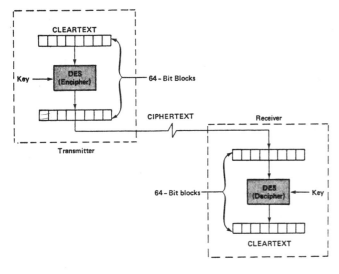

Fig. 4. The ECB mode of the DES.

In the CBC mode, as in the ECB mode, a message is first fragmented into block-sized pieces and then padded, if necessary. The first block is combined, via addition modulo 2, with an *initialization vector* (IV), and enciphered as in ECB mode. This ciphertext block is then combined, via addition modulo 2, with the second message block, and the result is enciphered as it would be in the ECB mode. This process is repeated until the complete message is enciphered. An error occurring in a ciphertext block will propagate throughout that block and a portion of the following block, but will not affect subsequent blocks.

Release of Message Contents

This section discusses how end-to-end encryption can be used to protect the contents of messages being exchanged by protocol entities. The amount of information that can be hidden from an intruder depends on the layer in which encryption is done. For example, if encryption is done by the session layer, all transport-layer protocol control information is visible to the intruder, whereas if encryption is done by the transport

Each bit in a ciphertext block is a function of each bit of the key and of each bit of the cleartext block from which it was generated. A change of as little as 1 bit in either the key or the cleartext results in ciphertext, in which each bit is changed with approximately equal probability. Conversely, a change in 1 bit of either the key or ciphertext will produce changes in an average of 50 percent of the bits of deciphered cleartext. Although this error propagation is extensive, it is strictly limited to the block in which the error occurs—decryption of other blocks is unaffected.

CBC Mode

In the ECB mode (Fig. 4), each block of ciphertext is independent of all other ciphertext, that is, it is a function only of the key and the cleartext block that produced it. This independence limits the types of modification detection codes that can be employed. Also, note that identical cleartext blocks produce identical ciphertext blocks. This exposure of block-size data patterns that fall on block boundaries is often unacceptable. A second DES mode, known as the *cipher block chaining* (CBC) mode, can be used to eliminate these problems.

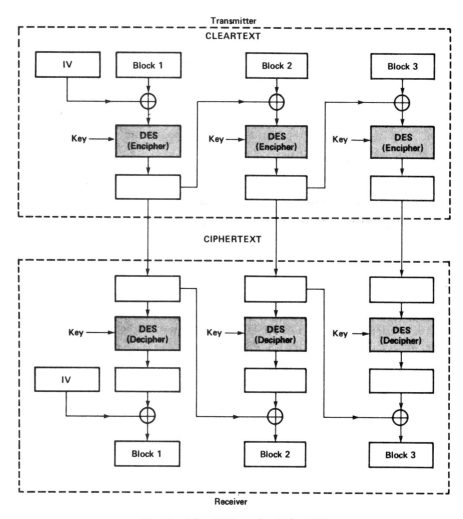

Fig. 5. The CBC mode of the DES.

layer, only network-layer (and below) information can be seen. Note, however, that having encryption done by the network layer, rather than by the transport layer, will not provide any additional end-to-end protection. This is because network-layer protocol control information must, by its very nature, be visible at each node (packet switch or gateway) that a network-PDU traverses. Thus, the transport layer is the lowest layer in which the adoption of encryption would provide additional end-to-end protection.

Key Granularity

A unique key can be used for each association, or a coarser granularity of key distribution can be employed. For example, a different key can be used between each pair of communicating protocol entities, or a single key can be used among an entire group of protocol entities. As the range of use of a single key increases, the amount of information exposed in the case of disclosure of that key also increases, but the task of distributing keys becomes easier. The granularity of key distribution also affects the design of countermeasures against active attacks. A unique key for each association is a powerful tool for constructing such countermeasures.

When an entity receives an encrypted PDU, it must be able to determine the key under which the PDU was encrypted. How this is done depends on the granularity of key distribution. For example, suppose a different key were used for each pair of communicating entities. Because no two pairs communicate on the same association, the association on which the PDU arrives implicitly identifies the sending entity, and therefore the key to use for decryption.

Masking Data Patterns

In The CBC mode, the pattern exposure problems of the ECB mode can be overcome. In this mode, the ciphertext produced for a cleartext block is a function of that block and of all preceding blocks in the message. Because of this dependence, identical cleartext blocks in two messages result in identical ciphertext blocks only if they have identical prefixes—that is, only if all preceding cleartext blocks in those messages were also identical. Thus, all data patterns can be masked in the CBC mode by ensuring that every message encrypted under the same key begins with a unique prefix. The following requirements must hold for CBC IV's:

- a different IV must be used for each association.
- IV's must be pseudorandomly chosen.
- IV's must either be protected from disclosure or be different for each PDU of each association.

These requirements hold even if a unique key is used for each association.

Traffic Analysis

Traffic analysis countermeasures are concerned with masking the frequency, length, and origin–destination patterns of the message traffic between protocol entities. The precision with which an intruder can analyze these patterns determines the amount of information that he can gain from that analysis. Appropriate link encryption techniques can mask all such patterns and prevent all traffic analysis attacks. This is not true with end-to-end techniques. It is easy to achieve a certain level of protection, but beyond this the techniques become clumsy and increasingly expensive, and cannot, in any case, completely prevent all forms of traffic analysis.

In an open-system environment, end-to-end techniques can limit the precision of origin–destination analysis but cannot entirely prevent it. The precision with which such analysis can be done depends on the layer in which encryption is performed. For example, if encryption were performed in the presentation layer, an intruder could determine which presentation, session, and transport entities were involved in a given association. Performing encryption in the transport layer would limit the intruder to observing patterns at the network-address level. That is, he could tell which transport-layer entities were exchanging messages, but not which (or how many) higher level entities were doing so.

Masking these host-level patterns is infeasible in an open-system environment. Doing so would involve encrypting the actual destinations of network PDU's using a network-wide key and sending all PDU's to all hosts on the network. This would, of course, cause an extreme reduction in the effective bandwidth of the network and waste large amounts of processing power in the hosts. Thus, the most that end-to-end measures can practically do is to limit origin–destination analysis to the host level.

End-to-end measures can also limit the precision of message frequency and length pattern analysis. If encryption were performed in the transport layer (to limit origin–destination analysis, for instance), the intruder would already be limited to examining such patterns at the host level. That is, he could determine how many messages were sent from one host to another, at what rate they were sent, and what their lengths were, but he could not relate this to higher level entities residing on those hosts.

In summary, end-to-end techniques can effectively and efficiently limit all forms of traffic analysis to the host level. Beyond the host level, further limitations on information release become increasingly expensive and are probably not necessary in non-military environments.

Message Stream Modification

In this section, we discuss methods that can be used to detect message-stream-modification (MSM) attacks.

Message-stream modification refers to attack on the integrity, authenticity, and ordering of PDU's passing on an association. Integrity means that a PDU has not been modified while passing on the association. Authenticity means that the source of the PDU is the entity at the other end of the association, and ordering means that the PDU can be properly located in the stream of PDU's moving from the source to the destination entity.

The need to provide protection from passive attacks is apparent. It could be argued that most users and many application programs can easily detect MSM attacks without the inclusion of explicit countermeasures in the communications protocols involved, especially when an encryption scheme with suitable error propagation characteristics is used. But, many application programs are not prepared to detect attacks of this sort, and many message streams do not contain the proper kind of redundant information to allow such detection. Even messages directed to a user may admit a wide range of "meaningful" contents. In addition, providing detection measures in a communications protocol obviates the need for each application programmer to devise an application-specific means of detection. It also makes it unnecessary to check many sets of security measures for correctness. Finally, it ensures that the correctness of security measures need not be rechecked each time an application program is changed.

MSM attacks can cause PDU's to arrive out of order or to be modified, lost, or duplicated. Restoring cryptographic synchrony after such events can be difficult and expensive if the ability to decrypt a PDU depends on having successfully decrypted all previously sent PDU's. For this reason, protocols that implement countermeasures to MSM attacks will generally encrypt each PDU independently. Independent PDU encryption is assumed in the discussion that follows.

Overview

Measures to detect the three forms of MSM attacks are hierarchically organized. The most fundamental measures are those that ensure message integrity. These measures involve cryptographically binding an error detection code to a PDU so that changes to that PDU are detected with high probability, as are PDU's decrypted with the wrong key. Such measures are the foundation on which authentication measures are built. Ordering measures rely on both integrity and authentication measures.

Measures to ensure message authenticity are based on the ability of the receiver to determine, with high probability, the association to which a PDU belongs, regardless of what an intruder does. They involve uniquely identifying an association for all time and binding this unique ID (either implicitly or explicitly) to every PDU passing on that association. The integrity measures are relied on to ensure that the binding is inalterable by an intruder.

Measures to ensure message ordering are based on the ability of the receiver to determine, with high probability, the position of a PDU in the stream of PDU's moving in one direction on an association. They involve binding to each PDU a sequence number that identifies that PDU's position in the stream. The integrity measures are relied on to ensure that the binding is inalterable by an intruder. The authentication measures are relied on to filter out PDU's that were not sent by the other end of the association at all.

Message Integrity

As mentioned above, message integrity measures involve cryptographically binding an error detection code to each PDU in such a way that:

Property I—changes made to an encrypted PDU as it traverses the network will be detected with high probability when the PDU is decrypted.

Property II—a PDU that has been decrypted using the wrong key will be detected with high probability.

Measures that ensure Property I generally ensure Property II also. This is because decrypting a PDU with the wrong key produces a result at least as garbled as that produced by decrypting a PDU that has been modified en route. However, Property II is explicitly stated because it is one of the foundations on which authentication measures are based.

Communication protocols have long used error detection codes to detect transmission errors. A code is generally attached to each PDU. It allows the receiving protocol entity to detect which PDU's were modified en route by a transmission error. This, of course, does not protect the integrity of the PDU against a deliberate attack. An intruder can make an arbitrary change to a PDU, compute what the new value of the error code should be, and replace the old error code with the. new. Message integrity measures involve binding the error code to the PDU in a way that prevents an intruder from doing this.

A fundamental requirement of message integrity mechanisms is that an intruder change to an encrypted PDU must generate a change in the decrypted PDU that is not invariant under the error detection algorithm being employed. The CBC mode of the DES has this property when used with an appropriate error detection algorithm. Inverting a ciphertext bit affects 64 bits of decrypted cleartext unpredictably. That is, each of those 64 bits has a probability of approximately one half of being changed. Thus, a bit inversion to an encrypted PDU introduces, in effect, a random burst error into the decrypted PDU. If each PDU includes an error code that has good burst error detection properties, such attacks on message integrity have a high probability of being detected.

Message Authenticity

Attacks on message authenticity involve the insertion of spurious PDU's into the stream of PDU's moving in one direction on an association. Such attacks include:

- inserting a PDU synthesized by the intruder.
- playing back a valid PDU from another association.
- playing back a valid PDU that had previously been sent in the opposite direction on the same association.

The goal of message authentication measures is to detect such attacks, by making it possible for the receiving entity to reliably determine the association to which a PDU belongs and the direction in which it is moving.

The approach to detecting the first two types of attack is to uniquely identify an association for all time, and to attach inalterably (either implicitly or explicitly) this unique ID to every PDU passing on that association. An association may be sequentially assigned a number of unique ID's; that is, it may have a different unique ID at different times in its life. However, no unique ID will ever be used for more than one association. Thus, from the unique ID, one can reliably determine to which association a PDU belongs.

If a separate key is used for each association, the key provides an implicit unique ID. That is, the key used to encrypt a PDU uniquely identifies the association to which it belongs. Thus, Property II of the message integrity measures ensures that PDU's from other associations will be detected. In this context, synthesized PDU's are equivalent to PDU's from other associations and will also be detected.

The unique ID allows the receiver to determine which association a PDU belongs to, but it does not indicate the direction in which the PDU is moving. Thus, an additional mechanism is needed to detect the third type of attack on PDU authenticity. There are several approaches to this problem.

One approach relies on the way in which IV's are chosen. Distinct IV's or sets of IV's may be used in each direction on an association. In such protocols, if an entity receives a PDU that is a playback of one it previously sent, it will decrypt it with the wrong IV. Property I of the integrity measures ensures that this will be detected, since changing the IV is equivalent, in this sense, to changing the encrypted PDU itself. Thus, such protocols automatically detect the third type of attack on PDU authenticity.

A different approach must be found for protocols that do not use distinct IV's for each direction on an association. The simplest approach is to add a field to each PDU indicating the direction in which it is moving. Property I of the message integrity measures ensures that an intruder cannot undetectably alter this field. In many protocols, the association specifier indicates in which direction a PDU is moving. This is sufficient if that specifier is not sent in the clear, and if specifiers are unique for the life of the key. Otherwise, a separate direction indicating field is needed in each PDU.

Message Ordering

Attacks on message ordering involve disrupting the stream of PDU's moving in one direction on an association. Such attacks include:

- deleting PDU's from the stream.
- altering the order of PDU's in the stream.
- duplicating PDU's in the stream, that is, recording a legitimate PDU from the stream and later playing it back into that stream.

The goal of message-ordering measures is to detect such attacks by making it possible for the receiving entity to reliably determine the position of each PDU in the stream of PDU's being sent by its correspondent peer. (The message authenticity measures are relied on to filter out PDU's that do not belong to this stream at all.)

Message ordering is achieved by including a sequence number in each PDU, that indicates the position of the PDU in the stream of PDU's moving in one direction on an association. Property I of the integrity mechanisms ensures that any attempt to change a sequence number will be detected. In this way, the receiving entity can detect missing, duplicated, or out-of-order PDU's.

To ensure that the third type of ordering attack is detected, sequence numbers may not be reused during the life of an association unique ID. This ban on reuse prevents an intruder from undetectably playing back an old PDU after the sequence numbers have cycled.

Summary of Message-stream Modification

It has been shown that to detect MSM attacks, a protocol must be able to detect deleted, duplicated, and out-of-order PDU's, as well as spurious PDU's from other associations and PDU's whose contents have been modified. To recover from transient MSM attacks, the protocol must further be capable of retransmitting missing or modified PDU's, throwing away spurious and duplicate PDU's, and resequencing out-of-order PDU's. This capability requires fairly elaborate protocol mechanisms.

Most protocols above the transport layer rely on that layer to ensure that PDU's arrive in order, with no duplicates or losses. Thus, they are not able to cope with MSM attacks. Changing one of these protocols to cope with such attacks would complicate it considerably, and would duplicate mechanisms already present in the transport layer to deal with transmission errors.

This argues that the proper way to handle MSM attacks is to augment the existing transmission error-recovery mechanisms of the transport layer. Since countermeasures to MSM attacks can also protect against release of message contents, it would seem that the proper placement for all end-to-end security measures discussed so far is the transport layer.

Denial of Message Service

As mentioned above, denial-of-message-service attacks can be viewed as persistent MSM attacks. Such attacks include:

- discarding all PDU's passing on an association in either or both directions.
- delaying all PDU's passing on an association in either or both directions.

The countermeasures previously discussed can detect some, but not all, forms of denial-of-message-service attacks. In particular, they cannot reliably detect such attacks if they begin while the association is quiescent, that is, when no PDU's are outstanding in either direction. In general, in such a situation, a protocol entity at one end of an association has no way of determining when the next PDU should arrive from its correspondent peer entity. The entity is thus unable to detect a denial-of-service attack that completely cuts off the flow of PDU's from its peer entity.

In many cases, the entity attempting to send PDU's will detect the attack but it has no way of notifying the other entity. The receiving entity will remain unaware of the attack until it attempts to send PDU's itself. In some situations, such an event may never occur. This could happen, for example, if one entity were an editor program waiting for a user request and the correspondent peer were a user at a terminal. The user would be able to detect such attacks, since the editor would not respond. The editor, on the other hand, would wait forever for the next user request.

An additional countermeasure is needed to detect such attacks. It entails adding a request–response mechanism [1] to the MSM countermeasures. This mechanism can be incorporated either into the same layer as the MSM countermeasures or into a higher layer.

The request–response mechanism involves the periodic exchange of a pair of PDU's between peer entities to verify that an open path exists between them. To do this, a timer is added to each end of the association; each timer periodically triggers the transmission of a request PDU that forces a response from the other end. Lack of a response indicates that a denial-of-service attack is taking place.

Increasing the frequency with which request-response PDU's are exchanged will reduce the time interval during which a denial-of-service attack will remain undetected. Unfortunately, this increased mes-sage traffic also reduces the effective bandwidth of the network.

Spurious Association Initiation

Active attacks that can occur during the association initiation process are referred to as spurious association initiation attacks and fall into two categories:

- attempting to establish an association under a false identity.
- playing back a recording of a previous legitimate association initiation sequence.

To counteract the first type of attack, an association must be initiated in a way that supports secure identification of the principals at each end. Verification of identity is a complex issue that interacts with issues of user authentication and access control that are beyond the scope of this paper. As is seen below, though, a portion of the identification problem must be dealt with during association initiation itself.

To counteract the second type of attack, association initiation must include a mechanism to verify the time integrity of the association; that is, to verify that the association initiation attempt is being made in real time. Both types of attacks are similar in nature to MSM attacks; however, the context of association initiation requires the use of additional counter-measures.

Authentication of Principals

To detect the first kind of attack, it must be possible to authenticate the identities of the principals involved in an association initiation attempt. The ability to encipher messages under a specific key carries with it an implicit form of authentication. In particular, only a possessor of a given key is able to encipher messages under it. Thus, authentication of principals can be based on the appropriate distribution and protection of secret encryption keys.

The precision with which a principal can be identified depends on the granularity of key distribution. For example, if a single key is employed by a subset of the principals in a network, then these principals form a secure virtual subnet. Knowledge of the key identifies the members of the subnet without distinguishing among them. To be able to authenticate the identity of each individual principal, a finer level of granularity is needed. This can be achieved by using a different key for communication between each pair of principals. Such a scheme is known as *pairwise disjoint key distribution*.

Hierarchic Key Distribution

If pairwise disjoint key distribution is used, each principal involved in an association can reliably verify the identity of the principal at the other end. But this approach, by itself, has the problem that two principals always use the same key (call it the long-term key) when communicating with each other. To extend this approach to allow a per-association key, the key must be securely distributed to each end of the association. One method of distribution is to transmit the per-association key at association initiation time, encrypted under the long-term key.

Keys held for long periods of time and used exclusively for the transmission of per-association keys are referred to as *master, primary,* or *key-encrypting* keys. One or more keys used during the course of a single association are referred to as *working, secondary,* or *data-encrypting* keys. Thus, master keys are used to authenticate principals, and to protect transmitted working keys, while working keys are used exclusively to encrypt PDU's on a single association. Using a master key as a bootstrapping mechanism in the distribution of working keys is referred to as *hierarchic key distribution.*

In order to ensure security, working keys must be pseudorandomly chosen from the key space. A number of approaches may be used to generate keys. For example, one can encrypt a non-repeating value under the master key and use the resulting ciphertext as the working key. This paper does not consider key generation issues in detail.

A problem with pairwise disjoint distribution of master keys is that the number of master keys needed tends to increase rapidly as the size of the network increases, and the granularity of the keys decreases. For example, if pairwise disjoint distribution is carried out at the level of individual hosts, complete communication among N hosts requires on the order of N^2 keys. If this form of key distribution is carried out at the level of terminals, or of individual users, the number of master keys involved can become staggering.

Managing such large numbers of keys can be cumbersome and expensive. For example, if the master key list on a host is subverted, all users on that list must be notified. If a user loses his list of master keys, all hosts on that list must be notified. In order to reduce the proliferation of master keys significantly, the concept of trusted intermediaries known as *key distribution* centers has been developed [5], [9].

Key Distribution Centers

A key distribution center (KDC) is a secure host dedicated to acting as a trusted intermediary in the establishment of secure associations. A conventional KDC (that is, a KDC that handles conventional ciphers) holds one master key for each principal that uses its services. A principal that wants to initiate an association first contacts the KDC and indicates the target of the association. The KDC generates a working key and sends it to the initiator and the target. The copy of the working key sent to the initiator is enciphered under the master key of the initiator, while the copy sent to the target is enciphered under that of the target. In this way, each association participant need hold only one master key, and yet mutually suspicious participants are protected, just as if pairwise disjoint key distribution were employed.

Key distribution centers are needed for public-key ciphers as well. It has been suggested that telephone book listings of public keys would suffice [10]. Unfortunately, such a static approach is not appropriate in an open-system environment. First and most important, the frequency of key changes, additions, and deletions will be high owing to changing user populations, the need to replace lost keys, and the need to change keys periodically to reduce the impact of key exposure. Second, as the use of open systems becomes widespread, the size of such key phone books would become unmanageable. Finally, public keys tend to be very long, so manual key entry would be cumbersome and error-prone. For these reasons, the automated key distribution and maintenance services of a KDC are necessary.

Both conventional and public-key KDC's require an initial "face-to-face meeting" with a representative of each principal they serve. At this meeting, the principal's representative first establishes his identity with the KDC. Then, if the meeting is with a conventional KDC, he receives (or presents) his master key. Otherwise, he presents his public key and receives, in turn, the public key of the KDC. Note that while both procedures involve a tamper-free key exchange, only the former requires secrecy in the exchange as well.

Once this initial meeting has taken place, a principal can establish an association with any other principal with the assistance of the KDC, as described above. A response message from the KDC must be reliably bound to the request that generated it. It can be bound by having the request contain a unique identifier, which the KDC then attaches to the associated response. Failure to employ such a mechanism exposes the principal to attacks in which recordings of prior principal/KDC interactions are played back, possibly resulting in the use of old, exposed keys and subsequent masquerading and/or data release. The preceding discussion assumes that the KDC and the principal communicate using a transaction-oriented mechanism. Another approach to this problem would be to maintain a secure connection between the principal and the KDC.

Detecting Playback Attacks

The second type of spurious association initiation attack is to play back a recording of a previous legitimate association initiation sequence. Counteracting such attacks involves verifying that the association initiation attempt is being made in real time.

One way to do this is to make use of a challenge-response mechanism. This mechanism is employed after the two sides have agreed on a key to use, but before the transmission of user data begins. At this point, each side sends the other an encrypted challenge PDU containing a unique bit pattern (perhaps a real-time clock reading). The other side must send an encrypted response PDU containing a value that is some predefined transformation of the unique bit pattern contained in the challenge. When both pairs of challenge-response PDU's have been exchanged, each side knows that the other has replied in real time.

Note that the above mechanism involves the exchange of four PDU's over and above those needed to establish the key to be used. By integrating this mechanism with the key distribution mechanism, the total number of messages involved can be reduced.

Summary

Threats to communication security fall into two general categories: passive attacks and active attacks. The purpose of a passive attack is to bring about the unauthorized release of information; the purpose of an active attack is to cause either unauthorized modification or unauthorized denial of use of resources.

There are two basic approaches to communication security: link-oriented security measures and end-to-end security measures. The former measures provide security by protecting message traffic independently on each communication link, whereas the latter provide uniform protection for each message from its source to its destination. End-to-end measures seem to be more appropriate for use in an open-system environment.

Data encryption is the fundamental technique on which all communications security measures are based. Encryption directly prevents passive attacks by preventing an intruder from observing data in the clear. Data patterns can be masked by using a unique key for each association and by exercising care in the selection of IV's. The protocol layer in which encryption is performed determines the precision with which traffic analysis can be done.

Active attacks fall into three categories: message-stream modification (MSM), denial of message service, and spurious association initiation. All of these attacks can be detected by using an encryption algorithm with appropriate error propagation characteristics.

Measures to detect the three forms of MSM attacks are hierarchically organized. The most fundamental measures are those that ensure message integrity. Measures that ensure message authenticity rely on the integrity measures, and measures that ensure message ordering, in turn, rely on both of the previous measures. MSM countermeasures are based on the use of a unique key for each association, a unique sequence number for each PDU, and an error detection code that can be inalterably bound to each PDU.

Denial of message service is an important type of active attack that is often overlooked. MSM countermeasures can detect some, but not all, forms of this attack. To detect denial-of-message-service attacks that begin when an association is quiescent, some form of request-response mechanism must be employed.

Spurious association attacks take two forms: attempting to establish an association under a false identity, and playing back a recording of a previous legitimate association-initiation attempt. To counteract the first kind of attack, an association must be initiated in a way that supports secure identification of the principals at each end. This can be done through hierarchic key distribution. To counteract the second kind of attack, association initiation must include a mechanism that verifies that the initiation attempt is being made in real time. One way to do this is by using a challenge-response mechanism similar to the request-response mechanism used to detect denial of message service attacks.

Acknowledgments

Douglas Hunt and Gregory Pearson made numerous useful suggestions and comments throughout the preparation of this paper. Dennis Branstad and James Moulton, contract monitors for the NBS contract, provided useful feedback during preparation of the manuscript. Rachel Rutherford made numerous suggestions that significantly improved the readability of this paper.

The work described in this paper was sponsored in part by the Institute for Computer Sciences and Technology of the National Bureau of Standards under Contract SB80NBS0015. A longer version of this paper appeared in *Computing Surveys*, vol. 15, no. 2, June 1983.

References

[1] S. Kent, "Encryption-based protection protocols for interactive user-computer communication," LCS-TR-162, MIT Laboratory for Computer Science, Cambridge, MA, 1976.

[2] National Bureau of Standards, "Data encryption standard," Federal Information Processing Standards Publ. 46, Government Printing Office Washington, D.C., 1977.

[3] National Bureau of Standards, "DES modes of operation," Preliminary Copy of Federal Information Processing Standards Publ., Government Printing Office, Washington, D.C., 1980a.

[4] National Bureau of Standards, "Telecommunications: interoperability and security requirements for use of the Data Encryption Standard in data communication systems," Proposed Federal Standard 1026, Government Printing Office, Washington, D.C., 1980b.

[5] D. K. Branstad, "Encryption protection in computer data communications," *IEEE Proc. 4th Data Communications Symp.*, Quebec, pp. 8-1–8-7, Oct. 7–9, 1975.

[6] H. Feistel, W. Notz, and J. Smith, "Cryptographic techniques for machine to machine data communications," *Proc. IEEE*, 63, 11, pp. 1545-1554, Nov. 1975.

[7] D. Kahn, *The Code Breakers*, Macmillan, New York, 1967.

[8] S. T. Kent, "Encryption-based protection for interactive user/computer Communication," *IEEE Proc. 5th Data Communications Symp.*, Snowbird, UT, pp. 5-7-5-13, Sept. 27-29, 1977.

[9] D. Branstad, "Security aspects of computer networks," *Proc. AIAA Computer Network Systems Conf.*, Huntsville, AL, Apr. 1973.

[10] R. L. Rivest, A. Shamir, and L. Adleman, "A method for obtaining digital signatures and public-key cryptosystems," *Commun. ACM*, 21, 2, pp. 120-126, Feb. 1978.

[11] International Organization for Standardization, "Data processing—open systems interconnection—basic reference model," ISO/TC 97/SC 16 N537, rev. Available from American National Standards Institute, New York, 1980.

[12] R. M. Needham and M. D. Schroeder, "Using encryption for authentication in large networks of computers," *Commun. ACM*, 21, 12, pp. 993-998, Dec. 1978.

[13] V. Voydock and S. Kent, "Security in higher level protocols: approaches, alternatives, and recommendations," BBN Rep. 4767, Bolt Beranek and Newman, Cambridge, MA. Also available as National Bureau of Standards, Rep. ICST/HLNP—81-19, Government Printing Office, Washington, D.C., 1981.

Victor Voydock is a Senior Software Designer at Microcom, Inc. where he leads the development of communication products for personal computers. Previously at Bolt Beranek and Newman, he was involved in research in the areas of network security and network interprocess communications mechanisms. At SofTech, he managed the Software Development Tools section. Prior to this, he managed the Standard Service System group of the Multics development project at M.I.T. He has a broad range of experience in the areas of computer networks, operating systems, software development tools, and user interface design. He has a B.S. in Mathematics from M.I.T., and an M.S. in Mathematics from the University of Illinois.

Stephen Kent received the B.S. degree (summa cum laude) in Mathematics from Loyola University, New Orleans, LA in 1973, and the S.M., E.E., and Ph.D. degrees in Computer Science from the Massachusetts Institute of Technology in 1976, 1977, and 1980, respectively. He joined Bolt Beranek and Newman in 1980, where he has served as project leader or principal investigator for projects involving the development of end-to-end encryption systems for packet switched networks, design of a secure transport layer protocol, design of personal authentication systems, and performance analysis of end-to-end network security systems. He is now the Chief Scientist of BBN Communications Corporation, a subsidiary of Bolt Beranek and Newman.

Dr. Kent is the author of a book chapter and numerous papers on the topic of packet network security. He is the communication security editor for the *Journal of Telecommunication Networks*, a member of the Board of Directors of the International Association for Cryptologic Research, and the Chairman of the DARPA Internet Task Force on Privacy. He has served as a National Lecturer for the ACM and has lectured on the topic of network security in the United States and Western Europe for George Washington University, USC, MIT, the Department of Defense, and several private firms. He is a member of the ACM, Delta Epsilon Sigma, Pi Mu Epsilon, and Sigma Xi. ∎

Section 3.5: Network Applications

Why Discuss Network Applications

Because this is the final section in this tutorial, as expected, it serves to integrate all of the material presented thus far. Few new concepts are introduced. Rather, the discussion attempts to summarize and the papers are selected to exemplify. If you find the discussion simplistic and the papers clear and obvious, then all objectives have been achieved!

The Importance of Standards

A good deal of this tutorial has been concerned with standards, either directly or indirectly. By *standard* we mean a set of specifications for the construction and operation of a device, mechanism, or procedure established by an organization officially empowered to establish such standards. These are *de jure* standards, not to be confused with *de facto* common practices established by informal common consent or market forces, especially not by commercial market domination. One benefit of standards is interoperability of hardware and software built by diverse organizations (although the current trend toward multiple options and subsets is diminishing this attribute).

Another benefit of standards is the ability to rely on experts. This aspect is especially important in matters of computer and network security. Some standards are established by public organizations such as ANSI in order to satisfy a publically felt need. Adaption of such a standard is a voluntary action indicating recognition of the value added by compliance. Noncompliance, including adaption of a nonstandard practice, might be construed as imprudent behavior. Some standards are established within organizations by entities established for that purpose; often they also have enforcement powers. Within the U.S. federal government, the National Bureau of Standards has certain authority to establish Federal Information Processing Standards (FIPS) and the Department of Defense (including various subsidary organizations) establishes standards within its domain. These standards organizations can also disseminate expert judgment without publicizing the basis for that judgment.

Reprints

In his paper, "Automated Distribution of Cryptographic Keys Using the Financial Institution Key Management Standard," David M. Balenson provides an opportunity to learn about a standard without having to separate for yourself what it does from how it does it. The standard discussed is ANSI X9.17, Financial Institution Key Management (Wholesale). In addition to its use among banks and other financial institutions (that is what the "wholesale" in the title means), it has been adopted by the U.S. Department of the Treasury for use in all Federal government electronic funds transfer.

As discussed in Greenlee [GREE85] in Section 3.2, X9.17 employs a message authentication code (MAC) for data authentication which is cryptographically based on the *Data Encryption Standard* Algorithm (DES/DEA). It provides for the secrecy and integrity of *keying material* encompassing generation, distribution, storage, entry, use, destruction, and archiving. A physical *key management facility* (KMF) is specified along with requirements for control of keying material, secure distribution of keys, ensured integrity of keys and KMF, and failure recovery.

A hierarchy of keys is specified: (1) manually distributed key-encrypting keys (KKMs), (2) automatically distributed key-encrypting keys (KKs), and (3) automatically distributed data keys (KDs). The KKM and KK may be used in pairs according to a specified algorithm for additional protection. At a minimum, the KKM is used to encrypt the KD for distribution; optionally, the KKM encrypts the KK for distribution, which in turn encrypts the KD.

Key counters prevent replay and out of sequence messages; *key offsetting* adds reuse protection. *Key notarization* restricts key use to the intended parties. A set of fixed-format cleartext cryptographic service messages (CSMs) are provided as protocols for establishing and disestablishing keys and related information. Three environments are specified: point-to-point (PTP) (the minimum), key distribution center (KDC), and key translation center (KTC).

Five CSMs are defined for PTP environment: request for service initiation, key service message, response service message, error service message, and disconnect service message. In the KDC environment, two CSMs are added: response to request message and request for service message. Both KDC and KTC support an error recovery service message.

In his paper, "Space Shuttle Security Policies and Programs," not only does Ernest Keith provide insight into the development of computer and network security policies, but he also provides insight into the larger programmatic environment of the space shuttle. He sees security as a tradeoff between resource protection, mission requirements, and budgetary constraints. Restrictions on information release have required organizational policy and management instructions. As requirements change, so will the protective mechanisms. The value of a good security audit is emphasized.

Protected information includes mission critical voice circuits, crew medical data, and proprietary rights, including sufficient time for a principal investigator to publish results. With the shuttle being designated an essential national resource, evolving requirement exist for survivability, safety, and operational capability. As a result of threat assessment, telemetry and command data links are encrypted; on the other hand, there is no operational security (OPSEC) or countermeasures. National defense classified operations necessitated development of a management feedback loop with the U.S. Air Force. Dedicated secured facilities are minimized; time sharing or offline approaches have been developed.

This is a report on work in progress, so the interested reader should ascertain the current status of the local area network described by Mr. Schnackenberg in his paper, "Development of a Multilevel Secure Local Area Network." This product is targeted for evaluation under the *Trusted Computer System Evaluation Criteria* (TCSEC), discussed in Section 2.3, at the highest available (A1) level. This is an exciting development worthy of careful study.

The physical layer employs wavelength division multiplexed fiber optics and the IEEE 802.4 Token Bus protocol. Access to the bus is through a secure network server (SNS), which provides U.S. Department of Defense transmission control protocol (TCP), virtual terminal TELNET protocol, file transfer protocol (FTP), and the host to front end protocol (HFE). A need has been identified for a end-to-end user identification and trusted path; the Defense protocol suite presently does not support this functionality. Network services such as file server and mail server are also planned.

Security design goals include a uniform host interface, exclusion of the upper layer protocols from the trusted computer base (TCB) (which must be sufficiently small to be proveably secure), and development of a security model independent of the protocol suite. The network separates all communications objects, relying on multiple microprocessors in the SNS so that the TCB can provide complete isolation of user sessions and provide all the necessary support functions. Packet sensitivity labels are employed.

In addition to treating host computers as subjects, the security policy defines untrusted tasks performing communications functions as internal network subjects; other extensions to the TCSEC security policy are mentioned. Formal proof of security correctness employs a state model written in the Ina Jo language. An exerpt is included as an appendix.

Automated Distribution of Cryptographic Keys Using the Financial Institution Key Management Standard

David M. Balenson

This article describes the important features of the ANSI Key Management Standard including the requirements it addresses, and the internal structure, cryptographic techniques, and protocols it uses

Reprinted from *IEEE Communications Magazine*, September 1985, pages 41-46. U.S. Government work not protected by U.S. copyright.

Existing and potential threats to computer network security raise concern for protecting the integrity and secrecy of data in the network. Cryptography has proven to be an effective means for providing high levels of data communications security. The Data Encryption Standard (DES) was published in 1977 by the National Bureau of Standards (NBS) for use by the Federal government to protect valuable and sensitive, but unclassified, data. The standard was subsequently adopted by the American National Standards Institute (ANSI) as the Data Encryption Algorithm (DEA). Several high-speed DES devices have been developed, and many public and private institutions now rely on DES based cryptographic equipment for data communications security.

Since DES was published, NBS has been committed to helping develop additional standards based on DES, and in particular, standards for integrating cryptography into computer networks. The most recent effort includes the ANSI Financial Institution Key Management (Wholesale) Standard (X9.17). Developed jointly by the banking industry, federal government, and private industry, the standard is in response to the growing security requirements identified by financial institutions, which collectively transfer trillions of dollars in funds and securities by electronic means. Used in conjunction with the ANSI Data Encryption Algorithm (X3.92) and the ANSI Financial Institution Message Authentication Standard (X9.9), financial messages and other sensitive information can be protected to insure their accuracy and their secrecy. The standard has been adopted by the U.S. Department of Treasury for use in all systems which originate, transmit, relay, receive, or process, Federal Government Electronic Funds Transfers (EFT). This paper will highlight the important features of the ANSI Key Management Standard, including the key management requirements it addresses, and the internal structure, cryptographic techniques, and protocols it uses to automatically distribute cryptographic keys over a computer network in a secure manner.

Computer Network Security Based on Cryptography

The objective of classical cryptography is to transform original data, called *plaintext*, into an unintelligible form, called *ciphertext*, before transmitting it over a network. The rules for transforming the plaintext into ciphertext, called *encryption*, and recovering plaintext from ciphertext, called *decryption*, are expressed by a *cryptographic algorithm*. The NBS Data Encryption Standard (DES) specifies a cryptographic algorithm to encrypt and decrypt 64-bit blocks of data under the

This paper is a contribution of the National Bureau of Standards.

control of a unique 56-bit key. If the key is randomly selected from the set of approximately 70 quadrillion possible 56-bit keys and kept secret, then an unauthorized receiver who does not have the key cannot decrypt the ciphertext to recover the underlying plaintext, while the intended, authorized receiver who has the secret key, can easily do so.

Data authentication is another cryptographic technique, based on encryption, used to assure that the integrity of data is maintained when it is transmitted over a computer network. A message authentication code (MAC) is computed by the originator of the data using a secret key shared with the intended recipient. The MAC, which is a cryptographic function of every data bit, is transmitted along with the data. The recipient of the data uses the same key to compute another MAC that is compared with the one received with the message. If the MAC's are identical, then there is a very high probability that the data was not altered during transmission. If the MAC's differ, then the data has been altered, possibly by no more than a single bit, or the key is incorrect.

A crytographic system combining encryption and authentication can be integrated into a computer network to protect the integrity and secrecy of transmitted data. However, since the cryptographic algorithm specified by DES is public knowledge, the level of protection provided depends on the level of protection afforded the secret keys used. The secure management of these keys is a critical element of a cryptographic system, for even the most sophisticated system will be ineffective if the key management is weak. The primary function of *key management* is to provide keys when they are needed for data encryption and authentication, and to protect the key's secrecy and integrity. Key management encompasses all of the procedures for *generating*, *distributing, storing, entering* and *using*, and *destroying* or *archiving* cryptographic keys. Until recently, the distribution of cryptographic keys was performed only by manual means, which are time consuming, expensive, and subject to errors. Automating the distribution of keys on large computer networks allows keys to be exchanged quickly and transparently with increased efficiency and flexibility, lower cost, and improved security. Some manual key distribution is still required, but the number of keys is significantly reduced.

The same cryptographic techniques used to protect data transmitted over a computer network can also be used to protect the integrity and secrecy of keys transmitted over the network. Encrypting keys before transmitting them protects their secrecy by preventing the unintentional or unauthorized *disclosure* of the keys. Authenticating keys protects their integrity by detecting any *modification* of the keys, including transmission errors. When used in conjunction with a key numbering system, authentication can also detect *substitution* or *deletion* of keys, *insertion* of false keys, and *replay* of old keys.

The Financial Institution Key Management Standard

General Key Management Requirements

The ANSI Financial Institution Key Management (Wholesale) Standard (X9.17) describes a standard level of protection to assure the security of *keying material*, which includes the cryptographic keys and other related information needed to manage the keys, and the *key management facility* (*KMF*), which is the physical enclosure (for example, device or room) containing the cryptographic elements—hardware, software, firmware, keys, and so forth. The minimum requirements specified by the standard include:

- *Control of keying material* during the entire life of the keys. Keys must be randomly generated. To protect keys from unintended or unauthorized disclosure they must either be physically secured or encrypted. To protect keying material from unintended or unauthorized modification it must either be physically secured or cryptographically authenticated. When physical protection is not possible, keying material must be cryptographically authenticated in conjunction with a counter to protect it from unintended or unauthorized substitution, insertion, replay, and deletion.
- *Secure distribution of keys to permit interoperability* between communicating parties and their various cryptographic equipment or facilities. To support the varying needs of financial institutions and to permit interoperability, the standard defines both manual and automated methods for the exchange of cryptographic keys.
- *Ensuring integrity of keys and the KMF.* Overall key management must be put in place with the proper procedural controls. The keys, KMF, and procedural controls must be continually tested and monitored to ensure that the entire key management process is secure.
- *Recovery in the event of failure*, that is, ability to maintain level of protection when the integrity of a key or the key management process is compromised.

Automated Key Management Architecture

The X9.17 standard is based on a hierarchically structured set of cryptographic keys designed for automated distribution of keys over a computer network. Three distinct classes of keys form the hierarchy:
1) Manually distributed key encrypting keys (KKM's)
2) Automatically distributed key encrypting keys (KK's)
3) Automatically distributed data keys (KD's)

Key encrypting keys (KKM's and KK's), which may be single keys or key pairs, encrypt other keys for distribution. Since key encrypting keys typically have longer cryptoperiods than data keys, *key pairs*, which are simply two keys used for multiple encryption, may be

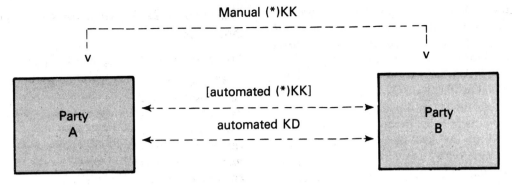

Fig. 1. *Keying relations in the point-to-point environment*

used for increased protection. *Data keys* (KD's), which must be single keys, authenticate the messages used to distribute keys as well as encrypt or authenticate data.

The KKM's form the basis for a *keying relationship* between two communicating parties. In order to automatically exchange keys over a computer network, both parties must either share a single KKM or KKM pair as shown in Fig. 1, or each share a KKM key pair with a common mutually trusted third party, usually a key center as shown in Fig. 2. These keys must be generated and exchanged in a physically protected form and manually entered into the KMF's of both parties.

Once a KKM is shared between two parties or with a common key center, it can encrypt additional keys for automatic distribution over a computer network. At a minimum, the standard requires a two-layer architecture in which KKM's encrypt KD's for distribution. Optionally, a three-layer architecture may be used in which KKM's encrypt KK's for distribution and KK's encrypt KD's for distribution. In both cases, *initialization vectors* (IV's), which are required for certain data encryption operations, may also be automatically exchanged. If the IV's are encrypted, they must be encrypted by KD's.

Key Generation

The methods used to generate new keys and IV's must be secured. If the methods involve manual procedures,

then they must take place in protected areas and **under** dual control (that is, two independent sources). **Auto-mated** procedures must be physically and logically protected. New keys and IV's must be generated so **that** they are random, or if a deterministic algorithm is **used,** so that they are pseudorandom. Any one of the possible keys or IV's must be equally likely to be generated, **and** each key or IV generated must have no apparent relationship to its predecessors or successors. The protec-tion provided to the key generation process must be **at** least as great as that required for the data so that **the** cryptographic protection obtained by encryption **and** authentication with the generated keys is not compro-mised by the key generation process.

Key and IV Encryption and Decryption

The standard recommends using the ANSI **Data** Encryption Algorithm (DEA) to encrypt and **decrypt** keys and IV's for automated distribution. Single **key** encrypting keys (KKM's and KK's) encrypt and **decrypt** other single keys using DEA in the Electronic Codebook (ECB) mode. Single keys may not be used to encrypt **and** decrypt key pairs. Key encrypting key pairs (KKM's **or** KK's) may be used to encrypt and decrypt single keys **and** other key pairs using DEA in the ECB mode to perform multiple encryption. To perform multiple encryption of

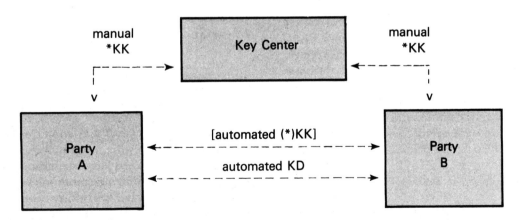

Fig. 2. *Keying relations in the key center environments*

a key with a key pair, first the key is encrypted by the first key in the key pair, then the result is decrypted by the second key in the key pair, and finally the second result is encrypted again by the first key in the key pair. To perform multiple decryption of a key with a key pair, the key is first decrypted by the first key in the key pair, then encrypted by the second key in the key pair, and finally decrypted again by the first key in the key pair. Even if a KMF is designed to use key pairs, it can perform encryption by a single key by using the same key as both the first and second keys of a key pair. If IV's are encrypted, then data keys (KD's) encrypt and decrypt the IV's using DEA in the ECB mode.

Key Counters and Key Offsetting

The standard requires *key counters* to be used to control the automated distribution of encrypted keys. By counting the messages transmitted over a computer network to distribute encrypted keys, the replay of previously transmitted messages can be detected and messages received out of sequence can be recognized. When two communicating parties exchange keys directly between themselves, two separate counters, a transmit count and a receive count, must be maintained by both parties so that keys may be simultaneously exchanged in both directions. The counters are kept with the key encrypting keys used to encrypt keys for distribution. Each time a message containing encrypted keys is transmitted, the count associated with the key encrypting key used is included in the message. Under normal conditions, the originating party's transmit count should equal the receiving party's receive count and the message is accepted. Then both counts are incremented for the next message. However, if the transmit count included in the message is less than the count expected by the receiving party, then the message is determined to be a duplicate and is rejected. When a wrong count is received, an expected count is exchanged so that both party's counters can be resynchronized for subsequent messages.

The standard requires that all keys encrypted for distribution be protected by key offsetting. *Key offsetting* simply combines (by exclusive-or'ing) the transmit count associated with a key encrypting key with the key encrypting key before it encrypts other keys for distribution. Then, to decrypt the encrypted keys the receiver must also offset the key encrypting key with the same count. This prevents previously distributed encrypted keys, whose contents may have been disclosed for some reason, from being retransmitted since the encrypted key must be transmitted with a new count, but can only be decrypted using the original count.

Key Notarization

Another protective cryptographic feature of the standard is the support of *key notarization*. Key notari-zation is similar to the actions of a notary public who first requires a customer to be identified before the customer's signature is notarized on a document with a notary stamp. For automated key distribution, electronic notarization seals encrypted keys with the identities of the originator and the intended recipient. A notary seal is formed by combining the key encrypting key to be used with the identities of the two parties. This notary seal is then offset by the counter associated with the key encrypting key to form a notarizing key which finally encrypts keys for distribution. Once keys are sealed, or notarized, they can only be decrypted by the same notarizing key, again a combination of the key encrypting key used and the identities of the originator and intended recipient. Thus, key notarization is similar to having a notary public for both the originator and intended recipient of keys distributed over a computer network. The standard requires that all keys generated by a key center for use by two particular parties be notarized with the identities of those parties. Security is increased since the notarized keys cannot be decrypted and used by any other parties.

Automated Key Distribution Protocols

cryptographic service messages and authentication

Cryptographic Service Message (CSM's) are exchanged between two communicating parties to establish new keys and discontinue existing keys. These fixed-format messages, which are transmitted in plaintext, may carry encrypted keys, IV's, and other keying material including the identities of the two parties, the identities of keys, and counts. To guarantee the integrity of a CSM when it is transmitted over a computer network, its originator must authenticate the entire contents of the message in accordance with the X9.9 Message Authentication Standard, and include the resulting MAC in the CSM where it can be verified by the recipient. Certain CSM's must be authenticated with the KD's they are establishing or discontinuing. Since these KD's will be encrypted, and therefore must be decrypted, with a secret key encrypting key shared only between the actual originator and intended recipient of the KD's, the identitiy of the actual originator of the CSM can be verified by its recipient.

point-to-point environment

The standard specifies three environments for key distribution: *Point-to-Point (PTP)*, *Key Distribution Center (CKD)*, and *Key Translation Center (CKT)*. The PTP environment is the minimum requirement of the standard for automated key distribution. It specifies the protocol that permits two communicating parties who share a key encrypting key, either a single key or a key pair, to directly exchange additional KD's, IV's, and possibly KK's between themselves (see Fig. 1). At least one of the parties must be able to generate or otherwise acquire the new keys and IV's.

There are five different types of CSM's defined by the standard for the PTP environment. If one party wishes to establish keys with another party, but is unable to generate or otherwise acquire the keys, they may request new keys from the other party with a *Request for Service Initiation (RSI)* which includes a field for indicating the types of keys desired. A *Key Service Message (KSM)* permits one party to send new keys to another party, either spontaneously or in response to an RSI. The KSM must contain at least one KD, and may optionally contain a KK, a second KD, and an IV. If the recipient of a KSM can correctly authenticate the KSM and the count is correct, then the recipient returns a *Response Service Message (RSM)* to the originator of the KSM. Since the MAC used to authenticate the RSM will be a function of the keys received in the KSM, the originator of the KSM can verify that the keys were correctly received. If the recipient of a KSM cannot correctly authenticate the KSM, a count error occurs, or some other error is detected, then the recipient returns an *Error Service Message* (ESM). The ESM includes a code indicating the type of error that occurred, and, if a count error occurred, the expected count. The originator of the KSM may retransmit the KSM an arbitrary number of times until it is correctly received by its intended recipient. If either party wishes to terminate the keying relationship or discontinue the use of specific keys, then they may send a *Disconnect Service Message (DSM)* which includes the identities of the keys to be discontinued. Like a KSM, the recipient of the DSM returns either an RSM or an ESM to indicate the success or failure of the received DSM.

In the PTP environment every party must manually exchange at least one KKM with every other party with whom they wish to exchange additional keys, IV's, and encrypted or authenticated data. In a large network of computers the number of KKM's that need to be manually distributed and stored will be quite large. However, since key encrypting keys may be key pairs for increased protection, and since key encrypting keys typically have longer cryptoperiods than KD's, the frequency at which KKM's must be distributed is reduced.

key center environments

The CKD and CKT environments permit centralized control of key management functions within a computer network. They permit two communicating parties, who may not share a KKM or may not be able to generate or otherwise acquire new keys, to exchange keys with the assistance of a mutually trusted third party, or key center (see Fig. 2). The two parties must each share a KKM pair with this center, which may be administered by the network owner or some other trusted party.

If one party wishes to establish keys with another party, but neither party is able to generate or acquire keys, they may request keys from a CKD with an RSI. The CKD generates the desired keys and returns them in a *Response to Request Message (RTR)* to the originator, who then sends them to the actual party they are to be shared with (the ultimate recipient). The RTR includes two identical sets of keys. One set is notarized and encrypted with a key encrypting key pair shared with the originator, and the other set is notarized and encrypted with a key encrypting key pair shared with the ultimate recipient.

If one party wishes to establish keys with another party, but wants to generate the new keys themselves, they may encrypt the keys with a key encrypting key shared with a CKT and send them to the CKT in a *Request for Service Message (RFS)*. The CKT decrypts the keys, then notarizes and re-encrypts them with a key encrypting key pair shared with the ultimate recipient, and returns them to the requesting party in a RTR. The requesting party then sends the encrypted keys to their ultimate recipient.

In both the CKD and CKT environments, if the requesting party sends keys to their ultimate recipient and an error is detected, then an *Error Recovery Service Message (ERS)* is sent to the center so that the process can be repeated. All keys exchanged between a party and a key center must be notarized so that they cannot be used with any party other than their ultimate recipient.

The key center environments provide the greatest flexibility and efficiency for automated key distribution. Each party is no longer required to share KKM's with every other party in a computer network. Instead, each party only needs to share a KKM with each key center with which they need to communicate. Thus, the number of KKM's that need to be manually distributed and stored is greatly reduced. Typically, the cost of using a key center will be greater than the cost of exchanging keys directly. To minimize these costs, two parties can first exchange a KK with the help of a key center, and then use the PTP protocols to directly exchange KD's and IV's between themselves.

Summary

The use of cryptographic techniques to provide secure key management functions has been recognized. The techniques specified by the X9.17 Key Management Standard provide a uniform process for automatic distribution of keys throughout networks of incompatible computers systems and cryptographic devices. The development of these techniques will continue as the use of computer networks continues to grow. An addition to the standard is already being developed to provide support for multiple key centers within a computer network.

NBS played a major role in the development of the X9.9 and X9.17 standards, and is providing support to the banks, Treasury, and vendors as they integrate the standards into their computer systems and products. A key management facility based on the X9.17 standard is being developed at NBS for further study. This facility will ultimately be integrated into an experimental secure local area network to demonstrate the feasibility of implementing high quality, yet low cost, secure key management functions, especially those of a key center, using microcomputer technology.

Copies of the X9.17 Key Management Standard may be obtained by contacting the American Bankers Association at 1120 Connecticut Ave, N.W., Washington D.C., 20036.

Acknowledgment

The author would like to express his appreciation to Miles Smid for his encouragement and his many valuable suggestions.

References

[1] American National Standard X3.92-1981, *Data Encryption Algorithm,* American National Standards Institute.

[2] American National Standard X3.106-1982, *Modes of Operation of the DEA,* American National Standards Institute.

[3] American National Standard X9.9-1982, *Financial Institution Message Authentication,* American National Standards Institute.

[4] American National Standard X9.17-1985. *Financial Institution Key Management (Wholesale),* American National Standards Institute.

[5] Dennis K. Branstad, "Security of computer communications," *IEEE Communications Society Magazine,* pp. 33-40, Nov. 1978.

[6] Department of the Treasury, *Criteria for Testing and Evaluating Message Authentication Technology,* EFTC Task Force, Jan. 28, 1985.

[7] Federal Standard 1027, General Services Administration, *General Security Requirements for Equipment Using DES,* Apr. 14, 1982.

[8] National Bureau of Standards, *Data Encryption Standard,* Federal Information Processing Standards Publication (FIPS PUB) 46, Washington, D.C., 1977.

[9] Miles E. Smid, "Integrating the data encryption standard into computer networks," *IEEE Trans. on Comm.,* vol. Com-29, no. 6, p. 762-772, June 1981.

David M. Balenson has been designing and implementing the X9.17 standard (Financial Institution Key Management) in "C" on the IBM PC, evaluating numerous PC security devices, and assisting in developing a local area network, since beginning work at the National Bureau of Standards in May, 1984. He is presently enrolled at the University of Maryland as a graduate student in Computer Science. He has taught computer programming and worked at the University in various programming tasks. He was director of computing activities at the University Career Development Center.

Mr. Balenson has a B.S. in Computer Science from the University of Maryland. ∎

SPACE SHUTTLE SECURITY POLICIES AND PROGRAMS

Ernest L. Keith

NASA Headquarters, Shuttle Operations Division,
Washington, D. C., 20546

ABSTRACT

For many years, the National Aeronautics and Space Administration (NASA) was operating under a very open door policy as established by its charter.[1] Information concerning space technology, science and applications was readily available and space operations were open to the public. Because of increased restrictions in allowing disclosure, various accommodations have been established through policy and management instructions to implement the desired levels of protection within the Space Shuttle program.

INTRODUCTION

Throughout all written material, reference may be made either to the Space Shuttle, Space Transportation System or National Space Transportation System. The latter is more perferred when all of the production facilities, elements and uses are included. Since this paper is more oriented to the operational phase, Space Shuttle was chosen as a more appropriate and more familiar title.

The Space Shuttle vehicle consist of the orbiter, external tank and two solid rocket boosters. It facilities include the launch pads, preparation facilities, control centers, simulators and all the supporting elements essential for its operations.

In dealing with security, we are concerned with two major protective categories. One category is resource protection and the other is information protection. These two major categories may become interrelated, because the level of protection for one may dictate the level of protection for the other. The information that details vulnerabilities of a resource must be protected at least to an equivalent level of effort or security that is being applied to the protection of the resource. Any imbalance in the levels of protection will introduce another element of security risk.

In dealing with information protection, there are three major aspects with any disclosure restrictions. These are the procedures which culminate in an authorized release, the protective requirements prior to the release authorization and the implemented capability to respond to the protection requirements. All of the above must be well defined and documented in the program policies and implementing instructions. Many of the policies and instructions for Space Shuttle are, in fact, NASA wide across all programs. However, due to some of the special features of the Space Shuttle, (e.g., homosapiens are essential operating elements and that it has been declared an essential national resource because it is committed to support both civil and national defense classified missions) there are many factors which are strictly oriented to the Space Shuttle situation.

An examination of various protective requirements and implementing policies will provide one with an overview of the many complex managment approaches and decisions required to implement an adequately secure system. When dealing with security, "adequate" becomes a preplexing confrontation all by itself. In many cases, adequacy is bounded by budgetary constraints, and the real result may be inadequate security. The only saving factor, which is possible in an inadequate security system, is the lack of an immediate desire or means by an adversary to penetrate the supposedly secure system. With no security viloations, the overseers of the inadequate security system then may erroneously conclude that their security is indeed adequate. These are hard facts not to be denied, but rather to be examined by a good security audit.

Within the Space Shuttle program, resources and information protection are required to satisfy four basic programs as follows:

1. Science and Technology Transfer
2. Sensitive and Private
3. National Resources Protection
4. National Defense Classified Operations

Each of the above programs will be reviewed separately and where applicable, implementation techniques for computer security will be identified.

SCIENCE AND TECHNOLOGY TRANSFER

In response to laws and regulations, the restrictions for the transfer of science and technology information are covered under various NASA Management Instructions (NMI's). Contained within these NMI's are five availability categories for information disclosure as follows:

1) Security Classified
2) Export Controlled
   a) International Traffic in Arms Regulation
   b) Export Administration Regulations
3) NASA Restricted Distribution
   a) Early Domestic Dissemination for near term domestic benefit
   b) Limited Distribution for long term development
4) Disclosure of an Invention
5) Publicly Available

Even with the above restrictions, "It is NASA policy to make the widest practicable and appropriate dissemination of the results of its

activities. Under that policy NASA disseminates, or authorizes others to disseminate, NASA produced or sponsored documentary reporting the results of NASA developed or supported scientific and technical activities to the widest practical and appropriate extent consistent with U.S. laws and national policy."[2]

The Space Shuttle is, of course, subject to all of the above restrictions; however, it has no security classified, technological developments. There have been several reviews of possible classification of specific operational characteristics, but no such restrictions have been imposed. Documents describing every detail of the Space Shuttle and its operational characteristics are readily available in government and public publications.

SENSITIVE AND PRIVATE

There were really two major events which influenced the protection of sensitive and private information on the Space Shuttle program. The first event was the manned space flight accident, and the second was the enactment of a congressional bill to establish the rights of privacy. On January 27, 1967, a fire erupted within the Apollo command module on Pad 34 at Cape Canaveral, Florida, and three astronauts lost their lives. The ensuing investigation was somewhat hindered by extraneous voice communications contained in the recordings of operational, voice circuits. This event initiated voice access control instructions. The NASA Policy for Space Transportation Systems states, "Authorizations will be controlled for access terminations on voice circuits where unauthorized voice instructions or interruptions could disrupt critical operations····."[3]

The second event was the Privacy Act of 1974. This law provided for the protection of information where disclosure would constitute an unwarranted invasion of personal privacy. Associated with privacy is priviledged information, and provisions for the protection of proprietary rights.

For the Space Shuttle, the implementing program is divided between two distinct parts--institutional and operational. Contained within the institutional arena are personnel records, especially crew medical data, information which may reveal proprietary rights, and data which is restricted for general distribution in order to provide a principal investigator first rights of publication. Of course, there is much information associated with contract negotiations and source evaluation board assessments that are protected due to the potential injurious effects on the vendor.

Crew medical data has special interest for manned space flight. The data is essential for the continuing understanding of homosapians reaction to zero "g" and their overall space orientation adaptation. In order to maintain private medical data, the identity of the subject is disassociated from the data. This allows many medical doctors access to the space medical data. Where a specific subject is needed to perform special medical experiments aboard the Space Shuttle, the subject must provide a waiver as an element of the qualifications to perform the experiment.

Owners of experiments or payloads must be able to protect their proprietary rights. NASA will enter into a contractual obligation to protect the data and turn this data over to the owner. The only data that NASA requires are safety related. At the owners option and expense, the remaining data may be encrypted.

For principal investigators who are not owners, an agreement is established with NASA to protect the data for a period of approximately one year. This allows the principal investigator sufficient time to publish the experimental results.

The protection of sensitive and private information during operations requires communications discipline. Voice communications between crew members and doctor, family or principal investigator must be protected. Since the digitized voice signal is processed in the Mission Control Center at Johnson Space Center in Houston, Texas, distribution of the voice communications can be controlled. Communication technicians may hear parts of the conversation, but they are obligated not to discuss what they hear with anyone.

Distribution control may also be used by program management personnel during a contingency situation. This tends to restrict speculation on the condition of the Space Shuttle or its crew based on limited information, which may be easily misinterpreted.

In all of the above, the data storage media for telemetry and voice data is carefully logged and placed in bonded storage. Request for copies of the data are routinely processed, and only those with proper authorization are honored.

NATIONAL RESOURCE PROTECTION

Protection of government property has always been a predominate responsibility of government employees. However, the protection of the Space Shuttle took on new meaning with the issuance of Presidental Directive No. 42. Contained within this directive are statements to the effect that the Space Shuttle, associated upper stages and related facilities are the primary national launch capability and, as such, will be provided the protection necessary for an essential national resource. Accordingly, efforts were initiated to determine exactly what was required beyond that which was normally being provided to protect government property.

To implement Presidental Directive No. 42, an internal NASA Management Instruction (NMI) was issued. This NMI established a basic implementing policy as follows: "...the STS is a vital element of the United States space program and is the primary space launch system for both United States national security and civil government missions. In order to protect this capability, the STS will be afforded the degree of survivability and security protection required for a critical national space resource. Therefore, it is a NASA policy to meet this responsibility by implementing reasonable and affordable protection for STS resources within acceptable risks."[5]

Survivability is the primary goal of the protective effort, and the terms of survivability must be established by the program office. It should determine the allowable tolerances in survivability to sustain the program at some specified level. For the Space Shuttle, there are two primary levels of protection. The first is to protect an ongoing flight in order to bring it to a safe conclusion. The second is to maintain operational capability in order that program objectives are not adversely affected. A thirty-day down time was determined to be an acceptable condition for sustaining program objectives. This is an initially set condition and is subject to change as the national resource protection program matures.

There are two major functions that influence the capability to survive. These are the threats on the system to be protected and the vulnerabilities of the system. The level of vulnerability is a function of operational capability and security provisions which can off-set threats and provide the desired level of survivability. Figure 1 illustrates these very dependent relationships.

Threats to any operating system can come from many different sources; however, our primary concern here is threats from adversaries. It is essential to identify all possible adversaries, to review all potential weapon systems and techniques of employment, and to develop probabilities of attack. The latter is most difficult to determine

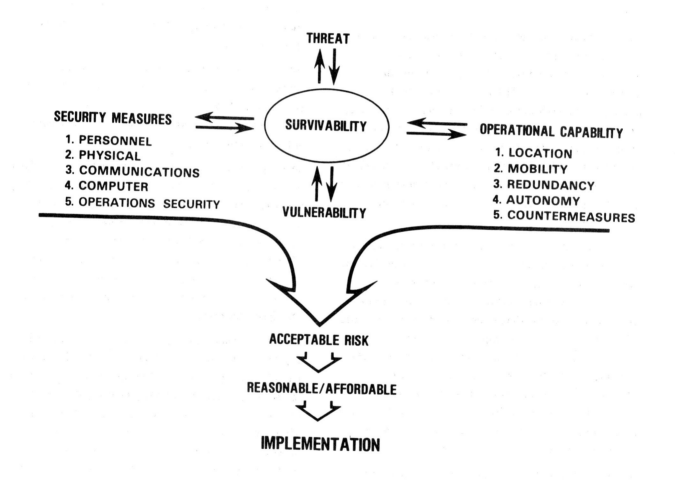

Figure 1. Space Shuttle National Resource Protection

because there are no adversary absolutes. The threat may come from within an organization as well as from without. To obtain an understanding of the threat, a special threat assessment study is essential.

With a generic threat assessment, each element of the program operations must be examined. Where single point failures would cause the most disruption of program progress, the threat probabilities are more likely to be higher. Of course, this is highly dependent on the character of the adversary. If the adversary is unsophisticated, the threat is more likely to occur anywhere with readily available weapons. If the adversary is sophisticated, the attack is more likely to occur at the most vulnerable points with more appropriate weapons.

Another major consideration in assessing threats and vulnerabilities is the level of program activity at a specific facility. For example, a launch pad by itself has a lower vulnerability than a launch pad with a fully fueled launch vehicle on it. In these cases, the level of security protection may vary with the program activity to off-set the threat. If the threat supersedes the available protection, then the survivability requirement may dictate multiple launch pads or even multiple launch sites.

To better understand the protection requirements for the Space Shuttle, its assets were divided into two categories--mission critical and mission essential. Mission critical assets are defined as: "Those assets whose loss could cause the loss of an orbiter, crew or capability to process or launch a mission. These assets must receive the maximum protection consistent with policy constraints."[5] Whereas mission essential assets are: "Those assets whose loss would significantly delay, degrade or hamper the ability to process, launch or complete an STS mission."[5]

Having established the survivability requirements for the Space Shuttle, planning was initiated to implement additional security measures or operational capability. Operational communications with the Space Shuttle via the tracking and data relay satellite system were determine to have a high vulnerability. An adversary could receive both command and telemetry data, decode the digital data into useful information and generate and transmit its own commands. Although the software aboard the Space Shuttle already had command check processing to reject erroneous command data, a decision was made to encrypt both the telemetry and command data links to provide additional protection. This action denies an adversary access to clear text, operational data in real time.

Development of Space Shuttle software for the general purpose computers aboard the orbiter has always been protected by allowing only select personnel to work the final software package. With controlled handling and validation test procedures, all software programs for the Space Shuttle have survived and have operated according to their specifications.

For computer systems, the primary methods of protection as a national resource were personnel screening, physical access control, internal partitioning, internal limited access and validation testing of mission critical software.

Operational security could be used to accommodate national resource protection. For example, a bogus mission software package could be developed to divert an adversary's attention away from the actual software package. In order to be really effective, the fewer personnel involved in the operations security plan the better its chances of success. No such activity has been required for the Space Shuttle.

Additional operations capabilities have played an important part with all manned space flights to sustain the operations. Backup capability such as an emergency mission control center, diversity communications routing and contingency landing sites, provide an element of national resource protection by extending the survivability of the Space Shuttle from both an adversary or a failure of part of the operating system.

With four orbiters, Columbia, Discovery, Challenger and Atlantis, there is survivability in numbers.

However, many of the NASA programs managers believe it would be wiser to acquire a fifth orbiter to off set any loss of the main fleet.

One of the original goals of the Space Shuttle program was for an automonus operation. Since the operations are very complex, the current system requires much ground support to execute its operations with a high order of accuracy and safety. One option to gain more automony is to transfer the ephemerous determination from the ground to the orbiter. The first major step in this implementation is to provide the interface for receiving and processing position data from the Global Positioning System, which is under the development by the Department of Defense. With a complete software package for the orbiter, the on-board ephemeris determination would add a major step in automony, thereby increasing its survivability.

Countermeasures have had very little employment within the Space Shuttle program and then only under very special circumstances. There are no plans to develop any countermeasure techniques to protect computer systems.

Once it has been determined what the operational capabilities and security measure options are to protect the system, the final steps are to assess the risk for acceptability, evaluate the options for being reasonable, determine if the program can afford the costs and make the decisions to implement the selected options.

One major problem in dealing with internal vulnerabilities is personnel. Even with excellent screening procedures, there is the ever present possibility that one individual will intentionally or unintentionally go astray. Then all of the expenditures to protect the system would be wasted. Long ago, NASA recognized this problem and established a personnel reliability program.[6] This program goes beyond the normal security clearance requirements, which validates one's law abiding attitude and national loyalty. The personnel reliability program includes National Agency checks, which verifies the name of the individual with the FBI finger print records. Also, local

agency checks may be conducted. Performance is assessed during training, simulations and job activities. Medical evaluations are done to ensure no performance constraints are present. In addition, the psychological background of each individual, who has a critical operating function, is evaluated. This includes an individual's volunteering for temporary removal from the critical position when they are unable to give one hundred percent because of personal problems. It also requires each supervisor to stay alert to the performance of their personnel to detect any underlying emotional stress. This combined effort drives down the unintentional threat. And finally, the personnel reliability program has had some serendipidy by detecting undesirable personnel.

Another major consideration for national resource protection is its application at sites not under NASA control. The Space Shuttle launch site for polar orbits is located at Vandenberg Air Force Base in California, and it was developed and is being operated by the Air Force. Therefore, the Air Force and NASA jointly agreed to accept two principles as follows: one, each agency has the responsibility for national resource protection at its facilities; and two, an equivalent level of protection will be implemented at both launch sites. This joint effort will provide a balanced program between the two agencies for protection of the Space Shuttle.

NATIONAL DEFENSE CLASSIFIED OPERATIONS

The introduction of national defense classified operations into the Space Shuttle operations was indeed a new experience for NASA. Through early Manned Space Flight programs, NASA worked with the DoD to obtain launch support from the Redstone, Atlas and Titan II boosters. With NASA's development of the Saturn launch vehicles for the Apollo, Skylab and Apollo-Soyuz programs, classified data in the civil operations were nil. The combining of civil and military operations was not an easy task. A great joint technical management effort, however, has resulted in a dual Space Shuttle capability--unclassified and classified operations.

To obtain an appreciation of how this was accomplished, one needs to examine the agreements and management interfaces between the two agencies. The top management agreement states that the Air Force as the DoD agent will "... provide the requirements and funds for unique facilities and equipment required for national security space operations, and ensure their compatibility with the STS."[7] Within the same agreement, NASA did accept the responsibility to implement and operate the Space Shuttle in a classified mode.

The basic implementing interfaces between the two agencies are depicted in figure 2. The classification interface was established at the secret level, thereby requiring only a very few personnel within NASA to be knowledgeable about the details of the classified DoD payload for safety evaluations and certification.

The first step was for the Air Force to establish the security requirements.[8] Each NASA center involved in Space Shuttle operations interpreted these security requirements as they applied to their facilities and operations. The developed implementation requirements and plans were reviewed with the Air Force and as approved were funded by them.

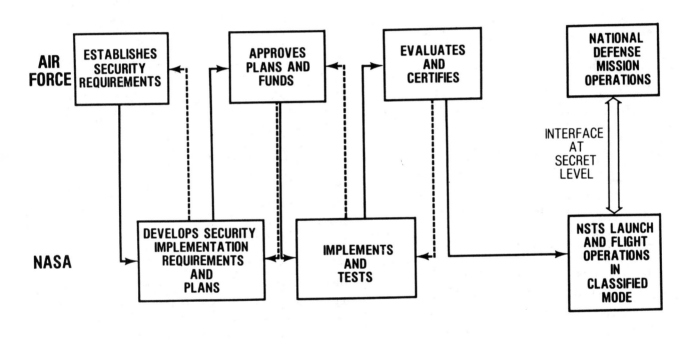

Figure 2. Space Shuttle Joint Management Interfaces for National Defense Security Systems

The primary implementation concept had two principles as follows: one, minimum impact to NASA operations, and two, minimum dedicated secured facilities. It is believed that both principles were satisfied. For operational impact, only the experience of combined civil and military operations will determine their compatibility. For dedicated secure facilities, only a few were required. One major secure facility is the Space Shuttle software development lab located at the Johnson Space Center in Houston, Texas. Due to the overall security requirements, it was not possible to accommodate the classified software production in a time sharing mode within the existing facility.

In other cases at major facilities, time sharing was acceptable. The third launch control room located within the Launch Control Center at the Kennedy Space Center in Florida and the third floor flight control area located within the Mission Control Center at the Johnson Space Center in Houston Texas, were developed with a "swing" capability. That is, prior to each classified operation these facilities are configured for secure operations and security swept. After each classified operation, these facilities are purged of all classified data and reconfigured for unclassified operations. However, to maintain the security integrity of these facilities, physical security is active for all operations.

The Space Shuttle program had developed over the years many information management systems with terminals located at contractor facilities, universities and even in other countries. To secure the entire system such as the Baseline Accounting and Reports System (BARS), which contains the specifications and configuration data of each orbiter, and other program management information, would have been very difficult and very expensive. The accepted solution was to implement an off-line delta system with a secure data base, limited distribution, controlled and secured terminal locations, and encrypted communications.

On the other hand, the solution for the Automated Support Requirements System was off-line manual.

This system contains all of the inter-center and inter-agency support requirements for all Space Shuttle and associated payload operations. Support requirements include tracking and data acquisition, communications, data records distribution, photography, meteorological data, etc.

When an information management system was localized at a center, a popular solution was off-line isolated. This required a secure facility to contain the entire data system and, in most cases, the containment was within a single room. Individuals requiring information from these data systems would either go to the facility and acquire the data from an internal terminal or request the data from the system operator.

Another more sophisticated approach is under development by the Goddard Space Flight Center, Greenbelt, Maryland. They not only support the Space Shuttle, but many other space operations. Their data base is accessed by many remote terminals and is very interactive, thereby making this entire system secure or even a delta secure system very impractical. To protect unencrypted data within the data base from unauthorized remote access, a front end processor, Restricted Access Processor (RAP), is under Development. The RAP will be used to screen requestors and direct proper routing of classified data for encryption. The RAP is more descriptively referred to as the "traffic cop."

Once the implemented security measures for classified Space Shuttle operations were in place and operationally tested, the Air Force conducted security tests and evaluations of the overall security system. If they were satisfied with the results, the system was certified by the Air Force for classified data entry and operations.

SUMMARY OF IMPLEMENTATION TECHNIQUES

Throughout this paper many techniques to protect information and systems were addressed. These are summarized within figure 3 as applicable to the four basic programs which affect the Space Shuttle. It is not intended to be all inclusive, but a representative illustration of the various

	WAIVER	OFF-LINE MANUAL	OFF-LINE CODED	OFF-LINE ISOLATED	OFF-LINE DELTA	INTERNAL PARTITIONING	INTERNAL LIMITED ACCESS	COMBINATION OF PRIOR TWO	EXTERNAL "TRAFFIC COP"	FULL-UP SECURE	DOUBLE ENCRYPTED	TIME SHARED	VALIDATION TESTS
SCIENCE AND TECHNOLOGY												X	
SENSITIVE AND PRIVATE	X	X	X	X		X	X	X				X	
NATIONAL RESOURCE						X	X	X					X
NATIONAL DEFENSE	X	X		X	X				X	X		X	

Figure 3. Summary of Implementation Techniques

applications for one program.

There are really two types of waivers. One waiver is a verification that protecting is not required and the other is to avoid a complex or expensive implementation approach for an acceptable risk workaround. In both cases, waivers should be explored to avoid unnecessary protection or implementation.

The off-line approach like the waiver is usually ignored until the data system plan indicates that a major problem exists. In addition, a pure computer systems engineer likes to see a neat and all inclusive tidy package. This approach may be a disservice to the customer, because he/she may be mislead and thus acquire more resources then are absolutely needed. Therefore, off-line applications need to be evaluated.

The double encrypted technique only applies to DoD payloads and is, therefore, not an integral part of the Space Shuttle. Classified DoD payload data not required for safe Space Shuttle operations are encrypted aboard the payload and encrypted again by the Space Shuttle communications system. It is possible for a commercial user to adapt this technique for protection of proprietary rights.

Although it is clearly illustrated in the Space Shuttle application that there is no singularly superior technique to resolve all protection requirements, a single specific solution for other programs might be the highest order of protection required as the most desirable and acceptable approach based on practicality. This, of course,

401

is very sensitive to the overall application for a specific program.

CONCLUSION

There are many restrictions imposed upon the Space Shuttle program in the release of information. Each restriction has required organizational policy and management instructions to guide its appropriate implementation. The impact on automated and computerized data systems resulted in the utilization of various techniques to protect not only the information but also the resources to process the information. Threats must be formally assessed and special attention is required to screen critical personnel.

Since the Space Shuttle is in a very dynamic world, additional requirements to restrict information flow or provide more resource protection are more than likely on the horizon.[9] As each of these new requirements is validated, existing techniques or additional and possibly new techniques will be used to implement them.

In conclusion, each protective requirement needs specific implementing guidance to establish an acceptable risk level and to assure appropriate applications of implementing techniques. Even in an automated or computerize data system, waivers, off-line systems and manual operations are not to be ignored.

REFERENCES

1. The National Aeronautics and Space Act of 1958, as amended.

2. NASA Management Instruction 2230.1, "NASA Scientific and Technical Document Availability Authorization," as amended.

3. NASA Management Instruction 8610.11A, "Control of Access to Operational Voice Communications Circuits - Space Transportation Systems," dated: December 29, 1982.

4. NASA Management Instruction 1382.17B, "Protection of Personal Privacy - NASA Privacy Regulations," dated: September 24, 1979.

5. NASA Management Instruction 8610.19, "Space Transportation Systems National Resource Protection," dated: March 31, 1984.

6. NASA Management Instruction 8610.13, "Space Transportation Systems Personnel Reliability Program," dated: July 6, 1979.

7. Memorandum of Agreement between NASA and the Air Force for "Management and Operation of the Space Transportation System," dated: March 27, 1980.

8. "Space Transportation System (STS) Security Classification Guide," issued by Headquarters Space Division (AFSC), Los Angeles, California, dated: August 8, 1984.

9. National Security Decision Directive (NSDD) 145, dated September 17, 1984 to form a committee to develop an "National Policy on Application of Communications Security to Civil (U.S. Government and Commercial) Space Systems,".

Development of a Multilevel Secure Local Area Network

D.D. Schnackenberg

Mail Stop 8H-35
Boeing Aerospace Company
P.O. Box 3999
Seattle, WA 98124

Boeing Aerospace Company is developing a multilevel secure (MLS) local area network (LAN), designed to meet the A1 criteria of DoD Trusted Computer System Evaluation Criteria (1). The development effort is funded under internal research and development. This paper will present an overview of the MLS LAN development, and will discuss security design issues (e.g., protocol `security), security architecture, security policy, formal security policy model, current status and future directions for our MLS LAN.

OVERVIEW

The MLS LAN is a high performance network that supports simultaneous transmission of digital (150 Mbps), voice and analog video data, using a wavelength division multiplexed fiber optics communications medium. Figure 1 shows the system diagram for the MLS LAN. The MLS LAN comprises network access units (called Secure Network Servers or SNSs) and a management node. The network trusted computing base (TCB) is distributed across the SNSs and the network management node. The SNS provides network security functions to ensure that data is not sent or received at an inappropriate sensitivity level for the subjects the SNS controls. The network management node provides the administrator interface to the network, and maintains the network configuration and security databases. The SNS provides embedded upper layer protocols (e.g., Transmission Control Protocol (TCP), TELNET and File Transfer Protocol (FTP)), supports the connection of terminals to the network, and will eventually support embedded user services (e.g., file server and mail server).

There are 5 types of users of the network:
1. human users on a network terminal (or workstation configured as a terminal);
2. host processes acting on the behalf of some human user (the network view of host processes is a host-to-network logical channel);
3. voice devices;
4. analog video devices; and
5. high bandwidth digital stream devices.

The demonstration system will provide four optical channels on the fiber optics medium. The terminal, host and voice traffic is transmitted using one of these channels. Access to this channel is gained using the IEEE token passing bus protocol. The remainder of the channels are used to transmit circuit-switched analog video and high bandwidth digital stream data. The circuit switching is controlled by users at terminals through the digital network.

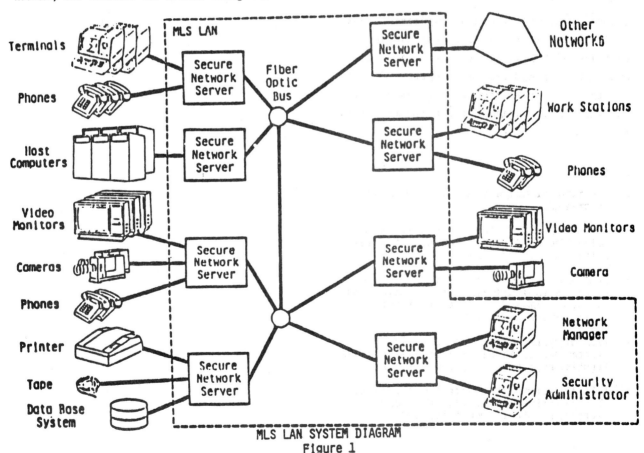

MLS LAN SYSTEM DIAGRAM
Figure 1

An SNS comprises multiple 286s, hardware for the subscriber interfaces, link control hardware and a fiber optics interface. A multi-CPU executive provides dynamic domains for the tasks within an SNS across multiple CPUs. This executive acts as a separation kernel, and enforces a policy of complete isolation of user data streams.

SECURITY DESIGN ISSUES

The security design goals include providing a uniform interface to hosts, excluding upper layer protocols from the TCB, and developing a uniform security policy and model independent of the protocol set and subscriber device (e.g., host, terminal, or video camera).

The philosophy for the MLS LAN is to provide sufficient protection mechanisms supporting separation of host process communication, as specified by the host. The goal is to ensure that communication between host processes meets the mandatory and discretionary policies specified in CSC-STD-001-83 at the system level. To meet this requirement, access control to the network is provided at or above the transport layer. Within the network, complete separation of communication objects (datagrams, connections, and sessions) is provided. This implies that network software outside the TCB be dedicated to a single communication object (connection or session). To support separation of host process connections, the TCB assumes responsibility for all addressing within the network, so that correct delivery is assured by the TCB.

The network makes some security assumptions about the host in areas that are outside the scope of network control. It is the responsibility of the security administrator to ensure that only hosts with these characteristics are attached to the network. The following assumptions are made:

1. each host will authenticate its users, and will provide the network with the correct user identity when a network service is requested on behalf of the user;
2. each host will correctly label packets sent to the network within the range that the host is assigned;
3. the host will control the process-to-process covert channels available through the modulation of network resources;
4. each host provides adequate protection for data within the host's range, and provides adequate discretionary and mandatory access controls for the users of the host;
5. the host will perform access checks based on the network provided user identity when a remote user is attempting to gain access to host resources through the network (i.e., the network does not control access to host resources, but rather to the host); and
6. the host will control host process utilization of the network, so that host processes cannot deny access to other host processes.

The software architecture allows the major part of TCP and all of TELNET to reside outside the TCB. To limit the size of the TCB, each TCP connection is single-level. However, multiple concurrent TCP connections can be active within an SNS at differing security levels. The TCB not only separates data by security level, but also provides complete isolation of user sessions. This separation is enforced at both the network and host-to-network interfaces, and within the SNS. The User Datagram Protocol (UDP) is provided as a multilevel service to hosts. The design supports reliable file transfer (through FTP) between hosts at different security levels. To provide this capability requires that a major part of FTP resides within the SNS. The data transfer between the SNSs is reliable (uses TCP). When the destination host is at a higher sensitivity level than the FTP session, there would be limitations placed on the control information passed from the host to the non-TCB FTP functions.

An issue that arises at the system level is the provision of end-to-end user identification and end-to-end trusted path. The network must be able to support these requirements. This implies that the TCB components must be capable of detecting modification of information passing through an end-to-end trusted path.

NETWORK TCB

Figure 2 shows the network TCB. The TCB includes the SNS security functions, the network management software, the executive, and the network hardware.

The SNS security functions include the access control functions, and support functions for network management and security control. These include executive, multiplexing/demultiplexing, access control, session management, startup, shutdown, audit and performance monitoring. Network management functions include auditing, performance monitoring, network and security administrator support, network configuration and reconfiguration, authentication, maintenance of access control tables, recognition and notification to the security administrator for security alarm conditions These functions are provided in a dedicated network device that is assumed to be physically protected from unauthorized tampering.

Within an SNS there are two or more Intel 286 microprocessors. The tasks (Intel 286's concept of process) in these processors provide the network protocol and management services. These tasks are controlled by an executive, which provides memory management, task management, timer management, signal management, and intertask communication services to these tasks. For intertask communication and signals, the communicating tasks may or may not be within the same processor of the SNS. This is transparent to the tasks.

SECURITY DESIGN

The network level security design is illustrated in figure 3. Each packet placed on the network has an attached sensitivity label provided by the TCB. When a packet is received at an SNS, the TCB checks to make sure that the packet destination is active, and is permitted to receive a packet at the provided sensitivity level. For terminals attached directly to the network, the SNS provides login and authentication services. The overall network security control resides at the network management node.

Within an SNS the executive acts as a separation kernel (3). It enforces complete separation of the non-TCB processes that support different user sessions. Figure 4 illustrates the software architecture for the SNS. Each active service (e.g. TCP) is logically separated by the TCB from all other services within an SNS. There is a different processing stream for each active service. This is similar to the software architecture for the Communications Operating System Network Front End (2). The separation of these services is supported by the multiplexing/demultiplexing functions in both TCP and the WWMCCS HFE protocol. The session managers enforce the access control policies at the interface between the network and external devices, and control the creation and deletion of the processing streams that perform the non-TCB protocol functions. The security design uses the Intel 286 processor features to provide task separation and separation of TCB from non-TCB functions within an SNS.

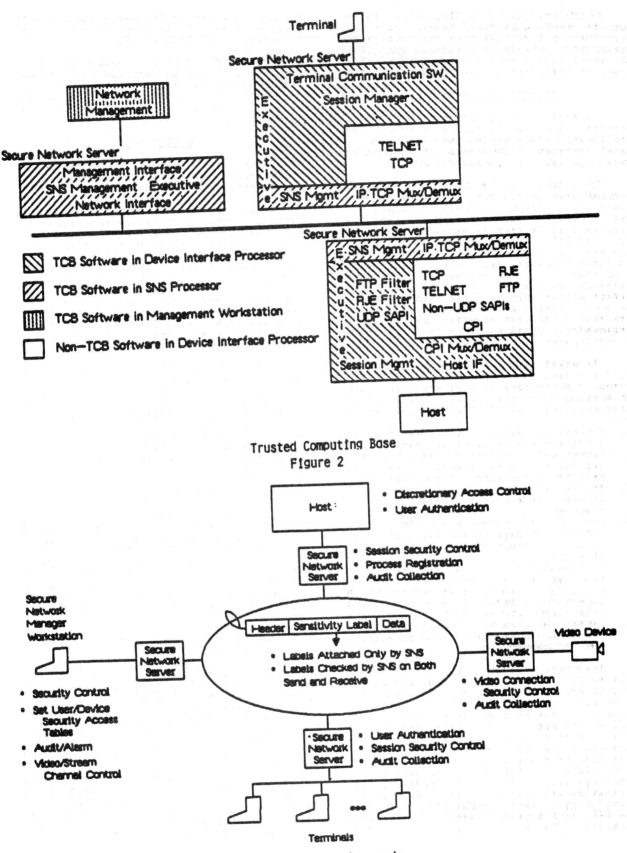

Trusted Computing Base
Figure 2

MLS Design Approach
Figure 3

Secure Network Server

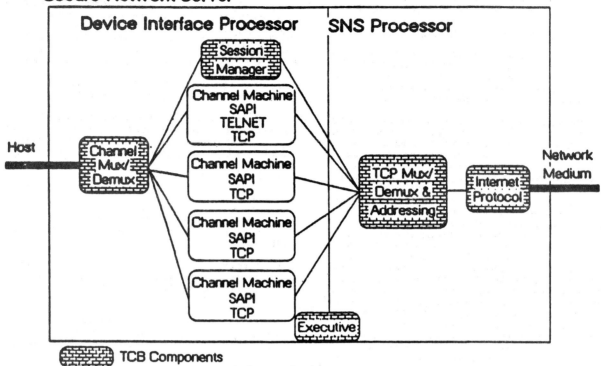

Software Architecture
Figure 4

SECURITY POLICY

The policy and model for the MLS LAN address the control of access to network communication objects by network subjects. In addition to the external subjects listed above, there are internal network subjects -untrusted tasks performing communication functions. The policy for these internal subjects is complete isolation of processing for different user sessions.

The policy enforced at the external interface to the network is an extension of the policy defined in the DoD Trusted Computer System Evaluation Criteria for Class A1. The extensions address multilevel subscribers and multilevel services for these subscribers.

Discretionary Access Control Policies

The policies enforced by the network TCB at the network external interface are as follows:

1. if a subject has send access to a communication object, then the communication object and subject are active and the subject has send discretionary access rights to the communication object; and

2. if a subject has receive access to a communication object, then the communication object and subject are active and the subject has receive discretionary access rights to the communication object.

Mandatory Access Control Policies

The policies enforced by the network TCB at the network external interface are divided into two cases: multilevel subjects and single-level subjects. In either case, each subject is associated with a device, and the maximum and minimum sensitivity levels for a subject must be within the range of levels for the associated device. The multilevel subjects (currently UDP processes

are the only multilevel subjects) are permitted concurrent access to multiple communication objects at different sensitivity levels. The single-level subjects are given a range of sensitivity levels, but can connect to only one communication object at any time. This is used to model services such as a TELNET server on a multilevel host. The server is announced to the network by the host along with the range of sensitivity levels that the host is willing to support for the server. The TELNET service (and server) is single-level, so that when a TELNET session request is received at the SNS, the session sensitivity level must be within the range for the server. The server's sensitivity level will be the same as the session level for the duration of the session.

Multilevel Subjects

1. If a subject has send access to a communication object, then the communication object is active and the communication object's current sensitivity level is within the subject's range of sensitivity levels.

2. If a subject has receive access to a communication object, then the communication object is active and the communication object's current sensitivity level is at or below the subject's maximum sensitivity level.

Single-Level Subjects

1. If a subject is single-level, then the subject's current level is between it's maximum and minimum levels.

2. If a subject has send access to a communication object, then the communication object is active and the communication object's current sensitivity level is equal to the subject's current sensitivity level.

3. If a subject has receive access to a communication object, then the communication object is active and

the communication object's current sensitivity level is at or below the subject's current sensitivity level.

FORMAL SECURITY POLICY MODEL

The principle state components in the MLS LAN security model are the attributes of the active communication objects and subjects. Of particular interest are the sensitivity levels of the objects and subjects, and the discretionary access control lists for the objects.

The system may change state when a subject requests activation of a communication object, a subject requests access to a communication object, a subject requests disconnection from a communication object, a subject requests that subjects be added to a communication object's discretionary access control list, a communication object becomes inactive, a subject becomes active, or a subject becomes inactive. When a subject requests communication object activation, that subject becomes the owner of the communication object. The owner is the sole subject able to modify the discretionary access control list. When the communication object is initialized, the subject specifies a sensitivity level for the object (or this can be set to the subject sensitivity level if the subject is single-level), and an initial list of subjects and modes of access for the discretionary access control list. The specified level must be within the subject's range. The discretionary access control list will typically be specified as the remote socket (or logical name for a remote process) for a TCP connection. The state invariants (Ina Jo criterion) for the model are formalizations of the policy defined above. When a subject attempts to connect to a communication object, the state invariants are enforced to ensure that the subject has the appropriate authorization for that object.

When a subject becomes active, a range of sensitivity levels is set for that subject, and this range must be within the range specified for the associated device. For host processes, the host TCB is responsible for providing the network with this range of sensitivity levels. This range must be within the limits placed on the host by the network security administrator.

Excerpts from our formal security policy model written in the Ina Jo language are included as an appendix to this paper. The part of the model presented describes the policy enforced at the network external interface. The formal verification approach is (1) to use the Ina Jo tool to prove the theorems required for the model, (2) to develop the formal top-level specification (FTLS) required by the Criteria as an Ina Jo second level specification, and (3) to use the Ina Jo tool to prove consistency of the FTLS with the formal model.

CURRENT STATUS AND FUTURE DIRECTIONS

We currently have prototype hardware, and a large part of the network software is complete. Network functionality will be added in increments, with a full scale demonstration system completed by the end of 1985.

The major protocol security issue encountered was determining the degree of support provided within the LAN for system-wide session layer security. There is a need for end-to-end user identification and trusted path to support the system level security requirements. The DoD protocol suite does not have a session layer supporting these requirements. We are addressing these issues as part of this research program, and plan to provide this capability as part of our MLS LAN product. We are also investigating the incorporation of encryption into the MLS LAN.

Enhancements are planned for the MLS LAN to approach the functionality shown in figure 1. In 1986, we plan to develop a file server, mail server and gateway to DDN. An effort is underway to address the packaging issues for the MLS LAN. Provision of higher data rates (up to 300 Mbps) is being investigated.

References

(1) DoD Computer Security Center, "DoD Trusted Computer System Evaluation Criteria," CSC-STD-001-83, 1983.

(2) Grossman, G., "A Practical Executive for Secure Communications," Proceedings of the 1982 Symposium on Security and Privacy, Oakland California, IEEE Computer Society, April 1982.

(3) Rushby, J., "A Trusted Computing Base for Embedded Systems," Proceedings of the DoD/NBS Computer Security Conference, Gaithersburg Maryland, September 1984.

Appendix

Formal Security Policy Model for an MLS LAN

Type

        Level,
        Ext_User,
        Subject < Ext_User,
        Device < Ext_User,
        Subjects = Set of Subject,
        Comm_Object,
        mode = (send, receive),
        Security_Mode = (sl, mls)

Constant

        Lteq(Level, Level) : Boolean,
        Resides_On(Subject) : Device

Variables

        Active_Comm_Object(Comm_Object) : Boolean,
        Send_DAC_List(Subject, Comm_Object) : Boolean,
        Receive_DAC_List(Subject, Comm_Object) : Boolean,
        Object_Level(Comm_Object) : Level,
        Connection(mode, Comm_Object, Subject) : Boolean,
        Active_Subject(Subject) : Boolean,
        Subject_Mode(Subject) : Security_Mode,
        Current_Level(Subject) : Level,
        Min_Level(Ext_User) : Level,
        Max_Level(Ext_User) : Level,
        Owner(Subject, Comm_Object) : Boolean

Initial

    A" c : Comm_Object
     (~Active_Comm_Object(c))
    & A" s : Subject, c : Comm_Object
     (~Send_DAC_List(s, c) & ~Receive_DAC_List(s, c) & ~ Owner(s, c))
    & A" s : Subject, c : Comm_Object, m : mode
     (~Connection(m, c, s))
    & A" s : Subject
     (~Active_Subject(s))

Criterion

    A" m : mode, c : Comm_Object, u : Subject
      (Connection(m, c, u) - >
        Active_Comm_Object(c) & Active_Subject(u)
        & (m = send - >Send_DAC_List(u, c))
        & (m = receive -> Receive_DAC_List(u, c)))

    & A" m : mode, c : Comm_Object, u : Subject
      (Connection(m, c, u) & Subject_Mode(u) = mls - >
        (m = send - >
         Lteq(Object_Level(c), Max_Level(u))
          & Lteq(Min_Level(u), Object_Level(c)))
       & (m = receive - >Lteq(Object_Level(c), Max_Level(u))))

    & A" m : mode, c : Comm_Object, u : Subject
      (Connection(m, c, u) & Subject_Mode(u) = sl - >
        & (m = send -> Current_Level(u) = Object_Level(c))
        & (m = receive - >Lteq(Object_Level(c), Current_Level(u)))
        & A" c1 : Comm_Object, m1 : mode (c1 ~ = c - >~Connection(m1,c1,u)))

    A" u : Subject
       (Lteq(Max_Level(u),Max_Level(Resides_On(u)))
         & Lteq(Min_Level(Resides_On(u)), Min_Level(u))
         & Lteq(Min_Level(u), Max_Level(u))
         & (Active_Subject(u) & Subject_Mode(u) = sl - >
          Lteq(Min_Level(u), Current_Level(u))
          Lteq(Current_Level(u), Max_Level(u))))

Transform Set_Up_Comm_Object(u : Subject, c : Comm_Object, l : Level,
                                        S : Subjects, R : Subjects) External

Effect

Lteq(Min_Level(u), l) &¬ Active_Comm_Object(c) & Active_Subject(u)
& (Subject_Mode(u) = sl - >
    (A" c1 : Comm_Object, m : mode
      (¬Connection(m, c1, u))))
& A" c1 : Comm_Object, u1 : Subject
    ((N"Active_Comm_Object(c1) <-> c1 = c │ Active_Comm_Object(c1))
    & (N"Send_DAC_List(u1, c1) <->
        u1 <: S & c1 = c │ Send_DAC_List(u1, c1))
    & (N"Receive_DAC_List(u1, c1) <->
        u1 <: R & c1 = c │ Receive_DAC_List(u1, c1))
    & (N"Object_Level(c1) = (c1 = c =>l
                                    < > Object_Level(c1)))
    & (N"Owner(u1, c1) <-> u1 = u & c1 = c │ Owner(u1, c1)))
  │NC"(Active_Comm_Object, Send_DAC_List,
            Receive_DAC_List, Object_Level, Owner)

Transform Connect_to_Comm_Object(u : Subject, c : Comm_Object, m : mode)
                              External

Effect

(Active_Comm_Object(c) & Active_Subject(u)
& (Subject_Mode(u) = sl - >
    (A" c1 : Comm_Object, m1 : mode
        (Active_Comm_Object(c1) & Connection(m1, c1, u) - >c1 = c)))
& ((m = send & Send_DAC_List(u, c)
        & Lteq(Min_Level(u), Object_Level(c))
        & Lteq(Object_Level(c), Max_Level(u)))
    │ (m = receive & Receive_DAC_List(u, c)
        & Lteq(Object_Level(c), Max_Level(u))))
& A" m1 : mode, c1 : Comm_Object, u1 : Subject
    (N"Connection(m1, c1, u1) <->
        m1 = m & c1 = c & u1 = u │ Connection(m1, c1, u1))
& (Subject_Mode(u) = sl - >(m = send & N"Current_Level(u) = Object_Level(c) │
    m=receive&Lteq(object_Level(c),N"Current_Level(u)))
& A" u1 : Subject (u1¬ = u -> N"Current_Level(u1) = Current_Level(u1)))
│ NC"(Connection, Current_Level)

Transform Disconnect_from_Comm_Object(u : Subject, c : Comm_Object,
                                      m : mode) External

Effect

A" m1 : mode, c1 : Comm_Object, u1 : Subject
    (N"Connection(m1, c1, u1) <->
                (m1 ¬= m │ c1 ¬ = c │ u1 ¬ = u) & Connection(m1, c1, u1))
  │ NC"(Connection)

Transform Add_to_DAC_List(u : Subject, c : Comm_Object, S : Subjects,
                          R : Subjects) External

Effect
Owner(u, c) & Active_Subject(u) & Active_Comm_Object(c)
& (Subject_Mode(u) = sl = >Lteq(Current_Level(u), Object_Level(c))
                        < > Lteq(Min_Level(u), Object_Level(c)))
& A" u1 : Subject, c1 : Comm_Object
    ((N"Send_DAC_List(u1, c1)< - >
        u1 <: S & c1 = c │ Send_DAC_List(u1, c1))
    & (N"Receive_DAC_List(u1, c1) <->
        u1 <: R & c1 = c │ Receive_DAC_List(u1, c1)))
  │NC"(Send_DAC_List, Receive_DAC_List)

Transform Release_Obj(u : Subject, c : Comm_Object) External

Effect

(Receive_DAC_List(u, c) │Send_DAC_List(u, c)) & Active_Subject(u)
& (Subject_Mode(u) = sl = >Lteq(Current_Level(u), Object_Level(c))
                        < > Lteq(Min_Level(u), Object_Level(c)))
& A" u1 : Subject, m : mode
    (¬Connection(m, c, u1))
& (A" c1 : Comm_Object, u1 : Subject
    ((N"Active_Comm_Object(c1) <-> c1 ¬ =c & Active_Comm_Object(c1))

409

        & (N"Send_DAC_List(ul, cl)< -> cl ~= c & Send_DAC_List(ul, cl))
        & (N"Receive_DAC_List(ul, cl) <-> cl ~= c & Receive_DAC_List(ul, cl))
        & (N"Owner(ul, cl) <-> cl ~= c & Owner(ul, cl))))
   |NC"(Active_Comm_Object, Send_DAC_List, Receive_DAC_List, Owner)

Transform Activate_Ext_Subject(u : Subject, l1 : Level, l2 : Level,
                                      sm : Subject_Mode) External

Effect

    ~Active_Subject(u)
    & Lteq($\overline{l1}$, Max_Level(Resides_On(u)))
    & Lteq(Min_Level(Resides_On(u)), l2)
    & Lteq(l2, $\overline{l1}$)
    & A" ul : Subject
      ((N"Active_Subject(ul) <-> ul = u | Active_Subject(ul))
      & (N"Subject_Mode(ul) = (ul = u = >sm
                            < > Subject_Mode(ul)))
      & (ul = u => (Lteq(l2, N"Current_Level(ul))
              & Lteq(N"Current_Level(ul), l1))
         < > (N"Current_Level(ul) = Current_Level(ul)))
      & (N"Max_Level(ul) = (ul = u => l1
                      < > Max_Level(ul)))
      & (N"Min_Level(ul) = (ul = u => l2
                      < > Min_Level(ul))))
   |NC"(Active_Subject, Subject_Mode, Current_Level, Max_Level, Min_Level)

Transform Deactivate_Ext_Subject(u : Subject) External

Effect

    A" c : Comm_Object, m : mode
    (~Connection(m, c, u) &~ Owner(u, c))
    & A" ul : Subject,
    (N"Active_Subject(ul) <-> ul ~= u & Active_Subject(ul))
    |NC"(Active_Subject)

Conclusions

Computer security is a relatively new discipline dating back to the early 1970s. Although computer security had a slow start, several developments in the 1970s within the National Bureau of Standards and the U.S. Department of Defense provided a basis for further federal guidance to the public and private sectors. For example, the National Bureau of Standards issued the *Data Encryption Standard* on January 15, 1977. In the same year, the U.S. Department of Defense Computer Security Initiative was started. These efforts continued into the 1980's, producing additional computer security guidance from the National Bureau of Standards and resulting in the formation, in 1981, of the National Computer Security Center (NCSC), formerly named the Department of Defense Computer Security Center.

We suggest that computer security has reached a "critical mass." The computer security discipline has, in our opinion, experienced classic "learning curve" rates of growth. For approximately 10 years, until around 1977, computer security was primarily a research and development topic. Developments began to occur at an increased rate of growth in the 1980s, with the formation of groups such as the NCSC in 1981. The current rate of growth is relatively rapid. Examples demonstrating this rate of growth include the expanding use of the *Orange Book* as the basis of the security certification process for the NCSC's *Evaluated Products List* and the substantial growth in attendance at the Annual National Computer Security Conference.

An overview of current security concepts and developments is presented in the sections on computer system security and network security. These security concepts form the foundation for the continued research developments and associated security applications.

When compared with the state of the computer security discipline 10 years ago, the current rate of growth is substantial. We recognize that this situation exists in part, by generally emphasizing the more current reprints in this book and moving the older work to a recommended readings list. As we go to press, new literature from the many security conferences and symposiums, as well as recent announcements of products receiving new security certifications and being placed on the *Evaluated Products List* continue to appear.

Although we present information system security as composed of separate sections on issues pertaining to computer and network security, we believe that the central theme of this book is the continued merging and interfacing of the computer and network security developments. This conversion is a natural parallel result of similar merging and interfacing of automated hardware, software, and communication systems in the respective computer and network industries. Since the terminology in the computer and network literature is neither uniform nor standard, we strive to provide a bridge between the two aspects of the security discipline: computer and network security. For example, when we discuss concepts that are shared in common, such as access control and authentication in Section 3.3, we mention the interrelationships between the sections.

The sections in this book provide building blocks for the construction of an integrated overview of the principle computer security and network security concepts, interrelationships and developments. Sections 1.1 and 2.1 provide an integrated overview and set of management issues that serve as a framework for computer security.

In Section 2.2 we discuss formal models from a computer security viewpoint, upon which we build in the discussions in Section 2.3. The key point is that when we present network security standards and guidance development, we extend the basic computer security concepts. For example, the Trusted Computing Base in Section 2.2 could possibly be the Trusted Computing Base or Trusted Network Base in Section 2.3, depending on whether we are discussing computer or network security issues.

Sections 2.4 and 2.5 emphasize hardware/software security issues, with only limited mention of network issues. However, in Section 2.6, we provide a more explicit bridge between computer and network security. The bridge is SCOMP, a secure communications processor certified as an A1 product on the *Evaluated Products List*.

We continue developing selected interrelationship issues between computer and network security in Section 3.1. For example, when we discuss security services for a network security architecture, we mention that access control depends on labels. We further state that labels relate to mandatory access control as presented in the *Orange Book*. In Section 3.2 concerning encryption, we also present the interrelationship. Here, we discuss the advances in very large scale integration that are essential for effective implementation of the cryptographic function on a single chip which is highly resistant to reverse engineering (i.e., demonstrating the dependence of encryption on computer technology). The interrelationships between computer and network security in Section 3.3 access control and authentication were already mentioned.

EH0255-0/87/0000/0411$01.00 © 1987 IEEE

Interrelationships are continued in the discussions of protocols in Section 3.4 and network applications in Section 3.5. For example, in Section 3.4, open system interconnection networks are discussed as a collection of nodes connected by communication links. These nodes may contain a wide variety of data terminating equipment, including computers. The last section (3.5) presents network applications that pertain to network security. Each network security application contains a variety of computers that require computer security capabilities. For example, the discussion of a multilevel secure local area network presents a secure network server that is based on Intel 286 microprocessors.

In many respects, the interrelationships we discuss between computer and network security are a function of the evolving digital technology. However, there is a secondary trend that reinforces the interrelationships: the gradual development of network guidance that will in varying degrees be highly dependent upon existing computer security guidance. Since computers are the main components of network nodes, the *Orange Book* applies to their trusted functions.

We expect the merging of computer and network security to continue. Possible impacts could include: (1) closer working relationships in the development and operation of automated information systems within the organization between computer security and network security officials and (2) gradual development of a unified computer and network security budget for the organization.

Glossary

Introduction

Every area of technical specialization has its own vocabulary. Furthermore, many areas of subspecialization create alternative and conflicting definitions. Computer and network security certainly experiences this problem. The very title is compound, indicating the merger of two communities of interest. In addition, we have attempted to present both civilian and military viewpoints.

Several authoritative glossaries have been consulted and their definitions extracted, selected, and merged. When necessary, this glossary contains multiple definitions for a term, separately numbered. In some cases we have synthesized definitions; be alerted to the possibility of divergent usage. The glossary of any specific document should, of course, take precedence in defining the terminology used in that document.

— A —

ACCESS. (1) A specific type of interaction between a subject and an object that results in the flow of information from one to the other. (2) The ability and the means necessary to approach, to store, or to retrieve data, to communicate with, or to make use of any resource of an ADP system.

ACCESS CONTROL. (1) The limiting of rights or capabilities of a subject or principal to communicate with other subjects, or to use functions or services in a computer system or network. (2) Restrictions controlling a subject's access to an object.

ACCESS CONTROL LIST. (1) A list of subjects or principals authorized for specific access to an object. (2) A list of entities, together with their access rights, which are authorized to have access to a resource.

ACCESS MODE. An indication of a specific action that can be applied to an object (e.g., read, write, and execute).

ACCESS PERMISSION. The definition of which subjects have the ability to change access modes and/or the ability to pass the ability to another subject.

ACCESS PORT. A logical or physical identifier that a computer uses to distinguish different terminal input/output data streams.

ACCOUNTABILITY. The quality or state that enables violations or attempted violations of ADP system security to be traced to individuals who may then be held responsible.

ACCREDITATION. The managerial authorization and approval, granted to an ADP system or network to process sensitive data in an operational environment, made on the basis of a certification by designated technical personnel of the extent to which design and implementation of the system meet pre-specified technical requirements for achieving adequate data security. Management can accredit a system at a higher/lower level than the certification. If management accredits the system at a higher level than it is certified, management is accepting the residual risk (difference between the levels of accreditation and certification).

ACTIVE THREAT. The threat of an unauthorized change to the state of the system. Examples of security relevant active threats may be modification of messages, replay of messages, insertion of spurious messages, masquerading as an authorized entity, and denial of service.

ACTIVE WIRETAPPING. The attaching of an unauthorized device, such as a computer terminal, to a communications circuit for the purpose of obtaining access to data through the generation of false messages or control signals or by altering the communication of legitimate users.

ADD-ON SECURITY. The retrofitting of protection mechanisms, implemented in hardware or software, after an ADP system has become operational.

ADMINISTRATIVE SECURITY. The management constraints, operational procedures, accountability procedures, and supplemental controls established to provide an acceptable level of protection for sensitive data. Synonymous with procedural security.

APPLICATION CONFIDENTIALITY. The state that exists when application source and object code and documentation is held in confidence and is protected from unauthorized disclosure.

APPLICATIONS INTEGRITY. The state that exists when the source and object code are the same as originally developed and certified/accredited or have been modified and tested in accordance with established standards and procedures and recertified/reaccredited, and have not been exposed to accidental or malicious alteration or destruction.

413

APPLICATION PROCESS. (1) An untrusted process performing end-user computation. (2) A part within an open system that processes information and uses Open Systems Interconnection communication services to communicate with other application processes in other open systems. See Open System and Open Systems Interconnection.

ATTRIBUTE. In a relational database, the subset of a domain which corresponds to the values in a column of a relation.

AUDIT TRAIL. (1) A set of records that collectively provide documentary evidence of processing used to aid in tracing from original transactions forward to related records and reports and/or backward from records and reports to their component source transactions. (2) Information collected or used to facilitate a Security Audit. See Security Audit and Security Audit Trail.

AUTHENTICATION. (1) To establish the validity of a claimed identity. (2) To provide protection against fraudulent transactions by establishing the validity of message, station, individual, or originator. See Data Origin Authentication, Message Authentication, Message Authentication Code (MAC), and Peer Entity Authentication.

AVAILABILITY. (1) The state that exists when required automated services can be obtained within an acceptable period. (2) The property which requires the resources of an open system to be accessible and usable upon demand by an authorized entity.

— B —

BACK-UP PLAN. Provides the ability to conduct, by alternate means, the critical data processing workload.

BACKUP PROCEDURES. The provisions made for recovery of data files and other system assets and for restart or replacement of ADP equipment after the occurrence of a system failure or of a disaster.

BANDWIDTH. A characteristic of a communication channel that is the amount of information that can be passed through it in a given amount of time, usually expressed in bits per second.

BELL-LaPADULA MODEL. A formal state transition model of computer security policy that describes a set of access control rules. In this formal model, the entities in a computer system are divided into abstract sets of subjects and objects. The notion of a secure state is defined and is proven that each state transition preserves security by moving from secure state to secure state, thus, inductively proving that the system is secure. A system state is defined to be "secure" if the only permitted access modes of subjects to objects are in accordance with a specific security policy. To determine whether or not a specific access mode is allowed, the clearance of a subject is compared to the classification of the object and a determination is made as to whether the subject is authorized for the specific access mode. The clearance/classifications scheme is expressed in terms of a lattice. See also Lattice, Simple Security Property, *-Property.

BETWEEN-THE-LINES ENTRY. Access, obtained through the use of active wiretapping by an unauthorized user, to a momentarily inactive terminal of a legitimate user.

— C —

CALL BACK. A procedure for identifying a terminal dialing into a computer system by disconnecting the calling terminal and reestablishing the connection by the computer system's dialing the telephone number of the calling terminal.

CAPABILITY. (1) In a computer system, a ticket or token that cannot be forged, which when presented can be taken as incontestable proof that the presenter is authorized to access the object named in the ticket. (2) In a network, a token used as an identifier for a resource such that possession of the token confers access rights for the resource.

CATEGORY. A grouping of objects to which a nonhierarchical restrictive label is applied (e.g., proprietary, compartmented information). Subjects must be privileged to access a category.

CERTIFICATION. The technical evaluation of a system's security features, made as part of and in support of the approval/accreditation process, that establishes the extent to which a particular system's design and implementation meet a set of specified security requirements.

CHANNEL. An information transfer path within a system. May also refer to the mechanism by which the path is effected. See also Covert Channel and Overt Channel.

CIPHERTEXT. Unintelligible text or signals produced as the result of encryption or encipherment. Notes: (1) The International Standards Organization uses the term encipherment, because encryption does not translate adequately into French. (2) Ciphertext may, itself, be input to encipherment, producing superenciphered output.

CIRCUIT. A communications link between two or more points.

CLASSIFICATION. A determination that information requires a specific degree of protection against unauthorized access together with a designation signifying that such a determination has been made. Classification is performed according to a stated policy.

CLEARANCE. The authorization of a system user to access sensitive data. A clearance implicitly encompasses lower clearance levels (e.g., a secret-cleared user has an implicit confidential clearance). Each organization has its own definition of clearance and the associated levels. The U.S. Department of Defense uses several clearance levels, which require varying background investigations. The extent of investigation required for a particular clearance varies based both on the background of the individual under investigation and on derogatory or questionable information disclosed during the investigation. Identical clearances are assumed to be equivalent; however, despite differences in the amount of investigation performed. The increasing levels of clearance or authorization follow: (1) *Uncleared (U):* personnel with no clearance of authorization. Permitted access to any information for which there are no specified controls, such as openly published information. (2) *Unclassified information (N):* Personnel who are authorized access to sensitive unclassified (e.g., for official use only (FOUO)) information, either by an explicit official authorization or by an implicit authorization derived from official assignments of responsibilities. (3) *Confidential clearance (C):* requires U.S. citizenship and typically some limited records checking. In some cases, a national agency check (NAC) is required (e.g., for U.S. citizens employed by colleges or universities). (4) *Secret clearance (S):* Typically requires a NAC, which consists of searching the U.S. Federal Bureau of Investigation fingerprint and investigative files and the Defense Central Index of Investigations. In some cases, further investigation is required. (5) *Top secret clearance based on a current background investigation (TS(BI)):* Requires an investigation that consists of a NAC, personal contacts, record searches, and written inquiries. A BI typically includes an investigation extending back 5 years, often with a spot check investigation extending back 15 years. (6) *Top secret clearance based on a current special background investigation (TS(SBI)):* Requires an investigation that in addition to the investigation for a BI includes additional checks on the subject's immediate family (if foreign born) and spouse and neighborhood investigations to verify each of the subject's former residences in the United States where the subject resided six months or more. An SBI typically includes an investigation extending back 15 years. (7) *One category (1C):* In addition to a TS(SBI) clearance, written authorization for access to one category of information is required. Authorizations are the access rights granted to a user by a responsible individual (e.g., security officer). (8) *Multiple categories (MC):* In addition to TS(SBI) clearance, written authorization for access to multiple categories of information is required.

CLEARTEXT. Used in a cryptographic context for data in intelligible processable form that can be read or acted upon without the application of an decipherment.

CLOSED HOT SITE. A facility which is owned by a consortium or which was otherwise constructed for a specific set of companies to satisfy part of the need for back-up capability.

CLOSED SECURITY ENVIRONMENT. An environment that includes those systems in which both of the following conditions hold true: (1) Developers and maintainers of software outside the security kernel have sufficient clearances and authorizations to provide an acceptable presumption where the maximum classification of data to be processed is Confidential or below (developers are cleared and authorized to the same level as the most sensitive data) or where the maximum classification of data to be processed is Secret or above (developers have at least a Secret clearance). (2) Configuration control provides sufficient assurance that this software is protected against the introduction of malicious logic prior to and during operation. Compare with Open Security Environment.

CLOSED USER GROUP. A closed user group permits users belonging to a group to communicate with each other but precludes communications with other users who are not members of the group.

COMMUNICATION LINK. The physical means of connecting one location to another for the purpose of transmitting and/or receiving data.

COMMUNICATIONS MEDIUM. Those circuits that interconnect networks, terminals, or network physical devices. The circuits may be logical or physical and provide end-to-end paths between communicating processes.

COMPARTMENTALIZATION. (1) The isolation of system resources and assets from one another to provide protection against unauthorized or concurrent access by other users or programs. (2) The subdividing of sensitive data into small, isolated blocks for the purpose of reducing risk to the data. (3) The separation of sensitive data in such blocks based on a need-to-know and privileges to access the data granted by a cognizant authority. See Category.

COMPARTMENTED SECURITY MODE. The mode of operation that allows the system to process two or more types of compartmented information (information requiring a special authorization) or any one type of compartmented information with other than compartmented information. In this mode, all system users need not be cleared for all types of compartmented information processed but must be fully cleared for at least Top Secret information for unescorted access to the computer.

COMPONENT. A device, consisting of hardware, along with its firmware and/or software that performs a specific function on a computer communications network. Examples include modems, telecommunications controllers, message switches, technical control devices, host computers, gateways, etc. Components typically do not implement all protocol layers.

COMPROMISE. A violation of the security system such that an unauthorized disclosure, modification, or destruction of sensitive information may have occurred or that a denial of service condition has been induced.

COMPUTER ARCHITECTURE. (1) Computer architecture is often used to mean the organization and design of computers. (2) Computer architecture can also be described as six architectural levels: three software and three hardware levels. The six-level model of computer architecture presents an abstract picture of a computer system. The simplest operations and functions are on the bottom and the most complex, user-dependent operations on top. Each level uses the functions provided by the level below. Architecture can be viewed as the boundary or interface between the levels. Conceptually, an architecture is the functional appearance of the system below an interface to a user above the interface. In general, we are not concerned with the details of the system below the architecture at which we are operating. Rather, we are concerned with the function of the system at the interface immediately below us. There are exceptions for computer security. For example, we want to know the effectiveness of access controls at one or two levels below the general user level (System Architecture level). The six levels are (1) *System architecture:* The interface between the whole computer system and the outside world. (2) *Programming language architecture:* The interface between the application program and the high-level programming language itself (assuming the application is written in a high-level language). (3) *Operating system architecture:* The interface between the language and various run-time resource management functions usually provided by operating systems. (4) *Instruction set architecture:* The interface that defines the boundary between hardware and software. It is the level at which elementary, machine-recognized instructions are decoded and executed. (5,6) *Microcode architecture* and *gate-level architecture:* Define more primitive (fundamental) functions.

COMPUTER SECURITY. The protection of computers and their services from all natural and human-made hazards and provides an assurance that the computer performs its critical functions correctly and there are no harmful side-effects. Includes providing for information accuracy. See Information Security, Network Security, and Security.

COMPUTER SOFTWARE QUALITY (OR SOFTWARE QUALITY). The degree to which the attributes of the software enable it to perform its specified end item use.

CONFIDENTIALITY. The property that information is not made available or disclosed to unauthorized individuals, entities, or processes.

CONFIGURATION CONTROL. Management of changes made to a system's hardware, software, firmware, and documentation throughout the development and operational life of the system.

CONTINGENCY PLAN. Describes the appropriate response to any situation which jeopardizes the safety of data or of data processing and communications facilities to a degree that threatens meaningful harm to the organizations supported by those data and facilities.

CONTINUITY OF OPERATIONS. A system architecture that provides ADP availability within a predefined time period after system failure, as measured by the restart/recovery time (e.g., continuous for redundant components, 30 milliseconds, 30 minutes, or 30 hours). Note: The major security risks during the continuity of operations process include bypassing security controls during restart/recovery operations.

CONTROLLED SECURITY MODE. The mode of operation that is a type of multilevel security mode in which a more limited amount of trust is placed in the hardware/software base of the system, with resultant restrictions on the classification levels and clearance levels that may be supported.

CONVERSATION. An interactive exchange of information between two systems or systems users.

CORRECTNESS. The extent to which a program satisfies its specifications and fulfills the user's mission objectives.

COVERT CHANNEL. A communications channel that allows a process to transfer information in a manner that violates the system's security policy.

COVERT STORAGE CHANNEL. A covert channel that involves the direct or indirect writing of a storage location by one process and the direct or indirect reading of the storage location by another process. Covert storage channels typically involve a finite resource (e.g., sectors on a disk) that is shared by two subjects at different security levels.

COVERT TIMING CHANNEL. A covert channel in which one process signals information to another by modulating its own use of system resources (e.g., CPU time) in such a way that this manipulation affects the real response time observed by the second process.

CREDENTIALS. Data passed from one entity to another that are used to establish the sending entity's access rights.

CRITICAL DATA PROCESSING WORKLOAD. That portion of the total workload which will generate serious loss if disrupted for a specified period of time.

CRYPTANALYSIS. The analysis of a cryptographic system and/or its inputs and outputs to derive confidential variables and/or sensitive data including Cleartext.

CRYPTOGRAPHIC CHECKFUNCTION (ALSO CHECK-SUM). Information derived by performing a cryptographic process on the data unit. Note: The derivation of the checkfunction or checksum may be performed in one or more steps and is a result of a mathematical function of a key and a data unit. It is usually used to check the integrity of a data unit. See Message Authentication Code (MAC).

CRYPTOGRAPHIC DEVICE. An implementation of a cryptographic procedure.

CRYPTOGRAPHY. The discipline involving principles, means, and methods for the mathematical transformation of data to hide its information content, prevent its alteration, disguise its presence, and/or prevent its unauthorized use. This transformation employs confidential variables, such as keys, to map between cleartext and cyphertext. Note: Cryptography determines the methods used in encryption or encipherment and decryption or decipherment. An attack on a cryptographic principle, means, or method is cryptanalysis.

— D —

DATA. Information represented within a computer or network.

DATA CONFIDENTIALITY. The state that exists when data are held in confidence and is protected from unauthorized disclosure.

DATA DICTIONARY/DIRECTORY. Data management functions often associated with a DBMS. A Data Dictionary explains the semantic meaning of the date. A DAta Directory locates the physical and/or logical position of the data.

DATA INTEGRITY. (1) The state that exists when computerized data are the same as that in the source documents and has not be exposed to accidental or malicious alteration or destruction. (2) The property that data have not been exposed to accidental or malicious alteration or destruction. (3) In a database system, avoidance of simultaneous update where two concurrently executing transactions, each correct in itself, may interfere with each other so as to produce incorrect results.

DATA ORIGIN AUTHENTICATION. The collaboration that the source of data received is as claimed. See Authentication.

DATABASE. An organized collection of data.

DATABASE MANAGEMENT SYSTEM (DBMS). The software or firmware that facilitates the use and control of large information files normally maintained on external storage devices. A DBMS permits the insertion, deletion, retrieval, and modification of the data maintained in the database.

DECIPHER. To convert, by use of the appropriate key, encrypted text into its equivalent plain text.

DEDICATED SECURITY MODE. The mode of operation in which the system is specifically and exclusively dedicated to and controlled for the processing of one particular type or classification of information, either for full-time operation or for a specified period of time.

DENIAL OF SERVICE. The prevention of authorized access to system assets or services or the delaying of time critical operations.

DESCRIPTIVE TOP-LEVEL SPECIFICATION (DTLS). A top-level software specification that is written in a natural language (e.g., English), an informal program design notation, or a combination of the two.

DIGITAL SIGNATURE. A mechanism that allows a recipient of data to prove the source and integrity of information to a third party. This mechanism is used to protect against forgery and repudiation.

DISCRETIONARY ACCESS CONTROL (DAC). A means of restricting access to objects based on the identity of subjects and/or groups to which they belong. The controls are discretionary in the sense that (1) a subject with a certain access permission is capable of passing that permission (perhaps indirectly) on to any other subject; (2) DAC is often employed to enforce need-to-know; and (3) access control may be changed by the owner of the object. Compare to Mandatory Access Control.

DISCRETIONARY SECURITY. Those aspects of security policy that involve the provision of security services as a result of a request by an entity requiring an instance of communication.

DOMAIN. The set of objects that a subject has the ability to access.

DOMINATE. Security level S1 is said to dominate security level S2 if the hierarchical classification of S1 is greater than or equal to that of S2 and the nonhierarchical categories of S1 include all those of S2 as a subset.

— E —

EAL. (1) Expected annual loss, generally derived by: EAL = (cost) * (probability of occurrence). The EAL is developed during a risk analysis.

EFFICIENCY. The amount of computing resources and code required by a program to perform a function.

EMERGENCY RESPONSE PLAN. Provides procedures to respond promptly and well to a potential disruption so as to limit the damage.

ENCIPHERMENT. See Encryption.

ENCRYPTION. The (usually) reversible transformation of data from plain text to ciphertext by a cryptographic device so as to drastically increase the amount of work required to gain access to the information. The purpose is usually to increase the confidentiality of the information, although encryption may be employed as the basis of other security services. Also known as encipherment. Note: Encryption may be irreversible, in which case the corresponding decryption process cannot feasibly be performed.

END-TO-END ENCRYPTION. Encryption at or within two systems considered the end points of a system incorporating intermediate subsystems. The corresponding decryption occurs only within or at the destination end system. End-to-end encryption occurs at protocol layers 4 and above. Compare with Link Encryption.

ENVIRONMENT. The aggregate of external circumstances, conditions, and objects that affect the development, operation, and maintenance of a system. See Open Security Environment and Closed Security Environment.

EXPLOITABLE CHANNEL. Any channel that is usable or detectable by subjects external to the trusted computing base.

EXPORTATION. (1) The process that causes data to flow from one network component to an adjacent network component.

— F —

FLAW. An error of commission, omission, or oversight in a system that allows protection mechanisms to be bypassed.

FLAW HYPOTHESIS METHODOLOGY. A system analysis and penetration technique where specifications and documentation for the system are analyzed and then flaws in the system are hypothesized. The list of hypothesized flaws is then prioritized on the basis of the estimated probability that a flaw actually exists and, assuming a flaw does exist, on the ease of exploiting it and on the extent of control or compromise it would provide. The prioritized list is used to direct the actual testing of the system.

FLEXIBILITY. The effort required to modify an operational program.

FORGERY. The fabrication of information by one individual, entity, or process and the claim that such information was received in a communication from another individual, entity or process.

FORMAL PROOF. A complete and convincing mathematical argument, presenting the full logical justification for each proof step, for the truth of a theorem or set of theorems. The formal verification process uses formal proofs to show the truth of certain properties of formal specification and for showing that computer programs satisfy their specifications.

FORMAL SECURITY POLICY MODEL. A mathematically precise statement of security policy. To be adequately precise, such a model must represent the initial state of a system, the way in which the system progresses from one state to another, and a definition of a "secure" state of the system. To be acceptable as a basis for a TCB, the model must be supported by a formal proof that if the initial state of the system satisfies the definition of a "secure" state and if all assumptions required by the model hold, then all future states of the system will be secure. Some formal modeling techniques include state transition models, temporal logic models, denotational semantics models, and algebraic specification models. See also Bell LaPadula Model, Security Policy Model.

FORMAL TOP-LEVEL SPECIFICATION (FTLS). A top-level specification that is written in a formal mathematical language to allow theorems showing the correspondence of the system specification to its formal requirements to be hypothesized and formally proven.

FORMAL VERIFICATION. The process of using formal proofs to demonstrate the consistency (design verification) between a formal specification of a system and a formal security policy model or (implementation verification) between the formal specification and its program implementation.

FUNCTIONAL TESTING. The portion of security testing in which the advertised features of a system are tested for correct operation.

— G —

GENERAL-PURPOSE SYSTEM. A computer system designed to aid in solving a wide variety of problems.

GRANULARITY. The size of an object protected is referred to as its granularity. Traditionally the granularity has been on the order or a file or device, but database management systems may support much finer granularity at the record or item level.

— H —

HIERARCHICAL DECOMPOSITION. The ordered, structured reduction of a component to its most elementary security property.

HOST ACCESS CONTROL. A means of restricting access at ISO protocol level 3 based on the identity of hosts and/or groups to which they belong.

HOST COMPUTER. A computer connected to a network which provides end-user service.

— I —

INFERENCE. The inference problem occurs in database retrieval when the classification of the response returned by a query permits data to be released to the used even though the the user is not authorized to access that data. The user can infer the unauthorized data from the authorized response.

INFORMATION SECURITY. The sum of computer security and network security.

INTEGRITY. (1) For software quality, the extent to which access to software or data by unauthorized persons can be controlled. (2) For computer, database, and network security, see Data Integrity.

INTEROPERABILITY. The ability and extent to which one system can exchange information with another. The limits on interoperability are often related to the extent of data structure.

— J —

JOURNAL. An audit trail of database activities.

— K —

KEY. A sequence of symbols that controls the operation of encryption and decryption.

KEY MANAGEMENT. The generation, storage, secure distribution, and application of encryption keys in accordance with a security policy.

— L —

LABEL. See Security Label for network systems, and see Sensitivity Label for computer systems.

LATTICE. A partially ordered set for which every pair of elements has a greatest lower bound and a least upper bound.

LEAST PRIVILEGE. This principle requires that each subject in a system be granted the most restrictive set of privileges (or lowest clearance) needed for the performance of authorized tasks. The application of this principle limits the damage that can result from accident, error, or unauthorized use.

LIMITED ACCESS. A security mode in which not all users are fully cleared or authorized access to all sensitive or classified data being processed and/or stored in the system.

LINK ENCRYPTION. The individual data encryption or encipherment on one or all individual links of a data communications system. Note: The implication of link encryption is that data will be in cleartext form in relay entities. Compare to End-to-End Encryption.

— M —

MAINTAINABILITY. The effort required to locate and fix an error in an operational program.

MALICIOUS LOGIC. Hardware, software, or firmware that is intentionally included in a system for the purpose of causing loss or harm.

MANDATORY ACCESS CONTROL. A means of restricting access to objects based on the sensitivity (as represented by a label) of the information contained in the objects and the formal authorization (i.e., clearance) of subjects to access information of such sensitivity.

MANIPULATION DETECTION. A mechanism used to detect whether a data unit has been modified (either accidentally or intentionally).

MASQUERADE. An attack on a system that involves an unauthorized entity pretending to be an authorized one in order to gain access to system assets.

MESSAGE AUTHENTICATION. A procedure that when established between two or more communicants allows each party to verify that received messages are genuine. Communicants can be people, devices, or processing functions. Typically, a communicant acts as both a sender and receiver of messages, although it is possible for a communicant to participate only as a sender or receiver. It is not necessary for the communication to take place in real-time: messages may be received on a delayed basis, as in an electronic mail system. See Authentication.

MESSAGE AUTHENTICATION CODE (MAC). A cryptographic checksum or checkfunction. See Cryptographic Checkfunction.

MULTILEVEL DEVICE. A device used in a manner that permits it to process data of two or more security levels simultaneously without risk of compromise. To accomplish this, sensitivity labels are normally stored on the same physical medium and in the same form (i.e., machine-readable or human-readable) as the data being processed.

MULTILEVEL NETWORK SUBJECT. A network subject that causes information to flow through the network at two or more security levels without risk of compromise. To accomplish this, sensitivity labels are transmitted along with the data.

MULTILEVEL SECURE. A class of system containing information with different sensitivities that simultaneously permits access by users with different security clearances and needs-to-know, but prevents users from obtaining access to information for which they lack authorization.

MULTILEVEL SECURITY MODE. The mode of operation that allows two or more classification levels of information to be processed simultaneously within the same system when some users are not cleared for all levels of information present.

MUTUALLY SUSPICIOUS. The state that exists between processes each of which contains sensitive data which must extract data from the other and protect its own data.

— N —

NEED-TO-KNOW. A determination made by the processor of sensitive information that a prospective recipient, according to security policy, has a requirement for access to, knowledge of, or possession of the sensitive information in order to perform official tasks or services.

NETWORK. A network is composed of a communications medium and all components attached to that medium whose responsibility is the transference of information. Such components may include, but are not limited to, hosts, packet switches, telecommunications controllers, key distribution centers, access control centers, technical control devices, and other components used by the network. Network delimitation is best expressed in terms of the protocol layers. See Network Architecture.

NETWORK ARCHITECTURE. (1) Defines protocols, formats, and standards that different hardware/software must comply with to achieve stated objectives. (2) The International Organization for Standardization (ISO) provides a framework for defining the communications process between systems. This framework includes a network architecture, which consists of seven layers. The architecture is referred to as the open systems interconnection (OSI) model or reference model. Services and the protocols to implement them for the different layers of the model are defined by international standards. From a systems viewpoint, the bottom three layers support the components of the network necessary to transmit a message, the next three layers generally pertain to the characteristics of the communicating end systems, and the top layer supports the end users. The seven layers are (1) *physical layer:* includes the functions to activate, maintain, and deactivate the physical connection and defines the functional and procedural characteristics of the interface to the physical circuit; the electrical and mechanical specifications are considered to be part of the medium itself. (2) *Data link layer:* Formats the messages and covers synchronization and error control for the information transmitted over the physical link, regardless of the content. "Point-to-point error checking" is one way to describe this layer. (3) *Network layer:* Selects the appropriate facilities and includes routing communications through network resources to the system where the communicating application is, segmentation and reassembly of data units (packets), and some error correction. (4) *Transport layer:* Includes such functions as multiplexing several independent message streams over a single connection and segmenting data into appropriately sized packets for processing by the network layer. Provides end-to-end control of data reliability. (5) *Session layer:* Selects the type of service. Manages and synchronizes conversations between two application processes. Two main types of dialogue are provided: two-way simultaneous (full-duplex) or two-way alternating (half-duplex). Provides control functions similar to the control language in computer system. (6) *Presentation layer:* Ensures that delivered in a form that the receiving system can understand and use. Communicating parties determine the format and language (syntax) of messages: translates, if required, and preserves the meaning (semantics). (7) *Application layer:* Supports distributed applications by manipulating information. Provides resource management for file transfer, virtual file and virtual terminal emulation, distributed processing, and other functions.

NETWORK DISCRETIONARY ACCESS CONTROL (NETWORK DAC). Discretionary access control applied to network components at protocol layer 3. Network DAC is employed to control access between network components. It is one mechanism for establishing a closed user group.

NETWORK SECURITY. The protection of networks and their services from all natural and human-made hazards. Provides an assurance that the network performs its critical functions correctly and there are no harmful side-effects. Includes providing for information accuracy. See Computer Security, Information Security, and Security.

NETWORK SECURITY ARCHITECTURE. A subset or network architecture specifically addressing security-relevant issues. The OSI Security Architecture encompasses security services and mechanisms for the OSI seven-layer model. These services and mechanisms may be included in the OSI architecture and in implementation of the services and protocols of the architecture. An example of a security service is peer-entity authentication. An example of a specific security mechanism is encryption or encipherment.

NETWORK SECURITY MODEL. A model implementing the concepts of the network security architecture. An extension of the OSI basic reference model covers security aspects, which are general architectural elements of communications protocols. The general security-related architectural elements can be applied appropriately in the circumstances for which protection of communication between open systems is required. Existing standards may be improved or new standards developed, using the the guidelines and constraints in the network security model.

NOTARIZATION. The registration of data with a trusted third party that provides for future recourse to the data and assures accuracy concerning its characteristics such as content, origin, time, and delivery of the data.

— O —

OBJECT. A passive entity that contains or receives information. Access to an object potentially implies access to the information it contains. Examples of objects are records, blocks, pages, segments, files, directories, directory trees, and programs, as well as bits, bytes, words, fields, processors, video displays, keyboards, clocks, printers, etc. See also Passive.

OBJECT REUSE. The reassignment to some subset of a medium (e.g., page frame, disk sector, magnetic tape) that contains one or more objects. To be securely reassigned, such media must contain no residual data from the previously contained object(s).

OPEN HOT SITE. A data processing facility operated for profit by making available to otherwise unaffiliated companies a site on which they can conduct their data processing after loss of the use of their own facility.

OPEN SECURITY ENVIRONMENT. An environment that includes those systems in which one of the following conditions holds true: (1) Application developers (including maintenance) do not have sufficient clearance or authorization to provide an acceptable presumption that they have not introduced malicious logic. (See the definition of Closed Security Environment for an explanation of sufficient clearance.) (2) Configuration control does not provide sufficient assurance that applications are protected against the introduction of malicious logic prior to and during the operation of system applications.

OPEN SYSTEMS INTERCONNECTION (OSI) MODEL. See Network Architecture.

OUTPUT. Information that has been exported by a trusted computer base (TCB).

OVERT CHANNEL. An overt channel is a path within a network that is designed for the authorized transfer of data.

— P —

PASSIVE. (1) A property of an object or network object that lacks logical or computational capability and is unable to change the information it contains. (2) Those threats to the confidentiality of data which, if realized, would not result in any unauthorized change in the state of the intercommunicating systems (e.g., monitoring and/or recording of data).

PASSIVE THREATS. Threats of unauthorized disclosure of information without changing the state of the system.

PASSWORD. A private character string that is used to authenticate an identity.

PEER-ENTITY AUTHENTICATION. The corroboration that a peer entity in an association is the one claimed. See Authentication.

PENETRATION. The successful compromise of a protected system.

PENETRATION TESTING. The portion of security testing in which the penetrators attempt to circumvent the security features of a system. The penetrators may be assumed to use all system design and implementation documentation, which may include listings of system source code, manuals, and circuit diagrams. The penetrators work under no constraints other than those that would be applied to ordinary users.

PERSONNEL SECURITY. The procedures established to ensure that all personnel who have access to any sensitive information have the required authorities as well as all appropriate clearances.

PHYSICAL SECURITY. The measures used to provide physical protection of a system's assets against malicious and accidental attacks. Such measures include the use of locks, guards, and similar administrative mechanisms.

PLAIN TEXT. Intelligible text or signals that have meaning and that can be read or acted upon without the application of decryption. Compare with Ciphertext.

POLICY. See Security Policy.

PORTABILITY. The effort required to transfer a program from one hardware configuration and/or software system environment to another.

PRINCIPAL. The entity in a computer system to which authorizations are granted; thus the unit of accountability. Essentially synonymous with Subject.

PRIVACY. (1) The ability of an individual or organization to control the collection, storage, sharing, and dissemination of personal and organizational information. (2) The right to insist on adequate security of, and to define authorized users of, information or systems. Note: The concept of privacy cannot be very precise and its use should be avoided in specifications except as a means to require security, because privacy relates to "rights" that depend on legislation.

PROFILE. A list of protected objects and access rights associated with each subject. A profile is a row-based projection of an access control matrix.

PROCESS. A program in execution. It is completely characterized by a single current execution point (represented by the machine state) and address space.

PROTECTED SUBSYSTEM. (1) User-provided (layer 7) programs that control access to objects at a finer granularity than provided by the kernel. (2) A collection of procedures and data objects encapsulated in a domain of its own so that the internal structure of the data object is accessible only to the procedures of the protected subsystem. The procedures may be called only at designated domain entry points and only be designated subjects.

PROTECTION. Mechanisms and techniques that control access to stored information.

PROTECTION-CRITICAL PORTIONS OF THE TCB. Those portions of the TCB whose normal function is to deal with the control of access between subjects and objects. See also Subject, Object, Trusted Computer Base.

PROTECTION PHILOSOPHY. An informal description of the overall design of a system that delineates each of the protection mechanisms employed. A combination (appropriate to the evaluation class) of formal and informal techniques is used to show that the mechanisms are adequate to enforce the security policy.

PROTOCOL REFERENCE MODEL. See Network Architecture.

PROTOCOL SUITE. A collection of protocol implementations properly (but in practice, not always) based on a protocol reference model.

— R —

READ. A fundamental operation that results only in the flow of information from an object to a subject.

READ ACCESS. Permission to read information.

RECOVERY PLAN. Guides the return to full and normal data processing capability.

REFERENCE MONITOR CONCEPT. An access control concept that refers to an abstract machine that mediates all accesses to objects by subjects. The implementation of the reference monitor concept in a computer system is called a security kernel that mediates every computer system object access to ensure that the security policy is maintained.

RELATION. (1) In mathematical language, given sets S1,S2,. . .,Sn (not necessarily distinct), R is a relation on these n sets if it is a set of n-tuples each of which has its first element from S1, its second element from S2, and so forth. (2) Relations correspond to tables with tuples as the rows and attributes as the columns. At the intersection of each row and column is a value.

RELIABILITY. The extent to which a program can be expected to perform its intended function with required precision.

REPUDIATION. Denial by one of the entities involved in a communication of having participated in all or part of the communication.

RESOURCE. Anything used or consumed while performing a function. The categories of resources are time, information, objects (information containers), or processors (the ability to use information). Specific examples are CPU time, terminal connect time, amount of directly-addressable memory, disk space, number of I/O requests per minute.

REUSABILITY. The extent to which a program can be used in other applications and is related to the packaging and scope of functions that programs perform.

RISK ANALYSIS. An analysis of system assets and vulnerabilities to establish an expected annual loss (EAL) or equivalent for certain events based on costs and estimated probabilities of the occurrence or a ranking of the categories of risk of those events.

RISK INDEX. The disparity between the minimum clearance or authorization of system users and the maximum classification of data processed by the system.

RISK MANAGEMENT. An approach to balance the risk of developing and operating cost-effective automated information systems.

— S —

SANITIZE. To erase or alter sensitive data in order to reduce its sensitivity or the sensitivity of its storage media.

SCHEMA. Definitions of the various types of records in the database, the data-items they contain, and the sets into which they are grouped. Specifically related to the network database model.

SECURITY. Mechanisms and techniques that control access to system assets. Protection is against, for example, unauthorized modification, destruction, denial or service or theft. Security is an important aspect of broader concepts, such as computer security, information security, and network security. These broader terms address many concerns that are outside the scope of technical and communications security criteria (e.g., managerial, physical, and administrative controls).

SECURITY ARCHITECTURE. The subset of computer architecture dealing with the security of the computer or network system. See Computer Architecture, Network Architecture.

SECURITY AUDIT. An independent review and examination of system records and activities in order to test for adequacy of system controls, to ensure compliance with established policy and operational procedures, and to recommend any indicated changes in controls, policy, or procedures. See Audit Trail.

SECURITY AUDIT TRAIL. See Audit Trail.

SECURITY KERNEL. The hardware, firmware, and software elements of a trusted computing base that implement the reference monitor concept. It must mediate all accesses of subjects to objects, be protected from modification, and be verifiable as correct.

SECURITY LABEL. A sensitivity indicator permanently associated with protected data, processes, and other open systems interconnection (OSI) resources and which may be used in enforcing a security policy. See also Sensitivity Label for computer systems.

SECURITY LEVEL. The combination of a hierarchical classification and a set of nonhierarchical categories that represents the sensitivity of information.

SECURITY POLICY. The set of laws, rules, and practices that regulate how an organization manages, protects, and distributes sensitive information. A complete security policy will necessarily address any concerns beyond the scope of computers and communications. See, for example, Bell-LaPadula Model.

SECURITY POLICY MODEL. An informal presentation of a formal security policy model.

SECURITY TESTING. A process used to determine that the security features of a system are implemented as designed and are adequate for a proposed application environment. This process includes hands-on functional testing, penetration testing, and verification. See also Functional Testing, Penetration Testing, Verification.

SENSITIVE INFORMATION. Information that, as determined by a competent authority, must be protected because its unauthorized disclosure, alteration, loss, or destruction will at least cause perceivable damage to someone or something.

SENSITIVITY. The characteristic of an asset (object) that implies its value to the organization using it and the asset's vulnerability to accidental or deliberate threats.

SENSITIVITY LABEL. (1) A sensitivity indicator, associated explicitly and incorruptibly with protected data, processes, or other resources, which may be used in carrying out a security policy. (2) A piece of information that represents the security level of an object and that describes the sensitivity (e.g., classification) of the data in the object. Sensitivity labels are used by the TCB as the basis for mandatory access control decisions. See also Security Label for network systems.

SIGNATURE. See Digital Signature.

SIMPLE SECURITY PROPERTY. A Bell-LaPadula security model rule allowing a subject read access to an object only if the security level of the subject dominates the security level of the object.

SINGLE-LEVEL DEVICE. A device used to process data of a single security level at any one time. Since the device need not be trusted to separate data of different security levels, sensitivity labels do not have to be stored with the data being processed.

STANDBY FACILITY. A facility which does nothing until the primary one is lost. Possible variations include a facility doing routine work ready to take over in an emergency.

*-PROPERTY (STAR PROPERTY). A Bell-LaPadula security model rule allowing a subject write access to an object only if the security level of the subject is dominated by the security level of the object. Also known as the Confinement Property.

STORAGE OBJECT. An object that supports both read and write accesses.

SUBJECT. An active entity, generally in the form of a person, process, or device that causes information to flow among objects or changes the system state. Technically, a process/domain pair. See also Principal.

SUBJECT SECURITY LEVEL. A subject's security level is equal to the security level of the objects to which it has both read and write access. A subject's security level must always be dominated by the clearance of the user with which the subject is associated.

SUBSCHEMA. (1) A consistent and logical subset of the schema from which it is drawn. (2) A sub-schema consists of a specification of which schema record types the user is interested in, which schema data-items he or she wishes to see in those records, and THE schema relationships linking those records. Specifically related to the network model.

SYSTEM. An assembly of computer and/or communications hardware, software, and firmware configured for the purpose of classifying, sorting, calculating, computing, summarizing, transmitting and receiving, storing, and retrieving data with a minimum of human intervention.

SYSTEM HIGH SECURITY MODE. The mode of operation in which system hardware/software is only trusted to provide need-to-know protection between users. In this mode, the entire system, to include all components electrically and/or physically connected, must operate with security measures commensurate with the highest classification and sensitivity of the information being processed and/or stored. All system users in this environment must possess clearances and authorization for all information contained in the system. All system output must be clearly marked with the highest classification and with all system caveats until the information has been reviewed manually by an authorized individual to ensure appropriate classifications and that caveats have been affixed.

SYSTEM USERS. Users with direct connections to the system and also those individuals without direct connections who receive output or generate input that is not reliably reviewed for classification by a responsible individual. The clearance of systems users is employed in the calculation of the Risk Index.

— T —

TEMPEST. The study and control of spurious electro-magnetic signals emitted from ADP equipment.

THREAT. A potential violation of system security.

TOP-LEVEL SPECIFICATION (TLS). A nonprocedural description of system behavior at the most abstract level. Typically, a functional specification that omits all implementation details.

TRAFFIC ANALYSIS. The inference of information from observation of traffic flows (presence, absence, amount, direction, participants, and frequency).

TRAFFIC FLOW SECURITY. Protection against Traffic Analysis.

TRAFFIC PADDING. The generation of spurious instances of communication to reduce or circumvent Traffic Analysis.

TRAPDOOR. A hidden software or hardware mechanism that permits system protection mechanisms to be circumvented. It is activated in some nonapparent manner (e.g., special "random" key sequence at a terminal).

TROJAN HORSE. A computer program with an apparently or actually useful function that contains additional (hidden) functions that surreptitiously exploit the legitimate authorizations of the invoking process to the detriment of security. For example, making a "blind copy" of a sensitive file for the creator of the Trojan Horse.

TRUSTED COMMUNICATIONS PATH. A mechanism by which a network subject can communicate directly with the TNB. This mechanism can only be activated by the network subject or the TNB and cannot be imitated by untrusted software.

TRUSTED COMPUTER SYSTEM. A system that employs sufficient hardware and software integrity measures to allow its use for processing simultaneously a range of sensitive or classified information.

TRUSTED COMPUTING BASE (TCB). The totality of protection mechanisms within a computer system—including hardware, firmware, and software—the combination of which is responsible for enforcing a security policy. The TCB creates a basic protection environment and provides additional user services required for a trusted computer system. The ability of a trusted computing base to correctly enforce a security policy depends solely on the mechanisms within the TCB and on the correct input by system administrative personnel of parameters (e.g., a user's clearance) related to the security policy.

TRUSTED FUNCTIONALITY. That which is perceived to be correct with respect to some criteria (e.g., as established by a security policy). The functionality shall neither fall short of nor exceed the criteria.

TRUSTED PATH. A mechanism by which a person at a terminal can communicate directly with the trusted computing base. This mechanism can only be activated by the person or the trusted computing base and cannot be imitated by untrusted software.

TRUSTED SOFTWARE. The software portion of a trusted computing base.

TRUSTED SUBJECT. A subject trusted to bypass the security kernel (specifically, the *-property of the Bell-LaPadula model) but not the security policy model.

TUPLE. In a relational database, a single row of a relation. Corresponds to a record in a network database.

— U —

USABILITY. The effort required to learn, operate, prepare input, and interpret output of a program.

USER. (1) Any person who interacts directly with a computer system. (2) Used imprecisely to refer to the individual who is accountable for some identifiable set of activities in a computer system. See also Principal, Subject.

— V —

VERIFICATION. The process of comparing two levels of system specification for proper correspondence (e.g., security policy model with top-level specification, TLS with source code, or source code with object code). This process may or may not be automated.

VIEW. A virtual set of records. A dynamic picture of a query.

VIRUS. Malicious software, perhaps a Trojan horse, which reproduces itself in other systems.

— W —

WORK FACTOR. An estimate of the amount of time or effort that can be expected to be expended to overcome a protective measure by a would-be penetrator with specified expertise and resources.

WRITE. A fundamental operation that results only in the flow of information from a subject to an object.

WRITE ACCESS. Permission to write an object.

References/Other Readings

[ABRA84] Abrams, Marshall, and Cotton, Ira W., *Computer Networks: Tutorial,* IEEE Computer Society, Washington, D.C., 1984.

[AKL83] Akl, Selim G., "Digital Signatures: A Tutorial Survey," *Computer,* February 1983, pp. 15-24.

[ANDE85] Anderson, Howard M., "Resolving the Conflict: User Friendliness vs. Effective Security," *The Twelfth Annual Computer Security Conference,* Computer Security Institute, November 4-7, 1985.

[ANSI82] X9.9-1982, *Financial Institution Message Authentication (Wholesale),* 1982.

[ANSI85] X9.17-1985, *Financial Institution Key Management (Wholesale),* 1985.

[ATHA85] Athanasiou, Tom, "DES Revisited," *Datamation,* October 15, 1985, pp. 110-114.

[BELL74] Bell, David E., *Secure Computer Systems: A Refinement of the Mathematical Model,* MITRE Technical Report 2547, Vol. 3, April 1974.

[BELL76] Bell, D. Elliot and Leonard J. LaPadula, *Secure Computer Systems: Unified Exposition and Multics Interpretation, Foundations and Model,* The MITRE Corp., Bedford, Mass. MTR-2997 Rev. 1, March 1976.

[BLOT86] Blotcky, Steven, Kevin Lynch, and Steven Lipner, "SE/VMS: Implementing Mandatory Security in VAX/VMS," *Proceedings of the 9th National Computer Security Conference,* National Computer Security Center, September 15-18, 1986, pp. 47-54.

[BRAN85] Brand, Sheila, "A Status Report on the Development of Network Criteria," *Proceedings of the 8th National Computer Security Conference,* National Computer Security Center, September 30–October 3, 1985, pp. 145-151.

[BROW79] Browne, Peter S., *Security: Checklist for Computer Center: Self-Audits* (Introduction), AFIPS Press, Reston, Va., 1979, pp. 1-7.

[CAMP80] Campbell, Robert P., *A Guide to Automated Systems Security,* Advanced Information Management Incorporated, Woodbridge, Va. 1980.

[CHAU85] Chaum, David, "Security Without Identification: Transaction Systems to Make Big Brother Obsolete," *Communications of the ACM,* October 1985, pp. 1030-1044.

[CHEH81] Cheheyl, Maureen Harris, Morrie Gasser, George A. Huff, and Jonathan Millen, "Verifying Security," *Computing Surveys,* Vol. 13, No. 3, September 1981, pp. 280-339.

[COLB85] Colby, Wendelin, "The Security Vow," *Infosystems,* March 1985, pp. 94-98.

[COUR84] Courtney, Robert H. Jr., and Mary Anne Todd, "Problem Definition: An Essential Prerequisite to the Implementation of Security Measures," *Second International Congress and Exhibition on Computer Security,* Toronto, September 10-12, 1984, p. 4.

[COUR86] Courtney, Robert H., Jr. "An Economically Feasible Approach to Contingency Planning," *Proceedings of the 9th National Computer Security Conference,* National Computer Security Center, September 15-18, 1986, pp. 237-244.

[CRAN77] Crane, Hewitt D., Daniel E. Wolf, and John S. Ostrem, "The SRI Pen System for Automatic Signature Verification," *Proceedings Trends & Applications 1977: Computer Security and Integrity,* IEEE Computer Society, Washington, D.C., pp. 32-40.

[CSCD85] *Department of Defense Trusted Network Evaluation Criteria: Draft,* Department of Defense Computer Security Center, July 29, 1985.

[CSCG85] *Department of Defense Password Management Guideline,* Department of Defense Computer Security Center, CSC-STD-002-85, April 12, 1985.

[CSCS83] *Department of Defense Trusted Computer System Evaluation Criteria,* Department of Defense Computer Security Center, CSC-STD-001-83, August 15, 1983.

[CSCS85] *Computer Security Requirements: Guidance for Applying the Department of Defense Computer System Evaluation Criteria in Specific Environments,* Department of Defense Computer Security Center, CSC-STD-003-85, June 25, 1985.

[CSCT85] *Technical Rationale Behind CSC-STD-003-85: Computer Security Requirements,* Department of Defense Computer Security Center, CSC-STD-004-85, June 25, 1985.

[CSCW85] *Proceedings of the Department of Defense Computer Security Center Invitational Workshop on Network Security,* National Computer Security Center, New Orleans, La., March 19-22, 1985.

[CSID85] *1985 Directory: Computer Security Products,* Computer Security Institute; The 1985 National Computer Security Exhibition, Hyatt Regency O'Hare, Chicago, Ill., November 4-5, 1985.

[DATA85] *Datamation,* Hardware, Off-Line, May 15, 1985, p. 145.

[DAVI81] Davies, Donald W., *Computer Securiy: Tutorial,* IEEE Computer Society, Washington, D.C., 1981.

[DAVI83] Davies, Donald W., "Applying the RSA Digital Signature to Electronic Mail," *Computer,* February 1983, pp. 55-62.

[DEMI83] DeMillo, Richard and Michael Merritt, "Protocols for Data Security," *Computer*, February 1983, pp. 39-50.

[DENN83] Denning, Dorothy E., "Protecting Public Keys and Signature Keys," *Computer*, February 1983, pp. 27-35.

[DDN85] *Defense Data Network Evolution of Security Services: 1986–1992*, Defense Data Network Program Management Office, Defense Communications Agency, Code B610, Washington, D.C., drafts of August 6, 1985.

[DODS85a] *Military Standard: Software Quality Evaluation*, Department of Defense, DOD-STD-2168 (Draft), April 16, 1985, Superseding MILS-52779A, August 1, 1979.

[DODS85b] U.S. Department of Defense, *Trusted Computer System Evaluation Criteria*, DOD 5200.28-STD, December 1985.

[DPRM83] *DoD Protocol Reference Model, System Development Corporation Report TM-7171/201/02*, for the Defense Communication Agency, January 1983.

[DRUC54] Drucker, Peter F., *The Practice of Management*, Harper & Row Publishers, New York, N.Y., 1954.

[EVAL86] *Evaluated Products List for Trusted Computer Systems*, National Computer Security Center, 1986.

[GOLD85] Goldberg, Eddy, "DP Nightmare Hits N.Y. Bank," *Computerworld*, December 2, 1985, pp. 1 and 7.

[GUID77] *Data Encryption Standard*, U.S. Department of Commerce, National Bureau of Standards, FIPS PUB 46, January 15, 1977.

[GUID79] *Guideline for Automatic Data Processing Risk Analysis*, U.S. Department of Commerce, National Bureau of Standards, FIPS PUB 65, August 1979.

[GUID83] *Guideline for Computer Security Certification and Accreditation*, U.S. Department of Commerce, National Bureau of Standards, FIPS PUB 102, September 27, 1983.

[GUID84] Ruthberg, Zella G. and William Neugent, *Overview of Computer Security Certification and Accreditation*, U.S. Department of Commerce, National Bureau of Standards, NBS Special Publication 500-109, April 1984.

[GUID85] Steinauer, Dennis D., *Security of Personal Computer Systems: A Management Guide*, U.S. Department of Commerce, National Bureau of Standards, NBS Special Publication 500-120, January 1985.

[GUID85a] *Password Usage Standard*, U.S. Department of Commerce, National Bureau of Standards, FIPS PUB 112, May 30, 1985.

[GUID85b] Neugent, William, John Gilligan, Lance Hoffman, and Zella Ruthberg, *Technology Asessment: Methods for Measuring the Level of Computer Security*, Special Publication 500-133, U.S. Department of Commerce, National Bureau of Standards, October 1985.

[HORW86] Horwitt, Elizabeth, "GM, Other Giants Join COS, Aim to Protect Users' Rights," *Computerworld*, May 19, 1986, p. 45.

[JOHN86] Johnson, R.E., "Data Security Products Roundup: Loose Lips Sink Ships," *Infosystems*, April 1986, pp. 28-34.

[KAHN67] Kahn, David, *The Codebreakers*, Macmillan, New York, N. Y., 1967.

[KAHN80] Kahn, David, "Cryptology Goes Public," *IEEE Communications Magazine*, March 1980, pp. 19-28.

[KATZ85] Katzke, Stuart W. "Summary of Key Issues," *Minutes of the Federal Information Systems Risk Analysis Workshop*, The Air Force Computer Security Program Office, Gunter AFB, Al., January 22-24, 1985, pp. 17-1–17-5.

[KENT82] Kent, Stephen T., Peter J. Sevcik, and James G. Herman, "Personal Authentication System for Access Control to the Defense Data Network," *Conference Record EASCON 82*, IEEE, New York, N.Y., pp. 89-93.

[LAND81a] Landwehr, Carl E., *A Survey of Formal Models for Computer Security*, Naval Research Laboratory, Washington, D.C., NRL Report 8489, September 30, 1981.

[LAND81b] Landwehr, Carl E. "Formal Models for Computer Security," *Computing Surveys*, Vol. 13, No. 3, September 1981, pp. 247-278.

[LAND83] Landwehr, Carl, "The Best Available Technologies for Computer Security," *IEEE Computer*, July 1983, pp. 86-95.

[LAND84] Landwehr, Carl E., Constance L. Heitmeyer, and John McLean, "A Security Model for Military Message Systems," *ACM Transactions on Computer Systems*, Vol. 2, No. 3, August 1984, pp. 198-222.

[LAND85] Landwehr, Carl E. and H.O. Lubbes, "Determining Security Requirements for Complex Systems with the *Orange Book*," *Proceedings of the 8th National Computer Security Conference*, National Computer Security Center, September 30–October 3, 1985, pp. 156-162.

[LEE86] Lee, J.A.N., Gerald Segal, and Rosalie Steur, "Positive Alternatives: A Report on an ACM Panel of Hacking," *Communications of the ACM*, Vol. 29, No. 4, April 1986, pp. 297-299.

[LEMP79] Lempel, Abraham, "Cryptology in Transition," *Computing Surveys*, Vol. 11, No. 4, December 1979, pp. 285-303.

[LIPN82] Lipner, Steven B., "Non-Discretionary Controls for Commercial Applications," *Proceedings: 1982 Symposium Security and Privacy*, IEEE Computer Society Press, Washington, D.C., 1982, pp. 1-10.

[MIL1777] *Military Standard Internet Protocol*, U.S. Department of Defense, MIL-STD-1777, August 12, 1983.

[MIL1778] *Military Standard Transmission Control Protocol*, U.S. Department of Defense, MIL-STD-1778, August 12, 1983.

[MILL84] Millen, Jonathan K., "A1 Policy Modeling," *Proceedings of the 7th National Computer Security Conference*, September 24-26, 1984, pp. 137-145.

[MILL85] Millen, Jonathan K., *The Interrogator: Protocol Security Analysis*, MITRE Technical Report 9912, September 1985.

[NCSC85] *Personal Computer Security Considerations*, National Computer Security Center, NCSC-WA-002-85, December 1985.

[OMB85] Executive Office of the President, Office of Management and Budget, *Management of Federal Information Resources*, OMB Circular No. A-130, December 12, 1985.

[OSI84] *Information Processing Systems–Open Systems Interconnection: Basic Reference Model*, International Standard 7498, 1984, pp. 10-15.

[OSI85] *Rapporteur's Report–Proposed Changes to Addendum to ISO 7498 on Security Architecture*, ISO/TC97/SC21/WG16.1 Ad Hoc Group on Security, London, June 1985 (or most recent version).

[OTA86] U.S. Congress, Office of Technology Assessment, *Federal Government Information Technology: Management, Security, and Congressional Oversight*, OTA CIT-297, U.S. Govenment Printing Office, February 1986.

[ROSE86] Rosenberg, Robert, "Slamming the Door on Data Thieves," *Electronics*, February 3, 1986, pp. 27-31.

[RUSH85] Rushby, John, "Networks Are Systems; A discussion Paper," *Proceedings of the Department of Defense Computer Security Center Invitational Workshop on Network Security*, National Computer Security Center, March 19-22, 1985.

[SALT75] Saltzer, Jerome H. and Michael D. Schroeder, "The Protection of Information in Computer Systems," *Proceedings of the IEEE*, Vol. 63, No. 9, September 1975, pp. 1278-1308.

[SCHE85] Schell, Roger R., "Designing the GEMSOS Security Kernel for Security and Performance," *Proceedings of the 8th National Computer Security Conference*, National Computer Security Center, September 30-October 3, 1985, pp. 108-119.

[SCHE86] Schell, Roger R. and Dorothy E. Denning, "Integrity in Trusted Database Systems," *Proceedings of the 9th National Computer Security Conference*, National Computer Security Center, September 15-18, 1986, pp. 30-36.

[SHAN77] Shankar, K.S., "The Total Computer Security Problem: An Overview," *IEEE Computer*, June 1977, pp. 50-73.

[SHIR83] Shirey, Robert W., *Security Architectures for Long-Haul Packet-Switching Networks*, MITRE Technical Report 83W00163, December 1983.

[SIII85] Horgan, John, "Thwarting the Information Thieves," *IEEE Spectrum*, July 1985, pp. 30-41.

[SORK79] Sorkowitz, Alfred G., "Certification Testing: A Procedure to Improve the Quality of Software Testing," *IEEE Computer*, August 1979.

[STAL85] Stallings, William, *Tutorial: Computer Communications: Architectures, Protocols, and Standards*, IEEE Computer Society, Washington, D.C., 1985.

[TNEC85] *Department of Defense Trusted Network Evaluation Criteria Draft*, Department of Defense, Computer Security Center, July 29, 1985.

[TOMP83] Tompkins, Frederick G., *Guidelines for Developing NASA ADP Security Risk Management Plans*, The MITRE Corporation, McLean, Va., August 1983.

[TOMP84] Tompkins, Frederick G., *NASA Guidelines for Assuring the Adequacy and Appropriateness of Security Safeguards in Sensitive Applications*, MITRE-MTR-84W179, Falls Church, Va., September 1984.

[TROY85] Troy, Eugene F., "Dial-up Security Update," *Proceedings of the 8th National Computer Security Conference*, National Computer Security Center, September 30–October 3, 1985, pp. 124-132.

[VOYD83] Voydock, Victor L. and Stephen T. Kent, *Security in Higher Level Protocols: Approaches, Alternatives, and Recommendation*, BBN Report 4767, Bolt Beranek and Newman, Cambridge, Mass. Also available as National Bureau of Standards, Report ICST/HLNP-81-19, 1981.

[VOYD85] Voydock, Victor L. and Stephen T. Kent, "Security in High-Level Network Protocols," *IEEE Communications Magazine*, July 1985, pp. 12-24.

Recommended Readings

Section 1.1: Overview

[SALT75] Saltzer, Jerome H. and Michael D. Schroeder, "The Protection of Information in Computer Systems," *Proceedings of the IEEE*, Volume 63, Number 9, September 1975, pages 1278-1308.

[SHAN77] Shankar, K.S., "The Total Computer Security Problem: An Overview," *Computer*, June 1977, pages 50-73.

[KATZ85] Katzske, Stuart W., *Minutes of the Federal Information Systems Risk Analysis Workshop*, The Air Force Computer Security Program Office, Gunter Air Force Base, Ala., January 22-24, 1985, pages 17-1—17-5.

Section 1.2: Society and Policy

[GLIC84] Glickman, Dan, *Computer and Communications Security and Privacy*, The Subcommittee on Transportation, Aviation, and Materials, Committee on Science and Technology, U.S. House of Representatives, Washington, D.C., April 1984.

[TOMP84] Tompkins, Joseph B., Jr., James R. Jorgenson, Nathaniel E. Kossack, and Marcia L. Proctor, *Report on Computer Crime*, American Bar Association, 1984.

[OTA86] U.S. Congress, Office of Technology Assessment, *Federal Government Information Technology: Management, Security, and Congressional Oversight*, OTA-CIT-297, U.S. Government Printing Office, Washington, D.C., February 1986.

Section 2.1: Computer System Security

[BROW79] Browne, Peter S., *Security: Checklist for Computer Center Self-Audits*, AFIPS Press, Reston, Va., 1979, pages 1-7.

[LAND85] Landwehr, Carl E. and H.O. Lubbes, "Determining Security Requirements for Complex Systems with the *Orange Book*," *Proceedings of the 8th National Computer Security Conference*, National Computer Security Center, September 30—October 3, 1985, pages 156-162.

[TOMP84] Tompkins, Fredrick G., *NASA Guidelines for Assuring the Adequacy and Appropriateness of Security Safeguards in Sensitive Applications*, The MITRE Corporation, MTR-84W179, September 1984. (Available from NTIS.)

Section 2.2: Formal Models

[LAND81a] Landwehr, Carl E., *A Survey of Formal Models for Computer Security*, Naval Research Laboratory Report 8489, September 30, 1981.

[LIPN82] Lipner, Steven B., "Non-Discretionary Controls for Commercial Applications," *Proceedings of the 1982 Symposium on Security and Privacy*, Oakland, Calif., April 26-28, 1982, pages 2-10.

[LAND84] Landwehr, Carl E., Constance L. Heitmeyer, and John McLean, "A Security Model for Military Message Systems," *ACM Transactions on Computer Systems*, Volume 2, Number 3, August 1984, pages 198-222.

Standard 2.3: Standards

[CSCS85] U.S. Department of Defense Computer Security Center, *Computer Security Requirements: Guidance for Applying the Department of Defense Computer System Evaluation Criteria in Specific Environments*, U.S. Department of Defense Computer Security Center, CSC-STD-003-85, June 25, 1985.

[CSCG85] U.S. Department of Defense Computer Security Center, *Department of Defense Password Management Guideline*, U.S. Department of Defense Computer Security Center, CSC-STD-002-85, April 1985.

[GUID83] National Bureau of Standards, U.S. Department of Commerce, *Guideline for Computer Security Certification and Accreditation*, Federal Information Processing Standard Publication 102, National Bureau of Standards, U.S. Department of Commerce, September 27, 1983.

[GUID84] Ruthberg, Zella G. and William Neugent, *Overview of Computer Security Certification and Accreditation*, Special Publication 500-109, National Bureau of Standards, U.S. Department of Commerce, April 1984.

[GUID85b] Neugent, William, John Gilligan, Lance Hoffman, and Zella Ruthberg, *Technology Assessment: Methods for Measuring the Level of Computer Security*, Special Publication 500-133, National Bureau of Standards, U.S. Department of Commerce, October 1985.

[SCHA85] Schaefer, Marvin and D. Elliott Bell, "Network Security Assurance," *Proceedings of the 8th National Computer Security Conference*, National Computer Security Center, September 30—October 3, 1985, pages 64-69.

Section 2.4: Technology and Methodology

[LAND83] Landwehr, Carl, "The Best Available Technologies for Computer Security," *Computer,* July 1983, pages 86-95.

[CHEH81] Cheheyl, Maureen Harris, Morrie Gasser, George A. Huff, and Jonathan Millen, "Verifying Security," *ACM Computing Surveys,* Volume 13, Number 3, September 1981, pages 280-339.

Section 2.6: Computer System Applications

[ASHL85] Ashland, R.E., "B1 Security for Sperry 1100 Operating System," *Proceedings of the 8th National Computer Security Conference,* National Computer Security Center, September 30—October 3, 1985, pages 105-107.

[LIPN85] Lipner, Steven B., "Secure System Development at Digital Equipment: Targetting the Needs of a Commercial and Government Customer Base," *Proceedings of the 8th National Computer Security Conference,* National Computer Security Center, September 30—October 3, 1985, pages 120-123.

Section 3.2: Cryptography

[KAHN80] Kahn, David, "Cryptology Goes Public," *IEEE Communications Magazine,* March 1980, pages 19-28.

[LEMP79] Lempel, Abraham, "Cryptology in Transition," *ACM Computing Surveys,* Volume 11, Number 4, December 1979, pages 285-303.

[ATHA85] Athanasiou, Tom, "DES Revisited," *Datamation,* October 15, 1985, pages 110-114.

[ROSE86] Rosenberg, Robert, "Slamming the Door on Data Thieves," *Electronics,* February 3, 1986, pages 27-31.

Section 3.3: Access Control and Authentication

[DENN83] Denning, Dorothy E., "Protecting Public Keys and Signature Keys," *Computer,* February 1983, pages 27-35.

[CRAN77] Crane, Hewitt D., Daniel E. Wolf, and John S. Ostrem, "The SRI Pen System for Automatic Signature Verification," *Proceedings of the Trends and Applications 1977: Security and Integrity Conference,* Gaithersburg, Md., May 19, 1977, pages 32-40.

[MCCA86] McCalmont, Arnold M., "End-to-End Encryption in X.25 Packet Switched Networks," *Proceedings of the 1986 Phoenix Conference on Computers and Communications,* 1986, pp. 53-56.

[KENT82] Kent, Stephen T., Peter J. Sevcik, and James G. Herman, "Personal Authentication System for Access Control to the Defense Data Network," *Conference Record EASCON 82,* Washington, D.C., September 20-22, 1982, pages 89-93.

[AKL83] Akl, Selim G., "Digital Signatures: A Tutorial Survey," *Computer,* February 1983, pages 15-24.

[CHAU85] Chaum, David, "Security without Identification Transaction Systems to Make Big Brother Obsolete," *Communications of the ACM,* October 1985, pages 1030-1044.

[TROY85] Troy, Eugene F., "Dial-up Security Update," *Proceedings of the 8th National Computer Security Conference,* National Computer Security Center, September 30—October 3, 1985, pages 124-132.

[NEED78] Needham, Roger M. and Michael D. Schroeder, "Using Encryption for Large Networks of Computers," *Communications of the ACM,* Volume 21, Number 12, December 1978, pages 993-999.

Session 3.4: Protocols

[DEMI83] DeMillo, Richard and Michael Merritt, "Protocols for Data Security," *Computer,* February 1983, pages 39-50.

[STAL85] Stallings, William, *Tutorial: Computer Communications: Architectures, Protocols, and Standards,* IEEE Computer Society Press, Washington, D.C., March 1985.

4274

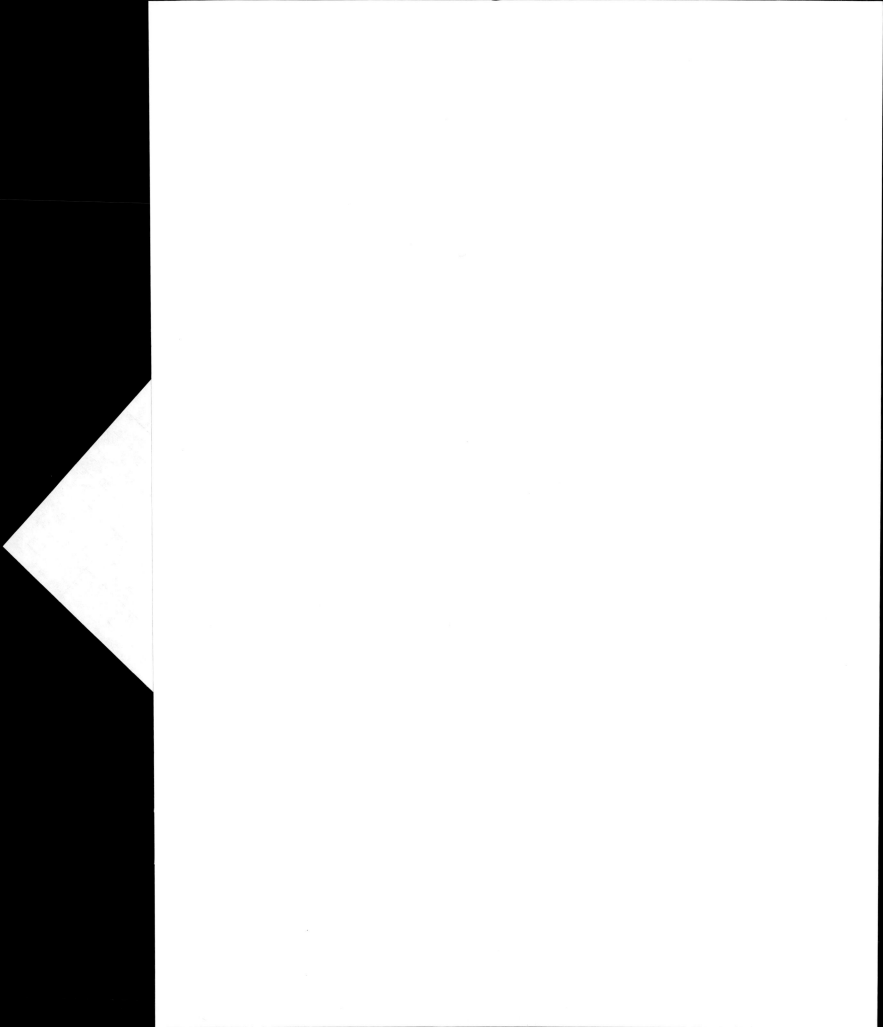

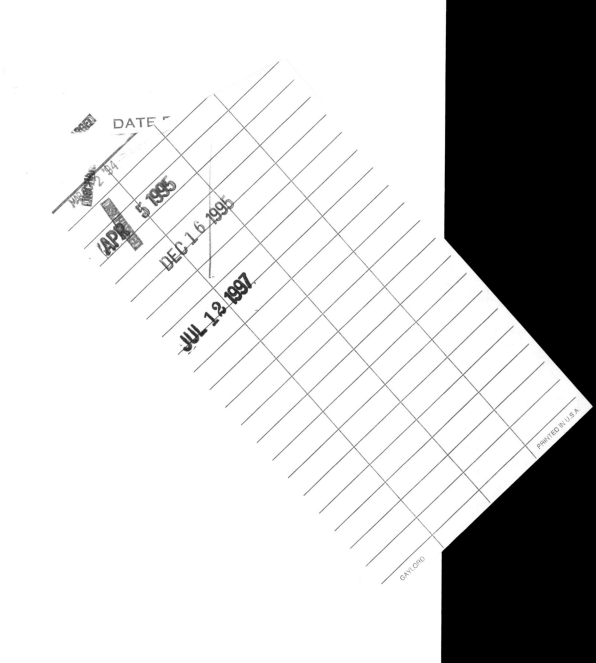